P9-CMF-648

MESSAGE OF THE FATHERS OF THE CHURCH

General Editor: Thomas Halton

Volume 11

MESSAGE OF THE FATHERS OF THE CHURCH

PREACHING THE WORD

by

Thomas K. Carroll

Michael Glazier, Inc.
Wilmington, Delaware

ABOUT THE AUTHOR

Thomas K. Carroll holds doctorates in theology and liturgy, was a peritus at Vatican II, and has written and lectured widely on patristic topics. He is presently on the faculty of the University of Dallas.

First published in 1984 by Michael Glazier, Inc.,
1723 Delaware Avenue, Wilmington, Delaware 19806

Library of Congress Catalog Card Number: 83-81840
International Standard Book Number:
Message of the Fathers of the Church series:
(0-89453-312-6, Paper; 0-89453-340-1, Cloth)
PREACHING THE WORD
(0-89453-322-3, Paper)
(0-89453-351-7, Cloth)

Cover design by Lillian Brulc
Typography by Joyce Cartagena

Printed in the United States of America

CONTENTS

LIST OF ABBREVIATIONS

CCL	Corpus Christianorum, series latina
CSEL	Corpus Scriptorum Ecclesiasticorum Latinorum
FC	Fathers of the Church
GCS	Die griechischen christlichen Schriftsteller
LCL	Loeb Classical Library
OECT	Oxford Early Christian Texts
PG	Migne, Patrologia Graeca
PL	Migne, Patrologia Latina
PLS	Patrologia Latina, Supplementum, ed. A. Hamman
SC	Sources chrétiennes

EDITOR'S INTRODUCTION

The *Message of the Fathers of the Church* is a companion series to *The Old Testament Message* and *The New Testament Message.* It was conceived and planned in the belief that Scripture and Tradition worked hand in hand in the formation of the thought, life and worship of the primitive Church. Such a series, it was felt, would be a most effective way of opening up what has become virtually a closed book to present-day readers, and might serve to stimulate a revival in interest in Patristic studies in step with the recent, gratifying resurgence in Scriptural studies.

The term "Fathers" is usually reserved for Christian writers marked by orthodoxy of doctrine, holiness of life, ecclesiastical approval and antiquity. "Antiquity" is generally understood to include writers down to Gregory the Great (+604) or Isidore of Seville (+636) in the West, and John Damascene (+749) in the East. In the present series, however, greater elasticity has been encouraged, and quotations from writers not noted for orthodoxy will sometimes be included in order to illustrate the evolution of the Message on particular doctrinal matters. Likewise, writers later than the mid-eighth century will sometimes be used to illustrate the continuity of tradition on matters like sacramental theology or liturgical practice.

An earnest attempt was made to select collaborators on a broad inter-disciplinary and inter-confessional basis, the chief consideration being to match scholars who could handle the Fathers in their original languages with subjects in which they had already demonstrated a special interest and competence. About the only editorial directive given to the selected contributors was that the Fathers, for the most part, should be allowed to speak for themselves and that they should speak in readable, reliable modern English. Volumes on individual themes were considered more suitable than volumes devoted to individual Fathers, each theme, hopefully, contributing an important segment to the total mosaic of the Early Church, one, holy, catholic and apostolic. Each volume has an introductory essay outlining the historical and theological development of the theme, with the body of the work mainly occupied with liberal citations from the Fathers in modern English translation and a minimum of linking commentary. Short lists of Suggested Further Readings are included; but dense, scholarly footnotes were actively discouraged on the pragmatic grounds that such scholarly shorthand has other outlets and tends to lose all but the most relentlessly esoteric reader in a semi-popular series.

At the outset of his *Against Heresies* Irenaeus of Lyons warns his readers "not to expect from me any display of rhetoric, which I have never learned, or any excellence of composition, which I have never practised, or any beauty or persuasiveness of style, to which I make no pretensions." Similarly, modest disclaimers can be found in many of the Greek and Latin Fathers and all too often, unfortunately, they have been taken at their word by an uninterested world. In fact, however, they were often highly educated products of the best rhetorical schools of their day in the Roman Empire, and what they have to say is often as much a lesson in literary and cultural, as well as in spiritual, edification.

St. Augustine, in *The City of God* (19.7), has interesting reflections on the need for a common language in an expanding world community; without a common language a man is more at home with his dog than with a foreigner as far as intercommunication goes, even in the Roman Empire, which imposes on the nations it conquers the yoke of both law and language with a resultant abundance of interpreters. It is hoped that in the present world of continuing language barriers the contributors to the series will prove opportune interpreters of the perennial Christian message.

Thomas Halton

INTRODUCTION

FROM SYNAGOGUE TO SANCTUARY

The Gospel according to Matthew ends with the Lord's command to the eleven:

> ... go, therefore, and make disciples of all the nations. Baptize them in the name of the Father and of the Son, and of the Holy Spirit. *Teach* (*didaskontes*) them to carry out everything I have commanded you. And know that I am with you always, until the end of the world. (Mt 28:19)

The fulfilment of this command Mark expresses with another word:

> The Eleven went forth and *preached* (*ekèruxan*) everywhere. The Lord continued to work with them throughout and confirm the message through the signs which accompanied them. (Mk 16:20)

Preaching and teaching, or *Kerygma* and *Didache*, are here the key words. In Old Testament usage there was no distinction between them: in the New Testament they were no less synonymous for the disciples sent out by Jesus "to preach the Good News" (Mk 3:14) return and report to him "all that they had done and what they had taught." (Mk 6:30). Furthermore when Paul, for example, said that, "it pleased God to save those who believe through the absurdity of the preaching of the gospel" (1 Cor 1:21) it is unclear whether he was speaking about the absurdity of the act of preaching or of the message preached. Nevertheless if one were to assess from New Testament sources where the weight of meaning generally falls one would conclude that preaching or kerygma invariably contains the primary notion of the dynamic activity of preaching: yet no context ever excludes the idea of content which must therefore always be included within the general connotation of the term. This identity of act and message is well expressed by the Matthean promise of the presence of Christ in the teaching of disciples "until the end of the world" and the Markan comment that "the Lord continued to work with them throughout." Thus the effective and mysterious presence of Christ as divine Word or power in the human words of his disciples marks a new beginning in the act of preaching and teaching, and clearly brings Christian Preaching within the tradition of the synagogue and the context of worship. Consequently the well-known account of Jesus in the synagogue of Nazareth is the biblical starting point for any study of Christian preaching and teaching:

> He came to Nazareth where he had been reared, and entering the synagogue on the sabbath as he was in the habit of doing, he stood up to do the reading. When the book of the prophet Isaiah was handed him, he unrolled the scroll and found the passage where it was written: "The spirit of the Lord is upon me; therefore he has anointed me. He has sent me to bring glad tidings to the poor, to proclaim liberty to captives, recovery of sight to the blind and release to prisoners, to announce a year of favor from the Lord." Rolling up the scroll he gave it back to the assistant and sat down. All in the synagogue had their eyes fixed on him. Then he began by saying to them, 'Today this Scripture passage is fulfilled in your hearing.'

> All who were present spoke favourably of him; they marvelled at the appealing discourse which came from his lips. They also asked, 'Is not this Joseph's son'? He said to them, 'You will doubtless quote me the proverb, 'Physician, heal yourself,' and say, 'Do here in your own country the things we have heard you have done in Capernaum.' 'But in fact,' he went on, 'no prophet gains acceptance in his native place.' (Lk 4:16-24)

In this vivid account of Jesus preaching and teaching the worshipping community in his own home town, little is revealed about "the appealing discourse which came from his lips" but four elements seem to emerge with distinct clarity and may be identified accordingly as homiletic, exegetical, liturgical and prophetic.[1] These basic elements can be likewise seen in the preaching of the Apostolic Church and in that of the early Christian Fathers, both Greek and Latin, as the divine command is fulfilled of preaching the Gospel to the ends of the earth.

1. The Homiletic Dimension

That form of discourse known to the Greeks as diatribe in which the Cynic philosophers perfected the art of communicating at a popular level was the forerunner in Old Testament times of synagogue preaching and teaching and in New Testament times of Greek homily and Latin sermon. It began in the confusion and fear that followed in the wake of the Greek city state when Hellenism lost its walls of security and revealed its manifold problems. In those days the man who was listened to was the man who had entered into dialogue with his audience in familiar terms and retained throughout his discouse a firm pragmatic concern as he delivered his message to his hearers as an antidote to the perplexities of their situation. Bion of Borysthenes was the

[1]Brilioth, Y. *A Brief History of Preaching*, pp. 1-15.

great master of this new form of diatribe or familiar discourse and in his hands it became 'un dialogue monologue'; a discourse on a moral subject given by a preacher before an audience but retaining the mannerisms and devices of animated conversation:

> Therefore we should not try to alter circumstances but to adapt ourselves to them as they really are, just as sailors do. They don't try to change the winds or the sea but ensure that they are always ready to adapt themselves to conditions. In a flat calm they use the oars; with a following breeze they hoist full sail; in a head wind they shorten sail or heave to. Adapt yourselves to circumstances in the same way. Are you old? Do not long for youth. Again, are you weak? Do not hanker after the prerogatives of the strong ... Are you poor? Do not seek the ways of the wealthy. ... [2]

These talks were conversation and not formal discourses. Hence the chosen name of diatribe, or homily, with its connotation of informality. In keeping with this impromptu character was the pose of informal planlessness, an intimate and confidential tone and divagations from, and returns to, the main theme. In Roman imperial times the diatribe or homily surfaced again with the Stoicism of Zeno, Seneca and Marcus Aurelius. But the real master of the "Bionei Sermones" was Horace who called his satires *sermones* or *diatribae*. A resume of his satire or sermon on the faults of our neighbors will illustrate the genre:

> Like other singers Tigellius would not sing when asked, but when not asked would never stop: he was all inconsistency. 'Well, have *you* no faults'? Yes, and I admit them. Instead of condoning our own faults and condemning those of others, we should imitate lovers who find charm even in blemishes; usually we reverse this, turning virtues

[2]McDonald, J.I.H. *Kerygma and Didache*, p. 40.

> into faults. But if we would be forgiven we must forgive, particularly small faults. The Stoic says there are no small faults, all offences are equal. But if Nature makes a sharp cleavage between virtue and vice, what becomes of law? Punishment should discriminate according to the gravity of an offence. 'If I were king,' says the Stoic, 'I would punish severely,' Why, according to your sect you *are*: the wise man, you know, is the only king! Yes, and the very children in the street jeer at you, while I, the outsider, enjoy the respect and affection of dear friends.[3]

Whatever cultural cross-fertilization may have taken place during the Hellenistic period two major factors in particular differentiate popular preaching in the Jewish tradition from the Graeco-Roman homily or sermon. In the first place Jewish preaching was related to a Scripture-using tradition or sacred text which evolved its own distinctive hermeneutic and in the second place it operated within the cult of the synagogue. These factors transformed the Cynic-Stoic diatribe into the Jewish diatribe in which in keeping with the sacred text and the solemn setting the witticisms and humor of the earlier form disappear and dialogue seldom occurs. Indeed the style of the Jewish diatribe is much heavier and more serious and religious and lacks in particular the vivacity and rhetoric of the earlier Greek preachers. In other words the Jewish intent modified the Greek form as Scripture and synagogue left their mark and influence.

2. *The Exegetical Dimension*

In reading the text that was handed to him, Jesus acted in accordance with the tradition of the synagogue, for the central concern of Jewish preaching was in fact the interpretation and contemporization of the scriptural message. *Midrash*—the technical term for this hermeneutical

[3]McDonald, *op. cit.* p. 160.

process—denotes, at least by the time of the Destruction, an interpretative and paraphrastic commentary on the Scriptures which proceeds by comparing one text of Scripture with a variety of others and by relating the biblical meaning to the contemporary situation. Essential to it is the reciprocal relations between personal experience and text. "Has not every word of the Scripture seventy aspects?" These aspects were latent and, as generation after generation found expression for some or other of them, they revealed again and anew the *Torah* or Law which Moses received on Sinai. Such *midrashim* are traditionally divided into two recognized types: *midrash halachah*, designed to elucidate the fundamental principles of the legislative parts of the *Torah*, and *midrash haggada* providing homiletic commentary on the rest of Scripture.

Apart from a few central dogmas, such as the existence of God who revealed Himself to Israel and made his will known to his people through the Torah, there were no doctrinal prescriptions, no 'systematic theology' to which believing Jews were obliged to subscribe. Judaism was more interested in living out ethical values than in elaborating theological formulations, and its sages put the accent on correct interpretation of the law rather than on abstract speculation. Consequently the *Halachah*, the authoritative application of the divine will to the daily lives of Jews, was much more systematically developed than the *Haggadah*, the Rabbis' homiletic interpretation of Scripture. The *Halachah* was law and had to be observed in all its details. The goal of *Haggadah* was instruction, exhortation and edification and it contained a rich variety of folk tales, narratives, parables and bizarre interpretations and applications of Scripture that stemmed from the fertile imaginations of innumerable teachers who were steeped in their own lore. In either case one can see how the Greek form of homily was specifically modified by its attachment to a scriptural text, and in its Jewish form became characteristically exegetical.

3. The Liturgical Dimension

Jesus' sermon was clearly within the context of worship according to Luke: "entering the synagogue on the sabbath as he was in the habit of doing, he stood up to do the reading." (4:16.) Indeed the reading of the Scriptures was the very source from which the first Jewish liturgical assemblies sprang. Certainly the synagogue liturgy centered around the *Reading* which is a technical term for the public reading of Scripture in a religious assembly. As regards the *Reading* two categories are to be distinguished: one was the reading or *seder* from the Pentateuch; the other was composed of passages or *haftarah* taken from the other books of Scripture but introduced as commentaries on the *seder*. These two readings in this order explain the New Testament formula *the Law and the Prophet* to signify the Old Testament as a whole. This *Reading* was no mere reading: it was a community's celebration of the sacred Scripture and it expressed itself in a highly liturgical manner. In the first place the very taking of the Scripture rolls and the replacing of them was a ceremony in itself performed with due solemnity. Secondly, both readings, *seder and haftarah*, were proclaimed in a traditional chant by three or four members of the assembled community. Thirdly, these chantors were called upon by the chief of the synagogue to take their places in turn at the reading desk on a platform or bench in the center of the synagogue; nor could the chief himself read without the invitation of the community. Fourthly, the readings were not haphazardly chosen, for the Pentateuch was divided into 54 portions or *seders* of which one was read on each sabbath in dawn worship. On the other hand, one cannot say for certain that the *haftarah*, or reading from the prophets, was equally determined by officially established order. Finally, they were proclaimed in Hebrew and since the reading and exposition of Scripture was the very purpose of the synagogue it was therefore necessary to resort to the use of *targum* since some did not understand Hebrew, and to the homily so that the message of Scripture could be understood in contemporary perspective.

Because the homily emerged as an integral part of the synagogue liturgy its nature was determined accordingly. Surviving Jewish homiletic *midrashim* indicate two broad types whose liturgical dimensions are equally clear. The *yelammedenu* homily is distinctive in that it starts with a question put by the leaders of the liturgical assembly—*yelammedenu rabbenu*: let our teacher instruct us. The teacher's answer followed customary midrashic practice and usually included an appeal to *hallachah*. The *proem* homily, on the other hand, begins with a *proem* or introductory text, chosen with care in order to interpret and, in a sense, bind together the readings from the Law and the Prophets. Although this text was not selected from either, it usually linked the *seder* with the *haftarah* by means of word-play or other linguistic form, and the evidence suggests that the preacher kept the *haftarah* constantly in mind. In both forms of homily, the theme was developed by means of a string of cited texts (*haruzin*: pearl stringing) giving as a result a characteristic 'list' structure to the homily. Considerable substance, however, was introduced by means of appropriate stories, parables or other illustrative material which formed part of the homiletic convention. The overall unity of structure, however, was preserved or secured by the fact that the preacher controlled the interpretative development so as to lead to a conclusion related to the Law or the *seder*. Bowker summarises well when he says:

> The homilies in a sense move from the circumference of a circle to its center. They start from a *proem* text outside the *seder* and the *haftarah* of the day, but linguistically related to the *haftarah*; they proceed by *hazurin* which implies the *haftarah* and may perhaps quote from it; and the *hazurin* leads directly to a text from, or pointing to, the *seder*.[4]

[4]Bowker, A. "Speeches in Acts," *NTS*. 14. (1967), pp. 96ff.

Thus one can see how the Greek homily already modified in Judaism by the connection with the Scripture text and becoming as a result exegetical was further modified by its liturgical setting and became as a result cultic.

4. The Prophetic Dimension

Prophecy is perhaps the most significant element in the formation of the holy address and in the veneration of the holy word. Like cultic speech it emerged from a sacral form as it placed ecstatic inspiration in the service of both religious renewal and the personal life of the spirit. In its most proper sense prophecy asserted itself as a holy address—a compelling word of God put into the mouths of the servants and messengers. In this context one can appreciate the clarity and brevity of Luke's comment: "all in the synagogue had their eyes fixed on him. Then he began by saying to them, 'Today this Scripture passage is fulfilled in your hearing.' The content of Jesus' preaching was summed up in this prophetic declaration, which retained the characteristic crisp lapidary style of the oracles. This sermon was prophetic in the deepest sense inasmuch as it is the essential nature of prophecy to speak to the present with divine authority and to transform the historical revelation into a contemporaneous dynamic reality. The captivating feature of this summary account of Jesus' sermon is that it shows us how the prophetic word with its creative elemental religious power and with its supernatural demands finds a place within the framework of the sabbath sermon in the synagogue while at the same time victoriously breaking these shackles. Jesus' words have thus given the highest authorization to the claim of the Christian preacher that he also stands in the prophetic succession. Furthermore, they have placed upon the preacher the overwhelming responsibility of being more than a commentator on a text. He is to interpret every text so that out of its swaddling clothes the Lord of Scripture and the fulfiller of prophecy appears as the contemporary teacher and Lord. This Lord is the one who gives to every text its interpretation and its address for every time and place; he is the one who gives to every text its eternal content.

Conclusion

The story of what Jesus did in the synagogue in Nazareth gives us the key to what the Fathers in the immediate generations after Him did in the Churches of the Greek and Roman world. Within the experience of the divine liturgy they too preached on the sacred scriptures in a prophetic and homiletic manner, and thus brought into being within the first two centuries of the Church a unique type of rhetoric, which came to full flower in the time of Origen (185-253) and was named by him a homily in Greek, afterwards called a sermon in Latin. That the early Church Fathers, like Christ and His Apostles before them, also preached outside the liturgical setting is beyond dispute: in every age the Church has practised missionary preaching to convert, parenetic preaching to inculcate her moral precepts, and catechetical to instruct and explain. But these types of preaching lack that specific uniqueness which marks the homily or sermon as a form of address which has not only developed within the liturgical life of the church but also developed such a fixed form in that context that it can be differentiated with ease from other rhetorical types.

In classical usage this Greek word homily (*homilia*) had a social connotation and meant primarily a being together or a communion. In Hellenistic Greek it frequently means speech and therefore connotes the idea of a meeting of minds and hearts. Thus it quickly took on the meaning of familiar speech with someone, of conversation, and of familiar discourse with a gathering. Ironically as a noun the word 'homily' occurs only once in the New Testament and then in a direct quotation from the comic poet, Menander:

> Do not be led astray any longer. "Bad company (*homiliai kakai*) corrupts good morals." Return to reason as you sought and stop sinning. (1 Cor 15:33)

On the other hand, it is in keeping with the notion of preaching as divine act that the word appears in its verbal form also in the New Testament:

> discussing (*homiloun*) as they went all that had happened. In the course of their lively exchange (*en tō homilein*) Jesus approached and began to walk along with them. (Lk 24:14)

and again:

> At the same time, he hoped he would be offered a bribe by Paul, so he used to send him frequently to converse (*homilei*) with him. (Acts 24:26)

This verbal use of the word leads our search for its meaning in the right direction for it inclines us away from any over-structured or set-form connotation that might tempt us to distinguish in a material way between *Kerygma*, *didache* and homily, as if they were three really distinct and independent types of early preaching, rather than different dimensions of the one divine activity. In the same way other Biblical and non-Biblical terms of the time, such as *paraclesis*, *paraenesis*, *catechesis* and *paradosis*, further specified and qualified the very act of preaching and teaching, and thus contributed to the developing pattern of the homily:

> After the reading of the law and of the prophets, the leading men of the synagogue sent this message to them: Brothers, if you have any exhortation (*logos parakleseos*) to address to the people, please speak up. (Acts 13:15);

and again:

> My brothers, I beg you to bear with this word of encouragement (*tou logou tes parakleseos*) for I have written to you rather briefly. (Heb 13:22)

Isocrates to Demonicus writes: "So it is not a piece of *paraclesis* that I have produced for your benefit, but rather *paraenesis*,"[5] and Paul expresses the same idea: but in the Church I would rather say five intelligible words to instruct (katecheso) others than ten thousand words in a tongue. (1 Cor 14:19)

In other passages Paul expresses his notion of *paradosis* or tradition which can also be included within the developing notion of homily:

> I praise you because you always remember me and are holding fast to the traditions (*paredoka humin tas paradoseis*) just as I handed them on to you. (1 Cor 11:2)

and again:

> Therefore, brothers, stand firm. Hold fast to the traditions (*tas paradoseis has edidachthete*) you received from us, either by our word or by letter. (2 Thess 2:15)

The use of preaching in the worship of the Church is a practice that unites Judaism and Christianity, and brings the Christian preacher into the legacy of the prophets of the Old Testament and the tradition of the synagogue where the scriptures were read and explained. There are parallels in other religions but they are remarkably few, as rite sacrifice and liturgical formulae are usually the dominant feature of this cult. Only Judaism and Christianity make the freely or itegral part of their worship. Thus the homily or sermon holds a central place in the life of the Church for it has continued from the beginning the Lord's activity and Gospel.

[5]McDonald. *op. cit.* p. 69.

1. THE GREEK HOMILY IN HELLENISTIC CULTURE

The widespread growth of Christianity on coming into contact with the Greek world at the dawn of the second century caused a radical development in Church Order and Worship, and consequently in the act and form of Preaching. Written and detailed evidence of this two-fold development is indeed scant: nevertheless the surviving documents of this age indicate (a) a transition in the notion of preacher from charismatic prophet to hierarchic priest, (b) an equally significant change in the notion of worship from Jewish *synaxis* to Christian eucharist, (c) a totally new form of exegesis from Jewish allegory to Christian typology, and (d) a new style of presentation as classical rhetoric replaces biblical diatribe.

By these developments the act of preaching was radically altered as the person of the homilist became hierarchically defined and classically formed, and the character of the homily became scripturally centered and liturgically confined. Such developments on account of their influence on both homily and homilist alike must be further analyzed and illustrated under the following headings—prophet and priest, word and worship, allegory and type, classical rhetoric and second sophistic.

1. Prophet and Priest

The relation of the prophet to the priest in the primitive Christian community is as obscure in the history of Christian origins as is the problem of the hierarchy in general. Nevertheless the documents of this age, expecially the *Didache* and the *Shepherd of Hermas*, give us some indications, however faint, of the developments. The *Didache* (c. 100) is our earliest and most important witness:

> C. 11.3.[1] As regards the apostles and prophets you should act in line with the gospel precept and welcome every apostle on arriving, as if he were the Lord. But he must not stay beyond one day: in case of necessity, however, a second day too. If he stays three days, he is a false prophet ... Every genuine prophet who wants to settle with you 'has a right to his support.' Similarly, a genuine teacher himself, just like a 'workman, has a right to his support.' Hence take all the first fruits of vintage, and harvest, and of cattle and sheep, and give these first fruits to the prophets. For they are your high priests ...

The *Shepherd of Hermas* (c. 100-150) also speaks of "Apostles and teachers who preached unto the whole world" and of prophets in similar terms to those of the *Didache*. Indeed in this document there is a clear distinction between "the Apostles and the teachers" on the one hand and the "Episcopoi" on the other hand. This distinction is already expressed in the *Didache*:

> C.15.1.[2] You must, then, elect for yourselves bishops and deacons who are a credit to the Lord, men who are gentle, generous, faithful, and well tried. For their ministry to you is identical with that of the prophets and teachers. You must not, therefore, despise them, for along with the prophets and teachers they enjoy a place of honor among you.

[1]Text: SC. 248. 184.

[2]Text: SC. 248. 192.

Thus, there seems to have existed side by side in the early Church a ministry of universal preaching involving Apostles, prophets and teachers, and a ministry of local leadership involving Bishops, Priests, and Deacons. The distinction here is between a stable priesthood, that of the presbyters and bishops, and a missionary priesthood, that of the *apostoloi.* The various roles assigned to these *apostoloi* are all related to this primary and distinct vocation. They are essentially preachers, and this aspect of their ministry is indicated by the terms prophet and *didaskalos*. As prophets they announce the Kerygma to the pagans; as *didaskaloi* they prepare those pagans who have decided to receive baptism. Yet as early as the *Didache* there is already some indication that the preacher was no longer the traveling prophet and had been replaced by the residential bishop who had appropriated his role:

> 4.1.[3] My child, day and night 'you should remember him who preaches God's word to you,' and honor him as you would the Lord. For where the Lord's nature is discussed, there the Lord is. Every day you should seek the company of saints to enjoy their refreshing conversation.

Ignatius of Antioch (c. 107) is the first clear witness of this early development in the understanding of the bishop as both prophet and priest, which he expresses in numerous passages and in extravagant language. Consequently, for him the Chair of the Bishop was in reality "the throne of God." Thus, the Bishop seated upon his throne as an inspired teacher preached from a "teacher's chair," or *cathedra*, which he shared with no one else but inherited from all his predecessors back to the first apostolic missionaries to his Church. On the other hand, he exercised his office of priesthood away from his throne and standing at the altar as the exclusive representative of Christ to the people.

[3]Text: SC. 248. 156.

This twofold notion of the bishop possessing through his ordination not only the power of priesthood but also that of prophecy appeared in numerous authors of this century but especially towards its close in Irenaeus (c. 200) in his *Against Heresies*:

> Bk. 4. C. XXVI.[4] We should listen to those elders who are in the church and who have their succession from the apostles for with their succession in the episcopate they have received the unfailing spiritual gift of the truth according to the Father's wish.

This understanding of the homilist had a profound effect on the nature of the homily. In this context prophecy was no longer the dominant dimension of preaching and was replaced by *didache* or teaching with its emphasis on the unity and authority of tradition as handed down from bishop to bishop. Another passage in Irenaeus sheds much light on this development:

> Bk. 1. C. X.[5] On account of this office of preaching, the Church, although she is scattered all over the earth, unanimously believes with one soul and the same heart, and thus she preaches and teaches her traditions with harmony and with one and the same voice as if living in one house. For although the tongues of earthly speech differ, yet is the force of tradition ever one and the same . . . Just as the sun, God's creature, is one and the same for all the world, so does the preaching of the truth everywhere shine and enlighten all men who are willing to come to the knowledge of the truth . . . For since their faith is one and the same, neither does he who can say a great deal about it actually add to it, nor does he who can say but little diminish it.

[4]Text: PG. 7. 1055.

[5]Text: PG. 7. 550.

2. Word and Worship

The hierarchial and sacramental development of the "homilist" naturally transformed the whole character of the homily, restricted as it was to the official congregation of the Church at the Sacred Liturgy, with the bishop presiding. Here

> "the delivery of the sermon was as much the bishop's 'special liturgy' and proper function at the *synaxis* as the offering of the eucharistic prayer was his 'special liturgy' at the eucharist. As we have seen, the bishop at his consecration received a special 'gift of grace' (charisma) for the office not only of high-priest of the church's prayers and offerings, but also of quasi-inspired 'prophetic teacher' of the Church's faith. He is the Church's mouthpiece, as it were, towards man as well as towards God. Except in emergencies, therefore, he was irreplaceable as preacher at the *synaxis*, the solemn corporate 'church,' even by the ablest of his presbyters. It was the 'special liturgy' of the bishop's 'order,' without which the action of the whole church in its *synaxis* was felt to be incomplete. The presbyters and other Christian teachers might expound their ideas at other gatherings to as many as would hear them, but the *synaxis* had a different character from even the largest private gathering of Christians. It was the solemn corporate witness of the whole church to the revelation of God recorded in the scriptures. At this the bishop, and the bishop only, must expound the corporate faith which his local church shared with the whole Catholic Church and the whole Christian past, back to the Apostles themselves. It was this, the unchanging 'saving' truth of the gospel, and not any personal opinion of his own, which he must proclaim in the liturgical sermon, because he alone was endowed by the power of the Spirit with the 'office' of speaking the authentic mind of his church." G. Dix, *The Shape of the Liturgy*, 40.

1. JUSTIN

The earliest description of this Christian congregation, and of the place of the homily within it, is to be found in Justin (c. 150) in his *First Apology*:

> C. 67.[6] On the day which is called Sunday there is a common assembly of all who live in the cities or in the neighboring outlying districts, and the memoirs of the Apostles or the writings of the Prophets are read, for as long as time permits. When the reader has finished, the president of the assembly verbally admonishes and invites all to imitate such examples of virtue. Then we all stand up together and offer up our prayers, and, as we said before, after we finish our prayers, bread and wine and water are presented. He who presides likewise offers up prayers and thanksgivings, to the best of his ability, and the people express their approval by saying 'Amen.' The Eucharistic elements are distributed and consumed by those present, and to those who are absent they are sent through the deacons ... Sunday, indeed, is the day on which we all hold our common assembly because it is the first day on which God, transforming the darkness and (prime) matter, created the world; and our Savior Jesus Christ arose from the dead on the same day. For they crucified Him on the day before that of Saturn, and on the day after, which is Sunday, He appeared to His apostles and disciples, and taught them the things which we have passed on to you also for consideration.

2. SECOND CLEMENT

From this text it is clear that a *synaxis* normally preceded the Eucharist in the regular Sunday worship of churches in the second century. Apart from Justin's casual and perhaps loose-fitting comment on the reading of either the memoirs of the Apostles (canonical gospels) or the writings of the

[6]PG. 6. 429.

prophets, and the possible implications of this choice of readings for preaching, nothing more can be inferred about the nature of the homily.

The so-called *Second Letter of Clement*, which has been described as our earliest sermon, is a document from the same period which illustrates the shape and content of a second century homily. It is a sober tract concerning Christ's deed of love which ought to compel the Christian to confess him not only in word but also in deed:

> 19. "So, my brothers and sisters, after God's Word I am reading you an exhortation to heed what was there written, so that you may save yourselves and your reader."[7]

The Scripture Lesson was *Isaiah* 54 for he takes the first verse of this chapter as his text: "Rejoice, you who are barren and childless; cry out and shout, you who were never in labor; for the desolate woman has many more children than the one with the husband."

With hardly any trace of the prophetic spirit he develops this text in a simple and direct manner without any claim to style or clear organization. He then passes on to exhort his hearers to a life of moral purity and steadfastness in persecution, emphasizing the need to repent in the light of the coming judgment. He is addressing Gentile converts who are in danger of falling a prey to Gnostic teachings. In consequence he stresses the divinity of Christ, the resurrection of the flesh, and the way in which the Church is the continuity of the Incarnation:

> 14.[8] So, my brothers, by doing the will of God our Father we shall belong to the first Church, the spiritual one, which was created before the sun and the moon. But if we fail to do the Lord's will, that passage of Scripture will

[7]Text: Lightfoot, J.H., *The Apostolic Fathers*, London 1893, 52, 93.

[8]Text: Lightfoot, *op. cit.*, 49, 91.

> apply to us which says, 'My house has become a robber's den.' So, then, we must choose to belong to the Church of life in order to be saved. I do not suppose that you are ignorant that the living 'Church is the body of Christ.' For Scripture says, 'God made man male and female.' The male is Christ; the female is the Church. The Bible, moreover, and the Apostles say that the Church is not limited to the present, but existed from the beginning. For it was spiritual, as was our Jesus, and was made manifest in the flesh of Christ, and so indicates to us that if any of us guard it in the flesh and do not corrupt it, he will get it in return by the Holy Spirit. For this flesh is the antitype of the spirit. Consequently, no one who has corrupted the antitype will share in the spirit. Now, if we say that the Church is the flesh and the Christ is the spirit, then he who does violence to the flesh, does violence to the Church. Such a person, then, will not share in the spirit, which is Christ. This flesh is able to share in so great a life and immortality because the Holy Spirit cleaves to it. Nor can one express or tell 'what things the Lord has prepared' for His chosen ones. (*Second Clement*)

Thus, at the beginning of the second century, preaching became the bishop's prerogative as the possessor of the teaching office. This second century preaching, on its way to becoming a third century homily, has been well described as follows: "Broadly speaking a homily represents an address or discourse delivered to a congregation in the context of worship and characterized, as the words *homilia* and *homileo* indicate, by a tone of intimacy, persuasive argumentation and didactic concern. It is to be distinguished, on the one hand, from prophetic proclamation or sermon characterized by kerygmatic authority and pneumatic intensity, and on the other hand from the more fragmented forms of *didache* or *paraenesis*. The basic forms of Christian communication, however, are fluid and none more so than the homily, the genius of which lies in its adaptability and appropriateness to the occasion . . . Normally it is introduced by a theme statement of a more or less precise type, and the theme is developed in several stages, either in a straight-forward, systematic manner or by means of sections standing in antithesis to each other. Frequently, a conclusion brings the message home to the hearers, with eschatological urgency in its tones of admonition or with a surge of praise." (J. H. McDonald, in *Studia Patristica, TU*, 115, 107).

3. Allegory and Type

Though sociologically disengaged from Judaism, Hellenistic Christianity retained the Jewish scriptures and was thus exposed to the Jewish tradition of exegesis, which ranged from the crudest literalism to the wildest flights of allegory. Neither of these schools could alone express the new and essential element in the Christian approach which lay in the relation between the Old and New Testaments. The interrelation of the Testaments on this level was not the discovery of any particular school but the insight or faith of the new Church. Thus Christian exegesis corresponds neither to what is called literal exegesis, namely that which is concerned with the events, characters and institutions of the Old Testament in themselves, nor to allegorical exegesis, which covers the many possible uses to be made of Scripture considered as a complex of symbols. Rather it deals with the historical interrelation of any two given moments in the divine plan; and the exegetical method which establishes the theological affinities between these two moments in order to elucidate the law of God's action is known in accordance with patristic usage as typology.

1. JUSTIN

Such is the essential difference between Allegory and Typology as methods of exegesis. Typological exegesis is the search for divine intentional links between events, persons or things within the historical framework of revelation, whereas Allegory is the search by man for a secondary and hidden meaning underlying the primary and obvious meaning of a narrative. This secondary sense of a narrative, discovered by allegory, does not necessarily have any connection at all with the historical framework of revelation: indeed it is only when the secondary allegorical sense has an accidental reference to God's self-revelations in history that there is an accidental resemblance between allegory and typology. On the other hand, typology is the corrollary of prophecy, for biblical types (*tupoi*) are as much the inspired events of the Holy Spirit as parables (*logoi*) are his inspired utterances. This distinction is clearly expressed by Justin in his *Dialog with Trypho*, the Jew:

> 90[9] 'Prove this from the Scriptures, therefore,' said Trypho, 'that we, too, may believe you. Indeed we know well that He was to endure suffering, and to be led as a sheep to the slaughter. But what we want you to prove to us is that He was to be crucified and subjected to so disgraceful and shameful a death ... 'Then, please listen,' I said, 'to what I am going to say. Moses was the first to make known this apparent curse of Christ by the symbolic acts which He performed.' 'What acts do you mean'? asked Trypho, 'When your people,' I answered, 'waged war with Amalec, and Jesus (Josue), the son of Nun, was the leader of the battle, Moses himself, stretching out both hands, prayed to God for help. Now, Hur and Aaron held up his hands all day long, lest he should become tired and let them drop to his sides. For, had Moses relaxed from that figure of outstretched hands, which was a figure of the cross, the people would have been defeated (as Moses himself testifies) but as long as he remained in that position Amalec was defeated, and the strong derived their strength from the cross. Indeed, it was not because Moses prayed that his people were victorious, but because, while the name of Jesus was the battle front, Moses formed the sign of the cross. (*Dial. Trypho*)

[9]Text: PG. 6. 689.

2. IRENAEUS

Irenaeus, however, and not Justin, was the first to lay down the fundamental principle of the relationship between the two Testaments for he was not content to treat figures of the Old Testament as prefigurations of Christ but went on to elaborate a theology of history on the basis of this exegesis. In his *Against Heresies* the same God and the same Word of God have been active throughout the whole course of history:

> Bk. 4. C.14.[10] Thus it was God who in the beginning created man on account of his own bounty, chose the patriarchs for their salvation, and singled out his first people, teaching them, stubborn as they were, to serve God; again he provided that there should be prophets on earth. He accustomed man to bear his Spirit, and to have communion with Him (not as needing anyone himself, but as granting communion with him to those who need him.) And to those who pleased him, he was an architect—designing the fabric of salvation—offering himself as a guide to those who were in Egyptian darkness, and giving a law adapted to the needs of those who were wandering in the desert and a worthy inheritance to those who entered the promised land. For those who return to the Father he kills the fatted calf and bestows the best robe, and in many different ways he organises the human race into a harmony of salvation. And the Word visited all of them and freely bestowed what was necessary on those who were submitted to him, thus writing a Law adapted to, and suitable to, every condition . . . through things of a secondary nature he called them to the higher: and through the temporal to the eternal.

This important text, one from many, shows the special contribution of Irenaeus to the science of typology as he

[10]Text: PG. 7. 1011.

integrates into it his personal thesis of a progressive economy of salvation. It is the same gracious God, who, by his Word, strives from the beginning to obtain life for the creature whom he made to receive his gifts; this love, however, adapts itself to man's nature, taking him as he was originally made, and making him gradually more fit to receive ever greater benefits: such is the educative conception of mankind which is so characteristic of Irenaeus:

> Bk. 5. C. XXXVI.[11] Since men are real, they must have a real existence, not passing away into things which are not, but advancing to a new stage among things that are. Neither the substance nor the essence of the created order vanishes away, for he is true and faithful who established it: but the form of this world passes away, that is, the things in which the transgression took place, since in them man has grown old. Therefore, God, foreknowing all things, made this pattern of things temporary, . . . But when this pattern has passed away, and man is made new, and flourished in incorruption, so that he can no longer grow old, then there will be new heavens and a new earth. In this new order man will always remain new, and in communion with God.

3. EPISTLE OF BARNABAS

From the exegetical point of view, the *Epistle of Barnabas*, (c. 130), is of particular importance for our understanding of the development of the homily. Its peculiar form of exegesis is different from the historical typology of Justin and the more developed typology of Irenaeus with his understanding of salvation history and the unity of both Testaments. Emphasising the value and the meaning of the Old Testament revelation in itself, Barnabas seeks to show that the Jews completely misunderstood the law because they interpreted it literally. Repudiating this approach, he presents what is in his opinion the genuinely spiritual mean-

[11]Text: PG. 7. 1221

ing which he calls *teleia gnosis*. This consists of an allegorical explanation of Old Testament doctrines and commandments. God does not desire material gifts of bloody sacrifices but the offering of one's heart in the form of repentance:

> 9. 3.[12] So he circumcised our ears that we might hear the word and believe but the circumcision in which they trust has been abolished. For He said that circumcision was not of the flesh: but they did not understand because an evil angel was misguiding them in their vanity.

But nowhere, perhaps, is his allegorical approach more obvious than in his interpretation of Genesis I, where he is clearly a follower of chiliasm. The six days of creation mean a period of six thousand years because a thousand years are like one day in the eyes of God. (The Greek word *chilioi*=1,000). In six days, i.e. in six thousand years, everything will be completed, after which the present evil time will be destroyed and the Son of God will come again and judge the godless and change the sun and the moon and the stars and He will truly rest on the seventh day. Then will dawn the Sabbath of the millennial Kingdom.

> 15. 8.[13] To the Jews he says your new moons and your sabbaths, I cannot bear. Consider what he means by this. Not the sabbaths of the present era are acceptable to me, but that which I have appointed to mark the end of the world and to usher in the eighth day, that is the beginning of the other world. Wherefore we joyfully celebrate the eighth day on which Jesus rose from the dead, and having manifested himself to his disciples he ascended into heaven.

This extensive use of the allegorical method of interpretation in the *Epistle of Barnabas* reflects the mental frame-

[12]Text: SC. 172. 144.

[13]Text: SC. 172. 186.

work of the Hellenistic world in which the Christian gospel was being preached. The same tension between gospel and culture can be seen especially in the influence of Greek rhetoric on the Christian homily. Thus, in the developing church of the second century, prophet and allegory took on new shades of meaning and were called respectively, bishop and type, and homily and homilist were influenced accordingly.

4. Classical Rhetoric and Second Sophistic

In the four centuries preceding the Christian era, the solid foundations of an authentic art of persuasion had been laid in Greek and Roman treatises. Ideally conceived by Plato in the *Phaedrus* and philosophically analysed by Aristotle in the *Rhetoric* it was studied in its practical applications by Cicero in seven separate works on the subject, and construed as a complete system of education by Quintilian. The composite aim of his study was to give persuasive impact to the cause of truth and justice and accordingly it was divided into five tracts, on (1) invention, (2) arrangement, (3) style, (4) memory, and (5) delivery. In our early Christian centuries this functional rhetoric, or old sophistic as it had been called, became overlaid by the new, contrived art of the Second Sophistic.

The term Second Sophistic denotes the aesthetic decline and pervasive extravagances in oratory and other literary genres, both pagan and Christian, that took place between the third and fifth centuries. This period of decadence was marked by the recrudescence of the spirit of self-display and an obsession with stylistic ornament against which Plato had striven centuries earlier. In this world of the Second Sophistic, Christian preaching appeared as a force unique in its origin, content, aim and spirit. It had originated in a divine mandate, contained a divinely revealed message, aimed at the radical conversion of the hearers, and breathed a spirit of earnestness and power. From these features arose the abiding problem of determining the relation of the theory of preaching to the theory of rhetoric, of maintaining the supernatural character and divine efficacy of the act of preaching, while yet perfecting the natural eloquence of the preacher, and of utilizing effectively principles of general rhetoric without succumbing to the superficiality and ostentation of Second Sophistic. The *Peri Pascha* of Melito of Sardis (c. 150) is certainly indicative of this rhetorical influence:

> 18.[14] For the whole of Egypt, plunged in pain and plague, in tears and beatings of the breast, went to Pharaoh all in mourning, not in outward appearance only but also in the heart, rending not just their outer garments but also their wanton breasts. It was a terrible sight: on one side, these beating their breasts, on the other, those bewailing, and in their midst Pharaoh grieving, seated in sackcloth and ashes, in a funeral robe of deep darkness, for Egypt draped him like a funeral garb. Such was the tunic woven for this tyrant's body; such was the garment which the angel of justice put on the hard-hearted Pharaoh: bitter mourning, and groping darkness, and the loss of children, and the angel's domination of the firstborn, for rapid and insatiable was the death that struck them.

Such preciosities of style do not merely present a display of architectonic virtuosity but constitute an impressive fusion of rhetoric and theology, and belong to a tradition of Greek oratory that goes back to Gorgias in the 4th century and develops through the Hellenistic declamations to influence Byzantine and Oriental literature. Indeed Melito may thus be seen introducing to Christian circles—perhaps clumsily and extravagantly—the rhetorical style to which his compatriots were greatly addicted:

> 8.[15] For born Son-like, and led forth lamb-like, and slaughtered sheep-like, and buried man-like, he has risen

[14]Text: SC. 123. 70.

[15]Text: SC. 123. 64.

> God-like, being by nature God and man. He is all things: in as much as he judges . . . Law; in as much as he teaches . . . Word; in as much as he saves, . . . Grace; in as much as he begets, . . . Father; in as much as he is begotten . . . Son; in as much as he suffers, . . . sheep; in as much as he is buried, . . . man; in as much as he has risen, . . . God.

Like classical rhetoric in general, the rhetorical dimension of the *On the Pascha* is lyrical and poetical:

> 26.[16] By one blow the firstborn of the Egyptians fell—the first sown, the first begotten, the long desired—on the ground, not only the men but also the brute beasts. And in the plains of the earth was heard the bellowing of beasts mourning their young, the cow her sucking calf, the mare her colt, and the other beasts who had brought forth, groaning and bitterly bewailing their firstborn. And among men there was lamentation and beating of the breast at the disaster because of the death of the firstborn. The whole of Egypt stank of the odor of unburied corpses. It was a dreadful sight: Egyptian mothers with dishevelled hair, fathers distracted in spirit, wailing woefully in Egyptian . . .

At times, however, the rhetoric is extravagant, showing, perhaps, the influence of the Second Sophistic and probably deserving the disparaging comment of Tertullian—*elegans et declamatorium ingenium*:

> 72.[17] He was put to death. Where? In the heart of Jerusalem. Why? Because he cured their lame, and cleansed their lepers, and restored sight to their blind, and raised to life their dead. That is why he suffered . . . Why Israel, have you committed this strange injustice? You have

[16]Text: SC. 123. 74.

[17]Text: SC. 123. 100.

> dishonored him who honored you. You have despised him who glorified you. You have denied him who confessed you. You have rejected him who proclaimed you. You have killed him who gave life to you. What have you done, Israel? . . . But I, says Israel, have slaughtered the Lord. Why? 'Because he had to suffer.' You are wrong, Israel, in quibbling thus about the sacrifice of the Lord. He had to suffer, but not by you. He had to be humiliated but not by you. He had to be judged, but not by you. He had to be crucified, but not by your right hand.

In spite of such obvious extravagance, *On the Pascha* of Melito is nevertheless the first clear example of the use of rhetoric in preaching the Christian mystery. At all times there is a definite awareness of the primacy of this mystery that is present and preached: rhetoric is at its service and is never an end in itself.

2. The Greek Homily In The Alexandrian Church

The third century broke on the Church with a whole new challenge: the deeper the new religion penetrated the ancient world, the more the need was felt for a scientific exposition of its tenets. Thus there came into being at Alexandria under Clement the first and foremost of those theological schools which were destined to have an enormous impact on the homily and homilist alike. In this center of intellectual life Clement experienced the new civilization emerging from the commingling of Oriental, Egyptian, Greek and Jewish culture. In particular he was exposed to the interaction of Greek thought and Jewish scripture as Philo, the Jewish exegete, had earlier brought into being a whole new synthesis of philosophy and religion, as a result of his allegorical exegesis. To him the literal sense of Holy Scripture was as a shadow is to the body: the allegorical and deeper meaning alone represented the true reality. In the Gnosticism of his day Clement experienced the same emphasis on the allegorical and as a result was obliged to pay less attention to historical typology. The ultimate effect of this new approach was the gradual fusion of allegory with historical typology which became the exegetical characteristic of Alexandria. Nevertheless, the main axis of his exegesis remains the traditional typology, around which he displays, on the one hand, an array of moral and physical symbols borrowed from Philo, and on the other hand a Gnostic type of exegesis of mixed Alexandrian and Palestinian origin. In the end, however, he succeeds in organizing all these elements in a coherent vision which expresses his own thought, based as it is on the relationship between the two Testaments. His exegesis of the burning bush makes the point.

1. Clement of Alexandria (150-215)

> 11. 8. 75.[1] There is here another mystery that I wish to make known to you. When the Lord God first began to give his laws through the Logos and wished to manifest his power to Moses He gave him a heavenly vision of light as He appeared in the form of a burning bramble-bush. Now remember that the bramble is a plant full of thorns. Remember, too, that when the Logos had finished his law-giving and his sojourn among men (at that very moment when he left the world to return to that from which he came down) he was mysteriously crowned with thorns again and in this way recapitulated what he had done in the beginning when he came in the light of the bramble-bush. Thus, having been revealed on the first occasion by the light of the bramble-bush the Logos when restored to heaven through the crown of thorns proved clearly that all these events were the work of one and the same power. (*Paedagogus*)

Clement, therefore, in no sense equates Greek allegory and Christian typology even when he includes them under the one heading of symbolic method. Nor, indeed, does he wholly dissociate them. Rather it would seem that in accordance with his central concept of the series of covenants he arranges them according to a historical pattern or

[1]Text: SC. 108. 149.

design: "Before Christ, there is on the one hand, Greek allegorism, consisting of cosmic symbolism, by which the pagans knew something of God through his manifestation of himself in the world, and moral symbolism by which they knew through his revelation in the human conscience; on the other hand, there is biblical typology, which corresponds to the historical revelation of God to the people of Israel, where the actions of Yahweh in the Old Testament are types of the actions of Christ in the New. Since Christ, however, there is the final stage of apocalyptic exegesis, the revelation of the world to come, the secrets of which are being worked out in the life of the Church. In this way, Clement is able to incorporate Greek allegorism organically into his vision of salvation history, and it becomes easier to understand why the *Protrepticus*, which is addressed to pagans, is largely based on Greek mythology, the *Paedagogus*, which is catechetical, on the bibilical types, and the *Stromateis*, which is Christian gnosis, on Pauline revelation of mysteries. The three books respectively represent the three stages in the history of salvation and in the conversion of souls—a first saving change from paganism to faith and a second from faith to gnosis."[2]

Thus, Clement extends the typology of Justin and Irenaeus in two directions: firstly by a Gnostic exegesis, with its emphasis on the communication of higher knowledge which he inherited partly from Judaeo-Christianity and partly from Philonian exegesis; and secondly by a cosmic and moral exegesis corresponding to God's universal covenant with mankind and serving to root the history of salvation firmly in the religious life of the world. Here again, he is to a great extent dependent on Philo; but by introducing typological exegesis into exegesis of the Platonic kind, he gives the whole an historical perspective to which Philo was a total stranger. Thus, it would appear that Clement's understanding of the relation between Scripture and philosophy,

[2]Daniélou, J. *Gospel Message and Hellenistic Culture*, p. 255.

and that in both cases his vision of salvation-history is the determining factor. Such was the vision of that Christian School in Alexandria in which Clement was succeeded by Origen—"the outstanding preacher and teacher of the early Church, a man of spotless character, encyclopaedic learning, and one of the most original thinkers the world has ever known." (Quasten, J. *Patrology, Vol. 11.* p. 37.)

2. Origen (185-253)

Preaching was as much the crucial problem in the life of Origen as it was his exclusive prerogative, for he was caught in the struggle between Prophet and Priest and was made and broken accordingly. Unlike his native Alexandria in which he spend the first part of his life as the school's most famous teacher, Jerusalem and Caesarea had preserved the primitive practice which went back to the Synagogue of allowing anyone—priest or layman—who was gifted with the Spirit to address the congregation. Having preached in those ancient churches on the invitation of their bishops, Origen was considered by Demetrius, his own bishop, to be in violation of Church Order and was banished accordingly. Thus, at Caesarea, and not at Alexandria, he began in mid-life his second career as preacher and was later ordained there a priest. But for him ordination was merely an enlargement of the teaching office which he had earlier been prevailed upon to accept by the invitation of the bishops and thus as preacher he remained more prophet than priest.

According to Socrates, the historian, he preached on every Wednesday and Friday but Pamphilus who was his biographer tells us that "he preached nearly every day at Church." Eusebius says: "It was only after he had passed the age of 60 and had acquired a very great facility that he allowed stenographers to take down the addresses he gave in Church: previously he had not allowed this."

Unfortunately there is no record of the majority of his sermons. Nevertheless, what remains is considerable, constituting the most ancient body of homilies to have come down to us from Christian antiquity and numbering about two hundred. For the most part, these are based on Old Testament texts, excepting the thirty-nine *Homilies on Luke* which Origen himself describes by the name of "homily" and thus gives the word for the first time in Christian usage description and precise definition as a distinctive form of preaching. In the first place, these homilies were preached in a liturgical setting; secondly, they have an indubitable prophetic quality spoken as they were by one of the most prophetic of all Christian preachers; thirdly, they have the character of a running or continuous exposition of the biblical text, and finally their conversational and direct homiletical style does not exclude the influence of contemporary rhetoric nor does it become a victim of it. It now remains to illustrate these four characteristics of third century preaching from the homilies of the first and foremost of all Christian homilists, Origen.

1. THE LITURGICAL DIMENSION

This dimension of the homily is especially clear in Origen's understanding of preaching as a mutual search by preacher and congregation—a seeking after the voice of God which inflects towards them and a praying together for the Holy Spirit to give them understanding of its utterance. Accordingly, Origen sometimes pauses in a homily to invite the community to join with him in prayer that the Holy Spirit might enlighten him:

> 4. 3.[3] On that question, if the Lord in answer to your prayers grants me understanding, and if at least we are worthy to receive the Lord's meaning, then I shall say to you a few words . . . (*Hom. Ez.*)

[3]Text: GCS. VIII. 363.

This act of praying while preaching expresses the very heart of Origen's thought and occurs again and again throughout his homilies:

> 6. 1.[4] . . . No one can find it easy to discover all the allegories contained in this story of Abimelech and Sara. All the same we must pray that the veil covering our hearts (as they strive to turn to the Lord) may be removed by the Spirit. The Lord is the Spirit. We must pray Him to lift from us the veil of the letter and show us the brightness of His Spirit. (*Hom. Gen.*)

This idea is very dear to Origen:

> 9. 8.[5] We shall understand the meaning of the Law if it is Jesus who reads it to us and makes its spiritual significance clear. Do you not believe that in this way the meaning was grasped by those who said: 'did not our hearts burn within us while he talked with us along the way and while he opened to us the Scriptures' (Lk 24:32). (*Hom. Jos.*)

Thus Scripture must be lit from within by the Holy Spirit or else the letter will remain in possession, as in the case of the Jews, and the mystery which Scripture contains and proclaims will remain hidden:

> 12. 1.[6] Unless Christ himself opens our eyes, how shall we be able to behold the great mysteries that are fulfilled in the patriarchs and are figured by the nights, births and taking of wives. (*Hom. Gen.*)

This understanding of the Scriptures was the fruit of grace as only those who had the spirit of Jesus could under-

[4]Text: PG. 12. 195.

[5]Text: SC. 71. 26.

[6]Text: PG. 12. 225.

stand their spiritual meaning. Here again Origen inherited a body of traditional doctrine taught everywhere in the Church but more clearly expressed by him:

> 4. 3.[7] The things belonging to the Word are hidden away in the sanctuary and only priests are allowed to approach them. Access to them is denied to all men leading animal lives and even to those who apparently had a certain amount of learning and accomplishment, if their merits and their lives have not yet raised them to the grace of the priesthood. (*Hom. Num.*)

Such had been the teaching of his predecessors: Justin in particular thought the grace of God essential for any understanding of Scriptures, while Clement of Alexandria regarded the gnosis, the operation that probes the mysteries of Scripture, as something bound up with spiritual perfection. No wonder then that at times during the homily, Origen pauses to pray:

> 19. 14.[8] O Lord Jesus come again to explain these things to me and to those who are here in quest of spiritual nourishment. (*Hom. Jer.*)

Preaching for him is an actual coming of Christ and it is Christ himself who grows present in the midst of the congregation gathered together in his name:

> 32. 6.[9] And now if you so wish in this Church and in this congregation your eyes can behold the Lord. For when you direct your loftiest thoughts to contemplate Wisdom and Truth, which are the Only Son of the Father, your eyes see Jesus. Blessed is the community of which it is written that the eyes of all—catechumens and faithful,

[7]Text: SC. 29. 108.

[8]Text: SC. 238. 230.

[9]Text: SC. 87. 390.

> men, women and children—saw Jesus not with eyes of the flesh, but with those of the spirit. (*Hom. Lk.*)

Here the presence of Jesus is linked with the community. This is a point of the greatest importance for it stresses the liturgical dimension of the act of preaching as understood by Origen, by which the Word is made flesh again in the community of faith and worship. Consequently the synaxis for Origen is a visible expression and representation of the invisible Church:

> 23. 8.[10] I do not hesitate to say it: in our congregation angels too are present. If we say anything consonant with the Word, they rejoice and pray with us. And it is because angels are present in Church, in that Church at least which is Christ's, that women are called upon to have their heads covered and men are bound to bow in veneration. (*Hom. Lk.*)

Such an allusion to angels is certainly in keeping with Origen's whole theology. To him the invisible world is everywhere present and more real than the visible, and by the presence of angels he signifies the divine character of the official liturgical congregation which participates in the heavenly liturgy. Thus the ministry of a preacher in this divine assembly is likewise divine and therefore Origen preaches not as a private doctor but in the name of the Trinity and in the presence of angels and calls upon the world to repent because of the divine judgment to come on man. Preaching is therefore a liturgical act of which the preacher is not only minister but also priest:

> Bk. X. II.[11] To announce the Gospel is a sacerdotal office. Even as the Priest had to see while officiating that the victim was without blemish, and hence agreeable to God,

[10]Text: SC. 87. 320.

[11]Text: PG. 14. 1268.

> so he who carries out this sacrifice of the Gospel and announces the words of God must watch that his preaching is without blemish, his instruction without fault, and his magisterium perfect. But that means that he is, as far as possible, first to offer up himself in sacrifice and to make his members dead to sin, so that, not only through his doctrine, but also by the example of his life, he shall ensure that his oblation, in being accepted by God, wins the salvation of those who hear him. (*Com. Rom.*)

Thus, preaching is truly a liturgical and sacerdotal act and accordingly the preacher is the high priest whose function it is to sacrifice the victim—the Logos—in such a way as to reveal its inner meaning and then to share it out on the spiritual altar on the souls of the faithful. The priest who flays the burnt offering is a figure of the one who removes the veil of the letter from the Word of God, and brings to light its inward members which are its spiritual interpretations.

2. THE PROPHETIC DIMENSION

Origen's understanding of the priestly dimension of preaching in no way diminished his conception of the preacher as prophet who must not only instruct minds but must also convert hearts: hence, his emphasis on the moral sense which presents the interior and individual meaning of the mystery to be preached while the mystical sense emphasizes the collective and universal message. Accordingly, he draws practical lessons to meet the needs of his particular community and searches the Old Testament not only for a figure of Christ but also for one of Christian life. Having shown in the fall of Jericho Christ's victory over the city of Satan, he then applies the moral to every Christian:

> 7. 2.[12] Those are things each one of us should fulfill in himself. You have within you Jesus as your leader by faith. If you sound the trumpet which is the word of Scripture; if you bear around the city the Ark of the Covenant, which figures the precepts of the Law, then shall you be able to give a cry of triumph, for the world in you will have been destroyed and annihilated. (*Hom. Jos.*)

With the privilege of the prophet who speaks in God's name Origen denounced the faults of his community:

> 12. 8.[13] Some people set themselves up above the rest because they are the children of leading citizens and belong to families which have produced men who are considered great because they have held public office. Such people are proud of a thing indifferent in itself and independent of the will; they have no justification for their pride. Others think highly of themselves because they have power over human lives and have attained the eminence, as they call it, of having the right to cut off men's heads; others pride themselves on their wealth, though it is not real wealth but is good only for this world. Others again are proud of having a fine house or vast estates. (*Hom. Jer.*)

In the homilies he delivered at Caesarea just before the persecution of Decius, he wistfully harked back to the days of the martyrs when Christians were less numerous but more fervent:

> 4. 3.[14] . . . if we judge by people's attitude of mind and not by the crowds we see assembled, we shall see that nowa-

[12]Text: SC. 71. 200.
[13]Text: SC. 238. 32.
[14]Text: SC. 232. 264.

> days we are not real believers at all. The days of real faith were the days when there were many martyrs, the days when we used to take the martyrs' bodies to the cemetery and come straight back and hold our assembly. They were the days when the whole Church was in mourning and the instructions the Catechumens received were meant to prepare them for martyrdom and help them to acknowledge their faith right up to the moment of their death, without wavering or faltering in their belief in the living God. Christians saw amazing signs and wonders then. There were few believers then but they were real ones; they followed the narrow road that leads on to life. Now there are many of us who believe but since many cannot be chosen, few get as far as election and beatitude. (*Hom. Jer.*)

In many other places, he portrays the faults of the various groups within the community in greater detail. Few find grace with the prophet as he reproaches the mass of the faithful for their want of assiduity in hearing the Word of God:

> 10. 1.[15] The Church sighs and grieves when you do not come to the assembly to hear God's Word. You go to Church hardly ever on feast-days, and even then not so much out of desire to hear the word as to take part in a public function . . . The Lord has entrusted me with the task of giving his household their allowance of food, i.e. with the ministry of the word at the appointed time . . . But how can I? Where and when can I find a time when you will listen to me? The greater part of your time, nearly all of it in fact, you spend on mundane things, in the marketplace or the shops; . . . Nobody, or hardly anybody, bothers about God's Word . . . But why complain about those who are not here? Even those of you who are, are paying no attention. (*Hom. Gen.*)

[15]Text: PG. 12. 215.

> 12. 2[16] ... There are some of you who leave as soon as you have heard the lessons read ... without making any effort to get at their meaning ... by comparing one text with another as is done in the homily; others have not even the patience to wait until the reading of the lessons is over ... others do not even know that the lessons are being read but stand in the most distant corners of the Lord's house and talk about secular things ... (*Hom. Ex.*)

> 13. 3.[17] Some do take to heart what is being read but others ... have their hearts and minds set on business matters ... on what is going on in the world or on financial matters and affairs while women think about their children, their needlework and their household duties ... (*Hom. Ex.*)

Again:

> 13. 3.[18] Indeed I often encourage young people to apply themselves to the study of the Sacred Scriptures but as far as I can see I am only wasting my time for I have never succeeded in inducing any of them to the study of the Bible. (*Hom. Ez.*)

In Origen's time the role of prophet, though originally a specific office in the community, was being slowly absorbed by the clerical hierarchy. Origen's own history shows that the period was one in which the organization of the Church was becoming more uniform. Lay doctors or *didaskaloi*, as the prophets were called, still had the right to preach to the Church in Palestine—they had no such right in Alexandria, as Origen painfully discovered and never forgot:

[16]Text: PG. 12. 383.
[17]Text: PG. 12. 390.
[18]Text: GCS. VIII. 448.

> 14. 3.[19] It ofttimes happens that a man who has been rejected by his local Church remains interiorly within it, while the man who seems exteriorly within may oftentimes be without. (*Hom. Lev.*)

This bitter experience of clericalization of the prophet's role by his own bishop explains many of Origen's outbursts against the hierarchy in general and against clerical ambition in particular:

> 16. 8.[20] There are times when we are even more overcome by pride than the pagan princes, worldly and wicked though they are, and we all but give ourselves bodyguards, like kings. We terrify people and make ourselves inaccessible especially if they are poor . . . You can see this happen in many a well-known Church, especially in the big cities. (*Com. Matt.*)

On the other hand, a man might occupy the pulpit as a prophet, a special position or office in the Church, and be as unworthy of this position as many a priest or bishop. This fact Origen, the prophet, did not hide:

> 2. 1.[21] It often happens that men with a low, mean outlook and a relish for the things of earth belong to the upper ranks of the priesthood or occupy the pulpit as prophets or doctors. Others may be spiritual in their outlook and not at all earthbound in their lives—and yet they will belong to one of the lower orders of the ministry or even still be among the common people. (*Hom. Num.*)

3. THE EXEGETICAL DIMENSION

Origen's homilies were always preceded by a reading of Scripture which was for him the essential source of revela-

[19]Text: PG. 12. 556.

[20]Text: PG. 13. 1393.

[21]Text: SC. 29. 83.

tion. On each occasion, the passage read was of a certain length but he did not necessarily expound the whole text: for instance in his *Homily on Samuel* he asks the presiding bishop to select from the reading the pericope for the homily. But the reading was always of primary importance, for Scripture was the centre of his life and preaching the highest form of ministry: anybody can carry out the solemn office of the liturgy before the people, but few men are instructed in doctrine and able to impart knowledge of the faith. For Origen, the Bible as a reflection of the invisible world, was first and foremost the Word of God; not a dead word imprisoned in the past but a living word spoken in the present. Secondly, the Old Testament in his eyes was illuminated by the New, just as the New only revealed its mystery when it was opened by the Old. The bond between the two was determined by typology and allegory, but ultimately seen and understood only by Divine grace:

> Bk. 1. Praef. 8.[22] Then there is the doctine that the Scriptures were composed through the spirit of God and that they have not only that meaning which is obvious, but also another which is hidden from the majority of readers . . . On this point the entire Church is unanimous that while the whole law is spiritual, the inspired meaning is not recognised by all, but only by those who are gifted with the grace of the Holy Spirit in the Word of Wisdom and knowledge. (*On Princ.*)

Elsewhere, he distinguishes three senses of Scripture—literal, moral and mystical corresponding to the three parts of man—body, soul and spirit:

> Bk. IV. 2.4.[23] The sense of Holy Scripture must therefore be given a threefold clarification in accordance with the nature of one's own life. The simple man has to be edified,

[22]Text: SC. 252. 84.

[23]Text: GCS. IV. 312.

> starting from what may be called the flesh of Scripture, for such we term its obvious meaning; the man who has made some moral progress may start from what we may call the soul of Scripture; and the perfect man . . . from the spiritual law which has a shadow of the good things to come. For just as man is composed of the body and soul and spirit, so is the Scripture which was designed by God to be given for the salvation of mankind. (*On Princ.*)

A passage from the *Homily on the Book of Numbers* clarifies the precise content of these three senses:

> IX. 7.[24] In the school of Christ the teaching of the Law and the prophets is clearly like a nut. On the outside it is bitter and unripe; it prescribes circumcision of the flesh and sacrifices. Then comes the second or inner layer which is moral instruction in continence; these things are necessary but they must one day vanish. Finally, enclosed and hidden within all the layers, as in the very core, will be found the secret—the meaning of the mysteries of the Wisdom and Knowledge of God, which nourishes and restores the souls of the saints. (*Hom. Num.*)

Elsewhere there is the same emphasis on the mystical sense:

> Bk. 4. 1. 6.[25] The light was indeed hidden and veiled in the Law of Moses. But, when Jesus came, it shone out, for the veil was lifted and the blessings which were merely foreshadowed in the letter were instantly and really revealed. (*On Princ.*)

Again:

> 1. 6. 36.[26] The gospel, the New Testament, saves us from the old order, the order of the letter, and reveals the

[24]Text: SC. 29. 180.

[25]Text: GCS. IV. 302.

[26]Text: SC. 120. 79.

> splendor of the new order. This is the order of the spirit realized by the light of gnosis and properly belongs to the New Testament but is found also hidden in the Scriptures of the Old. (*Comm. John*)

With this emphasis on the mystical sense of Scripture, Origen attacked literal-minded Christians and likened them to the Jews:

> 6. 1.[27] Whoever should interpret the Scriptures literally had better class himself with the Jews rather than with the Christians. But whoever wants to be a Christian and a disciple of Paul should listen to the words of Paul who said that the Law was something spiritual. (*Hom. Gen.*)

In another passage he condemns the literal interpretation of Scripture and compares it to the leaven of the Pharisees:

> 12. 5.[28] We can justly apply this phrase to those who live like Christians but desire to live like Jews as well. There are some who will not admit that the Law is spiritual and that it contains a mere shadow of the good things that are to come. They refuse to find out the future blessings which the various details of the Law foreshadow. They have no vision and thus do not avoid the leaven of the Pharisees. (*Comm. Matt.*)

Indeed, Origen himself was often the victim of those who defended the literal interpretation.

> 1. 1.[29] Sometimes certain people of our own religion pressure me to follow the literal meaning and to interpret what the Lawgiver says without any *stropha verbi*, or cloud of allegory, to use the sarcastic expression that they

[27]Text: PG. 12. 195.

[28]Text: PG. 13. 988.

[29]Text: PG. 12. 405.

> themselves use. If I were to do what they would wish me to do (although I am a member of the Church living by my faith in Christ and set in the midst of the Church) I should be forced to sacrifice calves and lambs and offer myrrh with incense and oil on the ground that the Commandments of God ordered me to do so.

In virtue of the same carnal outlook the Jews persecuted the Prophets, put Christ to death, and were still persecuting the defenders of the spiritual method of interpretation. But Origen did not allow himself to be worn down by these attacks.

> 13. 3.[30] Whenever I explain the words that these men used long ago and look for a spiritual meaning in them, that is, when I try to lift the veil that hides the Law I am doing what I can to bore a well. Yet, immediately the friends of the literal meaning take up the slanderous cry against me. They attack me and say that there can be no truth if it does not rest upon the earth. But for our part (since we are the servants of Isaac) we must prefer wells of running water and living springs. We must keep far away from these men with their literal untruths. We will leave them the earth since they love it so, while we will reach for the heavens.

Thus, Scripture is the field where the treasure mentioned by Christ is hidden:

> 10. 5.[31] The treasure hidden in the field is the various interpretations discovered by that wisdom which is concealed in the mystery—interpretations veiled and concealed by the things we see and feel, yet no less real, for the things of Heaven and the Kingdom of Heaven are buried but pictured in the Scriptures.

[30]Text: PG. 12. 232.

[31]Text: PG. 13. 845.

This hidden treasure, or spiritual meaning, of the Scriptures had been hitherto known only to the spiritually advanced but when Christ came He made it clear to everyone. Nevertheless we are still like blind men whose eyes are always in need of unsealing:

> 7. 6.[32] We should be careful, for we are often near the wells of running water—God's Scriptures, and yet we fail to recognize them for what they are ... We should be always weeping and beseeching the Lord to open our eyes. The blind man sitting by the roadside at Jericho would not have had his eyes opened if he had not shouted after the Lord. And yet why am I talking about the opening of our eyes as if that were something still to come? Already our eyes have been opened. Jesus came to open the eyes of the blind and the veil that covered the Law has already been lifted.

This theme of healing the eyes of the blind in their attitude to the interpretation of the Scriptures recurs in many other passages:

> 15. 7.[33] The Lord laid his hands physically upon a blind man's eyes. He also stretched out His hands spiritually over the eyes of the Law. Those eyes had been blinded by the carnal interpretation of the Scribes but the Lord restored sight to those whom he chose to reveal the Scriptures by enabling them to see and understand the Law spiritually. (*Hom. Gen.*)

Commentators on Origen's doctrine of the scriptural senses sometimes subdivide his mystical sense into the allegorical and anagogical, and thereby see in him the basis for the four-fold exegesis that later flourished in the Middle Ages. Certainly he was an innovator in the traditional typol-

[32]Text: PG. 12. 203.
[33]Text: PG. 12. 246.

ogy, for in the time of the Church he saw the New Testament realities as new types of the new realities that are already here and at the same time always dawning. With his keen eye for biblical and ecclesial analogies, he was able to find new meanings and realities in the similarities of the New Testaments, the Church's sacraments and the *eschaton*. In his homilies he makes use of all the themes found in traditional typology before his time: "Jesus is our Noah, the spiritual Noah who gives rest to mankind (*Hom. Gen.* 11:3); the sacrifice of Isaac prefigures that of Christ (*Hom. Gen.* VIII, 8-9); the marriage of Isaac and Rebecca, and the marriage of Jacob and Rachel, together with the wells which figure in the two stories, are types of the marriage of Christ and the Church in baptism. (*Hom. Gen.* X. 5); the words "and Joseph shall lay his hand upon thine eyes" (Gen 46:4) signify that the true Joseph is Christ who opens the eyes of the blind men of Jericho (Mt 20:34) by touching them with his hands (*Hom. Gen.* XV. 7); the death of Joseph coincided with the multiplication of Israel as the death of Christ ushered in the increase of the Church (*Hom. Ex.* 1.4); and our Lord Jesus Christ is indeed the true Moses and real Lawgiver (*Hom. Num.* VII. 2)."[34]

The belief that single verses, and even single words, of Scripture contained meanings hidden deep beneath the literal sense filled his homilies with uncontrolled allegory at times: here is the point of departure from biblical typology which prompted, perhaps, the exaggerations of medieval allegorism. Thus it is by reason of the Philonian impact on his thought that Origen sees a spiritual sense in each and every passage of Scripture and that some of his allegorical expositions become fantastic:

> XV. 34[35] Someone will ask how it is that it is not only to those who are idle but to those who have remained standing all day, that is, all the time up to the eleventh hour,

[34]Daniélou, J. *Gospel Message and Hellenistic Culture*. p. 275
[35]Text: PG. 13. 1352.

> that the master, when he came out, said at about the eleventh hour: Why stand ye here all the day idle? I sense that there is hidden here a secret teaching on the subject of the soul, when it said that they had done nothing all day until the eleventh hour, even though they wished, as they affirm, to work in the vineyard, and said that no one had hired them ... (but) ... the master hired them, because they remained patiently standing all day, and waited for someone to come to hire them in the evening. (*Comm. Matt.*)

In this way Origen transformed the careful philological scrutiny of exegesis into an uninhibited spiritualization: "the dearly loved child has many names, according to Origen; the hidden meaning must be discovered, one must reflect more carefully, one must think deeper and higher, one must see the divine, the inexpressible. As far as external form was concerned, the Roman and Greek laws were vastly superior to the laws which God himself had given the chosen people: only the spiritual interpretation could make the superiority of the divine law evident. Thus the oxen in the text must be a sign of earthly desires, the sheep, of foolish thoughts, and doves, of dangerous fancies. Thus the account of how Rebecca came to the well included a profound lesson on how man must daily come to the well of the Scripture and draw out the overflow of the Spirit." Brilioth, *op. cit.*, 24.

4. THE HOMILETICAL DIMENSION

The familiar and direct style of Origen, in sharp contrast to the Second Sophistic of his day, came to be a distinguishing mark of his preaching. This style is basically that of the diatribe, formed through usage by Jewish Rabbi and Christian Prophet to proclaim the Word of God. The simplicity of this form suited the urgency of Origen's message as he strove with zeal to reach every level of his congregation—"sinners who must be brought to repent; simple Christians content to obey the commandments; souls hungry for perfection and needing guidance; true friends of God who are already alive to spiritual things." To all these various levels Origen adapted his message and his utterance:

> 1. 4.[36] To adapt certain scriptural texts to beginners, others to those whose faith in Christ is already advanced, others to those who are already perfect in charity—that is to cut the victim limb by limb. Those who are little children in Christ should be taught with the milk of the Word, those who are weak in faith should gather strength from more solid nourishment, while the athletes of Christ require strong meat: the true *didaskolos* or preacher is he who with spiritual understanding cuts those things one by one. (*Hom. Lev.*)

Again:

> 4. 3.[37] A priest is one who has the secret vessels, i.e. the secrets of the mysteries of wisdom, entrusted to him. He ought to take a lesson from them and realize that he should keep them behind the veil of his conscience and not be too ready to show them in public. If circumstances require him to transmit them to the initiated, he should not present them without some concealment or he will be committing homicide and destroying the people. (*Hom. Num.*)

Elsewhere, the same idea occurs:

> 12. 7.[38] The homilists are those who dispense God's Word in the Church. They should therefore listen to make sure that they will not be entrusting God's Word to the polluted . . . in simple faith they should choose souls that are

[36]Text: PG. 12. 410.
[37]Text: SC. 29. 106.
[38]Text: PG. 12. 543.

> pure and virgin . . . and confide to them the secret mysteries, the Word of God and the hidden truths of the faith . . . that Christ may be formed in them by faith. (*Hom. Lev.*)

Again:

> 23. 5.[39] Perhaps the story of the publican has a more eminent meaning according to anagogy. But I do not know that I ought to expose anything so mysterious to my present hearers, especially to people who do not penetrate to the marrow of the scriptures, but are content to taste their surface. (*Hom. Lk.*)

This concern to adapt the message of the Scriptures to the spiritual capacity of his congregation must have spared him the temptation of floundering in the rhetoric of the Second Sophistic:

> 1. 10.[40] I readily impart to you an idea which a wise and faithful man gave me and which often occurs to my mind: of God it is dangerous to speak even truthfully. For it is not only the false that is dangerous but also the true; if it be spoken with exaggeration. (*Hom. Ez.*)

Gregory Thaumaturgos, his most famous student, is likewise his greatest witness on this point:

> XIII.[41] Origen deemed it right for us to study philosophy in such wise that we should read with utmost diligence all that has been written, both by the philosophers and the poets of old; yet he was wary of rhetoric and its fascination. (*Panegyric.*)

[39]Text: SC. 87. 316.

[40]Text: GCS. VIII. 444.

[41]Text: SC. 148. 158.

Accordingly, the outline, disposition and external form of Origen's homilies are simple and without any trace of rhetorical elaboration. The conversational tone is predominant, and the surviving homilies betray the marks of the spoken word as it was taken down by stenographers. Unlike the *Peri Pascha* of Melito of Sardis, there is simply no evidence of any rhetorical adornment in Origen, much less the more pronounced influence of the Second Sophistic. Thus the term 'homily' itself took on after him the technical meaning of an explanation of a scriptural passage and the verse-by-verse explanation that his exegetical method required has become known as "the first form" of homily, or "the lower homily," or "the versicular homily." Spoken within the liturgical assembly for the edification of that assembly, his homily has a very clear structure of exordium, mystical exegesis of a scriptural text, practical application, and final exhortation.

Conclusion

In his day Origen was indeed an acknowledged master in Christendom. Through him exegesis and preaching were so united that for long afterwards they remained one and the same. As preacher and exegete he was the foremost homilist of history's Christian mystery. For him, preaching was in reality a spiritual ministry in which the preacher was only an instrument and the active power was God's grace. Consequently men of little eloquence could touch the heart while learned men might leave it cold. Thus Origen distinguished with one stroke the real substance of Christian preaching and the subordinate role of the preacher. Gregory Thaumaturgos is again his witness:

> XV. D.[42] He used to interpret and explain all obscurities and difficulties as they occurred—and there are many of them in the Holy Scriptures, whether it is that God

[42]Text: PG. 10. 1093.

> decided to conceal certain things by that means, or whether we only find obscure what is not so in itself. Of all men now living, I have never known or heard of one who had meditated as he had on the pure and luminous words and had become so expert at fathoming their meaning and teaching them to others. I do not think he could have done that unless he had had the Spirit of God in him, for the same grace is needed for understanding the prophecies as for making them. No one can understand the prophets unless the Spirit who inspired the prophets himself gives him understanding of his word. The divine Logos opens what he had shut up when he enables us to understand the mysteries. Origen possessed the sovereign gift, which he got from God, of being the interpreter of God's words to men. He had the power to listen to God and understand what he said, and then to explain it to men that they too might understand. (*Panegyric*)

Something more of Gregory's admiration for his master can be heard in the opening paragraph of the *Panegyric Addressed to Origen* by Gregory before departing the school at Alexandria and becoming the founder of the Church at Cappadocia:

> VI. B.[43] Like some spark being kindled within my soul there was kindled and blazed forth in me my love both toward Him, the Word Holy and Wonderful, and toward this man Origen, his friend and prophet. Deeply stricken by it, I was led to neglect all that seemed to concern me: affairs, studies, even my favorite study of law, home and friends, no less than those among whom I was sojourning. One thing only was dear to me and consumed me: philosophy and its teacher, this divine man, Origen. (*Panegyric*)

[43]Text: PG. 10. 1072.

3. The Greek Homily In The Fourth Century

The Peace of Constantine in 313 brought the Church into a new set of circumstances which greatly affected the character of her preaching, as the liturgy, of which the homily was an integral, if loose-fitting, part, became more developed and well-defined. Several factors contributed to this development. In the first place, the increased number of catechumens brought about a clear distinction between the liturgy of the catechumens and the liturgy of the faithful. Secondly, the theological controversies of the age, trinitarian and christological, were naturally aired in the pulpit. Thirdly, to the same degree that prophecy definitely had become silent in this era, preaching became the official act of the bishop, who sometimes delegated the responsibility to the presbyters. Fourthly, as the Church year grew complete in her liturgical seasons and in the various festivals of saints and martyrs, there arose the need for thematic preaching and panegyrics. Finally, the appointment as bishops of men who had once studied in the ancient schools of rhetoric, and the spacious new buildings in which they addressed their large congregations were twin factors that called for new and more vigorous forms of eloquence. It now remains to illustrate these new features of preaching, namely, the rhetorical, thematic, catechetical and mystagogical, from the most prominent preachers of this new age, and to show the change in the exegetical homily of the third century which automatically followed.

1. The Rhetorical Dimension

GREGORY NAZIANZUS (329-389)

In the Greek Church during the 4th Century, Sacred Eloquence reached a summit (never surpassed in subsequent ages) in the province of Cappadocia which produced Basil of Caesarea (c. 330-379), his friend Gregory of Nazianzus (c. 329-389), and his brother Gregory of Nyssa (c. 330-395) known as "the Three Great Cappadocians." These men had been trained in the schools of the rhetors, and accordingly carried with them into the pulpit that extraordinary facility of extempore speech and that florid exuberance of style which characterized the Asiatic School more than the sober Attic. Gregory of Nazianzus, the most fascinating, perhaps, of all the Greek Fathers, is the great example.

Born the son of wealthy aristocratic family in Cappadocia, he might well be called the humanist among the theologians of the 4th Century as he was also called their greatest poet. In Byzantine times he was called "the Christian Demosthenes," and his literary bequest of orations, poems and letters has fascinated scholars for over a thousand years, especially the humanists of the Renaissance. His varied career is much more colorful than successful as, in that world of theological controversy, ecclesiastical intrigue and political unrest, he moves, and is moved, from the episcopal palace of his father in Nazianzus to his own Byzantine patriarchal chair in Constantinople. From Constantinople he returned to his hometown, broken and disappointed by his experience as Patriarch, and finally he retreated for the last years of his life to the isolation of an Anchorite and his literary pursuits on his family's estate at Arianzus. His entire life was one of flight to and from the world, as if he had neither the will nor the inclination to cope with its machinations, and, in so far as he had any success, he owed it chiefly to the power of his eloquence.

The Funeral Oration

His mastery of the rhetorical tradition can be seen at its best in the funeral oration which is one of the most elaborate of Christian literary forms, It represents an attempt to adapt to Christian usage a pagan form with many hundreds of years of tradition behind it; a form which in itself is only one example of the literary genre known as the Encomium. This genre developed out of the praise of those that had fallen in battle. The famous funeral speech of Pericles as presented by Thucydides (c. 450 BC) is probable the earliest extant example of this *epitaphios logos*, "epitaph" for the dead, whose schema or basic structure may be presented as follows: (1) Exordium or Introduction; (2) Encomium or Laudation proper, combined with lament and developed under the following headings—family, birth, upbringing, education, natural gifts, moral qualities, achievements, fortune, and especially comparison with the great and famous; (3) Final Exhortation and Prayer. In the Greek schools of rhetoric this form was much cultivated, especially in the second half of the fourth century A.D., when it was taught in theory and in practice at Athens, Constantinople, Antioch and other centers by such famous sophists as Libanius, Himerius and Themistius. Libanius, the most famous rhetorician of his age, was undoubtedly one of the principal teachers of Gregory Nazianzus in rhetoric as he was also of Julian the Apostate. It is not surprising, then, to find the influence of the pagan Encomium so marked in the first great Christian funeral orations, of which Gregory is the great exponent.

The Greek treatise on grief or consolation was a closely related genre and had a profound influence on the development and content of the funeral oration. Although many of the great Greek philosophers, including Plato and Aristotle, dealt with the problem of death and the possibility of consolation, the first treatise on grief as such was written in the fourth century B.C. by a certain Crantor. Throughout antiquity this work was regarded as the most comprehensive and model of its kind. His treatise was cast in the form of a letter to a certain Hippocles on the death of his children, and, both in form and in content, it exercised a great influence on all later works on the consolation theme.

Gregory's funeral orations reflect both these dimensions, laudation and consolation, but, at the same time, also exhibit modifications and new elements which give them their specific Christian character with their emphasis on Christ, the resurrection of the body and life everlasting. The commonplaces of the Greek funeral oration, even when influenced by the consolation literature, were on the whole, little more than a litany of platitudes. On the other hand, Christians in their divine scriptures possessed a consolation literature of unique power and beauty, one that enjoyed unique authority as the Word of God and gave new life to the old forms. In this field of adaptation, Gregory Nazianzus was a pioneer and there are extant four of his orations: (1) On his brother, Caesarius; (2) On his sister, Gorgonia; (3) On his father, Gregory the Elder, Bishop of Nazianzus; and (4) On his friend, Basil the Great, Bishop of Caesarea—the masterpiece of Christian Greek funeral orations.

The *Oration on Caesarius* follows the classical structure of Exordium, Encomium and Conclusion. In the Exordium or introduction, he introduces the notion of grief and consolation:

> VII. 1.[1] Perhaps you think, my friends and brethren and parents, ... that I eagerly undertake this address, and that I intend to pour forth lamentations ... We shall not lament the departed more than is proper, since we do not approve of such pagan excess; nor shall be bestow immoderate and unmerited praise. Yet, for an orator, who particularly loved my speeches, a eulogy would be, if anything could, a dear and brotherly gift. But in our tears

[1]Text: PG. 35.756

> and admiration we must observe the law concerning such matters, and this is in full accord with out philosophy which says: "The memory of the just is with praises," and "Shed tears over the dead, and begin to lament as if thou hadst suffered some great harm." Thus we are equally free from insensibility and immoderation.

Then follows the extended Encomium in praise of ancestry and parentage; physical endowments; upbringing and education; occupation and achievements; his struggles against Julian, the Apostate Emperor, and other enemies of the Church. The following excerpt in praise of his father is typical of his message and manner of presentation:

> VII. 3.[2] Our father was well engrafted from the wild olive into the cultivated olive, and so much did he share its richness that the engrafting of others and the care of souls was entrusted to him. Holding high office, and in a becoming manner, he presided over his people, a second Aaron or Moses, considered worthy to draw near to God and impart the divine voice to those standing far off. He was gentle, not given to anger, of a calm mein, warm in spirit, rich in externals, but richer still in what is hidden from the eye. Why should I describe one who you know? Even if I should make an extended speech, I could not do justice to the subject and give an account satisfactory to the knowledge and demands of each of you.

In the Encomium nothing worthy of praise is forgotten: even the performance of Caesarius, the student, in his public debate with the young Emperor Julian in the school of Alexandria, "a workshop of all kinds of learning," is remembered and magnified:

[2]Text: PG. 35.757

> VII. 12.[3] Caesarius was not terrified at the sight, . . . The masters of the contest were no less present: on one side Christ, arming His athlete with His own sufferings; on the other the dread tyrant, fawning upon him by the familiarity of his words and terrifying him by the weight of his power. The spectators on both sides, those who yet remained on the side of piety and those who were snatched from it, were also looking down to see how the contest would go and who would conquer, and they were in greater anxiety than they upon whom they gazed . . .
>
> I should like above all to present each single point of what was stated and proposed at the time but this would be wholly outside the scope of this occasion and this discourse. When Caesarius had foiled all his verbal subtleties, pushing them aside as child's play, he proclaimed in a loud and clear voice that he was a Christian and would so remain.

In conclusion Gregory contrasts "the vanity of the flesh" with "the worth of the soul" and addresses Caesarius directly with these words:

> VII. 16.[4] This, Caesarius, is my funeral offering to you. These are the first fruits of my oratory . . . This is your adornment at my hands, and it is to you, I well know, the dearest of all adornments. It is not the soft flowing folds of silk, in which, even while alive, you did not delight after the manner of most men, since you were adorned with virtue alone; . . . Away with libations, and first fruits, and garlands, and freshly plucked flowers, with which the pagans honor their dead, following ancestral law and unreasoning grief rather than reason! My gift is a speech. Perhaps even future time will keep it, and it will

[3]Text: PG. 35. 769

[4]Text: PG. 35. 773

> continue to live, and will not suffer the departed to be utterly gone, but will ever preserve our honored brother in men's ears and souls, setting forth more clearly than pictures the image of our beloved.

The consolation motif then appears with the light of Christian faith dispelling the darkness of the pagan commonplace:

> VII. 18.[5] What yet remains? Through words to offer consolation to the mourners . . .
>
> Let us not, then, bewail Caesarius, knowing from what evils he had his release, but ourselves, knowing to what evils we have been left . . . Let us look at the matter thus: Caesarius will not rule? No, but neither will he be ruled by others . . . He will not gather wealth? No, but neither will he suffer loss to his soul by always seeking to acquire as much again as he has acquired . . . He will not study the works of Hippocrates and Galen and their adversaries? No, but neither will he be afflicted by diseases or experience personal grief at others' misfortunes . . . He will make no display of the doctrines of Plato or Aristotle . . . No, but neither will he be worried about solving their specious arguments.

The oration ends with a prayer which reflects the authentic liturgical spirit of that age with its recognition and praise of the creative Word:

> VII. 24.[6] O Lord and Maker of all, and especially of this body of ours! O God and Father and Pilot of your own mankind! O Master of life and death! O Guardian and Benefactor of our souls! O you maker of every season by your creative Word, receive Caesarius now, the first fruits

[5]Text: PG. 35. 776.

[6]Text: PG. 35. 788

> of our pilgrimage! And if the last is first, we yield to your Word, by which the universe is ruled. And receive us also afterwards in due time, having directed us in the flesh as long as it is for our advantage. And receive us, ready and not troubled by fear of you, nor turning away in our last days, nor forcibly drawn from things of earth, as is the misfortune of souls loving the world and the flesh, but eagerly drawn to the heavenly life, everlasting and blessed, which is in Christ Jesus our Lord, to whom be glory forever and ever. Amen.

But it is in his *Funeral Oration on St. Basil* that Gregory shows his complete mastery of the genre and his originality in adapting it to a most independent and specifically Christian use. The pagan funeral oration is here transformed into a masterpiece of Christian eloquence in which the pagan elements do not assume undue importance but are harmoniously subordinated to Christian use. Again the following excerpts will illustrate the traditional structure and style of the oration on the one hand and the new Christian elements or dimensions on the other hand. The Exordium is typical of the rhetorical structure:

> 43. 1.[7] It was inevitable that the great Basil, who constantly used to furnish me with subjects for my discourses . . . should now present me in the person of himself with the loftiest theme ever given to those who have engaged in oratory . . . So difficult a task is the eulogy of this man, not only for myself, who long ago put aside all love of glory, but even for those who have devoted their lives to eloquence, and made their one and only object the gaining of distinction from subjects such as this . . . Yet I do not know in what subject I could be eloquent if not in this, or in what better way I could satisfy myself, or the admirers of virtue, or eloquence itself, than by honoring such a

[7]Text: PG. 36. 493

> man. For myself, it will be a convenient way of paying a debt that is due. And, surely, a discouse is due above all else to those who have excelled especially in eloquence.

On this occasion, the Encomium was long and extended and may be analysed as follows: in praise of the ancestors of Basil; their piety and its proofs; his parents; physical endowments; his education in Caesarea, Cappadocia, Constantinople, and Athens; his life as a priest; his persecution—struggle compared to Joseph's; his election as bishop and conception of the office; his administration of his church; his moral qualities—poverty, austerity, celibacy, solicitude for the poor and sick; his intellectual qualities—eloquence, writings and teachings; finally there are extended comparisons with more than twenty biblical characters from Adam to St. Stephen. The following selected and truncated excerpts from the Encomium are indicative to some degree of what he had to say and of the manner in which he said it:

(a) In praise of Basil's ancestors:

> 43. 3.[8] On his father's side, Pontus furnishes us with many stories in no way inferior to the ancient wonders of that place in which all history and poetry abound. Many, too, are furnished by this, my native land, noble Cappadocia, goodly nurse of youth no less than horses. Hence, we can match his mother's family with that of his father. As for military commands, high civil offices, and power in imperial courts, and again, as to wealth and lofty thrones and public honors, and splendors of eloquence, what family has been more often, or more highly, distinguished?

[8]Text: PG. 36. 497

(b) In praise of Basil, the man:

> 43. 10.[9] Let me now proceed to Basil himself, stating at the outset . . . that his own voice itself would be required to eulogize him. For he is at once a magnificent subject for eulogy and the only one with powers of eloquence adequate to deal with it. Beauty, and strength, and size, in which I see most men delight, I shall leave to those who are interested in them . . . I therefore shall proceed to praise what no one will consider either superfluous or outside the scope of my discourse.

(c) In praise of Basil's training:

> 43. 23[10] Who was like him in rhetoric, though his character differed from that of the rhetoricians? Who was like him in grammar, which makes us Greeks in language, which composes history, which presides over meters, and makes laws for poems? Who was like him in philosophy, that truly sublime science which soars aloft, . . . As for astronomy, geometry, and mathematics, he was content with a knowledge sufficient to avoid being confused by those who were clever in these sciences. Anything beyond that he scorned as useless for those who wished to lead a pious life.

(d) In praise of Basil, the Bishop:

> 43. 37.[11] As he had previously shown himself to surpass others, he now appeared to surpass himself . . . For he thought that the virtue of a private individual consisted in avoiding vice and being good in a certain measure, but that in a ruler and chief it was a vice, especially in such an office as his, if he did not far surpass most men, manifest

[9]Text: PG. 36. 508
[10]Text: PG. 36. 528
[11]Text: PG. 36. 548

constant progress, and raise his virtue to the height demanded by his dignity and throne ...

(e) In praise of Basil's sense of duty:

43. 59.[12] For, while in general I admire this man far more than I can say, of this one thing I cannot approve, I mean his strangeness and distrust toward me, a cause of pain which not even time has effaced. This has been responsible for all the inconsistency and confusion in my life ... He recognized the respect due to friendship and he disregarded it only where the honor of God had prior claim and when he had to esteem the object of our hopes as more important than what he set aside.

(f) In praise of Basil's asceticism:

61. 1.[13] A great thing is virginity and celibacy—a state to be ranked with that of the angels; I shrink from saying with Christ's, who, having willed to be born for us who are born, was born of a virgin, giving the force of law to virginity to detach us from this life and cut off the world, or, rather, to put away one world for another, the present for the future. Who, more than he, either esteemed virginity or imposed laws on the flesh, not only by his own example but by the objects of his zeal? Whose are the convents and the written rules by which he subjected all the senses and regulated all the members, and urged the practice of true virginity, turning the eye of beauty inward, from the visible to the invisible, ... showing what is hidden to God, who alone is the pure bridegroom of souls, ...

The conclusion of this oration is typical in that it gives vent to the sorrow of death on the one hand, and expresses

[12]Text: PG. 36. 572

[13]Text: PG. 36. 576

the consolation of Christian Exhortation and Prayer on the other hand:

> 81.[14] Come hither, now, and stand about me, all you who made up his choir, ... assist me in my eulogy, ... Let those of you who have supreme authority consider the lawgiver; you public officials, the founder of the city; you of the people, his orderliness; you men of letters, the teacher; you virgins, the groom; you married people, the counselor; you hermits, him who gave you wings; you cenobites, the judge; you who are simple and sincere, your guide; you contemplatives, the theologian; you exuberant souls, the bridle; you unfortunate, your consolation; old age, its staff; youth, its preceptor; poverty, its relief; wealth, its dispenser. It seems to me also that widows should praise their protector, orphans their father, the poor, the lover of the poor, strangers, their host; brothers, the lover of brothers; the sick, their physician, ... the healthy, the guardian of their health; and, finally, all men, him who became all things to all men that he might gain all, or at least as many as possible ... This Basil, ... is my discourse in your honor.

The Second Oecumenical Council was held in Constantinople in 381, while Gregory was Patriarch. His episcopacy of the local church during the two previous years made this Council possible, for his eloquence in the *Five Orations on the Divinity of the Logos* had silenced that Arian city. But the politics of the Council occasioned not only his immediate retirement but also his famous oration, the Last Farewell, delivered before the general congregation of Fathers and people:

> 42. 26.[15] Farewell, ye lovers of my discourses, ... Farewell, Emperors, and palace, and ministers, and household of the Emperor, whether faithful or not to him, I

[14]Text: PG. 36. 604

[15]Text: PG. 36. 492

> know not, but, for the most part, unfaithful to God ... This pestilent and garrulous tongue has ceased to speak to you ... Farewell, mighty Christ-loving city ... Our separation renders us more kindly. Approach the truth: be converted at this late hour. Honor God more than you have been wont to do. It is no disgrace to change, while it is fatal to cling to evil ... Last of all, and most of all, I will cry, ... Farewell, O Trinity, my meditation, and my glory. May you be preserved by those who are here, and preserve them, my people: for they are mine, even if I have my place assigned elsewhere; and may I learn that you are ever extolled and glorified in word and conduct.

Gregory represents, to a certain extent, the flowering of an art which had found in the Christian message a worthier theme than the fanciful topics of pagan times on which it had so long spent itself. He was not, however, unaware of the dangers of this sophistic style whose rhetorical exaggerations and pagan dependence can be seen to a much greater degree in the orations of his friend and colleague, Gregory of Nyssa; at times, however, he is equally guilty of these same aberrations.

2. The Thematic Dimension

GREGORY OF NYSSA

In the middle of the 4th Century, controversy raged over the nature of Christ and the Holy Spirit, and consequently about the triune nature of God Himself. Inevitably such controversy was carried over into the pulpit and as a result the exegetical homily took second place to this new need for doctrinal exposition and rhetorical expression. Gregory of Nyssa was the least of the three great Cappadocians as a preacher but the most versatile and successful of them as a theologian and writer: consequently his homilies, more than those of his brother and friend, reflect the Platonic thought and sophistic rhetoric of his pagan contemporaries. Born in Caesarea about 335 in a family no less renowned for its Christian spirit than for its nobility and wealth, he spent his early married years as a teacher of rhetoric and the later part of his life as the Bishop of Nyssa.

His preaching is of varying value both in content and in form, but is nonetheless representative of the new approach to preaching in his day. Among the large number of surviving homilies are, in the first place, his *Homilies on the Canticle of Canticles*, in which there is high praise for the mystical exegesis of Origen; secondly, Panegyrics on Martyrs and Saints, and Funeral Orations with their fondness for rhetorical ornamentation; thirdly, moral and ascetical homilies, which are the most natural and unaffected; fourthly, dogmatic homilies, dealing with the divinity of Christ and the Holy Spirit; and finally, the festal homilies which are devoted to the solemn days of the ecclesiastical year including Christmas, Epiphany, Easter, Ascension and Pentecost. All of these homilies emphasize the thematic approach, and the allegorical method of exegesis is used in support of the theme to the extent that exegesis is invoked. Even the festal homilies reflect this tendency as can be seen in the sermon *On the Baptism of Christ*: "a homily for the Day of Lights," which was probably delivered on the feast of the Epiphany 383. Here the extempore nature of his rhetoric can be heard in the Exordium, in which he expresses his joy at the crowded congregation on this occasion which fills him "with enthusiasm and eagerness to preach":

> 1.[16] But when things are otherwise, and you are straying in distant wanderings, as you did but lately, the last Lord's Day, I am much troubled, and glad to be silent; and I consider the question of flight from hence, and seek for the Carmel of the prophet Elijah, or some rock with-

[16]Text: PG. 46. 577

> out inhabitant; for men in depression naturally choose loneliness and solitude. But now, when I see you thronging here with all your families, I am reminded of the prophetic saying, which Isaiah proclaimed from afar off, addressing by anticipation the Church with her fair and numerous children:—"Who are these that fly as a cloud, and as doves with their young to me?" (Isa 60:8)

The notion of a theme or topic for the particular festival dominates his approach and baptism is the theme chosen for this feast of the Epiphany:

> [17] Therefore let us leave the other matters of the Scriptures for other occasions, and abide by the topic set before us, offering, as far was we may, the gifts that are proper and fitting for the feast: for each festival demands its own treatment . . . Christ, then, was born as it were a few days ago . . . Today He is baptized by John that He might bring the Spirit from above, and exalt man to heaven, . . .

Renovation and regeneration, purification and remission, innocence and rebirth—such are the divine realities prefigured by Christ for Jew and Gentile alike:

> [18] Baptism, then, is a purification from sins, a remission of trespasses, a cause of renovation and regeneration. By regeneration, understand regeneration conceived in thought, not discerned by bodily sight. For we shall not, according to the Jew Nicodemus and his somewhat dull intelligence, change the old man into a child, nor shall we form anew him who is wrinkled and gray-headed to tenderness and youth, if we bring back the man again into his mother's womb: but we do bring back, by royal grace,

[17]Text: PG. 46. 580
[18]Text: PG. 46. 580

> him who bears the scars of sin, and had grown old in evil habits, to the innocence of the babe ... And this gift is not bestowed by the water, but by the command of God, and the visitation of the Spirit that comes sacramentally to set us free.

His incarnational approach to the sacraments stresses on the one hand their natural significance and on the other hand the importance of the biblical word of revelation. Consequently he invokes the notion of ontological signification without enunciating the principle and thus avoids all discussion on the "how" of sacramental efficacy:

> [19] ... water, though it is nothing else than water, renews the man to spiritual regeneration, when the grace from above hallows it. And if any one answers me by continually asking and inquiring how water and the sacramental act that is performed therein regenerate, I most justly reply to him, ... How does heaven exist? how earth? how sea? how every single thing? For everywhere men's reasoning, perplexed in the attempt at discovery, falls back upon this syllable "how," as those who cannot walk fall back upon a seat. To speak concisely, everywhere the power of God and His operation are incomprehensible, and incapable of being reduced to rule, easily producing whatever He wills, while concealing from us the minute knowledge of His operation.

This incarnational emphasis draws him more deeply into the typological setting of the sacramental rites and accordingly he sees baptism prefigured in a great many Old Testament events including the contest of Elijah with the priests of Baal: "vainly praying and crying aloud to non-existing gods" for the power to sacrifice without fire:

[19]Text: PG. 46. 584

> [20] For he did not simply by prayer bring down the fire from heaven upon the wood when it was dry, but exhorted and enjoined the attendants to bring abundance of water. And when he had thrice poured out the barrels upon the cleft wood, he kindled at his prayer the fire from out of the water, that by the opposition of the elements, concurring in a friendly cooperation, he might show with superabundant force the power of his own God. Now herein, by that wondrous sacrifice, Elijah clearly proclaimed to us the sacramental rite of Baptism that should afterwards be instituted. For the fire was kindled by water thrice poured upon it, so that it is clearly shown that where the mystic water is, there is the Kindling, warm and fiery Spirit, that burns up the ungodly, and illuminates the faithful.

These Old Testament types of baptism in deeds and acts he distinguishes from Old Testament prophecies of it in word and language:

> [21] Let us for the rest consider the prophecies of it in words and language. Isaiah cried saying, "Wash you, make you clean, put away evil from your souls"; and David, "Draw nigh to Him and be enlightened, and your faces shall not be ashamed." And Ezekiel, writing more clearly and plainly than them both, says, "And I will sprinkle clean water upon you, and ye shall be cleansed: from all your filthiness, and from all your idols, will I cleanse you. A new heart also will I give you, and a new spirit will I give you: and I will take away the stony heart out of your flesh, and I will give you a heart of flesh, and my Spirit will I put within you." Most manifestly also does Zechariah prophesy of Joshua, who was clothed with the filthy garment (to wit, the flesh of a servant, even ours), and stripping him of his ill-favored raiment adorns him with the clean

[20]Text: PG. 46. 592

[21]Text: PG. 46. 593

> and fair apparel; teaching us by the figurative illustration that verily in the Baptism of Jesus all we, putting off our sins like some poor and patched garment, are clothed in the holy and most fair garment of regeneration. And where shall we place that oracle of Isaiah, which cries to the wilderness, "Be glad, O thirsty wilderness: let the desert rejoice and blossom as a lily: and the desolate places of Jordan shall blossom and shall rejoice"? For it is clear that it is not to places without soul or sense that he proclaims the good tidings of joy: But he speaks, by the figure of the desert, of the soul that is parched and unadorned, even as David also, when he says, "My soul is unto Thee as a thirsty land," and, "My soul is athirst for the mighty, for the living God."

Application and exhortation then follow by way of conclusion: "let you all, as many as are made glad by the gift of regeneration, show me after the sacramental grace, the change in your ways that should follow it."

> [22] The man that was before Baptism was wanton, covetous, grasping at the goods of others, a reviler, a liar, a slanderer, and all that belongs to these things, and comes from them. Let him now become orderly, sober, content with his own possessions, and imparting from them to those in poverty, truthful, courteous, affable—in a word, following every laudable course of conduct. For as darkness is dispelled by light, and black disappears as whiteness is spread over it, so the old man also disappears when adorned with the works of righteousness.

The final note is an extended doxology in which the *magnalia* or *mirabilia Dei* are proclaimed and proposed as the object of our praise and thanksgiving, from Adam "cowering in the thicket of Paradise . . . to the creation that was

[22]Text: PG. 46. 596

once at variance with itself but is now knit together in friendship—we men are made to join in the Angels' song."

> [23] For all these things then let us sing to God that hymn of joy, which lips touched by the Spirit long ago sang loudly: "let my soul be joyful in the Lord: for He hath clothed me with a garment of salvation, and hath put upon me a robe of gladness: as on a bridegroom He hath set a mitre upon me, and as a bride hath He adorned me with fair array." And verily the Adorner of the bride is Christ, Who is, and was, and shall be, blessed now and for evermore. Amen.

In his five homilies *On the Lord's Prayer*, and eight homilies *On the Beatitudes*, there is the same development of theme and allegorical approach to the scriptures but they lack the congregational contact of the baptismal homily for the *Day of Lights* and were doubtfully ever delivered in Church; nonetheless they give a very definite picture of Gregory: "it is that of a man thoroughly conversant with human nature in general and the needs of his contemporaries in particular; not a desert father living in isolation from the world around him, but steeped in its culture and interested in all it has to offer. At the same time, the former rhetor has found that, attractive though this world may often be, the only goal worth living for is the Kingdom of Heaven; and having become a bishop and shepherd of souls, he uses all his powers and knowledge to imbue others with the same conviction," Hilda Graef.

In Gregory of Nyssa the simple and direct exegesis of Origen has been abandoned and the homily moves in the direction of the synthetic method of a later date, taking its theme from liturgical practice, pastoral needs or theological controversy: accordingly it may be trinitarian, christological, pneumatic, sacramental or ascetical.

[23]Text: PG. 46. 600

3. The Catechetical and Mystagogical Dimensions

CYRIL OF JERUSALEM

The peculiar circumstances of the 4th Century after the Peace of Constantine in 313 occasioned the catechumenate as a center for the instruction and formation of the new converts of the rapidly growing Church, and Lent as the appropriate season of this new formation. Under the name of Cyril, Bishop of Jerusalem, there is extant a collection of twenty-four sermons, one of the most precious treasures of Christian antiquity, addressed to the catechumens of Jerusalem on these occasions, commonly called the *Mystagogical Catecheses.* The liturgical setting in which these homilies were preached was described by Etheria, the pilgrim nun, whose diary, discovered in this century, gives the detailed account of the Holy Week liturgy of the Church in Jerusalem in the 4th Century:

> 46.[24] Then they place a chair in the Martyrium for the Bishop, and all those who are to be baptized sit in a circle around him, both men and women, and their godfathers and godmothers, and also all those who wish to hear, provided they are Christians. During these forty days, the Bishop goes through all the Scriptures, beginning with Genesis, explaining first the literal and then the spiritual sense: this is what is called catechesis. At the end of five weeks of instruction, they receive the Symbol or Creed, and its teaching is explained to them phrase by phrase, as was that of all the Scriptures; first the literal sense and then the spiritual.

The *procatechesis*, or introductory homily, which must have been preached on the first Sunday in Lent, opens with an enthusiastic welcome for the catechumens:

[24]Text: CCL. 175. 87

> [25] Already, my dear candidates for Enlightenment, scents of paradise are wafted towards you; already you are culling mystic blossoms for the weaving of heavenly garlands; already the fragrance of the Holy Spirit has blown about you; already you have arrived at the outer court of the palace: may the King lead you in! Now the blossom has appeared on the trees; God grant the fruit be duly harvested! You have walked in procession with the tapers of brides in your hands and the desire of heavenly citizenship in your hearts.

In the first five homilies the great themes of the Christian life are developed with special emphasis on the reality of sin and the devil:

> 11. 4.[26] The chief author of sin, then, is the devil, the begetter of all evil . . . This is not my teaching, but that of the inspired Prophet Ezechiel . . . "Blameless you were in your conduct from the day you were created until evil was found in you." The phrase, "was found in you," is most appropriate, for the evil was not brought in from without, but you yourself begot it.

On the other hand the creative and cleansing power of the waters of baptism is also emphasized:

> 111. 5.[27] With water the world began; the Jordan saw the beginning of the Gospel. The sea was the means of Israel's liberation from Pharaoh, and freedom for the world from sin comes through the laver of water in the Word of God. Wherever there is a covenant there also is water. After the deluge, a covenant was made with Noe; it was given from Mount Sinai, but "with water and scarlet wool and hyssop." Elias was taken up, but not without water; for first

[25]Text: PG. 33. 332

[26]Text: PG. 33. 385

[27]Text: PG. 33. 433

> he crosses the Jordan, and only then mounts to heaven in a chariot. The high priest washes himself, then offers incense; for Aaron was first washed, then became high priest. For how could one who had not yet been cleansed by water pray for others? Further, the laver had been set within the tabernacles, as a symbol of baptism.

The approach throughout these early catecheses is scriptural and the method of exegesis is allegorical. But a more doctrinal and theological approach can be seen in the body of this collection of homilies:

> V. 12.[28] In learning and professing the faith, embrace and guard that only which is now delivered to you by the Church and confirmed by all the Scriptures. For since not everyone has both the education and the leisure required to read and know the Scriptures, to prevent the soul perishing from ignorance, we sum up the whole doctrine of the faith in a few lines. This summary I wish you to commit to memory, word for word, and to repeat among yourselves with all zeal, not writing it on paper, but engraving it by memory on the heart . . . For the present, just listen and memorize the creed as I recite it, and you will receive in due course the proof from Scripture of each of its propositions. For not according to men's pleasure have the articles of faith been composed, but the most important points collected from the Scriptures make up one complete teaching of the faith. And just as the mustard seed in a small grain contains in embryo many future branches, so also the creed embraces in a few words all the religious knowledge in both the Old and the New Testament.

The rule of secrecy which was imposed on the candidates for baptism at the very beginning of those pre-baptismal instructions, called the *disciplina arcani*, surrounded the

[28]Text: PG. 33. 520

Christian sacraments in mystery in this age. Something of this mystery approach is evident in the preaching of the sacraments and can be sensed in the introductory words of Cyril, spoken on the Monday of Easter Week to his neophytes fresh from the font and still clad in their white garments of redemption:

> XIX. 1.[29] It has long been my wish, true-born and long-desired children of the Church, to discourse to you upon these spiritual, heavenly mysteries. On the principle, however, that seeing is believing, I delayed until the present occasion, calculating that after what you saw on that night I should find you a readier audience now when I am to be your guide to the brighter and more fragrant meadows of this second Eden. In particular, you are now capable of understanding the divine mysteries of divine, life-giving baptism. The time being now come to spread for you the board of more perfect instruction, let me explain the significance of what was done for you on that evening of your Baptism.

This distinctive quality, commonly called mystagogical, dominates the last five Catecheses (Nos 19-23) in which the hidden realities or mysteries of the different Rites of Initiation are revealed. In the case of each sacrament, Baptism, Confirmation, and Eucharist, Cyril first considers its figures in the Old Testament, then the symbolism of the sacramental rite in itself, and finally explains the nature of its mystery. These three aspects of his preaching, namely, scriptural, liturgical and dogmatic constitute that mystagogical development of exegetical preaching that took place in the liturgy of the 4th Century catechumenate as mystery-presence and sacramental rite are seen as one, and explained accordingly. The following examples show the preacher interpreting every aspect of the sacramental action with the same sense

[29]Text: SC. 26. 82

of typology and allegory which he heretofore applied to the scriptural word:

(a) The Mystery and Rite of Baptism

XX. 5.[30] The extraordinary thing is that we did not really die, nor were we really buried or really crucified; nor did we really rise again: this was figurative and symbolic; yet our salvation was real. Christ's crucifixion was real, His burial was real, and His resurrection was real; and all these He has freely made ours, that by sharing His sufferings in a symbolic enactment we may really and truly gain salvation. Oh, too generous love! Christ received the nails in His immaculate hands and feet; Christ felt the pain: and on me without pain or labor, through the fellowship of His pain, He freely bestows salvation.

(b) The Mystery and Rite of Confirmation

XXI. 5.[31] Once privileged to receive the holy Chrism, you are called Christians and have a name that bespeaks your new birth. Before admission to Baptism and the grace of the Holy Spirit you were not strictly entitled to this name but were like people on the way towards being Christians. You must know that this Chrism is prefigured in the Old Testament. When Moses, conferring on his brother the divine appointment, was ordering him high priest, he anointed him after he had bathed in water, and thenceforward he was called "christ" ("anointed"), clearly after the figurative Chrism ... But what was done here in figure was done to you, not in figure but in truth, because your salvation began from Him who was anointed by the Holy Spirit in truth.

[30]Text: SC. 26. 112

[31]Text: SC. 26. 128

(c) The Mystery and Rite of the Eucharist

> XXII. 3.[32] In the figure of bread this Body is given to you, and in the figure of wine His Blood, that by partaking of the Body and Blood of Christ you may become of one body and blood with Him ... Once, speaking to the Jews, Christ said: "Unless you eat my flesh and drink my blood, you can have no life in you." Not understanding His words spiritually, they "were shocked and drew back," imagining that He was proposing the eating of human flesh. The Old Covenant had its loaves of proposition, but they, as belonging to the Covenant, have come to an end. The New Covenant has its heavenly bread and cup of salvation, to sanctify both body and soul. For as the bread is for the body, the Word suits the soul. Do not then think of the elements as bare bread and wine; they are, according to the Lord's declaration, the Body and Blood of Christ. Though sense suggests the contrary, let faith be your stay. Instead of judging the matter by taste, let faith give you an unwavering confidence that you have been privileged to receive the Body and Blood of Christ ... the mystical and spiritual table which God has prepared for us.

The *Catechetical Homilies* of Theodore of Mopsuestia (d.428) lead us a little later to Antioch about the end of the century. Again the Mystery-reality of the sacramental symbol is a real feature of his preaching and can be seen especially in the three homilies on baptism and the two on the Eucharist that constitute his Mystagogical Catecheses properly so-called. But Theodore, unlike Cyril, rejects typology because he refuses to see a relationship between historic realities. Consequently he was forced to interpret sacramental symbolism in a vertical sense as the the relationship of the visible to the invisible rather than the relationship

[32]Text: SC. 26. 136

between things past and things yet to come which is the true meaning of typology. In the Eucharistic Rite, for example, he sees the heavenly sacrifice rather than the sacrifice of the Cross rendered visible in the sacrament. But we always come back to the parallelism of these two aspects. To quote Danielou:

> "Although in the food and the drink we make commemoration of the death of Our Lord, it is clear that in the liturgy it is as if we accomplished a sacrifice, without its being anything new, nor its being His own sacrifice that the Pontiff carries out, but it is a kind of image of the liturgy taking place in heaven . . . Each time, then, that the liturgy of this dread sacrifice is carried out—which is obviously the likeness of earthly realities—we must consider that we are like one who is in heaven; by faith it is the vision of heavenly realities of which we see the outlines in our understanding, considering that Christ, Who is in heaven, Who for us died, rose again, ascended into heaven; it is He Himself Who even now is immolated by means of these figures." (*The Bible and the Liturgy*, 137).

Allegory is thus his preoccupation and *ritual* imitation his discovery. Others after him will exaggerate his approach and as a result will fail to distinguished between symbolic reality and symbolic representation. Thus, we are here at the beginning of a line of sacramental preaching which would develop in the East with Cabasila and in the West with Amalarius and which laid the foundation for those disastrous expositions of the Mass and sacraments that were so popular in medieval times.

4. The Exegetical Dimension

BASIL THE GREAT

The rhetorical, thematic, catechetical and mystagogical aspects of the 4th Century preaching modified but in no way replaced completely the biblical exegesis of earlier times as can be so clearly seen, for example, in the exegetical homilies of Basil. In the *Vita Macrinae*, the life of his saintly sister, Gregory of Nyssa gives us a further insight into his remarkable family by relating in all candor how Macrina rescued her brother Basil for the ascetical life from the dangers of the rhetorical:

> 6.[33] He was puffed up beyond measure with the pride of oratory and looked down on the local dignitaries, excelling in his own estimation all like leading men of rank and position. Nevertheless, Macrina took him in hand and with such speed did she draw him also toward the love of truth that he forsook the glories of the world and despised fame gained by speaking.

Basil differs from his great contemporaries in that he did not write any scholarly commentaries on the sacred Scriptures. His exegetical skills appear in his numerous homilies, in which he also employed the artifices of ancient rhetoric in general and the devices of second sophistic in particular, especially metaphor, comparison, ecphrasis, gorgianic figures and parallelism.

More restrained, however, than the two Gregorys he is always the pastor and the prophet who wants more to preach than to please. The most notable of his homilies are the nine on the Hexaemeron which he delivered during one week in Lent, preaching sometimes in the morning and again in the evening. Considered by some to be the finest specimens of late Greek literature they are also landmarks in the history of preaching, illustrating, on the one hand, the primary place of exegesis and, on the other hand, the relative value of rhetoric. On the exegetical side he makes it clear to his congregation that he is not interested in the allegorical interpretation of scripture:

[33]Text: SC. 178. 160

[34]Text: SC. 26. 478

> IX. 1.[34] I know the laws of allegory, although I did not invent them of myself, but have met them in the works of others. Those who do not admit the common meaning of the Scriptures say that water is not water, but some other nature, and they explain a plant and a fish according to their opinion. They describe also the production of reptiles and wild animals, changing it according to their own notions, just like the dream interpreters, who interpret for their own ends, the visions seen in their dreams. When I hear "grass," I think of grass, and in the same manner I understand everything as it is said—a plant, a fish, a wild animal, and an ox.

These homilies are expositions of texts taken from the first chapter of Genesis but while the exegesis is literal, the rhetorical presentation takes flight in various directions:

> 1. 2.[35] "In the beginning God created the heavens and the earth." Astonishment at the thought checks my utterance. What shall I say first? Whence shall I begin my narration? Shall I refute the vanity of the heathens? Or shall I proclaim our truth? The wise men of the Greeks wrote many works about nature, but not one account among them remained unaltered and firmly established, for the later account always overthrew the preceding one. As a consequence, there is no need for us to refute their words; they avail mutually for their own undoing . . . It is because they did not know how to say: "In the beginning God created the heavens and the earth." They were deceived by the godlessness present within them into thinking that the universe was without guide and without rule, as if borne around by chance. In order that we might not suffer this error, he who described the creation of the world immediately in the very first words, enlightened our mind with the name of God, saying: "In the beginning

[35]Text: SC. 26. 92

> God created." How beautiful an arrangement! He placed first "the beginning," that no one might believe that it was without beginning. Then he added the word, "created," that it might be shown that what was made required a very small part of the power of the Creator . . . If, then, the world has a beginning and was created, inquire: "Who is He that gave it the beginning, and who is the Creator"? Rather, lest in seeking through human reasoning you might perhaps turn aside from the truth, Moses has taught us beforehand, imprinting upon our hearts as a seal and a security, the highly honored name of God, saying: "In the beginning God created." The blessed Nature, the bounteous Goodness, the Beloved of all who are endowed with reason, the much desired Beauty, the Origin of things created, the Fount of life, the spiritual Light, the inaccessible Wisdom, He is the One who "in the beginning created the heavens and the earth."

In spite of this obvious use or abuse of rhetoric, Basil maintains through the extempore comment that vital contact with his audience that was typical of the homilist's simplicity or conversational style:

> IX. 1.[36] How did my morning repast of words appeal to you? Indeed, it has occurred to me that I should compare my talk with the kindness of a certain poverty-stricken host, who was ambitious to be among those that offer a good table, but, lacking costly foods, annoyed his guests by laying his poor fare upon the table in such abundance that his ambition was changed in him into disgraceful lack of taste. Well, such has been our method, unless you say differently. Yet, however it was, you must not disregard it. Elisha was by no means rejected as a poor host by his contemporaries, in spite of the fact that he feasted his friends on wild plants.

[36]Text: SC. 26. 478

And again:

> III. 1.[37] It has not escaped my notice, however, that many manual workers who, with difficulty provide a livelihood for themselves from their daily toil, are gathered around us. These compel us to cut short our discourse in order they may not be drawn away too long from their work. And what do I say to them? That the portion of time lent to God is not lost; He gives it back with a great increase .... Therefore, free your heart of all solicitude for your livelihood and give yourself wholly to me. There is no advantage from mere bodily presence if the heart is busy about earthly treasure.

In these homilies Basil intends to provide a Christian conception of the world in contrast to ancient pagan notions and to Manichaeanism which was still an influence in his day. His aim is to show the Creator in all his creation, in the rhythm and forces of nature, the germination of the earth and the birds of the air as a lesson for man who alone is made in the image of God:

> VIII.5.[38] Let no one bewail his poverty; let no one who possesses little at home despair of his life, when he looks at the inventiveness of the swallow. When building her nest, she carries the dry twigs in her beak, and not being able to raise the mud in her claws, she moistens the tips of her wings with water, then rolling in the very fine dust, she thus contrives to secure the mud. After gradually fastening the twigs of wood to each other with mud as with some glue, she raises her young in this nest .... Let this warn you not to turn to evil-doing because of poverty, nor in the harshest suffering to cast aside all hope and remain idle and inactive, but to flee to God; for, if He

[37]Text: SC. 26. 190

[38]Text: SC. 26. 454

bestows such things upon the swallow, how much more will He give to those who call upon Him with their whole heart?

Again:

VIII. 5.[39] The halcyon is a sea bird. It is accustomed to build its nest along the very shores, depositing its eggs in the sand itself; and it builds its nest almost in the middle of winter, a time when the sea is being dashed against the land by violent windstorms. Nevertheless, all the winds are calmed and the waves of the sea become quiet for seven days when the halcyon is sitting upon her eggs. In exactly that number of days it hatches its young. But, since there is need of food for the nestlings so that they may grow, the bountiful God provides for the tiny creatures seven more days. As all the sailors know this, they call these the halcyon days. Divine Providence has ordained these laws concerning the irrational creature to encourage you to ask from God what pertains to your salvation.

And yet again:

VIII. 6.[40] They say that the turtledove, when once separated from her mate, no longer accepts union with another, but, in memory of her former spouse, remains widowed, refusing marriage with another. Let the woman hear how the chastity of widowhood, even among the irrational creatures, is preferred to the unseemly multiplicity of marriages. The eagle is most unjust in the rearing of her offspring. When she has brought forth two nestlings, she drops one of them to the ground, thrusting it out by blows from her wings; and, taking up the other one, she claims it alone as her own. Because of the labor

[39]Text: SC. 26. 456

[40]Text: SC. 26. 458

> of rearing it, she rejects one which she has hatched. The lammergeyer, however, as it is said, does not allow it to perish, but, taking it up, rears it along with her own nestlings. Such are those parents who expose their children on a pretext of poverty, or who are unfair to their offspring in the distribution of the inheritance . . . Do not imitate the cruelty of the birds with crooked talons, who, when they see their own nestlings already attempting flight, throw them out of the nest, striking and thrusting with their wings, and for the future take no care of them. The love of the crow for its offspring is laudable. She even accompanies them when they have begun to fly, and feeds and nurtures them for a very long time.

In the last homily he announces another on man as the image of God: "We shall tell later, if God permits, in what respect man is in the image of God and how he shares in His likeness." This homily seems never to have been delivered, but Gregory of Nyssa composed his *De hominis opificio* with the special purpose of completing his brother's work, which he admired so much: "All who have read that divinely inspired exposition of our Father on this same subject (the creation of the world as handled by Moses) admire it no less than the writing of Moses, and in my opinion they do well and remarkably."

Nor was this judgement of Gregory of Nyssa prejudiced on his brother's behalf: the high esteem with which the ancients regarded these homilies of Basil is well known and well expressed by Gregory Nazianzus:

> 43. 67.[41] Whenever I take up the Hexaemeron and read it aloud, I am with my Creator, I understand the reasons for creation, and I admire my Creator more than I formerly did when I used sight alone as my teacher . . . When I

[41]Text: PG. 36. 585

> read his other explanations of Scripture, which he unfolds for those who understand but little, writing in a threefold manner on the solid tablets of my heart, I am prevailed upon not to stop at the letter, not to view only the higher things, but to pass beyond, and to advance from depth to depth, calling upon abyss through abyss, finding light through light, until I reach the loftiest heights.

Conclusion

From this survey of 4th Century preaching it is clear that the exegetical approach of Origen and his age was greatly modified by the changing circumstances of this new age. The basic four-fold structure of preaching, already described as liturgical, prophetical, exegetical and homiletical, remained, but became more rhetorical, thematic, catechetical, mystagogical and less exegetical. Accordingly there were theological and thematic homilies to explain doctrines and events which were burning issues; panegyrics and funeral orations to proclaim the deeds of holy men and women and to sing their praises, as festivals became a part of the ever growing church year; catechetical homilies to explain the Christian religion to the crowds that came flocking into the 4th Century catechumenate, and mystagogical homilies for the faithful of the ever developing *Disciplina Arcani.* But by far the most significant of all was the fact that the preachers of this new age inherited the legacy of the recent revival of ancient rhetoric, which experienced its last great flowering in their times. Consequently, in the rhetoric of the Cappadocians, the art of Christian preaching reached a dangerous crossroads: on the one hand, it might well be termed the final incarnation of the great rhetorical tradition of antiquity as the Bible added a new message and richer imagery; on the other hand, it might just as easily be termed the first incarceration of the Judaic Christian revelation as rhetoric received a new inspiration and greater temptation.

4. St. John Chrysostom Greek Homilist *Par Excellence*

The Greek homily, shaped by the preaching of Origen and developed by the Cappadocians, was given its final form by John, the patriarch of Constantinople, appropriately known as Chrysostom, or John of the Golden Mouth (350-407). He was the very embodiment of his age and place, and in him all the tensions meet—East and West, Hellenism and Christianity, asceticism and hierarchy, ethical heroism and ecclesiastical intrigue. His sermons tell it all and they tell it in the rhetoric of the day. At Antioch he was the prize student of Libanius, the rhetor; there, he was ordained in 386 and entrusted by his aged bishop with the almost exclusive mission of preaching. There, too, he remained for 12 years and won his reputation as preacher which brought him in 397 to the Patriarchal Chair of Constantinople. In the hectic atmosphere of this atmosphere of this half-oriental world capital with its political struggles and dogmatic strifes the life of Chrysostom as preacher and champion of righteousness was both turbulent and tragic, and ended in exile and death in 407 in faraway Pontus. Thirty years later his bones were returned in triumph and he received in death the recognition he was denied in life.

1. The Preacher's Guide

The theory behind Chrysostom's conception of preaching can be clearly seen in his treatise *On the Priesthood*, in which the office of Christian preaching is analysed theologically for the first time. This short work in six books or chapters was written as an apology for his reluctance to accept ordination on account of his exalted notion of the priesthood. On such notions he built his exalted conception of the preacher which is expressed in books 4 and 5 with its recognition of the power and purpose of rhetoric. In those days in Antioch and in Constantinople rhetoric was fashionable and people thronged to hear the preachers; they applauded, or refrained from applauding if unsatisfied by the performance, and left the church before the holy mysteries were offered. It was no less, and sometimes no more, than public entertainment:

> V. 8.[1] Or do you not know what a passion for oratory has nowadays infatuated Christians? Do you not know that its exponents are respected above everyone else, not just by outsiders, but by those of the household of the faith? How, then, can anyone endure the deep disgrace of having his sermon received with blank silence and feelings of boredom, and his listeners waiting for the end of the sermon as if it were a relief after fatigue; whereas they listen to someone else's sermon, however long, with eagerness, and are annoyed when he is about to finish and quite exasperated when he decides to say no more? (*On Priesthood*).

Naturally in such an age, when training in rhetoric was taken for granted, Chrysostom in his treatise discussed the qualities of a preacher rather than the techniques of preaching. In discussing the primacy in the preacher of theological

[1]Text: PG. 48. 677

orthodoxy he attacks the "nonsense taught by Valentinus and Marcion"; "the madness of Sabellius" and "the ravings of Arius"; nor does he forget "the idle speculations" of some within the church community:

> IV. 5.[2] Need I mention the idle speculations of our own people? . . . Some people, out of restless curiosity, want to elaborate idly and irresponsibly doctrines which are of no benefit to those who understand them, or else are actually incomprehensible. . . . You will find that few are deeply concerned about faith and conduct, but the majority go in for these elaborate theories and investigate questions to which there is no answer and whose very investigation rouses God's anger. (*On Priesthood*).

Secondly, he criticizes the inactivity or laziness of others who in their mistaken interpretation of Paul's Letter to the Corinthians belittle the role of rhetoric in the defense of truth or orthodoxy:

> IV. 6.[3] To establish this fact Paul carefully made the distinction by saying that he was inadequate in speech, but not in knowledge. Now if I were demanding the polish of Isocrates, and the grandeur of Demosthenes, and the dignity of Thucydides, and the sublimity of Plato, it would be right to confront me with the testimony of Paul. But in fact I pass over all those qualities and the superfluous embellishments of pagan writers. I take no account of diction or style. Let a man's diction be beggarly, and his verbal composition simple and artless, but do not let him be inadequate in the knowledge and careful statement of doctrine. And do not let him misrepresent the apostle to cloak his own idleness. IV. 7. Tell me, how did he confound the Jews dwelling in Damascus, when he

[2]Text: PG. 48. 667

[3]Text: PG. 48. 669

> had not yet begun his miracles? How did he confute the Grecians? Why was he sent to Tarsus? . . . For at that time his only power was the power of speech.

Nevertheless rhetoric in the defense of orthodoxy is indispensable: otherwise the preacher fails his congregation:

> IV. 9.[4] That is the chief reason why anyone who has the responsibility of teaching others must be competent in the art of debates. For though he himself stands secure and is not injured by his opponents, yet, when the multitude of simple folk who are set under him see their leader unable to answer his opponents, they do not blame his rhetorical incompetence for the defeat, but his unsound doctrine. So through the incompetence of one man the whole congregation is brought to ultimate disaster.

The third quality recommended in a preacher by Chrysostom is almost a self-portrait of the Greek homilist himself and aptly described accordingly as "the contempt of praise and the power of eloquence":

> V. 2.[5] If either is lacking, the one left is made useless through divorce from the other. If a preacher despises praise, yet does not produce the kind of teaching which is "with grace, seasoned with salt," (Col 4:6) he is despised by the people and gets no advantage from his sublimity. And if he manages this side of things perfectly well, but is a slave to the sound of applause, again an equal damage threatens both him and the people, because through his passion for praise he aims to speak more for the pleasure than the profit of his hearers. The man who is unaffected by acclamation, yet unskilled in preaching, does not ruckle to the people's pleasure; but no more can he confer

[4]Text: PG. 48. 672

[5]Text: PG. 48. 673

> any real benefit upon them, because he has nothing to say. And equally, the man who is carried away with the desire for eulogies may have the ability to improve the people, but chooses instead to provide nothing but entertainment. That is the price he pays for rounds of applause.

Finally, while the ministry of the word in one sense was committed to all alike within the body, at the same time Paul acknowledged a distinct ministry of the word for priests:

> IV. 8.[6] Let the elders that rule be counted worthy of double honor, especially those who labour in the word and in teaching ... (1 Tim 5:17) ... And this statement is not mine, but the Saviour's own. For he says, 'Whosoever shall do and teach, he shall be called great.' Now if to do were the same as to teach, the second word would be superfluous ... But in fact by distinguishing the two he shows that example is one thing and instruction another, and that each requires the other for perfect edification ... 'Wherefore, watch ye, remembering that for three years I did not cease to admonish every one of you night and day with tears.' What need was there of tears or of verbal admonition, when the apostle's life shone so brightly? For the keeping of the commandments his holy life might be a great help to us ... But when conflict arises on matters of doctrine and all the combatants rely on the same scripture, what weight will his life carry then?

Thus, in the eyes of Chrysostom, preacher and priest are one, and accordingly there is a clear distinction between the preacher and the congregation:

[6]Text: PG. 48. 671

> V. 4.[7] The priest should treat those whom he rules as a father treats very young children. We are not disturbed by children's insults or blows or tears; nor do we think much of their laughter and approval. And so with these people, we should not be much elated by their praise nor much dejected by their censure, when we get these things from them out of season.

This exalted notion of the preacher and his prominence was certainly at odds with the religious indifference of the congregation and the secular nature of their expectations:

> V. 5.[8] For the congregation does not sit in judgement on the sermon as much as on the reputation of the preacher, so that when someone excels everyone else at speaking, then he above all needs painstaking care. He is not allowed sometimes not to succeed—the common experience of all the rest of humanity. On the contrary, unless his sermons always match the great expectations formed of him, he will leave the pulpit the victim of countless jeers and complaints. No one ever takes it into consideration that a fit of depression, pain, anxiety, or in many cases anger, may cloud the clarity of his mind and prevent his productions from coming forth unalloyed; and that in short, being a man, he cannot invariably reach the same standard or always be successful, but will naturally make many mistakes and obviously fall below the standard of his real ability ... If it happens that a preacher weaves among his own words a proportion of other men's flowers, he falls into worse disgrace than a common thief. And often when he has borrowed nothing at all, he suffers on bare suspicion the fate of a convicted felon. But why mention the work of others? He is not allowed to repeat his own compositions too soon. For most people usually

[7]Text: PG. 48. 674

[8]Text: PG. 48. 675

> listen to a preacher for pleasure, not profit, like adjudicators of a play or concert. The power of eloquence, is of greater demand in church than when professors of rhetoric are made to contend against each other!

Chrysostom's literary output which has survived and which illustrates his theory of preaching is still immense and consists of exegetical and expository homilies, thematic homilies, homilies for the great festivals of the Church, and eulogies in honor of the saints. All these compositions were either written to be spoken, or recorded by stenographers while they were being spoken and afterwards revised by Chrysostom himself. Unlike his contemporaries, Chrysostom was first and foremost the preacher and he wrote few theological treatises. Consequently the basic outline of the homily as identified in the work of Origen, and developed in the preaching of the Cappadocians, is everywhere visible in all Chrysostom's works. Accordingly the following dimensions can be distinguished—liturgical, prophetical, exegetical, thematic, mystagogical, and rhetorical. Such dimensions are not mutually exclusive but together they form a useful sort of map that can guide us purposefully through a vast, though not wholly uncharted, sea.

2. *The Liturgical Dimension*

The influence of the liturgy upon the homilies of Chrysostom is not obvious at first glance, for the half-instructed converts of that new Christian age were often present more for the entertainment of the occasion than for the worship of God. Their exclamations and regular applause, whenever they were pleased by the preachers' performance, is indicative of their mentality:

> II. 4.[9] The church is not just a theater, to which anyone goes to amuse himself ... what is the benefit of this

[9]Text: PG 49. 38.

> applause to me, or what does the praise and fuss profit me? It will be my praise if you transmute all my words into deeds ... (*On the Statues*)

Nevertheless, a sense of the liturgical occasion dominates in spite of the secular confusion in the homily, *I have seen the Lord*:

> I. 1.[10] In heaven, choirs of angels praise the glory of God, and here on earth, choirs of men are preparing to do the same in the life to come. There the seraphim are singing: *Holy, Holy, Holy*; here on earth the same song resounds from countless human lips. The same praise of God resounds in heaven and on earth, one and the same hymn of thanksgiving, a song of jubilee, a chorus of joy. Therefore I rejoice when I see how the praises of God are sung; I exult when I behold such piety in your hearts, such spiritual triumph, this exultation in God. Nothing makes my life so full of joy as the sight of you flocking so joyfully to the Church. In the Church the joyful will preserve their joy; in the Church the disconsolate will find courage; in the Church the troubled will become happy; in the Church the spiritually weary will find rest; in the Church, refreshment beckons to the heavy laden ...

But the liturgical assemblies at Antioch to which Chrysostom preached, like those at Constantinople over which he later presided, were as human as they were divine, and as earthly as they were heavenly. Consequently there is frequent lamentation whenever he notices a restless and distracted congregation:

> VII.[11] How can anyone with courage and with hope take upon himself the task of preaching when he sees that no fruit comes from it? Indeed my own sermons are

[10]Text: PG. 56. 97

[11]Text: PG. 48. 1045

> applauded merely out of custom because everyone rushes off to the circus immediately and gives far more applause to the jockeys, thereby displaying an entirely uncontrolled passion for them. At the circus they cuddle together and with great interest and concentration discuss their chances saying 'this horse did not run well or the other one stumbled': again one favors this jockey while another prefers the other. At any rate no one thinks about my sermons nor indeed of the holy and awesome mysteries that are celebrated in this sacred place. (*On Lazarus*)

Elsewhere there is the same lamentation:

> 41. 1.[12] It is with doubt and trepidation that I begin this day my sermon to you when I consider the fact that I preach daily and admonish you and set before you this spiritual nourishment, and that many of you who are here to partake of this very teaching, or to approach the awesome Table of the Lord, at the same time attend horse races all day, and they draw no further benefit from our celebration.

This same note of lamentation and condemnation is struck again and again; yet he always draws attention to the liturgical setting in which the sermon was preached:

> 4. 5.[13] I have no idea what I shall say to you today. I see that since the Feast of Pentecost the attendance at divine service has fallen off, the Prophets are neglected, the Apostles are little valued, the Fathers are set aside ... There is divine service once a week, and even this day you cannot spend without the cares of business. Some say they are poor and must take care of making their living, while others have urgent business. As a matter of fact the

[12]Text: PG. 54. 374

[13]Text: PG. 54. 660

> whole city is at the circus ... No poverty stands in the way there, no urgent work, no illness, no weakness of the feet, nothing of all these is able to hold back the unruly passion. The old men run with the youths to the betting in order to find a place, and expose their gray hairs to shame and ridicule. And if they occasionally come here to the Church, they experience seizures, and listening to the sermon gives them fainting spells. (*On Anna*)

There were some, according to Chrysostom, who shamelessly associated with all and sundry and brought the awesome mystery of the sacraments and liturgy into contempt. Addressing himself to such as these he warned that the Church still celebrated the mysteries behind closed doors and still forbade attendance at them by the uninitiated because the majority were not really prepared for them:

> XIX. 12.[14] For our disrespect at Divine Service, if for nothing else, we deserve to undergo the utmost punishment. For when Prophets are chanting, and Apostles singing hymns, and God is discoursing, we wander around and invite upon us a turmoil of worldly business. And we do not give to the laws of God as much respect as the spectators in the theatres give to the emperor's letters, keeping silence for them ... But here, when the letters from heaven are being read, great is the confusion on all sides. And yet both He who sent the letters is much greater than this our king, and our assembly more venerable: for not men only, but angels too are in it; and these triumphs of which the letters bear us the good tidings, are much more awful than those on earth ... Nevertheless, we make an uproar and disturbance as though we were in the midst of a public forum, and we spend the entire time of our sacred assembly discussing things that are of no value to us. (*On Matt.*)

[14]Text: PG. 57. 285

But it is in Chrysostom's understanding of the preacher as priest that the liturgical dimension of his preaching is most clearly expressed; for him the preacher is always a priest and preaching is always an exercise of that priesthood. Indeed he is consumed with this sense of being ordained to preach; consequently nothing, not even sickness, should prevent him from the exercise of his ministry.

> [15] Preaching improves me. When I begin to speak weariness disappears; when I begin to teach fatigue too disappears. Thus neither sickness itself nor indeed any other obstacle is able to separate me from your love ... For just as you are hungry to listen to me, so too I am hungry to preach to you. My congregation is my only glory and every one of you means much more to me than anyone of the city outside. (*Hom. Earthq.*)

Again:

> I. 1.[16] Did you even think of me as long as I was away from you? For my part, I have never been able to forget you. Rather your image was always before my eyes ... With me it was as it was with Solomon, for I too slept but my heart kept watch. The power of sleep closed my eyes but the power of love opened the eyes of my soul. Oftentimes in my dreams I see myself in the pulpit speaking to you ... And even though I could not see you with the eyes of my body, nevertheless I plainly saw you with the eyes of my heart ... You kept crying to me begging me to come to you and indeed urging me to break off my rest before the proper time. In fact because of you I now see health, rest and all that concerns myself in relation to you. (*On Pentecost*)

[15]Text: PG. 50. 713

[16]Text: PG. 49. 277

3. The Prophetical Dimension

If we define the prophetical element as an attempt to actualize the gospel by making the scriptural text a living work of contradiction in an actual historical situation, then we will find rich source material in Chrysostom. In the midst of a corrupt capital and at the degenerate court of the eastern emperor he was heard as such and in his different exiles and early death he received accordingly the prophet's reward. His moralism was by no means abstract for in his preaching he applied himself to the reform of his people. Accordingly his homilies reflect his mission and as a result are paranetic in their exhortation. In Chrysostom, as in the prophetical tradition, the joy and sorrow of the preaching office is everywhere felt and he corrects and encourages his audience as he would his own children:

> 31. 1.[17] With all my heart I thank you, for yesterday you listened to my exhortation on prayer so eagerly that you came with enthusiasm again to the sermon. For this gives us more courage again, and inspires us to prepare more richly this spiritual banquet. So it is with the farmer: when he sees that his field and the seed which he has sown in it bring abundant fruit, and the crops flourish, he spares himself no trouble, taking care day and night that his work shall not be in vain. So it is with me. When I see that this spiritual field stands blooming, and the spiritual seed is sown in the furrows of your souls, then I rejoice and am glad, and weary myself in the battle, because I know well the malice of my enemy, who lies in wait for your souls' health. (*On Genesis*)

Fervent admonitions were borne patiently by those who needed them least and probably lost on those in the greatest need:

[17]Text: PG. 53. 283

> 3. 1.[18] I do not have to admonish you to pay careful attention to the sermon. Your frequent visits, your unvarying attention, and the fact that you even push and shove one another in order to come as near as possible to the pulpit, (where my voice may be heard better, and that it does not even discourage you when someone treads on your feet in the crowd and you endure to the end until this spiritual drama is finished,) your loud applause and everything else, proves sufficiently what zeal animates you, and how gladly you listen to the sermon. (*Hom. John*)

His own sense of mission compels him to proclaim a sense of apostleship to his congregation:

> 1. 12.[19] I beg you for this favor as a reward for my sermon: Reform anyone in the city who curses and slanders. If you hear anyone blaspheming God on the street or in the middle of the market place, go to him and rebuke him, and if you have to beat him, do not shrink from it. Give him a slap in the face, hit him in the mouth ... and if he abuses you and brings you into court, go and say quietly to the judge, that he had insulted the King of the angels! (*Hom. Statues*)

The people of Antioch, according to Procopius, thought only of good living, and of continuous theater and circus plays. Against this paganism Chrysostom did battle with very little success and a great deal of distress:

> 6. 1.[20] I am disconsolate, discouraged and confused—a cloud lies over my spirit ... When I think that the devil needs only to sound the trumpet a little, in order to make you forget all the good teaching and the daily admoni-

[18]Text: PG. 59. 37

[19]Text: PG. 49. 32

[20]Text: PG. 53. 54

tions which I have always given you; ... how shall I be able any more to preach to you with confidence, since my previous words have so quickly flown away? ... Believe me, the blush of shame rises to my face when I see that all my labors are in vain, and that I have sowed the seed among stones ... For my part I have done everything I could, I have fulfilled my duty, I have admonished and warned. (*On Genesis*)

Nevertheless the prophet's desire to forgive and to encourage in spite of his own distress is always present:

6. 3.[21] My reproach of you to-day is severe but I beg you to pardon it. It is just that my soul is wounded. I do not speak in this way out of enmity but out of care for you. Therefore I will now strike a somewhat gentler tone ... I know that your intentions are good, and that you realize your mistakes. The realization of the greatness of one's sins is the first great step on the way to virtue ... I can now read your feelings from your faces, and comprehend the remorse of your souls. But you must offer assurance that you will not fall into the same sins again, and after this earnest admonition, that you will not again run to the same devilish games. (*On Genesis*)

In the theater at Antioch "Mimes" in which women were allowed to play were as popular as comedies, and against these Chrysostom railed in great style:

5. 4.[22] Let me tell you why young people so often lose their innocence. In this it is not youth that is to blame, it is because we ourselves willingly spring into the fire. When you go into the theater and delight yourselves by looking at the naked limbs of women; ... then a mighty passion grips you. When you see men appearing in women's

[21]Text: PG. 53. 54

[22]Text: PG. 62. 428

> parts; when you attend plays and hear songs that are concerned with nothing but indecent love adventures, where it always goes like this,—this woman loved that man and did not get him so she ended her life in the water ... and when even old men appear in the masks of women, tell me, will you still be able to remain chaste? (*Hom. I Thess.*)

Again:

> 1.[23] The theater is a constant temptation; yet no one hesitates to go there nor remains away from it; no one alleges lack of time. They are all prepared for it, and they all run there as though they had no cares at all. The old man is not ashamed of his gray hair, the youth pays no attention to the heat of nature and passion, and it does not occur to the rich man to wish to maintain his dignity. It is only when he is going into the church that he acts as though he had to come down from the high throne of his dignity; then he moves slowly and allows himself time, and imagines himself to be something, as though he had done God a favor. (*Inscrip. Altar.*)

Something of the prophet's vitriolic eloquence can be likewise heard in his denunciation of actors:

> 88. 4.[24] Our gospel is that Christ has accomplished a great work, in which He has made angels out of men. If someone then demands and requires proofs from us, that we should produce examples from our flocks, we must be silent for fear of actually bringing out swine and asses from the stall, instead of angels. I know this wounds you, but my words do not apply to every individual, only to the guilty, and I do not speak so much against them as

[23]Text: PG. 51. 68

[24]Text: PG. 58. 780

rather more for them, if only they comprehend it. Truly, in the present time, everything is brought down and destroyed;... (*Hom. Matt.*)

The same sharpness of tongue can be felt in his denunciation of the guilty on their return to Church:

3. 1.[25] To-day there are many present who ... have recently committed sin, because they have been going to the theater of sin. Let all these know that I shall send them back from the holy gates, not that they may remain away forever, but that they may better themselves before they return here again. Therefore I should like to know the names of those I have in mind. If I cannot distinguish them with the eyes of the body ... then may their own conscience urge them to depart from here! ... Therefore I beseech and pray you: Cleanse yourselves through repentance and sorrow from the sins with which you have burdened yourselves by looking at such things, and then come and hear the word of God! ... Are you not ashamed, to hear with the same ears the filthy conversation of loose-living women, and the mysterious revelations of the prophets and apostles? (*Hom. David and Saul*)

On the first day of the year things were at their liveliest in Antioch with Saturnalia and all its festive implications. Such celebrations were the last vestiges of paganism which many of the new Christians were as reluctant to relinquish as the older pagans were determined to preserve. In the face of such opposition, where Bacchus was the city's prefect and Venus his faithful spouse, Chrysostom was powerless but nonetheless undaunted:

1. 1.[26] All who have been ordained for the Ministry of the Word have received from the dear God the command

[25]Text: PG. 54. 695

[26]Text: PG. 48. 963

> never to abandon our duty, and never to be silent, whether anyone listens to us or not. Thus I am determined ... as long as I live, and as long as God pleases to leave me in this life, to fulfil this duty and carry out this command, whether anyone pays attention or not. There are those who make merry over us and say: Stop the good advice, skip the admonitions; they will not listen to you, let them go. What are you saying? Have we promised to convert all men in one day? If only ten, or only five, or indeed only one, repents, is not that consolation enough? ... What is not accomplished today, can be accomplished tomorrow or if not tomorrow, then the day after tomorrow or later. So a fisherman may draw in his net all day long without any catch: yet, in the evening, at the very moment when he is about to depart for home he often catches a fish that had avoided him all day long ... The very same is true of each and every calling. (*On Laz.*)

The teeming oriental cities of Antioch and Constantinople furnished Chrysostom with abundant moral problems. Consequently his biblical expositions, especially the homilies on the Sermon on the Mount, widen into an ethical paranesis in which salutary moral lessons are driven home in a candid and practical style:

> XVII. 7.[27] Let no rich or powerful man sit here before me with contempt, puffing at me and frowning. Such gestures are lost on me—mere fables or dreams. For none of the rich or powerful will speak up for me on the day of judgement when I am called to account for my preaching of the laws of God ... Therefore that neither you nor I may be condemned I entreat you to do what I tell you and free yourselves from the habits and ways of the world. (*Ser. Mount*)

[27]Text: PG. 57. 264

Such is the dauntless spirit of this prophetic preacher:

> 5. 1.[28] For this reason the preacher must proclaim the divine word or sow the seed whether anyone listens to him or not for God has entrusted to him His treasures and will demand a reckoning. Thus have I reproached you, reprimanded you, prayed for you and admonished you. In this way by my preaching our heavenly Father has not punished you for your sins but has opened the door of His house and prepared the spiritual banquet for you. (*On Anna*)

4. The Exegetical Dimension

For Chrysostom preaching was essentially the interpretation of a text from scripture and its application to a particular congregation. Exegesis is, therefore, the starting point of his preaching as exhortation is its conclusion. In his exegesis he continues the tradition of the Eastern Church, especially that of Origen, but he did so in his own specific way. He is the typical representative of the Antiochene school of exegesis. Sobriety and restraint were its characteristics in contrast with the more imaginative allegorical approach of the school of Alexandria. In origin it belongs to the tradition of the literal and historical interpretation represented by the rabbis rather than the allegorical interpretation of Philo. A 9th century explanation of the different approaches states the problem exactly: "People ask what the difference is between allegorical exegesis and historical exegesis. We reply that it is great and not small; just as the first leads to impiety, blasphemy, and falsehood, so the other is conformed to truth and faith. It was the impious Origen of Alexandria who invented this art of allegory. Just as poets and geometricians, when they wish to raise their disciples

[28]Text: PG. 54. 669

from material and visible things to things hidden and invisible, erring in regard to the eternity of incorporeal matter and to indivisible atoms, say: 'Just as it is not these visible signs which are signs for reading, but their hidden meanings, so from created natures one must rise by the image of thought to their eternal nature'; just so, Origen taught ... The psalms and the prophets who spoke of the captivity and the return of the soul far from truth and its return to faith ... They do not interpret paradise as it is, or Adam, or Eve, or any existing thing."[29]

The advocates of allegory could point to its use within the New Testament itself, especially to the allegorical interpretation of the difference between Sarah and Hagar in Galatians:

> You want to be subject to the Law? Then listen to what the Law says. It says, if you remember, that Abraham had two sons, one by the slave-girl, and one by his free-born wife. The child of the slave-girl was born in the ordinary way; the child of the free woman was born as the result of a promise. This can be regarded as an allegory: the women stand for the two covenants. The first who comes from Mount Sinai, and whose children are slaves, is Hagar—since Sinai is in Arabia—she corresponds to the present Jerusalem that is a slave like her children. The Jerusalem above, however, is free and is our mother, since Scripture says: Shout for joy, you barren women who bore no children! Break into shouts of joy and gladness, you who were never in labor. For there are more sons of the forsaken one than sons of the wedded wife. Now you, my brothers, like Isaac, are children of the promise, and as at that time the child born in the ordinary way persecuted the child born in the Spirit's way, so also now. Does not scripture say: Drive away that slave-girl and her son; this slave-girl's son is not to share the inheri-

[29]Pelikan, J. *The Preaching of Chrysostom*, Philadelphia, 1967, p. 14.

> tance with the son of the free woman? So my brothers, we are the children, not of the slave-girl, but of the free-born wife. (Gal 4:21-31)

But by the time of its encounter with Antioch, allegory had more than Pauline precedent on its side: "Against Marcion it had won the day as a vindication of the Christianization of the Old Testament; in the conflict with Gnosticism it had proved that the truly 'spiritual' interpretation of the mystery of Christ did not reside only with Valentinus, Basilides, and their disciples, but was being set forth by the orthodox exegesis of the church catholic. And in the course of the controversy with Arianism allegory had marshalled the evidence of both Testaments in support of the consubstantiality of the Son with the Father, citing the Psalter, the eighth chapter of the Book of Proverbs, and the prologue to the Gospel of John as parts of the same Scripture, regardless of their chronological difference."[30] On the other hand, Chrysostom's realistic and historical exegesis could not, and did not, involve him in any rejection of the typological sense:

> 3. 7.[31] Blood and water flowed from his side ... Beloved, do not pass over this mystery without thought; it has yet another hidden meaning, which I will explain to you. I said that water and blood symbolized baptism and the Holy Eucharist. From these two sacraments the Church is born: from baptism, the cleansing water that gives rebirth and renewal through the Holy Spirit, and from the Holy Eucharist. Since the symbols of baptism and the eucharist flowed from his side, it was from his side that Christ fashioned the Church, as he had fashioned Eve from the side of Adam ... Do you understand, then, how Christ has united his bride to himself and what food he

[30]Pelikan, J. *op. cit.* pp. 14-15.

[31]Text: SC. 51. 61

gives us all to eat? By one and the same food we are both brought into being and nourished.

Furthermore, in his homily, *The Grave and Cross*, it is even difficult to distinguish between typology and allegory:

> [32] Beloved, you know the achievement of Christ and the glorious victory of the Cross ... Now let me tell you something even more remarkable, the manner in which he gained his victory, and you will marvel all the more. Christ conquered the devil using the same means and the same weapons that the devil used to win. Let me tell you how this occurred. The symbols of our fall were a virgin, a tree and death. The virgin was Eve (for she had not yet known man); then there was the tree; and death was Adam's penalty. And again these three tokens of our destruction, the virgin, the tree, and death became the tokens of our victory. Instead of Eve there was Mary; instead of the tree of knowledge of good and evil, the wood of the cross; instead of Adam's death, the death of Christ. Do you see, then, that the devil was defeated by the very means he used to conquer?

The inclination to be more sober than imaginative in interpreting a text can be seen more clearly in his paranetic homilies, especially those *On the Sermon on the Mount.* Here there is conflict only when Chrysostom attacks an excessively allegorical view:

> XV. 5.[33] Blessed are the meek for they shall inherit the earth. Tell me, what kind of earth? Some say a figurative earth, but it is not this, for nowhere in Scripture do we find any mention of an earth that is merely figurative. But what can the saying mean? He holds out a sensible prize;

[32]Text: PG. 49. 396

[33]Text: PG. 57. 229

> . . . Thus he does not incite us by means of future blessings only, but by the present ones as well, on account of the human needs of his congregation . . .

The most striking illustration within the paranetic homilies of the antithesis between the two styles of exegesis comes in the interpretation of the fourth petition of the Lord's Prayer, "Give us this day our daily bread." Origen spoke for many when he protested against the physical meaning of bread in this passage. On the basis of the Bread of Life discourse of Jesus in John 6 he argued that Christ himself was the true bread and therefore he concluded that this petition was actually a prayer for the only bread that was in the fullest sense the divine substance. On the other hand, Chrysostom's interpretation was much more literal: for him the whole prayer like the whole sermon was addressed to men of flesh and blood. Therefore, the Lord's Prayer included not only requests for spiritual blessings but also the prayer for the daily requirement of the body—daily bread for the sustenance of the physical body:

> XIX. 5.[34] 'Daily bread.' What is this? Bread for one day . . . because He was preaching to men of flesh and blood who were subject to the laws of nature and its every need . . . it is neither for riches, nor for delicate living, nor for costly raiment, nor for any other such thing, but for bread only, that he commanded us to make our prayer. And for 'daily bread,' so as not to 'take thought for the morrow.' Because of this he added, '*daily* bread,' that is, bread for one day. And not even with this expression is he satisfied, but qualified it afterwards, saying, 'Give us *this* day'; so that we may not, beyond this, wear ourselves out with the care of the following day.

Chrysostom emphasized the material and the historical as part of God's good creation, and opposed accordingly the

[34]Text: PG. 57. 280

false spiritualism of the Gnostics and the Manichaean dualists more than allegorical exegesis as such. In this way he replaced Origen's elaborate system of symbols with a very literal verbal exposition. Whereas Origen saw a succession of types and prototypes in which the material world of experience mirrored the reality of the spiritual world of God, Chrysostom saw the goodness of the created world of God, marred by the sin of man but redeemed by the blood of Christ. Thus he did not wholly reject the allegorical approach but resorts to it to draw forth moral and ethical lessons: "Like no exegete in ancient times Chrysostom grasped the essential nature of parable and understood the difference between parable and allegory."

His 88 *Homilies on the Gospel of St. John* are a splendid example of his preaching style as he begins with the exegesis of a scripture text and concludes with the parable or moral of the story for his particular congregation. Throughout each of these homilies an identical pattern is consistently followed. By way of preface he quotes the text with which he intends to begin his commentary. There follows a brief introduction, rather formal in tone, with a few apt reflections suggested by the text of the day. The commentary on the text follows, rambling in style, often repetitious, and wandering easily from the subject in hand. This part of the homily is not cast in any set form, but can be engagingly informal, or relentlessly logical, as occasion demands. With the dramatic instinct of the born orator, he urges his audience to 'see' what is taking place as he graphically unfolds the Gospel story.

He makes frequent use of the device of the dialog in which he himself and an imaginary member of his audience parry question and answer with one another, or with one of the Gospel personalities, such as Peter, or Pilate. Though this commentary bulks large in each homily, a considerable part of each one is also devoted to the moral exhortation which directly follows it. The teeming oriental city of Antioch furnished abundant matter and consequently all the capital sins are castigated in turn, in the form in which they were most prevalent. Nearly every phase of human morality receives its share of praise or blame: the good use of time (hom 58), the evil of adultery (hom 63), bearing wrongs patiently (hom 83), avoiding bad companionship (hom 57), imitating Christ's meekness and gentleness (hom 60), to mention but a few samples. Finally, the homily always concludes with a brief prayer ending in a doxology. Though the latter is made up of stereotyped phrases, it is not always identical, but there are several recurring formulae.

5. The New Dimensions

The new dimensions of preaching already identified as thematic, catechetical, mystagogical, and rhetorical determined many of Chrysostom's themes, especially his frequent outbursts against Arianism and Eunomianism:

> 11. 3-4.[35] What utter madness' . . . The Prophets exhaust all available metaphors to express the insignificance of man, as compared with God. Men are 'dust and ashes,' 'grass,' and the 'flower of grass,' 'a vapor,' 'a shadow.' Inanimate creation acknowledges the irresistible supremacy of his power; 'if He does but touch the hills they shall smoke,' . . . 'He established the sky like a roof, and stretched it out like a tent over the earth.' The solid, durable earth He made, and all the nations of the world, even as far as the British isles, are but as a drop in a bucket; and shall man, who is but an infinitesimal part of this drop, presume to enquire into the nature of Him who made all these forces and whom they obey'? . . . (*Incomp. Nature of God*)

[35]Text: PG. 48. 712-4

Again:

> IV. 4.[36] But the different forms under which God is said to have appeared, proves that these manifestations were merely condescensions to the weakness of human nature, which requires something that the eye can see and the ear can hear. They were only manifestations of the Deity adapted to man's capacity; not the Divine Nature itself which is simple, incomposite, devoid of shape. So, also, when it is said of God the Son that He is 'in the bosom of the Father,' when He is described as 'standing', or 'sitting on the right hand of God', these expressions must not be interpreted in too material a sense; they are expressions accommodated to our understandings, to convey an idea of such an intimate union and equality between the two Persons as . . . is in itself a mystery. (*Incomp. Nature of God*)

Jews and pagans were influential in the life of Antioch and their festivals were popular among the Christians but denounced by Chrysostom:

> 1. 8.[37] In the words of Moses, I call upon Heaven and earth record against you this day, that if any of you now present or absent, attend the Feast of Trumpets, or enter a synagogue, or observe a fast, or a sabbath, or any Jewish rite whatever, I am innocent of your blood. (*Against the Jews*)

The feast of Saturnalia of the pagans, which ushered in the new year, was likewise denounced:

> 2.[38] The joy of the Christian year was not determined by the observation of particular feasts, but by the amount of

[36]Text: PG. 48. 732-3

[37]Text: PG. 48. 712-4

[38]Text: PG. 48. 955

> goodness which we put into it. Sin was the only real evil, virtue the only real good; therefore, if a man practised justice, almsgiving, and prayer, his year could not fail to be propitious; for he who had a clean conscience carried about with him a perpetual holy day, and without this, the most brilliant and joyous festival was obscured by darkness. (*On the Kalends*)

On the other hand the festivals of the martyrs and saints had multiplied in his day and there are extant many of the homilies which he delivered at their martyries or places of commemoration on their feast days:

> 3.[39] We should visit the martyrs and their shrines . . . with faith embrace their reliques, that we may derive some blessing therefrom; . . . Not only on their festival, but at other times, let us resort to them and invoke them to become our protectors; for they can use much boldness of speech when dead, more, indeed, than when they were alive, for now they bear in their bodies the marks of Jesus Christ . . . let us therefore procure for ourselves, through them, favor from God. (*On Juv. Max. Mart.*)

The most famous of Chrysostom's discourses were probably the twenty-one *Homilies On The Statues* preached after the riots in Antioch in which the Royal Statues had been torn down. As the people were fluctuating between hope and fear awaiting the return of Flavian, their bishop, who had gone to Constantinople to beg the Emperor's forgiveness, Chrysostom preached. He exerted all his powers to console and encourage the vast crowds that thronged the Churches out of fear but seized the opportunity to castigate at the same time the vices and offences that had brought upon them the wrath of God. Constantinople, on the other hand, with its scarcely assimilated western and oriental

[39]Text: PG. 50. 576

elements and its court of luxury and intrigue was a far cry from Antioch however turbulent and confused the latter might at times have been. Here, reform was the message of the new Patriarch and when he stripped the episcopal residence of all the adjuncts of luxurious living he thereby served notice on the clergy. The avarice and luxury of the wealthy were also themes of his indignant invective, just as the plight and poverty of the poor were occasions of his pathetic appeal:

> V. 1.[40] Oh! the sheer horror of money which drives many of our brethren from the fold! For it is nothing but that grievous disease, that never quenched furnace, which drives them hence; this mistress, more ferocious than any barbarian or wild beast, fiercer than the very demons, taking her slaves with her, is not conducting them round the Forum, inflicting upon them her oppressive commands, nor suffers them to take a little breath from their destructive labors ... May you derive great good from the zeal with which you listen to these words, for your groaning and the smitings of your foreheads prove that the seed which I have sown is already bearing fruit. (*Sermon on the Mount*)

Denunciation was certainly the major theme practised and preached by this new patriarch and prophet. Nothing escaped his eye and no one escaped his tongue:

> Hom. XLIX. 4.[41] How ridiculous and absurd to thread your shoes with silk laces ... What form of madness can be worse? ... He who ought to bend his thoughts and eyes heavenwards casts them down upon his shoes instead. His chief care, as he walks delicately through the Forum, is to avoid soiling his boots with mire or dust.

[40]Text: PG. 63. 485

[41]Text: PG. 58. 501

> Will you let your soul grovel in the mire while you are taking care of your boots? Boots were made to be soiled; if you cannot bear this, take them off and wear them on your head instead of on your feet. You laugh when I say these words, but I rather weep for your folly. (*On Matt.*)

This truncated litany of themes is merely intended to illustrate a certain development that took place in the manner of preaching in the 4th century to meet the particular needs of the Church in that age. Like the exegetical homily properly so-called the thematic approach also begins with a Scripture text and its interpretation; but it develops and widens in its application and the preacher judges the human situations in which he finds himself by the light of the Divine Word he preaches. Herein the balance is struck: but the balance is upset whenever the theme outweighs the Word.

It is impossible to read the homilies of Chrysostom without being constantly reminded that he was both Christian prophet and Greek orator. Antioch with her rhetorical traditions shaped his compositions as Chrysostom, the first and greatest orator of Christian antiquity, sat at the feet of Libanius the last great rhetorician of pagan antiquity. It was an age of rhetoric and the Word. In Chrysostom's opinion rhetoric alone was not sufficient to convert the disorderly and unprofitable delight of ordinary people and to divert their attention to something more useful. In addition, the preacher must be as indifferent to praise as he is skilled in oratory. It is in his attitude to praise that Chrysostom reveals his attitude to rhetoric and this can be seen in a great number of passages.

> XVII. 7.[42] Are you in praise of what I have said? For my part I care not for I need neither your applause nor your noisy praise. This only I ask of you that with quiet and

[42]Text: PG. 57. 264

> wisdom you listen to me and do what I say. Such is the applause that I ask of you. This is the panegyric that pleases me. But if you praise simply what I say, but do not do what I say, great will be your punishment. (Sermon on the Mount)

In his homilies on the Sermon on the Mount Chrysostom tried to discern the rhetoric of Christ and sought to conform his own preaching accordingly. Christ, the skilled rhetorician, knew how to adapt his words to his message and in this way to produce the desired effect in his audience. Chrysostom, his prophet and priest, would do likewise with the rhetoric of Libanius. For this reason critical evaluation of his rhetorical gifts is not easy and usually varied. Some have on occasion classified him as a true Atticist continuing the noblest tradition in Greek prose. Others on account of the metaphorical influence of the Bible upon him point to the extravagance in him and label him more Asian than Attic. More accurately, perhaps, he is both Attic and Asian, as he is also prophet and rhetor, for he uses and deliberately changes the various stylistic arts depending on his purpose. For example he seems to consider the diatribe the natural form of the homily and it appears especially in paranetic applications, in the use of short sentences and rhetorical questions. On the other hand, rhetoric plays a leading role in the panegyrics on the saints and in the thematic discourses where the meaning of the text is not of primary importance. It is this combination of prophet and rhetor that made John of Antioch known to posterity as Chrysostom. Nothing that he accomplished as exegetic author or bishop brought him this distinction but what he accomplished as a pulpit orator, or preacher of the Word of God. That was what obviously appeared to his contemporaries as most noteworthy in him:

> 1. 1.[43] Since I preached for a longer time than ever before, many believed that your zeal would grow cool on account

[43]Text: PG. 49. 245

> of my speaking at such length. But the opposite happened: your hearts became still warmer and your longing more ardent. How did I know that? By this, that your applause near the end of the sermon grew stronger and your exclamations louder. It happened then as it does with a burning fire. In the beginning the fire is but small: but if it seizes on wood, it leaps up to a greater height. So also was it with us. In the beginning this assembly was not especially excited. But as the sermon grew longer and laid hold of the material, and the wood of instruction came to it in ever increasing quantity, then your anxiety to hear what I had to say grew and grew and produced louder applause. Thus it happened that I went on and on much longer indeed than I originally planned. Actually, never before did I preach for such a length—for excellence in preaching should not be measured by the length of the sermon but by the interest of the congregation. (Rule of Demons)

Conclusion

In his own day Chrysostom, "the golden lyre of the Holy Spirit" was a living legend in the west as in the east. "When he poured out his words his splendid images and striking comparisons in lavish abundance before his listeners, it soon became clear why the multitude listened voiceless and often breathless before the magic of his oratory, and were sometimes held in such suspense that their feelings suddenly released themselves in enthusiastic and universal applause."[44] Rhetoric, perhaps, killed the homily! Certainly it contributed to the death of the homilist. On the feast of St. John the Baptist, June 404, he began his homily with the words: "Again Herodias raves; again she rages; again she dances; again she asks for the head of John upon a charger." His enemies regarded this sensational introduction as an allusion to Eudoxia, the Empress, angered earlier by a

[44]Baur, C. *John Chrysostom and His Time*, Vol. 1, p. 207.

similar outburst from the Golden-Mouth. Exile was the reward and death the result but not before the final homily:

> [45] The waters are raging and the winds are blowing but I have no fear for I stand firmly upon a rock. What am I to fear? Is it death? Life to me means Christ and death is gain. Is it exile? The earth and everything it holds belongs to the Lord. Is it loss of property? I brought nothing into this world and I will bring nothing out of it. I have only contempt for the world and its ways and I scorn its honours.

[45]Text: PG. 52.427.

5. The Latin Sermon In The African Church

The preeminence of the Roman Church in those early centuries enjoyed no similar influence in the development of Christian thought in that same period. Unlike Alexandria or Caesarea, Rome fostered no school whose memory has outlived the passage of time), and produced only two divines worthy of mention, Hippolytus (d. 235) and Novatian (c. 250), both antipopes and probably martyrs. In the former she could boast a savant almost the equal of Origen; in the latter the first theologian to write in Latin. But the undisputed Greek background and Greek writings of Hippolytus placed him outside the ambience of the Latin sermon, while the remains of Novatian's Latin writings cannot be considered as sermons. Strangely enough it was the Church of Africa and not the Church of Rome that gave us Tertullian (155-c. 220) and Cyprian (c. 200-258), the founding fathers of Latin theology, whose works represent the beginnings of Latin Christian literature and consequently the starting point for any study of the Latin sermon.

1. Early Latin Exegesis

The writings of Tertullian and Cyprian are of particular importance for the origin and development of the Latin sermon on account of their distinctive approach to the Bible. Devoted to the literal sense of the text, and distrustful of any allegorical interpretation, they acknowledged only one spiritual sense, namely the typological. Accordingly the traditional types of Christ and the Church abound in their writings, but are much more developed than in Justin or Irenaeus. However, the unique contribution of these fathers to the science of typology is best seen in their exposition of the sacraments for they are the earliest Christian authors to have studied and expounded sacramental typology for its own sake. In Tertullian is found a great variety of baptismal figures—the primordial waters; the flood; the waters of Marah sweetened the wood; the rock of Horeb; the iron axehead which Elisha caused to float in the Jordan. Cyprian, on the other hand, was the first of all the early Christian writers to elaborate on the typology of the eucharist. In the sacramental bread, for example, he sees a symbol of the bond between Christ and the faithful and also a symbol of ecclesiastical unity. The mixture of wine and water had the same significance for him. But his eucharistic typology, for the most part, centers around the significance of the cup:

> LXIII. II.[1] The Chalice of Benediction intoxicates by leading our souls back to spiritual wisdom, by leading us back from a taste for the world to a spiritual understanding of it. Just as the spirit is relaxed by ordinary wine, and the soul is loosened and all sadness is vanished, so too does drinking the Lord's blood and the cup of salvation dispel the memory of the old man, make us forget our past life in the world, and spread the joy of God's forgiveness in hearts made sad by the pain of sin. (Letters)

[1]Text: CSEL. 3. (2). 709

In his work *On Purity*, Tertullian expounded his principles of exegesis:

> VIII. 9.[2] We do not take the parables as our source of doctrine, but rather we take doctrine as our norm for interpreting the parables. Thus we make no effort to twist everything in order that it fits our own explanation. We strive to avoid every discrepancy. Why a 'hundred' sheep? and why, indeed 'ten' drachmas? and what does that 'broom' stand for? When he wanted to show how pleased God is at the salvation of one sinner, he had to mention some numerical quantity from which one could be described as 'lost.' And in view of the ordinary practice of a woman who looks for a drachma in the house, he had to supply the assistance of a broom and lamp. Strange questions of this sort lead to conclusions which are suspect and, as a rule, they seduce men from truth through the subtleties of an artificial exegesis. There are some things, however, which are introduced into the parable with a view to its literal sense, as elements of its structure, design and essential constitution, so that they may lead us to that which it is intended to illustrate.
>
> The two sons are obviously introduced for the same reason as the drachma and the sheep, for they have their origin in the same situation as the parables with which they are united, that is, in the same grumbling of the Pharisees against our Lord's association with the heathen. But if anyone does not believe that in Judea, subjected as it was long since by the power of Pompey and Lucullus, the publicans were pagans, let him read Deuteronomy: There shall be no weigher of tribute from among the sons of Israel. The name 'publican' would not have been so odious before the Lord, had it not been of aliens who demanded toll for passage through the very air itself, and over land and sea. And when sinners are mentioned in the text, along with publicans, this does not prove

[2]Text: CSEL. 20. 235-240

immediately that they were Jews, even though some of them may have been. Rather, only one group is distinguished, the heathens, since the text places side by side some who are sinners by reason of their office, that is, the publicans, and others who are sinners by reason of their character, that is, those who are not publicans. Moreover, He would not be blamed for taking food with Jews but rather with pagans, since the Jewish law forbids communicating with them at table.

With regard to the prodigal son, we must consider, first of all, that which is more useful, since typology cannot be tolerated if it is dangerous to salvation, even though it may balance as perfectly as a scale. We see, however, that the interpretation put forward by our opponents destroys the whole economy of salvation, which is founded on the preservation of discipline. For if it is a Christian who, wandering far from his Father and living like a pagan, wastes the substance which he has received from God his Father (this means, of course, Baptism and the Holy Spirit and, in consequence, the hope of eternity), and if, stripped of his soul's good gifts, he has even given himself over in bondage to a prince of this world (who else but the devil?), and been appointed by him to herd swine (this means, of course, to serve unclean spirits), and if he has recovered his senses so as to return to his Father—then, according to this parable, not only adulterers and fornicators, but idolaters also, and blasphemers, and renegades, and apostates of every kind may make satisfaction to the Father. Truly, a similitude such as this destroys the whole substance of the sacrament. For who will hesitate to throw away what he is able, afterwards, to recover? Who will try to keep for ever whatsoever he is able to lose for a time? Security in sin stimulates the very desire to commit it.

Thus, the apostate may also recover his former garment which is the cloak of the Holy Spirit and receive, once more, the ring which is the seal of Baptism. For him Christ will be slain once again and he will recline upon that couch from which those who are unworthily attired (to say nothing of those who have been stripped of their garments) are wont to be taken by the executioners and cast out into the darkness. Therefore we have taken a step forward, if it is inexpedient that the account of the prodigal son be referred to a Christian.

Should the figure of the dutiful son, however, not apply to the Jew, then our interpretation will be determined simply by the intention of the Lord. We know that the Lord came to save the lost, and was a physician more necessary for the sick than for the healthy. This he taught symbolically in parables and preached openly in His discourses. What man is lost who is sick if not the man who is ignorant of God?

Who is safe and sound if not the man who knows God? These two types, who are brothers by birth, are symbolised in this parable each in his own way. Ask yourself if the pagan has, as his portion, his origin in God, the Father, and a natural knowledge and understanding of that heavenly Father. Therefore, the apostle clearly says 'in the wisdom of God, the world, through wisdom, has not known God,' that wisdom which it has received from God.

Such, indeed, is the substance which the prodigal wasted, being far away from the Lord by his unruly passions, and lost in the delusions, temptations and lusts of the world. Here, overcome with hunger for the truth, he gave himself over to the prince of this world who put him in charge of swine (to tend that herd which is the child of the devil) where, on the one hand, he would not have sufficient food for life and, on the other hand, where he would see the friends of God being nourished richly with bread from heaven. Then, he remembers his heavenly Father and, having made due satisfaction to Him, he returns to Him. His former garment is restored to him, that garment which Adam lost by his sin. For the first time he receives a ring, and this ring seals the covenant of faith. Then is open to him the larder of the Lord which is the Table of the Holy Eucharist.

Such is the real understanding of this parable. At no time was the prodigal ever virtuous. From the beginning he was prodigal, because from the beginning he was not a christian. This is the one the pharisees saw in the persons of the publicans and sinners, returning from the world to his Father's house. In this sense the envy of the elder brother is meaningful because the Jews were neither virtuous nor obedient to the laws of God but they, nonetheless, begrudged with envy salvation to the Gentiles. They deplored the first call of the christian and not his second salvation; for the former is evident even to the pagans while the latter is not even known to the Jews, since it takes place in the secrecy of the Church's mysteries.

It seems to me that my interpretations are more in harmony with the substantial teaching of the parables and the unity of their disparate elements. Should our opponents wish to make the sheep, the drachma, and the prodigal son types of the christian sinner in order to grant forgiveness to adultery and fornication, then other capital sins should also be forgiven: otherwise adultery and fornication, which are on a par with them, should not be forgiven.

It is more important, however, to avoid extending a text beyond its limit by reading into it what is not there. Were it permissible to read into the parable of the prodigal unlimited forgiveness we would be proclaiming a forgiveness that should be confined to the martyr. For this alone will be able to re-instate the son who has wasted all his substance. It will proclaim that the drachma has been found ... even in the dunghill; it will restore the sheep to the flock on the master's shoulder, even though it wandered through every kind of wasteland. But, if needs be, I would prefer an incomplete understanding of the Scripture to an incorrect one. In the same way, we should respect the words of the Lord as much as his commands. Bad exegesis is no less worse than bad conduct. (*On Purity*)

In addition to typological exegesis the Latin Fathers also practised a special form of *moral* exegesis in which they drew attention to various virtues on the basis of models derived from the Bible. With the figure of Job, for example, we meet a new form of Latin moral exegesis, especially prominent in treatises on patience—a theme that was commonplace in Latin Stoic philosophy, especially in Cicero and Seneca. The story of the righteous man put to the test is ancient and indeed prebiblical; but the Book of Job gave it a monotheistic perspective. In his exegesis of this book Clement of Alexandria gave us a Hellenistic Job while Tertullian presented us with a Latin one and pictured Job between a laughing God and a devil grinding his teeth. For Cyprian, Job is not just the model of the righteous man who is persecuted but the very idea of the righteous man as such. This interest in the moral aspect of the Old Testament, and especially in its hagiographical elements, was characteristic of Cyprian and of the general concern of the Latins with the moral sphere:

> X.[3] After the loss of his wealth and the death of his children, Job was grievously afflicted with every kind of bodily sore. Nevertheless, he was never overcome. Rather he emerged from his struggles tried and true and displayed the patience and power of a truly religious mind saying 'naked I came from my mother's womb and naked I shall return to mother earth for the Lord gave and the Lord took away as it seemed fit to Him to do: blessed be the name of the Lord forever! When his wife urged him to speak against God with a complaining and envious voice he answered her saying 'you speak as a foolish woman. If we have received such good things from the hand of the Lord why shall we not suffer in patience our misfortunes.' Never in speech did Job offend the Lord in spite of everything that happened to him. For this reason the Lord God made of him an example saying: 'have you not considered my servant, Job? There is none like him in all

[3]Text: CSEL. 3. 302-3

the earth; he is a man without complaint and a true worshipper.' And Tobias, after his many wonderful works and the glorious manifestation of his merciful spirit, grew in worship and praise in spite of the loss of his sight and his bodily afflictions. His wife also tried to pervert him saying 'where is your righteousness and happiness and behold the magnitude of your sorrow.' But he, firm and steadfast in his fear of the Lord and strengthened by his faith to endure all suffering, did not yield an inch to the weakness of his wife and grew accordingly in patience and resignation. Afterwards, Raphael, the Angel of God, praised him saying 'it is right and good to manifest and confess the works of the Lord for when I heard your prayer and the prayer of Sara, your daughter-in-law, I proclaimed it in the presence of the glorious Lord. And when in singleness of heart you did not hesitate to bury your dead without murmur or complaint ... God sent me to heal both you and Sara ... for I am Raphael one of the seven Holy Angels, a presence in the glory of God and a light in the darkness of man.' ...

XI. Righteous men have always possessed this spirit of endurance. The Apostles ... never murmured in adversity and accepted bravely and patiently whatever happened to them in the world. On the other hand, the Jews always offended in this matter and constantly complained as the Lord God bears witness in the Book of Numbers, saying 'let their murmuring cease for Me and they shall not die.' We should never murmur in adversity, beloved children, but we must bear with patience and courage whatever happens since it is written by the psalmist 'the sacrifice to God is a broken spirit and a contrite and humble heart God does not despise.' Again in Deuteronomy, the Holy Spirit warns us and says 'the Lord your God will try you and bring hunger upon you; then you will know in your heart if you have kept faith in Him' ...

XXV. Much more ought we now to live steadfastly in the faith since the world around us is collapsing and is oppressed with the mischievous ways of men. We see the terrible things that surround us and we know that still more terrible things are to come, nevertheless we continue to believe and regard death as the way of salvation. If the walls of your home were shaken with age, the roof above you trembling ... and threatening an immediate collapse, would you not depart with all speed? If an angry and raging storm ... foretold the wreckage of your ship, would you not quickly make for the harbor? So, too, we should read the signs of the times and recognise that this world is changing and passing away. And for this vision of faith we should give thanks to God for already He has delivered us from the shipwrecks and the disasters that are yet to come ...

XXVI. Dearly beloved brethren, we should always remember that we have renounced this world and are now living here as mere guests and strangers. Let us salute the day which assigns to each of us his true home and which snatches us from here and sets us free from the snares of the world and restores us to Paradise and the true Kingdom. Surely the exile would not hesitate to return to his own land? Who is there that would not desire favorable wind to speed him to the companionship of his friends? Paradise is the country of faith, and the Patriarchs are our fathers in faith: why then do we not hasten to behold our country to greet our parents? There, a host of friends are waiting for us—parents, brothers, children are all there in that paradise and anxiously awaiting our arrival. What a joy for them and for us when we are together for ever and a day. What happiness there must be in that Kingdom which is free from the fear of death ... there the glorious company of the Apostles is reigning; there, too, are the Prophets, the innumerable multitude of the Martyrs, the triumphant Virgins (who overcame the lust of the flesh by the strength of their continence) and the many and wonderful merciful men

> and women who ... keeping the Lord's precepts, have transferred their earthly patrimonies to the heavenly treasuries. To these, let us hasten to go; let us beg to be with them ... may God behold our desire and may Christ his Lord look upon the plan of our hearts and souls.

2. Early Latin Theology

As a theologian Tertullian is astonishingly original and personal, and displays those very qualities which were forever to characterize Latin Christianity: "a realism which knows nothing of the Platonic devaluation of matter; a subjectivity, which gives special prominence to inner experiences; and a pessimism which lays more stress on the experience of sin than on transfiguration."[4]

Accordingly law, and not philosophy, permeated his whole understanding of theology and of the relationship between God and man. Thus for Tertullian God is the giver of the Law and the judge who administers this Law. The Gospel is the Law of the Christian, and sin is a breach of this Law. Likewise, the fear of the Lawgiver is the beginning of wisdom and the ultimate in faith, and the merit of man is the satisfaction of God.

In fact the words debt, satisfaction, guilt, compensation occur frequently throughout his disciplinary, moral and ascetical writings, with their sweeping and scathing condemnations:

> BK. 2. C. 5.[5] All who refresh their bodies with perfume, color their cheeks with rouge and enlarge their eyes with soot, sin gravely against the Lord. To them, I suppose the creative power of God is displeasing and in their own persons they convict and censure the Artificer of all things. (*On the Cult of Women*)

[4]Daniélou, J. *Latin Christianity*, Vol. 3. p. 341

[5]Text: CSEL. 70. 79

In this light his famous address to the prisoners awaiting martyrdom must be read:

> 2.[6] If we realise that this world is really and truly a prison, we shall see that you have gone out of a prison rather than into one ... It is full of darkness, but you yourselves are light; it has bounds, but God has made you free ... You are about to pass through a noble struggle, in which the living God acts the part of umpire, in which the Holy Spirit is your trainer, in which the prize is an eternal crown, citizenship in the heavens, glory everlasting. Therefore your Master, Jesus Christ, before the day of conflict, has imposed on you a harder treatment, that your strength might be greater. For the athletes, too, are set apart to a more stringent discipline, that they might have their physical powers built up. They are kept from luxury, from daintier meats, from more pleasant drinks; they are pressed, racked, worn out; the harder their labors in the preparatory training, the stronger is the hope of victory. (*To the Martyrs*)

Tertullian's realist and anti-Platonic attitude to the material universe in contrast with his Manichaean surroundings can be seen especially in his writings on the sacraments. In his *On Baptism* we read:

> [7] Happy sacrament of water, in which the sins of our former blindness are washed away and we are set free for everlasting life ... All waters, therefore, in virtue of the pristine privilege of their origin, do, after invocation of God, attain the sacramental power of sanctification; for the spirit rests over the sanctifying waters.

Cyprian, on the other hand, is different from Tertullian, but is not less characteristic. He is above all conscious of the unity of the Church as a social reality. Whereas the Greek Fathers of the Second Century were equally interested in

[6]Text: CCL. 1. 3

[7]Text: CCL. 1. 277

ecclesiology, but emphasized the mystery of the Church as an eternal reality outside of time, Cyprian stresses the concrete reality of the Church in time as a community of people with its need for unity and charity. Here again, from another viewpoint it is the Latin church of later centuries which is nourished *in embryo*, at least in its major features:

> 4.[8] The Lord speaks to Peter, saying, 'I say unto thee, that thou art Peter; and upon this rock I will build my Church,...' And although to all the apostles, after His resurrection, He gives an equal power,... yet that He might set forth unity, He arranged by His authority the origin of that unity, as beginning from one... This unity we ought firmly to hold and assert, especially those of us that are bishops... The episcopate is one, each part of which is held by each one for the whole. The Church also is one, which is spread abroad far and wide into a multitude... since from one spring flow many streams, although the multitude seems diffused in the liberality of an overflowing abundance, yet the unity is still preserved in the source... cut off the stream from its fountain, and that which is cut off dries up. Thus also the Church,... She broadly expands her rivers, liberally flowing, yet her head is one, her source one; and she is one mother, plentiful in the results of fruitfulness: from her womb we are born, by her milk we are nourished, by her spirit we are animated.

Such is the distinctive approach of these two Latin Fathers of teaching and preaching. Each in his own way left on Latin theology at its very conception that indelible mark which has made it *sui generis* and which distinguishes it from the theology of the Greeks. Their biblical exegesis and original typology were no less distinctive. In those circumstances there is reason to suppose that the first Latin preachers reflect the influence of those first Latin teachers.

[8]Text: OECT, ed. Bevenot, 61

3. *Early Latin Sermons*

The earliest evidence for the existence and nature of the Latin Sermon is found in the *Apologeticum* of Tertullian. In a single chapter can be seen the characteristics of Christian preaching already recognized in Origen and identified as the mark of those discourses called homilies:

Liturgical:

> 39.[9] We are a society with a common religious feeling, unity of discipline, and a common bond of hope. We meet in gatherings and congregations to approach God in prayer ... We pray also for the Emperors, for their ministers, and for those in authority, for the security of the world, for peace on earth, and for postponement of the end.

Exegetical:

> We meet to read the books of God, if anything in the nature of the times bids us look to the future or open our eyes to facts. In any case, with those holy words we feed our faith, we lift up our hope, we confirm our confidence; and no less we reinforce our teaching in inculcation of God's precepts.

Prophetic and Homiletic:

> There is, besides, exhortation in our gatherings, rebuke and divine censure. For judgment is passed and it carries great weight, as it must among men certain that God sees them; and it is a notable foretaste of judgment to come, if any man has so sinned as to be banished from all share in our prayer, our assembly, and all holy intercourse. Our presidents are elders.

[9]Text: CCL. 1. 150

6. The Latin Sermon In The Fourth Century

The surviving evidence for such Latin Sermons in the third century is scant but at the beginning of the fourth century the scene changes with Hilary of Poitiers (315-367), the Rhone of Latin eloquence, Gregory of Elvira (357-392) famous for his sermons on the Canticle of Canticles, and Zeno of Verona (d. c. 375) the first preacher in Latin whose sermons survive in any appreciable number. However, on Ambrose of Milan (339-397) must rest the mantle of honor for he was without doubt the most prodigious in output and prestigious in name of the early Latin preachers:

> 6. 4.[1] I was glad . . . that the ancient writings of the Law and the Prophets were no longer put before me to be read with that vision whereby they had heretofore seemed absurd, when I charged Thy holy people with thinking in a certain way, though they did not actually hold such opinions. And I listened with joy to Ambrose, saying often in his sermons to the people, as though he were most carefully commending it as a rule: 'the letter kills but the spirit gives life.' (2 Cor 3:6) Having lifted the mystic veil, he laid bare the spiritual meaning of those things

[1]Text: LCL, ed. Watts, 1. 278

> which seemed to teach error when taken literally, he said nothing that offended me, though I still did not know whether his statements were true. (*Conf. Augustine*)

In Ambrose, especially, can be seen the basic fourfold structure of the sermon as it was preached by Origen and described by Tertullian; but in Ambrose also can be seen, as has already been seen in the Cappadocians, that further development of the basic structure as the sermon became more rhetorical, thematic, catechetical, mystagogical, and less exegetical. The same spirit which occasioned this fourth century development in the East was equally at work in the West. It now remains to illustrate these new features of Latin preaching from the sermons of the first Latin preachers.

1. The Rhetorical Dimension

AMBROSE OF MILAN (339-397)

In the Christian funeral orations of the Greek Fathers we saw something of the interaction of Christianity and paganism that took place in the fourth century as the schools of rhetoric informed the eloquence of the Fathers, and the Fathers transformed the eloquence of the schools. Like the Greek *Encomium* the Latin *Laudatio Funebris* was also influenced by Latin consolation literature whose commonplaces were no different from those of the Greek. Once again the loss of wealth, health, power, friendship, beauty and vigor was softened by vision and insight. Men were reminded of the transience of the living and the repose of the dead. Grief was tempered by reason, and emotion controlled accordingly. Time alone was the great solace for it cured all ills and healed all things.

To such commonplaces of consolation Christianity added the incomparably superior means of consolation furnished by the Christian faith with its emphasis on the central doctrines of the Christian religion. Furthermore, in the

Psalms and Prophets of the Old Testament Christians possessed a consolation literature of unique power and beauty which also enjoyed unique authority as the Word of God Himself.

The three funeral orations of Ambrose on the Emperor Valentinian, on Theodosius, and on his brother Satyrus are the only known examples of this genre in ancient Christian Latin literature. In these Ambrose, for the most part, followed the classical rhetorical structure of Exordium and Lament, Encomium and Consolation, Exhortation and Prayer, canonized in a sense by Gregory Nazianzus; but already in contrast with the orations of the Greeks there can be detected in those of Ambrose the conciseness and brevity of the Latin language, and a new humanism which is the fruit of Christian faith. The oration on Satyrus illustrates the point:

Exordium and Lament:

> [2] We have here ... beloved brethren, my sacrifice in the person of my lord and brother Satyrus, an untainted victim and one acceptable to God ... I have considered nothing, dear brethren, in human relationships more priceless than such a brother, nothing worthier of my affection, nothing more dear. But public concerns come before personal matters ... Why, indeed, should I weep for you, my dearest brother, when you were thus taken away from me that all might have you in common? I have not lost you; I have simply changed my way of enjoying you. Before, we were inseparable in a physical sense; now, we are undivided in our affection. For you abide in me, and you will abide with me forever. When you were living among us, our country never took you away from me. You yourself never preferred our country to me, and now you have given me our other country. For I have begun to

[2]Text: CSEL. 73. 7. 209

> be no longer a stranger in the land where the better portion of myself now is. I really never lived for myself alone, since the better part of both of us was in each other. Yet we were both in Christ, in whom is the sum of all things and the portion of every individual. This grave, within which is the fruit not of nature but of grace, is more precious to me than our native soil. In your body, which now lies lifeless, is the better effort of my life, and in this body also, which I carry about, the richer portion belongs to you.

The grief of the Exordium is extended into the Encomium by way of a prolonged lamentation in which he grieves for his personal loss but is consoled by the sympathy of his people.

> 28.[3] Naturally, I am deeply grateful to you, beloved brethren, my holy people, that you participate in our sorrow as your own sorrow, that you think that our bereavement has fallen upon yourselves, and that with this new and wonderful demonstration of affection you are offering the tears of the whole city, of every age, and of all orders. This is not the sorrow proper to private sympathy, but a public offering and service inspired by general good will. Yet, if you feel any sympathy for me personally because I have lost such a brother, I derive a rich recompense from this, since I have the pledge of your love. I wish my brother were alive. But I must grant that, while proof of public kindness is pleasant in prosperity, it is especially welcome in adversity.

In the *Encomium* he sings the praises of his brother and extols his virtues. The loss of such a soul is then lamented but the notion of Christian consolation is dominant:

[3]Text: CSEL. 73. 7. 224

> 64.[4] Mine are the tears of longing for . . . the loss of a man who exemplified such virtues and has been rescued from dangers. The very timeliness of his death suggests that we attend his funeral more with gratitude than with sorrow. For it is written, that private grief should cease in time of public mourning. Now, the Prophet does not offer consolation to that one woman only who is figured there, but to each and every one, since he seems to have addressed the Church . . . Therefore, I too, am addressed, and holy Scripture asks 'Is this what you teach? Do you not know that your example is a danger to others? Or is it possible that you are complaining that God has not heard your prayer? In the first place, your wish to merit alone what you know has been denied even to many saints is shameless arrogance, for everyone knows 'that God is not a respecter of persons.' Even if God is merciful, were He always granting the prayers of all He would seem no longer to act freely, but, as it were, like someone under constraint. Then, (since all ask, if He were to hear all, none would die.) How many things do you not ask for daily? Must God's design be destroyed because of you? When you know that a petition cannot always be granted, why do you grieve that sometimes your petition is not granted?

Thus Christian faith and human sorrow are both acknowledged: They dwell together in the heart of the pilgrim Christian, for belief and grief are fellow travelers in the Christian odyssey:

> 78.[5] But why am I tarrying, brother? Why am I waiting for my address to die with you and, as it were, be buried with you? Even though the sight and form of your lifeless body give solace, and your abiding and unchanging grace

[4]Text: CSEL. 73. 7. 242
[5]Text: CSEL. 73. 7. 249

and beauty comfort my eyes, I will delay no longer, I repeat; let us proceed to the tomb. But first, before all of the people, I bid you the last farewell. I give you peace, and I pay the last kiss. Precede us to that common abode to which we must all go, and for which I long beyond everything else. Prepare a common dwelling for us, and just as here we had all things in common, so there let us also have all things in common.

Conclusion:

79.[6] Please do not abandon one who pines for you; expect one in a hurry, help him as he hastens, and if you think he tarries too much, urge him on. Never, indeed, were we really long separated from each other, and you always came to us on your return. Now, since you can no longer come back to me, I will go to you. It is only fair that I should repay your kindness and now take my turn. There was never much difference in the way we lived, and we were always well or ill together. When one of us got sick, the other ran a fever, too; and when one recovered, both were up and about. Why have we lost our common right? Even recently we were both sick together. Why did we not both die together?

Final Prayer:

80.[7] Almighty God, I now commend to you an innocent soul ... a true oblation. Accept favorably and kindly a brother's gift, the sacrifice of Thy priest. By anticipation, I now offer these libations of myself. I am coming to you with my brother as a surety, not with a pledge of money but of a life. Do not make me remain in debt for so great a sum too long. The interest on a brother's love is high and nature's principal is large when both accumulate through

[6]Text: CSEL. 73. 7. 250
[7]Text: CSEL. 73. 7. 250

increments of virtue. I can bear the burden if I shall be required to pay quickly.

2. *The Thematic Dimension*

Again as in the East so also in the West controversy raged over the nature of Christ and the Holy Spirit and consequently over the triune nature of God. Inevitably these theological themes were also carried into the pulpit though the evidence in the West is scant in comparison with that of the East. Hilary of Poitiers is the first dogmatic theologian and eminent exegete of our western world whose sermons have reached us. An accomplished stylist who loved literary beauty and was well versed in the philosophical and rhetorical culture of his time, he was probably the first to announce the principle that sacred subjects should be presented in dignified form.

1. HILARY OF POITIERS (315-367)

In Hilary, Eastern and Western styles come together. Something of this style can be seen in the following excerpt from his *Treatise on the Trinity*:

> VIII. 14.[8] We believe that the Word became flesh and that we receive His flesh in the Lord's Supper. How then can we fail to believe that He really dwells within us? When He became man, He actually clothed Himself in our flesh, uniting it to Himself forever. In the sacrament of His body, He actually gives us His own flesh, which He has united to His divinity. This is why we are all one, because the Father is in Christ, and Christ is in us. He is in us through His flesh and we are in Him. With Him we form a unity which is in God. The manner of our indwelling in Him through the sacrament of His body and blood is

[8]Text: PL. 10. 247

evident from the Lord's own words: 'This world will see me no longer but you shall see me. Because I live you shall live also, for I am in my Father, you are in me, and I am in you.' (Jn 14:19) Were it a question of mere unity of will, why should He have given us this explanation of the steps by which it is achieved? He is in the Father by reason of His divine nature; we are in Him by reason of His human birth, and He is in us through the mystery of the sacraments. This, surely, is what He wished us to believe; this is how He wanted us to understand the perfect unity that is achieved through our Mediator, who lives in the Father while we live in Him, and who, while living in the Father, lives also in us. This is how we attain to unity with the Father. Christ is in very truth in the Father by his eternal generation; we are in very truth in Christ, and He likewise is in us. Christ Himself bore witness to the reality of this unity when He said: 'He who eats my flesh and drinks my blood lives in me and I in him.' No one will be in Christ unless Christ Himself has been in him; Christ will take to Himself only the flesh of those who have received His flesh. He had already explained the mystery of this perfect unity when He said: 'As the living Father sent me and I draw life from the Father, so he who eats my flesh will draw life from me.' We draw life from His flesh just as He draws life from the Father. Such comparisons aid our understanding, since we can grasp a point more easily when we have an analogy. And the point is that Christ is the well-spring of our life. Since we who are in the flesh have Christ dwelling in us through His flesh, we shall draw life from Him in the same way as he draws life from the Father.

2. ZENO OF VERONA (d. c. 375)

The earliest and largest collection of Latin sermons that has come down to us belongs to Zeno, the Bishop of Verona. A trained Latin rhetor, he was well acquainted with the classical literature of Rome and also with the theological writings of Tertullian and Cyprian. The trinitarian and christological themes of the fourth century appear in his sixteen long sermons and seventy-seven shorter ones that survive: in fact all his sermons are thematic and show a great propensity for the allegorical approach to Scripture and the symbolic approach to the sacraments; likewise they reflect the moral exegesis of the North African theologians with their preference for certain Old Testament types like Job and Tobit as we have already seen:

> 1. 15.[9] Is Job a type of Christ? Listen to the Scriptures: 'The sun of justice will arise for you.' (Mal 4:2) Job was called truthful, but the Lord is, as he says in the Gospel, 'the way and the truth.' (Jn 14:16) And while Job was rich, the Lord is far richer, 'for the earth is the Lord's and everything in it; the world and all who dwell in it.' (Ps 23:1) But we may compare Job and Christ in many ways. As Job was tempted by the devil three times, so too Christ was tempted three times. The Lord set aside his riches out of love for us and chose poverty so that we might become rich, while Job lost all that he possessed. A violent wind killed Job's sons, while the sons of God, the prophets, were killed by the fury of the Pharisees. Job became ulcerated and disfigured, while the Lord, by becoming man, took on the defilement of the sins committed by all mankind. The wife of Job tempted him to sin, much as the synagogue tried to force the Lord to yield to corrupt leadership. And as Job sat on a dunghill of worms, so all the evil of the world is really a dunghill which became the Lord's dwelling place. The restoration of health and riches to Job prefigures the resurrection, which gives health and eternal life to those who believe in Christ. And just as Job fathered other sons, so too did Christ, for the apostles, the sons of the Lord, succeeded the prophets. Job died happily and in peace, but there is no death for

[9]Text: CCL. 22. 61

> the Lord. He is praised forever, just as he was before time began, and as he always will be as time continues and moves into eternity.

3. The Catechetical and Mystagogical Dimension

AMBROSE OF MILAN (339-397)

The same circumstances which occasioned the development of the catechumenate in the East in the fourth century were equally felt in the West after the peace of Constantine. Thus in the *De Mysteriis* of Ambrose there is the equivalent in Latin of the Mystagogical Catecheses attributed to Cyril of Jerusalem. Again, they are the addresses given to the newly baptized during Easter week and they treat of the rites and meaning of the sacraments of baptism, confirmation and eucharist. Another work, *De Sacramentis*, very similar in content to the *De Mysteriis*, is, however, a more detailed presentation of the same material and it too is now recognized as the work of Ambrose. Like the catecheses of Cyril of Jerusalem, the *De Mysteriis* of Ambrose also clearly distinguishes between the daily lenten sermon on morals and the mystagogical catecheses:

> 1. 1.[10] We have given a daily sermon on morals, when the deeds of the Patriarchs or the precepts of the Proverbs were read, in order that, being informed and instructed by them, you might become accustomed to enter upon the ways of our forefathers and to pursue their road, and to obey the divine commands, whereby, renewed by baptism, you might hold to that manner of life which befits those who are washed.

As at Jerusalem, the mystagogical catecheses of Ambrose were also delivered during Easter week to the neophytes fresh from the font and clad in their garments of white:

[10]Text: SC. 25. (2). 156

> 1. 2.[11] Now is the time to speak of the mysteries and to set forth the very meaning of the sacraments. Had we thought that this should have been explained to those not yet initiated before baptism, we would have betrayed rather than portrayed the mysteries.

This new dimension of preaching, commonly called mystagogical, was probably developed in the first place to safeguard the transcendent Christian mystery from the dangers of popular exposure and in the second place to proclaim the deeper understanding of the sacraments which theologians like Tertullian and Cyprian had earlier expressed. Theologically, this development is the result of typology properly understood and seen as something different, if not really distinct, from prophecy. Again this typological approach can be, and in fact often has been, the victim of excessive allegory, as with Theodore of Mopsuestia, for this danger is ever present to the degree that the sacramental sign is isolated in its significance and divorced from the biblical word of explanation. But in Ambrose, as in Cyril, there is no such separation. In fact the mystagogical instructions of each are clearly an integral part of what was called the Mass of the Catechumens which at that time still centered upon the Word of God celebrated and explained.

The multiplicity of biblical references in the catecheses of Ambrose is indicative of the place and importance of the Scriptures in the explanation of the sacraments in the catechumenate at Milan. Here word and sacrament are perfectly intertwined, and are intrinsically bound up with each other. As a result the works performed by God in the history of salvation show forth and bear out the doctrine and realities signified by the words; the words, for their part, proclaim the works and bring to light the mystery they contain.

[11]Text: SC. 25. (2). 156

This blend of Divine Word and human symbol, of Mystery and sacrament, of Spirit and matter, of God and man, of Word made flesh, of Christ and his Church, is a new vision and a new experience. The catecheses of Ambrose are a sharing of this vision with his new faithful. Something of their distinctive quality can be seen in the following schematic summary:

> I. 3.[12] effetha, that is, be opened . . . open then your ears . . . enjoy the fragrance of eternal life breathed on you by means of the sacrament . . .
>
> II. 5.[13] the holy of holies was opened up for you . . . you entered into the sacred place of regeneration . . . you renounced the world and its dissipation and sensuality . . .
>
> II. 6.[14] then you saw the priest . . . he is an angel whose message is the Kingdom of Christ and eternal life . . . judge him not by his appearance but by his office . . .
>
> III. 8.[15] What did you see in the baptistry? Water certainly, but not water alone . . . believe that the presence of the Godhead is there. Consider how ancient the mystery is . . . prefigured as it was in the flood . . . Noah sent first a raven, then a dove, which came back with an olive branch . . . you see water . . . you see wood, you look on a dove . . . and you hesitate to believe the Mystery? The water is that in which the flesh is dipped . . . to wash away all its sin: the wood is that to which the Lord Jesus was fastened when he suffered for us: the dove is the one in whose likeness the Holy Spirit descended; the Spirit who

[12]Text: SC. 25. (2). 156

[13]Text: SC. 25. (2). 158

[14]Text: SC. 25. (2). 158

[15]Text: SC. 25. (2). 158

breathes into you ... peace of soul ... tranquility of mind ... the raven is the figure of sin ... it goes out and does not return.

III. 16.[16] Learn from the readings ... Naaman ... was a leper ... the rivers of his own country had better waters ... he refused to obey the prophet's instructions ... he yielded and bathed and was instantly made clean ... then he realized that it is not waters that make clean but grace ... you are already made clean and so ought to have no doubt.

V. 28.[17] You went down into the water ... Remember what you said ... I believe ... in the Father ... in the Son ... in the Holy Spirit ... You are committed by this spoken understanding to believe the same of the Son as of the Father, and the same of the Holy Spirit as of the Son, with this one exception: you proclaim that you must believe in the cross of the Lord Jesus alone.

VII. 29[18] After this you went up to the priest ... This is the oil spoken of by Solomon: Your name is oil poured out, so that the maidens loved you and attracted you ... How many souls reborn today have loved you, Lord Jesus and have said: draw us after you; we shall make haste to follow you, in the fragrance of your garments ... to breathe the fragrance of the Resurrection ... the oil flows down ... on the grace of youth ... we are all anointed with spiritual grace ... to share in God's kingdom and in the priesthood.

VII. 34.[19] Then you received white garments ... as a sign ... that you had cast off the clothing of sin ... and put

[16]Text: SC. 25. (2). 164

[17]Text: SC. 25. (2). 170

[18]Text: SC. 25. (2). 172

[19]Text: SC. 25. (2). 174

on the chaste garment of innocence . . . because Christ's garments were white as snow when in the Gospel he revealed the glory of the resurrection . . . and the Church says . . . in the Song of Songs . . . I am black, but beautiful: black through human frailty, beautiful through divine grace.

VII. 37.[20] When Christ sees his Church clothed in white . . . When he sees the soul washed clean by the waters of regeneration, he cries out: how beautiful you are, my beloved, how beautiful you are; your eyes are like the eyes of a dove, for it was in the likeness of a dove that the Holy Spirit came down from heaven . . .

VII. 40.[21] And the Church answers him . . . Who shall give thee to me, my brother . . . I shall find thee . . . and shall kiss thee . . . I shall take hold of thee and bring thee into my Mother's house . . . into the secret place of her who conceived me . . . you will teach me.

VII. 40[22] Do you see how . . . She desires to attain to the inner mysteries . . . to consecrate all her affections to Christ? She still seeks . . . She still rouses His love and asks that it be roused for her . . . She desires that her spouse be provoked to a richer love for her . . . and Lord says . . . put me as a seal upon thy heart . . .

VII. 42.[23] So recall . . . That you have received a spiritual seal . . . and preserve what you have received . . . God the Father sealed you . . . Christ, the Lord, confirmed you, or gave a pledge . . . the Spirit in your heart . . .

[20]Text: SC. 25. (2). 176

[21]Text: SC. 25. (2). 178

[22]Text: SC. 25. (2). 178

[23]Text: SC. 25. (2). 178

As regards the Eucharist, Ambrose, in his *De Mysteriis* as in *De Sacramentis*, introduces two new features, more philosophical than mystagogical, to Latin theology: (1) a pronounced emphasis on the conversion of the elements into the body and blood of Christ; (2) a similar emphasis on the words of institution as effecting this conversion or consecration. Nonetheless this form of his preaching reflects the same biblical language and imagery of the baptismal sermons as he continues with the rites and types, and passes through them to the heavenly realities, the divine mysteries. Again, the following schematic summary illustrates his approach:

> VIII. 43.[24] Fresh from the waters and resplendent in white garments ... God's holy people hasten to the altar of Christ ... that heavenly banquet ... the sacred altar ... a table against those who afflict me.
>
> IX. 50.[25] How do you tell me that I receive the body of Christ ... this is not what nature formed but what benediction consecrated ... the power of benediction is greater than that of nature ... even nature is changed by the benediction ... of a prophet ... will not the words of Christ have power enough to change the nature of the elements ... He spoke and they were done; He commanded and they were created.
>
> IX. 53.[26] But why do we use arguments ... did the process of nature precede when the Lord Jesus was born of Mary? ... this is indeed the true flesh of Christ ... which was crucified and buried ... this then in truth is the sacrament of his flesh.

[24]Text: SC. 25. (2). 178

[25]Text: SC. 25. (2). 184

[26]Text: SC. 25. (2). 184

IX. 54.[27] The Lord Jesus himself declares . . . This is my body . . . This is my blood . . . and you say Amen . . . that is . . . it is true . . . What the mouth speaks let the mind within confess . . . What words utter, let the heart feel.

IX. 55.[28] Christ . . . feeds his Church . . . and says . . . How beautiful your breasts have become, my sister, my spouse . . . how beautiful they have become . . . from wine . . . A garden enclosed is my sister, my spouse, . . . the mystery should remain sealed with you . . .

IX. 56.[29] The Church . . . calls . . . to the Bridegroom . . . Arise, O Northwind, and come; . . . O Southwind blow through my garden . . . let my brother go down into his garden . . . and eat the fruit of his apple trees . . . it has good trees . . . fruitful ones . . . their roots in the waters of the sacred fountain.

IX. 57.[30] The Lord . . . replies . . . I have entered into my garden . . . I have eaten my food with honey . . . I have drunk my drink with milk . . . in us He himself eats and drinks.

IX. 58.[31] The Church, therefore, invites her neighbors . . . Eat, my neighbors, and drink and be inebriated my brethren . . . Taste and see that the Lord is sweet . . . Christ is in that sacrament . . . that food strengthens our heart . . . that drink rejoices the heart of man . . . no order of nature is here, where there is the excellence of grace.

This mystagogical dimension certainly represents a development that took place in 4th century preaching in keeping

[27]Text: SC. 25. (2). 184

[28]Text: SC. 25. (2). 184

[29]Text: SC. 25. (2). 184

[30]Text: SC. 25. (2). 185

[31]Text: SC. 25. (2). 185

with the development of sacramental theology in general. Nevertheless, the homily was not endangered by it as it was much more theological than rhetorical.

4. The Exegetical Dimension

ST. JEROME (347-430)

The sermons of Jerome (347-430), the father of the Latin Vulgate Bible, are uniquely indicative of the place of exegesis in the early Latin sermon. More exegete, scholar and hermit than preacher, this ascetic from Dalmatia received his grammatical, rhetorical and philosophical education at Rome; at Antioch on his way to Jerusalem, he attended the exegetical lectures of Apollinaris and acquired a thorough knowledge of Greek; in the desert of Chalcis, east of Antioch, he lived for three years as a hermit and learned Hebrew; at Constantinople he attended the lectures of Gregory of Nazianzus and became an enthusiastic admirer of the exegesis of Origen. Later at Rome this *vir trilinguis*, as he was called, began his literary career but was soon forced to flee the city; as the center of an ascetical circle of rich Roman ladies his familiar relations with Paula, a wealthy widow and her family became suspect. From Rome he returned to Jerusalem and settled eventually at Bethlehem. Paula's wealth enabled her to build three convents for women at Bethlehem of which she was the superior and one monastery for men directed by Jerome. Thus, Bethlehem for thirty-four years was the home of Jerome's unceasing literary activity, biblical scholarship, and extempore preaching. His fifty-nine Homilies on the Psalms illustrate the homiletic style of the great exegete:

> [32] The Psalter is like a stately mansion that has only one key to the main entrance. Within the mansion, however,

[32]Text: CCL. 78. 3

> each separate chamber has its own key. Even though the great key to the grand entrance is the Holy Spirit, still each room without exception has its own small keys and each room without exception has its own small key. Should any one accidentally confuse the keys and throw them out and then want to open one of the rooms, he could not do so until he found the right one. Similarly, the psalms are each like single cells, every one with its own proper key. The main entrance to the mansion of the Psalter is the first psalm.

Something of his approach can be seen in the following schematic summary as he comments exegetically on each verse of this first psalm:

[33]*Happy the man who follows not the counsel of the wicked* . . .

> Some commentators think that the key to this first psalm must be the person of Christ our Lord, interpreting 'the happy man' to be the man, Christ. They mean well, of course, but such an interpretation certainly shows a lack of experience and knowledge, for is that happy man is Christ, and Christ gave the law, how can the words: 'But delights in the law of the Lord,' apply to Christ? Do you see, then, that the psalm cannot refer to the person of the Lord, but rather refers in general to the just man. Here Scripture describes the three usual ways of committing sin: we entertain sinful thoughts; we commit sin in act; or we teach what is sinful. 'Happy the man who follows not the counsel of the wicked'—who thinks no evil; 'nor has stood in the way of sinners'—who does no evil; 'nor sits in the company of the insolent'—who has not taught others to sin.

[33]Text: CCL. 78. 3. = FOTC. 48. 3-13

Nor walks in the way of sinners . . .

Scripture did not say happy the man who has not sinned, but rather, happy the man who has not persevered in sin. 'Nor walks in the way of sinners.' Yesterday I committed sin. I am not happy. If, however, I do not remain in the state of sin, but withdraw from sin, I become happy once more. 'Nor sits in the company of the insolent.' Why does it say 'sits' in this verse and 'walks' in the preceding one? For this reason: just as he who has not walked—persisted—in sin is happy, so he who has not sat—persisted—in evil doctrine is happy. What does that mean? You see yourselves that the three determinants of beatitudes consist in not thinking evil, in not perservering in it and in not teaching it.

And meditates on his law day and night . . .

Meditation on the law does not consist in reading, but in doing. Even if I merely stretch forth my hand in alms giving, I am meditating on the law of God; if I visit the sick, my feet are meditating on the law of God.

He is like a tree planted near running waters . . .

There are many who interpret these words very simply to mean that just as a tree, if planted near water, will take root and grow and not wither away because it has enough moisture, so in like manner one who meditates on the law of God will derive strength and life from his meditation. This is their simple interpretation. But we shall combine spiritual things with spiritual things and read of the tree of life that was planted in Paradise, the tree of life and the tree of the knowledge of good and evil. Likewise we read in Solomon . . . 'She is a tree of life to those who grasp her,' he is speaking of wisdom. Now, if wisdom is the tree of life, Wisdom itself, indeed, is Christ. You understand now that the man who is blessed and holy is compared to this tree, that is, he is compared to Wisdom. Consequently, you see, too, that the just man is like the tree that is planted near running water. He is, in other words, like Christ you see too, that because this tree has been planted in the Garden of Eden, we have all been planted there together with Him.

That yields its fruit in due season . . .

This tree does not yield fruit in every season, but in the proper season. This is the tree that does not yield its fruit in the present day, but in the future, that is, on the day of judgement. This is the tree that bears blossoms now, that buds forth now, and promises fruits for the future. This tree bears twofold: it produces fruit and it produces foliage. The fruit that it bears contains the meaning of Scripture; the leaves, only the words. The fruit is in the meaning; the leaves are in the words. For that reason, whoever reads Sacred Scripture, if he reads merely as the Jews read, grasps only the words. If he reads with true spiritual insight, he gathers the fruit.

And whose leaves never fade . . .

The leaves of this tree are by no means useless. Even if one understands Holy Writ only as history, he has something useful for his soul . . . Because he cannot pluck the fruit, he plucks only words, the leaves for the healing of the nations, for it is written: 'and the leaves are for the healing of the nations.' One who belongs to the nations, who is not a disciple, who is as yet only one of the crowd, gathers only leaves from the tree; he receives from Scripture plain words for a healing remedy.

Not so the wicked, not so . . .

The psalmist did not say, not so the sinners, for if he had said 'sinners,' we would all then be excluded from reward. 'Not so the wicked.' There is a difference between the wicked and sinners. The wicked deny God altogether; the sinner acknowledges God and in spite of his acknowledgement commits sin.

They are like chaff which the wind drives away . . .

Holy Writ says the wicked man will be so unhappy that he is not even chaff from the earth. Chaff does not seem to have any substance, but it does, of course, have a kind of existence of its own. There is no body to it, yet what substance it does have is really by way of punishment. It is scattered here and there and is never in any one place; wherever the wind sweeps it, there its whole force is spent. The same is true of the wicked man. Once he has denied God, he is led by delusion wherever the breath of the devil sends him.

Therefore in judgement the wicked shall not stand, nor shall sinners, in the assembly of the just . . .

They shall not rise to be judged because they have already been judged, for 'he who does not believe in Me is already judged.' 'Nor shall sinners in the assembly of the just.' It does not say that sinners shall not rise again: but that they shall not stand in the assembly of the just; they do not deserve to stand with those who are not to be judged. If they believe in Me, says the Lord, they would rise up with those who do not have to be judged.

For the Lord watches over the way of the just . . .

Why is it so extraordinary that the Lord knows the way of the just? The Scriptures also say that God knows those whom He deigns to know. In regard to the wicked, it says: 'I never knew you. Depart from me, you workers of iniquity.' Moreover, the Apostle says: 'If anyone acknowledges the Lord, the Lord will acknowledge him.' 'For the Lord knows the way of the just.' The Lord does not know the sinner, but the just man He does know.

But the way of the wicked vanishes . . .

> That does not mean that the wicked will perish. If they repent and do penance, they too will be saved. When the Apostle Paul was persecuting Christ and His Church, he was wicked. If the wicked perish, there is no chance for their repentance. It does not say that the wicked shall perish, but that the way of the wicked vanished, that is, wickedness sshall perish. Not the wicked, but wickedness itself; not the man who was wicked will perish, but while he is repenting, wickedness vanishes.

This sermon shows the exegete respecting the literal word of his text but at the same time always moving spiritually beyond it. The summary with which he concludes this sermon shows his simple and direct style—so much more in the tradition of the earlier homiletical approach than in the later rhetorical development:

> God vouchsafes to instruct us that there are three things we must not do, and two things that we must do. Let us be the just man compared to the tree of life; let us not be the wicked who are compared to dust; let us not be sinners, for sinners shall not stand in the assembly of the just. Let us take heed that the path of evil may vanish; and let us bless God to whom be glory forever and ever. Amen

Conclusion

The Latin Sermon and the Greek Homily bear the same marks of their common origin. They developed in the same thematic and mystagogical directions and presumably for the same reasons. Nonetheless fundamentally they are different and they differ in the way that a Latin differs from a Greek, not only in seeing but also in believing. In style they are not less different and this difference becomes clearly visible in the use or abuse of rhetoric. The nine sermons preached by Ambrose on the *Six Days of Creation*, contrasted with the nine homilies of Basil on the *Hexaemeron*, illustrate this point. Following in the footsteps of Basil, his master and model, Ambrose has made his sermons into a series of Christian and humanistic observations on nature and man in their relationship to their Creator. But he does so with the mind, and taste, and style of a Latin, and with over a hundred reminiscences from his beloved Latin poet: Virgil's theocentric philosophy as expressed especially in the *Georgics* became an object of fascination to his fellow countryman. In these sermons on the *Six Days of Creation* can be seen especially the language of the Roman poet who also marvelled at the wonders of the created world with "all the charm of all the Muses often flowering in a lovely word." Many of these "lovely words" Ambrose embedded in his mosaic on creation, which shows the "genius" of the early Latin Sermon and the humanism of the first Latin preacher in Italy:

> 1. 4.[34] In order to show that the creation of the world took place in the spring, Scripture says: 'This month shall be to you the beginning of months, it is for you the first months of the year,' (Ex 12:2) calling the first month the springtime. It was fitting that the beginning of the year be the beginning of generation, and that generation itself be fostered by the gentler breezes. The tender germs of matter would be unable to endure exposure to the bitter cold of winter, or to the torrid heat of summer . . . Then there was the mild temperature of spring . . . a season suitable for all things . . . The sons of Israel left Egypt in the season of the spring . . . At that time each year the Pasch of Jesus Christ is celebrated, that is to say, the passing over from vices to virtues, from the desires of the flesh to grace and sobriety of mind, from the unleavened bread of malice and wickedness to truth and sincerity.

[34]Text: CSEL. 32. 1. 11

Accordingly, the regenerated are thus addressed: 'This month shall be to you the beginning of months; it is for you the first in the months of the year.' The person who is baptized leaves behind and abandons in a spiritual sense that prince of the world when he says: 'I renounce thee, devil, both thy works and thy power.' No longer will he serve him, either by the earthly passions of his body, or by the errors of a corrupt mind. On this occasion every evil deed of his sinks to the bottom like lead. Protected as he is by good works on his right and his left, he endeavors to cross over the waters of this life with step untainted . . .

7. Augustine
Latin Preacher *Par Excellence*

Augustine in his pulpit was the heir of Cicero and Quintilian as Chrysostom was of Demosthenes and Isocrates. To these Fathers belong more than half of the three thousand sermons and catecheses that are extant from this period between Nicaea and Chalcedon, modern research assigning about eight hundred to Chrysostom and over a thousand to Augustine.

In Augustine the Latin sermon for the first time shed its Grecian form and assumed its own distinctive character. This is probably the most significant moment in the history of preaching for it is the Latin sermon more than the Greek homily that has influenced Western preaching. Like Chrysostom, he too was ordained to preach as the aged Bishop of Hippo needed the help of this rhetor, philosopher and exegete. In his background lay the whole development which is described in the *Confessions* as he moves through the rhetorical studies and extensive experience as a teacher into the art of oratory. Nor can one forget the inner development which led him from his youthful life in Carthage to the ascetical ideal in Milan and beyond as he moves through Manicheism and Platonism into the theology of faith.

1. The Preacher's Guide

The Bible was the book Augustine preached. It is no coincidence, then, that his short homiletic guide should be the fourth book, or conclusion, of his *De Doctrina Christiana*, for the full study of the scriptures involved him in two actions: the art of discovering what we are to preach, and the art of preaching what we have discovered. This fourth book of *De Doctrina Christiana* is not so much a practical guide on the techniques of preaching as a discussion on the basic relationships of rhetoric and preaching. Like Cicero he assumed in most a knowledge of the rules or rhetoric from their school training. Otherwise there was little point in bothering about them, for the right approach could be easily acquired by an intelligent reading of the great authors of the Church like Cyprian or Ambrose or by simply listening to good preachers at work. Thus Augustine places very little emphasis on the conscious study of the preacher's art: "Eloquence grows upon those who read and listen eagerly and intelligently to the eloquent more easily upon those who strive merely to imitate the rules for eloquence." With these words the liveliest speaker of the old school impatiently throws overboard all the useless antique ballast that cluttered up his subjection. Thus wisdom, and not eloquence, was for Augustine the soul of the preacher:

> IV. 5.[1] He helps his hearers more by his wisdom than his oratory; although he himself is less useful than he would be if he were an eloquent speaker also. But the one to guard against is the man whose eloquence is no more than an abundant flow of empty words. His listener is more easily charmed by him in matters that are unprofitable to hear about and, all too frequently, such eloquence is mistaken for truth. Moreover, this opinion did not escape the notice of those who believed that the art of rhetoric

[1]Text: CCL 32. 120 = FOTC 4. 173.

> should be taught. They acknowledged that 'wisdom without eloquence is of small benefit to states, but eloquence without wisdom is frequently very prejudicial, and never beneficial' ... Furthermore, a man speaks more or less wisely in proportion as he has made more or less progress in the Holy Scriptures."

Nevertheless, Augustine in no way belittled the place of eloquence in preaching. In fact he claims that the writers of the sacred scriptures possess an eloquence of their own as divine wisdom gives to human speech an unmistakeable exaltation of style. By way of illustration he quotes from the second epistle to the Corinthians in which Paul, "The companion of wisdom and the leader of eloquence ... contradicts certain false apostles among the Jews who were disparaging him":

> I repeat, let no one think me foolish. But if so, then regard me as such, that I also may boast a little. What I am saying in this confidence of boasting, I am speaking according to the Lord, but, as it were, in foolishness. Since many boast according to the flesh, I too will boast. For you gladly put up with fools, because you are wise yourselves! For you suffer it if a man enslaves you, if a man devours you, if a man takes from you, if a man is arrogant, if a man slaps your face! I speak to my own shame, as though we had been weak. But wherein any man is bold—I am speaking foolishly—I also am bold. Are they Hebrews? So am I! Are they Israelites? So am I! Are they offspring of Abraham? So am I! Are they ministers of Christ? I—to speak as a fool—am more: in many more labors, in prisons more frequently, in lashes above measure, often exposed to death. From the Jews five times I received forty lashes less one. Thrice I was scourged, once I was stoned, thrice I suffered shipwreck, a night and a day I was adrift on the sea; in journeyings often, in perils from floods, in perils from robbers, in perils in the city, in perils from my own nation, in perils from the Gentiles, in perils in the wilderness, in perils in

> the sea, in perils from false brethren; in labor and hardships, in many sleepless nights, in hunger and thirst, in fastings often, in cold and nakedness. Besides those outer things, there is my daily pressing anxiety, the care of all the churches! Who is weak, and I am not weak? Who is made to stumble, and I am not inflamed? If I must boast, I will boast of the things that concern my weakness." Attentive souls can see how much wisdom is in these words. Even one who is deep in sleep can observe also with what a noble flow of eloquence they rush on. (2 Cor 11:16-30).

Augustine's analysis of this passage according to the rules of rhetoric shows this rhetor's feel for the eloquence of biblical language:

> VII. 13.[2] Further, anyone who has learned about them observes that, inserted with a most suitable variety, those *caesa*, called *commata* by the Greeks, and the *membra* and periods of which I spoke a little while ago, created the whole figure and expression, so to speak, of a style which charms and arouses even the unlearned. From the place where I began to introduce this passage there are periods. The first is the smallest, that is, it has two *membra* (periods cannot have less than two *membra*, although they may have more). The first, then, is: 'I repeat, let no one think me foolish.' The second follows with three *membra*: 'But if so, then regard me as such, that I also may boast a little.' The third, which comes next, has four *membra*: 'What I am saying, in the confidence of boasting, I am not speaking according to the Lord, but as it were in foolishness.' The fourth has two: 'Since many boast according to the flesh, I too will boast.' The fifth has two: 'For you gladly put up with fools, because you are wise yourselves'! The sixth also has two: 'For you suffer it if a man enslaves you.' Three cases follow: 'If a

[2]Text: CCL 32. 125 = FOTC. 4. 179-181

man is arrogant.' Then comes three *membra*: 'If a man slaps your face! I speak to my own shame, as though we had been weak.' A period of three *membra* follows: 'But wherein any man is bold—I am speaking foolishly—I also am bold.' From this point on, after several *caesa* have been proposed as questions so separate *caesa* are given back in answer; three answers to three questions: 'Are they Hebrews? So am I! Are they Israelites? So am I! Are they offspring of Abraham? So am I!' Although the fourth *caesum* has been expressed with the same interrogation, he does not reply with the balance of another *caesum*, but of a *membrum*: 'Are they ministers of Christ? I—to speak as a fool—am more.' Then, after the form of interrogation has been properly set aside, the four following *caesa* are poured forth: 'in many more labors, in prisons more frequently, in lashes above measure, often exposed to death.' A short period is then inserted, because by the elevation of our voice we must distinguish 'From the Jews five times,' making it one membrum to which is joined the other: 'I received forty lashes less one.' Then he returns to *caesa* and uses three: 'Thrice I was scourged, once I was stoned, thrice I suffered shipwreck.' A *membrum* follows: 'a night and a day I was adrift on the sea.' Then fourteen *caesa* flow forth with appropriate vigor: 'in journeyings often, in perils from floods, in perils from robbers, in perils from my own nation, in perils from the Gentiles, in perils in the city, in perils in the wilderness, in perils in the sea, in perils from false brethren; in labor and hardships, in many sleepless nights, in hunger and thirst, in fastings often, in cold and nakedness.' After these he inserts a period of three *membra*: 'Besides those outer things, there is my daily pressing anxiety, the care of all the churches!' And to this we join two *membra* as a question: 'Who is weak and I am not weak? Who is made to stumble, and I am not inflamed'? Finally, this whole passage as if panting for breath, is completed by a period of two *membra*: 'If I must boast, I will boast of the things that concern my weakness.' After

> this outburst, because he rests as it were, and makes his hearer rest by inserting a little narrative, it is impossible to describe adequately what beauty and what charm he produces. For, he continues by saying: 'The God and Father of our Lord Jesus, who is blessed for evermore, knows that I do not lie.' And then he tells briefly how he has been exposed to danger and how he escaped. (*Christ. Doct.*)

In the same way he analyzes the eloquence of the prophet Amos when "he was reproving the wicked, the proud, the voluptuous, and those who are careless about fraternal charity":

> VII. 16.[3] Woe to you that are wealthy in Sion, and to you that have confidence in the mountain of Samaria: ye great men, heads of the people, that go in with state into the house of Israel. Pass ye over to Chalane, and see, and go from thence into Emath the great: and go down into Geth of the Philistines, and to all the best kingdoms of these: if their border be larger than your border. You that are separated unto the evil day: and that approach to the throne of iniquity: You that sleep upon beds of ivory, and are wanton on your couches; that eat the lamb out of the flock, and the calves out of the midst of the herd: You that sing to the sound of the psaltery: they have thought themselves to have instruments of music like David: that drink wine in bowls, and anoint themselves with the best ointment: and they were not concerned for the affliction of Joseph.' Would those men who, as if they themselves were learned and eloquent, despise our prophets as illiterate and unskilled in speaking—would they have wished to express themselves otherwise, if they had been obliged to try something like this to such people—those of them, at least, who would not have wanted to act like madmen? (*Christ. Doct.*)

[3]Text: CCL 32. 128 = FOTC. 4. 183

What more could be desired from this outburst of eloquence in which the invective is hurled against senses that were numbed in sleep and in torpor. Augustine hears this discourse adorned with the sound of such names as Sion, Samaria, Chalane, Emath the Great, and Geth of the Philistines: even the words used in these places are very appropriately varied—"you are wealthy," "you have confidence," "pass ye over," "go," and "go down." Again one senses in his analysis something of the rhetor's sensitivity to the very sound of the word:

> VII. 21.[4] Indeed, many points which apply to the rules of eloquence can be discovered in this very passage which I have used as an example. A sincere reader is not so much instructed when he carefully analyzes it as he is set on fire when he recites it with glowing feeling. For, not by human effort were these words devised; they have been poured forth from the Mind of God both wisely and eloquently, so that wisdom was not bent upon eloquence, nor did eloquence separate itself from wisdom. As some very eloquent and intelligent men could observe and maintain, if those principles which are learned in the art of oratory could not be respected, observed, and brought to these teachings, unless they were first discovered in the natural ability of orators, is it any wonder that they are discovered in those men sent by Him who creates natural abilities? Therefore, let us admit that our canonical writers and teachers were not only wise, but truly eloquent, with such an eloquence as was appropriate for persons of this kind. (*Christ. Doct.*)

For Augustine even the obscurity of certain passages of scripture was spread by God to exercise the spirit of man. The preacher must therefore respect this obscurity: at the same time he must cultivate clarity of exposition if the

[4]Text: CCL 32. 131 = FOTC. 4. 187

congregation is to understand the message. But understanding is not enough: "even the very food without which we cannot live must be seasoned in order to satisfy the taste of the majority." Thus the necessity of eloquence to season wisdom. Accordingly he applies to preaching the rules of classical rhetoric concerning the purpose of the address and the use of various styles of presentation. In doing so, he makes Cicero his master who thought that "an eloquent man should speak in such a way that he teaches, pleases and persuades or speaks to intellect, feeling and will." For Augustine as a Christian preacher this means to explain, to edify and to convert. To these three categories correspond three kinds of delivery, namely, the subdued, the moderate, and the grand which in their turn again are means of instructing, holding the attention, and convincing:

> XII. 27.[5] Of these three, the one mentioned first, that is the necessity of teaching, depends upon what we say; the other two depend upont the manner in which we say it. Therefore, a man who speaks with the intention of teaching should not think that he has said what he intended to the person he is trying to instruct, so long as he is not understood. Although he has said what he himself understands, he thus is not to be regarded as having yet spoken to the man who has not understood him. However, if he has been understood, he has spoken, no matter how he expressed himself. But, if he is also trying to please or persuade the one to whom he is speaking, he will not succeed by speaking in any way whatsoever, for the manner in which he speaks is important in order that he may produce this effect. Just as the listener must be pleased in order that he may be kept listening, so he must be persuaded in order that he may be influenced to act. And, just as he is pleased if you speak attractively, so he is moved if he finds pleasure in what you promise, dreads

[5]Text: CCL 32. 135 = FOTC. 4. 193

> what you threaten, hates what you condemn, embraces what you praise, grieves over what you emphasize as deplorable, rejoices when you say something he should rejoice at, pities those whom in your discourses you set before his eyes as objects of pity, avoids those whom you by awakening fear point out should be avoided. Whatever else can be accomplished through grand eloquence to influence the hearts of one's listeners, they must be persuaded not that they may know what should be done, but to do what they already know they should do. (*Christ. Doct.*)

Ideally, according to Augustine, preaching should usually involve an intermingling of the three styles, for each one has its advantages and disadvantages. Interpretative passages, for example, should dispense with decorative elaborations but should glow with clarity of argument. Exaltation on the other hand can be made more effective by rhetorical elaboration whereas an exalted theme demands the passion of declamation to move the hearers and to spur them to action:

> XXIV. 53.[6] However, if a preacher is applauded repeatedly and eagerly, we should not for that reason believe that he is speaking in the grand style. It is the keenness of intellect in the subdued style and the ornaments of the moderate style which also have this effect. The grand style usually restrains voices by its own weight, yet it elicits tears. Indeed, at Caesarea in Mauritania when I was dissuading the people from civil war, or worse than civil war—which they called *Caterva* (for not only fellow-citizens, but even relatives, brothers, yes, parents and children, divided into two factions, and, according to custom, fought one another with stones for several successive days at a certain time of the year and each one

[6]Text: CCL 32. 159 = FOTC. 4. 224

> killed whomever he could)—I pleaded in the grand style as powerfully as I could that I might extirpate and banish by my speech such a barbarous and deep-rooted evil from their hearts and customs. However, it was not when I heard them applauding, but when I saw them weeping, that I realized I had accomplished anything. By their applause they signified that they were instructed and pleased, but by their tears they showed they were persuaded. When I saw these, I believed, before they demonstrated it by fact, that the frightful custom handed down from their fathers and grandfathers, and from their far-off ancestors, which was besieging their hearts like an enemy, or rather was in possession of them, had been completely conquered. As soon as my speech was finished, I directed their hearts and lips to thank God. And, behold! for nearly eight years or more, by the grace of Christ, nothing like that has been attempted there. (*Christ. Doct.*)

Examples of the three styles are then quoted from the writings of Saint Paul:

(a) The Subdued Style

> XX. 39.[7] Tell me, you who desire to be under the Law, have you not heard the Law? For it is written that Abraham had two sons, the one by a slave-girl and the other by a free woman. And the son of the slave-girl was born according to the flesh, but the son of the free woman in virtue of the promise. This is said by way of allegory. For these are the two covenants: one indeed from Mount Sinai, bringing forth children unto bondage, which is Agar. For Sinai is a mountain in Arabia, which corresponds to the present Jerusalem, and is in slavery with her children. But that Jerusalem which is above is free, which is our mother, and so on.

[7]Text: CCL 32. 144 = FOTC. 4. 205

(b) The Moderate Style

XX. 40.[8] Do not rebuke an elderly man, but exhort him as you would a father, and young men as brothers, elderly women as mothers, younger women as sisters; as it is in these words: 'I exhort you, therefore, brethren, by the mercy of God, to present your bodies as a sacrifice, living, holy, pleasing to God.'

Almost the entire passage in which this exhortation occurs employs the moderate style of eloquence. There is more beauty in those portions where, as if in payment of a just debt, things that belong together proceed fittingly from one another; for example: 'But we have gifts differing according to the grace that has been given us, such as prophecy to be used according to the proportion of faith; or ministry, in ministering; or he who teaches, in teaching; or he who exhorts, in exhorting; he who gives, in simplicity; he who presides, with carefulness; he who shows mercy, with cheerfulness.'

(c) The Grand Style

XX. 42.[9] Now, the grand style of eloquence differs from this moderate style principally in the fact that it is not so much embellished with fine expressions as it is forceful because of the passionate feelings of the heart. It adopts nearly all those ornaments of style, but it does not search for them if it does not have them at hand. In fact it is driven on by its own ardor and, if it chances upon any beauty of style, carries it off and claims it, not through a concern for beauty, but because of the force of the subject matter. It is sufficient for the purpose that appropriate words conform to the ardent affection of the heart; they need not be chosen by carefulness of speech. For, if a brave man, eagerly bent upon battle, is armed with a golden and jewel-studded sword, he certainly achieves

[8]Text: CCL 32. 146 = FOTC. 4. 207

[9]Text: CCL 32. 148 = FOTC. 4. 210

> whatever he does with these weapons. Yet, he is the same man and is very powerful even when 'anger provides a weapon for him as he casts about for one.' The Apostle is endeavoring to persuade us, for the sake of the preaching of the Gospel, to endure patiently all the misfortunes of this life with the consoling help of the gifts of God. It is a noble subject delivered in the grand style, and it does not lack the ornaments of eloqence.
> 'Behold,' he says, 'now is the acceptable time; behold, now is the day of salvation! Giving no offense to anyone, that our ministry may not be blamed. On the contrary, conducting ourselves in all circumstances as God's ministers, in much patience; in tribulations, in hardships, in distresses; in stripes, in imprisonments, in tumults; in labors, in sleepless nights, in fastings; in innocence; in knowledge, in long-suffering; in kindness, in the Holy Spirit, in unaffected love; in the word of truth, in the power of God; with the armor of justice on the right hand and on the left; in honor and dishonor, in evil report and good report; as deceivers and yet truthful, as unknown and yet we are well known, as dying and behold, we live, as chastised but not killed, as sorrowful yet always rejoicing, as poor yet enriching many, as having nothing yet possessing all things.' See him still aflame: 'We are frank with you, O Corinthians; our heart is wide open to you' and the rest which is too long to quote. (*Christ. Doct.*)

Those three aims of preaching, according to Augustine, should be no more exclusive of each other than the three styles already discussed:

> XXVI. 56.[10] They are not to be understood as if each is to be attributed to one of the three styles of eloquence in such a way that being understood pertains to the subdued style, giving pleasure, to the moderate style, and being

[10]Text: CCL 32. 161 = FOTC. 4. 227

> heard with persuasion, to the grand style. Rather they are to be applied in such a way that the speaker always keeps in mind and uses these three as much as possible, even when he is concerned with each one of them separately. We do not wish even what we say in the subdued style to be boring, and, therefore, we are anxious not only to be listened to with understanding, but also with pleasure. (*Christ. Doct.*)

In conclusion, he utters a warning:

> XXIX.[11] If the preacher lacks eloquence let him live in such a way that he will not only prepare a reward for himself but will also furnish an example for others. Let his beauty of life be as it were his most powerful ceremony.

Prayer and its importance in the life of the preacher is his last word on this subject:

> XXX. 63.[12] Whether he is just about to speak before the people or before some smaller group, or whether he is going to compose something to be spoken before the people, or read by those who are willing and able to do so, he should pray that God will put a good sermon into his mouth. For, if Queen Esther, who was about to speak before the king in behalf of the temporal well-being of her nation, prayed that God would put 'a well-ordered speech' in her mouth, how much more should he pray to obtain such a gift who is laboring 'in the word and in teaching' for the eternal well-being of men?
>
> Those who are going to preach what they have obtained from others, even before they received it should pray for those from whom they are obtaining it, that they may be granted what they wish to receive themselves.

[11]Text: CCL 32. 165 = FOTC. 4. 232

[12]Text: CCL 32. 167 = FOTC. 4. 234

> And, when they have received it, they should pray that they may preach it profitably and that those to whom they preach may accept it. They should give thanks for a favorable outcome of their speech to Him from whom they are aware they have received it, that 'he who takes pride, may take pride' in Him in whose 'hands are both we and our words.' (*Christ. Doct.*)

2. Liturgical and Prophetic Dimensions

Augustine's sermons all reflect the traditional four-fold structure of Christian preaching, but by his time the liturgical and prophetic dimensions had been forged together in the person of the bishop or priest as the preacher-president of the liturgical assembly. Thus, by the fourth century, prophecy was completely absorbed into the liturgy of the Word and the Mass of the Catechumens, and accordingly it was exercised and controlled by the presiding bishop or by the priest who presided and preached in the Bishop's name. But the most powerful influence on the content and shape of Augustinian preaching was that of the liturgy itself in which his sermons had their origin as he brought to light for his people the Mystery of the Scriptures and the sacraments which they were celebrating. This inner Mystery was Augustine's primary concern and not the external rite. Thus when preaching at the consecration of a new basilica he has very little to say about the structure and its form and hastens from the dead stones to the living congregation, from the physical church to the mystical one:

> We are gathered together to celebrate the dedication of a house of prayer . . . but we too are a house of God. If we are a house of God, its construction goes on in time so that it may be dedicated at the end of time. The house, in its construction, involves hard work, while its dedication is an occasion for rejoicing. What was done when this church was being built is similar to what is done when believers are built up into Christ. When they first come to

> believe they are like timber and stone taken from woods and mountains. In their instruction, baptism, and formation they are, so to speak, shaped, leveled and smoothed by the hand of carpenters and craftsmen . . . The work we see complete in this building is physical; it would find its spiritual counterpart in your hearts. We see here the finished product of stone and wood; so too your lives should reveal the handiwork of God's grace. Let us then offer our thanksgiving above all to the Lord our God, from whom every best and perfect gift comes. Let us praise his goodness with our hearts and souls.

Church building as such did not interest Augustine, and ambo and altar were not important except in so far as they were signs of the Word of God announced and the Word of God made flesh. Indeed, his sermons were no more important and his teacher's chair was even less so if not entirely irrelevant: " . . . external instruction is only a means to an end, a reminder, and the one who truly teaches our hearts has his cathedra or chair in Heaven." Consequently he was often heard to begin a sermon with the typical invitation: "We have heard the words, let us now seek the meaning of the Mystery." Thus the first thought that comes to him when his mind turns to the subject of worship in Church is not the ritual, nor the sacramental side of the cultus, but the eternal dialog between God and man. The *Confessions* say so with classical brevity:

> V. 9.[13] My mother went to Church twice a day; she went in the morning and the evening without ever allowing anything to keep her away, and she went not to hear idle tales and the gossip of old women, but that she might hear you, O Lord, in your sermons, and that you might hear her in her prayers.

[13]Text: LCL. 1. 240

In church, then, God speaks in the lessons, while we speak in our prayers for the Church in the place where the feast of the Holy Scriptures is always ready. That is why Augustine's emphasis is always on the speaking God, for God has his Word, and when we pray in Church we do so by means of rites and expressions that are taken from God's Word. Yes, we even pray in the very person of the Word made flesh, as we are gathered around his altar and into his body, which is the Church. Thus the preaching of Augustine owes its very flesh and bones and marrow to the Word of God in the Scriptures: "A late Roman man of letters to the core, even the world of nature was for him only God's 'dumb show': what interested him far more was the spoken word, the speech of God committed to a book, an eloquence teaching salvation, perfectly adjusted to stir the hearts of all learners." P. Brown, *Augustine of Hippo*, 263.

Yet, for all that, the value he attached to the sacraments was never disproportionate. He knew that the Word of God could express itself equally well through Scripture and sacrament and could achieve the same results both as to the objective infusion of grace and the power of its impression on the minds of those who truly believed. He knew that we can hear this Word equally well when it is proclaimed at the ambo, explained at the chair and represented on the altar. He also quite sincerely believed that the all-embracing Word of God, which manifests to us the reality of the fullness of Christ, is presented to us both in the Scriptures and in the sacraments under the same moving and uplifting disguise of the symbol and must therefore be explained in the sermon. For Augustine, Scripture, sacrament and sermon formed an indissoluble unity, for he interpreted Scripture and he both read it and saw it shown forth in the sacraments. He interpreted it, that is to say, as an all-embracing allegory. This is the element that unites his celebration of the Mystery in Word and Sacrament with his preaching, and it provides the real explanation of both.

3. Catechetical and Mystagogical

In Augustine's time the liturgical mystery of Scripture and sacrament was further enriched as the liturgical year was already complete in its seasons: accordingly Scripture and sacrament were absorbed, so to speak, into the cyle of Anno Domini and presented according to season to express the different aspects of the saving Mystery. The bulk of Augustine's sermons, especially those delivered to his catechumens, follow and reflect this temporal unfolding of the Mystery which chosen scriptural texts proclaim and fixed sacramental rites represent. From the dawn of Christianity Easter Sunday was the first day of this Mystery and its eventual season: but in the 4th century catechumenate it was already preceded by the forty days of Lenten preparation. For Augustine with his catechumens these days of Lent were above all others and were celebrated by a daily preaching in which the catechetical dimension dominates. On Palm Sunday this dimension is particularly obvious as Augustine listens to the catechumens recite the Creed which he had asked them some days previously to memorize, for in his words it contained the truths upon which the faith of Mother Church was solidly established.

But with the celebration of the Great Mystery the mystagogical dimension replaced the catechetical one. On Saturday evening, when darkness fell and the lamps were lit, the Holy Pasch began. For Augustine and the faithful the mysteries of this night were not the objects of a gentle piety; they were the celebrations of a mighty victory, and Easter, the nocturnal feast of light, represented triumph over demons, sin and death. He has a profound conviction of the sheer power of this night: in fact he says that the Church in her Easter liturgy is not only commemorating the death and resurrection of her Lord as she does his birth at Christmastide, but is actually engaging in a sacred action attesting all the happenings surrounding those momentous days and revealing their sacred meaning. The liturgy of this night is therefore for Augustine the source of renewal in all Christians by what he calls *memoria salutaris*, or a memorial of salvation:

> I.[14] Our Lord Jesus by his resurrection has made glorious the day which he had made doleful by his death. Let us recall both days in a solemn manner. Let us keep vigil as we recall his death. Let us rejoice as we celebrate his resurrection. This is our yearly feast and our Pasch, not in anticipation by the sacrifice of a lamb as it was for the people of the Old Law, but for us, the new people, it is fulfilled by the death of our Savior. For Christ our Passover has been sacrificed (I Cor 5:7) and the former things have passed away; behold, they are made new (II Cor 5:17). Our sins are solely responsible for our distress and our justification by grace is solely responsible for our joy: he was handed over for our sins and raised up for our justification (Rom 4:25). Let us feel distress on account of our sins; let us be joyful on account of the resurrection. Therefore let us rejoice. Let us not forget. Let us celebrate with gratitude Christ's sufferings on our behalf and be glad. Let us keep vigil then . . . This night, of course, is regarded as part of tomorrow, which is called the Lord's Day. By his resurrection he enlightened our darkness. It is for this reason that it took place at night. That is why the psalmist cried out: Thous shalt enkindle my lamp, O Lord, my God; thou shalt enlighten my darkness (Ps 18:28). In this celebration the great mystery is present. By faith we keep this night of vigil; . . . by the same faith . . . we see its mystery . . . May the light of this mystery flood our hearts and minds that we may think and love with the light of the Church and be freed from the darkness of the world. For all of us who are here present in the name of Christ . . . the sun has set, but this day has not ended since it has been replaced by an earth made glorious by the light of Christ . . . Tonight's vigil is so special that it deserves

[14]Text: SC. 116. 210

> to appropriate to itself the common title of vigil ... (because) ... the holy Gospel proclaims that on this night Christ, the Lord, rose from the dead. Everybody knows that the entire day begins on the preceding night, and is not reckoned according to the order of days in Genesis, although even there night took precedence: Darkness covered the abyss when God said, Let there be light, and there was light (Gen 1:2-3). But this darkness was not night yet, for no day had yet preceded it. God separated the darkness (Gen 1:4), and first called the light day, and then called the darkness night. From the creation of light to the following morning was called one day. It is clear that those days began with light and ended the following morning. However, once man fell from the light of justice into the darkness of sin ... days began to be reckoned from nightfall. Since we try to pass from darkness to light rather than from light to darkness the words of the Apostle proclaim our hope and desire: 'The night is far spent; the day draws near. Let us cast off the deeds of darkness and put on the armor of light' (Rom 13:12). Thus the day of our Lord's passion ... succeeded the night of which it was part, and was ended by the Parasceve, or "unblemished supper." The observance of the Sabbath also began at nightfall. Likewise the Sabbath, beginning at night, ended at the following sunset which was the beginning of the Lord's Day, glorious on account of the resurrection. It is this night which begins the Lord's Day that we now celebrate in solemn *memorial.* ... Therefore may Christ, the Risen Lord, arise in this vigil *memorial*, more solemn than any other vigil, and make us live with Him in His kingdom of grace. For he slept that we might keep vigil; and he died that we might live. (The Vigil of Vigils)

His numerous sermons for Easter day, the day which the Lord has made, resound with images of the new day, the new chant, and the blessed Alleluia, as he reminds the neophytes that the glory of God shines forth not so much in the splendor of the universe as in the perfection of man:

> Ser. 8. 1.[15] Every day belongs to the Lord and remains so. The day belongs to the Lord for 'he makes the sun rise on the evil and on the good and sends rain on the just and on the unjust (Matt 5:45) ... It is not the ordinary day, common to the good and the wicked, which is referred to in the text: 'This is the day which the Lord has made.' The reference is to some more illustrious day and our attention is drawn to some special day: 'This is the day that the Lord has made.' What a wonderful day it must be: 'Let us be glad and rejoice in it.' It must be good; ... as holy Jeremiah said: 'nor have I desired the day of man, you know' (Jer 17:16). What then is this day which the Lord has made? Live well and you will be that day. When the apostle said: 'Let us conduct ourselves becomingly as in the day' (Rom 13:13) he was not thinking of the day that lasts from sunrise to sunset. Likewise: 'For they who are drunk, are drunk at night' (1 Thess 5:7). Drunkenness occurs at night, not at lunchtime and not in the day that the Lord has made. It is day for those who live a holy and religious life; it is night for those who live in a luxurious way in a spirit of haughtiness and irreligion: 'The day of the Lord will come like a thief in the night.' (1 Thess 5:2). The apostle was referring to those to whom he had previously said: 'You know, brethren, that the day of the Lord will come like a thief in the night.' He also said: 'But you are not in darkness for that day to surprise you like a thief. For you are all sons of light and sons of the day; we are not of the night or of darkness' (1 Thess 5:4-5). Our hymn, then, exalts the good life. If we all exclaim in harmony 'This is the day which the Lord has made,' let our lips and our conduct be in harmony.

Again:

> Ser. 34. 1.[16] We are advised to sing a new song to the Lord and the new man should know this new song. This song is

[15]Text: PLS. 2, 556-558

[16]Text: PL. 38. 210

> the expression of joy: furthermore it is the expression of love. Therefore the man who knows how to love the new life knows how to sing the new song. In order to learn what the new song is we must first learn what the new life is for all things belong to one and the same realm, namely the new man, the new song, the New Testament. Therefore the new man will know the new song and he will belong to the New Testament ... O Catholic sons and daughters, O heavenly offshoots, O all you who have been reborn in Christ, listen to me, or rather hear from me the words of the psalmist: 'Sing to the Lord a new song.' 'I am singing,' you may answer. 'Yes, you are singing for I hear you,' I reply. But let not your life make little of your words. Sing with the voice, sing with the heart, or sing with the mouth, but above all else sing with your whole life: 'sing to the Lord a new song.'

Again:

> Ser. 256. 2.[17] The Lord our God has allowed me to be with you in this solemn night ... Let us sing Alleluia. Then the word of the Scripture will be realized ... 'Death has been swallowed up in victory.' Let us sing Alleluia. 'O death, where is your sting'? Let us sing Alleluia here in the midst of trial and temptation. Let us sing Alleluia for man is guilty, but God is faithful ... O blessed Alleluia of heaven! No more anguish or adversity ... but praise to God who is above, and praise to God who is here below. Here on earth praise mingled with fear, but in heaven praise without fear. Here on earth the one who sings must die, but in heaven he who sings lives forever. Here he sings in hope, there he sings in love. Here it is Alleluia on the way, there it is Alleluia on the spot. Now let us sing Alleluia to lighten our burden. Sing like a man upon a journey, but keep time as you keep step. Sing to sustain your effort and do not give in to laziness. Sing in tune and

[17]Text: PL. 38. 1190

> march to the tune you sing. I mean make progress in good, and advance in virtue, for as the apostle tells us there are those who progress in evil. As for you ... progress in integrity of faith and in purity of life. Sing and march. March in step and don't turn back. Onward, onward to Christ.

4. Thematic and Exegetical

In the sermons of Easter Week, like those of the Great Week itself, the mystagogical dimension dominates as the neophytes, or newly born infants of that virginal but fruitful Mother, the Church, enter the final stage of instruction about the mysteries of their initiation. Faith, baptism and eucharist naturally emerge as the major themes of this week of grace and glory. Nevertheless this thematic concern in no way diminished his exegetical approach, for Augustine clung closely to the fixed readings of the day and there is hardly a sermon which does not refer to the epistle, the psalm or the Gospel of that day. Indeed he was wont to begin his every sermon with some variation of his familiar introduction: "We have heard, and sung, and have reverently followed the reading of the Gospel; let us now seek the mystery":

> Ser. 251.[18] There are two occasions when the disciples of Christ went fishing at the command of the Master. The first occasion was when He chose them and made them apostles, and the other shortly after He arose from the dead. Now, let us compare these two events, if you will, and note very carefully how they differ. If we do so, our faith will be all the stronger for it. On the first occasion, when our Blessed Savior came upon these fishermen, we are told that He had not known them, that they had fished all night and had caught nothing, and that their

[18]Text: PL. 38. 1167

> labor was in vain. Nevertheless He ordered them to let down their nets. In this account he did not tell them to cast to the right, nor to the left but simply said: 'Let down your nets.' And so they did . . . with the result that both of their boats were filled with so many fish that they almost sank. And so great was the number of fish that the nets broke. That is what happened the first time they went fishing. But what happened on the second occasion? 'Cast the net on the right side of the ship,' our Lord told them. Before the Resurrection the nets are thrown out here or there; after the Resurrection the right side is chosen. Moreover, the first time they went fishing the boats almost capsized and the nets broke; but the time after the Resurrection, neither was the boat imperiled nor did the dragnet break. The first time no mention is made of the number of fish; but the time after the Resurrection a definite number is given.

Here he contrasts both instances in order to understand better the second. It is in a sense typology within the New Testament; nonetheless it is not far removed from allegory with its explanation of the nets of God's Word broken by heresy and the bad life.

> Ser. 251.[19] On the occasion of the second fishing perfect unity prevails, for there is a right side only and not a left. This signified the holy Church now made up of a few that are laboring among the many wicked. She is to consist of a definite and limited number, with no sinner found in her ranks. She is the right side and has no left. And the fish will be large ones, and all will be immortal, and all will be victors forever. But what is so great that it has no end? The Evangelist has written about it, if you will keep in mind the first occasion. Why else does he add in the second instance, 'And although there were so many, the

[19]Text: PL. 38. 1168

> net was not broken'? It is as though he wished to say: Remember the first fishing event, when the nets broke. Heaven will be where no heretic will bellow or schismatic cause dissension: heaven will be where all are of one heart and soul, and where peace will be in plenty.

This exegetical approach is less evident in Augustine's preaching throughout the remainder of the Paschal season and gives way somewhat to the thematic which is indicative of the theological and liturgical developments of the fourth century. Already by the time of Augustine the Ascension was a well-established biblical feast although it was of recent liturgical origin. Still, even though he preached frequently on the feast and there are extant a number of Ascension sermons, he is in no way clear on its theological significance. On one occasion he speaks about two glorifications of the Lord, one by the Resurrection and another by the Ascension, and consequently about two different givings of the Spirit in association with each glorification, but he is unable to explain further:

> Ser. 265. 8.[20] Listen to this, my dearly beloved brethren: someone of you may ask me this question: 'Why did the Lord give the Holy Spirit twice'? . . . I do not know the answer. Nevertheless, although I do not yet know what to think about this question, I still hold it as a fact that He gave the Holy Spirit on each occasion. Because I am so convinced of the fact I cannot cease from trying to explain it. If my explanation is correct, I pray that the Lord may confirm it as such: if, however, I am wrong and another explanation appears more plausible and closer to the truth then I pray the Lord again that He may grant me this knowledge. My view is that the Holy Spirit was given on two occasions for the purpose of teaching us the two precepts of charity. For although there are two precepts,

[20]Text: PL. 38. 1222

> there is however only one love . . . thus there is also only one Spirit but there are two bestowals of this Spirit . . .

Feasts other than the biblical ones of the Easter cycle have an altogether different significance for Augustine, as can be seen in his preaching of Christmas and Epiphany. In the strict sense Christmas, which was of recent origin in the time of Augustine, did not commemorate a divine mystery in the liturgical sense but rather a particularly unique birthday that fell on an especially suggestive day, the birthday of Sol Invictus, the Unvanquished Sun:

> Ser. 186. 1.[21] Brethren, let us be happy! Let the nations rejoice and be glad! Not the visible sun, but the sun's invisible Creator gave us this holy day, when the Virgin Mother, from the fruitfulness of her womb and with perfect virginity gave us Him who became visible for our sake and by whom she herself was created. A virgin conceives, yet remains a virgin; a virgin is heavy with child; a virgin brings forth her child, yet she is always a virgin. Why are you amazed at this, O man? It was fitting for God to be born thus when He deigned to become man . . .

Epiphany was in Augustine's view a kind of counterpart to Christmas and belonged to those natalia which were not celebrated as "sacraments" by means of a mystical dramatization, but as ordinary commemorative anniversaries:

> Ser. 203. 1.[22] That this event took place is a truth spoken by the gospel; that it happened on this day can be deduced from the fact that this glorious feast is everywhere observed. For it has seemed just, and it really is just, that, since the Magi were the first of the Gentiles to know

[21]Text: PL. 38. 773

[22]Text: PL. 38. 1035

> Christ the Lord and since they, not yet influenced by His speech, followed the star which appeared to them and, like a tongue from heaven, distinctly spoke to them in behalf of the Speechless Word, then, I repeat, it is just that the Gentiles should recognize this day as the occasion of salvation for their first-fruits and that, with solemn observance, they should consecrate it to Christ the Lord in a spirit of thanksgiving . . .

In developing such themes, Augustine avoids the temptations of Greek rhetoric by remaining close to the scriptural text: "Today we celebrate the feast of the Holy Martyr Laurence; the readings which you heard just now were most fitting for this feast." For someone who had hoped to train himself for the vision of God by means of the liberal arts Augustine came at last to rest on the solid intractable mass of the Christian Bible. In this time of distance the scripture became for Augustine the very countenance of God, and through the use of the allegorical method he came to a whole new awareness of the Bible, and found in it all the satisfactions of philosophy and poetry together. On allegory his exegesis rested. This idea was nothing new to Augustine, the Platonist. Already in common usage it had come to sum up a serious attitude to the limitations of the human mind, which is forever threatened by that patina of the obvious. But Augustine the preacher gave to this old idea of allegory a new meaning. For him allegory is necessary on account of man's fall from the direct knowledge through signs. Consequently, the Bible, like nature itself, has been similarly veiled by God in order to exercise the seeker. It was an acid test in just the same way as a philosophical problem might be: the superficial would be content with the obvious, with the letter; only the profound man could grasp the deeper meaning, the spirit.

5. Homiletical and Rhetorical

Augustine's theory of preaching was drawn from his practice of preaching and can be seen throughout the vast legacy of his sermons. Everywhere in these sermons it is evident that the trained rhetorician is the master of his art. Consequently the message alone is audible and the rhetoric is simply its mode of being. But it is there and can be heard when isolated: it is obvious, for example, in the short sentences of his fiery temperament and the enhanced intensity evoked by his questions and exclamations, as it is in his repetitions and word play:

> Ser. 224.[23] Will you reform? Will you change? When? Today? 'Tomorrow,' (in Latin, *cras*). Behold, how often you say: 'tomorrow, tomorrow,' (*cras, cras*); you have really become a crow (*cras, cras,* approximately the cawing of a crow.) Behold, I say to you that when you make the noise of a crow, ruin is threatening you. For that crow, whose cawing you imitate, went forth from the ark and did not return. Instead, my brother, return to the church, which the ark then represented. O you who are newly baptized, hear me; you who have been re-born through the blood of Christ, hear me. I beg you by the name which has been invoked upon you, by the altar to which you have approached, by the sacraments which you have received, by the future judgment of the living and the dead, I beg you, I put you under obligation in the name of Christ, not to imitate those persons who you know are such as I described. On the contrary may the sacraments of him who did not wish to come down from the cross, but who did wish to rise from the tomb endure.

Normally he speaks the living North African Latin used by his congregation and he is well aware of his divergence from classical usage. At other times, especially in his festal

[23]Text: PL. 38. 1095

sermons, he rises from the simple exposition to a rapturous artistry which transcends the boundary between poetry and prose:

> Ser. 191. 1.[24]When the Maker of time . . . was made flesh He reserved for Himself one day. With His Father He precedes all the cycles of time but on this day, born of an earthly mother, he stepped into the very course of the years. Man's maker was made man . . . the maker of time appeared in time . . . that he, Ruler of the stars, might be nourished at the breast; that he, the Bread, might be hungry; that he, the Fountain, might thirst; that he, the Light, might sleep; that he, the Way, might be wearied by the journey; that he, the Truth, might be accused by false witness; that he, the Judge of the living and the dead, might be brought to trial by a mortal judge; that he, Justice, might be condemned by the unjust; that he, Discipline, might be crowned with thorns; that he, the Foundation, might be suspended upon a cross; that Courage might be weakened; that Security might be wounded; that Life might die.'

The Scripture is always his text and consequently determines and influences his sermon both in content and in style. Its mood is his mood, its rhetoric is his rhetoric because its message is his message. Thus he avoids the elaborate introductions of the Greeks as he does their development of particular or peripheral biblical themes. As a result his sermons are more conversational than declamatory, more homiletical than rhetorical. At times they even give the impression of being spontaneous outpourings which very often end abruptly:

[24]Text: PL. 38. 1009

[25]Brilioth. op. cit. p. 54

> [25] I believe I have talked long enough, but nevertheless I have not come to the end of the Gospel reading. Were I to complete the rest, I would tire you too much, and I fear that what you have learned would be lost. Therefore this much must suffice.

Such unexpected endings only heightened the overall effect:

> [26] I have forgotten how long I have been speaking. The psalm is ended and I attribute my perspiration to the fact that I have delivered a long address but I cannot do enough to answer your enthusiasm. You have a violent effect upon men: would that you had the same enthusiasm for the Kingdom of God.

The free and easy conduct of the congregations in those times contributed in no small way to the more familiar or homiletical approach of the preacher. Talking and laughing were indulged in freely, and conduct was, in general, unrestrained in those churches that were as much social as liturgical centers. Thus there was a constant need on the part of the preacher to demand silence and attention from his congregation before beginning his sermon just as the pagan orators did of their hearers before beginning their orations. Augustine is no exception to this practice: On one occasion when the talking continued he wryly commented:

> [27] I have no doubt but that many of you have understood; but I judge from the talking that those who have understood are trying to explain the matter to those who failed to grasp it. Accordingly next time I will speak more plainly so that you may all understand!

[26]Brilioth. op. cit. p. 54

[27]FOTC. 4. 208

Conclusion

In the range and quality of his homiletic achievement, Augustine in the West was the Latin counterpart of Chrysostom in the East. In each case the Bible was the book preached and Augustine's intimate and extensive knowledge of it put at his disposal its every verse for spontaneous use and made his language entirely biblical. Furthermore in his preference for allegorical exegesis Augustine was able, unlike Chrysostom, to treat in a biblical manner the great themes of Christian life without upsetting the basic fourfold structure of Origen's homily. Nor did his preaching suffer at the hands of rhetoric, convinced as he was that "one who is not himself first a hearer in his inner being will be only a hollow preacher." Indeed, in his detailed treatment of the form of preaching he established the Christian preacher's ultimate independence of rhetoric. More heavily than all rhetorical brilliance on the one hand, or the displeasure of the grammarians because of unpolished diction on the other hand, there weighed on Augustine the duty of explaining the Word of God in so plain a manner that the less gifted could also grasp it.

To this end he delighted to give to his preaching the homiletic character of a dialogue, of the intimate conversation between the bishop at his *cathedra* and the congregation, which hung on his words and ingenuously replied to his questions. Augustine's lively spontaneity, his superior gift of improvisation, and his pedagogical skill were of uncommon benefit to such a manner of preaching. His biographer, Possidius, called special attention to the powerful impression which his method of preaching made on his hearers, and his successor in the preaching office at Hippo repeats this impression in his own way: 'now the cricket chirps, for the swan is silent.'

8. The Latin Sermon In Roman Tradition

1. Leo the Great (d. 461)

"And so . . . to Rome" but not before the middle of the 5th century by which time the cultural and ritual growth of the papal liturgy had greatly diminished the space of the sermon and determined its character. The ninety-six extant sermons of Leo the Great, Pope and Prince of the Church, belong to this period. They are indeed liturgical for they are, for the most part, expositions of the recently completed liturgical cycle but they are sadly lacking in the note of prophecy. Leo no longer stands in the prophetic tradition of Origen, Chrysostom, or Augustine. Secondly, they are much more thematic than exegetical as the complete faith of Chalcedon is defended like a dogmatic fortress and the tendency to moralize becomes everywhere dominant. Thirdly, they are more rhetorical than homiletical but the rhetoric is of a new and distinct Roman type: he loves antithesis and original stylizations and enthusiastically embellishes his addresses with sober but nonetheless rhetorical flourishes. This attention to language, often expressed in assonance and rhythmical cadence, is known as the *cursus leoninus* and became normative for the style of the Roman curia and set its stamp on the construction of the Roman collect or prayer.

Any student of these sermons is immediately struck by Leo's sacramental or liturgical realism: Easter is the central salvific event, not simply a past event which we should remember but rather a present reality which we should honor.

> Ser. LXXII. III.[1] Thus, my friends, if without faltering we believe in our hearts what we profess with our lips then in Christ we are crucified, we are dead, we are buried; on the very third day, too, we are raised. Hence the Apostle says, 'If ye have risen with Christ, seek those things which are above, where Christ is, sitting on God's right hand: set your affections on things above, not on things on the earth ... But that the hearts of the faithful may know that they have that whereby to spurn the lusts of the world and be lifted to the wisdom that is above, the Lord promises us His presence, saying, 'Lo! I am with you all the days, even till the end of the age.' (*On Resurrection*)

The language in which Leo expresses this sacramental realism is a new development: what has not been appreciated is the relationship between this sacramental language and patristic exegetical language. In Leo's perspective the historical events of Jesus' life are related to the liturgical renewal of those events as letter in the patristic exegetical sense is related to spirit. Once the spiritual faith-activity of the worshippers is engaged, the historical event is no longer simply historical. It is then seen as present—indeed objectively present—in the life of the church. Thus, the historical event itself is past and gone but the *virtus operis* or power remains and the mystery of the historical event is made present. In this sense Christmas, or the Lord's birth, like Easter itself, becomes more a present event which we can actually see than a past event which we simply recall:

[1]Text: PL. 54. 391

> Ser. XXVI. II.[2] Although with the passing of time the infancy of Christ naturally gave way to the fullness of his manhood ... nevertheless today's feast of Christmas renews for us the sacred beginning of Jesus' life, his birth from the Virgin Mary. In the very act in which we are reverencing the birth of our Savior, we are also celebrating our own new birth. For the birth of Christ is the origin of the Christian people; and the birthday of the head is also the birthday of the body. Though each and every individual occupies a definite place in this body to which he has been called, ... nevertheless as the whole community of the faithful, ... was crucified with Christ in the passion, raised up with him in the resurrection and at the ascension placed at the right hand of the Father, so too it is born with him in this Nativity, which we are celebrating today. (*On Nativity*)

In this understanding of the liturgical action as a *sacramentum* Leo advanced beyond Augustine. For him faith enables the Christian to transcend the limitations of historical time: listening to the liturgical readings, the man of faith can "see" what happened in the time of Jesus in such a way that there is no opposition between past and present. Thus the liturgical celebration provides an opportunity for the man of faith to be present at past events. This makes sense only because Leo integrates the sacramental language which speaks of *renewal* of the mysteries of Christ's life with the patristic exegetical principle of spiritual understanding. To miss this understanding of liturgy is to miss Leo's understanding of preaching. The feast of the Epiphany offers a good illustration of this point as Leo insists that the event has not really passed away. The assembly should not restrict itself to an imaginative reconstruction of the original event; this purely literal understanding of scripture is inadequate because it leaves one in the past. We must also realize how "our own age daily experiences" the Epiphany events in a

[2]Text: PL. 54. 213

still abundant way. The star continues to shine through grace leading darkened hearts to God; the Magi exist in all believers who come to adore the Lord in our time; Herod lives on in the person of the devil, who attacks the faith of the baptized just as Herod tried to kill Jesus:

> Ser. XXXVI. I.[3] Beloved, today we must celebrate with solemn ceremony the first appearance of Christ, the Savior of the world to the nations . . . and to-day those joys must be entertained in our hearts which existed in the breasts of the three magi, when, aroused by the sign . . . of a new star, . . . they fell down in presence of the King of heaven and earth. For that day has not so passed away that the mighty work, which was then revealed, has passed away with it, and that nothing but the report of the thing has come down to us for faith to receive and memory to celebrate; . . . therefore, although the narrative which is read to us from the Gospel properly records those days on which the three men, . . . came to acknowledge God from the furthest parts of the East, yet we behold this same thing more clearly and abundantly carried on now in the enlightenment of all those who are called . . . Hence when we see men who are devoted to worldly wisdom and far from belief in Jesus Christ, brought out of the depth of their error and called to an acknowledgement of the true Light, it is undoubtedly the brightness of the Divine grace that is at work . . . (*On Epiphany*)

There is perhaps no better example of the unity between exegetical and liturgical language in Leo than his teaching on Christ as a *sacramentum* and an *exemplum*:

> Ser. LXXII. I.[4] The Gospel narrative, dearly beloved, describes for us the whole Paschal mystery and thus by

[3]Text: PL. 54. 233

[4]Text: PL. 54. 390

> way of our bodily ears it has reached the ear of our soul, so that there are none among us who have not formed a picture of the events that took place . . . for the text of the Divinely-inspired story has clearly shown the treachery of the Lord Jesus Christ's betrayal, the judgment by which He was condemned, the barbarity of His crucifixion, and glory of His resurrection. But a sermon is still required of us, that the priests' exhortation may be added to the solemn reading of Holy Writ, as I am sure you are with pious expectation demanding of us as your accustomed due. Because, therefore, there is no place for ignorance in faithful ears, the seed of the Word, which consists of the preaching of the Gospel, ought to grow in the soil of your heart, so that, when choking thorns and thistles have been removed, the plants of holy thoughts and the buds of right desires may spring up freely into fruit. For the cross of Christ, which was set up for the salvation of mortals, is both a mystery and an example: a sacrament whereby the Divine power takes effect, an example whereby man's devotion is excited: for to those who are rescued from the prisoner's yoke Redemption further procures the power of following the way of the cross by imitation. (*On Resurrection*)

Leo preaches his *sacramentum-exemplum* sermon in a variety of ways. In one place he links it with his christological teaching: as true God Christ can be our cure; as true man he can give an example: "For, the Almighty Physician, had prepared a two-fold remedy for us in our misery—one part consists of mystery and the other of example—that, by the one, Divine powers might be bestowed, and, by the other, human weaknesses driven out. Because God is the Author of our justification, man is a debtor to pay Him devotion." Consequently the liturgical celebration of times of fasting such as Lent, "bring back to us" the mystery of the cross which is the mystery of our redemption and invite us to imitate Christ and to conform ourselves to Him:

> Ser. XLII. I.[5] Dearly beloved, now is the time to preach to you this saving and august fast ... How shall I begin more fitly than by quoting the words of the Apostle, in whom Christ Himself was speaking, and by reminding you of what we have read: 'Behold, now is the acceptable time, behold now is the day of salvation.' For though there are no seasons which are not full of Divine blessings, ... nevertheless in this season all men should be moved with greater zeal to spiritual progress, when the return of the day, on which we were redeemed, invites us to all the duties of godliness. ... Divine Providence has with great beneficence taken care that the discipline of the forty days should heal us and restore the purity of our minds, during which the faults of other times might be redeemed by pious acts and removed by chaste fasting. (*On Lent*)

The same stress on "exemplum" by way of imitation is found in his nine sermons on the December fast; his twelve on the fast of Lent and his four on the Ember days in September:

> Ser. XV. II.[6] Beloved, it is at all times profitable to fast. Nevertheless it is particularly appropriate and entirely apt for us in this present season ... Our holy fathers, being Divinely inspired, sanctioned the Fast of the tenth month, that when the gathering of crops was complete, ... each might remember so to use his abundance as to be more abstinent in himself and more open-handed towards the poor. For forgiveness of sins is most efficaciously prayed for with almsgiving and fasting, and supplications that are winged by such aids mount swiftly to God's ears: ... For that part of his material possessions with which a man ministers to the needy, is transformed

[5]Text: PL. 54. 275

[6]Text: PL. 54. 175

> into eternal riches, and such wealth is begotten of this bountifulness as can never be diminished or in any way destroyed. (Fast of 10th Month)

But nowhere is *exemplum* preached at the expense of *sacramentum*: O wondrous power of the Cross! O ineffable glory of the Passion, in which is contained the Lord's tribunal, the world's judgment, and the power of the Crucified! ... because your cross is the fount of all blessings, the source of all graces, and through it the believers receive strength for weakness, glory for shame, life for death. Indeed, Easter, Ascension and Pentecost are all preached as the sacramental presence of the saving Mystery:

> Ser. LXXIII. II.[7] These days, dearly beloved, which followed between the resurrection of the Lord and His ascension were not passed in simple idleness. During them great sacramental mysteries were confirmed, great truths revealed. In those days the fear of death with all its horrors was taken away, and the immortality of both body and soul affirmed. Throughout the whole period between the resurrection and ascension, God's providence was at work to instill this one lesson into the hearts of the disciples, ... that our Lord Jesus Christ, who was truly born, truly suffered and truly died, should be recognized as truly risen from the dead. (*On Ascension*)

Nor was the celebration of the Ascension as confusing in its significance for Leo as it was for Augustine:

> Ser. LXXIV. I.[8] At Easter time the resurrection of the Lord was then the cause of our joyful celebration: in this solemnity our present rejoicing is on account of his ascension into heaven. In solemn ceremony we are now commemorating that day on which our poor human nature

[7]Text: PL. 54. 395

[8]Text: PL. 54. 397

> was carried up, in Christ, above all the hosts of heaven, above all the ranks of angels, beyond the highest heavenly powers to the very throne of God the Father . . . Our faith is nobler and stronger because sight has been replaced by a doctrine whose authority is accepted by believing hearts, enlightened from on high. This faith was increased by the Lord's ascension and strengthened by the gift of the Spirit; . . . Even the blessed apostles, . . . took fright at the cruel suffering of the Lord's passion and could not accept his resurrection without hesitation. Yet they made such progress through his ascension that they now found joy in what had terrified them before. They were able to fix their minds on Christ's divinity as he sat at the right hand of his Father, since what was presented to their bodily eyes no longer hindered them from turning all their attention to the realization that he had not left his Father when he came down to earth, nor had he abandoned his disciples when he ascended into heaven. The truth is that the Son of Man was revealed as Son of God in a more perfect and transcendent way once he had entered into his Father's glory; he now began to be indescribably more present in his divinity to those from whom he was further removed in his humanity. A more mature faith enabled their minds to stretch upward to the Son in his equality with the Father; it no longer needed contact with Christ's tangible body, in which as man he is inferior to the Father. For while his glorified body retained the same nature, the faith of those who believed in him was now summoned to heights where, as the Father's equal, the only-begotten Son is reached not by physical handling but by spiritual discernment. (*On Ascension*)

Leo's sermons on Pentecost Day reflect the same liturgical realism:

> Ser. LXXV. I.[9] Beloved, indeed all Catholics are fully aware that today's solemnity is to be venerated as one of

[9]Text: PL. 54. 400

> the great feasts of the Church. In truth we have no doubt that great respect is due to this day, which the Holy Spirit has hallowed by the miracle of His most excellent gift. For from the day on which the Lord ascended up above all heavenly heights to sit down at God the Father's right hand, this is the tenth which has shone and the fiftieth from His Resurrection, ... and contains in itself great revelations of mysteries both new and old, by which it is most manifestly revealed that Grace was fore-announced through the Law and the Law fulfilled through Grace. (*On Pentecost*)

Such was the sacramental and exegetical language of Leo the Great as he proclaimed and explained the liturgical mystery. But he did not always confine himself to the sacramental liturgy for he loved to celebrate the *memoria* of Peter and Paul and other Roman saints: nor was he unmindful of his own anniversaries especially his elevation to the Episcopal See of Rome:

> IV. II.[10] Dearly beloved, with all due respect and in sincerity of heart we celebrate today's feast in such a way that in my humble person he may be recognized and honored, in whom abides the care of all the shepherds, together with the charge of the sheep commended to him, and whose dignity is not abated even in so unworthy an heir ... When therefore we utter our exhortations in your ears, holy brethren, believe that Peter is speaking whose representative we are: because it is his warning that we give, nothing else but his teaching that we preach, beseeching you to 'gird up the loins of your mind,' and lead a chaste and sober life in the fear of God, and not to let your mind forget his supremacy and consent to the lusts of the flesh ... For though the whole Church, which is in all the world, ought to abound in all virtues, yet you

[10]Text: PL. 54. 149

> especially, above all people, it behooves to excel in deeds of piety, because founded as you are on the very citadel of the Apostolic Rock, not only has our Lord Jesus Christ redeemed you in common with all men, but the blessed Apostle Peter has instructed you far beyond all men.

With such a sacramental and hierarchical notion of preaching it is small wonder that in Leo's opinion *no one* was allowed to preach but the priest:

> Ep. CXIX. VI.[11] This too it behooves you, beloved, to guard against, that no one except those who are the Lord's priests dare to claim the right of teaching or preaching, be he monk or layman, who boasts himself of some knowledge. Because although it is desirable that all the Church's sons should understand the things which are right and sound, yet it is permitted to none outside the priestly rank to assume the office of preacher, since in the Church of God all things ought to be orderly, that in Christ's one body the more excellent members should fulfill their own duties, and the lower not resist the higher. Dated the 11th of June, in the consulship of the illustrious Opilio (453). (Letter to Maximus of Antioch)

2. Peter Chrysologus

The history of preaching after Leo is on the whole one of decline. Nevertheless the duty to expound the Gospel lesson *inter missarum sollemnia* was not forgotten but the place occupied by the sermon was greatly narrowed by the growth of the liturgical service. Already, for example, in Leo one can detect the secondary role of preaching as he is anxious to spare his congregation from a long sermon but at the same time unaware of the tiresome ceremonial. Likewise in

[11]Text: PL. 54. 1045

Ravenna, Peter Chrysologus declares during Lent (which was the great season of preaching) that the labor of the vigils and the weariness of the fast have made him desist from preaching during Holy Week. On another occasion he suspended his preaching during a period of intense heat. The 176 extant sermons of this "Unknown Doctor" have earned Chrysologus the distinction of "The Golden Word" but they also place him in the tradition of the *exemplum* more than that of the *sacramentum*. With him the aim of the sermon is primarily ethical: it must discourage sin and encourage good works. With something of the ostentatious rhetoric of Chrysostom in Constantinople though with much more restraint he preached assiduously to reform the low moral standards of the capital city of the western empire and its corrupt court. Such was the ethical dimension of preaching at the dawn of later antiquity and it continued to grow throughout the Middle Ages:

> Ser. LIII.[12] Blessed are the peacemakers, the evangelist said, dearest brethren, for they shall be called sons of God. Truly Christian virtues grow in a man who enjoys the unchangeable possession of Christian peace, nor does one come to the title of son of God except through that of peacemaker. Peace, dearest brethren, rescues man from servitude, provides him with the name of a free man, changes his identity before God together with his condition, from a servant to a son, and from a slave to a free man. Peace among brethren is the will of God, the joy of Christ, the completion of holiness, the rule of justice, the teacher of truth, the guardian of morals and a praiseworthy disciplinary in every regard. Peace lends strength to our prayers; it is the way our petitions can reach God easily and be credited; it is the plenitude which fulfills our desires. Peace is the mother of love, the bond of concord and the manifest sign of a pure soul, . . . We must keep

[12]Text: PL. 52. 347

> peace before all other virtues, since God is always in peace. Love peace, and all the world will be tranquil and quiet. By doing so you store up rewards for me, and joy for yourselves, that the Church of God may be founded on the bond of peace and may cling to perfect observance in Christ. (*On Peace*)

3. Caesarius of Arles (d. 542)

The year 529 has special significance for the history of preaching in the Latin Church as Caesarius of Arles presided over the Council of Vaison which granted priests the right to preach, "for the edification of all the churches and the benefit of all the people not only in the cities but also in the rural areas. If, because of illness, the priest is unable to preach let the homilies of the holy fathers be read by the deacons." Juridically this canon marked the end of the bishops' monopoly of preaching in the Latin Church and acknowledged the *de facto* situation of the preaching priests. According to Caesarius "the Word should not be honored less than the Body of the Lord":

> Ser. 1. 20.[13] Now, someone may say: I lack a memory, and have not the eloquence to preach the word of God. I am afraid, pious soul of the Lord, that perchance this excuse will not be able to protect us at that dreadful judgment. We know very well that by preference our Lord did not choose learned men or orators, but unlettered fishermen and shepherds, poor and obscure men, to preach the word of God ... Therefore, all my priests of the Lord should preach to the people in simple, ordinary language which all the people can grasp, fulfilling what the Apostle says: 'I became all things to all men, that I might gain all.' Moreover, according to the holy and salutary advice of St. Jerome: 'When a priest preaches he ought to arouse

[13]Text: SC. 175. 272

> groans of compunction rather than applause.' Your holiness should carefully notice, too, that not without great fear should we reflect and consider that in the Gospel we have deserved to be called 'the salt of the earth.' Now, what should be understood as salt except the teaching of priests, and what as the earth but the people entrusted to them? Therefore, with God's help, we ought to labor as much as we can so that we may not, perchance, merit to be tasteless salt if—we are excessively impeded by earthly occupations and take the salt of doctrine away from Christ's flock. (*To Bishops*)

The life of Caesarius states that "he preached every Sunday and all feast days as long as his health permitted and had his deacons read the homilies of Ambrose, Augustine and his own (which he also readily passed on to every would-be taker) whenever illness prevented him from preaching in person:

> Ser. 1. 15.[14] If, perchance, it is difficult for some of my lords the bishops themselves to preach, why should they not introduce the ancient custom of the saints which is still observed with profit today in parts of the Orient, whereby sermons are read in church for the salvation of souls? Are we perhaps to think that some of you might disdain even to enjoin this upon your priests? . . . I say in truth that it is not unsuitable or unbecoming for a deacon to be charged to read the sermons of the holy Fathers publicly in church. If any deacon is worthy to read what Christ said, he should not be considered unworthy to read what St. Hilary, St. Ambrose, St. Augustine, or the rest of the Fathers preached ... Indeed, if we do not endeavor to fulfill our obligations of preaching, either ourselves or through some of our brethren, it is to be feared that what the Lord threatens in terrible words

[14]Text: SC. 175. 254

> through His Prophet may be fulfilled in us: 'I will send forth a famine into the land: not a famine of bread, nor a thirst of water, but a famine of hearing the word of God.' Since, according to the testimony of the Gospel, we and our servants have received a measure of wheat that is to be dispensed, what excuse will we be able to allege at the Lord's coming, then, if we have neglected to distribute what was entrusted to our care? We ought to fear that the souls of as many as have perished through a famine of the word of God due to our negligence will be demanded of our soul at the day of judgment ... Now, if our holy Fathers of old with such great zeal and pious labor wrote innumerable volumes for the benefit of all the churches, how will we appear among or before them if we neglect to distribute to our children what we find has been compiled by them? If we are unable to compose our own books, should we not ... make known in public ... what we find already written by the holy Fathers, ... Without any doubt, if the dew or rain of the word of God is provided too late, the fruits of the souls will be the same as earthly fruits which do not receive rain. So that you may understand it better, the divine word declares that the word of God can be compared to the dew and the rain: 'Let my speech be awaited as the rain, and my words as the dew.' ... how much more solicitous should we be for the Lord's garden, that is, the Church of God, that the dry places be watered and the hard places softened by the rivers of sacred Scripture and the spiritual streams or fountains of the ancient Fathers, ... According to the Apostle Paul, whose successors, although less capable, we are seen to be: 'I have planted, Apollos watered, but God has given the growth.' Therefore, with God's help, let us do what belongs to us, let us continually plant and water; if we thus fulfill our duty, God will confer His favor. (*To Bishops*)

Thus by the time of Caesarius preaching was in the process of becoming a mechanical trade. Indeed Caesarius himself, as we have seen, was by no means a stranger to the practice of using borrowed materials and he gladly furnished sermon manuscripts to his weaker brethren which comprise the 238 sermons that survive:

> Ser. II.[15] With the intuition of paternal devotion and the solicitude of any pastor we have written in this little book simple admonitions that are necessary for parishes. These the holy presbyters or deacons should read on the major feasts to the people entrusted to them. By taking care to do this with a kindly spirit, I have absolved my conscience in God's sight. If through negligence presbyters or deacons fail to read these sermons to the people, they should realize that they will plead their case with me before the tribunal of Christ, when both they and I will render an account to the eternal Judge for the flock committed to our care. Therefore, each year review this little book with all diligence, . . . if necessary . . . make more books out of these simple admonitions in better handwriting and on parchment . . . They may also be given to other parishes for transcription, . . .

4. Gregory the Great (d. 604)

In January 590 Gregory the Great was called from the quiet of his monastery on the Coelian Hill to be Bishop of the City of Rome, "once the hub of the world, now a mere shadow of her former self, crouched amid the ruins of its departed splendor. . . . Then there was long life, continual health, opulence in material things, fecundity of offspring, tranquility in lasting peace . . . Now this world has withered within itself . . . Everywhere there is death, everywhere mourning, everywhere desolation; on all sides are we stricken, on all sides filled with bitterness; and yet with minds blinded by carnal concupiscence we love the very

[15]Text: SC. 175. 280

bitterness, follow what is fleeting, cling on to what is falling."

At this time the Church herself, even in her word and worship, was also in urgent need of reform, and in Gregory she found the man that the times demanded—part prince, part monk, part landlord, total saint. But even he was no stranger to the practice of reading at Mass a sermon from an acknowledged Father of the Church and his own sermons were usually read by a priest or deacon on account of his feeble condition. However, on an Easter Sunday in the Basilica of St. Mary Major he noticed the adverse effect on his congregation of his sermon when read by another and accordingly he resolved "within the solemn context of the Mass to interpret the Gospel lesson, not by means of a written speech but by the spoken word which should grasp the hearers like a solicitous hand—*quasi quadam manu sollicitudinis.*" Thus he issued his *Liber Regulae Pastoralis, or Pastoral Care*, a western counterpart to Chrysostom's book *On the Priesthood*, which became the classic source for pastoral theology in the Church, and contained his directions for preaching and preachers:

> Pt. 1. C. VII.[16] Sometimes there are those who laudably desire the office of preaching, whereas others no less laudably are drawn to it by compulsion. This can be clearly perceived by all in the example of the two prophets . . .; for Isaiah, when the Lord asked whom He should send, offered himself of his own accord, saying, 'Here I am; send me' (Isai 6:8). But Jeremiah is sent, yet humbly pleads that he should not be sent, saying, 'Ah Lord God! behold I cannot speak: for I am a child (Jer 1:6). From these two men different voices proceeded outwardly, but they flowed from the same fountain of love. For there are two precepts of charity; the love of God and of our neighbor. Wherefore Isaiah, eager to

[16]Text: PL. 77. 20

> profit his neighbors through an active life, desires the office of preaching, Jeremiah, longing to cleave sedulously to the love of his Creator through a contemplative life, remonstrates against being sent to preach. Thus what the one laudably desired the other laudably declined; the latter, lest by speaking he should lose the gains of silent contemplation; the former, lest by keeping silence he should suffer loss for lack of diligent work. But this in both bases is to be nicely observed, that he who refused did not persist in his refusal, and he who wished to be sent saw himself previously cleansed by a coal of the altar; . . . (*Pastoral Care*)

Later an interesting distinction is drawn between those who are capable but reluctant to preach and those who are incapable but anxious to do so:

> Pt. III. C. XXV.[17] Those who can preach worthily but fear to do so out of excessive humility are to be admonished in one way; while in another way those who are handicapped by age but impelled by enthusiasm should be considered . . . Let them consider therefore with what punishment they must be visited who, when souls are perishing from famine of the word, supply not the bread of grace which they have themselves received. Whence also it is well said through Solomon, 'He that hideth corn shall be cursed among the people' (Prov 11:26). For to hide corn is to retain with one's self the words of sacred preaching . . . Let them see, then, in how great guilt they are involved who, knowing the sores of souls, neglect to cure them by the lancing of words . . . Let these, therefore, when they keep to themselves the word of preaching, hear with terror the divine sentences against them, to the end that fear may expel fear from their hearts . . . Let them hear what is said by the bridegroom in his colloquy

[17]Text: PL. 77. 96

> with the bride; 'Thou that dwellest in the gardens, thy friends hearken: make me to hear thy voice.' For the Church dwells in the gardens, in that she keeps in a state of inward greenness the cultivated nurseries of virtues. And that her friends hearken to her voice is, that all the elect desire the word of her preaching; which voice also the bridegroom desires to hear, because he pants for her preaching through the souls of his elect ... But, on the other hand, those whom imperfection or age debars from the office of preaching, and yet enthusiasm impels to it, are to be admonished ... to consider that young birds, if they try to fly before their wings are fully formed, are plunged low down from the place whence they fain would have risen on high ... Hence it is that our Redeemer though in heaven the Creator, and even a teacher of angels in the manifestation of His power, would not become a master of men upon earth before His thirtieth year in order to infuse into the enthusiastic the force of a most wholesome fear, He Himself, did not preach the grace of a perfect life until He was of perfect age ... And ... when Jesus at twelve years of age is spoken of as sitting in the midst of the doctors, He is found, not teaching, but asking questions. By which example it is plainly shown that none who is weak should venture to teach, ... (*Pastoral Care*)

Elsewhere he discusses the preacher's need to adapt his message to his congregation:

> Pt. III. C. XXXVI.[18] Preaching to the proud of heart should be tempered with such skill that it pass straight through the midst of their passion after the manner of a two-edged sword; on the other hand fear should not be struck into the heart of the timid; ... that confidence be so infused into the timid, that unbridled licence grow not

[18]Text: PL. 77. 121

> wild in the proud . . . that liberality in giving be so infused into the niggardly that the reins of profusion be in no wise loosened to the prodigal; that frugality be so preached to the prodigal that concern for perishable things be not increased in the niggardly; that marriage be so praised to the incontinent that those who are already continent be not called back to voluptuousness; that virginity of body be so praised to the continent that fecundity of the flesh be not despised by the married . . . The highest good is so to be praised that the lowest be not despaired of: The lowest is so to be cherished that there be no cessation of striving for the highest . . . (*Pastoral Care*)

However, tact and caution must be practiced by the preacher who should not preach what his congregation cannot understand:

> Pt. III. C. XXXIX.[19] The preacher should be sensitive to the mind of his hearer and never overtax it, for the string of the soul, so to speak, when stretched more than it can bear can very easily snap . . . For all deep things should be covered up before a multitude of hearers, and scarcely opened to a few . . . Hence it is said to the blessed Job, 'Who hath given understanding unto the cock'? For a holy preacher, crying aloud in time of darkness, is as the cock crowing in the night, when he says, 'It is even now the hour for us to arise from sleep.' And again, 'Awake ye righteous, and sin not.' But the cock is wont to utter loud chants in the deeper hours of the night; but, when the time of morning is already at hand, he frames small and slender tones; because, in fact, he who preaches aright cries aloud plainly to hearts that are still in the dark, and shows them nothing of hidden mysteries, that they may then hear the more subtle teachings concerning heavenly things, when they draw nigh to the light of truth . . . thus

[19]Text: PL. 77. 124

> every preacher should give forth a sound more by his deeds than by his words; by good living he should imprint footsteps for men to follow rather than by speaking show them the path of truth. For that cock, too, whom the Lord in his manner of speech takes to represent a good preacher, when he is preparing to crow, first shakes his wings, and makes himself more awake; thus it is surely necessary that those who give utterance to words of holy preaching . . . should first shake themselves up by lofty deeds, and then make others solicitous for good living; that they should first smite themselves with the wings of conscience . . . and then at length set in order the life of others by speaking; that they should take heed to punish their own faults by bewailings, and then denounce what calls for punishment in others; and that, before they give voice to words of exhortation, they should proclaim in their deeds all that they are about to speak. (*Pastoral Care*)

Finally and by way of conclusion to the entire book a note of warning is sounded for the salvation of the preacher lest having preached to others he himself become the castaway:

> Pt. IV. I.[20] It sometimes happens that the preacher is carried away by his own performance: self-display is the temptation of the gifted preacher: . . . great care is therefore needed that he chastise himself with the laceration of fear, lest he who calls the diseases of others to health by remedies should himself swell through neglect of his own health; lest in helping others he desert himself, lest in lifting up others he fall. For in the case of some the greatness of virtue can be the occasion of vice, . . . and it happens that the soul of a successful man casts aside the fear of limitation, and rests secure in self-confidence; . . .

[20]Text: PL. 77. 125

> Whence it is brought about, that before the eyes of the just judge the very memory of virtue can be a pitfall of the soul because, in calling to mind what it has done well, it falls before the author of humility ... Thus under the figure of Jerusalem the soul proud in virtue is reproved, when it is said, 'Thou wert perfect in my comeliness which I had put upon thee, saith the Lord, and having confidence in thy beauty thou hast committed fornication in thy renown.' For the mind is lifted up by confidence in its beauty, when, glad for the merits of its virtues, it glories within itself in security. But through this same confidence it is led to fornication; because, when the soul is deceived by its own thoughts, malignant spirits defile it through the seduction of innumerable vices ... it desires to spread abroad the glory of its own reputation, and busies itself to become known as one to be admired by all. In its renown, therefore, it commits fornication, because, forsaking the wedlock of a lawful bed, it prostitutes itself to the defiling spirit in its lust of praise. Hence David says, 'He delivered their virtue into captivity, and their beauty into the enemy's hands, when the old enemy gets dominion over the deceived soul because of elation in well doing. And yet this elation in virtue tempts somewhat, though it does not fully overcome, the mind even of the elect. (*Pastoral Care*)

On the other hand Divine Wisdom sometimes chastens a soul with the knowledge of self-weakness before raising it for greater things:

> Pt. IV. I.[21] When flattery abounds it is indeed salutary if the eye of the soul should acknowledge its own weakness; ... that it should look, not at the right things that it has done, but at those that it has left undone; so that, while the heart is bruised by recollection of infirmity, it may be

[21]Text: PL. 77. 126

> the more strongly confirmed in virtue before the author of humility. For it is generally for this purpose that Almighty God, though perfecting for the most part the minds of rulers, still to some small degree leaves them imperfect, in order that, when they shine with wonderful virtues they may pine with disgust at their own imperfection, and by no means lift themselves up for great things, while still laboring in their struggle against the least . . . (*Pastoral Care*)

Conclusion

Gregory the Great is remembered on the one hand as "the last of the Romans" and on the other hand "as the foremost intermediary between antiquity and the Middle Ages." Accordingly he marks a watershed in the history of preaching as the age of the Fathers gives way to the age of the Church and the emphasis passes from Word to Worship, that is from the Word of God announced to the Word of God made flesh. His "preaching leaves a poor impression in contrast to that of Augustine or even of Leo the Great. It has little of the formal elegance which characterized his predecessors, and the sweep of thought which characterizes Augustine is entirely lacking. The eclipse of the Latin sermon has to a degree been conditioned by the decayed state of rhetorical training. Gregory interprets his pericopes, which seem to have become solidly established, somewhat tritely; the texts themselves have been inserted in the written manuscript. First of all, he seeks to extract the ethical motifs from Scripture; his means is an unspiritual play on the 'hidden meaning,' an allegorizing, which very often dissipates the real content. No spirit of prophecy is found here, even though Gregory is anxious to present the demands of the times to his audience and his paraneses are sometimes characterized by the real warmth and seriousness of the shepherd of souls. The cultural decline he seeks to combat has settled upon his own world of thought."[22] Something of his style can be seen in the following:

Bk. 29. 2.[23] The Church is frequently and fittingly called Daybreak or the Dawn, for dawn or daybreak is a gradual transition from darkness into light ... While she is being led from the night of infidelity to the light of faith, she is opened gradually to the splendor of heavenly brightness, just as dawn yields to the day after darkness. The Song of Songs says aptly: 'Who is this who moves forward like the advancing dawn'? Holy Church, inasmuch as she keeps searching for the rewards of eternal life, has been called the dawn. While she turns her back on the darkness of sins, she begins to shine with the light of righteousness. This reference to the dawn conjures up a still more subtle consideration. The dawn intimates that the night is over; it does not yet proclaim the full light of day. While it dispels the darkness and welcomes the light, it holds both of them, the one mixed with the other, as it were. Are not all of us who follow the truth in this life daybreak and dawn? While we so some things which already belong to the light, we are not free from the remnants of darkness. In Scripture the Prophet says to God: 'No living being will be justified in your sight.' Scripture also says: 'In many ways all of us give offense.' When he writes, 'the night is past,' Paul does not add, 'the day is come,' rather is "at hand"; he shows that the period before full daylight and after darkness is without doubt the dawn, and that he himself is living in that period. It will be fully day for the Church of the elect when she is no longer darkened by the shadow of sin. It will be fully day for her when she shines with the perfect brilliance of interior light. This dawn is aptly shown to be an ongoing process when Scripture says: 'And you showed the dawn its place.' A thing which is shown its place is certainly called from one place to another. What is the place of the dawn but the perfect clearness of eternal vision? When the dawn has been brought there, it will retain nothing

[22]Brilioth. op cit. p. 66

[23]Text: PL. 76. 478

> belonging to the darkness of night. When the Psalmist writes: 'My soul thirsts for the living God; when shall I go and see the face of God?,' does he not refer to the effort made by the dawn to reach its place? Paul was hastening to the place which he knew the dawn would reach when he said he wished to die and to be with Christ. He expressed the same idea when he said: 'For me to live is Christ, and to die is gain.' (*Reflections on Job*)

Paradoxically the reform of worship which Gregory enthusiastically promoted contributed greatly to the decline of the Word in the Roman tradition. For one thing the practice grew of reading at Mass a patristic sermon and actually became the norm of preaching in the office of the canonical hours when it took definite shape. This widespread practice of homily reading is certainly indicative of the decadence that beset preaching as the fossilized remains of ancient sermons became an integral part of the Church's living worship. Such a practice could only happen in an age when exposition of Scripture had ceased and when the spirit of prophecy had departed the Church.

Select Bibliography

Baur, C., *John Chrysostom and His Time*, Vol. I., Newman Press, Westminster, MD. 1959.

Brilioth, Y., *A Brief History of Preaching*, Fortress Press, Philadelphia, 1965.

Daniélou, J., *The Theology of Jewish Christianity*, Vol. 1., Westminster Press, Philadelphia, 1964.

Daniélou, J., *Gospel Message in Hellenistic Culture*, Vol. 2., Westminster Press, Philadelphia, 1973.

Daniélou, J., *The Origins of Latin Christianity*, Vol. 3., Westminster Press, Philadelphia, 1977.

McDonald, J.I.H., *Kerygma and Didache*, Cambridge, 1980.

Quasten, J., *Patrology*, Vol. I., (The Beginnings of Patristic Literature), Newman Press, Westminster, MD, 1950.

Quasten, J., *Patrology*, Vol. II. (The Anti-Nicene Literature After Irenaeus), Newman Press, Westminster, MD, 1953.

Quasten, J., *Patrology*, Vol. III., (The Golden Age of Greek Patristic Literature), Newman Press, Westminster, MD, 1960.

Van Der Meer, F., *Augustine the Bishop*, Sheed and Ward, London, 1961.

The Fathers of the Church Series, Catholic University of American Press, Washington, D.C.:

Vol. 2: St. Augustine, Christian Instruction, (1947).

Vol. 17: St. Peter Chrysologus, Selected Sermons, (1953).

Vol. 22: St. Gregory of Nazianzen and St. Ambrose, Funeral Orations, (1953).

Vol. 31: St. Caesarius of Arles, Sermons 1-80 Vol. 1., (1956).

Vol. 34: St. Leo the Great, Letters, (1957).

Vol. 36: St. Cyprian, Treatises, (1958).

Vol. 41: St. John Chrysostom, Homilies 48-88 Vol. 2., (1960).

Vol. 42: St. Ambrose, Hexameron, (1961).

Vol. 44: St. Ambrose, Theological and Dogmatic Works, (1963).

Vol. 48: St. Jerome, Homilies 1-59 Vol. 1., (1964).

Vol. 61: St. Cyril of Jerusalem, Vol. 1., Lenten Lectures 1-12, (1969).

Vol. 64: St. Cyril of Jerusalem, Vol. 2., Lenten Lectures 13-18, Mystagogical Lectures, (1970).

The United States and the World Court, 1920–1935

To Pen,

Becky and Bronwen

The United States and the World Court, 1920–1935

Michael Dunne

St. Martin's Press, New York

St. Martin's Press, Inc., 175 Fifth Avenue, New York, NY 10010

First published in the United States of America in 1988

ISBN 0-312-02717-6

Library of Congress Cataloging in Publication Data
CIP applied for

Printed and bound in Great Britain

Contents

Foreign policies are not built upon abstractions

(Charles Evans Hughes, 1923)

Advisory opinions ... are ghosts that slay

(Felix Frankfurter, 1924)

Behind legal phrases and forms lie the active forces of national and international ... life

(Julius Curtius, 1931)

All law, of course, is political

(Louis Henkin, 1974)

Preface

In writing this study of United States foreign relations I have been helped and encouraged by many people. Above all I have benefited from the personal warmth and intellectual stimulus of my colleagues at the University of Sussex. Words can express only inadequately the depth of gratitude I feel to them; but they will know why I mention by name the following for their special help: Geoffrey Best, Sheila Brain, Colin Brooks, Steve Burman, Marion Cox, Stephen Fender, Rosemary Foot, Jane South, Christopher Thorne, Rupert Wilkinson.

Many librarians and archivists have helped me, as the Bibliographical Essay and footnotes will suggest. But this space allows me to thank formally the friendly and professionally outstanding staff of the University of Sussex Library. Once again I feel confident I can mention individuals, whose special assistance has helped produce this book. They and their colleagues will know that they carry the palm for the team as a whole: Marian Framroze and all in the Inter-Library Loans Division; Jenny Marshman; and John Burt.

Two libraries in London have been exceptionally helpful: the Royal Institute of International Affairs and the London Library; while a number of the constituent bodies and research centres of the University of London have treated me as one of their own: the main University Library, the LSE, the Institute of Historical Research, the Institute of United States Studies and the Institute of Advanced Legal Studies.

I have, of course, been helped by many librarians, here and abroad. For permission to use copyright material I am indebted to the Public Record Office, Kew; the University of Birmingham Library; the British Library; the Library of Congress; the Houghton Library and Harvard Law School Library; the Sterling Memorial Library, Yale; the Bancroft Library, University of California at Berkeley; the Hoover Institution on War, Revolution and Peace, Stanford University; the Hoover Presidential Library, West Branch, Iowa; the Franklin D. Roosevelt Library, Hyde Park, New York; the Lauinger Memorial Library, Georgetown University; and the Dinand Library, College of the Holy Cross, Worcester, Mass.

Many scholars in North America have helped me in various ways. The first was the late, beloved Armin Rappaport, who started me in 'diplomatic history'. For this present text I owe a special debt to the following: Robert D. Accinelli, J. Leonard Bates, Terry Deibel, Larry Gelfand, George Herring, Harold Josephson, James T. Kenny and Marshall Kuehl. They may not recognize (to anticipate my text) this 'offspring'; but they have all been part of its intellectual formation.

Warmest thanks, too, to those friends who have hosted and stimulated a peripatetic researcher: Diane Clemens, Bill Issel, Linda Kerber, Larry Levine, Tom Paterson and Jim Patterson. I hope they will think my transatlantic perspective adds something to their own deep historical insight.

To my other American friends, the McCarthys of Worcester and the Hortons of Berkeley, professionals in other fields, generous and kind beyond comparison, I send this wordy 'thank you'–overdue like all the others!

For financial aid I should like to thank the Arts Research Fund of the University of Sussex, the Trustees of the Herbert Hoover Presidential Library Association, and the US Embassy in London.

Vanessa Couchman, my editor, has been a constant source of encouragement and support to me in this project. I should like to think the finished text fulfils her best hopes.

My dear friends will read the hidden messages that run through these formal–though heartfelt–words. And they will also know that no words of mine can ever express my love for those to whom I offer this work.

Note on terminology and place-names

This is a study of American relations with the Permanent Court of International Justice (PCIJ), inaugurated in 1922 as part of the League of Nations system. Contemporaries and historians referred to the PCIJ as the World Court–or, more confusingly, as The Hague Court. Certainly the League-sponsored Court was established at The Hague in The Netherlands; but The Hague was also the organizational base of the Permanent Court of Arbitration (PCA), an arbitral system derived from the Peace Conferences held at The Hague in 1899 and 1907. The PCIJ and PCA co-existed, but they were quite distinct. The PCIJ was dissolved in 1946 and succeeded by the International Court of Justice (ICJ) as part of the United Nations Organization. The new court has also become known as the World Court; and, as in the interwar years, the ICJ has been called The Hague Court, while the PCA continued its separate existence.

In the following pages the term World Court is used to refer only to the PCIJ or the ICJ. Context and date will show which is involved.

Place-names

Place-names present a minor problem: Rome or Roma? Bern or Berne? Breslau or Wroclaw? In general I have used the form recognizable to English-speaking contemporaries. Linguistic consistency is, I think, impossible.

Where a publishing house gives two locations in the same country (e.g. Berkeley and Los Angeles), only one is cited for bibliographical purposes. Where two places in different countries are given (e.g. Vienna and Leipzig), then both are cited.

Abbreviations

ABA: American Bar Association
ABAJ: *American Bar Association Journal*
ACJ: Advisory Committee of Jurists
AF: American Foundation
AJIL: *American Journal of International Law*
Annals: *Annals of the American Academy of Political and Social Science*
APS: American Peace Society
APSR: *American Political Science Review*
BYBIL: *British Year Book of International Law*
CDT: *Chicago Daily Tribune*
CEIP: Carnegie Endowment for International Peace
CFR: Council on Foreign Relations
CPPA: Conference for Progressive Political Action
CR: *Congressional Record*
CSM: *Christian Science Monitor*
DBFP: *Documents on British Foreign Policy*
DSB: *Department of State Bulletin*
DWEA: Division of Western European Affairs
FCCCA: Federal Council of the Churches of Christ in America
FO: Foreign Office
FPA: Foreign Policy Association
FRUS: *Foreign Relations of the United States*
GPO: Government Printing Office, Washington, DC
HMSO: Her/His Majesty's Stationery Office
ICJ: International Court of Justice
LAT: *Los Angeles Times*
LEP: League to Enforce Peace
LNNPA: League of Nations Non-Partisan Association
LNOJ: *League of Nations Official Journal*
LWV: League of Women Voters
MD, LC: Manuscript Division, Library of Congress
NA: National Archives, Washington, DC
NCPW: National Council for Prevention of War
NWCC: National World Court Committee
NWP: National Woman's Party
NYH-T: *New York Herald-Tribune*
NYT: *New York Times*
PASIL: *Proceedings of the American Society of International Law*
PCA: Permanent Court of Arbitration
PCIJ: Permanent Court of International Justice
PRO: Public Record Office, Kew, England
PSQ: *Political Science Quarterly*

RIIA:	Royal Institute of International Affairs
RTAA:	Reciprocal Trade Agreements Act
SAFR:	*Survey of American Foreign Relations*
SCFR:	Senate Committee on Foreign Relations
SFC:	*San Francisco Chronicle*
SFE:	*San Francisco Examiner*
SIA:	*Survey of International Affairs*
USD:	*United States Daily*
USWA:	*United States in World Affairs*
WP:	*Washington Post*
WPF:	World Peace Foundation
WWCC:	Women's World Court Committee

1 The United States and the first World Court: history and historiography

On Tuesday, 29 January 1935 the US Senate voted on a resolution to effect American membership of the Permanent Court of International Justice. When the roll-call was completed, the Ayes numbered 52, the Nays 36. But the simple majority was not sufficient: under Article II, Section 2 of the Federal Constitution, a *two-thirds* majority was required for the approval of a treaty. With 88 votes being cast, the resolution was 7 votes short. In a phrase coined at the time and used ever since, the World Court had been defeated.[1]

In the United States and abroad the 'defeat of the World Court' was described as a mark, indeed a 'triumph' of American isolationism.[2] Diplomatic historians have broadly endorsed this contemporary judgment; and the episode is frequently cited in more general histories to exemplify a pattern in American interwar foreign relations.[3] Hesitant moves by internationalists inside the Roosevelt administration were thwarted by isolationists outside. Reduced to a brief sentence, this remains the dominant interpretation of the January 1935 vote.

The purpose of this study is to re-examine the Senate vote – and the fifteen preceding years. It might seem a daunting task. Not because the material is intractable; but rather because the indictment against the isolationists has been drawn in such lengthy and damaging terms. Since the 1935 vote only one monograph has been published on American relations with the World Court; and the reason for this neglect undoubtedly lies in the shared sense of historians that the Court defeat was a contributory factor in the outbreak of World War II and that the truth of this deplorable episode is well known.[4] Any attempt to offer a new account of the Court's history must begin by addressing this double prejudice, even if limitations of space mean that the counter-arguments will be put in the baldest language.

Despite the voluminous writings of 'new-left revisionists' in particular and political economists in general, American foreign relations during the interwar years continue to be schematized as follows:

— World War II was produced by the moral and material weakness of the Western democracies in the face of totalitarian aggression;
— such weaknesses would have been transformed into strength by American political and physical aid: complaisance would have become resistance;
— such emotional and practical aid was denied by the American isolationists;
— therefore, the isolationists brought about World War II, with its appalling loss of life, physical destruction and political upheaval.

This reasoning no doubt looks implausible when rendered schematically; but unless we appreciate that this basic pattern informs most American historiography we shall fail to understand either the professional inhibition against re-opening the Court issue or the consensus which characterizes the existing literature on the Court.[5] For however much Court scholars express their scepticism about the established aetiology of World War II, the tone and effect of their writing reinforce this explanatory model.

Against the few hundreds of pages of World Court historiography we are presented with many hundreds of thousand of pages on World War II and its origins. Obviously this study cannot provide a systematic analysis of such an enormous literature. It is possible, however, to pose a number of hypotheses to counter the conventional wisdom on the isolationists' responsibility for World War II. The following propositions refer specifically to the war in Europe and stress the role of the British government; for as contemporaries and historians have both acknowledged, the indictment against the isolationists has even less plausibility in the Pacific–Asiatic phases of World War II. (This was the major 'paradox of isolationism': its Asia-first quality.)[6]

— Until spring 1940, the British government sought to conciliate Hitler's Germany and Mussolini's Italy;
— such conciliation was prompted not just by economic and military considerations but in the hope of turning Nazi Germany and international fascism in general against the Soviet Union;
— American support for the British government, in these circumstances, would have been (as the isolationists pointed out) aid not *against* but *for* appeasement;
— the governments of the United Kingdom, France, Germany, Italy and the Soviet Union had little regard for the United States: at

> one extreme the British, under Prime Minister Neville Chamberlain, mistrusted the United States and wanted no interference; while Hitler's domination of German foreign policy ensured that the Wilhemstrasse's accurate assessments of American power and the commitment of policy-makers to prevent hostile control of the Atlantic were ignored in the Nazi high command.[7]

The first set of propositions above represents the essential case against the isolationists; the second offers a different perspective. More specifically, the former is the framework within which most historians continue to locate and analyse the World Court defeat; the latter schema is the conceptual grid into which the following analysis fits. With these markers in place, we can now review the history and literature of the World Court in the interwar years.

The story of American relations with the Permanent Court of International Justice (PCIJ) falls into five distinct stages. The first covers the years 1920–3 and begins with the establishment of the Court as part of the League of Nations system. Not surprisingly, the close connection of the Court with the League raised the possibility, frightening to some, encouraging to others, that American entry into the Court would be a large step towards membership of the League itself. But there was an added uncertainty. One of the drafters of the PCIJ's Statute (or constitution) was Elihu Root, the influential Republican politician who had played such an ambiguous role in compromising his party's divisions during the presidential election of 1920. We shall examine Root's actions closely later on; but the immediate effect of Root's involvement in the Court's creation was not in doubt. The new World Court was frequently referred to as the 'Root Court', with the implication that American adherence (or membership) should and would quickly follow – despite the Senate's recent rejection of the Treaty of Versailles and the Covenant of the League of Nations.

We all know that the Senate votes of November 1919 and March 1920 on the Treaty and its Covenant disguised American support for some sort of new international system – vague language, perhaps, but certainly compatible with the promotion of an international court. So despite the Senate votes and the Republican victory in the November 1920 general elections, the campaign for American adherence to the League-sponsored court continued. By the beginning of 1923 a set of conditions for American adherence had been devised by diplomats and jurists in Geneva (the home of the League), The Hague (the home of the Court), London and Washington; and these terms were presented by President Harding to the Senate with his warm endorsement. The first stage had been completed.

The second stage lasted from early 1923 to January 1926. As we shall see, the details were complicated but the net result was clear. In January 1926 the Senate easily approved the terms originally sponsored by Harding, but added a number of extra conditions. The additions caused no disagreement between the Senate and the Executive: the Coolidge administration identified itself completely with the enlarged terms for American adherence. However the consensus in Washington was countered by the League. Determined to refuse the American proposals, the League collectively responded with the offer of a compromise. The crucial area of conflict lay in the Court's advisory jurisdiction: its power of rendering a judgment when required by the League despite (it was said) the wishes of the disputants – a form of unqualified 'compulsory jurisdiction' which no Great Power was willing to surrender to any international body.

From 1926 to 1929 the US government and the League were at an impasse over the American demand for a veto on the advisory jurisdiction – a right the League simply would not concede. It was during this third stage that Root reappeared on the scene, his task being to break the acknowledged 'deadlock' between Washington and Geneva. The result was the so-called Root Protocol, which was less a method of resolving the deadlock than skirting the fundamental conflict. For the next two years (stage four) details of the Root Protocol were overshadowed by the onset of the Depression; and when the Senate resumed discussion of the proposed new terms, two foreign crises intervened to put the whole question of American adherence into serious doubt. The first was the Austro-German Customs Union scheme of March 1931; the second was the outbreak of war in Manchuria later that year.

The fifth stage in the Court history, from 1931 to 1935, was dominated by these two external events. Questions of the Court's jurisprudence and jurisdiction, questions which initially had seemed rather abstract perhaps to some, were now given immediate political force. Moreover a new domestic ingredient was added – or rather intensified. The partisanship present in the League controversy and never completely absent in its aftermath surfaced again in 1935 under the influence of Roosevelt's New Deal. As we shall see, this combination of foreign and domestic factors induced the Senate narrowly to reject in January 1935 almost the self-same terms it had approved in January 1926.

Not everyone will agree with every detail of this skeletal chronology; but its broad lines may be accepted provisionally. Its purpose, after all, is not to win converts but rather to provide a narrative framework for examining the historical literature on the Court issue in American politics. These last words are an important qualification. A number of major works appeared in the interwar years discussing the organization and activities of the Court, notably the English-language studies by M. O Hudson and A. P. Fachiri; but such legal treatises were not primarily concerned to describe the Court campaign in the United States.[8] Conversely a few monographs were written during the 1920s deliberately to influence that campaign. The leading authors for the proponents of adherence were Hudson and the Cuban jurist and judge of the Permanent Court, Antonio Sanchez de Bustamente y Sirven, whose work reached a wide audience in an English-language translation.[9] The opponents were more numerous, in book-form at least: the teams of Frances Kellor and Antonia Hatvany; James Giblin and Arthur Brown; and David Jayne Hill. Less partisan was the work of Edward Lindsey.[10] Much of this contemporary literature has faded from view and is rarely even cited by modern scholars, whose concern has focused on the final 1935 vote. Since then only one monograph has been published on the whole campaign; and that was by Denna Frank Fleming.

Today Fleming is best known for his criticism of American foreign policy in the making of the Cold War – a war he rightly traces to 1917 and the American response to the October Revolution in Russia.[11] Until the early 1960s, however, Fleming's reputation lay with the series of books and articles he had written damning American interwar isolationism. In Fleming's indictment the earliest, characteristic crime had been the rejection of the Versailles Treaty and the League of Nations; the major culprit had been the Senate; its weapon had been the unrepresentative and obstructionist provision of the Federal Constitution requiring a two-thirds majority for the approval of treaties.[12] For Fleming the defeat of the World Court in 1935 was only a stage in the terrible sequence which led from the American failures in the wake of World War I to the even greater tragedy of World War II. Such was the simple yet awesome argument of his monograph, *The United States and the World Court*, published in 1945. As we shall see, this small volume has influenced World Court historiography until the present day.[13]

Fleming was not the only critic of the procedures and decisions of the Senate. In the previous year Kenneth Colegrove had published his hostile study of *The American Senate and World Peace*. The roster of earlier critics included Eleanor E. Dennison, *The Senate Foreign Relations Committee* (1942); Wallace McClure, *International Executive Agreements: Democratic Procedure under the Constitution of the United States* (1941); George H. Haynes, with his massive two volumes on *The Senate of the United States: its History and Practice* (1938); and W. Stull Holt, *Treaties Defeated by the Senate: a Study of the Struggle between President and Senate over the Conduct of Foreign Relations* (1933). Even the few scholars with something to say 'in extenuation of the Senate' (as Colegrove put it), tend to share Fleming's criticisms on the Court campaign. Here the prime example is Royden J. Dangerfield, whose *Defense of the Senate* was published two years before the Court defeat.[14] This last citation shows that nuances can be distinguished between these different studies. Even so their basic agreement is not in doubt; nor indeed their cumulative effect. Together they reinforce the guilty verdict on the isolationists, not least by trivializing the case against American membership of the Court.

The group, with Fleming at their head, may be thought of as the First Generation of World Court scholars. Like any label, the term tends to minimize differences; but it is helpful in recording the common values and methods which united these critics. Collectively they deplored the American rejection of the League – and particularly its manner. In their judgment partisan, xenophobic Senators had exploited an archaic

Constitution to frustrate the public desire for a new system of international political co-operation. The two-thirds rule was singled out for special censure; and together they urged the elimination or severe curtailment of the Senate's so-called treaty-making power in favour of congressional joint resolutions and executive agreements as methods for obtaining legislative approval of inter-governmental undertakings.

Methodologically this First Generation also shared a number of characteristics. Perhaps the most striking was their neglect of arguments inside the Senate, particularly (even in the case of Dennison) those inside the Foreign Relations Committee. Less obvious and fractionally more excusable was their neglect of foreign sources, even the records of the Court itself and the League. Instead these scholars relied heavily – sometime exclusively – upon American pro-League sources, notably the *New York Times*. The results of this narrow range of source-material combined with pro-League prejudice can be seen at many points in the First Generation accounts. For example, it is the opponents of adherence who are both accused and convicted of 'obstructionism', of delaying and ultimately preventing adherence by procedural tricks and procrastination. In fact, as the public record clearly shows, the proponents were equally guilty. They too resorted to postponements and prevented legislative action, particularly after the League had refused to accept the American terms for adherence. A second, more famous instance of First Generation historiography is their version of the January 1935 vote. In their terms it was the 'violent, unscrupulous', and 'vicious propaganda campaign' which finally overwhelmed the Senate.[15] But, as we shall see, an examination of the contemporary evidence suggests that this powerful, long-lasting image has been grossly overdrawn.

One undeniable virtue of First Generation historiography was its coverage, where possible, of the Court campaign from beginning to end. So however skimpy the narratives, at least the broad outlines were presented. In recent decades, however, scholars have taken particular episodes discretely and, as a result, have failed to notice important points of continuity and change. Once again we can cite the 1935 vote. The resolution then closely lost was in substance the same as that passed by a comfortable majority in 1926. To understand the second, unsuccessful vote requires careful attention to the whole story of the Court campaign – not just the few weeks preceding the final defeat.

Until the late 1960s the influence of Fleming and the First Generation was transmitted partly through general diplomatic histories and hostile accounts of American interwar isolationism.[16] Even today Fleming's arguments and approach can be found setting the terms of discussion in works which have themselves become historiographical benchmarks. Here the most notable case is the recent literature on Roosevelt; and, in particular, the major biographies written by diplomatic historians such as Wayne Cole and Robert Dallek.[17] Yet the specific acknowledgement or simple echo of Fleming reveals a subtle paradox; for the Fleming of the anti-isolationist account is the same Fleming who later became a prolific critic of American 'globalism' in the Cold War and the 'destructive', anti-nationalist attempt to impose a 'pax Americana' in South-east Asia. It can only be assumed that Fleming's legatees have been able neatly to separate his politics from his historical writing. And, in fairness, they can cite Fleming's own practices in their defence. For one of the most remarkable features of Fleming's later career was his reissuing of earlier works with no adjustments made to previous arguments. So his account of the *United States and the World Court* was reprinted with a supplementary chapter inadvertently exposing the wishful thinking of Fleming's self-styled interwar internationalism and the narrowness of his attack upon the Senate and the isolationists.[18]

The reissue of Fleming's monograph coincided with the emergence of a definable Second Generation of World Court scholars. Leading the way was Robert Accinelli, with the completion of his doctoral dissertation on the early stages of the Court campaign. Since then has followed a series of articles from Accinelli on the remaining stages and the relationship of the Court issue to the question of American internationalism in general and the peace movement in particular.[19]

Each of these latter terms deserves quotation marks. What, after all, would we mean by a peace movement in the 1980s? Anti-nuclear unilateralists use the term to describe themselves; so do pro-nuclear multilateralists; and many in the first group are not pacifists. Historians would do well to remember Elihu Root's explicit attack on 'internationalism' – when this was the revolutionary cry of the Third International.[20] In an echo of the rhetoric of Progressivism, everyone claimed to be in favour of peace, certainly; internationalism, perhaps. Despite the volumes of writing on both peace and internationalism, the subjects continue to be treated unproblematically, with scholars bundling these ambiguous concepts into simplistic categories. As we shall see, far from setting a useful context for fresh insights into the Court campaign, such literature obscures the issues and repeats traditional misconceptions.[21]

Two other interrelated qualifications also need to be made before we discuss the Second Generation of Court scholars. The first is that for all his prominence, Accinelli has exerted nothing like the influence of Fleming. This is not surprising, once we realize that Accinelli has largely followed the contours of Fleming's historiography. Secondly, Accinelli forms part of a wider movement of recent historians and social scientists; and much material important for an understanding of the Court campaign has appeared in studies only tangentially concerned with the Court itself. To vary the metaphor slightly, the Second Generation can best be seen as an extended family. The primary, core group consists of such scholars as Accinelli, George Curtis, Terry Deibel, Gilbert Kahn and David Patterson, all of whom have written specifically on the first World Court and the United States. Then comes a larger group who have touched upon aspects of the Court as part of their broader interest with international judicial organization and peace research: scholars such as Charles Chatfield, Calvin Davis, Charles DeBenedetti, Martin Dubin, Sandra Herman, Roland Marchand and Warren Kuehl. Beyond them we can distinguish a third group, who have set the Court, international judicial organization and peace research in the context of political and military multilateralism – and by so doing, have themselves influenced the primary group. This third group includes such scholars as Ruhl Bartlett, Alexander DeConde, Robert Divine, Robert Ferrell, Harold Josephson, Robert Osgood, Gary Ostrower, Daryl Revoldt, Roland Stromberg, Barbara Stuhler and Lawrence Wittner.[22] This patterning, with its familial imagery, is not designed to set rigid categories but rather to suggest the range of scholarship relating to the Court – though without forgetting the continued historiographical dominance of Fleming. These considerations converge, moreover, when we notice the many ways in which First and Second Generations overlap in values and methods. Despite some differences of approach, the similarities between the two groups are more striking than the contrasts.

To take the differences first. Here the most obvious contrast is the nature and use of source material. Whereas Fleming & Company necessarily relied upon published materials in constructing their accounts, Accinelli & Company have worked widely in public and private archives. Within this area the best example comes from the study of the pro-Court lobbyists. Fleming's practice was simply to list campaigning organizations; Deibel and Kahn, however, have used the private records of individuals and groups to trace the dynamics of the extra-congressional forces promoting adherence.[23] But (as we have suggested) this exploitation of unpublished materials has not significantly altered the lines of debate set by Fleming. The archives support the view that public opinion was in favour of adherence – which was the contention of the First Generation. But this proposition has not been systematically tested. Moreover, if scholars take up this challenge, they should be encouraged to analyse the problem sociologically. For example, were there significant variations drawn along class, gender, ethnic or regional lines? Even if the answers to these and similar questions corroborate the claim for popular support, other questions will necessarily follow.

One would concern the conditions endorsed by public opinion for American adherence. Since the American Bar Association continually fluffed this crucial issue – not to mention the lobbyists, as we shall see – firm evidence will undoubtedly be difficult to find.[24] A second question is rather more philosophical than historical and methodological; but it is, if anything, more intractable and shows how little historians may reflect on the political systems they purport to analyse. Supposing public opinion, accurately defined, had favoured adherence and on precisely the terms set down for debate: should the Senate have concurred? The dilemma lies not just in the procedure of the two-thirds rule, which itself contradicts simple majoritarianism. The dilemma goes to the very heart of a representational system of government, especially (we should note) one in which senators are deliberately, constitutionally kept at a distance from the contemporary judgment of the people by the electoral phasing of the Senate's composition.

At the conceptual level, the most significant difference between the two generations lies in their analysis of the Executive–Senate relationship in the Court campaign. Whereas the First Generation portrayed the Senate as the major villain, with its weapon the two-thirds rule, the Second Generation has censured Roosevelt for contributing to the Court defeat. The chief exponent of this interpretation is Kahn, who argues that Roosevelt's reluctance to make adherence a 'salient' item on his legislative agenda increased the momentum towards failure. Kahn's analysis is a useful corrective to those who portray Roosevelt as a 'leader' on the Court campaign – a tradition which still appears strong.[25] But the leadership model creates its own problems. Here the test case is provided by Roosevelt's predecessor, Herbert Hoover. Hoover was by far the best informed of the presidents on the Court's complexities; he was also the Court's most consistent presidential advocate. But his own knowledge of the domestic and international difficulties made Hoover realize the obstacles to adherence on the terms demanded by the pro-Leaguers.[26] And it is this essentially pro-League vision which scholars continue to share.

It is, indeed, on the League issue that the First and Second Generations come closest together. Fleming correctly saw that the central question in the Court campaign was the League of Nations. That was why the advisory jurisdiction was so contentious. There were two aspects to the problem. It was not just the simple, understandable fear that the advisory jurisdiction might be used as a form of compulsory jurisdiction to hale the United States before the bar of the Court. There was also the possibility that an advisory opinion of the Court might be used to legitimate League policy and, through American membership of the Court, thereby commit the US government to enforcing a particular decision. Historians may scoff at this second fear as unjustified paranoia or simple scare-mongering; but it was exactly the kind of practical result that pro-League Court advocates wanted.

The Second Generation has acknowledged the centrality of the League connection; but they have not identified themselves (as Fleming conspicuously did) with the pro-League advocates. Like many other historians, notably Robert Dallek, the Court specialists have described the campaign as a 'symbolic' struggle – a form of wording which allows them to avoid the reality of the League itself.[27] Yet even before the appearance of Fleming's monograph a number of studies had appeared revealing the League in a critical light. The work of E. H. Carr and Robert Dell comes to mind. But in case such exposés are dismissed as hostile special-pleading, we should remember that corroboration appeared in the insider accounts of such pro-League actors as Alfred Zimmern and Robert Cecil.[28]

The historiography of the League of Nations is extensive – even if we confine ourselves to English-language material. To the critical and first-hand accounts just cited can be added the many excellent studies written since World War II, from Frank Walters's semi-official history through to the numerous monographs of James Barros.[29] Yet this richly informative literature seems to have had little influence upon recent Court scholarship, which continues to treat the League unproblematically. In similar fashion the Second Generation historians overplay the contribution of Elihu Root in the creation of the Court – another product, undoubtedly, of their dependence upon a rather narrow range of sources. But the most striking omission in the Second Generation historiography is not the work and nature of the League – but of its Court! We may allow the 'symbolic' allusion of the Court campaign to the League as rhetorical licence; but what can we make of histories of the Court campaign which have no discussion, scarcely even a mention of the jurisprudence and actions of the Court itself? In this staggering neglect, the Second Generation faithfully follows the First: studies written to attack the Senate for staying out of the Court are offered without any description, let alone evaluation, of the Court's role within the League system.

Perhaps this paradox is to be explained by the confident, unquestioned belief that the Permanent Court of International Justice was essentially an American creation. The premise which stands behind all the writing on the Court campaign is (to borrow Fleming's phrase) 'the American origins of the Court' – we may add, *exclusively* American origins.[30] Such origins have apparently been taken as a retrospective warrant for the Court's acceptability. The implication, therefore, is that any scrutiny of the Court would be debasing, a questioning of one's own heritage. This interpretation of a staggering silence in Court historiography may seem initially implausible; but it is surely the only defence available to those scholars who have neglected the work of an institution they implicitly praise. The rest of this chapter will examine the validity and implications of the Court's Americanness.

Fleming began his influential study with the assertion: 'The American demand for a world court is more than a century old.'[31] His readers were thereby invited to assume that such a tradition should have been consummated in American adherence to the Permanent Court of International Justice established and supported by the League of Nations. Other historians, before and after Fleming, have described at length the many proposals and detailed projects devised by Americans for international government and the judicial resolution of interstate conflict. The Federal Union created by the Constitutional Convention of 1787 is invariably cited as a historical and organizational model for such intergovernmental co-operation. Yet the best of such detailed historical accounts show that Americans were neither alone nor unanimous in their search for 'world order'. In other words, the simple fact that many Americans had demanded a world court (as Fleming put it) or even (in Warren Kuehl's claim) 'led the world' in 'agitation and planning' for intergovernmental leagues of various kinds was no guarantee that when a particular version of these goals was created, American legislators would or even should follow this logic by joining the new World Court or the new League of Nations.[32]

That such logic has been followed by American historians is remarkable. Of course we can all appreciate the rhetorical strength and political power of claiming that an event follows logically, inevitably from pre-existing conditions; but such pseudo-materialism disguises the real potential for political choice. Europeans may have the conceptual advantage here, simply because the examples are so plentiful. The most recent is the formation of the EEC. No one with *any* knowledge of European affairs, particularly schemes for interstate integration, could sensibly believe that the EEC is the only extrapolation from earlier history.[33] Rather the EEC is a particular form of integration (serving free-market capitalism and electorally powerful farmers), though it was frequently justified to prospective members by its alleged inevitability. Yet such deterministic arguments for the EEC would scarcely have found a voice unless there was some *prima facie* evidence, some basis in truth. The case of the American origins of the Permanent Court is no different – though the following analysis will trace this complex history selectively within a framework which anticipates the language and presumptions of the interwar debate on adherence.

We must begin by recognizing three crucial distinctions: first, the distinction between private and official action; second, between arbitration and adjudication; and third, between the executive and legislative branches of government. On the private, unofficial level it is relatively easy and uncontentious to list the individuals and groups which give weight to the claim that Americans have traditionally sought to create novel forms of international, even supranational legal and political organization. The activities of such campaigners as Noah Worcester (1758–1837), William Ladd (1778–1841) and William Ellery Channing (1780–1842), capped by the founding of the American Peace Society (APS) in 1828, are generally regarded as the opening, formative stage of a movement which reaches its acme at the turn of the century with the Lake Mohonk Conferences (1895–1916), the establishment of both the World Peace Foundation (WPF) and the Carnegie Endowment for International Peace (CEIP) in 1910, and the creation of the League to Enforce Peace (LEP) in 1915. It was just such a tradition which World Court advocates invoked to bolster their appeal for American adherence. However, a critical examination of what has been loosely called the 'modern American peace movement' shows that such private bodies, notably the APS and the CEIP, were internally divided on the merits of the new League Court – just as the LEP had split on the League itself.[34] Such private lobbyists were not apt to think their own existence was a warrant for the Court's acceptability – let alone the inevitability of American membership.

The traditional practices of the US government were equally problematical. There can, of course, be no denying that the United States had a full record of resolving international disputes by arbitral means: of submitting, in other words, international controversies to *ad hoc* panels for interim or final decision. The practice went back to the early years of the Republic with Jay's Treaty of 1794. Boundary and similar disputes with the British government constituted the material for such arbitrations throughout the nineteenth century. The settlement of the *Alabama* claims by the Treaty of Washington (1871) became a landmark case in the modern history of intergovernmental arbitration – a powerful argument that the most divisive controversies could be settled amicably between Great Powers. Once again, though, we need to study the other side of these encouraging episodes. Two qualifications are immediately relevant. The first and more general is that the cited record is one of diplomatic bargaining, in which the disputants defined the terms of the problem and thereby effectively determined the results of the arbitration. (The settlement of the Canadian border, especially the resolution of the Oregon dispute, confirms this general rule.) Secondly and relatedly: in these cases it was the United States which was negotiating from strength. Propagandists of the Anglo–American special relationship have interpreted these arbitrations as expressions of a fundamental common interest shared by the British and Americans. Such an interpretation is more politics than history. A more convincing explanation lies in the passage of power from the British Empire to the United States. When either side thought its interests would be served by arbitration, it would arbitrate; if not, other less pacific means were threatened. The history of the Isthmian Canal treaties from Clayton-Bulwer (1850) to the second Hay-Pauncefote (1901) on to the Hay-Herran (1903) bears out this interpretation over more than fifty years – as the various Venezuelan crises at the turn of the century do in the space of a decade.

But this is the history of arbitration – though with physical force never totally ruled out. What of the United States and adjudication: the submission of disputes to a permanent body of judges who would define the nature of the controversy and set their own terms for its resolution independently of the adversaries' claims? The lines between the processess of arbitration and adjudication may seem tenuous; and some legal and diplomatic authorities denied such a categorical distinction. But all students of the World Court know that the contrast was often drawn. That being the case, what follows from this separation?

Here the evidence is readily available and its implications unmistakable. The United States was indeed a participant in the First and Second Hague Peace Conferences of 1899 and 1907 which led to the establishment of a permanent court. But this was the Permanent Court of *Arbitration*.[35] As the title of the new court revealed, its diplomatic nature was undeniable. In the common language of the time, the system created by The Hague Conventions was a 'compromise'. Disputant governments selected judges *ad hoc* from an existing panel and set their own terms of reference. Meanwhile the contracting states proclaimed the virtues of 'permanency' in personnel and jurisprudence and envisaged a time when the initial voluntary status of the proceedings would be replaced by 'compulsion' on the model of domestic courts, where alleged wrongdoers could be haled before a bench *nolens volens*. Certainly there were Americans who wished to move further along the path of compulsory (or obligatory) jurisdiction and towards permanent judges; but so too did the nationals of other countries. There was nothing especially American about these goals. (We may remember that it was Tsar Nicholas II who had summoned the First Hague Conference.)

Where the United States did play a special role was in setting specific limits to the scope of the PCA and any successor. Here we do indeed find some powerful elements of tradition.

So far in this review we have spoken of the federal government as a unit. Now we must be more discriminating. Earlier on we alluded to the many hostile accounts of the Senate's treaty-making power, the notorious 'two-thirds rule' which allegedly 'produce[*d*] impotence and friction' in the conduct of foreign relations.[36] It is unnecessary to recapitulate the general criticisms of the Senate. The specific point to notice is the long history of the Senate requiring its own consent to diplomatic arbitrations and international judicial proceedings. (The terms do not need to be nuanced: the Senate was equally insistent in both areas.) Under Presidents McKinley, Roosevelt, Taft and Wilson any number of treaties were negotiated with foreign governments, only for the final text to carry a provision, proposed by the Executive or added by Senators, that a two-thirds vote would be needed to approve the exact terms of any particular proposal to arbitrate a dispute. Sometimes draft legislation would be rejected by the Senate (as with the Olney-Pauncefote Treaty of 1897); sometimes abandoned by the Executive after such senatorial amendment (as with the Hay Treaties of 1904–5); sometimes adopted (as with the Root Treaties of 1908–9). One principle was constant – and was to continue through to the Kellogg Treaties of the 1920s: the insistence of the Senate upon preserving a role for itself.[37] If indeed the United States had established a claim to being a world leader in the field of arbitration, the Senate had also shown a determination to retain its own prerogatives.

Senatorial insistence on a procedural matter undeniably created 'friction' with the Executive; but on certain substantive issues there was no disagreement between the Senate and Executive or between the two of them and the people-at-large. Another element of tradition lay in the consensus excluding certain topics from the competence of arbitral bodies and, *a fortiori*, from any court with power to determine its own jurisdiction. Chief among the excluded or 'reserved' topics were immigration, the tariff and the Monroe Doctrine. The same American delegates who had negotiated the Conventions of 1899 to 1907 at The Hague signed them only with such exclusions; and these principles were maintained by both friends and enemies of the Versailles Treaty in the battles of 1919–20. The succeeding Court campaign would preserve the tradition.

This brief review of American practice in the areas of arbitration and adjudication has been admittedly selective. Its purpose, like the previous references to isolationism and the outbreak of World War II, has been to establish a framework for a more detailed analysis of the Court campaign, particularly by anticipating some of the language and concepts of the contemporary debate. What is beyond dispute is that any American diplomatic traditions were, like the Monroe Doctrine itself, 'elastic' and could be adjusted to suit argumentative purposes.[38] With these caveats in mind, we can now turn to the Court itself: the Permanent Court of International Justice established by the League of Nations – the Court which soon came to be called the Root Court.

Notes

1 *Congressional Record*, 74th Congress, 1st Session (cited below as *CR*, followed by Congress and Session number), 1145–6 (in the following pages, references are to the consolidated Sessional volumes of *CR*); 'Defeat of the World Court', *Springfield Republican* (Massachusetts), 30 January 1935, 10.

2 'Rejecting the Court', *New York Times* (cited below as *NYT*), 31 January 1935, 18; 'A Disappointing Verdict', *Manchester Guardian*, 31 January 1935, 8; *Le Temps* (Paris), 31 January 1935, 1.

3 Dexter Perkins, *The New Age of Franklin Roosevelt, 1932–1945* (Chicago: Chicago University Press, 1957), ch. 4; William E. Leuchtenburg, *Franklin D. Roosevelt and the New Deal, 1932–1940* (New York and London: Harper & Row, 1963), ch. 9.

4 Ernest C. Bolt, Jr., 'Isolation, Expansion, and Peace: American Foreign Policy between the Wars', in Gerald K. Haines and J. Samuel Walker (eds.), *American Foreign Relations: a Historiographical Review*, Contributions in American History, no. 90 (Westport, Ct.: Greenwood Press, 1981), 133–57.

5 Keith L. Nelson and Spencer C. Olin, Jr., *Why War? Ideology, Theory, and History* (Berkeley and London: University of California Press, 1979), ch. 5; Jeffrey Kimball, 'The Influence of Ideology on Interpretive Disagreement: a Report on a Survey of Diplomatic, Military and Peace Historians on the Causes of 20th Century U.S. Wars', *History Teacher* 17 (May 1984), 335–84.

6 Drew Middleton, *Retreat from Victory: a Critical Appraisal of American Foreign and Military Policy from 1920 to the 1970s* (New York: Hawthorn Press, 1973); Howard Jablon, *Crossroads of Decision: the State Department and Foreign Policy, 1933–1937* (Lexington: University Press of Kentucky, 1983).

7 The essential evidence is in *Documents on German Foreign Policy, 1918–1945*, Series D (London: HMSO, 1949–), I. 634–732; ibid., II. 369–923 *passim*.

8 Manley O. Hudson, *The Permanent Court of International Justice, 1920–1942: A Treatise* (New York: Macmillan, 1943), an earlier version of which had been published in 1934; Alexander P. Fachiri, *The Permanent Court of International Justice: its Constitution, Procedure and Work*, 2nd ed. (London: Oxford University Press, 1932), the first edition of which had been published in 1925.

9 Manley O. Hudson, *The Permanent Court of International Justice and the Question of American Participation: with a Collection of Documents* (Cambridge, Mass.: Harvard University Press, 1925); Antonio Sanchez de Bustamente y Sirven, *El Tribunal Permanente de Justicia Internacional* (Madrid: Editorial Reus, 1925): trans. Elizabeth F. Read, *The World Court* (New York: Macmillan, 1925).

10 Frances Kellor and Antonia Hatvany, *The United States Senate and the International Court* (New York: Thomas Seltzer, 1925); James V. Giblin and Arthur L. Brown, *The World Court Myth* (Boston: Wright & Potter, 1926); David Jayne Hill, *The Problem of a World Court: the Story of an Unrealized American Idea* (New York: Longmans, Green, 1927); Edward Lindsey, *The International Court* (New York: Thomas Y. Crowell, 1931).

11 Denna Frank Fleming, *The Cold War and its Origins, 1917–1960*, 2 vols

(Garden City, NY: Doubleday, 1960).

[12] Denna Frank Fleming, *The Treaty Veto of the American Senate* (New York and London: Putnam's, 1930); *The United States and the League of Nations, 1918–1920* (New York and London: Putnam's, 1932); and *The United States and World Organization, 1920–1933* (New York: Columbia University Press, 1938).

[13] Denna Frank Fleming, *The United States and the World Court* (Garden City, NY: Doubleday, Doran, 1945).

[14] Royden J. Dangerfield, *In Defense of the Senate: a Study in Treaty Making* (Norman: University of Oklahoma Press, 1933); Kenneth Colegrove, *The American Senate and World Peace* (New York: Vanguard Press, 1944), 198.

[15] Colegrove, ibid., 20; Fleming, *United States and the World Court*, 136.

[16] Selig Adler, *The Isolationist Impulse: its Twentieth Century Reaction* (New York and London: Abelard-Schuman, 1957); Richard W. Leopold, *The Growth of American Foreign Policy: a History* (New York: Knopf, 1962); Robert A. Divine, *The Illusion of Neutrality* (Chicago: University of Chicago Press, 1962).

[17] Wayne S. Cole, *Roosevelt and the Isolationists, 1932–1945* (Lincoln and London: University of Nebraska Press, 1983); Robert Dallek, *Franklin D. Roosevelt and American Foreign Policy, 1932–1945* (New York: Oxford University Press, 1979).

[18] Denna Frank Fleming, *The United States and the World Court, 1920–1966* (New York: Russell & Russell, 1968), esp. 3–5; and *The United States and the League of Nations, 1918–1920,* enlarged ed. (New York: Russell & Russell, 1968). All subsequent references are to these later versions.

[19] Robert Domenic Accinelli, 'The United States and the World Court, 1920–1927', PhD dissertation, University of California at Berkeley, 1968. Accinelli, his predecessors and contemporaries, are discussed in Michael Dunne, 'Isolationism of a Kind: Two Generations of World Court Historiography in the United States', *Journal of American Studies* 21 (December 1987), 327–51.

[20] Elihu Root in *Proceedings of the American Society of International Law* (cited below as *PASIL*) (1921), 1–13, esp. 3–5.

[21] Warren F. Kuehl, 'Webs of Common Interests Revisited: Nationalism, Internationalism, and Historians of American Foreign Relations', *Diplomatic History* 10 (Spring 1986), 107–20; Lawrence S. Wittner, 'Peace Movements and Foreign Policy: the Challenge to Diplomatic Historians', ibid., 11 (Fall 1987), 355–70.

[22] Representative texts are cited in Dunne, 'Isolationism of a Kind'; and relevant works will be cited below.

[23] Terry Lattau Deibel, 'The League of Nations and American Internationalism, 1919–1929', 2 vols., PhD dissertation, Fletcher School of Law and Diplomacy, 1972, an elaboration of his earlier work, 'Struggle for Cooperation: the League of Nations Secretariat and Pro-League Internationalism in the United States, 1919–1924', Mémoire presented for the Diploma of the Institute, Graduate School of International Studies, Geneva, 1970; Gilbert N. Kahn, 'Pressure Group Influence on Foreign Policy Decision-Making: a Case Study of United States' Efforts to Join the World Court – 1935', PhD dissertation, New York University, 1973).

[24] Manley O. Hudson (ed.), *In re The World Court: the Judgment of the American Bar as Expressed in Resolutions of National, State and Local Bar Associations, 1921–1934* (Chicago: American Bar Association, 1934).

[25] Gilbert N. Kahn, 'Presidential Passivity on a Nonsalient Issue: President Franklin D. Roosevelt and the 1935 World Court Fight', *Diplomatic History* 4 (Spring 1980), 137–59; Walter LaFeber, 'The Constitution and United States

Foreign Policy: an Interpretation', *Journal of American History* 74 (December 1987), 695–717, esp. 710.

[26] Michael Dunne, 'Herbert Hoover and the World Court', unpublished paper to VI Hoover Symposium, Newberg, Oregon, October 1987.

[27] Robert D. Accinelli, 'Peace through Law: the United States and the World Court, 1923–1935', Canadian Historical Association, *Historical Papers/ Communications Historiques* (1972), 247–61, esp. 250–2; Robert Dallek, *The American Style of Foreign Policy: Cultural Politics and Foreign Affairs* (New York: Knopf, 1983), 114–18.

[28] Edward Hallett Carr, *The Twenty Years' Crisis, 1919–1939: an Introduction to the Study of International Relations* (London: Macmillan, 1939); Robert Dell, *The Geneva Racket, 1920–1939* (London: R. Hale, 1941); Alfred E. Zimmern, *The League of Nations and the Rule of Law, 1918–1935* (London: Macmillan, 1936); Edward Algernon Robert Cecil, *A Great Experiment: an Autobiography of Viscount Cecil (Lord Robert Cecil)* (London: Jonathan Cape, 1941).

[29] F. P. Walters, *A History of the League of Nations*, 2 vols. (London: Oxford University Press, 1952). James Barros's most recent monograph is *Britain, Greece and the Politics of Sanctions: Ethiopia, 1935–1936*. Royal Historical Society Studies in History Series, no. 33 (London: Royal Historical Society, 1982).

[30] Fleming, *United States and the World Court*, ch. 1.

[31] Ibid. 15.

[32] Warren F. Kuehl, *Seeking World Order: the United States and International Organization to 1920* (Nashville: Vanderbilt University Press, 1969), 3.

[33] Carl H. Pegg, *Evolution of the European Idea, 1914–1932* (Chapel Hill and London: University of North Carolina Press, 1983) provides a detailed bibliography, including work on post-World War II movements studied by Walter Lipgens, *Die Anfänge der europaïschen Einigungspolitik 1945–1950. I Teil: 1945–1947* (Stuttgart: Ernst Klett, 1977).

[34] The leading recent scholar is the late Charles DeBenedetti: see *Origins of the Modern American Peace Movement, 1915–1929* (Millwood, NY: KTO Press, 1978) and *The Peace Reform in American History* (Bloomington: Indiana University Press, 1980).

[35] Calvin DeArmond Davis, *The United States and the First Hague Peace Conference* (Ithaca: Cornell University Press, 1962) and *The United States and the Second Hague Peace Conference: American Diplomacy and International Organization, 1899–1914* (Durham: Duke University Press, 1976).

[36] W. Stull Holt, *Treaties Defeated by the Senate: a Study of the Struggle between President and Senate over the Conduct of Foreign Relations* (Baltimore: Johns Hopkins Press, 1933), 307. Holt, Dangerfield, *In Defense of the Senate*, and Quincy Wright, *The Control of American Foreign Relations* (New York: Macmillan, 1922), provide bibliographical details through World War I.

[37] L. Ethan Ellis, *Frank B. Kellogg and American Foreign Relations, 1925–1929* (New Brunswick, NJ: Rutgers University Press, 1961), ch. 8.

[38] Holt, *Treaties Defeated by the Senate*, 212.

2 League Court–Root Court: the United States and the establishment of the PCIJ, 1919–20

The Treaty of Versailles, including the Covenant of the League of Nations, came officially into effect on 10 January 1920. Six days later the first meeting of the Council of the newly constituted League took place in the Salle de l'Horloge of the Quai d'Orsay, in the same setting and almost exactly a year to the day from the opening of the Paris Peace Conference. As a matter of courtesy the chair was offered to Léon Bourgeois, former Prime Minister of France, delegate to the Peace Conference and recently elected President of the French Senate.[1]

Under the terms of the Covenant, Article IV, the Council was to comprise nine representatives: the five 'Principal Allied and Associated Powers' (the United Kingdom, the United States of America, France, Italy and Japan), together with four 'other Members of the League' (those nominated *ad interim* being Belgium, Brazil, Greece and Spain). In his opening remarks Bourgeois alluded to the obvious absence of any American representation and lamented the events which had prevented President Wilson from assuming his rightful place at the head of their deliberations. But Bourgeois was brief: the US Senate's rejection of the Treaty of Versailles two months previously would have even less chance of being reversed if European statesmen meddled in the congressional discussion, emphasized the complexities of the Treaty's provisions or dilated upon the obligations and implications of the Covenant.[2]

Little formal business was conducted at this inaugural meeting of the League Council. Bourgeois presented a political survey of the world focused upon the League; but the numerous problems directly facing the League would have to wait, Bourgeois concluded, for proper and detailed investigation to begin at the second Council meeting. Among these were the limitation of armaments; the establishment of the mandate system; the development of economic and social organizations; and the 'definite foundation of international justice'.[3]

On 11 February the League Council reconvened in London at St James's Palace, this time with Arthur Balfour in the chair. (Balfour, the British Foreign Secretary during the Paris Peace Conference, was now Lord President of the Council.) Almost immediately the delegates went into secret session to discuss the publication of eight separate Reports on matters of substance and procedure arising from the Covenant and the Treaty of Versailles. Two days later Bourgeois submitted a Report on the Organisation of a Permanent Court of International Justice.[4]

The *Report* began with the terms of Article XIV of the Covenant:

> The Council shall formulate and submit to the Members of the League for adoption plans for the establishment of a Permanent Court of International Justice. The Court shall be competent to hear and determine any dispute of an international character which the parties thereto submit to it. The Court may also give an advisory opinion upon any dispute or question referred to it by the Council or by the Assembly.

Bourgeois, as rapporteur, did not relate the very complicated history of Article XIV – a history he had helped to shape both before and during the Paris Peace Conference. Instead he sketched the antiquity of the 'idea of entrusting to a supreme tribunal the peaceable settlement of disputes between nations and between governments', an idea he traced to the institutions of classical Greece and Rome. Bourgeois was careful, however, to emphasize that this ancient record was one of 'arbitration, which alone seems consistent with the sovereignty of States'. It had to be distinguished from adjudication before a permanent court on the model of domestic or municipal law enforcement. Certainly there had been modern landmarks: the resolution of 'the *Alabama* affair [was] within the memory of many of' his fellow Council representatives. Yet even the limited scope of arbitration 'was still only an incident in the life of nations; it knew no law but the convenience of States which, sure of their right or distrustful of their military strength, would consent to accept its verdict'.

Bourgeois praised the Permanent Court of Arbitration (PCA) at The Hague, which had been established and maintained under the Conventions of 1899 and 1907. In so doing he was partly congratulating himself, for Bourgeois had been a delegate to both Hague Peace Conferences. Nevertheless Bourgeois admitted that the *ad hoc* nature of the PCA prevented its functioning as 'really a permanent tribunal' for arbitration; while its origins in the arbitration movement itself meant that it lacked the 'special character of a Court of Justice'.

To meet these inadequacies the delegates to the 1907 Hague Peace Conference had considered setting up, either within or alongside the

PCA, 'a really Permanent Tribunal... with the object of giving to the future decisions of international judges the unity and the stability which the awards of arbitrators had hitherto lacked'. The United States delegates had been prominent in urging the creation of such a body; and their theoretical arguments had been favourably received. The practical obstacle came (as Bourgeois noted) in the selection of the permanent bench of judges.

The number of judges had necessarily to be restricted, [for] there could be no question of giving a representative to each of the forty-four States which had taken part in the conference. How was a choice to be made between Powers of equal sovereignty, equally jealous of their prerogatives?

Bourgeois listed some possible methods: by free election regardless of nationality; by lot; by rotation. The 1907 Hague Conference had acknowledged the dilemma and referred it to the signatories of the Permanent Court of Arbitration.[5]

The impasse had remained as war broke out in Europe in 1914. But now, Bourgeois concluded, 'circumstances are singularly favourable for [*the*] immediate realisation' of the aspirations of 1907.

From all parts of the devastated and tormented world rises a cry for justice. The military and moral unity which for five years has held the free peoples together, and concentrated their efforts in the defence of the right, must survive with our victory; it can find no nobler expression nor a more splendid symbol than the establishment of a *Permanent Court of International Justice.*

This was understandable rhetoric. Surrounding remarks and allusions made clear the political arguments of Bourgeois, the representative of a victorious power, who was fusing the history of the arbitration movement with the success of the Allied and Associated Powers and implicitly discounting the role of Germany, Austria-Hungary and even Russia in the establishment of the PCA. The new court envisioned by Bourgeois would consummate centuries of international striving for the judicial resolution of conflict – as well as legitimate the subordination of the defeated Central Powers and continue the ostracism of States beyond the pale of the League.

The lapse was brief: a sentence in many hundreds of words. But it was indicative, as we shall see. Bourgeois closed on a less provocative note. Questions of the Court's composition, procedure, jurisdiction and siting could be most 'usefully... entrusted to a commission of legal experts', whose recommendations would be examined by the Council itself. Then, as proof of the great preparation and collaboration which had gone into the *Report* since the previous summer, Bourgeois offered the names of twelve men to constitute the advisory committee: Satsuo Akidzuki (Japan); Rafael Altamira y Crevea (Spain); Clovis Bevilaqua (Brazil); Edouard Descamps (Belgium); Luis Maria Drago (Argentina); Carlo Fadda (Italy); Henri Fromageot (France); Gregers Gram (Norway); Bernard Loder (The Netherlands); Walter Phillimore (United Kingdom); Milenko Vesnitch (Kingdom of the Serbs, Croats and Slovenes); and

Elihu Root (United States of America). As Balfour himself acknowledged when moving the Council's acceptance of the *Report's* list of nominees, the most striking inclusion was that of the American representative, Elihu Root.[6]

Root was arguably the most famous member of the proposed commission – at least in the general public's eyes. (Drago would, of course, be well-known to international lawyers and diplomats.) Root had been in the cabinets of Presidents McKinley and Roosevelt, first as Secretary of War from 1899 to 1904; later as Secretary of State from 1905 to 1909. He had then served a full term as Senator for New York (1909–15). This was the Root known nationally and internationally as a Republican. In the summer of 1917, however, he had accepted a non-partisan role as President Wilson's Ambassador Extraordinary to the Provisional Government in Russia. Yet Root's fame was perhaps even wider outside the scope of party politics. He had been the first President of the Carnegie Endowment for International Peace since its foundation in 1910; he had been a leading officer in the American Society for International Law since its foundation in 1906; he was a panel-member of the PCA. For these and many other reasons Root had been awarded the Nobel Peace Prize of 1912; and among the most famous examples of his prominence in the fields of diplomacy and arbitration was his attempt to develop the judicial element in The Hague Court. Indeed, Root's instructions to the American delegation at the Second Peace Conference in 1907 to pursue this goal attracted great, perhaps unjustified, publicity.[7]

In the period of US neutrality during World War I Root held 'pro-allied convictions' – the words of Root's younger confidant and major biographer, Philip Caryl Jessup. One aspect of his sympathies was shown by the close contact Root maintained with leading British proponents of international adjudication, notably James Bryce and Lassa Oppenheim. Since Root's beliefs and actions will form a major focus of this and succeeding chapters, it will be worth while to quote at length from a letter he wrote to Oppenheim in March 1915. As Root 'reflect[*ed*] upon the possibilities of the future' after the close of hostilities, he became all 'the more certain… that the establishment of adequate law [*was*] the essential of every proposal for a new condition of international affairs better than the old'. He continued:

> There can be no court without a law to guide it. Otherwise the judges would be irresponsible sovereigns. There can be no police force without the judgments of a court to enforce. Otherwise the police force would be the agent of an irresponsible majority reducing all sovereigns to vassalage and destroying national independence. At the basis of all reform… lies an agreement upon certain, definite, specific rules of national conduct, very general and very rudimentary at first but capable of being enlarged by continual additions. With a court to pass upon the conformity of national conduct to such rules and a tribunal of conciliation to supplement its jurisdiction with adequate power to enforce its judgments we may get away from the wretched policies and plans, intrigues and suspicions, which have brought about the present dreadful condition.[8]

Root was not, of course, the only American to be thinking along these lines. Nor, indeed, were Root's ideas on international politics and adjudication absolutely consistent or unambiguous, as we shall see. Nevertheless Root's reputation and authority were great – even in Democratic circles, as his appointment to the Russian mission had shown. In the early part of 1918 Root urged the Wilson administration to provide for an international court in any future League of Nations – a proposal which chimed in with the contemporaneous work of the so-called Phillimore Committee, which was reporting to the British War Cabinet on postwar organization. Wilson's close adviser, Colonel Edward Mandell House, had himself been persuaded by Root's arguments for such a court, going so far as to say to Wilson that such a 'court might well prove the strongest part' in the 'machinery' of the prospective league.[9]

Wilson was less confident. As his Secretary of State, Robert Lansing, phrased the difference: Wilson preferred to rely upon 'diplomatic adjustment' rather than 'strict legal justice' in resolving international disputes. Historians are well aware of the disagreements between Lansing and Wilson; and informed contemporaries knew in particular of Wilson's antipathy to lawyers as a group and to legalism as a mode of thinking and action. Yet if President Wilson could scarcely leave Secretary Lansing in the United States while he himself presided over the American delegation to the Paris Peace Conference, he could ensure that no other prominent lawyer would attend as a plenipotentiary. Root was, therefore, not offered a place on the delegation, even though House, Lansing and Wilson's son-in-law, Secretary of the Treasury, William G. McAdoo, supported his presence. Their arguments stressed Root's influence and contacts with leading Republicans: men such as Theodore Roosevelt; Roosevelt's presidential successor, William Howard Taft; Charles Evans Hughes, formerly Governor of New York and Associate Judge of the US Supreme Court and Wilson's opponent in the 1916 election; Philander Chase Knox, once a cabinet colleague of Root's, then Secretary of State under Taft and presently Senator from Pennsylvania; and Henry Cabot Lodge, an intimate of Roosevelt's, a man who had spent over thirty years in Congress (twenty-five of them in the Senate) and was soon to assume the chairmanship of the Senate Committee on Foreign Relations. Since, however, Root was to remain in the United States he would serve the Republican establishment as an authoritative counsellor on the terms of peace being negotiated at Paris.[10]

The first plenary session of the Peace Conference was held on 18 January 1919; and within a week a subcommittee called the Commission on the League of Nations was appointed to report a constitution. In the space of a fortnight the Commission held ten meetings; and on 14 February President Wilson formally presented the Draft Covenant of the League of Nations to the third plenary session 'for examination and discussion by all the interested Powers'.[11]

The text of the Draft Covenant ran to twenty-six articles. As one of its major authors, the American David Hunter Miller, commented: it appeared 'inconceivable that a [League] constitution could have been drawn in thirty hours'. But, as he acknowledged, this 'bald statement' failed to take into account 'all the thought which had previously been given to the subject'.[12] Wilson and House, the American representatives on the Commission, had themselves constructed a number of schemes. The representatives of the British Empire, Lord Robert Cecil and Lieutenant General Jan Christiaan Smuts, had also been engaged in formulating such plans, both before and after the Armistice of November 1918. So too had Bourgeois, one of the two French Commission members; while Miller himself had worked closely with officials from the British Foreign Office, notably Cecil Hurst.[13]

Miller, Cecil and Hurst were all eager to develop the judicial resolution of international disputes. Bourgeois, however, was less committed, for he placed greater reliance upon arbitration and enlarging the role of the Permanent Court of Arbitration. Smuts too was an advocate of arbitration and the political resolution of international controversies; but he lacked Bourgeois's personal and intellectual commitment to the PCA. As for Wilson and House, they were at best sceptical of the value of extending the scope of the PCA – House having reverted to the views he held before his temporary conversion by Root in the spring of 1918. Their fellow plenipotentiary, Lansing, favoured the development of the PCA; but he was not a member of the Commission on the League. Furthermore, Wilson did not permit him much discretion at the Conference and House had become a somewhat unsympathetic intermediary between the President and Secretary of State. Of the Commission members the Italians, represented by Prime Minister Vittorio Orlando and Senator Vittorio Scialoja, proffered the most detailed plans for advancing the work of The Hague Conferences and Court.[14]

Given these conflicting priorities and the numerous proposals for political leagues, international arbitration and legal adjudication sketched before and during the Peace Conference it was scarcely surprising that the relevant terms of the Draft Covenant of 14 February should constitute a compromise of those issues and thereby disappoint some expectant outside observers.[15] No one more so than Elihu Root.

Initially Root's criticisms of the Draft Covenant were centred on its political clauses rather than those concerning arbitration and adjudication. In particular he deplored Article X requiring the League to guarantee the 'territorial integrity and existing political independence' of Member States; and he faulted the Covenant's failure to acknowledge the Monroe Doctrine. Yet it was not until late March that Root published his most detailed and extensive criticisms of the Draft Covenant.

Root's analysis was offered by way of an open letter to the chairman of the Republican National Committee, Will Hays. The letter's origins were complex, but the main lines of the story can be stated briefly. From Paris the sole Republican among the American plenipotentiaries, Henry White, cabled Lodge to discover what amendments to the Draft

Covenant would satisfy the large Republican opposition in the Senate – an opposition which had declared itself in the famous Round Robin of 4 March 1919. Lodge contacted Root; he in turn consulted his own close friend, law partner and former Secretary of War, Henry Lewis Stimson; and between the three of them they decided that Hays should write publicly to Root (in a letter largely composed by Root) 'seeking the fullest information and best judgment to enable [*the American people*] to reach a correct conclusion' on the meaning and necessary modification of the February terms.[16]

Contemporaneously Taft and Hughes were broadcasting their objections to the Draft Covenant. Like Root they offered specific amendments for incorporation in the Covenant, notably on Article X and the Monroe Doctrine.[17] The striking and peculiar quality of Root's letter to Hays (and thus to the Peace Conference and US Senate) was the prominence given to Articles XIII and XIV of the Draft, articles concerning the arbitration and adjudication of international controversies.

Since Root's open letter to Hays sounded so many key words and raised so many central concepts it will be analysed and quoted at length. However, before this extensive discussion, it will be convenient to cite the full text of Articles XIII and XIV of the Draft Covenant. Article XIII stated:

1. The High Contracting Parties agree that whenever any dispute or difficulty shall arise between them which they recognise to be suitable for submission to arbitration and which cannot be satisfactorily settled by diplomacy, they will submit the whole subject matter to arbitration.
2. For this purpose the Court of arbitration to which the case is referred shall be the Court agreed on by the parties or stipulated in any Convention existing between them.
3. The High Contracting Parties agree that they will carry out in full good faith any award that may be rendered. In the event of any failure to carry out the award, the Executive Council shall propose what steps can best be taken to give effect thereto.

Article XIV (the final form of which we have already seen) ran as follows in the earlier February draft:

The Executive Council shall formulate plans for the establishment of a Permanent Court of International Justice and this Court shall, when established, be competent to hear and determine any matter which the parties recognise as suitable for submission to it for arbitration under the foregoing Article.[18]

Root began with some remarks on the tentative nature of the February Covenant (a Wilsonian term Root noticeably avoided) and the constitutional propriety of the Senate's offering amendments to the terms so far negotiated at Paris. After this introduction, the bulk of the letter (and the portion which is relevant to us) concerned arbitration and adjudication. Root started his case by arguing that the 'avowed object' of the Covenant was the avoidance of war. Then he insisted that the 'causes of war [*fell*] into two distinct classes'. The first consisted of 'controversies about rights under the law of nations and under treaties'; and these were 'in a general way... described as justiciable or judicial questions'. The second class of war-breeding disputes were those involving

> clashes between conflicting national policies, as distinguished from claims of legal right. They do not depend upon questions of law or treaty, but upon one nation or ruler undertaking to do something that another nation or ruler wishes to prevent. Such questions are a part of international politics.

The distinction was traditional but not without its difficulties; and the history of international law in the years between World Wars I and II would highlight this problematical categorization.[19] Nevertheless Root offered a number of familiar examples to support his analysis; and he was particularly concerned to prove the role of the United States government in mediating international disputes of both kinds. The *Alabama* arbitration of 1872 represented a triumph in the first category; the Algeciras Conference of 1906 a triumph in the second.

To Root's mind the tragedy of the recent war had occurred because the German government had 'refused to attend [*a*] conference' on the lines of Algeciras, as the British Foreign Secretary, Sir Edward Grey, had proposed in the last days of July 1914. Now, however, the 'great and essential thing' about the Draft Covenant was that it made 'international conferences on political questions compulsory in times of danger'; and Article XV 'relating to the submission of disputes to the Executive Council of the League or... to the body of delegates' was its 'central and controlling' provision. Root cited extensively from the terms of Articles XI, XII, XV and XVI to substantiate his case that a 'great step forward' had been made in the 'settlement of... political questions'. The combined effect of all these articles would be 'to make the sort of conference which ... Grey tried in vain to get for the purpose of averting this Great War obligatory, inevitable, automatic'. And, he added, 'everybody ought to be in favor of that'.

So much for the credit side. But against the articles dealing with political disputes had to be set Article XIII, which was 'merely an agreement to arbitrate when the parties choose to arbitrate' – in short, 'no agreement at all'. In general terms, the Draft Covenant had

> practically abandon[ed] all effort to promote or maintain anything like a system of international law, or a system of arbitration, or of judicial settlement, through which a nation can assert its legal rights in lieu of war.

The Draft Covenant had set the clock back two decades; and 'instead of perfecting and putting teeth into the... Hague conventions, it throws those conventions upon the scrap heap'. Neither the Executive Council nor the body of delegates was a 'judicial body or an arbitral body'; and naturally and rightly each was 'bound to recommend' political or expedient solutions to the disputes referred to them. Even the Court of International Justice mentioned in Article XIV was a prospect rather than a reality; and even if it were constituted, there was 'no agreement or direction' that any questions would be submitted to it. As Root summarized his major complaint:

> International law is not mentioned at all, except in the preamble [*to the Covenant*], no method is provided, and no purpose is expressed to insist upon obedience to law to develop the law, to press forward agreement upon its rules and recognition of its obligations. All questions of right are relegated to the investigation and recommendation of a political body to be determined as matters of expediency.

Root ended his letter to Hays with two amendments incorporating his criticisms of Articles XIII and XIV. The first proposed the complete deletion of Article XIII and its replacement by the following terms:

1. The high contracting powers agree to refer to the existing Permanent Court of Arbitration at [The] Hague, or to the Court of Arbitral Justice proposed at the Second Hague Conference when established, or to some other Arbitral Tribunal, all disputes between them (including those affecting honor and vital interests), which are of a justiciable character, and which the powers concerned have failed to settle by diplomatic methods. The powers so referring to arbitration agree to accept and give effect to the award of the Tribunal.
2. Disputes of a justiciable character are defined as disputes as to the interpretation of a treaty, as to any question of international law, as to the existence of any fact which if established would constitute a breach of any international obligation, or as to the nature and extent of the reparation to be made for any such breach.
3. Any question which may arise as to whether a dispute is of a justiciable character is to be referred for decision to the Court of Arbitral Justice when constituted, or, until it is constituted, to the existing Permanent Court of Arbitration at [The] Hague.

With Article XIII so drastically revised in the direction of what Root called 'obligatory' arbitration, he then offered an addition to Article XIV to consolidate the jurisprudence to be implemented by the competent international authorities.

1. The Executive Council shall call a general conference of the Powers to meet not less than two years or more than five years after the signing of this convention for the purpose of reviewing the condition of international law, and of agreeing upon and stating in authoritative form the principles and rules thereof.
2. Thereafter regular conferences for that purpose shall be called and held at stated times.[20]

One month after the publication of Root's letter to Hays, President Wilson presented a revised final text of the Covenant to the Plenary

Session of the Peace Conference on 28 April 1919. Both Articles XIII and XIV of the February Draft had been altered by the Commission on the League of Nations. Apart from minor changes of phraseology, Article XIII had been modified in two ways. The third and last clause had been amended to include an undertaking by League Members that they would 'not resort to war' against another Member State complying with an arbitral award. The other amendment was far more obvious. Between the original first and second paragraphs were now listed the sort of 'disputes... generally suitable for submission to arbitration'. The disputes were, in fact, those spelled out by Root in his own suggested revision of the Draft Article XIII. But whereas Root had spoken of such disputes as 'justiciable' and therefore properly to be referred to the PCA, its successor or an equivalent 'tribunal', the final text of the Covenant described such disputes as susceptible to *arbitration.*[21] Granted that adjudication and arbitration were terms often used synonymously; granted even that Root himself sometimes confused their usage while generally insisting upon their difference; there could be no doubt that the revised text of Article XIII fell far short of Root's hopes. Nor could he take bitter comfort from the Covenant's repetition – and then perversion – of his examples of 'justiciable' disputes. The language and definitions of the new Paragraph 2 owed their origins not to Root but rather more to Lord Bryce, to the Phillimore Committee and to Robert Cecil – the latter, in fact, submitting the agreed formula to the Commission on the League before the publication of Root's March open letter to Will Hays.[22]

The revisions to Article XIV (dealing with the establishment of a Permanent Court of International Justice) also failed to meet Root's previous criticisms. There was no amendment providing for the codification of international law. Miller (the leading historian of the drafting of the Covenant) and Jessup (important to us as Root's major biographer and confidant) justified the omission on grounds of realism – as did other advocates of the League and Court.[23] But it constituted a setback for Root at least. More important for the history of the proposed Court, and in particular for its relationship with the USA, was the addition of a clause to the February Draft of Article XIV. The wording was offered initially by Bourgeois's colleague and compatriot, Larnaude; it was then modified by Hurst and Miller; and finally it became the single most contentious sentence in the constitution and life of the Court:

> The Court may also give an advisory opinion upon any dispute or question referred to it by the Council or by the Assembly.[24]

In these brief words was written the issue which would ultimately defeat American membership in the new World Court.

The Treaty of Versailles, Part I of which contained the Convenant of the League of Nations, was formally signed on 28 June 1919. Despite the instructions of the Supreme Council at the Paris Peace Conference unofficial texts of the Treaty had leaked out; and the final terms of the peace settlement with Germany and the League Covenant were known in advance in the United States. Root once again consulted with leading members of the conservative Republican establishment (including Lodge, Knox and Senator Frank Brandegee of Connecticut) and then composed a second open letter, this time addressed to Lodge in his new capacity as chairman of the Committee on Foreign Relations.

Root's letter to Lodge repeated many of the points made earlier to Will Hays – not least because the amendments and revisions made to the Draft Covenant were 'very inadequate and unsatisfactory'. For the second time Root insisted upon the constitutional propriety of the Senate's incorporating reservations into the resolution of ratification; and he suggested specific formulations concerning Article I (withdrawal); Article X; (the new) Article XXI alluding to the Monroe Doctrine; together with provisions for the absolute and exclusive competence of the US government in respect of 'domestic' questions. The most notable contrast with his March letter lay in Root's present relative neglect of arbitration and adjudication. Three months previously he had devoted many hundreds of words to these questions. Now Root passed over them in a few regretful sentences.

> Nothing has been done to provide for the reestablishment and strengthening of a system of arbitration or judicial decision upon questions of legal right. Nothing has been done toward providing for the revision or development of international law. In these respects principles maintained by the United States without variation for half a century are still ignored, and we are left with a program which rests the hope of the whole world for future peace in a government of men, and not of laws, following the dictates of expediency, and not of right.

Yet rather than attempt to repair the inadequacies of the Covenant by amendments or reservations on these subjects, Root advised that Senate adopt contemporaneously 'a separate resolution' requesting the President

> without any avoidable delay to open negotiations with the other Powers for the reestablishment and strengthening of a system of arbitration for the disposition of international disputes upon questions of right, and for periodical meetings of representatives of all the Powers for the revision and development of international law.[25]

The Treaty of Versailles was submitted to the Senate on 10 July 1919; referred to the Committee on Foreign Relations; and Hearings were held from the end of July until the middle of September. The Hearings produced remarkable incidents: Secretary Lansing's obvious criticisms of the Treaty and his frequent confessions of diplomatic ignorance; the denunciatory testimony of William C. Bullitt, a member of the American Delegation to Negotiate Peace; and, surpassing all, the cross-examination in mid August of President Wilson himself at the White House by members of the Committee on Foreign Relations. One thing, however, stands out clearly to any student of the Permanent Court of International Justice. Whatever the details of the Shantung settlement, the obligations under Article X of the Covenant, the question of Irish independence, the mandates system, equal rights for American blacks, the future of the Baltic peoples or any of the other issues examined by the Committee during the Hearings, one topic escaped discussion. Apart from the tiniest allusions, Articles XIII and XIV of the Covenant might not have existed. When the Committee reported the Treaty to the full Senate not one of its proposed changes or qualifications related to these two articles. So also in the nine weeks of debate on the Senate floor: Articles XIII and XIV were passed over. Finally, on 19 November 1919, when the Treaty of Versailles failed to gather a two-thirds majority vote, not one of the fourteen reservations attached by the Senate referred to Articles XIII and XIV. The Covenant was rejected; but its references to arbitration, adjudication and the establishment of a Permanent Court of International Justice had been ignored rather than deliberately opposed.[26]

Earlier in the year and before the official publication of the final text of the Covenant, the recently appointed Secretary-General of the League of Nations, Eric Drummond, had proposed to his political superiors on the Supreme Council that a Committee of Jurists be appointed to draft a statute for the Permanent Court envisaged in Article XIV. Drummond's proposal was accepted; and President Wilson and Col. House discussed an American candidate. Ex-President Taft was one suggestion; Chief Justice Edward D. White another; finally they settled on Root – not, Wilson was reported as saying, 'because [*Root*] could do the work any better than [*the others*], but because of the prominent part he had taken in urging an international court'.

Hardly a week after the Wilson-House discussion, Root's critical June letter to Lodge was published. Nevertheless Drummond, House himself and his colleagues on the American delegation were even more keen for Root's participation. When an informal invitation reached Root he expressed 'deep interest' and appeared flattered; but he demurred. The Treaty of Versailles had not been submitted to the Senate; the terms of its ratification could not be known. If he were to 'consent [*to the invitation in advance*] both his motives and those of the President would be misconstrued'. It would, therefore, be advisable to await the establishment of the League Council and the actions of the Senate; then he could properly respond to the President's generous nomination. Drummond accepted Root's arguments; and throughout the summer of 1919 and despite Root's severe criticisms of the Covenant and its relationship to the Peace Settlement, Drummond was confident that Root would represent the United States on the Jurists' Committee.[27]

The first failure of the Senate in November 1919 to consent to ratification of the Treaty distressed Root, since there was 'in the Covenant a great deal of very high value which the world ought not to lose'. Even more important was the failure to conclude peace with Germany. Root feared revolution. As he had written to Lodge in the summer: 'Satan is finding evil work for idle hands to do in Europe – evil work that affects the whole world, including the United States.' Yet Root placed the blame for the Senate's action squarely on Wilson, with his 'self-sufficient pride', rather than on the (mainly Republican) 'Irreconcilables' – and certainly not on Lodge and the Reservationists. As Root wrote to Lodge in December to congratulate him on 'one of the greatest examples of parliamentary leadership', he was confident there could be 'some sort of compromise and adjustment' when the Treaty was resubmitted to the Senate. At all events, the publication of the Lodge Reservations, the attitude of Wilson, and the wish to salvage part of the 'value' of the Covenant led Root to modify his initial response to Secretary-General Drummond's informal soundings. By the beginning of the New Year and long before the second and final Senate rejection of the Treaty and Covenant, Root had let it be publicly known that he would accept a formal League invitation to serve on the Advisory Committee of Jurists. This came (as we have seen) in mid February.[28] With a grant of $50,000 from his own Carnegie Endowment to cover expenses; and with a staff which included its Secretary, James Brown Scott (a world-renowned legal scholar and negotiator), Root set sail for Europe and The Hague on 1 June 1920, not as an official representative of the US government but as a distinguished private American citizen undertaking a commission for the League of Nations.[29]

It hardly needs to be said that our summary of the Paris Peace Conference, the early months of the League and the American response to both has been highly selective. The primary focus of our discussion has been Elihu Root; for, as we noted in the previous chapter, Root's participation in the 1920 Advisory Committee of Jurists has been taken retrospectively by American historians as a major premise for their country's membership in the Permanent Court of International Justice. Such a historiographical tradition fairly represents the contemporary record. Commentators, colleagues and friends identified the Court with Root: he was its 'father', its 'spiritual genius'; the Court was his 'handiwork'. The metaphors were numerous – but all to the same purpose.[30] Even so two interrelated points must be borne in mind. First, there were other candidates for the title of creator to the Court: Robert Cecil; Walter Phillimore; Cecil Hurst; Léon Bourgeois – and even Root's present assistant, James Brown Scott.[31] But, as we shall see, each of the Europeans was too closely identified with the League to make his name a ready substitute for argument in the America of the 1920s. Second, Root's claims were grounded most firmly in the role he played on the Advisory Committee of Jurists. However, Root was not completely successful at The Hague; furthermore, some of his victories were later reversed by the League. Historians have largely ignored the mixed nature of Root's success; even more rarely have they tried to explain its causes. The second half of this chapter will attempt to rectify these omissions.

The Advisory Committee of Jurists (ACJ) assembled in the Peace Palace at The Hague on 16 June 1920. On 24 July, after nearly three dozen meetings, the Committee unanimously approved a Draft Scheme (or proposed Statute) of a Permanent Court of International Justice (PCIJ) and referred it to the League Council. The records of these meetings run to many hundreds of pages; there were, additionally, extensive memoranda and model constitutions submitted by the League Secretariat, former neutral Powers and even by the German and Austrian governments.[32] Regrettably it is beyond the scope of this study to provide a full analysis of the work and jurisprudence of the ACJ. Our concern must be more limited: the role of Elihu Root and the political context in which he and his colleagues acted.

Root himself deprecated anyone's attributing a 'political aspect' to his presence. The Committee's work was 'entirely technical' he asserted on his arrival at The Hague; and long afterwards he denied that his colleagues represented 'any country'. On the contrary. 'They were all there purely as experts, as if physicians were called together to consult about a case, or engineers to consult about a bridge.'[33] The statements were plausible in one sense; but naive if meant sincerely. Certainly the ACJ was only reporting to the League and therefore possessed a degree of independence. This was the substance behind Root's comments. But the League itself quite openly appointed a body to represent political interests. The ten members of the ACJ were carefully chosen to balance five Great Powers and five Smaller Powers – as Secretary-General Drummond's phrasing acknowledged. Consequently, though five of the original twelve nominees had been unable to attend, the 5:5 ratio had been achieved by finding substitutes for the Japanese, Italian and French nominees and neglecting to fill the vacancies caused by the absence of the Yugoslav and Argentinian. Furthermore Root was the only member of the Committee not currently holding high office in the executive, judicial or diplomatic service of his country. It was a significant exception.[34]

The assembly of the Committee of Jurists at The Hague was an obvious reminder of the 1899 and 1907 Conferences, as the Dutch Foreign Minister, Van Karnebeek, recorded in his address of welcome. He named individuals who had participated in one way or another in creating the tradition: Descamps, Hagerup, Root, Scott. But no one more so than Bourgeois, who was attending the opening ceremony as official representative of the League Council – Bourgeois, 'the statesman who has presided over the labours of the two Hague Conferences and whose services in the cause of international justice have entitled him to a position of authority universally recognized, and to an imperishable debt of gratitude'.[35]

Bourgeois accepted the compliments, but his task was to emphasize the development of tradition rather than its preservation. With many echoes of the *Report he* had presented to the February Council Bourgeois stressed the changes brought by the recent, horrific and devastating war. Men and women throughout the world now realized the need for 'the organisation of international justice' in order 'to guarantee the maintenance of peace', for true peace was 'founded on public right itself'. This was the purpose of the Covenant in general and Article XIV in particular.

Bourgeois insisted upon the changed circumstances in which this third Hague conference would take place. The League of Nations had become the political force which could alone realize the promise of those earlier attempts. The delegates to the first two conferences 'had not the power and did not even dream of establishing at a single blow and at once the sovereign power of right'. Now, however, there existed the Covenant and the Treaties of Peace; and soon there would be the Court. League and Court would be 'complementary', Bourgeois continued: 'of necessity being organised at the same time and… being unable, as long as they wish to preserve their existence, to live apart'. Bourgeois concluded his remarks by citing 'the decisive problem of sanctions'. Here the complementarity, or more accurately, interdependence of the League and Court was most clearly shown. For what, he asked rhetorically, 'would be the efficacy, what would be the reality of a sentence of justice if it did not find in a strong organisation of international institutions what one calls the executor of these decisions?' 'Military sanctions' could not be ruled out; 'the opposition of the force of right to the force of violence' would be a regrettable necessity for many years to come. Again and again Bourgeois rephrased the intimate relationship of the League and its Court, the Court and its League. He spoke 'in the name of the Council', and he did so

simply to show what a large place, in our eyes, the Court of Justice must take in the international organisation of the world. We wish to see it armed with the highest moral power and organised for a penetration as deep as possible into international relations.[36]

In the course of his address Bourgeois had suggested a number of problems for discussion and solution. Chief among them were the organization of the Court; the selection of the bench; the rules of procedure; and the nature and limits of the Court's jurisdiction.[37] In the following pages we shall examine only two subjects from this shortened list (namely, the selection of judges and the jurisdiction of the Court) – together with the question of codifying international law. Once again our focus will be Elihu Root; and our contention is that his successes and failures in the Committee have to be explained in terms of the congruence of his ideas and goals with the political forces represented by his colleagues and by the League, to which they were reporting.[38] Nowhere is the evidence for such a claim stronger than in the area of Root's universally acknowledged triumph: the solution of the seemingly 'insoluble' difficulty of devising a method for selecting the Court's bench.[39]

The problem had been touched upon by Bourgeois in his February *Report*. It could be expressed in a variety of ways; but its essence was simple. The Great Powers would not support a permanent international court whose judges they had not appointed; and without the support of the Great Powers a permanent international court would be a mere cipher. Yet a truly international court needed to represent not solely the

Great Powers. However, if all Powers sought to appoint their own separate representative, the number of judges would be unmanageable. It was, therefore, generally agreed that the desirable but elusive quorum of judges should be appointed on a suffrage combining elements of restriction and universality, equality and inequality. The solution devised by the ACJ comprised all these four principles; and it used the establishment of the League to provide the 'machinery'. With great relief at having conquered the problem which (in the words of one leading legal scholar) 'had baffled and defeated' previous attempts, the ACJ proposed 'the only possible system for the formation of the Court': namely, 'equal and simultaneous election [of the judges] by the Council and the Assembly'.[40]

The conceptual underpinning to the functional solution derived from harmonizing conflicting notions of State equality and inequality. In the Assembly all Member States of the League, whatever their actual power, had an equal voice. In the Council voting was also equal, but the Great Powers (or, in what became League language, the Permanent Members) were to predominate numerically as well as politically. Furthermore, of course, the Permanent Members, together with the non-Permanent Members, voted twice in any joint or concurrent voting of the Council and Assembly. The idea and its embodiment in the Committee's proposal were very neatly and idiomatically expressed by Alexander P. Fachiri, a leading British student of the Court and a member of its bar. The scheme for concurrent elections

> reconcile[d] the legal principle of the equality of States as subjects of international law with the reality of their political inequality, crystallized in the distinction between Great Powers and other States.[41]

It was Root who suggested the formula in its final terms; but he had worked closely with the British representative, Phillimore, and was keen to share the sponsorship with him. Indeed the proposal became known as the 'Root–Phillimore Plan'. Moreover a number of the Committee members had advanced similar schemes; and the many memoranda presented to the Committee had offered analogous suggestions. Root's contribution ought not to be minimized; but it has been decidedly overestimated by American scholars.[42] Where he offered valuable weight was in showing a historical precedent for harmonizing heterogeneous principles and thereby promising that such a solution would be acceptable to the United States.

The precedent came from the Federal Constitution. It was popularly known as the Connecticut Compromise; and it had been offered to the Philadelphia Convention of 1787, when 'precisely the same kind' of problem faced the delegates. Root described that dilemma and its resolution as follows.

> We were all independent, sovereign states – some large, some small. The large states were unwilling to permit the majority of the smaller ones the control which would come from equal representation, and, on the other hand, the

smaller states were unwilling to allow to the larger ones the preponderance of power which would arise from the recognition of their greater population and wealth.

That *impasse* was disposed of by the creation of two chambers, in one of which the states are represented equally, and another in which the population is represented without reference to the sovereign states in which the people reside.[43]

So Root explained the theoretical and practical origins of the bicameral Ferderal Congress. Ricci-Busatti, the Italian representative, who flattered himself as being something of a sociological jurist, welcomed the analogy as an ingenious solution to an age-old conflict between conflicting principles. His Prime Minister, Orlando, had spoken to similar effect when the Covenant was born at the Peace Conference.[44] American commentators and historians after them have been somewhat less cynical and rather stressed the procedural neatness of the electoral scheme Root legitimated rather than engendered. But even a rapid review of its origins and rationale highlights the substantive reasons for its favour with the Advisory Committee. Phillimore was its co-author; and he was frank enough to tell his colleagues that he had come to The Hague to 'establish… peace', which to him was 'even more important than justice'. In response Descamps, the president of the Committee, tried to suggest that the two might not be incompatible goals; but Phillimore was not softened. Far from it: he made distinctly condescending remarks to the Spaniard Altamira y Crevea when the latter protested against the predominance of Great Power thinking in the Committee.[45]

Phillimore, Ricci-Busatti, Adatci of Japan, Lapradelle of France all spoke with a common voice: the object of international jurisdiction was to recognise political inequalities and 'guarantee peace'. In the final Report of the Committee Lapradelle's words as Rapporteur echoed Bourgeois's opening address. It was absolutely essential that in the new World Court

the Great Powers would be represented by judges, with the free consent of the other Powers, as their great civilising influence and juridical progress entitle them to be, even though no weight were attached to the fact that it would be greatly to the interest of the Court to include them on the Bench, to increase respect for its sentences, which could not be put into execution without the all important support of their military, economic and financial powers.

Root's success, therefore, lay in providing (with Phillimore) a procedure for the selection of judges which (in his own words) both 'articulate[*d*] the new organization with the political organization of the League' and removed 'any possibility of unfairness' by giving 'small nations [*and*] large nations… a veto' on one another. It was a veto Phillimore was ready to claim and his country ready to invoke: the British Empire, after all, did expect to deploy six votes in the League.[46]

In the second area we shall discuss, namely the advancement and codification of international law, Root was outstandingly successful on the ACJ. This had been a concern in both his open letters of 1919; and though the final terms of the Covenant had disappointed his hopes for a court, he still urged the Senate to promote 'the revision and development of international law'. When the Committee was well embarked on the difficult subject of the future Court's jurisdiction Root and Descamps formally moved a resolution calling for a third Hague Conference to 'be held as soon as practicable for the following purposes':

1. To restate the established rules of international law, especially, and in the first instance, in the fields affected by the events of the recent war.
2. To formulate and agree upon the amendments and additions, if any, to the rules of international law shown to be necessary or useful by the events of the war and the changes in the conditions of international life and intercourse which have followed the war.
3. To endeavor to reconcile divergent views and secure general agreement upon the rules which have been in dispute heretofore.
4. To consider the subjects not now adequately regulated by international law, but as to which the interests of international justice require that the rules of law shall be declared and accepted.

International law associations throughout the world were called on to collaborate in preparing for this conference and briefing governments; and, perhaps most importantly, this conference was to be 'followed by further successive conferences at stated intervals to continue the work left unfinished'.[47]

The Root–Descamps resolution was adopted unanimously. After all, as Committee members and later commentators acknowledged, there was little sense in trying to advance 'compulsory jurisdiction' for the Court without supplying a corpus of law for enactment.[48] But Root's success was short-lived. The resolution remained an expression of the Committee's wishes; it was not put into practice. One clue to its brief life lay in its neglect of the League, to which the Committee was formally reporting. In bypassing the League the ACJ had sent the resolution into a cul-de-sac. There was also a second consideration, one which explains why the League did not try to rescue the proposal.[49] Whatever commentators said in later years about the impracticality of the resolution, its implications for the peace settlement were immediately apparent to the League.[50] Dionisio Anzilotti, a senior official in the League who acted as Secretary to the ACJ, wrote to Secretary-General Drummond that the codification of international law, especially in the neutral hands of a third Hague Conference, might well undermine the legitimacy of the Peace Treaties and thus the authority of the League itself.[51] One other major reason contributed to the Root–Descamps resolution's lack of impact: the nature of the jurisdiction finally accorded to the PCIJ. Not, indeed, the jurisdiction proposed by the Advisory Committee in its Draft Scheme but rather the jurisdiction set by the League Council and Assembly. This was by far the most contentious problem in drafting of the Court Statute; and it is the third and last area of Root's activities we shall discuss in this chapter.

The problems surrounding the jurisdiction (or competence) of the proposed court were complex and heterogeneous. (Competence was rather more the Continental expression; but legal scholars used the terms interchangeably.) Some of the problems, the ones we shall discuss, can be posed in the following basic terms:

1. Who was to appear before the court?
2. Would they come voluntarily? or could they be arraigned?
3. What law or body of law would the court expound?
4. What status would the court give to previous judgments of its own or other comparable bodies?

Our examination will fall into two halves, the first concerned with the court's so-called compulsory jurisdiction, the second concerned with its advisory jurisdiction. This twofold division does not neatly correspond with items 1–4 in the scheme just given, because the four sections cut across the distinction between the compulsory and advisory jurisdiction. In anticipation of our examination of Root's role we can say that in the area of the court's compulsory jurisdiction he was successful in the ACJ; while on the advisory jurisdiction he suffered a series of reverses.

The Draft Scheme devised by the ACJ ran to 62 Articles, arranged in three separate Chapters. Chapter I, on the Organization of the Court, consisted of 29 Articles; Chapter III on Procedure consisted of 26; Chapter II on jurisdiction contained just 6 Articles – one of which was taken up with the advisory jurisdiction. Rather than relate the debates in Committee and then print the agreed text, it will be more convenient to give the final terms of the Draft Scheme and then explain their origins and difficulties.

Chapter II – Competence of the Court

Article 31. The Court shall have jurisdiction to hear and determine suits between States.

Article 32. The Court shall be open of right to the States mentioned in the Annex to the Covenant, and to such others as shall subsequently enter the League of Nations.

Other States may have access to it.

The conditions under which the Court shall be open of right or accessible to States which are not Members of the League of Nations shall be determined by the Council, in accordance with Article 17 of the Covenant.

Article 33. When a dispute has arisen between States, and it has been found impossible to settle it by diplomatic means, and no agreement has been made to choose another jurisdiction, the party complaining may bring the case before the Court. The Court shall, first of all, decide whether the preceding conditions have been complied with; if so, it shall hear and determine the dispute according to the terms and within the limits of the next Article.

Article 34. Between States which are Members of the League of Nations, the Court shall have jurisdiction (and this without any special convention giving it jurisdiction) to hear and determine cases of a legal nature, concerning:

(a) The interpretation of a treaty;
(b) Any question of international law;
(c) The existence of any fact which, if established, would constitute a breach of international obligation;
(d) The nature or extent of reparation to be made for the breach of an international obligation;
(e) The interpretation of a sentence passed by the Court.

The Court shall also take cognizance of all disputes of any kind which may be submitted to it by a general or particular convention between the parties.

In the event of a dispute as to whether a certain case comes within any of the categories above mentioned, the matter shall be settled by the decision of the Court.

Article 35. The Court shall, within the limits of its jurisdiction as defined in Article 34, apply in the order following:

(1) International conventions, whether general or particular, establishing rules expressly recognized by the contesting States;
(2) International custom, as evidence of a general practice, which is accepted as law;
(3) The general principles of law recognized by civilized nations;
(4) Judicial decisions and the teachings of the most highly qualified publicists of the various nations, as subsidiary means for the determination of rules of law.

Article 36. The Court shall give an advisory opinion upon any question or dispute of an international nature referred to it by the Council or Assembly.

When the Court shall give an opinion on a question of an international nature which does not refer to any dispute that may have arisen, it shall appoint a special Commission of from three to five members.

When it shall give an opinion upon a question which forms the subject of an existing dispute, it shall do so under the same conditions as if the case had been actually submitted to it for decision.[52]

On the Court's proposed compulsory jurisdiction, the crucial Articles were 33 and 34; and those two Articles were adopted very much at the urging of Root, Phillimore and Descamps. Most of the Committee, with the notable exception of Adatci and Ricci-Busatti, were convinced that Articles XIII and XIV of the Covenant had confused adjudication and arbitration. Led by Root the majority of the Committee wanted to seize the opportunity of their appointment to cut through the political and expedient contradictions of the Covenant and establish the compulsory adjudication foreshadowed in the 1907 Hague Peace Conference. The wording of Articles 33 and 34 in the Draft Scheme was designed to effect that end. Where Adatci and Ricci-Busatti dissented was not over goals but over the meaning and purpose of the Covenant. Both confidently predicted that the League would not support a reading of the Covenant and consequently the organization of its Court which would permit one Member State to bring another willy-nilly before a judicial tribunal.[53]

The textual difficulties in Articles 33 and 34 of the Draft Scheme arose from the uncertainty with which the Committee approached the objections raised by Adatci and Ricci-Busatti. Article 33 suggested that the two were wrong in their analysis and that the Covenant did indeed contain an obligation on Member States to appear before a court on arraignment. Article 34, on the other hand, implied the obligation had never been precisely and explicitly acknowledged by the signatories to the Covenant. At all events, the Committee as a whole wanted to advance the Court's compulsory jurisdiction and Root was a leading figure in this movement.[54] Far more problematical was whether the League would accept the Jurists' arguments and desires. As a straw in the wind the British government had already made it absolutely clear that it believed the Covenant had not 'admit[*ted*] the principle of compulsory arbitration in any class of disputes'.[55]

In the light of the discussion preceding the drafting of Articles 33 and 34, together with the text of Articles 31–35 as a whole, we can now answer most of the questions in items 1–4 of our introductory scheme. Right of access to the Court was given to all present and future Members of the League, to non-Member States on special terms to be decided by the Council, and (specifically) to the United States of America, as one of 'the States mentioned in the Annex to the Covenant'. Between Members of the League the Court's jurisdiction could be invoked unilaterally as well as bilaterally and multilaterally. Article 35 governed the substance of the Court's law; while Article 34 concerned the scope of the Court's work. Both these Articles suggested that the Court could, but not necessarily would, follow the principle of *stare decisis* or precedent. In all these areas of the Court's contentious jurisdiction Root had seen his ideas win support. On the Court's advisory jurisdiction, however, Root suffered almost total defeat.

It is not unusual for historians to come across an event whose reverberations are felt only in later years. From 1924 until 1935 the advisory jurisdiction was the dominant jurisprudential issue in American discussion of membership of the Court and it formed the main source of controversy between the Court's members and the League on one side and the US government on the other. Yet in the Committee of Jurists the principle of the Court's rendering advisory opinions to the League Council and Assembly was agreed within a matter of minutes rather than days. It could scarcely have been otherwise, given the terms of Article XIV of the Covenant. Whether the English or French text was read (and in spite of discrepancies, both were of equal status: Treaty of Versailles, Article 440), the power if not the necessity of the Court's acting as judicial adviser to the League was unquestionable.[56]

Jessup, Root's biographer, and Scott, Root's assistant, passed in silence over their principal's actions and attitudes towards the advisory jurisdiction during The Hague negotiations. The omission is regrettable but understandable, for Root's failure was grave enough to counterbalance his success on the electoral college scheme. Even the Minutes of the ACJ are extremely brief: but they do state Root's initial and theoretical position quite clearly. He was

opposed to the Court's having the right to give an advisory opinion with reference to an existing dispute. In his opinion it was a violation of all judicial principles.

This paraphrase comes late in the Committee record, when the final terms of the Draft Scheme were being read and agreed line by line. In fact Root had compromised his basic objections some weeks earlier, when he had supported Phillimore's defence of the advisory function and joined him in devising a formula to give effect to the Covenant's provisions.[57]

The grounds of Root's fundamental opposition to a permanent judicial body's exercising an advisory role can be extracted from available if scattered evidence; and thus the scantiness of the official record and the silence of Root's partisans can be rectified. There were, essentially, four distinct yet related parts to his argument. First, Root desired a Court which could determine its own jurisdiction on application by a suitor in an existent dispute. Second, this determination should be made on the basis of codified international law and accepted precedent; by a mixture (in other words) of statute and common law, the method which the US Supreme Court and its inferior courts had evolved. Thirdly, for the proposed International Court to act in response to a body (i.e., the League) which was not a party to a dispute would make the Court subordinate to a political authority, unlike the United States, where the judiciary was co-ordinate with the executive and legislative branches of government. As later critics phrased the relationship: the advisory function turned the Court into the League's attorney rather than impartial judge between disputants. Finally, the advisory jurisdiction hindered the development of law through precedent in litigated and adjudicated cases, since judgments offered as advisory opinions would be of uncertain status and would inhibit subsequent contentious proceedings. For either the advisory opinions would be regarded as definitive; in which case the issues would not be submitted for litigation – there would simply be no sense in repeating a judgment. Alternatively, if the advisory opinions were truly provisional, they could be reversed during litigation. But this second possibility would tend to make the whole process self-stultifying, particularly as the interim status of the advisory opinions would be so lacking in authority and hence effectiveness.[58]

When Root raised his objections in the ACJ against the formula he and Phillimore had previously agreed, Lapradelle, acting as executive secretary to the drafting subcommittee, merely pointed to the terms of the Covenant (particularly Articles XII and XIII) and 'convinced' Root of the futility of his opposition by reminding him of the Council's need for a quasi-judicial body to help resolve politico-legal controversies.[59] However, in the massive Report presented by Lapradelle on the Draft Scheme as a whole, Article 36 covering the Court's advisory jurisdiction was warmly endorsed rather than excused as unavoidable. This function of the Court was 'completely judicial' and certainly 'highly desirable', since among its 'special advantages' it permitted the 'judicial' method to be applied 'to a case wrongly given a political aspect by the parties'.[60]

Though Root lost the major struggle over the advisory jurisdiction, he could claim two victories – while acknowledging two setbacks. He could congratulate himself that the final text of the Draft Scheme limited advisory opinions to questions 'of an international nature', whereas the Covenant referred to 'any dispute or question'. (The apparently narrow distinction would help to protect 'domestic questions' from foreign judicial scrutiny.)[61] Secondly, the dilemma concerning the juridical status of advisory opinions was recognized. However, the solution offered by the ACJ to this second problem highlighted the fundamental uncertainty. The Draft Scheme distinguished two procedures for applying the advisory function. If the court were consulted on a question which was not the subject of an existent dispute (what the Report called an abstract or hypothetical question) then a 'special commission' of 3–5 judges would render the judgment.

If, however, 'the question... form[ed] the subject of an existing dispute', then the Court would take cognizance and determine the issue 'under the same conditions as if the case had been actually submitted to it for decision' through a litigated suit. It was a procedural solution which constituted something of a pyrrhic victory for Root, for by its terms the substantive problem of authority and precedent would be aggravated rather than eased.[62]

The other setback for Root concerned the Court's obligation to render an advisory opinion. The English text of the Covenant made the power discretionary; conversely and confusingly, the Draft Scheme appeared to restrict the Court's discretion.[63] It was a principle of Root's that a court should decide its own competence (according to its peculiar statute and organization), as the PCIJ would do under all the other articles of Chapter II of the Draft Scheme and as the US Supreme Court did under the Federal Constitution and appropriate congressional legislation.[64]

This review of Root's achievements on the Advisory Committee of Jurists shows them to have been mixed; less than the 'considerable' success which a recent and careful historian has attributed to Root.[65] Our aim has not been simply and iconoclastically to belittle Root's performance; but rather to set his work in its proper political, jurisprudential and historical context.[66] Even from this inevitably cursory study it will be clear that American observers would not endorse the Statute of the PCIJ simply on the grounds of Root's earlier participation. Moreover, any initial scepticism extended by Americans towards the Draft Scheme might reasonably be expected to increase once it was appreciated that the League of Nations was to have the last word on the final terms of the Court's Statute.

On 24 July 1920 the Advisory Committee of Jurists transmitted its Draft Scheme to the League Secretariat. This procedure for cloaking the Committee's accountability to the League Council was adopted on the motion of Root – a fine example of the self-consciousness with which he performed his role at The Hague.[67] On 5 August Léon Bourgeois presented the Draft Scheme to the Council at its San Sebastian meeting. Once again he invoked the glories of the Permanent Court of Arbitration and stressed that the new court would be a partner not a successor to the former. More importantly he instanced a number of contentious areas within the Draft Scheme (the electoral college; the ambiguities surrounding the Court's jurisdiction) and formally proposed that the text should be transmitted to Member States for comments, which would in their turn form the basis for a full report to the October Council and the subsequent drafting of a final Statute to be presented to the First Assembly of the League later in the year.[68]

The Report presented by Bourgeois to the October Council meeting in Brussels well exemplified the collaboration between the League Secretariat and the Council Members. It ran to some five thousand words and covered nine 'essential points' for consideration. They were not of equal weight; but two are especially relevant to our study: the election of the judges and the jurisdiction of the Court. But before we turn to these, it is useful to remember the context in which the Council and Secretariat regarded the Draft Scheme for the League-sponsored Court. The Scheme, in the words of the October Report, was the product of honourable and 'mutual concessions' on the part of 'the most competent experts'. Unless the League Members could show such tolerance, the 'failure' of 1907 undoubtedly would be repeated. As the Report continued:

> The Council would regard an irreconcilable difference of opinion on the merits of the scheme as an international misfortune of the gravest kind. It would mean that the League was publicly compelled to admit its incapacity to carry out one of the most important of the tasks which it was invited to perform. The failure would be great, and probably irreparable; for if agreement proves impossible under circumstances apparently so favourable, it is hard to see how and when the task of securing it will be successfully resumed.[69]

This was a plea for unanimity, for the League Members to follow the Council and Secretariat; and it offered a reciprocal undertaking that the latter two would try to accept the ACJ Draft as far as possible. On balance the Council–Secretariat Report presented by Bourgeois did confirm the decisions of the Advisory Committee. This was strikingly true of the electoral college plan, which was endorsed without discussion. On the other hand Chapter II of the Draft Scheme governing the Court's jurisdiction was virtually rewritten.

The Report rejected the ACJ view that the Covenant was ambiguous on compulsory jurisdiction. Moreover, even if it were, any ambiguities in the Covenant ought not to be resolved in the terms of Article 33 and 34 of the Draft Scheme. By those articles, the discretion of the Council was being 'substituted' or replaced by the decisions of the Court. The principle, the 'advantages' of compulsory jurisdiction between States was not the issue, the Report allowed; but it was improper for the Council, following the Committee of Jurists, to present the First Assembly of the League with proposals for altering the Covenant. Improper – and dangerous, the Report added, in an unmistakable allusion to the Peace Settlement.

At the present moment it is most important in the interests of the authority of the League of Nations that differences of opinion should not arise at the very outset with regard to the essential rules laid down in the Covenant of the 28th April, 1919.

Consequently the Council proposed: first, to insert a clause explicitly reaffirming 'the Jurisdiction of the Court [*under*] Articles 12, 13 and 14 of the Covenant' (new Article 33); second, to delete the passages in Article 34 of the Draft Scheme extending compulsory jurisdiction to League Members; and, third, to add a clause stating the particular competence of the Court 'to hear and determine disputes, the settlement of which is by Treaties in force entrusted to it or to the tribunal instituted by the League of Nations'. This last provision was a vigorous if coded reference to the judicial enforcement of the Peace Treaties.[70]

In a less dramatic formulation (and one which was not explicitly defended by Bourgeois), the Report levelled a different challenge to the Draft Scheme's qualified promotion of compulsory jurisdiction. A new provision (Article 36 *bis*) encouraged disputants to refer controversies to the Court by *compromis* – the very essence of an arbitration system as distinct (Root would have argued) from a true court of justice and a proposal which (as its wording made clear) attempted to steer the new court in the direction of the 1907 Hague Convention.

Article 36 *bis* of the Council's counter-proposals was part of a consistent pattern, as other examples prove. The most notable instance was Article 57 *bis*, which stated: 'The decision of the Court has no binding force except between the parties and in respect of that particular case.' This was interpreted (by Scott, for example) as a deliberate blow to the development of international law through precedent and coherent jurisprudence; and it was a provision of the Council's which went against Root's own desires for an international court.[71]

Even where the Council deferred to American sensitivities, it had the effect of weakening the judicial quality of the Court. This was shown in the question of the Court's official language. Root apparently had raised no objections in the ACJ to French being the Court's official language – unless the contending parties requested another language and the Court agreed (Draft Scheme, Article 37). The Council proposed that both French and English should be the Court's official languages (Report, Article 37); and it was clear from external evidence that the possibility of American support for the Court helped determine the Council decision.[72] However, the move from a single language would impede the development of precedent and strengthen the arbitral, *ad hoc* role of the Court.

In only one area did the Council Report make suggestions which supported rather than undermined Root's ideal of judicial practice. Article 56 of the Draft Scheme had allowed the 'fact' of dissent or reservation by a minority of the bench to be published – but not the 'reasons'. In the corresponding article of the Council Report it was provided that 'Judges who do not concur in all or part of the judgment of the Court may deliver a separate opinion.' Thus dissenting opinions (in American terminology) were to be permitted – a characteristic of American courts which Root had not been able to preserve in the ACJ but which the League Secretariat and Council salvaged for him.[73]

Root's belated and vicarious victory on the issue of dissenting opinions was a small counterweight to the actions of the Secretariat and Council in producing their revisions of the Jurists' Draft Scheme. Root's collaborator at The Hague, James Brown Scott, was already expressing his dismay at the evolution of the Court's Statute.[74] Even so the final terms of that document remained to be written. The October Report was due for presentation to the assembled Member States of the League. Only when they had approved the wording would the Court Statute be properly engrossed. This third stage in the drafting of the Statute would be the final measure of the distance from the summer of 1920, when (as we shall see) friendly observers in the United States were speaking of the creation of the 'Root Court'.

The First Assembly of the League of Nations was held in Geneva from 15 November to 18 December 1920. The Report and revisions presented by Bourgeois had been unanimously approved at the October Council; and they now came before all the Member States of the League in accordance with the first clause of Article XIV of the Covenant. The procedure adopted for debating and finalizing the Court Statute was rather complicated. First the Council Report on the ACJ's Draft Scheme was referred to a very large committee of the whole Assembly, the Third Committee, detailed to discuss legal questions. The Third Committee in turn appointed a Subcommittee of ten delegates to scrutinize the various recommendations and report back to the Third Committee for transmission to the plenary Assembly.[75]

This intricate structure produced a series of bodies largely ratifying their own work and allowed prominent men to endorse their earlier decisions. Thus Bourgeois was appointed chairman of the Third Committee. Of the Subcommittee of Ten, five had served on the Advisory Committee of Jurists: Adatci, Fernandes, Loder, Ricci-Busatti, and Hagerup, the latter filling the important role of Rapporteur to both the Subcommittee and Third Committee. (The five newcomers were Doherty of Canada, Fromageot of France, Huber of Switzerland, Hurst of the United Kingdom and Politis of Greece.) Even so there was a sequence of modification from the ACJ through the Council, Subcommittee, Third Committee to the terms ultimately agreed by the plenary Assembly. Once again we shall be most selective in recording the changes made and the arguments advanced, our focus being the history of Root's contribution and the sensitivity of League members to the question of American participation in the nascent court.

The Subcommittee (repeating the bias of the ACJ) challenged the Council's interpretation of the Covenant and its effective opposition to compulsory jurisdiction between Members of the League. Nevertheless the Ten admitted the practical reality that the Assembly would not go against the Council's decision and that unanimity was 'necessary for the establishment of the Court'. Eventually a compromise was reached between the two positions. On the motion of Fernandes, the Assembly agreed to insert a clause into the Court's Statute permitting States to declare

> that they recognize as compulsory *ipso facto* and without special agreement, in relation to any other Member [of the League] or State accepting the same obligation, the jurisdiction of the Court in all or any of the classes of legal disputes [specified in Article 36 of the Court Statute].

This clause became known as the Optional Clause; and its force was to offer the Court the compulsory jurisdiction Root had sought – provided each sovereign State conceded this jurisdiction on a reciprocal basis to the Court.[76]

Against this qualified success for one Root desideratum, the final terms of the Court Statute allowed the Court 'to decide a case *ex aequo et bono*, if the parties agree thereto'.[77] This constituted yet another stage in the reinforcement of the Court's arbitral role. Neither the Subcommittee nor the Third Assembly offered any defence of this addition; but, in conjunction with the Assembly's acceptance of the Council's Article 57 *bis*, it was clearly another blow (in Hagerup's words) to the Court's 'power... to attribute the character of precedents to judicial decisions'.[78]

One more aspect of the Court's jurisdiction and procedure concerns us. We previously noted the ACJ's cursory handling of the advisory function.[79] It was, therefore, a most bizarre turn of events which led to the Court Statute's complete neglect of this topic. By a series of overwhelming votes the various drafting bodies at the First Assembly deleted all references to the advisory jurisdiction. The process began in the Subcommittee when Ricci-Busatti argued that the distinction drawn in the Draft Scheme between existent and hypothetical questions was untenable; and he urged the institution of a special chamber to deal with both categories. In contrast the other Subcommittee members insisted that the advisory procedure should be assimilated to that in litigated suits; but then added that since both jurisdictions were specifically provided for in Article XIV of the Covenant, there was no need to lodge either in the constitution of the Court. Thus it happened that the judicial function which was the centre of controversy for more than a decade of American debate on the Court was first incorporated in and then eliminated from the Statute – and on both occasions with minimal discussion.[80]

It was only with the lapse of years that the Court's advisory function became the insuperable obstacle to American membership of the new Court.[81] But even in 1920 both the ACJ and the League were sensitive to the position of the United States. Before the Jurists gathered at The Hague the Legal Section of the League Secretariat had filled its memoranda with numerous favourable references to American judicial practice, especially to the authority enjoyed by the Federal Supreme Court. Root's public statements calling for 'a genuine Court of [*International*] Justice' were often quoted. The Legal Section even inclined to Root's analysis of the scope for compulsory jurisdiction under the Covenant. Root had been nominated to the Advisory Committee partly – if not largely – to ease American acceptance of the proposals; and by the time the ACJ assembled (after the second Senate vote against the Versailles Treaty and League membership), the League Secretariat gave priority to devising a judicial organization open to non-Member States. During the meetings of the ACJ the political practice of the United States was instanced as often and as favourably as its judicial traditions. The Monroe Doctrine was frequently mentioned – but never challenged. Far from it: Lapradelle's comment that American presumptions in the Western Hemisphere should be indulged rather than resisted appeared to win unanimous approval.[82]

Like the Secretariat, the ACJ was keen to construct a Court which the United States could join, as a State mentioned in the Annex to the Covenant. To make their goodwill towards the United States even more obvious, the ACJ deliberately rejected accession-schemes which would permit ordinary non-Member States to join. Such openness would permit the entry of Germany, Austria, Hungary, Turkey – and thus potentially undermine the legitimacy of the Peace Treaties. In addition revolutionary States such as Soviet Russia or Mexico could use membership in the Court as a means of subverting bourgeois international legal doctrine.[83] It was generally agreed that the historical accident of American abstention from the League itself was not to stand in the way of the United States acceding to the League's Court.[84] With these goals in mind the text of the Court Statute was eventually drafted to read:

Article 34: Only States or Members of the League of Nations can be parties in cases before the Court.

Article 35: The Court shall be open to the Members of the League and also to States mentioned in the Annex to the Covenant….

[This meant the United States. Other States might be permitted to appear before the Court at the Council's discretion: Article 35 §2 §3.]

The extension of special consideration to the Americans continued into the autumn and winter of 1920. When Léon Bourgeois introduced the Draft Scheme to the Council he was concerned to stress the unlikelihood of any equally authoritative group of jurists achieving so comprehensive and persuasive an amalgamation of judicial principles and political realities. This allusiveness was made more precise later in the year when Hagerup joined Bourgeois in appealing to the First Assembly to follow the Council amendments as closely as possible, if there were to be any hope of the United States joining 'the League'. It was not a slip of the tongue: that was the ultimate goal, as some Latin American delegates quickly pointed out. Hagerup later supported the proposal of the Italian delegate, Anzilotti, that the Court Statute should be adopted by means of a multilateral treaty between individual, signatory States (rather than adopted only by an Assembly resolution) deliberately to conciliate the Americans and facilitate their participation in the Court and ultimate membership of the League.[85] Even when Bourgeois lost a vote (a rare occurrence), the outcome appeared a mark of deference to the United States. The classic example was the question of the official language of the Court. Bourgeois, following the ACJ's Draft Scheme, supported a single language: French. In the Council discussions Balfour (backed by Ishii of Japan) favoured English and overcame Bourgeois's objections. It was not, Balfour argued, simply that the Peace Treaties had placed English and French on equal diplomatic terms. It would plainly be foolish to decide the issue in a way which might prejudice American membership.[86]

The First Assembly approved the Statute of the Permanent Court of International Justice on 13 December; three days later, on 16 December 1920, a separate Protocol of Signature was adopted. When this latter document had been ratified by a majority of the Member States of the League the attached Court Statute would itself be formally brought into effect. Only then would the Statute be open for acceptance by 'States mentioned in the Annex to the Covenant' – most obviously and importantly, the United States of America.[87] Within two months a majority of the League Members had signed the Protocol of Signature. By the following autumn and the convening of the Second Assembly in September 1921, sufficient ratifications had been deposited with the League for elections to the bench to be held. The Permanent Court of International Justice had been established under Article XIV of the Covenant; and in February 1922 it held its inaugural session in the Peace Palace at The Hague.[88]

It is impossible in a single chapter to summarize fairly the distant origins and immediate antecedents of the Permanent Court of International Justice. The preceding pages have deliberately concentrated upon the activities and ideals of Elihu Root in order to correct the American historiography which gives him a pre-eminent role in the creation of the Court. The picture which emerges from this survey is more qualified. In certain areas Root met success, in others defeat; while all the time his role as representative of a United States outside the League was important – to the League Secretariat, to League representatives, to his fellow-members on the Advisory Committee of Jurists.[89] But, as we have seen, the creation of the PCIJ has to be understood as part of the history both of the prewar Hague system and the postwar League.[90] If, indeed, individuals are to be assigned key roles in the Court's creation then Léon Bourgeois has at least as great a claim as Root – with Phillimore and Cecil not completely outdistanced in the race.[91]

Historiography, however, can never deviate too far from the brute facts of history; and there is no denying the weight of contemporary evidence that simply recorded or argumentatively interpreted the presence of Root in the Advisory Committee of Jurists.[92] But the bias of American historiography has inclined too greatly to those contemporaries who advocated American membership in the new Court; who accentuated Root's victories and minimized if not totally ignored his defeats, whether in the Advisory Committee or later at the hands of the League; and who coloured their reportage to convince the doubters and rebut the critics.[93] Yet it could hardly be thought that the United States Senate, which had twice rejected the Covenant of the League – allegedly the handiwork of their own President – would uncritically endorse American participation in the League-sponsored Court on the argument that a former Secretary of State and Senator from New York had aided in its creation – especially when Root was seen to be playing a very crafty game to hold together a deeply divided Republican party in a presidential election year.

Notes

1 *League of Nations Official Journal* (cited below as *LNOJ*), February 1920, 17–25. Quotations from the *LNOJ* are from the English text, so far as possible. Sometimes, where the English version of a French original is unsatisfactory, I have made my own translation.

2 Léon Bourgeois, *L'Oeuvre de la Société des Nations, 1920–1923* (Paris: Payot, 1923), 9–20.

3 *LNOJ* (February 1920), 19, 24.

4 Ibid., March 1920, 30–7; Bourgeois, *Oeuvre*, 159–68.

5 Cf. P. J. Baker, 'The Permanent Court of International Justice', in H. W. V. Temperley (ed.), *A History of the Peace Conference of Paris*, 6 vols (London: Oxford University Press, 1920–4), VI. 481–99.

6 *LNOJ* (March 1920), 37.

7 For studies of the Conferences at The Hague and Root's role, see esp., James Brown Scott (ed.), *Instructions to the American Delegates to The Hague Peace Conferences and their Official Reports* (New York: Oxford University Press, 1916) and *Texts of the Peace Conferences at The Hague, 1899 and 1907* (Boston and London: Ginn, 1908). Scott is one of the relatively minor actors in the subsequent narrative.

8 Root to Oppenheim, 6 March 1915: quoted in Philip C. Jessup; *Elihu Root*, 2 vols (New York: Dodd, Mead, 1938), II. 375. For Second Generation studies of Root, see George Harry Curtis, 'The Wilson Administration, Elihu Root and the Founding of the World Court, 1918–1921' (PhD dissertation, Georgetown University, 1972); Martin David Dubin, 'Elihu Root and the Advocacy of a League of Nations, 1914-1917', *Western Political Quarterly* 19 (September 1966), 439–55; and David S. Patterson, 'The United States and the Origins of the World Court', *Political Science Quarterly* (cited below as *PSQ*) 91 (Summer 1976), 279–95.

9 For House's words, see Ray Stannard Baker, *Woodrow Wilson and World Settlement: Written from his Unpublished and Personal Material*, 3 vols (London: Heinemann, 1923), I. 218; for House's schemes, ibid., III. 79–87 and

Charles Seymour (ed.), *The Intimate Papers of Colonel House*, 4 vols (London: Benn, 1926–8), IV. chs 1, 2 and 9. For Root's uncertainties, see Elihu Root, 'The Real Monroe Doctrine', *PASIL* (1914), 6–22.

10 Robert Lansing, *The Peace Negotiations: a Personal Narrative* (Boston: Houghton Mifflin, 1921), 46; Baker, *Woodrow Wilson and World Settlement*, I. 284. The five US plenipotentiaries were Wilson, Lansing, House, General Tasker H. Bliss and Henry White.

11 A good introduction to a huge subject is Felix Morley, *The Society of Nations: its Organization and Constitutional Development* (London: Faber & Faber, 1932), ch. 3; copious documents and a narrative analysis are in David Hunter Miller, *The Drafting of the Covenant*, 2 vols (New York: Putnam's, 1928). Wilson's words are quoted in Morley, *The Society of Nations*, 80; the Minutes of the plenary session of 14 February are in Miller, *The Drafting of the Covenant*, II. 557–79; the Minutes of the Commission's first ten meetings are ibid., II. 229–335; and the Draft Covenant is printed ibid. II. 327–35.

12 Miller, ibid., I. 120.

13 Morley, *Society of Nations*, ch. 6; George W. Egerton, *Great Britain and the Creation of the League of Nations: Strategy, Politics and International Organization, 1914–1919* (Durham: University of North Carolina Press, 1978), esp. chs 4–6. The 'Draft adopted by the French Ministerial Commission for the League of Nations' (8 June 1918) is given in translation by Miller, *The Drafting of the Covenant*, II. 238–46. For Smuts, see ibid., II. 23–60 and Baker, *Woodrow Wilson and World Settlement*, III. 94–9.

14 'Schema di Atto Generale per Costituire la Società delle Nazioni', Titolo II, Capo II: 'Corte internazionale di giustizia', in Miller, *The Drafting of the Covenant*, II. 539–47. For the US delegation, see Lansing, *Peace Negotiations*, esp. chs 4 and 11; Seymour, *Intimate Papers of Colonel House*, IV, chs 1, 2, 9 and 10; Kuehl, *Seeking World Order*, esp. chs 12 and 14.

15 C.A. Kluyver (ed.), *Documents on the League of Nations* (Leiden: A.W. Sijthoff, 1920), chs 3 and 6.

16 Hays to Root, 24 March 1919 and Root to Hays, 29 March 1919. Texts were published in *International Conciliation*, Special Bulletin (April 1919), 72–95. See also Jessup, *Elihu Root*, II. 372 ff., esp. 385 ff.; and Will H. Hays, *The Memoirs of Will H. Hays* (Garden City, NY: Doubleday, 1955), ch. 15.

17 For Taft, see Theodore Marburg and Horace E. Flack (eds), *Taft Papers on the League of Nations* (New York: Macmillan, 1920), 228 ff.; for Hughes, speech of 26 March 1919: text in *International Conciliation*, Special Bulletin (April 1919), 39–71.

18 Miller, *Drafting of the Covenant*, II. 327–35 at 330–1. The final form of Article XIV has been given at p. 18 above. For the tentative nature of the Draft Covenant, see the comments of Cecil, Bourgeois and Orlando on 14 February 1919 in ibid., II. 565–73.

19 For a brief introduction to a complex subject see Thomas Willing Balch, *Legal and Political Questions between Nations* (Philadelphia: Allen, Lane & Scott, 1924).

20 Root offered four other amendments: on withdrawal; on arms control; on revision; and on the Monroe Doctrine and 'domestic questions'. On this latter pair, see chs 4 and 5 below.

21 Miller, *Drafting of the Covenant*, II. 699 ff. at 728–9.

22 Ibid., I. 327–30, 377–80; Jessup, *Elihu Root*, II. 395–6; James, Viscount Bryce, *Proposals for the Avoidance of War with a Prefatory Note by Viscount Bryce* (as revised to 24th February 1915), cited by Root in *PASIL* (1918–19), 50 ff.

23 Miller, *Drafting of the Covenant*, I. 380–1; Jessup, *Elihu Root*, II. 395; Morley,

Society of Nations, p. 181.

24 Miller, *Drafting of the Covenant*, I. 328–30, 390–418: Morley, *Society of Nations*, p. 185.

25 Root to Lodge, 19 June 1919: published in the *American Journal of International Law* (cited below as *AJIL*) 13 (July 1919), 596–602. For the background, Jessup, *Elihu Root*, II. 399–401; Hays, *Memoirs*, ch. 15.

26 The debate in the Senate can be traced in the *Congressional Record*, Sixty-sixth Congress, First Session; the Committee Hearings were published as *Treaty of Peace with Germany*. Hearings before the Committee on Foreign Relations, United States Senate. Senate Document no. 106, Sixty-sixth Congress, First Session (Washington, DC; GPO., 1919)

27 David Hunter Miller to Root, 7 July 1919; Root to Miller, 14 July 1919: Elihu Root Papers, Manuscript Division, Library of Congress (cited below as MD, LC); Curtis, 'Wilson Administration', pp. 84–92.

28 Root to Lodge, 19 June 1919 (cited at n. 25 above); Root to Lodge, 1 December 1919: Jessup, *Elihu Root*, II. 407; Drummond to Root, 16 February 1920; Root to Drummond, 11 March 1920; Joost van Hamel (of the League's Legal Section) to Root, 26 March 1920: Root Papers; and see generally Curtis, 'Wilson Administration', ch. 7.

29 Curtis, 'Wilson Administration' makes Root's position clear; cf. the many references to Root in Henry Merritt Wriston, *Executive Agents in American Foreign Relations* (Baltimore: Johns Hopkins University Press, 1929), where the formal contrast to Root's official though abortive Russian mission can be inferred. For the involvement of the Carnegie Endowment (cited below as CEIP), see James Brown Scott to Root, 6 May 1920: James Brown Scott Papers, Lauinger Library, Georgetown University. Scott had been Solicitor in the Department of State from 1906 to 1910, when Root was Secretary of State; he had also been a leading member of the US delegation to the Second Hague Peace Conference and had served on Wilson's staff in Paris.

30 Henry L. Stimson and McGeorge Bundy, *On Active Service in Peace and War* (New York: Harper, 1947), 276.

31 Walter Simons (President of the German Supreme Court) to Scott, 27 March 1929: Scott Papers.

32 The extensive records are in Permanent Court of International Justice: Advisory Committee of Jurists, *Procès-Verbaux of the Proceedings of the Committee: June 16th–July 24th 1920, with Annexes* (The Hague: Van Langenhuysen, 1920) and *Documents presented to the Committee relating to Existing Plans for the Establishment of a Permanent Court of International Justice* (London: League of Nations, 1920). These volumes are cited below as PCIJ, *Procès-Verbaux* and PCIJ, *Documents*, respectively. Scott provided a valuable (though selective and contentious) record for his sponsors: James Brown Scott, *The Project of a Permanent Court of International Justice and Resolutions of the Advisory Committee of Jurists: Report and Commentary*, CEIP, Division of International Law, Pamphlet no. 35 (Washington: CEIP, 1920).

33 *NYT* (13 June 1920), 4; Root to American Society of International Law, 26 April 1923, in *International Conciliation* 186 (May 1923), 113–35; Root to Jessup, 18 March 1929: typescript journal, 'World Court – Geneva Trip, 1929' (cited below as 'World Court–Geneva Trip'), Philip Caryl Jessup Papers, MD, LC.

34 Drummond, cited in James Brown Scott, 'A Permanent Court of International Justice', *AJIL* 14 (October 1920), 581–90 at 582.

35 *LNOJ* (July–August 1920), 227. Hagerup replaced his Norwegian colleague, Gram: see above at p.19.

[36] Ibid. 228–33; Bourgeois, *Oeuvre*, 169–76 for his speech of 16 June 1920. For the continuities and contrasts between the systems of The Hague and the League: Bourgeois, *Oeuvre*, 34–72. On military sanctions: PCIJ, *Procès-Verbaux*, 693–749, esp. 700 (this is the text of Lapradelle's Report); PCIJ, *Documents*, 133–9 (the Memorandum of the Austrian jurist Heinrich Lammasch).

[37] *LNOJ* (July–August 1920), 229; Bourgeois, *Oeuvre*, 171.

[38] Jessup is cursory and uncritical on Root and the ACJ: *Elihu Root*, II. 419 ff. Scott's *Project* is helpful; but it must be read in conjunction with Scott's later articles ('Permanent Court of International Justice'), which record the author's disillusionment: *AJIL* 15 (January and April 1921), 52–6 and 260–6.

[39] Alexander P. Fachiri, *The Permanent Court of International Justice: its Constitution, Procedure and Work* (London: Oxford University Press, 1925), 5. This is the 1st ed of the work cited above in ch. 1, n. 8.

[40] Manley O. Hudson, *The Permanent Court of International Justice, 1920–1942: A Treatise* (New York: Macmillan, 1943), 149 (see also ch. 1, n. 8). The description of the 'system' comes from the Report of Lapradelle: PCIJ, *Procès-Verbaux*, 700.

[41] *Fachiri, Permanent Court*, 5.

[42] For the 'Root-Phillimore Plan', see Scott, *Project*, 12–48, 218–23; for their collaboration, PCIJ, *Procès-Verbaux*, 542.

[43] PCIJ, *Procès-Verbaux*, 108–109; Scott, *Project*, 29–35, 59–62. Some of Root's remarks to the ACJ on these subjects were collected as 'The Constitution of an International Court of Justice', *AJIL* 15 (January 1921), 1–12.

[44] PCIJ, *Procès-Verbaux*, 107; Scott, *Project*, pp. 27–9; Miller, *Drafting of the Covenant*, II. 567–8.

[45] PCIJ, *Procès-Verbaux*, 125, 145–6. Ricci-Busatti, Adatci and Lapradelle replaced the original nominees: see above at pp. 19–20, 30.

[46] ACJ, Report, in PCIJ, *Procès-Verbaux*, 693–749 at 700: see also 106–9, 125–6, 148–51, 389, 535.

[47] Annex 1 to 23rd meeting: ibid. 519–20; Annex B, 'Resolutions of the Advisory Committee': Scott, *Project*, 168–72.

[48] PCIJ, *Procès-Verbaux*, 519–20; Scott, 'Permanent Court of International Justice', 265; (Sir) H. Erle Richards, 'The Jurisdiction of the Permanent Court of International Justice', *British Year Book of International Law* (cited below as *BYBIL*) (1921–2), 1–5.

[49] 'Recommendations of the Advisory Committee of Jurists': Report adopted by the League Council, *LNOJ* (November-December 1920), 20–1.

[50] David Hunter Miller spoke of a slightly earlier version of Root's proposals as 'hopelessly impossible': *Drafting of the Covenant*, I. 380–1.

[51] Anzilotti to Drummond, 11 February 1921: Deibel, 'Struggle for Cooperation', p. 93. Anzilotti was, of course, one of the most distinguished international legal scholars. His writings were gathered together as *Opere di Dionisio Anzilotti*, 4 vols in 5 (Padua: CEDAM, 1955–63). He was later a judge and president of the Court. His most famous opinion from the Court bench is discussed in ch. 7 below.

[52] Text of 'Draft Scheme' as Annex 1 to 32nd meeting: PCIJ, *Procès-Verbaux*, 673–85; *LNOJ*, Special Supplement 2 (September 1920); Scott, *Project*, Annex A, 149–68. The other Article (to total sixty-two) was a Preamble: Article 1.

[53] The views of Root, Phillimore, Descamps, Adatci and Ricci-Busatti consume much of the debate in the 7th–11th meetings of the ACJ: PCIJ, *Procès-Verbaux*, pp. 177 ff.; and they are analysed in the Report of Lapradelle: ibid. 694 ff., 725–9.

[54] Ibid. 229–45.

[55] Cmd. 151, Misc. no. 3 (1919), *The Covenant of the League of Nations with a Commentary thereon*. Presented to Parliament by Command of His Majesty, June 1919 (London: HMSO, 1919), 16. The legal section of the US Department of State shared the analysis of Adatci and Ricci-Busatti: F. K. Nielsen (Office of the Solicitor) to Secretary of State (Bainbridge Colby), 30 September 1920: Department of State Records (Record Group 59: National Archives, Washington, DC), Decimal File no. 500. C 114/43. (These voluminous records are cited below as NA 500. C114, i.e., file no. for the PCIJ, followed by/item no. The names of correspondents, rather than simply their office (as in the originals), are supplied.)

[56] The English text of Article XIV is given at p. 18 above. The relevant clause of the French text read: '[La Cour] donnera aussi des avis consultatifs sur tout différend ou tout point dont la saisira le Conseil ou l'Assemblée.' The following chapters and the Bibliographical Essay will attest to the voluminous literature on the Court's advisory jurisdiction. Useful introductions are Bustamente y Sirven, *World Court*, ch. 14; Hudson, *Permanent Court*, ch. 22; Horace A. Read, 'Advisory Opinions in International Justice', *Canadian Bar Review* 3 (April 1925), 186–95.

[57] PCIJ, *Procès-Verbaux*, 584–85. The crucial provision was Article 32: Scott, *Project*, p. 223.

[58] Root's ideas can be gleaned from Scott, *Instructions to the American Delegates, passim* and *Project*, 111–13. His Papers are unhelpful, Two useful articles (not least on the domestic antecedents) are Manley O. Hudson, 'Advisory Opinions of National and International Courts', *Harvard Law Review* 37 (June 1924), 970–1001; Albert R. Ellingwood, 'The Advisory Function of the World Court', *American Bar Association Journal* (cited below as *ABAJ*) 11 (February 1926), 102–8.

[59] PCIJ, *Procès-Verbaux*, 584–5. The 'Compte-rendu' of the proceedings (ibid. 595–605, at 605) states: 'Des objections soulevées par M. Root... ont été écartées par des arguments tirés de l'article 13 du Pacte'.

[60] Ibid. 689–749 at 701, 730 ff.

[61] See chs 4 and 5 below.

[62] Scott referred most favourably to the solution and its defence by Lapradelle: *Project*, 111–13.

[63] For the English text of Article 36, see p. 46 above. The corresponding French text ran: 'La Cour donne son avis....

[64] James Brown Scott never ceased to describe the United States of America as a truly *international* political organization: e.g., *Project*, 93, 102.

[65] Patterson, 'United States and the Origins of the World Court', pp. 292–3, n. 38; cf. Root's own Draft Report to the CEIP, 7 December 1920: copy in Scott Papers.

[66] The respective political and legal roles of Root and Scott were well expressed by one of their colleagues, the Spaniard Rafael Altamira y Crevea, *La Sociedad de las Naciones y el Tribunal Permanente de Justicia Internacional*, 2nd ed, Publicaciones del Instituto de Derecho Comparado Hispano-Portugués-Americano, no. 14 (Madrid: Bermejo, 1931), 73. Altamira y Crevea served on the bench throughout the life of the Court. Another good evaluation can be found in Jean Morellet, *L'Organisation de la Cour Permanente de Justice Internationale* (Paris, Pedone, 1921), 34–50. Not that Root was not credited by the League for his helpful (if limited) role: Drummond to Manley O. Hudson, 28 September 1920 and Joost van Hamel to Hudson, 28 June 1920: Manley O. Hudson Papers, Harvard Law School Library, Harvard University.

[67] PCIJ, *Procès-Verbaux*, 690–1.

68 *LNOJ* (September 1920), 318–21; Bourgeois, *Oeuvre*, 176–81.
69 *LNOJ* (November–December 1920), 12–18, esp. 13; Bourgeois, *Oeuvre*, 181–95.
70 *LNOJ* (November–December 1920), 15; Bourgeois, *Oeuvre*, 186.
71 Scott, 'Permanent Court of International Justice', 265–6.
72 Report by the Greek Council representative, Demetrius Caclamanos, 'The Official Languages of the Court': *LNOJ* (November–December 1920), 19–20; Bourgeois, *Oeuvre*, 194–5.
73 *LNOJ* (November–December 1920), 18; Scott, *Project*, 128–9 had skated over Root's belief in the value of dissenting opinions.
74 See n. 38 above; and Root's Draft Report to the CEIP, cited at n. 65 above.
75 The details can best be found in the voluminous compilation, League of Nations, *Permanent Court of International Justice: Documents concerning the Action taken by the Council of the League of Nations under Article 14 of the Covenant and the Adoption by the Assembly of the Statute of the Permanent Court of International Justice (not including material collected for, or the Minutes of, the Advisory Committee of Jurists)* (Geneva: League of Nations, 1921.) These records are cited below as League of Nations, *PCIJ Documents*.
76 League of Nations, *PCIJ Documents*, 226–9, 284–6. The text of the Optional Clause is taken from the final Statute: ibid. 258–66. This (new) Article 36 corresponded to ACJ, Draft Scheme Article 34, except that the latter's sub-paragraph (e) was deleted.
77 League of Nations, *PCIJ Documents*, 258–66. For the Assembly-Committee discussion of this (new) Article 38: ibid. 54 ff. The provision was never used by the PCIJ.
78 For Article 57 *bis* of the Council, see p. 41 above. Hagerup's words come from the Subcommittee annotations to the ACJ Draft Scheme Article 35: Fachiri, *Permanent Court*, 1st ed, p. 320.
79 See pp. 65 ff. above.
80 For the complex details: League of Nations, *PCIJ Documents*, 54 ff., 211 ff., 225 ff., 254–6.
81 Hudson, *Permanent Court*, 210–12, comments ruefully on these events.
82 PCIJ, *Documents*, 15–16, 37 ff., 53 ff., 109–11, 133–9; PCIJ, *Procès-Verbaux*, 314, 432, 704 ff., 724–5; League of Nations, *PCIJ Documents*, 86, 90–1, 229.
83 Kluyver, *Documents on the League of Nations*, pp. 184–9.
84 Eugène Borel, 'The United States and the Permanent Court of International Justice', *AJIL* 17 (July 1923), 429–37.
85 Adatci to Root, 25 January 1921: Root Papers. For Bourgeois *et al.*, see *LNOJ* (September 1920), 318–21; *LNOJ* (November–December 1920), 12–18; Bourgeois, *Oeuvre*, 176–95; League of Nations, *PCIJ Documents*, 86, 90, 229. Anzilotti's proposal is ibid. 166.
86 See citations at n. 72 above.
87 League of Nations, *PCIJ Documents*, pp. 225–56; the Statute is ibid. 258–66. This remained the constitution of the Court until 1936.
88 For the elections of 1921, see ch. 3 below.
89 Hagerup to Root, 15 December 1920: Root Papers; Adatci in PCIJ, *Procès-Verbaux*, 542.
90 For a study of the League–Hague systems written for an American audience *before* the ACJ assembled, see Carlton J. H. Hayes, 'The Historical Background', in Stephen P. Duggan (ed.), *The League of Nations: the Principle and the Practice* (Boston: Atlantic Monthly Press, 1919), 18–49.
91 For fair summaries by Second Generation Court scholars of the roles of Bourgeois, Phillimore and Cecil, see Davis, *United States and the Second Hague Peace Conference*, 347–52; Curtis, 'Wilson Administration,' ch. 2.

92 See ch. 3 below.

93 Counter-arguments to this bias can be found in Hill, *Problem of a World Court*, chs 1 and 2; Frances Kellor, *The United States of America in relation to the Permanent Court of International Justice of the League of Nations and in relation to The Hague Tribunal*, 2nd ed (New York: privately published, 1923), esp. 140–61.

3 Back door to the League: the Court in US–League relations, 1920–23

On the very day the Covenant of the League of Nations entered into effect, Raymond B. Fosdick, an American serving as a very high-ranking officer in the Secretariat, wrote a letter to Secretary-General Drummond. Both men were intensely keen for American membership in the League. Indeed, shortly after the first Senate vote in November 1919 against the Treaty of Versailles and the Covenant, Drummond had argued that the 'appalling' consequences of American abstention made it 'worth paying almost any price to obtain ratification', including the League's acceptance of 'very stiff reservations'. Fosdick's aim in writing to Drummond was to encourage him with the thought that the presidential election eleven months ahead could not provide a clear indication of public opinion or even future governmental policy towards the League. National electoral campaigns were not designed to pose deliberately or answer unambiguously questions of any complexity – least of all on foreign relations. The specific and comforting lesson to be drawn from campaign history was that the incoming administration and the League would have more scope for defining the terms of their mutual relationship than convention politics, party platforms, candidates' speeches and voting tallies would initially suggest.[1]

Fosdick did not employ the phrase, 'solemn referendum', the words used contemporaneously by President Wilson to describe his vision of the central issue before the electorate: 'the part the United States is to play in completing the settlements of the war and in the prevention in the future of such outrages as Germany attempted to perpetrate'.[2] Historians, however, particularly those sympathetic to Wilson and

American membership in the League, have largely endorsed Fosdick's general rule of electoral interpretation. For over fifty years the judgment of Walter Lippmann on the 1920 election has been repeated.

> The Republican majority was composed of men and women who thought a Republican victory would kill the League, plus those who thought it the most practical way to secure the League, plus those who thought it the surest way offered to obtain an amended League.[3]

Lippmann was a thoughtful observer – though not as neutral in his political judgments as his frequent citing in American historiography suggests. American entry into the war, the actions and attitudes of government and public, and most of all the terms of the Peace Treaties had deeply affected his progressive liberalism; and he carried the intellectual traces of his disillusionment into the 1930s.[4] Yet for all the plausibility of Lippmann's analysis of the 1920 election and its adoption by later writers, some historical qualifications are apposite.

First and most obvious are the bare words and obvious implications of the Democratic and Republican party platforms. While both tried to bridge disagreements within their parties, there was no mistaking the fundamentally different approach of each to the Covenant of the League and the Treaties of Peace. The Democratic platform

> favor[ed] the League of Nations as the surest, if not the only, practicable means of maintaining the permanent peace of the world and terminating the insufferable burden of great military and naval establishments. It was for this that America broke away from traditional isolation and spent her blood and treasure to crush a colossal scheme of conquest.

The rest of the long plank on the League continued to echo Wilson's language, and openly attacked Senator Lodge and his partisan colleagues, whose 'vicious' campaign of misrepresentation had dishonoured and endangered the nation. Certainly the Democrats tried to satisfy the proponents of both unconditional and conditional ratification by calling for

> the immediate ratification of the treaty without reservations which would impair its essential integrity [*and the acceptance of*] any reservations making clearer or more specific the obligations of the United States to the League associates.

But if this was a concession to the reservationists within the Democratic party, its partisan edge was sharp and unsheathed.

> Only by doing this may we retrieve the reputation of this nation among the powers of the earth and recover the moral leadership which President Wilson won and which Republican politicians at Washington sacrificed.[5]

The Republican national convention of 1920 met in Chicago, where eight years previously the party had split between Taft and Roosevelt.

Lodge, chairman of the 1920 convention, was determined to avoid a repetition which would return the presidency to the Democrats. He wanted a foreign relations plank which could unite mild Reservationists like Senators Kellogg, McNary and Lenroot; strong Reservationists like Senators Cummins, Fall and Harding; regular, old guard Irreconcilables such as Senators Brandegee, Knox and Moses; and progressive, irregular Irreconcilables such as Senators Borah, La Follette, Norris – and Johnson, Roosevelt's running-mate in 1912. Two months before the convention assembled, Lodge asked help of Elihu Root in drafting a satisfactory formula. Eventually, and in a most roundabout way, Root provided what was needed. As he himself neared The Hague to join the Advisory Committee of Jurists, Root's proposals were put to a deeply divided platform caucus in Chicago, gratefully accepted and 'adopted without a change'.[6]

The planks on the League of Nations came not first in the Republican platform (as they did in the Democrats') but last, third in line after an attack on Wilson's 'ineffective policy' towards the Mexican revolution and a firm rejection of a United States mandate for Armenia. Nevertheless, when the censure of the Treaty of Versailles came it was direct, though less bitter than the condemnation of Wilson's dictatorial demands that it be ratified 'without any modification'. Where the Democratic platform applauded the break with 'traditional isolation', the Republicans (following Root) censured the Wilson administration for repudiating

> to a degree wholly unnecessary and unjustifiable, the time-honored policies in favor of peace declared by Washington, Jefferson, and Monroe, and pursued by all American administrations for more than a century....

The weight of these and other remarks in the six paragraphs on the League of Nations was clearly against the terms negotiated and signed by Wilson at Paris and which had subsequently twice failed to command a two-thirds majority vote in the Senate, even with the addition of strong reservations. Yet neither Root nor many of the other leading Republican convention delegates could openly reject the idea of international co-operation whether for narrow partisan motives, ideas of national interest or more abstract, disinterested reasons. In the Republican platform the language of internationalism was ubiquitous – and ambiguous.

The first paragraph of the separate plank dealing with the League of Nations declared:

> The Republican party stands for agreement among the nations to preserve the peace of the world. We believe that such an international association must be based upon international justice, and must provide methods which shall maintain the rule of public right by the development of law and the decision of impartial courts, and which shall secure instant and general international conference whenever peace shall be threatened by political action, so that the nations pledged to do and insist upon what is just and fair may exercise their influence and power for the prevention of war.[7]

If the Democratic platform echoed Woodrow Wilson, the Republicans in their convention followed the lead and language of Elihu Root: their platform recalled his criticisms of the draft and final Covenant. As the Jurists were assembling at The Hague the Republican party in Chicago was uniting on a platform which could fairly be interpreted as a general endorsement of Root's participation and goals.

A tradition was being established. Just as the proposal for a permanent court of international justice contained in Article XIV of the Covenant had escaped the Senate's censure during nine months of scrutiny, so in the major party conventions of 1920 the ideal passed unscathed. The Democrats paradoxically avoided the topic altogether; the Republicans for their part were allusive rather than outspoken advocates.

On 12 June the Republicans formally nominated Senator Warren Gamaliel Harding of Ohio as presidential candidate. He was a surprise choice – though with the virtue of known flexibility and the advantage of a party united on its platform. In his acceptance message Harding followed Lodge in the latter's criticisms of Wilson's contemptuous attitude towards the Senate; and then paralleled Wilson in describing the forthcoming election as a 'referendum'. But it was to be a 'referendum... on the preservation of America', Harding's formula for describing the objectives of the strong Reservationists. This was the nearest he came to even qualified approval of the Covenant. Like the platform-drafters and their ghostwriter Root, Harding posed the issue as first, renegotiating the conditions of peace with the defeated enemy powers and second, constructing a new world order, one in which America could 'be the free and disinterested agent of international justice and advancing civilization'.[8]

Such rhetoric was initially encouraging to Root; but the situation did not take long to change. Senators Johnson, La Follette and Borah had not bolted from the Republican party and its candidate; but as the summer passed they began to suspect Harding's commitment to their position. They made it clear that their loyalty was not unconditional; and, gradually, Harding's campaign speeches sounded a more and more irreconcilable tone. In Europe Root watched the process with disgust. He wanted a 'treaty with reservations', while Harding appeared to be moving towards 'irreconcilable opposition to any league'. As Root cabled to senior Republicans: Harding had fallen for the deceptive way in which 'Wilson wish[ed] to frame [the choice:] League or no League instead of Wilson League against Americanized League'.[9]

On returning to the United States in the autumn the dilemma facing Root was even sharper. The work of the Advisory Committee had been completed; but Harding was still closer to the Irreconcilables than to Root's section of the Republican party. Eventually Root joined with other prominent Republicans to issue a statement endorsing Harding's candidacy while squaring it with his own commitment to joining the League with strong reservations. In the famous Declaration of Thirty-One Pro-League Republicans, Root and his colleagues advised the American people that they could 'most effectively advance the cause of International Co-operation to promote Peace by supporting' Harding against his Democratic opponent, James M. Cox.[10] As so often in these debates, the language was imprecise – and deliberately so. Root's biographers have rightly conceded that the Declaration's purpose was more prescriptive than descriptive, more an attempt to remind Harding and a wider world of the views and priorities of the Thirty-One, less an accurate or even plausible assessment of Harding's position and objectives.[11] Even so, Root and his co-signatories were more specific and less disingenuous in supporting Harding's straightforward opposition to Article X of the Covenant and endorsing his campaign pledge to promote a 'court of international justice' – the latter commitment being, after all, only a repetition of the 1916 Republican platform.

When the Third-One Republicans took their wishful stand for Harding only the Draft Scheme of the Advisory Committee had been proposed; the League Council and Assembly had still to dispose. Nevertheless the work of the Jurists was already referred to in the United States as the 'Root Plan', the 'Root Court'.[12] One purpose of such terminology was readily seen and denounced by Senator Knox of Pennsylvania. He warned Harding against using such language uncritically, as his Democratic rival, Cox, was doing. It was part of a cunning plot to 'put [the United States] in Wilson's League by the back door'.[13]

There was justification for Knox's warning. Inside the League Secretariat a highly placed American, Arthur Sweetser, used the same metaphor to describe his hopes. As he wrote to Dionisio Anzilotti in mid October: the Court project was 'generally accepted as the door through which the Republican party, if elected in the present campaign, will seek to enter the League of Nations'. Two months later and after Harding's victory at the polls, Sweetser changed the metaphor but argued to the same effect when he wrote to another senior League official, the Swede Åke Hammarskjöld: 'The Court is undoubtedly the League's strongest claim on America and will in time... serve as the entering wedge' to full American membership of the League.

Anzilotti and Hammarskjöld thought rather differently from Sweetser, about both the so-called Root Plan and the ultimate benefits of American participation in the Court. Hammarskjöld, who had acted as Anzilotti's assistant at the ACJ, was rather bitter. He believed that Root and his assistant, Scott, had prevailed upon their colleagues to create a statute 'calculated to satisfy the exigencies of the United States'; and that the Americans would employ it 'as a lever to reverse the Covenant'. Anzilotti agreed. As he wrote to Secretary-General Drummond after the Assembly's completion of the Court Statute: if it were 'satisfactory to the United States, they would accept it and try to reform the League, with the Court for a basis'.[14]

Even Sweetser could see these possibilities. He was well aware that the Republicans might be tempted to capitalize on Root's prominence and the excessive credit he had gained in the summer at The Hague. He too saw the danger of anti-League Americans trying to separate the Court from its parent organization. Fosdick had similar forebodings –

and so did a number of other well-placed Americans in the Secretariat.[15] Yet Sweetser was adamant that such an attempt would be stillborn; and with characteristic vigour he wrote from his League office to the Department of State deprecating any such illusions. It had to be

stated unequivocally that the Permanent Court is not only an essential part of the League, if not indeed the very backbone of the League, but beyond that is wholly inseparable from it. The two are intertwined and interdependent to such a degree that neither could function properly without the other.

For any one in the United States to believe otherwise was to suffer 'the most serious misapprehensions'; and Sweetser enclosed a copy of Bourgeois's opening speech to the ACJ to corroborate his argument. In the selection of judges, in the determination of the Court's jurisdiction, in effecting the Court's judgments, the Covenant and the League were indispensable. Root himself would have had nothing to do with the ACJ unless the Court was to have the protection and basis of the League. Sweetser concluded: it was

the crassest absurdity to try to separate two bodies, one of which is the offspring of the other, and both of which are mutually interdependent.[16]

The hopes and warnings of Sweetser, the rebukes of Knox, the forebodings of European and American officials in the League Secretariat carried the same basic message as the party conventions and electoral campaigns. The international court envisaged before the war and given a constitution by the ACJ had a peculiar hold over American public opinion.[17] This much is clear; but it would be a false deduction retrospectively to assume that the US government would endorse *in toto* the Draft Scheme – even less so changes deliberately made by the League Council and Assembly. Furthermore, even if the final Court Statute were acceptable to the American government, its use as a staging-post into the League or as an instrument to separate the two bodies were alternative possibilities and neither was inevitable. Inside the United States a thoughtful observer could see that even if the November presidential election were to be the referendum announced by both Wilson and Harding, the fate of the proposed Court still remained to be decided. A massive vote for Harding and the Republican party platform did not mean the Court's rejection by the electorate; nor did it suggest that the Court's final constitution would be endorsed without qualification. Whatever the impressionistic merit of Walter Lippmann's frequently quoted judgment on the election and the League issue, the huge popular vote for Harding in November 1920 gave no precise indication of public opinion or governmental action on the Court question.[18] The League, at least, drew favourable inferences. The First Assembly, which finally authorized the Court Statute, met nearly a fortnight after Harding's election – the election which (he claimed) had declared the League 'deceased'.[19]

Arthur Sweetser was only one of a number of American citizens who wrote to the Department of State lobbying for membership in the League and the Court. In the course of our analysis we shall encounter a number of such lobbyists, who frequently represented well-organized and quite vocal groups. The materials they produced enrich the files of the Department; and much work has been done and still remains to be done on their activities and influence.[20] In the following pages space precludes our treatment being systematic; but from time to time we shall have to correct some of the misapprehensions and mistakes which characterize the historiographical record of particular individuals and organizations concerned with promoting American adhesion to the Permanent Court of International Justice.

These comments, which are prompted by Lippmann's notorious judgment, the ambiguities and ambivalences of political campaigns and the manipulative purposes of phrases such as the Root Court, are not meant to suggest that the Department of State lacked its own official channels for the reporting and dissemination of news and opinions. On the contrary. Despite the direct slurs and frequent innuendo found in much historical writing on the American foreign service, the Department of State was well represented and well served by its overseas and home-based officers on the Court question.[21] For more than a dozen years membership of the Court was governmental policy, endorsed by Republican and Democratic administrations alike – though with varying salience. Throughout the period most Department of State officials displayed exceptional knowledge of the Court and the League, kept a good sense of political possibilities, accurately countered the exaggerations of propagandists on all sides and rarely appeared to indulge in partisanship, even though political patronage played a large role in the recruitment and appointment of officials.

On the Court question the tradition of full and intelligent reportage began as early as the summer of 1920, when the chargé d'affaires at The Hague, William Phillips, covered the evolution of the Jurists' Draft Scheme.[22] Later the work of the Council and Assembly was conscientiously transmitted to Washington. But perhaps the neatest example of the diligence and acuteness of the Department in these early days was shown by the Solicitor, Fred K. Nielsen in one of the areas we have already discussed. His memorandum on the Draft Scheme, particularly Chapter II (covering jurisdiction) was excellent; and many of his criticisms were later endorsed by the League. Yet it was his political sensitivity which was so impressive. Realizing the gaps between the thinking of the ACJ's Draft Scheme and the purposes of the Covenant, Nielsen warned against the dangers of dubbing the Jurists' proposals the 'Root Court'. Such an identification could only backfire if (and, he suggested, when) they were substantially modified by the League.[23]

Root's great triumph in 1920 had been his role in shaping the electoral machinery of the Court. This element of the Draft Scheme had been unconditionally endorsed by the Council, Bourgeois welcoming it with the comment that the process of concurrent voting by Assembly and Council preserved the principle of equality 'to exactly the same degree as in the Covenant'.[24] Under the terms of Chapter I of the Court Statute the eleven judges and four deputy-judges were to be elected from candidates 'nominated by the national groups in the [Permanent] Court of Arbitration [PCA]'. Thus the four American judges on the roster of the PCA were entitled to nominate up to four candidates for election, two of whom might be American citizens.

The four American panelists on the PCA were Root himself, John Bassett Moore, George Gray and Oscar S. Straus. When approached by the League Secretariat, the four men declined to offer any nominations and gave three conflicting reasons for their inaction. The two public ones were the less plausible. The first of these maintained that the invitation had come too late for them to meet the deadline for filing candidates' names. This explanation was rendered suspect by their second, in which they argued that their office as panellists of the PCA was a presidential appointment deriving from the 1907 Hague Convention; consequently they had no authority to perform functions arising from the League Covenant and Statute of the Court, neither of which had been ratified by the US government. Subsequent events were to expose this argument; but it did hint at the third and most substantial reason for the panellists' behaviour. As Root wrote privately to his colleagues, after consulting the new Secretary of State, Charles Evans Hughes:

> for the American group in the old Court of Arbitration to make nominations for the new Court under the covenant of the League of Nations would involve serious risk of immediate controversy which might be very injurious to the success of the important policies the government is now pursuing....[25]

Root's reference was imprecise; but one of the 'important policies' was the forthcoming Washington Conference, called to discuss naval armaments and political and strategic questions in East Asia and the Pacific. This conference had been sponsored by the Harding administration (following the congressional initiative of Senator Borah) partly to resolve issues arising from American rejection of the League and to complement the dispositions of the Paris Peace Conference. Its deeper origins lay in the steady rise of Japan as a world power and the attempts of previous administrations to accommodate Japanese expansion and pretensions on the Asiatic mainland and over the islands of the ocean. There was also the chronic American resentment at the Anglo-Japanese alliance – a grievance which the Pacific Dominions of the British Empire shared with the United States.[26]

Root's generalities also covered the firm decision of the Harding administration to steer 'clear of all unnecessary participation' in League activities, especially when many lobbyists were describing the Permanent Court of International Justice as the vestibule to the League.[27] Root's three colleagues on the PCA united behind his vague wording, not because they supported the administration politically; but in so far as they all desired eventual American membership in the 'new Court' they chose to do nothing to hazard that goal.[28]

Root himself had been nominated by a number of national groups as a candidate in the League elections to the Court's bench. He was flattered by the honour (for his election was assured) but he declined to stand. It was not simply his prior engagement as a plenipotentiary to the Washington Conference – for its work should be concluded before the Permanent Court began its sittings. There was also the question of his age. At seventy-six he felt 'too old to transplant' himself and his wife to Europe for the rest of their lives. However Root did have his own candidate in mind, his colleague on the PCA, John Bassett Moore: a man with 'an accurate mind, great learning in International Law, and practical experience in International affairs'.[29]

Moore was indeed an exceptional man. He was an outstanding authority on international law, arbitration and diplomacy; he had written a number of monumental works of legal scholarship; he was an experienced negotiator; he had served as Counselor in the Department of State in 1913–14, having begun his career as a law clerk in 1885. Moore was also a Democrat; equally he was an articulate though restrained critic of the Wilson administration's wartime policies on neutrality and belligerent rights. He supported the idea of the new Permanent Court of International Justice, but without illusions; at the same time he opposed American membership of the League and called for changes in the terms of the treaties imposed at Paris.[30] Moore could offer many qualities to the bench and appeal to a range of political persuasions off the bench – but without appearing complaisant. He was, above all, an American. With the endorsement of his PCA colleagues and on the nomination of the Italian group Moore was elected as a full judge at the joint Council-Assembly elections of September 1921.[31]

Earlier in the year President Harding had repeated his obituary on the League as an electoral issue and he deprecated the revival of this dead subject. He gave a familiar metaphor another polish.

> In compliance with its pledges the new Administration... definitely and decisively put aside all thoughts of entering the League of Nations. It doesn't propose to enter now, by the side door, back door, or cellar door.[32]

In the autumn of 1921 and on the eve of the Court elections David Hunter Miller (one of the drafters of the Covenant) remained convinced of the administration's hostility to the League. He warned a senior official of the League Secretariat, William Rappard, to build no hopes on the presence of Charles Evans Hughes and Herbert Hoover (co-signatories with Root of the Declaration of Thirty-One) in Harding's cabinet. Conversely Fosdick (who had recently resigned from the Secretariat) was that much keener to see an American candidate elected to the bench, since that would help 'a lot to tie [the USA] up' in the Court and eventually in the League. After the elections Sweetser tried to use Moore's success to relieve the misgivings of Hammarskjöld in the

Secretariat that American participation would harm the Court, undermine the Covenant and thus destroy the League. Far from it, thought Sweetser: the Court was the most convenient and likely means for Americans to approach and ultimately enter the League. Even so, nothing could be expected from the Harding administration until after the Washington Conference. That much had been made clear to Root by Harding himself shortly before the Court elections.[33]

The Conference opened on 12 November 1921 and ended after nearly three months of negotiations on 6 February 1922. Writing a few years afterwards, Arnold Toynbee described the 'constructive work achieved at Washington [as] second only to that accomplished [in] four years... by the League of Nations'. Among these accomplishments were the Four Power Treaty of 13 December between the United States, the British Empire, France and Japan, concerning their rights and possessions in the Pacific and committing the signatories to seek peaceful means for resolving controversies; the Five Power Treaty of 6 February (Italy this time included) relating to naval armaments and installations; and the Nine Power Treaty of the same date (with Belgium, China, The Netherlands and Portugal the additional signatories) pledging, inter alia, 'respect [for] the sovereignty, the independence, and the territorial and administrative integrity of China'.[34]

Before the treaties were submitted to the Senate President Harding reportedly staked his reputation upon the achievements of the Washington Conference.

> Every administration's name rests on one or two acts. If these treaties are ratified by the Senate, then this administration's name is secure in history.[35]

Harding was proved wrong. His two and a half years in the White House have gained a scurrilous reputation for events far removed from international politics. Even historians of the Conference are apt to identify fundamental weaknesses in the system designed in 1921–2.[36] We cannot here untangle the complexities or provide a balance-sheet of the Conference. What we can do is underscore a number of conditions affecting the passage of the treaties by the US Senate and also place the Conference in the context of the World Court – as the Permanent Court of International Justice had become to be called.

The Senate's handling of the Washington treaties showed the same principles which had generally informed and ultimately determined first the earlier debate and rejection of the Versailles Treaty and the League Covenant and then the subsequent passage of the Treaty of Berlin in the autumn of 1921. So it happened that the Four Power Treaty was passed by the Senate only after the inclusion of the Brandegee Reservation (itself an echo of a Harding pledgè) that ratification entailed 'no commitment to armed force, no alliance, no obligation to join in any defense' – what may be interpreted as the reassertion of the basic objection to Article X of the Covenant.[37] In spite of this explicit disclaimer, four of the original Republican Irreconcilables voted against the Four Power Treaty: Borah, Johnson, La Follette and France.

Conversely, twenty-three Democrats were recorded against final passage – which strongly suggested a partisan opposition and a wish to level scores after the League defeat – an allegation made explicitly by Senator John Sharp Williams of Mississippi, one of Wilson's most loyal supporters. Even the failure of the Senate to register any objections to the Nine Power Treaty may be understood as a belated victory for claims and protests made in 1919–20. The Open Door Policy, enunciated by Secretary of State John Hay in 1899, was formally accepted by the eight co-signatories, Japan included; while many of the complaints previously made about the Chinese clauses of the Versailles Treaty were now answered textually and at the cost of Japanese counterclaims (notably over Shantung).[38]

If the Senate behaved in a manner characteristic of its stance in 1919–20, the Harding administration and the Republican leadership in Congress had apparently learned something from the mistakes of Woodrow Wilson and the Democrats. The Washington Treaties were guided through the Senate by Lodge in his capacity as chairman of the Committee on Foreign Relations. He had been appointed one of the four American plenipotentiaries to the Conference. Oscar W. Underwood, Senator from Alabama and Minority leader, was another delegate; Secretary of State Hughes and Elihu Root were the remaining members. The contrast with the Paris Peace Conference delegation was striking. Whereas Robert Lansing had been overlooked during the Paris Conference and became an outspoken critic of the Treaty of Versailles, Hughes wholeheartedly endorsed the work of his delegation. Indeed he had begun the Conference with something of a *coup de théâtre*, delivering a keynote appeal for disarmament which attracted great attention.[39] Root was generally more restrained and circumspect; and he lived to see his misgivings realized. But simply in parliamentary terms and in marked distinction to 1919, the construction of the delegation was well-suited for final Senate approval. As Taft wrote to Root in mid September: Lodge's presence was 'indispensable'. Indispensable – indeed a guarantee of success. 'With him and Underwood any conclusion you reach will have the strongest support in the Senate...'. Taft was correct. The treaties were reported to the Senate by Lodge within days of the Conference's adjournment and all were approved by the end of March. Barely seven weeks had elapsed. Lodge congratulated himself on his achievement. As he told George Harvey, a former ally in the League fight and currently US Ambassador in London: 'it was on the whole pretty well done'.[40]

The negotiation and ratification of the Washington Treaties encouraged Sweetser to renew his representations to Secretary-General Drummond. The last few months had shown a willingness on the part of the American government to cooperate with League powers; and it was not utterly unrealistic to hope that one day the USA might adhere to the Covenant. Nor was Sweetser alone – or even first to resume the lobbying. From Harvard, Arthur N. Holcombe wrote to Rappard in

Geneva that the obligations undertaken by the United States through the Four Power Treaty were potentially more extensive and more binding than those of the Covenant. This promised much for the future, Holcombe concluded.[41]

It is striking how League Covenant and Court Statute were woven together in the minds of such lobbyists; but then this correspondence was addressed to League officials. It was not, however, unrepresentative of a type of thinking in the United States. By late spring 1922 a number of organizations had begun to petition the Harding administration to sign the Court Protocols, now that the Senate had completed its legislative the action on the Washington Conference. Much of this lobbying was discreet and good-humoured even though it was forcefully expressed.[42] Social and intellectual equals were speaking to one another on their own terms. In midsummer, however, the tone and methods altered.

The most dramatic example came in early July, when Hamilton Holt publicly upbraided Secretary Hughes; and Holt broadcast his censure to a wide audience. Holt was editor of *The Independent* and a prominent personality in the so-called peace movement. A Wilsonian Democrat, he had been a founding member of the League to Enforce Peace – the influential non-partisan organization established in 1915 with a collective-security philosophy and including in its leadership people such as Taft, Roosevelt and Root.[43] Holt attacked Hughes for his delay in carrying out the commitments implied in the Declaration of Thirty-One. In particular Holt complained of Hughes's neglect of the Permanent Court of International Justice: the Department of State's handling of the nominating process for the 1921 elections had been cowardly and disingenuous. With Holt's allegations appearing in the *New York Times*, Hughes had to respond equally openly to protect the Department and clear his own reputation. He used the columns of the *New York Times* to rebut Holt's charges as baseless and unworthy: Root, Straus, Gray and Moore had 'act[ed] on their own responsibility' in declining to nominate candidates. Hughes's explanation was true, but only part of the truth. Not every reader would be able to see that, however. More obvious and important were the other branches of Hughes's answer: first, the re-affirmation of American abstention from the League; second, the insistence that the United States would not adhere to the Court Protocols until it could participate in the election of the bench.[44]

There were two other aspects to Holt's allegations which Hughes chose to ignore in public. The first concerned the nature of the contact between the Department of State, the League and the Court; the second related to the steps Hughes had already taken towards participation in the Court. Since the early days of 1921 the Department of State had received correspondence and documents from the League and Court.[45] Part of Holt's criticism was that this material had been neglected by the US government; and historians have generally accepted this complaint. Where historians have been at fault is not in commenting on the inactivity of the Department but in suggesting that any inactivity stemmed from disdain, as Holt alleged.[46] Moreover, and this is the more serious but related fault, historians have not recorded the substance of the correspondence. For example, William Phillips at The Hague sent reports on the politicking surrounding the elections to the presidency of the Court.[47] Thus the more grievous and reprehensible historiographical failure has consisted in the suppression of the evidence for the League Powers' continuing determination to mould the Court to their individual and collective interests. In censuring the Department of State for an initial attitude of aloofness (which Drummond called 'most discourteous') historians have conducted a form of secret plea-bargaining to free the Court and League of a much graver indictment.[48]

The second point for commentary is less problematical but perhaps more startling. Despite Holt's denunciations Secretary Hughes had already begun to explore the possibility of the United States participating in elections to the Court's bench. With the next full elections not due until the end of the decade this seemed a remote goal, scarcely worth the trouble to hide the truth. That it might have a deeper meaning, one Hughes would wish to conceal from the public, was suggested by the name of the chosen intermediary. As Hughes wrote to a pro-League correspondent: the man he had briefed for the negotiator's role was 'one of the most eminent and influential friends of the League', William Howard Taft.[49]

Taft was a far more famous founding member of the League to Enforce Peace than Ham Holt. In the spring of 1919 he had criticized the Draft Covenant in similar terms to Hughes and Root; for, like them, he wanted the United States to join a modified League of Nations. In the summer of 1920 Taft was not entirely happy with the compromise Root offered to construct the League planks of the Republican electoral platform; but, as he admitted to an intimate, it was 'about as good a result as we could have expected'. Within a few weeks of Harding's nomination Taft expressed publicly his concern about the candidate's commitment to even a very modified Covenant. Later in the election campaign Taft would have signed the Declaration of Thirty-One in an attempt to stop Harding succumbing to the Irreconcilables in the Republican party. The evidence is indisputable: Taft was a vigorous though conditional supporter of American membership in the League of Nations – and a supporter who saw adherence to the Court as a huge advance towards that ultimate goal.[50] So far as Taft's relations with the Harding administration were concerned, the debate over the League had not worked against Taft. In the summer of 1921 Harding appointed him Chief Justice of the US Supreme Court – the one ambition left to a man who had been President.

Taft was due to visit Great Britain in the summer of 1922 to study judicial procedure. Through the columns of the *American Bar Association Journal* he let it be understood that as Chief Justice he would not involve himself in controversial political issues.[51] The remark was surely intended to deceive. Before Taft left the United States Hughes briefed him on the Court Protocols and asked him to explore the possibility of co-operation.[52] However, once in Great Britain, Taft was treated cautiously by Hughes, who appeared both to doubt Taft's discretion and to fear a reaction from anti-League Republicans. Conversely the leading British officials, Arthur Balfour and Robert Cecil, were aware of Taft's unofficial status and could well measure the distance between his original conception of the League and the public statements of the Harding administration and its nominal supporters in Congress. Thus Taft was somewhat abandoned by Hughes, his sponsor, but not unreservedly welcomed by his hosts. Eventually, however, certain conditions were agreed for an American approach to the Court; but in the negotiations as a whole Taft played first an introductory and then a subsidiary role.[53] Even Secretary Hughes left the centre of the stage, when he undertook an official visit to South America in the late summer; and in the detailed discussions which followed men who had been active in the earlier years of the Court's history returned to prominence. These were Root in the United States; Walter Phillimore, Cecil and Balfour acting for the British government; and Eric Drummond, officially representing the League Secretariat and unofficially inclining to the British view. Two other names need to be mentioned: John Bassett Moore and Manley Ottmer Hudson.

We have said a little about Judge Moore but nothing so far about Hudson. He will appear frequently in the following pages, for he became the leading American campaigner for membership of the Court. If Hudson's name is known today it is perhaps because of his career as a judge of the PCIJ in the latter half of the 1930s and his many books and articles on the history and jurisprudence of the Court (notably his *Treatise* and the *World Court Reports*), together with studies of other international organizations and arbitral-judicial procedures. Hudson, who had served on both the Inquiry and David Hunter Miller's legal team at the Paris Peace Conference, held a permanent Chair in the Harvard Law School but he spent much of each year in Geneva and The Hague working in the League Secretariat and the Court Registry. He was a prolific letter-writer and the Department of State received many communications and documents from him as he travelled and worked in Massachusetts, Switzerland and the Netherlands. Fragments of Hudson's biography will be scattered throughout the rest of this study; but one consideration is not out of place here. If indeed Elihu Root is seen as 'father of the Court', no-one has a greater claim than Manley Hudson to the title of benevolent guardian who struggled to win American recognition for the offspring.[54] That Hudson failed – at least in the interwar years – says a little bit about his tactics and personality; immeasurably more about the practical realities of the Court, the League and the US government. It says nothing against Hudson's determination and dedication.[55]

There was a great deal of circumspection during the negotiations initiated by Taft. To understand its origins and as a prelude to our own narrative it is useful to remember the broad context of the discussions. Some individuals already mentioned personify the differing perspectives on American adherence to the World Court. There were those like Hudson who saw American participation in the Court as a first step into the League. Cecil held somewhat similar views but he always treated

American adherence to the Court as subordinate to maintaining the integrity and vigour of the League – provided it was compatible with his sense of British interests. Drummond also put the League before the Court; but he was more realistic, less abstract about the League and its politics than Cecil. Then there were those, certainly few in number, who desired American membership of the PCIJ to defend its judicial independence against the political pressures of the League. Moore was such a person: but he realized how isolated he was, even on the Court's bench. Another group wanted American co-operation but not necessarily full membership in the League. Adherence to the Court was both a means to and sign of this measured involvement; but such collaboration was only one goal among many. On the British side Balfour represented such thinking; and in later years it became increasingly popular among senior British statesmen and diplomatists, most notably in the person of Austen Chamberlain. Their American counterparts were Taft, Hughes and Root, men who had adjusted to the improbability – if not impossibility – of the United States ever formally entering the League of Nations. Finally there were some highly placed officials who were sceptical even of the value of American participation in the Court and ultimately the Leage: men such as Anzilotti, Hammarskjöld and Joost van Hamel, the Dutch head of the Secretariat's Legal Section. Above all they wanted to avoid amending the Covenant and the Court Protocols to satisfy Washington – only to see their concessions rejected once again.[56]

Sweetser was thinking of such a dreadful outcome when he wrote to Fosdick in the summer of 1922. The League had 'more than opened the door' to the United States' entering the Court: first Root's invitation to serve on the ACJ; then the provision for non-League States to adopt the Protocol; the use of the Permanent Court of Arbitration to nominate candidates to the bench; the election of Moore; and (most recently) permitting ex-enemy States to adhere to the Court. Sweetser concluded the catalogue with a somewhat despairing appeal for an American response.

If there remains something that must be done to satisfy America, surely it is not too much to ask that [America] make a clear-cut statement of her desires?[57]

Sweetser wrote in early August 1922; the 'statement' appeared in February 1923. It was the product of converging activities.[58] On one side was Taft (with help from Root and with Hughes in the background) negotiating face to face and then corresponding with the British. Contemporaneously Hudson and Moore were offering suggestions, gaining the endorsement of League officials and then transmitting their ideas to Washington – as well as publishing them in journal form. A third centre of activity was the Department of State, where the Solicitor's Office under Fred K. Nielsen was drafting proposals independently of Taft's negotiations. Indeed, what is so striking about the whole proceedings was the degree of isolation in which the different teams worked. Only the League Secretariat seems to have maintained an overview of the separate activities. This is a remarkable testimony to the sensitivity of the issue. Moore, for example, did not want American adherence to the Court threatened by and subordinated to the goal of American adherence to the League; while Cecil did not want the League humiliated and embarrassed by snubs from importunate Americans. In the middle stood Drummond. It was a paradoxical fact, but only one of many examples of his intelligence and tact in diplomatic negotiations.

It must be remembered that there was no problem about the United States using the Court, that is being a willing litigant before the bench. This facility was 'open' to the United States as one of the 'States mentioned in the Annex to the Covenant' (Statute, Article 35). Nor was the United States debarred from having a national permanently on the bench itself. Provided one of the 'national groups' in the Permanent Court of Arbitration nominated an American citizen and that candidate was then successful in the concurrent elections of Council and Assembly, the USA could be said to have a representative on the bench (Statute, Articles 4 ff.). If no American citizen had been elected and the USA wished to appear before a bench containing an American judge, it was permitted *qua* litigant 'to select or choose a judge' *ad hoc* (Statute, Article 31).

The various negotiating and drafting teams at work in constructing the statement of American intentions identified a number of problems. All were agreed that the United States should participate in the election of judges. The obvious difficulty was that the Statute confined this function to Members of the League. Likewise only League Members contributed to the financing of the Court. It was also suggested, though with less assurance, that only League Members (rather than Signatories of the Court Protocol) could amend the Court Statute. However, even if this was a privilege of membership, it was not agreed that the power had to be exercised in the Assembly. After all, the Statute had been formally and finally approved by the Assembly, but its signature and ratification had been effected on an individual basis. It was, therefore, uncertain whether the adhesion of the USA would constitute the granting of a *de facto* veto power over future revision of the Statute. Finally there was the legacy of the 1919–20 debates. The Statute contained no provision for withdrawal, or more technically, the right of a State to revoke its ratification of the Protocol of Signature. Such an unqualified right had been a major demand of the Senate in its reservations to the Covenant – a demand which Taft, Hughes and Root had expressed much earlier. This in turn led directly to the overarching question of the obligations which flowed from adherence. Could the United States possibly adhere to the Court envisaged in one article of the Covenant without assuming commitments under the other clauses?

Since the negotiating teams worked very much independently of one another, a chronological review of their discussions and conclusions is less useful than a more conceptual analysis. Thus, though Moore and Hudson began drafting proposals later than Taft and the British, the two Americans with their widely differing goals soon constructed the elements of the final statement. By early August the outlines of the

Moore–Hudson scheme were approved by Drummond; and they were then despatched to the Department of State. There were four key points:

(1) the United States should participate in the concurrent Council-Assembly elections on equal terms with the Permanent Members of the Council;
(2) no obligations were to be assumed under the Covenant;
(3) the right of withdrawal from the Court was to be allowed; and
(4) the United States should contribute financially to the upkeep of the Court.

Drummond's approval was not easily won, for the terms met strong opposition from the Legal Section of the Secretariat and its chief, van Hamel. The latter particularly deprecated American participation in the elections, arguing that this would inevitably involve amending the Covenant (not simply the Court Statute), which was a most dangerous as well as impractical suggestion. Drummond countered this objection with a more hopeful consideration. As he later wrote to Cecil:

> America has gone far, and unexpectedly fast, in the past few months, so I think we may well be optimistic regarding a wider cooperation in the future.

Drummond's qualifications were tactical and procedural. First, it was important that the initiative for American participation be seen to come from the United States – certainly not from the League. Second, the form of American adherence must be as binding as possible.

> U.S. participation in the Court should be approved by the Senate and should not merely be an administrative act which can be altered at any time.[59]

The insistence of Drummond that the United States adhere to the Court Protocol by way of a formal treaty requiring a two-thirds majority in the Senate was striking but not idiosyncratic. Both Hudson and Sweetser had previously suggested this method – the former writing along these lines to Secretary Hughes, the latter offering the same advice to his colleagues in the League Secretariat. Far more surprising is the fact that the British negotiators had originally endorsed this procedure – and in the face of initial objections from Taft and Root.

Taft had begun his discussions with the British by proposing that the Court should be organizationally separated from the League. The idea was clearly a non-starter; and it certainly helps explain the caution with which the British approached Hughes's envoy. Balfour scotched the idea immediately, though courteously; and then Cecil, with help from Phillimore, was detailed to respond to the substantive issue of American participation in the existing League-sponsored Court. The final Cecil–Phillimore scheme had two main interrelated elements: (1) the preservation of the Court Statute textually, with (2) substantive changes introduced unilaterally by the Americans in the form of reservations to the ratification of the Court's Protocol of Signature. In other, non-technical words: the US government was to say it adhered to the Court but on terms and conditions peculiar to itself.[60]

The scheme nonplussed Taft and horrified Root. Taft had sought amendments to the Court Statute, for he believed textual changes were a 'psychological necessity in dealing with our Bitter Enders' – a favourite phrase of his to describe the anti-Leaguers. Root, however, was more outspoken and pessimistic. He feared a repetition of 1919–20 and the fate of the Versailles Treaty. Opponents of the Court would so load the resolution of ratification with wrecking amendments that its sponsors would abandon it. Alternatively the crippled resolution would be passed by the Senate and then prove abortive or be rejected outright by the original signatory States.[61]

By the latter part of October 1922 the League Secretariat, the British and American governments, and the prominent individuals Moore and Hudson were all agreed that the best method for American adherence lay in signing and ratifying the Court Protocol of Signature, with specific reservations or conditions governing (above all) participation in the League elections to the bench. As the Europeans then added: it would remain for the United States to propose further reservations, e.g., on withdrawal. In Cecil's judgment, 'any reasonable suggestion made by America would be immediately accepted' – by the League. (It was a significant qualification.) What was important was the substance of American co-operation, not its form.

League and congressional timetables meant that there was little if any possibility of action for another year. This did not trouble Taft. He had written to Balfour earlier that 'a year's delay may make matters more favorable in many respects'. The antagonisms of 1919–20 would have more time to die down. Cecil agreed: if the Harding administration went slowly it would avoid the impression of 'forc[ing] the League issue once more on the Senate'. Cecil was optimistic, particularly if the Americans were to adhere to the Court through a full treaty rather than by an executive agreement. The more exacting the legislative process, the greater the promise for the future. As Cecil wrote to Taft in late October:

> Such final endorsement by both branches of the American Government would give the Executive far greater freedom... in co-operating with the Court, and would demonstrate that co-operation with the Court had entered into the very fibre of American foreign politics.[62]

Cecil's language was guarded but evocative; its implication was clear. John Bassett Moore knew this sort of thinking and saw it in Hudson and many of his compatriots, especially and paradoxically in the hostile atmosphere of Geneva. (Sweetser was later to write of adherence connecting the United States 'in a very organic way with the *League*'.) At the very moment when Moore himself was working to bring the United States into the Court to develop its global and independent character, he felt it necessary to censure the peripatetic Americans in Europe who, 'while representing nobody but themselves, assume, as professed representatives of public opinion in the United States, to advise people over here ' that the United States was eager and poised to enter the League. So Moore wrote to William Phillips at The Hague, who happened to be a family friend. Later the letter found its way to Washington and into the files of the Department of State. But Moore was equally prepared to write directly to Secretary Hughes and make his comments even sharper. Moore's purpose was to warn Hughes against the League propagandists and the dangers of a congressional reaction. The Court had to 'be dealt with solely on its merits and independently of any other question', particularly 'the question of entrance into the League'. The cause of adherence to the Court was being damaged by American lobbyists who were 'chiefly preoccupied with the desire to participate in European and "world" affairs' and therefore asserted 'that a tide of pro-League sentiment [was] sweeping the country'. No doubt, Moore concluded (in a pointed jibe at the Republican Thirty-One), the same propagandists had made similar claims during the 1920 presidential campaign.[63]

What Moore perhaps did not know was the weight of the countervailing force upon Hughes. Ham Holt's July public attack was not an isolated incident, to be dismissed as the grumbling of a disagreeable but solitary individual. Early in August Hughes told Taft that '"friends of the League"', including Ray Fosdick, were 'gunning for him'.[64] Hughes was, in fact, tracing a narrow line between, on the one side, politically powerful Republicans and Democrats who wanted the United States to join the Court and then the League; and, on the other, those who were suspicious of the first movement as a step to the latter. A member of this second group was Lodge. Since he chaired the Senate Committee on Foreign Relations any prospective treaty of adherence would have to pass through his hands. It was, therefore, vital that Lodge stay at least neutral on any proposals put to the Senate. Lodge might be unable to stifle debate on a measure he disliked; but his open dissent would seriously undermine what administration control remained over the Senate.[65]

By the end of October Hughes was aware of the broad terms of adherence which would be acceptable to the League. It remained to prepare public and senatorial opinion – it being agreed that legislative action might not be started before the beginning of the Sixty-eight Congress in December 1923. On 30 October Hughes delivered a speech advocating adherence in Lodge's home town of Boston. Lodge was standing for re-election on a Massachusetts Republican platform which was intentionally vague: 'We stand for a Permanent Court of International Justice.' If Hudson in neighbouring Cambridge would not publicly acknowledge the ambiguity, neither did Lodge. He not only missed Hughes at the Symphony Hall ('laid up' with an unnamed malady); Lodge also avoided publicly endorsing or repudiating the terms of the speech itself.[66]

Lodge's silence is not difficult to explain. He had his own problems, the most immediate being an awkward re-election campaign, as Hudson informed Drummond.[67] Like Taft, Lodge's instincts were to separate the Court from the League; unlike Taft (and for different reasons), Lodge remained consistent. However, Lodge, Taft and Hughes were united on some foreign policy issues (the Washington Treaties being the most obvious and recent) and all three feared the growing power of the insurgent or irregular wing of the Republican party, a group led by such Irreconcilables as Borah, La Follette, Johnson and Norris. It would be unwise for Lodge to increase his difficulties by openly backing Hughes, even if he had sincerely believed in joining the League-sponsored Court. Conversely it would be gratuitously self-damaging for Lodge to distance himself from allies like Hughes and Taft, especially when legislative action was so remote. Silence was the appropriate answer.[68]

League officials responded appreciatively to Hughes's speech; and a little later Hudson's version of the argument appeared in the pages of the newly-established *Foreign Affairs*.[69] This was the journal of the Council on Foreign Relations, an elite policy-making group set up in the wake of the War which brought together Wilsonian Democrats and prominent pro-League Republicans, though the Council was not itself a strong lobbyist for the Court.[70] Hudson's article represented another stage in his emergence as a nationally known pro-Court advocate. Whereas Hughes had spoken in generalities, Hudson was more specific. After a survey of the Court's origins, Hudson offered a detailed discussion of the basic conditions for American adherence. They covered the main terms as we have already described them; and they were rounded off by an argument that the Department of State should effect membership through a formal treaty requiring a two-thirds vote of the Senate.

Everything that Hudson proposed was in line with Department of State thinking. Yet once again it is remarkable that Hudson and the Department appear not to have been collaborating consciously. Here is further evidence of the independence – even mutual isolation – of the proponents of adherence. What hints and allusions we do possess confirm a picture of the Department and the Harding administration in general distancing themselves from the 'friends of the League'.[71]

The caution is not surprising. While Hughes was denying any plans to move closer to the League itself, the unrestrained advocates of American membership were asserting the contrary. In the winter of 1922–23 Sweetser was in the United States and lending his support to a proposal to effect adherence to the Court by a joint resolution of Congress – a means of bypassing the two-thirds rule in the Senate which had been used only very rarely, notably to annex Texas and Hawaii. Early in January 1923 the League of Nations Non-Partisan Association (LNNPA) was formed to unite Republicans and others with Democratic supporters of League membership; and by mid February it was so successful that more than half the Republican Thirty-One had enrolled. Indeed the paradoxical result of this vigorous campaign was to frighten Sweetser and some of his highly placed colleagues in the League. They feared that the Court would be endorsed, the League abandoned; and that the American government would salve its conscience and discharge its international obligations by travelling to The Hague as an alternative to Geneva. As Florence Wilson, the League Librarian, expressed her forebodings to Drummond:

There are those in America only waiting to weaken the League and extend the scope of the Court. I fear this group more than any of the others.[72]

Moore, no less than Sweetser and Wilson, could see what was at stake. As he wrote to an intimate colleague on the World Court bench, Max Huber: the 'so-called "non-partisan" movement' was seeking to exploit the Court question 'for the entrance of the United States into the League'. Sweetser, for his part, was trying to reassure the Court's leading official, Registrar Hammarskjöld, that 'the bitterness of the anti-League campaign' in 1919–20 meant that Hughes and the administration would stress the complete separation of the Court from the League. Where Moore and Sweetser fundamentally agreed was in their common belief, approached from opposite sides, that if adherence to the Court were closely identified with American membership in the League then its chances of success would be minimal.[73]

On 24 February 1923, President Harding submitted the Court Protocols to the Senate. The *New York Times* (which Moore rightly described as a 'strenuous advocate' of American membership in the League) reported the Senate completely surprised by the move.[74] Clearly public opinion had been prepared, notably by Hughes, less so by Hudson; and, of course, the lobbyists had been active. What *was* surprising was less the substance than the timing of the action. There was less than one legislative week until the end of the congressional Session. Effectively there could be no Senate examination and discussion until the new Session convened in December. Nor is it wisdom after the event to realize that legislation on such a contentious issue might well be postponed throughout the coming Session, since senatorial and administration eyes would be looking to the party conventions and national elections of 1924.

Historians have tended to avoid the question of the administration's timing – and with some justification. Nothing in the relevant Department of State files explains the decision; there are few clues in the Harding and Hughes Papers – the latter's private account being, frankly, disingenuous; and the Hudson and Moore Papers are silent.[75] But these gaps should encourage speculation rather than quench it; and a number of interrelated items suggest the beginnings of an explanation.

First we must distinguish the actions of President Harding and Secretary of State Hughes. Harding formally submitted the Protocols on 24 February; but it was Hughes who composed the lengthy written argument for adherence. This document had been produced at least one week earlier and was dated 17 February. The date itself has significance, especially when seen in the physical circumstances of the brief's composition. Hughes had written it when 'laid up with the grippe' which had come on him a few days earlier.[76]

There were two paths converging upon these coincidental events. One requires us to reflect upon the general nature of the Harding administration and its relationship with Congress; and, in particular, the Senate's role in the conduct of foreign relations. The second shares some of the same ground and concerns the influence and future conduct of one of the Senate's leading members, Borah of Idaho.

The elections of 1920 had returned a Republican Congress and administration for the first time since the elections of 1908. The unity, however, was only nominal. The Republicans were divided between regular and insurgent wings; and the Regulars themselves were split between Harding's White House Gang (as it was pejoratively called) and a more established, traditional leadership. The gap between the Republican administration and its ostensible supporters was seen most clearly in the Senate – thus bearing out the general rule that the House is more docile, more amenable to party discipline than the Senate. But a particular keenness was given to the Executive–Senate friction by the opposition which arose against Hughes's nomination as Secretary of State. Chief among the opponents was William E. Borah. Not many months later the great international triumph of the administration, the Washington Conference, intensified the disagreement and mutual suspicion between its prime initiator, Borah, and its subsequent sponsors, Harding and Hughes – and this was on top of the split between the administration and Borah over the conclusion of the Treaty of Berlin. As Borah wrote in the midst of these struggles to Hiram Johnson, his great ally in the Irreconcilables' League fight: 'the Senate will now be suspicious of everything' emanating from an administration which was reneging on its earlier promise to avoid political commitments to the major League Powers.[77]

The justification for Borah's attitude is less important than its force. Nor was Borah alone, a mere voice, only one negative presence – as he is commonly described.[78] So far as Harding and his wing of the Republican leadership were concerned, the congressional and party situation was increasingly disturbing. The primaries of early 1922, followed by the mid-term elections at the end of the year had registered a definitive victory for the Insurgents in the Republican party. Even the recent historiographical attempts to rehabilitate Harding's presidential leadership acknowledge (sometimes inadvertently) the erosion of Harding's political base. His original self-denying ordinance not to impose himself on Congress, and especially the Senate, might not be sufficient: complaisance might not earn him re-nomination in 1924. The split of 1912 (still evident in 1916: it probably cost Hughes the presidency), barely bridged in 1920, might reappear with disastrous results in 1924. If it did, Harding would be lost. Since the Insurgents would not have him, perhaps he should move closer to Hughes and Hoover in the cabinet and conservative allies throughout the party, men like Taft and Root. Sponsorship of the Court Protocol would certainly help this strategy; and the greatest trick of all would be to delay the submission until legislative action became virtually impossible in the run-up to the 1924 conventions and elections.[79]

If a break came many political commentators tipped Borah to be its standard-bearer. His one great weakness lay in the electoral insignificance of his home-state, Idaho. Against this he had many assets. He was a national figure: his activities in 1919–20 had broadened, not created, his image. He had strong links with the insurgent, radical sections of the Republican party – yet he had never bolted and so preserved a claim upon the formal designation. Borah had often been endorsed by third-party movements in the Middle and Mountain West. He was reckoned to have a national constituency among industrial, urban voters as well as with independent farmers and agricultural workers. Borah was also highly popular in the South, where his opposition to federal anti-lynching legislation and defence of Prohibition were apparently well-received by the White electorate.[80]

Borah's Republicanism was not rhetorically of the 'bloody shirt' variety, but rather the sort of Republicanism he associated with Abraham Lincoln, the 'sainted Lincoln', who had sought to bind up the nation's Civil War wounds. Constantly in speeches and articles Borah alluded to the great political realignment of the pre-Civil War years: the Republican party had formed as a mass movement in the face of Whig and Democratic inadequacy and prevarication. His message in the 1920s was that a similar popular realignment was bound to occur if the reactionary elements in the Republican and Democratic parties continued to dominate national and local politics. And (it was thought) he might possess the personal qualities to preside over such a realignment. For perhaps the most striking aspect of Borah's character – at least to many observers – was his integrity. Even during the fierce and exhausting League debates he had managed to retain the respect of Woodrow Wilson for his principled, non-partisan opposition.

These were the broader aspects of Borah's appeal – particularly noticeable against the scandals emerging from Harding's White House entourage.[81] But it was in foreign affairs that Borah's prominence was most marked. After the Washington Conference had disappointed his hopes for real reductions (rather than stabilized ratios) in land and sea armaments, Borah issued another call for international negotiations on a huge agenda: debts and reparations; the restoration of world trade; land, naval and aerial disarmament. Once again Borah showed his skill in sounding a resonant note. Disillusioned Wilsonian Liberals such as Walter Lippmann supported the proposal; so did Wilson's confidant, Frank Cobb; so too James G. McDonald, a leading member of the Foreign Policy Association, a prominent pro-Court, pro-League organization.[82] Most recently and most importantly (as the possible explanation for the precise timing of the Hughes-Harding initiative on the Court Protocols), on 14 February 1923 Borah introduced Senate Resolution (S. Res.) 441.

The resolution was long and complex but its drift was unmistakable. It denounced 'all alliances, leagues, or plans which rely upon force as the ultimate power for the enforcement of peace'. Such schemes carried 'the seeds either of their own destruction or of military dominancy to the utter subversion of liberty and justice'. Borah was here obviously alluding to the League of Nations and its Covenant; and, like many of his compatriots, he implicitly contrasted these foreign schemes with the stable, peaceful American Union under its noble and pacific Constitution. The lesson of American history was that the world at large needed 'an international arrangement of such judicial character [which would similarly] not shackle the independence or impair the sovereignty of any nation'. Borah became more direct. In the 'Federal Supreme Court [Americans had] a practical and effective model for a real international court [since it possessed] specific jurisdiction to hear and decide controversies between [the] sovereign States'. For almost a century and a half the US Supreme Court had settled 'scores of controversies... judicially and peaceably', controversies which 'otherwise might have led to war'. Here before the eyes of all Americans, here in their own history they had 'a practical exemplar for the compulsory and pacific settlement of international controversies'.

After his analysis Borah turned to proposals. There were three. The first was to make war a 'public crime under the law of nations', with each country binding itself 'by solemn agreement or treaty... to indict and punish its own international war breeders' in the way envisaged by the Federal Constitution. Secondly Borah called for the codification of international law upon a basis of 'equality and justice'. His third proposal was by far the longest and most specific. In conjunction with the first two implicit criticisms of the League, the Covenant and the Paris Peace Settlement, the third branch of Borah's resolution provided a substitute for the League-sponsored Permanent Court of International Justice. The last clause of S. Res. 441 proposed:

> that a judicial substitute for war should be created (or if existing in part, adapted and adjusted) in the form or nature of an international court, modeled on our Federal Supreme Court in its jurisdiction over controversies between our sovereign States, such court to possess affirmative jurisdiction to hear and decide all purely international controversies as defined by the code or arising under treaties, and to have the same power for the enforcement of its decrees as our Federal Supreme Court, namely, the respect of all enlightened nations for judgments resting upon open and fair investigations and impartial decisions and the compelling power of enlightened public opinion.[83]

Borah's biographers have generally faulted most of his actions: utopian and idealistic are the most charitable adjectives given to this and similar initiatives.[84] Of course, the language and arguments of S. Res. 441 are not without problems. Knowledgeable lawyers, sympathetic to Borah, cited the Dred Scott case as the prime example of a judicial decision of the Supreme Court laying the ground for war.[85] Other elements in Borah's thesis were equally suspect. Contemporaneously the Eighteenth (Prohibition) Amendment was being widely violated, apparently with the active support of public opinion and the connivance of many officials; in the South, particularly, the Fourteenth and Fifteenth (Civil Rights) Amendments were virtually suspended – again as a reflection of the (White) majority's values.

The importance of Borah's resolution lay less in its claim to impeccable history, political analysis or logic but rather in providing an alternative vision of international order to that offered by the League advocates. Here was an expression – ponderous and problematical perhaps – which emphasized a number of equally uncertain aspects of the Permanent Court of International Justice: its relationship, even subordination to the League; its jurisdiction under the Peace Treaties; the nature of its sanctions; and its contrast to the American judicial tradition. In the skeletal language of a senatorial resolution Borah was exposing a set of assumptions concerning the Court and its functions, the most general of which was that the commitment of successive American governments to international arbitration and adjudication led in a straight line from the First and Second Hague Conferences through the Advisory Committee of Jurists to membership in the Permanent Court of International Justice established by the League of Nations.[86]

Borah's resolution, following closely upon the lobbying of prominent pro-League lawyers led by John Foster Dulles and Charles P. Howland, gave Hughes the final push to initiate legislative action.[87] It was important not to let the opposition capitalize upon Borah's initiative – especially with Lodge so non-committal. If the administration and in particular the Department of State did not seem to be in command, the prospects for all legislation in the coming Congress would be bleak. Confined at home with a cold, Hughes used his enforced absence from the Department to draft a brief on behalf of American adherence.

Hughes's argument was delivered in the form of a letter of some 3,000 words addressed to President Harding.[88] The first third sketched in familiar but not unexceptionable terms the history of the 'leading part' taken by the United States 'in promoting the judicial settlement of international disputes', particularly through The Hague Conferences of 1899 and 1907. The second section of the brief began with the Paris Peace Conference and the writing of Article XIV of the Covenant; and Hughes correctly stated that 'the advisability of establishing a permanent international court' did not become part of 'the subsequent controversy' over American membership of the League. For the second time Hughes referred to Elihu Root. The first occasion had been during the discussion of the Second Hague Peace Conference; now Root was mentioned as a participant in the Advisory Committee of Jurists. That was all – Hughes wisely refraining from asserting the special prominence or influence of Root on the Committee. Such remarks could backfire in a knowledgeable Senate, especially if Root's conservatism were brought into discussion. Hughes then carefully explained the constitution of the Court, whereby the Statute was attached to a Protocol of Signature individually subscribed to by Member States of the League and open to non-Member States, such as the United States of America. This arrangement, Hughes argued, was both a mark and a defence of the Court's essential independence from the League. Nevertheless there were formal, organizational links between the two bodies, notably in the electoral machinery; and Hughes surveyed the first elections and noted the success of John Bassett Moore, 'one of the most distinguished American jurists'. One other item covered in the brief's middle section was the Court's jurisdiction – though not its advisory function. Hughes stressed the non-obligatory character of the contentious jurisdiction and implied that the government had no intention of signing the Optional Clause.

The third and final section of Hughes's brief was the most substantial. History was no longer at issue; nor were procedures and organization. Now it was a question of the reasons and conditions for American adherence. Hughes acknowledged that the United States was 'already a competent suitor in the Court', as a State 'mentioned in the Annex to the Covenant'. But, he continued,

> it is not enough that the United States should have the privileges of a suitor. In view of the vast importance of provision for the peaceful settlement of international controversies, of the time-honored policy of this Government in promoting such settlements, and of the fact that it has at last been found feasible to establish upon a sound basis a permanent international court of the highest distinction and to invest it with a jurisdiction which conforms to American principles and practice, I am profoundly convinced that this Government, under appropriate conditions, should become a party to the convention establishing the Court and should contribute its fair share of the expense of maintenance.

Before Hughes detailed the 'appropriate conditions' he reverted to the relationship of the Court to the League and the League to the United States. Hughes insisted that none of the 'various procedural provisions' linking the Court and League 'impair[ed] the independence of the Court'; none 'create[d] any difficulty in the support of the Court by the United States', except the method of electing the judges. He would later enlarge on this topic; but before so doing he wished to summarize his judgment of the Court.

> It is an establishment separate from the League, having a distinct legal status resting upon the Protocol and Statute. It is organized and acts in accordance with judicial standards, and its decisions are not controlled or subject to review by the League of Nations.

Hughes's remarks on the election machinery add nothing to our previous reviews; his formal suggestions will be given below. Similarly all his other specific reservations will be recorded textually. There is, however, one condition he mentioned only in passing: the procedure for referring a case to the Court. As Hughes expressed the point: since the United States was not proposing to sign the Optional Clause conferring qualified compulsory jurisdiction on the Court, it was as well to note that they

> would not be required to depart from the position, which [the United States] has thus far taken, that there should be a special agreement for the submission of a particular controversy to arbitral decision.

In this guarded language Secretary Hughes alluded to the *compromis*, the very essence of a system of arbitration rather than legal adjudication. It was another example of the confusion which ran through Hughes's brief between the two methods of resolving controversies. Moreover it gave a lever to the Senate, which observers failed to detect at the time. But the conceptual mistake was not, of course, peculiar to Hughes: it was commonly made, especially in the formative years of the Court. What could be said in defence of Hughes was that not one of the other Great Powers had any intention of surrendering the principle of judicial sovereignty in its own case.

At the end of his long letter to the President, Secretary Hughes offered his statement of the four 'appropriate conditions' for American adherence. Formally they were the reservations to be attached to a Senate resolution assenting to the American signature of the Protocol of Signature of the Statute of the Permanent Court of International Justice. Tucked away in the preamble to the resolution was a disclaimer of the Court's compulsory jurisdiction over the United States. More important but far less obvious was a provision lodged in the closing words of Hughes's letter. Appended to the four 'appropriate conditions' was an obscure paragraph hazily stating that once the Senate had agreed to the proposed conditions the existing signatory States would be informed and on receipt of their acceptance of the Senate-approved conditions the United States would sign the Protocol of Signature. This roundabout method was to ensure that when the Executive signed the Protocol with specific conditions and reservations both the US Senate and the Signatories would have given a prior commitment to support them. In this way the Signatories and the United States government were to be spared the embarrassment of any possible mutual misunderstanding.

The four 'conditions and understandings to be made a part of the instrument of adhesion' were as follows:

I. That such adhesion shall not be taken to involve any legal relation on the part of the United States to the League of Nations or the assumption of any obligations by the United States under the Covenant of the League of Nations constituting Part I of the Treaty of Versailles;

II. That the United States shall be permitted to participate through representatives designated for the purpose and upon an equality with the other States members respectively of the Council and Assembly of the League of Nations in any and all proceedings of either the Council or the Assembly for the election of judges or deputy judges of the Permanent Court of International Justice, or for the filling of vacancies;

III. That the United States will pay a fair share of the expenses of the Court as determined and appropriated from time to time by the Congress of the United States;

IV. That the Statute for the Permanent Court of International Justice adjoined to the Protocol shall not be amended without the consent of the United States.

One week after Secretary Hughes completed his brief President Harding submitted it and the Court Protocol to the Senate. Though only a week remained before the close of the lame-duck final Session of the Sixty-seventh Congress, Harding stated that it 'would be well worth the while of the Senate to make such special effort as is becoming to record its approval'. This exhortation to speedy action was a sop for Hughes and Hoover in the cabinet; for Root outside; and for all the other like-minded advocates of adherence. It would have no credibility with Lodge and the overwhelming majority of Republicans in the Committee on Foreign Relations. As Harding wrote privately and more honestly to the veteran Ohio journalist, Walter Wellman: he did 'not really expect the assent of the Senate' in the short time before the adjournment.[89] Even so, the air of boldness in Harding's message was notable. Whereas Hughes wrote in a detached, official tone, Harding was more forthright and sounded more personal and committed, even when purporting to record stark facts.

> [D]eliberate public opinion of today is overwhelmingly in favor of our full participation, and the attending obligations of maintenance and the furtherance of [the Court's] prestige.

Harding refrained from 'repeating the presentation' of Hughes; but he did offer some points of his own. He admitted that the administration had been considering the terms of adherence since (and largely because of) the conclusion of the Washington Conference. If this was a hint of co-operation with the League Harding corroborated the impression by suggesting that Hughes's conditions had been approved by the League – though Harding used the less provocative term, 'signatory powers'. Nevertheless, Harding added, nothing could be done 'definitely... until the United States tenders adhesion with [the proposed] reservations'.[90] The Executive had made the first move; it now remained for the Senate to respond.

Notes

1. Drummond memo, 15 November 1919; Fosdick to Drummond, 10 January 1920: Deibel, 'Struggle for Cooperation', 11–12, 43. Some of Fosdick's correspondence during 1919–24 has been published as Raymond B. Fosdick, *Letters on the League of Nations: from the Files of Raymond B. Fosdick* (Princeton: Princeton University Press, 1966).
2. Message of 8 January 1920: Fleming, *United States and the League of Nations*, 404.
3. Walter Lippmann, *Public Opinion* (New York: Harcourt, Brace, 1922), 195–6; Gary B. Ostrower, *Collective Insecurity: the United States and the League of Nations during the Early Thirties* (Lewisburg, Pa.; Bucknell University Press, 1979), 15–16.
4. Lippmann to Fosdick, 15 August 1919: Fosdick, *Letters on the League*, 10–12; Ronald Steel, *Walter Lippmann and the American Century* (London: Bodley Head, 1980), chs 13 and 14.
5. Donald Bruce Johnson (ed.), *National Party Platforms, 1840–1976*, 2 vols

(Urbana and London: University of Illinois Press, 1978), I. 213 ff. This work, Vol. I, is cited below as *National Party Platforms.*

6 Will H. Hays to Root, 26 October 1925: Root Papers; Hays, *Memoirs*, ch. 19; Jessup, Elihu Root, II. 409–11.

7 Johnson (ed.), *National Party Platforms*, 229 ff.

8 *Official Report of the Seventeenth Republican National Convention held in Chicago, Illinois, June 8, 9, 10, 11 and 12* (New York: Tenney Press, 1920), 257–72 at 260. See the detailed study by Randolph C. Downes, *The Rise of Warren Gamaliel Harding, 1865–1920* (Columbus: Ohio State University Press, 1970), chs. 15 and 23.

9 Jessup, *Elihu Root*, II. 411–13; Root to Hays (August 1920); Hays to Root, 20 August 1920: Root Papers; Downes, *Rise of Warren Harding*, ch. 19.

10 The classic study, partisan yet informative, is Samuel Colcord, *The Great Deception: Bringing into the Light the Real Meaning and Mandate of the Harding Vote as to Peace* (New York: Boni & Liveright, 1921), esp. ch. 9. Among the signatories were Nicholas Murray Butler, Herbert Hoover, Charles Evans Hughes, Oscar S. Straus, Henry Lewis Stimson, Harlan Fiske Stone, George W. Wickersham – with William Howard Taft willing but unavailable. They will reappear in the following pages.

11 Jessup, *Elihu Root*, II. 413–14; Richard W. Leopold, *Elihu Root and the Conservative Tradition* (Boston: Little, Brown, 1954), 146–50.

12 'A Supreme Court for Quarreling Nations', *Literary Digest* (14 August 1920) 17–19; 'Root World Court', *New Republic* (29 September 1920), 105; Fosdick, *Letters on the League*, pp. 126–7.

13 Philander C. Knox to Harding, 16 September 1920: Downes, *Rise of Warren Harding*, 582.

14 Deibel, 'Struggle for Cooperation', 47, 92–3; Deibel, 'League of Nations', 374. Sweetser had been a press assistant to Ray Stannard Baker at the Paris Peace Conference. His Papers are in the MD, LC.

15 Cf. James G. McDonald (of the League of Free Nations Association) to Sweetser, 17 August 1920: Sweetser Papers.

16 Sweetser to G. Howland Shaw, 17 August 1920: NA500. C114/105.

17 E. M. Hood to Sweetser, 27 July 1920; Denys P. Myers (of the World Peace Foundation) to Sweetser, 25 September 1920: Sweetser Papers.

18 Calvin Coolidge said even the League issue was undecided: Fleming, *United States and the League of Nations*, 470. Hudson wrote along Lippmann's lines: Hudson to Drummond, 11 November 1920: Hudson Papers.

19 'The Landslide and its Meaning'; 'The "Now Deceased" League', *Current Opinion* 69 (December 1920), 757–61, 769–72.

20 I have developed some of these points in 'Isolationism of a Kind'.

21 For Secretary of State Hughes's own perspective, see *The Autobiographical Notes of Charles Evans Hughes*, ed. David J. Danelski and Joseph S. Tulchin (Cambridge, Mass.: Harvard University Press, 1973), 199–208.

22 Phillips's dispatches of 14 and 15 July 1920: NA500. C114/28, 34. The Phillips Papers are in the Houghton Library, Harvard University.

23 Nielsen to Secretary of State Bainbridge Colby, 30 September 1920: NA500. C114/43.

24 Hudson, *Permanent Court*, 152,

25 Drummond to Root *et al.*, 4 June and 13 August 1921: Root Papers; Root to Hughes, 13 and 14 August 1921; Hughes to Root, 16 August 1921: NA500. C114/127, 193; Root to Gray *et al.*, 12 September 1921: Hudson Papers.

26 Hughes to David Jayne Hill, 31 August 1921: Charles Evans Hughes Papers, MD, LC; Hughes, *Autobiographical Notes*, ch. 15

27 Harding to Root, 6 September 1921: Warren Gamaliel Harding Papers, Ohio

Historical Society, Columbus. I have used the microfilm edition.

28 Root to Hughes, 18 July 1923: Hughes Papers.

29 William Howard Taft to Root, 15 and 25 August 1921; Léon Bourgeois to Root, 13 September 1921; Root to Taft, 21 August 1921; to Walter Phillimore, 13 September 1921: Root Papers.

30 Moore is perhaps best known today for his two monumental analytical compilations: *History and Digest of the International Arbitrations to which the United States has been a Party, etc., etc.*, 6 vols (Washington, DC: GPO, 1898), published as House Misc. Document no. 212, Fifty-third Congress, Second Session; and *A Digest of International Law*, 8 vols (Washington, DC: GPO, 1906) Moore's Papers are in the MD, LC.'

31 The Court's origins and first elections are analysed by Moore in 'The Organization of the Permanent Court of International Justice', *Columbia Law Review* 22 (June 1922), 497–526.

32 Council on Foreign Relations, *Survey of American Foreign Relations*, (1928), (New Haven: Yale University Press, 1928), 300. For the Council, see above p.72.

33 Miller to Rappard, 29 August 1921; Sweetser to Hammarskjöld, 10 December 1921: Deibel, 'Struggle for Cooperation', 59, 94; Fosdick memo, 27 July 1921: Deibel, 'League of Nations', 372; Harding to Root, 6 September 1921: Root Papers; Hughes, *Autobiographical Notes*, 222–5.

34 Arnold J. Toynbee, *Survey of International Affairs, 1920–1923* (London: Oxford University Press, 1925), 419. (This series is cited below as *SIA*.) For the texts of the treaties and an official documentary record, see US Department of State, *Foreign Relations of the United States* (cited below as *FRUS*), 1922, I. 1–384.

35 Francis Russell, *The Shadow of Blooming Grove: Warren G. Harding in his Times* (New York: McGraw-Hill, 1968), 485–8.

36 Thomas H. Buckley, *The United States and the Washington Conference, 1921–1922* (Knoxville: University of Tennessee Press, 1970); John Chalmers Vinson, *The Parchment Peace: the United States Senate and the Washington Conference, 1921–1922* (Athens: University of Georgia Press, 1955).

37 Kurt and Sarah Wimer, 'The Harding Administration, the League of Nations and the Separate Peace Treaty', *Review of Politics* 29 (January 1967), 13–24; Peter H. Buckingham, *International Normalcy: the Open Door Peace with the Former Central Powers, 1921–29* (Wilmington: Scholarly Resources, 1983), esp. chs 1–3.

38 *CR* 67:2, 3855–6; Buckley, *United States and the Washington Conference*, 126–71, 178–83; Vinson, *Parchment Peace*, p. 194.

39 Manley O. Hudson (see above p.66) described Hughes's speech as the 'greatest document' in American history: Hudson to Huntington Gilchrist, 13 November 1921: Hudson Papers.

40 Taft to Root, 14 September 1921: Root Papers; Lodge to Harvey, 15 April 1922: Willis Fletcher Johnson, *George Harvey: 'A Passionate Patriot'* (Boston: Houghton Mifflin, 1929), ch. 32.

41 Sweetser to Drummond, 18 May 1922; to Fosdick, 31 May 1922: Sweetser Papers; Holcombe to Rappard, 17 April 1922: Deibel, 'Struggle for Cooperation', 82–3.

42 Incoming correspondence, May–June 1922: NA500. C114/172–82. The major lobby group was the Federal Council of the Churches of Christ in America (FCCCA).

43 Warren F. Kuehl, *Hamilton Holt: Journalist, Internationalist, Educator* (Gainesville: University of Florida Press, 1960), ch. 11.

44 The exchanges were republished in an untitled broadsheet by the Woodrow

Wilson Democracy of New York City, whose President was Holt: copy in Hudson Papers. For their impact, see Fosdick to Sweetser, 20 July 1922: Sweetser Papers; Bernardo Attolico to Hudson and to van Hamel, 28 July 1922: Hudson Papers.

45 Robert B. Machatee (US Vice-Consul, Geneva) to Hudson, 24 August 1921; Hammarskjöld to Hudson, 9 April 1922: Hudson Papers; incoming correspondence, February 1921–March 1922: NA500. C114/54–166 *passim*.

46 Vinson, *Parchment Peace*, p. 75; cf. Thomas A. Bailey, *Woodrow Wilson and the Great Betrayal* (New York: Macmillan, 1945), 352.

47 Phillips to Hughes, 18 January and 6 February, 1922: NA500. C114/169, 170.

48 Drummond, quoted in Sweetser to Fosdick, 20 July 1922: Sweetser Papers.

49 Hughes to Edwin F. Gay, 1 August 1922: Hughes Papers.

50 Taft to Gus Karger, 19 June and 30 July 1920: Alpheus Thomas Mason, *William Howard Taft: Chief Justice* (New York: Simon & Schuster, 1965), 138–39; 'Foreward' (23 July 1920) to *Taft Papers on the League*; Colcord, *Great Deception*, p. 124; Taft to Root, 15 and 25 August, 1921: Root Papers.

51 'The Chief Justice Abroad', *ABAJ* 8 (August 1922), 455–6.

52 Taft to Hughes, 21 July 1922; Hughes to Taft, 1 August 1922: NA500. C114/236.

53 A fraction of the documentation is printed in *FRUS* (1923), I. 1–10.

54 James W. Garner to Root, 1 November 1935; Sweetser to Fosdick, 5 November 1935; Fosdick to Newton D. Baker, 18 November 1935: Root Papers.

55 Hudson's biographer is James T. Kenny: see Kenny, 'The Contributions of Manley O. Hudson to Modern International Law and Organization', PhD dissertation, University of Denver, 1976.

56 Moore to Hughes, 27 September and 2 October 1922: NA500. C114/269, 241. This paragraph relies heavily upon the Hudson Papers for October–November 1922. Drummond is the subject of the fine biography by James Barros, *Office without Power: Secretary-General Sir Eric Drummond, 1919–1933* (Oxford: Clarendon Press, 1979).

57 Sweetser to Fosdick, 8 August 1922: Sweetser Papers.

58 These next few paragraphs are based upon two main sources: the Department of State files for August–October 1922: NA500. C114/196–243 and the Hudson Papers for July–November 1922, especially the writings of Attolico, Fosdick, Hammarskjöld, Nielsen, Sweetser, Taft and Hudson himself.

59 Drummond to Cecil, 25 October 1922; van Hamel memo, 12 October 1922; Hudson to Drummond, 1 November 1922: Hudson Papers.

60 Hudson to Cecil, 11 October 1922; to Drummond, 3 November 1922: Hudson Papers; the records of Cecil, Hudson, Phillimore, Root and Taft for July–November 1922 at NA500. C114/236–43; Deibel, 'Struggle for Cooperation', 99.

61 Taft to Root, 15 August and 14 September 1921: Root Papers; Taft to Cecil, 29 September 1922; Root to Taft, 9 September 1922: NA500. C114/237, 236½.

62 Cecil to Taft (late October 1922) in Taft to Hughes, 16 November 1922; Taft to Balfour, 14 September 1922: NA500. C114/240, 236½; Taft to Root, 16 November 1922: Root Papers.

63 Moore to Phillips, 13 September 1922; to Hughes, 2 October 1922: NA500. C114/361, 241; Sweetser to Fosdick, 13 February 1923: Sweetser Papers.

64 Hughes to Taft, 1 August 1922: NA500. C114/236.

65 Hughes to Harding, 6 October 1922; Samuel Colcord to Hughes, 13 April and 20 June 1924: Hughes Papers.

66 Lodge to Hughes, 1 November 1922: Hughes Papers; *NYT* (31 October 1922),

1, 4; Hudson, *The Permanent Court of International Justice and the Question of American Participation*, 208, 239.

[67] Hudson to Drummond, 9 November 1922: Hudson Papers; cf. Colcord to Hughes, 20 June 1924: Hughes Papers.

[68] For Lodge's notorious circumspection: *New York Herald*, 29 April 1923, 1, 2.

[69] Hammarskjöld to Hudson, 6 November 1922: Hudson Papers; Hudson, 'The United States and the New International Court', *Foreign Affairs* 1 (December 1922), 71–82.

[70] Robert A. Schulzinger, *The Wise Men of Foreign Affairs: the History of the Council on Foreign Relations* (New York: Columbia University Press, 1984), does not discuss the CFR's policy on the Court issue.

[71] Hudson to Hughes, 12 and 23 October 1922 and 22 November 1922: NA500. C114/242–4; J. W. Maynard (editor of the *Newark Evening News*) to Harding, 24 October 1922; Hughes to Maynard, 26 October 1922: Hughes Papers; Hudson to Hamilton Fish Armstrong (editor: *Foreign Affairs*), late November 1922; Armstrong to Hudson, 5 December 1922: Hudson Papers.

[72] Wilson to Drummond, 11 January 1923: Deibel, 'League of Nations', p. 389; Sweetser to John Hessin Clarke, 22 January 1923; to Cecil, 24 January 1923; to Fosdick, 13 February 1923; George W. Wickersham to Sweetser, 3 February 1923: Sweetser Papers. See also Wickersham, 'The Senate and our Foreign Relations', *Foreign Affairs* 2 (December 1923), 177–92. Wickersham was one of the Republican 31, prominent in the CFR and hostile to the two-thirds rule. Clarke had resigned from the US Supreme Court to campaign for the PCIJ.

[73] Moore to Huber, 31 March 1923; Sweetser to Hammarskjöld, 16 March 1923: Moore Papers.

[74] Moore to Huber, 31 March 1923: Moore Papers; *NYT*, 25 February 1923, 1, 2.

[75] Hughes, 'The Separate Peace with Germany, the League of Nations, and the Permanent Court of International Justice' (part of the Beerits Memoranda), 35a–35b: Hughes Papers.

[76] Hughes to Harding, 12 February 1923: Harding Papers; Hughes to Harding, 17 February 1923: NA500. C114/225a.

[77] Borah to Johnson, 24 August and (December) 1921: Hiram Warren Johnson Papers, Bancroft Library, University of California at Berkeley. Albert B. Fall, another Irreconcilable and now Harding's Secretary of the Interior, spoke likewise: Buckley, *United States and the Washington Conference*, 172.

[78] The literature is detailed in LeRoy Ashby, *The Spearless Leader: Senator Borah and the Progressive Movement in the 1920's* (Urbana and London: University of Illinois Press, 1972). It was, of course, Johnson who nicknamed Borah so disdainfully.

[79] William Allen White to Root, 22 March 1922; Harding to Root, 29 September 1922: Root Papers.

[80] The contemporary literature on Borah is enormous–and more helpful than any of his biographers except Claudius O. Johnson in his original 1936 study: *Borah of Idaho*, with a new Introduction by the author (Seattle and London: University of Washington Press, 1967). Borah's Papers are in the MD, LC.

[81] Charles W. Wood, *Collier's*, 28 October 1922, 7, 26–7; ibid., 9 December 1922, 15.

[82] Johnson, *Borah of Idaho*, chs 14 and 15; Robert James Maddox, *William E. Borah and American Foreign Policy* (Baton Rouge: Louisiana State University Press, 1969), chs 5 and 6. The Foreign Policy Association (FPA) had recently changed from being the League of Free Nations Association.

[83] S. Res. 441, Sixty-seventh Congress, Fourth Session: *CR* 67:4, 3605. A text is

printed in Johnson, *Borah of Idaho*, 392–4.

84 John Chalmers Vinson, *William E. Borah and the Outlawry of War* (Athens: University of Georgia Press, 1957). 'Outlaw[ing] war' was a potential electoral issue already in mid 1922: A. Lawrence Lowell to Hughes, 24 June 1922: Harding Papers. Lowell, President of Harvard, was another of the 31 Republicans.

85 Edwin M. Borchard (Professor of International Law at Yale) address to Academy of Political Science, New York, May 1923: reprinted in *CR* 68:1 1076–80; Moore to Senator Thomas J. Walsh, 19 January 1926: Moore Papers.

86 Borah's line of reasoning can be found in David Jayne Hill, *Problem of a World Court*; Kellor and Hatvany, *United States Senate and the International Court*; and Giblin and Brown, *The World Court Myth*.

87 Dulles and Howland to Hughes, 12 February 1923, enclosing 'An Opinion with Respect to Acceptance by the United States of the Permanent Court of International Justice: 'NA500. C114/246.

88 Hughes to Harding, 17 Feburary 1923: NA500. C114/225a (*FRUS*, 1923, I. 10–17).

89 Harding to Wellman, 5 March 1923: Harding Paper.

90 Harding to the Senate, 24 February 1923: NA500. C114/219a (*FRUS*, 1923, I. 17–18.)

4 The most intimate connection: the Court, the League and the advisory jurisdiction, 1922–25

Secretary Hughes's brief of 17 February had been very much his own composition, drafted during a bout of illness when he was absent from the Department. Nevertheless he was confident that his arguments would put the Harding administration in 'an impregnable position' by conciliating the vocal proponents of adherence and rebutting the critics. Within a fortnight Hughes was back at the Department and now working closely with his legal advisers to answer a set of detailed questions from the Senate Committee on Foreign Relations, which had taken charge of the Protocol. The questions had been framed by Borah and were primarily concerned with the Court's compulsory jurisdiction under the Optional Clause (Court Statute: Article 36). Privately Hughes described the questions as disingenuous and diversionary: it was ridiculous, he wrote to Harding, even to contemplate the Senate's agreeing to compulsory jurisdiction. After all, under the three previous Republican presidents the Senate had repeatedly rejected even 'limited' forms of 'compulsory adjudication'. (The terms were used interchangeably.) Nevertheless Hughes knew that his Department must appear fully informed and certainly not offhand towards the Senate. Consequently the questions from the Committee were answered promptly and exhaustively to the effect that the administration had no intention of signing the Optional Clause. Harding was well pleased. The submission of the Protocol had produced a universally 'favorable… newspaper reaction'; and Hughes's speedy, courteous and irrefutable response to the Foreign Relations Committee had 'put the administration in a position of advantage'.[1]

Shortly afterwards Hughes sent copies of the documents to Judge Moore at The Hague. Hughes did not apologize for the Protocol's late appearance on the Senate calendar. Rather it was a 'decided advantage', since it would allow 'all pertinent questions [to] find… expression.' Moore agreed. To his mind, however, the really worrisome and 'rather strange' fact was that the submission of the Court Protocol had 'revived the "League issue"…'. This could be attributed, Moore suggested somewhat obliquely, to the lack of logic in public life, even in the elite circles represented by such bodies as the Council on Foreign Relations. To Max Huber, however, his friend and fellow judge, Moore spoke more directly and prophetically:

> The principal danger in the present situation is the tendency to link or identify the question of adhesion to the Court with that of the acceptance of the League, and I do not hesitate to say that unless the two questions can be kept separate the United States will not adhere to the Court.[2]

A fortnight after the submission of the Court Protocol Moore had written to Arthur Sweetser that Secretary Hughes's proposed conditions and procedures closely corresponded to those suggested by Hudson in his December *Foreign Affairs* article. In this way Moore minimized his own responsibility and thus disclaimed the credit that Hudson was ready to extend to him.[3] Yet Hudson appeared just the kind of advocate that Moore so deplored, the sort of lobbyist who would wreck the chances of adherence.

A fine example of Hudson's actions and attitude comes from the record of William R. Castle, Jr. For over a decade Castle was the Department of State official most closely connected with the Court issue: first, in 1921–7, as Chief of the Division of Western European Affairs (the section dealing with League and Court matters); later, in 1927–33, as Assistant and then subsequently Under Secretary of State, when he maintained his initial interest. Castle began as a restrained supporter of adherence to the Court; later he became somewhat disillusioned and certainly sceptical of its value. He also grew decidedly impatient with most of the lobbyists for the Court, believing them to be both indulgent towards the League and ignorant of its role in (mainly) European politics; and there was, as a simple, practical matter, the sheer volume of legislative and executive energy and time consumed by the Court issue. Yet throughout all the period of his service in the Department and despite his changing feelings Castle remained an acute and well-informed observer: of the League, of the Court, of Congress and of domestic opinion in the United States. He did not exercise undue influence upon his superiors: in this sense he did play an ancilliary role. But his instincts were sure; and he himself personified a decided cooling among career officers in the Department during the Harding–Hoover years towards American adherence to the World Court.[4]

Castle came into contact with Hudson through their Harvard connections, a link they shared with William Phillips. In May 1923 Castle wrote to Phillips of the damage Hudson was doing to the cause of adherence by his unrestrained and very public campaigning. The man was 'more or less cracked... on American adherence to the League,' Castle explained; and though he had himself warned Hudson that he was 'injuring the chances of taking part in the... Court by insisting everywhere that this really meant joining the League of Nations itself', he very much doubted whether Hudson would ever 'stop his mouth', even though the culprit agreed 'theoretically' with Castle's criticisms.[5]

Only a day or so after the publication of Hughes's letter to Harding, Hudson had written joyously to Moore: 'At last we have opened the casket.'[6] By the end of spring 1923 it might appear to Moore something of a hornets' nest. Lord Robert Cecil was at that moment conducting a crowded lecture-tour of the United States and in numerous speeches he was treating the question of American entry into the Permanent Court of International Justice as purely subordinate to the larger interests of the League.[7]

In the late winter and early spring of 1923 President Harding was complaisant towards Hughes and Hoover, two of the most authoritative figures in his cabinet, advocates of the Court and once declared if qualified proponents of the League. Harding needed their prestige to ward off the attacks on the scandals of his administration. But other members of the cabinet were against joining the Court, let alone moving any closer to the League. These men were Secretary of the Treasury Andrew W. Mellon; Attorney General Harry M. Daugherty; Secretary of War John W. Weeks; Secretary of the Navy Edwin Denby; Secretary of the Interior Albert B. Fall; and Secretary of Labor, James J. Davis. Outside the Executive a number of influential regular and irregular Republicans were equally hostile to the Court as a staging-post to the League; and if Harding was not to be dumped or deserted in the 1924 election campaign he needed to satisfy both sets of opposing forces.[8]

This was the political setting in late April 1923, when Harding took the opportunity of an address to the Associated Press in New York to discuss international relations. His explicit theme was the distinction between the League and the Court; his major purpose was to unite the Republican party. Certainly, he declared, his administration supported adherence to the Court, but this was only the logical outcome of years, even decades of Republican internationalist thinking. As for the League, that had been overwhelmingly rejected by the electorate in 1920, when the Republicans had won on their unequivocal platform. That victory had 'definitely and decisively' closed the issue; and said Harding (in a favourite phrase), his administration had no intention to enter the League 'by the side door, the back door, or the cellar door'. The administration's goal was clear and limited; the method of approach was to be one of moderation. Harding's was the middle way and he deprecated 'unfounded hopes... [and] unjustifiable apprehensions...'.

Excessive friends of the League have beclouded the situation by their unwarranted assumption that it is a move toward League membership. Let them disabuse their minds, because there is no such thought among us who must make our commitments abroad. And the situation is likewise beclouded by those who shudder excessively when the League is mentioned, and who assume entanglement is unavoidable.[9]

Some weeks before Harding's New York speech Herbert Hoover had strongly argued for the Court in a well-publicized address delivered in Des Moines, Iowa. Only days after Harding spoke Hughes and Root used the annual meeting of the American Society of International Law in Washington to urge ratification of the Court Protocol. But in partisan terms all these speeches were counter-productive, since they raised the spectre of eventual League membership despite the explicit denials of such an outcome. Leading Irregulars such as Borah, La Follette and Johnson were dissatisfied; so too were senatorial Regulars such as Moses, James E. Watson of Indiana and, most importantly, Lodge. Outside Congress the Republican National Committee was increasingly worried that the Court issue would further split an already divided party.[10] Harding's efforts at unification had clearly failed. He could not successfully straddle the gap existing between Hughes, Hoover and Root on one side and the broad range of political forces represented by Borah and Lodge. By mid May this opposition had become so effective that Harding began to withdraw from the terms he had endorsed at the end of February, terms which had already become known as the Hughes–Harding conditions.

For some weeks Harding's retreat was performed privately, in response to particular pieces of lobbying. It was not until 21 June, in St Louis, Missouri, that Harding publicized his official retraction of the Hughes–Harding conditions. Circumstantial evidence suggests he was acknowledging the growing influence of Borah in the anti-Court campaign – a campaign whose first fear and enemy was the League of Nations. This campaign was gaining ground in the Middle West, particularly in the States of the Upper Mississippi Valley.[11] The recantation itself was apparently drafted with the help of George Harvey, James Brown Scott and another former Solicitor in the Department of State, J. Reuben Clark, Jr. – though Clark had little fondness for Scott personally.[12] Yet for all these men's efforts, Harding's speech was characteristically his own: superficially ambiguous, if not flatly self-contradictory; unmistakable in substance and intent.

In the St Louis speech Harding repeated his familiar analysis of the 1920 election, but his language was now sarcastic.

[B]y an overwhelming majority, the people rejected the proposal of the administration then in power to incorporate the United States in the League of Nations. To assert that those 16,000,000 voters did not know what they were doing is to insult their intelligence, and to deny the facts. Whatever other considerations may have influenced their judgment were purely incidental. The paramount issue, boldly, defiantly advanced in unmistakable terms by the Democratic Party and espoused by the Democratic candidate for President was indorsement of the demand of the then Democratic President.

Partisanship was obviously an element in Harding's rhetoric; but it would be an ignorant or very obtuse observer who failed to detect Harding distancing himself from Hughes, Hoover, Root and the other Thirty-One Republicans of the October 1920 Declaration – a point made forcefully by Samuel Colcord to Hughes and Hoover themselves.[13] Moreover Harding had already begun the retreat from the conditions he had approved in February. As he sketched the separation:

Though I firmly believe we could adhere to the court protocol, with becoming reservation, and be free from every possible obligation to the league, I would frankly prefer the court's complete independence of the league.

Earlier in the speech Harding had stated the two 'indispensable' conditions for American adherence:

First, that the tribunal be so constituted as to appear and to be, in theory and in practice, in form and in substance, beyond the shadow of doubt, a world court and not a league court.

Second, that the United States shall occupy a plane of perfect equality with every other power.

The first condition had not been specified in either February or April. Then the issue had been whether the relationship of the Court to the League harmed the Court and threatened the United States; but the relationship itself had been taken as given. The second condition was a veiled but hostile reference to the voting power of the British Empire – a vexed subject, undoubtedly, and one which agitated Lodge; but also one which had been handled graciously by both Hughes and Root in their own April speeches.[14] (The grievance had, of course, surfaced in the Senate debates on the Covenant and was the nub of the Fourteenth Reservation in both the November 1919 and March 1920 votes.)

From one side of his mouth Harding praised the 'abstract principle of a world court' and its 'concrete application... by the League'. He spoke as though 'its integrity, its independence, its complete and continuing freedom' were already established. The United States could, therefore, join with the appropriate conditions set forth in February. From the other side of his mouth Harding denied he was 'wedded irrevocably to any particular method' of adherence and suggested a fundamental reorganization of the Court itself 'as a basis for consideration, discussion, and judgment'.

Harding specified 'without excess of detail' four areas for reform, three of which were directed against the League itself, the fourth against a major League Power. First, the League should no longer elect the Court's bench, the role of Council and Assembly being replaced either by the judges themselves filling vacancies or by the Court's Signatories. Similarly financial responsibility for the Court should be transferred directly to the Signatories or to the Permanent Court of

Arbitration. Thirdly the League's 'exclusive privilege' of requesting advisory opinions should be ended, either through extension to other bodies or by abolishing the jurisdiction completely. Finally the power of the British Empire in the Assembly should be drastically reduced, on the principle that there should be no 'disparity in voting as between a unit nation and an aggregated empire'. These suggestions, Harding concluded, were the 'outline of the basis' on which he proposed, with the Senate's consent, 'to initiate negotiations with the powers which have associated themselves with the Permanent Court of International Justice'.[15]

Hughes's reaction to Harding's St Louis speech is difficult to discover but not hard to imagine. His own Papers contain no record of his impressions; the Department of State files are silent; the standard, rather indulgent biographers of Hughes have avoided the episode. Small wonder that Hughes increased his reputation as being a political trimmer.[16] It strains credulity to suggest that Hughes did not feel personally offended or professionally discouraged at Harding's rejection of his and the Department's efforts. Moreover, even if Hughes was magnanimous enough to accept Harding's disingenuous volte-face for simple partisan and electoral reasons, the operation itself had not been entirely successful. Johnson and Borah expressed differing degrees of dissatisfaction – as did the Hearst press, which usually acted as a Democratic counterweight to the many Democratic Senators who deplored Harding's pliability in the hands of the Republican Irreconcilables.[17] Abroad it was obvious that neither the League nor the Court would entertain Harding's four new conditions for a moment. As Hudson himself told the State Bar in Missouri later in the year:

> President Harding's [St Louis] address was greeted with utter coldness in European countries, and no disposition appeared on the part of the other governments to meet any of his proposals half way.

Not the least reason for this foreign reaction was that observers in the League understood that Harding's main purpose was to appease impossible demands from within his own party.[18]

President Harding's speech at St Louis was his first major engagement in a scheduled 15,000 mile, two-month 'Voyage of Understanding'.[19] He was trying to gain favourable public exposure and mend political fences in the West. His thoughts were fixed on the coming election year: something had to be done to cover the mess in Washington. His control over Congress was minimal and the scandals emanating from the White House were widely publicized. Yet six weeks after speaking at St Louis, Harding collapsed and died in San Francisco.

Vice-President Calvin Coolidge succeeded to Harding's office. Almost immediately he was presented with evidence of the strong Republican opposition to proceeding with the World Court Protocols on the terms sponsored by Secretary Hughes in February: the Hughes–Harding terms, as they were still called. The objections came from members of the cabinet, the Senate, the Republican National Committee and even farther afield.[20] Nevertheless Coolidge decided to seek further advice: after all, there were political pressures on the other side in favour of adherence. Not the least among these was the existence of vocal and powerful lobby-groups, notably the Foreign Policy Association (FPA), the World Peace Foundation (WPF) and, above all, the League of Nations Non-Partisan Association (LNNPA).[21]

On John Bassett Moore's autumnal return to the United States he was invited to the White House for lengthy discussions with Coolidge. Moore was delighted with the interviews: Coolidge had questioned him carefully and apparently without prejudice. Moore was impressed by Coolidge's resolution and principle: he was not a man like Harding to 'straddle' the question of adherence.[22] Yet Coolidge was also in touch with George Harvey. The truth seems to be that Coolidge, unlike Harding and without the legacy of the 1920 campaign, was confident he could promote adherence to the Court without increasing Republican divisions – but he would not pursue the former at the risk of the latter. Consequently Coolidge was able to listen to both sides (Moore, after all, was against American membership of the League) without arousing the suspicion of either.[23] Finally and most importantly for Moore, Coolidge shared Moore's opinion that American membership would contribute to the independence and authority of the Court – a goal of Moore's which was becoming increasingly irksome to influential figures in the League – and even, as we shall see, to some of his colleagues on the Court bench.[24]

Throughout the summer and autumn of 1923 the Department of State received thousands of letters from individuals concerning the Court Protocol. William Castle monitored this incoming correspondence; and in late November he calculated there had 'been perhaps four letters opposing the Court'. The miniscule opposition surprised Castle no less than it undoubtedly surprises historians; but Castle was more struck by the tone and substance of the support. 'Contrary to the insinuations' in the anti-League press, 'practically none of these [thousands of] letters [had] anything to say of the League in its connection with the World Court'. These words were written to Secretary Hughes, whom Castle was briefing on the electoral significance of the correspondence. There appeared to be no region of the nation which did not provide written testimony of support. Certain States however were particularly prominent: New York, Massachusetts and Connecticut in the North East; Michigan, Indiana and Iowa in the Middle West; and California on the Pacific coast. This was encouraging: there seemed to be no electoral risk in the administration's programme.[25]

Yet despite the concern of the Department to keep pace with effective public opinion, Castle's own actions both betrayed the embarrassment caused by Harding's retraction in June and pointed to the dangers of departmental reluctance to engage in a full debate on the terms and implications of adherence. The paradoxical result was that the Department appeared to endorse the ulterior schemes of pro-League lobbyists, the very situation Castle himself deprecated. The classic example is provided by Castle's response to questions from the public on the origins, organization and purposes of the World Court. Since Harding's St Louis speech had cut the ground from under Hughes's arguments of February and April 1923, Castle generally referred such detailed enquiries to the World Peace Foundation. This was an organization based in Boston, which published and distributed a great deal of literature on the Court and in support of American adherence. More pertinently, however, the Foundation was a strong advocate of American membership of the League of Nations and acted as its official documentary agency in the United States.[26] Castle's dilemma was acute; and it would not be resolved until Coolidge publicly endorsed the position advanced by Secretary Hughes in February and thereby repaired the damage done by Harding's June St Louis speech.

Coolidge did not delay long. In his first Annual Message delivered in December 1923 he 'commend [ed the Court Protocol] to the favorable consideration of the Senate with the proposed reservations', i.e. the original Hughes–Harding February conditions. Moore was delighted and felt his confidence in Coolidge had been vindicated. As he wrote to Huber: Coolidge's 'unequivocal declaration' had been 'characteristic' of the new President's 'precision'.[27] Meanwhile William King (Utah, Democrat) moved speedily to commit the Senate to the Hughes–Harding conditions – but not speedily enough to anticipate Senator Irvine Lenroot (Wisconsin, Republican). The latter's resolution proposed adherence on the base lines drawn by Harding at St Louis: the elimination of all links between the League of Nations and the Permanent Court of International Justice.[28] The key provision of Lenroot's resolution concerned elections to the Court bench. These were now to be conducted by all the signatory States through their diplomatic representatives at The Hague. Nevertheless the principle of concurrent elections by overlapping colleges was to be maintained. In Lenroot's new arrangement the League Assembly's role would be performed by all the signatory States, designated 'Group B'. Lenroot's 'Group A', corresponding to the League Council, would comprise 'the British Empire, France, the United States, Italy, Japan, Germany, and Brazil'.

In 1919–20 Lenroot had been a mild Reservationist in the debates on the Treaty of Versailles and the League of Nations. His present resolution was in keeping with that earlier position – though James G. McDonald of the Foreign Policy Association described Lenroot's action as a 'stab' from the 'Irreconcilables'.[29] German power and prestige were to be recognized in the substitute Council of Group A; and the voting power of the British Empire was to be reduced from six to one in the substitute Assembly of Group B. As for Brazil, she was the South American state *par excellence* in the League and Court. Neglect of her demands and pretensions would hasten the erosion of South American support for the Court – a possibility always feared by Judge Moore, not least for the implication that the Court was an 'old world' institution, different from and even hostile to the 'new'.[30]

Senator King's attempt in December 1923 to commit the Senate of the Sixty-eighth Congress to the Hughes–Harding terms was a repetition of his efforts in the previous February. Immediately after President

Harding submitted the Court Protocol to the Senate King had introduced resolutions to begin the legislative process. King appealed to Harding's public assertion that prompt senatorial consent was both appropriate and uncontentious. Lodge disagreed; and the Senate by a substantial majority supported Lodge's judgment. The Protocol must wait until the convening of the next Congress, i.e. until December 1923. King denounced the vote as partisan; yet even if the charge was justified, King and his fellow Democrats did nothing for five months after the assembly of the Sixty-eighth Congress towards legislative action on the Court Protocols. His and Lenroot's resolutions lay unexamined before the Committee on Foreign Relations until early May 1924. Then Claude A. Swanson, Senior Senator from Virginia and ranking member of the minority Democrats on the Committee, introduced a revised version of the King resolutions, in which the four 'conditions and understandings' specified by Secretary Hughes in February 1923 were repeated *verbatim*.[31]

Swanson's resolution of 6 May 1924 concluded the first stage of the Senate's progress towards approving the Hughes–Harding conditions. King's proposals dropped from the agenda. Indeed his subsequent behaviour exposed the shallowness of his charges of partisanship and obstructionism; for he himself swung away from the League–Department of State terms and towards the initial position of Lenroot.[32] Outside the Senate there were other signs of the bipartisanship common to proponents and opponents of adherence. In fact, the most spectacular had been a prelude to Swanson's resolution. On 30 April and 1 May more than forty pro-Court organizations and over fifty individuals had testified before a special subcommittee of the Foreign Relations Committee. The lobbyists were pleased with the impression they gave; and historians have marked the Hearings down as a great publicity success. But Judge Moore was less sure: the pro-League arguments of leading witnesses such as Taft's Attorney General George W. Wickersham, former Supreme Court Justice John H. Clarke and Manley Hudson, rendered them all, in Moore's words, 'unconscious... enemies of the Court'.[33]

Swanson would not have objected to the long-term goals of these advocates: he had himself been prominent in the fight for unconditional ratification of the Treaty of Versailles. (Swanson's leader in the Treaty fight, President Wilson, died in February 1924; and, true to 1919–20, Wilson deprecated the addition of a single condition to American acceptance of the Court Protocol.)[34] But the mood of the Foreign Relations Committee was different. Two days after Swanson submitted his resolution, Lodge proposed congressional legislation to sponsor a 'third Hague conference for the establishment of a World Court of International Justice'. Lodge was not content with a mere formula. Instead he submitted his own draft statute for such a court (S.J. Res. 122) comprising sixty-seven articles. Lodge had not worked alone. Among his collaborators was Chandler P. Anderson, Counselor in the Department of State when Knox had been Taft's Secretary of State, and still one of the most influential lawyers in the regular, conservative wing of the

Republican party. Lodge's other main helper was James Brown Scott, Root's disillusioned assistant on the 1920 Advisory Committee of Jurists.[35]

Lodge's resolution was technically a bill, requiring action and a simple majority vote in both Houses of Congress, followed by presidential signing. Perhaps its form and timing were sufficient grounds for its contemporary dismissal as a subterfuge: 'a red herring across the trail that leads to acceptance' of the Court Protocol. Senator King himself denounced the scheme as a 'torpedo'.[36] But such a charge could scarcely be brought against King's Democratic colleague, Thomas J. Walsh, the Senior Senator from Montana, and another leading proponent of the Treaty of Versailles and American membership of the League of Nations. The day after the Swanson resolution came before the Committee, Walsh proposed a fifth reservation to be added to the Hughes–Harding conditions. It concerned the Court's advisory jurisdiction, one of the subjects criticized by Harding in his St Louis speech and by now the focus of much anti-Court sentiment. Walsh's amendment ran:

> The United States shall be in no manner bound by any advisory opinion of the Permanent Court of International Justice not rendered pursuant to a request in which it, the United States, shall expressly join in accordance with the statute for the said Court adjoined to the protocol of signature of the same to which the United States shall become signatory.[37]

Walsh's language was inaccurate as well as tortuous. For example, the reservation suggested both that the Statute provided explicitly for an advisory function and that States were 'bound' by such advisory opinions. Neither was technically the case. Nevertheless, the Committee (for reasons we shall examine) adopted it unanimously and appended it to Swanson's resolution. Even so the revised resolution failed before the Committee. In the course of four days' discussions it was rejected by a vote of 10:8, Lenroot being the only Republican to support Swanson. Lenroot had indeed modified his initial opposition to the League's acting as the dual electoral college, but not to the multiple vote of the British Empire. In Committee Lenroot moved a compromise amendment along these lines, but found himself once again in a minority with the Democrats.[38]

The resolution eventually approved by the Committee on Foreign Relations and reported to the full Senate echoed Lenroot's December resolution but its actual author was George Wharton Pepper, the Republican Senior Senator from Pennsylvania. Pepper had introduced his proposals in response to Swanson's initiative; and their timing and success were both a sign and a result of the authority he had established during the brief five months he had served on the Committee. (Pepper had chaired the spring subcommittee Hearings.)[39]

Swanson and his allies described the Pepper resolution as a piece of 'unconcealed enmity', a 'studied affront' to the League of Nations.[40] The charge was not surprising; for Pepper had come to public prominence in 1919 as a leader in the anti-Wilson, anti-Covenant, League for the

Preservation of American Independence. Furthermore, the language of Pepper's resolution stopped any rebuttal. As Pepper himself insisted: the Senate should advise and consent to ratification of the Court Protocol only if they could achieve 'the disassociation of the Court from the League of Nations'. To an even greater extent than Lenroot in December and in a clearer manner than Harding at St Louis, Pepper (supported by the majority of the Committee) proposed the creation of a new court, modelled on the PCIJ but so totally 'disassociat[ed] from the League... as would make [it] a complete and independent international institution' and thus able to survive 'absolutely unaffected by [the] discredit or... dissolution' of the parent League.

That Pepper's plan of 'disassociation' was attached to a resolution formally requesting senatorial approval of the existing Court Statute was only one of many contradictions and paradoxes. A second lay in the revival of Lenroot's original electoral-college scheme. But whereas Lenroot had merely alluded to the League Council in his scheme for 'Group A', Pepper now boldly if somewhat disingenuously described the composition of his upper chamber in language drawn from the Treaty of Versailles. A third surprise came in the selective citing of long passages from the Secretary of State's April 1923 speech (the eloquent address to the American Society of International Law), in which Hughes had praised the Court and justified American adherence.[41].

Such idiosyncrasies were the side of Pepper which dazzled some observers by their brilliance – and which worried Judge Moore: perhaps Pepper was essentially a superficial legislator who could not be trusted? Certainly Hudson's earlier expectations of Pepper's goodwill had been disappointed.[42] Time would tell. But the catalogue of Pepper's conditions and reservations has not been completed. A number of provisions paralleled Lodge's recent bill, the most obvious from a varied list being the explicit reservation of the Monroe Doctrine from the Court's jurisdiction and the reduction of British voting power to a single unit. One more must be given; for it showed a common concern of Pepper, Lodge, Swanson and Walsh. The first clause of the fifth paragraph of Pepper's resolution stated:

> That the signature of the United States of America shall be understood to be affixed subject to the declaration that the United States disclaims all responsibility for the exercise by the court of the jurisdiction to render advisory opinions....

The explanation for the Committee's unanimous and intensified disquiet at the advisory jurisdiction is to be found in the actions of the Court and League in 1922 and 1923. Later, in 1925 and on the eve of the Senate debate of the Protocol, the issue would be revived in ominous circumstances. It will be more convenient to examine these events after completing our present analysis of proceedings in the Senate. The subject of the advisory jurisdiction was raised by the Senate in the spring of 1924 virtually without introduction. It then remained in abeyance for nearly a year and a half. Consequently our narrative will not be distorted if we first survey briefly the election campaign of 1924 and the lame-duck Session of the Sixty-eighth Congress before we turn to address at some length the complex jurisprudential and political background to the Senators' agreement to limit the scope of the Court's advisory role.

When Senator King had originally complained of the partisan opposition to his legislative proposals, he conveniently ignored the equally partisan support he had received from his fellow Democrats.[43] (In Committee the voting was distinctly partisan, with only Lenroot occasionally voting with the Democrats.) Such countervalence does not disprove, of course, his contention; rather it corroborates it in a circuitous way. However, he himself was backing a proposal of the Republican administration; and a more accurate analysis would have spoken of the congressional Democrats and their party establishment overwhelmingly endorsing American membership of the World Court on the Hughes–Harding terms; while the Republicans were deeply divided on the issue, with the Senate and irregular forces outside Congress generally opposed to adherence.

In April 1924 these intra-party divisions led a group of Republican women from Minneapolis (where the State Republican party was split on the related League-Court issues) to pose a direct question to Secretary Hughes: 'Does the Republican Party stand for a World Court or not?' The phrasing was, of course, ambiguous. As we have seen, Lodge had managed to stand on such a shaky platform when campaigning in 1922. But the Department of State did not enter directly into such subtleties. Instead it offered its own implicitly confusing answer by despatching texts of speeches by Hughes and Coolidge, but not Harding's notorious St Louis address, which had been the intellectual precursor of the schemes introduced into the Senate by the Republicans Lenroot, Lodge and Pepper.[44] At most the Department's reply answered affirmatively in respect of the administration. But if anyone had drawn broader inferences they should have been quickly qualified by the acrimonious and public argument between the pro-Court Wickersham and the anti-Court Anderson, which filled a number of columns in the mid May editions of the *New York Times*.[45]

A historian of the Permanent Court of International Justice must admit frankly that the Republican party had more pressing concerns on its collective mind in the summer of 1924 than the question of American adherence. One of the most serious was the possibility of Coolidge's being dumped at the June convention in Cleveland. His place at the head of the Republican ticket could then go to an Insurgent: a man such as Hiram Johnson, Robert La Follette, Gifford Pinchot, Governor of Pennsylvania – perhaps even Borah. In the event, Coolidge was easily renominated, with General Charles G. Dawes as his surprising running-mate. (Coolidge had initially hoped for a progressive Westerner.) Thereupon much of the insurgent energy in the Republican party was transferred to the independent campaign of the Conference for

Progressive Political Action (CPPA), which La Follette came to lead.[46]

The relatively brief La Follette platform ignored the Court while calling for revision of the Treaty of Versailles. The Republican platform repeated its 1920 rejection of the League but supported American membership of the Court 'as recommended by President Coolidge'. Whether this phraseology referred to Coolidge's recent implicit approval of the revised Swanson resolution or was simply a blank cheque for future engrossing was unclear – and consequently extremely shrewd. Once again the Republicans had Elihu Root to thank for some skilful drafting. Yet this much was obvious, even behind the ambiguities. As in 1920, so in 1924: the Republicans distinguished the Court from the League and conditionally supported the former while denouncing the latter.[47]

The Democratic Party platform of 1924 was by far the longest of the election manifestos. This was one reflection of the internecine struggle at the New York City convention, where John W. Davis and Charles W. Bryan were eventually chosen as presidential and vice-presidential candidates, with the former representing (in part) pro-League, pro-Court interests. (Davis, who had served under Wilson, first as Solicitor General and later Ambassador in London, was on the governing councils of numerous foreign-policy lobby groups.) The plank on the League was itself extensive. In it the Democrats

> renew [ed their] declarations of confidence in the idea of world peace, the league of nations and the world court of justice as together constituting the supreme effort of the statesmanship and religious conviction of our time to organize the world of peace.

This was grandiloquent, noble in sentiment – and even dull minds would see the close identification of Court and League. Nevertheless the journey from Court to League would not be immediate; not the 'back door', as some fearfully said. On the League, at least, the Democrats proposed to hold a special

> referendum election, advisory to the government [and] free from all other questions and candidacies [on the question whether the United States should] become a member of the league of nations upon such reservations or amendments to the convenant of the league as the president and the senate of the United States may agree upon.[48]

This plank was clearly a compromise bound up with a federal constitutional innovation. But it was no less worthy for that. It fairly stated the broad goals of the party while acknowledging political disagreements, constitutional proprieties and legislative impediments. For the historian of the Court Protocol, however, the main lesson of the party conventions in 1924 is unmistakable. American membership of the PCIJ was an objective, more or less qualified, of both major parties, and one which was shared or simply ignored by the third and minor parties.

The national elections of November 1924 returned Coolidge to the

White House and Republican majorities in Congress. Coolidge won nearly 16 million popular votes (54% of the total) and 382 electoral college votes; Davis polled nearly 8.4 million (29%) and 136 college votes; La Follette nearly 5 million (16%) and the thirteen electoral votes of his home-State, Wisconsin. La Follette and the Progessives were not disgraced: they had run second in eleven States and polled the highest third-party percentage of the popular vote since 1860 – excluding the Taft–Roosevelt split in 1912. (Taft was so scarred by the 1912 Bull Moose campaign that in 1924 he feared the Republicans would lose *every* State west of the Mississippi!)[49] But so far as the Court Protocol was concerned, the elections had meant 'little'. So Hudson correctly evaluated their significance in a letter to a friend and compatriot in the League Secretariat, Huntington Gilchrist – the latter having himself predicted exactly such an outcome in the aftermath of Harding's St Louis speech.[50] Indeed from the time of Swanson's resolution in early May until the assembling of the Second, lame-duck Session of the Sixty-eighth Congress in December, scarcely anything had happened to attract public attention to the Court. Nevertheless, a number of discrete and heterogeneous events took place which combined to shape the direction of Senate actions.

The first concerned the behaviour of Lenroot and Pepper, both of whom appeared to move close to Swanson's position. Lenroot, of course, had begun his shift earlier in the year; but by the autumn it was pronounced and he was depicted collaborating with Swanson.[51] Pepper was more guarded; but the process seemed underway – though the evidence is more circumstantial and will be discussed in the next chapter. Secondly, on 9 November (less than a week after the elections) Henry Cabot Lodge died; and in the new Session Borah was confirmed as his successor in the Chair of the Committee on Foreign Relations. There were two rather different public consequences of Borah's promotion. The more important, short-term result was to emphasize the disagreements between the Republican administration and its nominal supporters in the Senate over foreign policy.[52] The other was Borah's unsolicited recruitment of one of the sharpest minds in contemporary international law. For not long after Lodge's death, Edwin Borchard of Yale placed himself 'unreservedly at [Borah's] disposal' as his legal counsel. (Borchard was a close friend of Moore's, having studied under him at Columbia and worked as his Assistant Solicitor in the Department of State.)[53] A third item came with the President's December Annual Message, when Coolidge clarified the Republican platform by endorsing the four Hughes–Harding reservations to the Court Protocol and aligning his administration with the spirit if not the letter of the fifth or Walsh reservation governing the advisory jurisdiction. Coolidge rephrased and shortened the reservation to read:

> our country shall not be bound by advisory opinions which may be rendered by the court upon questions which we have not voluntarily submitted for its judgment.[54]

The fourth event in this disparate calendar came to light only after the opening of the Session – but its reverberations have continued into the most recent historiography. At issue was the agreement struck between the proponents of Swanson's resolution, the regular Republican leadership and the newly installed chairman of the Foreign Relations Committee that the Court Protocol should be kept off the Senate agenda during the lame-duck period. Effectively this meant that no substantive proceedings towards approval would take place before March 1925 – or, more likely, not before December 1925. Contemporary and retrospective criticism of Borah and the Committee monopolizes the historical record. [55] But it is clear that the proclaimed champions of the Court were following the path begun by Hughes and Root in 1921 and continued by Harding in February 1923 before he defected. Indeed Hughes's timing in the winter of 1922–3 virtually guaranteed no action until 1925; and Hudson had privately told both Court and League officials that the opening of 1926 was the earliest likely date for serious legislative proceedings.[56] Furthermore, the actions of Borah's adversaries would soon show that his responsibility for postponement was one they shared in fact while avoiding the odium in public.

The Second Session of the Sixty-eighth Congress convened on Monday, 1 December 1924. The Republicans were in a majority, not because of their successes in the recent elections but as a legacy of the turbulent elections held in 1922. Yet this was a 'shadow majority' (the phrase of one informed analyst); and there was little likelihood of 'any effective leadership from the White House ...'.[57] On one issue, however, there was agreement between the Republican and Democratic leaders: the Court Protocol would not be debated, much less put to a vote. The decision did not please or bind Henrik Shipstead, a Farmer–Labor Senator from the radical wing of Minnesota politics. He had been elected in 1922 by defeating the regular Republican Senator and 'mild Reservationist', Frank B. Kellogg; had taken his seat in 1923; and was then immediately appointed to the Committee on Foreign Relations – a testimony both to his drive and to his acceptability to Republicans such as Lodge, Pepper, Borah and Johnson. Shipstead became perhaps the most imaginative and profound critic of American adherence; but the public proof of that was to come later. In the winter of 1924–5 his concern was rather more for a gesture. He reminded the Senate that the Pepper proposals were still on the calendar; and he threatened to force a direct vote. Once again King of Utah intervened – though now to speak for postponement. The Democratic and Republican floor leaders supported King; and there was no further Senate action on the Protocol before the Session closed on Tuesday, 3 March 1925.[58]

In the House of Representatives the mood was different and valuable legislative time was not at risk. Early in February the veteran legislator, Theodore E. Burton of Ohio, introduced a motion endorsing American membership of the Court on the Hughes–Harding–Coolidge terms. Burton's resolution was entirely exhortatory – though there were already legislative gestures to bypass the Senate's monopoly of the treaty-making power.[59] The Committee on Foreign Affairs took charge of the Burton resolution; Hearings were held; and the resolution was favourably reported and returned to the House calendar. Finally, in the closing hours of the Session the Representatives debated and passed the Burton resolution by a vote of 303:28. So it happened that two years after Secretary Hughes's submission of the Protocol, Congressman Burton, himself a former Senator and member of the Committee on Foreign Relations, far outdistanced any of his senatorial counterparts in registering congressional support for American adherence to the Permanent Court of International Justice.[60] (This was lobbying of a practical if problematical kind. Burton was President of the American Peace Society, which was divided on the Court and opposed to the League.)

According to tradition the final Session of the Sixty-eighth Congress adjourned *sine die* on 3 March. The following day a Special Session of the incoming Sixty-ninth Congress assembled to receive President Coolidge's Inaugural Address; while the new Vice-President, Charles Dawes, assumed his duties as permanent chairman of the Senate, whose constitutional task on these occasions was to advise on and consent to presidential appointments. Immediately the weakness of the Republican leadership became apparent. Charles B. Warren's nomination to the post of Attorney General was rejected by the Senate, the first time a potential cabinet member had been rebuffed since the 1860s. Warren is now perhaps best known as a constitutional historian, and he was at the time a prominent advocate of American membership in the World Court. The latter consideration was not crucial as the joint opposition of Borah and Walsh to Warren's nomination showed. At issue in March 1925 was Warren's identification with the 'Sugar Trust'; and Progressives such as Walsh and Borah were anxious not to repeat the senatorial laxity which had allowed Harry M. Daugherty's nomination to the same office in 1921 to go unopposed.[61]

So far as the court Protocal was concerned the Special Session of March 1925 was encouraging. In his Inaugural Coolidge recommitted his administration to ratification on the Hughes–Harding conditions, adding (as before) his own phrasing of Walsh's fifth reservation on the advisory jurisdiction. Thereupon Frank B. Willis (Ohio, Republican) introduced a resolution, S. Res. 6, to give effect to Coolidge's position on advisory opinions – and thereby reversed his own earlier support of Pepper's far more radical opposition. Even more important legislatively, however, was Swanson's reintroduction of his motion from the previous Congress. The terms of this new resolution, S. Res. 5, were 'similar' to the earlier version, but not exactly the same. They now contained a rider added discreetly during the Committee stage. This clause (never formally numbered) had its germ in Hudson's 1922 *Foreign Affairs* article and had been developed by Secretary Hughes in February 1923. The additional clause stated:

The signature of the United States to the said protocol shall not be affixed until the powers signatory to such protocol shall have indicated, through an exchange of notes, their acceptance of the foregoing reservations and understandings as a part and a condition of adhesion by the United States to the said protocol.

The amended Swanson resolution was formally referred to the Committee on Foreign Relations; and on 13 March, just before the close of the Special Session, the full Senate voted that it, rather than Pepper's scheme of 'disassociation', should be made 'special order of business' ten days after the start of the First (regular) Session of the Sixty-ninth Congress. The effect of this agreement, fully supported by all the remaining Irreconcilables, was to fix Thursday, 17 December 1925 as the date upon which all other legislative action in the Senate would be subordinated to debating Swanson's proposed terms for American adherence to the Permanent Court of International Justice.[62]

Like so many other details in the history of the World Court, the significance and consequences of Swanson's new reservation would emerge only gradually. But it would be a forgetful observer who did not recall a similar provision forming the preamble to the Lodge reservations during the debates of 1919–20 on the Treaty of Versailles and League Covenant. As to making the Protocol first order of business, it might take a more discerning mind to realize (as Moore did) that no date had been set for a final vote; consequently there was no senatorial bar agreed against a filibuster.[63] Even so, these kinds of considerations and an analysis of the Senate debate itself must wait for the next chapter. The rest of this chapter will offer an examination of the Court and League since 1922 to explain the increasing and widespread concern in the Senate and administration at the jurisdictional reach and political uses of advisory opinions.

Among the many issues discussed in Chapter 2 was the contentious matter of the Court's advisory jurisdiction and its origins in Article XIV of the League Covenant. From the intricacies of that discussion it will be remembered that Elihu Root's objections to such a judicial function had been overcome in the Advisory Committee of Jurists; and the Draft Scheme reported to the League Council had contained procedures for discharging this responsibility. It will also be remembered that the First Assembly had displayed more vigour and variety than the Jurists' Committee and the Council; and the Assembly delegates had finally agreed upon an advisory role for the Court while deciding to omit from the Court's Statute procedures for operating the jurisdiction.

Almost a year elapsed from the League's approval of the Court Statute until the election in September 1921 of the first bench of eleven full judges and four deputy-judges. The new Court was not officially inaugurated at The Hague until 15 February 1922; but in the meanwhile a preliminary session was held, partly to begin drafting the Court's forms of procedure. These became known as the Court's Rules; and among the most troublesome questions facing the judges and the officials in the Court Registry was whether and in what ways the Rules should provide for the handling of requests from the League for advisory opinions. As John Bassett Moore himself recalled some years later: 'No subject... caused so much confusion [and none] proved to be so baffling' as the advisory jurisdiction. Indeed, for the first months of his tenure on the bench Moore devoted the major part of his physical and intellectual energy to persuading his colleagues to decline the exercise of an advisory function.[64]

Moore's arguments were presented to his colleagues in a long memorandum. In themselves the arguments were scarcely original, since they were mainly an examination of the cursory debates in the Advisory Committee of Jurists and the far weightier and more detailed discussions of the First Assembly. As such they add very little to the analysis offered in Chapter 2. Of the ten 'propositions... for consideration' advanced by Moore only two have so far escaped our attention. One raised the dangerous possibility of States' intervening in the Court's conduct of an advisory opinion for fear a judgment on either an instant dispute or hypothetical question might prejudice established rights or traditional claims. The other and assuredly less justified worry of Moore's was the demeaning image of the Court touting for quasi-judicial business from a litigious League.[65]

Moore's colleagues were not persuaded by his lengthy arguments, though Registrar Hammarskjöld praised him for his scholarly efforts and personal tact.[66] Like a number of leading figures in 1920 they saw no way nor any reason to avoid the provisions of Article XIV of the Covenant creating the advisory jurisdiction. Nor were they disturbed that such a role undermined the purity of their judicial function – a conclusion which Moore inadvertently allowed in his own favourable references to the practices of the Judicial Committee of the British Privy Council.[67] Procedurally, however, Moore was successful in many of his goals. The Rules of the Court adopted in 1922 contained four paragraphs (Articles 71–4) governing the advisory jurisdiction and these differed quite radically from the approach taken by the Advisory Committee of Jurists in 1920. Textually the Rules provided that advisory opinions would be given by the full bench, not by a separate, smaller chamber. Dissenting opinions could be published at the discretion of the dissenter. The request and its terms had to be publicly stated; secrecy was not permitted. Third parties were to be invited to submit testimony; and such parties could be States and international organizations. Lastly, the opinions themselves were to be published in serial form, as part of a developing corpus of law.

These were the explicit provisions of the Rules. Later it would appear that some procedures had been left implicit. Bargains had in fact been made but the terms had not been published. For example, Moore believed that his colleagues had decided (1) that no secret or confidential advice (as distinct from formal advisory opinions rendered in open court) should be given to the League; and (2) that the Court might decline to render an opinion.[68] For historians, therefore, the significance of Moore's memorandum has to be carefully estimated. Certainly it contained an extensive articulation of the kind of arguments Root had failed to publicize in 1920. Even Moore's inability to persuade a majority of his colleagues is enlightening; for we can see how Moore's initial forebodings were first justified and then relieved by the Court's behaviour. Finally, the memorandum's substantive failure and procedural success lead us to examine the connection between the Court and the League, and thus to understand the paradox that Moore's trepidation about this connection made him all the keener to see the United States adhere to the Court.

Judge Moore quite clearly disapproved of the Court's exercising an advisory jurisdiction; and in his jurisprudential views he appeared to be initially aligned with Judges Huber, Finlay and Loder. Moore's respected colleague and friend, the Cuban Bustamente y Sirven, on the other hand, warmly advocated such a function for the Court; and the latter had allies in Altamira y Crevea and Anzilotti. Yet both sides fundamentally agreed with the commonly held view that this function brought the League and Court into intimate contact; indeed it was the point at which the two bodies most closely joined. Nevertheless the Court's lack of compulsory jurisdiction (except under the Optional Clause and, far more importantly, the Peace Treaties), combined with the continued preference of States to seek alternative means for resolving international controversies meant that initially the great bulk of the Court's activity derived from the League's (or more precisely, the Council's) resort to the advisory jurisdiction. By the spring of 1925 (when the Senate at last agreed to debate the Protocol) the Court had delivered only five judgments in litigated cases as against ten advisory opinions.[69]

Such a ratio became a weapon for American opponents of adherence, who asserted that it confirmed their original charges of the Court's subordination to the League. Against these allegations the proponents (well represented by Registrar Hammarskjöld) contended that the Court's handling of the advisory jurisdiction demonstrated its political independence of the League and its continued determination to maintain the highest judicial standards.[70] By the time Moore resigned from the bench in the spring of 1928 the ratio had not altered significantly; but he had moderated, though not entirely abandoned, his earlier objections. The 'prestige' of the Court had not been diminished but rather enhanced by its discharge of the advisory function. He did not wish to be misunderstood: this result was entirely due to the Court's initial decision 'deliberately and advisedly [to] assimilate… its advisory procedure to its contentious procedure'. The prize had been won and would be kept only by constant effort and by continued independence.

That, after all, was why he wished the United States to join: the adherence of a great, neutral Power and leading judicial force would contribute to the independence and thus integrity of the Court. But the United States would be impotent on its own if the Court deferred to the political interests of the League; and it would be rendered contemptible as well as ineffectual if it placed itself in an inferior position to the League Members. The advisory jurisdiction, invoked only by the League, posed both these dangers: in the first instance against the Court's independence; in the second, vis-à-vis the United States as a non-

League Power. In a short but tight circle Moore's argument ran: the Court could most successfully preserve its independence if the United States entered; the United States should enter only if the Court preserved its independence.[71] Not surprisingly, Moore's attitude seemed somewhat complacent and nationalistic to important League officials, notably Drummond and van Hamel; and following Harding's scuttling and the growing unease in Washington over the advisory jurisdiction, such men expressed grave doubts about the benefits – let alone the practical possibility – of American adherence.[72]

The cycle of Moore's pessimism and optimism, the misgivings of League officials and the numerous senatorial-executive proposals on the advisory jurisdiction can best be understood by examining the three most important advisory opinions delivered by the Court in the years 1923–5. They were Advisory Opinion no. 4 of 7 February 1923; Advisory Opinion no. 5 of 23 July 1923; and Advisory Opinion no. 12 of 21 November 1925. As this bare chronology shows, Opinion no. 12 was delivered on the eve of the Senate debate yet long after the original reservations had been laid before the Foreign Relations Committee or the full Senate. Nevertheless that twelfth Opinion illuminated contentious areas in the preceding Opinions and was prominent in the minds of knowledgeable Senators during the debate. Indeed not one of the Opinions mentioned even alluded to the United States of America; yet each contributed much to the forthcoming debate. Two final, related points: though these Opinions played a large part in the politics of the League and the developing jurisprudence of the Court and though they determined the course and nature of American policy, they have been neglected – scarcely even mentioned – in the historiography of the Court Protocols.[73] Worse still, the few scattered allusions to the cases show misunderstanding of the political and jurisprudential issues involved.[74]

The first three advisory opinions requested of the Court by the League Council arose from the Labour Clauses of the Peace Treaties; and all three opinions were handed down in the Court's First (Ordinary) Session during the summer of 1922.[75] Advisory Opinion no. 4, relating to the Tunis and Morocco Nationality Decrees, was requested by the League Council in October 1922 and delivered by a unanimous Court at the Second (Extraordinary) Session on 7 February 1923.[76] Though the case did not arise directly from provisions of the Peace Treaties, it did turn upon the meaning and effect of two clauses in the League Covenant: Paragraphs 1 and 8 of Article XV. Article XV, Paragraph 1 stated (in part):

> If there should arise between Members of the League any dispute likely to lead to a rupture, which is not submitted to arbitration in accordance with Article XIII, the Members of the League agree that they will submit the matter to the Council.

Article XV, Paragraph 8 stated (in full):

If the dispute between the parties is claimed by one of them, and is found by the Council to arise out of a matter which by international law is solely within the domestic jurisdiction of that party, the Council shall so report, and shall make no recommendation as to its settlement.

Since late in 1921 the British and French governments were at odds over the publication by the French and their protected rulers in Tunis and French Morocco of decrees regulating (*inter alia*) the nationality of certain inhabitants claiming to be British subjects. The British government sought a direct reference of the dispute of the Permanent Court of International Justice under Article XIII of the Covenant or to the Permanent Court of Arbitration under a Franco-British convention of 1903. The French declined both alternatives for a variety of reasons, the weightiest of which insisted upon French sovereignty in domestic questions and the pure optionality of the jurisdiction exercised by the Permanent Court of International Justice. The British persisted in their objections, for allegedly British subjects were liable to be drafted into the French Army. The French government was equally adamant. Finally, in August 1922, the British formally notified the League Council of the existence of a dispute in the terms of Article XV, Paragraph 1 of the Covenant. Thereupon a compromise was reached; and in early October the Council forwarded a request to the Court that it decide the prior question whether the Nationality Decrees were (as the French maintained) 'by international law solely a matter of domestic jurisdiction' according to Paragraph 8 of Article XV of the Covenant. A second element in the compromise provided that if the Court found against the French contention, 'the whole dispute [*would*] be referred to arbitration or to judicial settlement under conditions to be agreed between the governments'.

The Court took evidence and heard oral pleadings at an Extraordinary Session in mid January 1923. On 7 February it delivered its advisory opinion. The Court found unanimously against the French government and advised the Council that the dispute had arisen 'out of a matter which, by international law, is not solely within the domestic jurisdiction of France'. In reaching their opinion the judges acknowledged the 'principle' that 'questions of nationality' are within the domain of exclusive domestic jurisdiction. Nevertheless the sovereign right of discretion in such cases could be limited by the obligations which that same sovereign State had undertaken through international agreements. Such engagements dismantled any protective wall around a set of pre-existent privileges. In the instant case it was a series of obligations entered into by France, the United Kingdom and other parties prior to the Nationality Decrees which brought those selfsame regulations out of the 'reserved domain' of domestic jurisdiction and into the scope of international adjudication.

In itself, this conclusion was not startling: the unanimity of the bench suggested as much. But there were two other elements in the Court's opinion which were ominous – certainly to those, Americans or not, who feared the encroachment of the Court and League upon the general principle of State sovereignty. The first line of judicial reasoning was found in the Court's analysis of the relationship between Paragraphs 1 and 8 of Article XV of the Covenant. The two clauses (the judges held) were not equivalent: while Paragraph 8 was important, it was ultimately subordinate to Paragraph 1. In the language of the unanimous opinion:

> Article XV, in effect, establishes the fundamental principle that any dispute likely to lead to a rupture which is not submitted to arbitration in accordance with Article XIII shall be laid before the Council... [Nevertheless H] aving regard to this very wide competence possessed by the League of Nations, the Covenant contains an express reservation protecting the independence of States [i.e., Paragraph 8]... Without this reservation, the internal affairs of a country might, directly they appeared to affect the interests of another country, be brought before the Council.... Under the terms of Paragraph 8, the League's interest in being able to make such recommendations as are deemed just and proper in the circumstances with a view to the maintenance of peace must, at a given point, give way to the equally essential interest of the individual State to maintain intact its independence in matters which international law recognises to be solely within its jurisdiction.
>
> It must not, however, be forgotten that the provision contained in Paragraph 8, in accordance with which the Council, in certain circumstances, is to confine itself to reporting that a question is, by international law, solely within the domestic jurisdiction of one Party, is an exception to the principles affirmed in the preceding paragraphs and does not therefore lend itself to an extensive interpretation.

Thus (the Court declared) any balance struck by Paragraphs 1 and 8 between the claims of the individual State and the corporate interest of the League must ultimately be tilted towards the latter.[77]

This argument should not have been surprising, coming from a Court required to declare the meaning of the Covenant. There were many other authoritative voices stating that in the difficult choice between peace and justice, the League must choose the former and impose its will on recalcitrant pretensions for the latter.[78] We certainly cannot resolve the dilemma here; for it was essentially a contest in political semantics, with various adversaries seeking to claim the stable ground from which actions could be effectively legitimated. American observers – certainly those who addressed the Court Protocol with a critical mind – were well aware of these problematical distinctions and identifications. And, indeed, it is the American perspective which we have to bring to the Tunis and Morocco Nationality Decrees Opinion. For the significance of the equation between Paragraphs 1 and 8 of Article XV becomes clearer when brought into conjunction with a second set of statements in the Opinion. Taken together the two interdependent arguments constituted rich resources for advancing the scope of international adjudication.

In an earlier part of its Opinion the Court had affirmed:

> The question whether a certain matter is or is not solely within the jurisdiction of a State is an essentially relative question; it depends upon the development of international relations.[79]

This passage was seized upon by those lawyers, politicians and analysts who wished to challenge (what has been called) the 'traditional pretensions', 'the dogma' of State sovereignty.[80] Together with the Court's interpretation of Article XV and the material parts of its decision against the French government's claim of exclusive competence, this affirmation of change and relativity – of jurisprudential 'dynamism' – rendered suspect the ability of any individual State to oust the Court's jurisdiction from traditionally reserved areas of domestic questions and matters of governmental or political policy.[81]

For twenty years and more the Executive and Senate of the United States had agreed upon excluding (or 'reserving') a number of issues from the general competence or jurisdiction of international adjudication and arbitration. Among these can be listed the Monroe Doctrine; tariff legislation; immigration restriction; and debts contracted by some of the Confederate States during the Civil War. As we noted in Chapter 1, reservations incorporating such specific exemptions had accompanied senatorial legislation from at least the time of The Hague Conferences to the debate on the Treaty of Versailles. The Tunis and Morocco Nationality Decrees Opinion both prompted the re-emergence of such disclaimers and suggested a strong challenge to their validity – at least before the bar of the World Court.[82]

Such a conclusion might appear an unwarranted inference – conjuring up bogies on insubstantial grounds. After all, the United States could not be arraigned before the Court as a litigant, because the Court's contentious practice depended upon the voluntary submission of parties in dispute. This was the kind of argument complacently put by American Court lobbyists with a pro-League bias, such as Samuel Colcord.[83] But what of the Court's advisory jurisdiction? Could American counsel resist the developing jurisprudence – some might say encroaching jurisdiction – of the Court if this were raised through the advisory function? This was the question partly posed and ambiguously answered by the Court's decisions over the status of Eastern Carelia and the border between Iraq and Turkey; and it was a line of reasoning brilliantly explicated by Moore.[84]

Throughout the 1920s and into the 1930s the decision in the question of the status of Eastern Carelia played a major role in American discussion of the Court Protocols and the conditions of adherence. The substance of the Opinion was generally well-received; much less attention was paid to its reasoning, context and final reception by the League Council. Before we disentangle the complexities of the Opinion itself, some words need to be said about its antecedents. These were complicated enough; and our background sketch is inevitably broadly drawn.

The status of Eastern Carelia was the subject of 'acute controversy' between Finland and the Russian Soviet government. It had its immediate origins in the breakup of the Tsarist Empire and the warfare accompanying the establishment of the Soviet State. The Peace Treaty of Dorpat (1920) between Finland and Russia, together with various protocols and unilateral declarations regulated (*inter alia*) the boundaries and local authority of the contracting parties; in particular, the autonomy of Eastern Carelia within Soviet Russia. For more than a year the Finnish government pressed the League Council to take action under Articles XI and XVII of the Covenant (relating to war and non-Member States) to enforce its interpretation of Soviet obligations. The Soviet government rebuffed the representations of the League, insisting that the question was legally one of 'Russian domestic jurisdiction'; and that the hostility of the dominant Powers in the League and Court to the Soviet government invalidated their pretensions of impartiality. Eventually, in April 1923, the League Council voted to request an advisory opinion from the Court as to whether the Soviet government had indeed undertaken 'engagements of an international character which place Russia under an obligation to Finland...?'

There was, perhaps, only one major element of similarity between the Court's handling of this reference and the preceding Nationality Decrees Opinion. In neither instance did the Court determine the merits of the dispute; rather it addressed its international character. In the words of the Court discussing the Eastern Carelia question: the 'point really in controversy' had been put 'with perfect clearness' by the League Council:

> Is there or is there not a contractual obligation between Finland and Russia with regard to Eastern Carelia, and, if no such obligation exists, do the requests put forward by Finland constitute acts of interference in the internal affairs of Russia? [85]

Thereafter it is the contrasts between the two cases which are so striking. The more important – if somewhat neglected as a technical consideration – was the refusal of the Court formally to give an advisory opinion. The so-called Advisory Opinion no. 5 was in fact a reply to the Council declining to offer an advisory opinion. Secondly, the unanimity present in the Nationality Decrees Opinion had disappeared. The Court's demurrer was supported by seven judges, with four judges challenging its validity. This division within the Court was public but little regarded in the United States. There attention focused on the effect of the Court's decision, not on its reasoning and structure; nor, indeed, upon the League's reaction to the Court's conclusion.

When American observers welcomed the decision of the Court in the Eastern Carelia reference, they did so because they agreed with its majority judgment that the Court found it 'impossible to give its opinion on [the] dispute' as presented to it. But this formulation registered a compromise between seven of the eleven judges; and the grounds on which the seven judges reached agreement were categorically different. The text of the majority's decision shows two lines of argument, parallel in effect and leading to the same conclusion; but each was constructed of different, even contradictory theory. Some judges argued that the resolution of the Council's question depended upon the Court's possession of factual information which could be obtained only from the obstinate Soviet government. This form of argument implied but did not openly state that the Court's jurisdiction or competence to entertain the Council's question was judicially unimpeachable but practically challenged and ultimately defeated by lack of evidence. Alongside this reasoning ran that of those judges who denied the competence of the Court in the instant case on purely theoretical grounds.[86]

It was this second branch of the Court's argument which was so frequently invoked in the United States. In the formulation of the majority:

> It is well established in international law that no State can, without its consent, be compelled to submit its disputes with other States either to mediation or to arbitration or to any other kind of pacific settlement.

States could give this consent 'once and for all in the form of an obligation freely undertaken', as Member States of the League had done through accepting the Covenant. Alternatively States could do so *ad hoc* 'in a special case apart from any existing obligation'. Such general or specific

> consent, however, [had] never been given by Russia. On the contrary, Russia [had], on several occasions, clearly declared that it accepts no intervention by the League of Nations in the dispute with Finland.

Proponents of the Court were pleased that the Court had so carefully preserved the conventions of contentious litigation even when reviewing a dispute referred for an advisory opinion. Indeed the Court offered just such a defence of its actions.

> The Court is aware of the fact that it is not requested to decide a dispute, but to give an advisory opinion. This circumstance, however, does not essentially modify the... considerations [to demurr]. The question put to the Court is not one of abstract law, but concerns directly the main point of the controversy between Finland and Russia, and can only be decided by an investigation into the facts underlying the case. Answering the question would be substantially equivalent to deciding the dispute between the parties. The Court, being a Court of Justice, cannot, even in giving advisory opinions, depart from the essential rules guiding their activity as a Court.

This was encouraging language when read at a distance; but closer scrutiny showed a faint blending of the two categorically different approaches. Moreover the substantive part of the Court's compromise answer to the Council had begun by leaving open the 'topic' whether

> questions for an advisory opinion, if they relate to matters which form the subject of a pending dispute between nations, should be put to the Court without the consent of the parties.[87]

The significance of this passage would not be seen by many observers until late in 1925. For the most part the effective decision of the Court was applauded – the lack of unanimity and consequent reversibility were generally neglected. In public Judge Moore cited the decision eagerly and at length to

> refute the forecasts and ... dispel the apprehensions of those who have reiterated that the Court would, as the creation or creature of the League, enforce the League's organic law, the Covenant, above all other law, without regard to the rights under international law of nations not members of the League.[88]

These words from Moore himself seem a powerful rebuttal of our analysis; but they too require careful study and location. The first point to note is their appearance soon after the Court's response: the Council had not yet commented. Secondly, Moore was well aware of the politics of publicity: his interpretation of the case was prescriptive as much as descriptive. If his voice (coming soon after President Harding's St Louis criticisms) affirmed the independence of the Court, he might thereby help confirm that independence. This seems the likely explanation for Moore's private and generous interpretation of Harding's scheming; and a study of his later correspondence corroborates this analysis.[89] For there we find Moore insisting upon the precariousness of the Eastern Carelia decision, all the more so in a Court not committed to a system of precedent. For two judges to have changed their minds would have placed him and the other 'independents' in a minority. Yet even this, he recalled in a letter to a fellow 'independent', Max Huber, 'was not the most alarming phase'.

> What counted most was the attempt of the Council, by means of the advisory-opinion function, to use the Court as a weapon against a non-Member State, not subject to the jurisdiction of the League or the Court, and the scarcely veiled admonition levelled at the Court in the Council's subsequent report.[90]

For the Council had not received the Court's demurrer with good grace. In September 1923 (that is, after Moore's triumphant public words) the Council had adopted a report rebuking the majority for their decision and exhorting them to reconsider their duties when questions of war and peace were at stake. While 'noting the view of the Court' the Council refused to entertain the idea that the Court's reasoning

> exclude[d] the possibility of resort by the Council to any action, including a request for an advisory opinion from the Court, in a matter in which a State non-member of the League, unwilling to give information, is involved, if the circumstances should make such action necessary to enable the Council to fulfil its functions under the Covenant of the League in the interests of peace.[91]

Even our cursory review of the Nationality Decrees and Eastern Carelia cases shows the grounds for unease in the American government – the Executive no less than the Senate. The Court's advisory opinion in the Franco-British dispute had posed a serious challenge to the American tradition of reserving areas from the competence of arbitration and adjudication. In the words of James W. Garner, a leading American proponent of adherence: 'what may be regarded as a domestic matter today, may be a matter of international concern tomorrow'.[92] Secondly, and equally importantly, the Council's resort to the advisory procedure (albeit with the consent of the disputant parties) was itself charged with possibilities. As Fachiri (himself Counsel in the Nationality Decrees case) argued in his treatise:

> the advisory jurisdiction offers, in cases of a legal nature, an indirect means of access to the Court which, in practice, is capable of being used as a not ineffective substitute for direct compulsory jurisdiction.
>
> [The advisory] jurisdiction has proved in the past, and is likely to prove in the future, one of the most fertile opportunities for extending the Court's field of activity and usefulness.[93]

The Eastern Carelia decision might appear to allay some of the forebodings arising from the Nationality Decrees Opinion. After all, in the subsequent case the Court had declined to take jurisdiction of the dispute between Finland and the Soviet government. But (as we have seen) this was a majority decision – and the majority itself embraced conflicts of judicial reasoning. Furthermore, the Court left open the question of a disputant State's objection invalidating the mere reference of a dispute for an advisory opinion. Finally, the League Council had reprimanded the Court for its response and thus answered this open question and directly contradicted both lines of judicial reasoning within the majority. No: it was for the League to decide the validity of the reference, which *ipso facto* demanded a full determination from the Court of the substantive dispute, whatever the pleas against the jurisdiction raised by an interested party.

In the Eastern Carelia case the League had sought a judicial response to a set of demands brought by a Member-State, Finland, against a non-Member State, Soviet Russia. The favourable American interpretation of the events stressed the Court's demurrer and ignored the League's rebuke. In later years Moore stressed this second stage in the interchange and saw it as the fundamental reason why the United States should exercise some control over the actual reference of questions to the Court rather than seek to intervene at the bar of the Court with pleas against the jurisdiction. As Moore analysed the true significance of the Court's action and the League's censorious reaction, he insisted that the whole Eastern Carelia episode

> was a sudden and startling revelation of the possibilities that lurked in the advisory-opinion function; and a Power, like the U.S., having interests and rivalries all over the world, with the jealousies and enmities that inevitably result, will hardly consent to rely, for the preservation of its rights and interests at the hands of a vast political combination, including its chief competitors, upon mere opinions, neither binding nor irreversible, rendered by a body the entire personnel of which is periodically subject to change.[94]

Here Moore elided League and Court; and his defence would be that the advisory jurisdiction itself produced the close and dangerous relationship between the two. It was a judgment he maintained all the more firmly as a result of the Court's Opinion no. 12, the Mosul Question, delivered only weeks before the opening of the Senate debate on the American conditions for signature and ratification of the Court Protocol.

The immediate origins of the Mosul question lay in the dissolution of the Ottoman Empire, the abortive Peace Treaty of Sèvres (1920) succeeded by the final Treaty of Lausanne (1923), and the subsequent dispute between the British and Turkish governments over the northern boundary of Iraq, a British mandate. Involved in the territorial controversy were complex issues concerning religious and ethnic minorities, the authority of new regimes in Ankara and Baghdad, and vast oil reserves and financial interests. In the summer of 1924 the British government referred the boundary dispute to the League Council. For a year the Council took responsibility for determining the border, with Turkey (a non-Member State) participating in the discussions by virtue of Article XVII of the Covenant, which permitted such *ad hoc* membership. In September 1925, however, substantive negotiations came to a stop before two prior legal and jurisdictional obstacles. The first concerned the competence of the Council: was its final decision on the boundary-line to be binding on all parties? Secondly, was the decision to be reached unanimously, that is with the inclusion of the British and Turkish votes? On 19 September the Council referred both questions to the Permanent Court of International Justice for an advisory opinion; and two months later, on 21 November 1925, the Court delivered its answer.[95]

Advisory Opinion no. 12 was one of the most important and far-reaching decisions of the Court, since it included an interpretation of voting procedures under the Covenant of the League.[96] It was, moreover, unanimous – a remarkable characteristic, given the weight of this central question. But unanimity did not guarantee the Opinion's acceptability: lawyers and politicians who welcomed its reasoning and deductions were matched by those who did not share its premises or follow its logic; and (as we shall see) the disagreement accompanied the Court throughout its existence. The particular relevance of the Opinion for the history of the Court campaign in the United States consisted in the procedural and jurisdictional challenge it presented to the common understanding of the Eastern Carelia case. If this consideration comes as a shock, the surprise will be partly relieved by knowing that Judge Moore, who was in poor health, had not contributed to framing the Opinion in the Mosul case.

The Court's answer to the first question posed by the Council need not be discussed at length. The unanimous Opinion stated clearly that under the Treaty of Lausanne, the relevant parties (namely the British and Turkish governments) envisaged a 'definite settlement of the frontier' by the arbitral body they were to appoint. In the instant case that body was the League Council; and, the Court concluded, the

> 'decision to be taken' by the Council... in virtue of... the Treaty of Lausanne will be binding on the Parties and will constitute a definitive determination of the frontier between Turkey and Iraq.

This part of the Court's answer did not please the Turkish government; but there could be no mistaking its meaning. It was the second question posed by the Council and answered by the Court which generated so much controversy in later years, particularly in the debate over American adherence. Even so it must be noted that while the British government welcomed the Court's answer to the first question, it never committed itself to endorsing the second limb of the Court's advisory opinion.

The Council had framed its second question in the following manner: 'must the decision [to be taken by the Council on the boundary-line] be unanimous or may it be taken by a majority?' Either way, could 'the representatives of the interested Parties take part in the vote?' The Court answered the tripartite question by assenting to all three propositions and then resolved the apparent contradiction. Under the explicit and implicit terms of the Covenant, the 'rule of unanimity' was paramount; 'exceptions' had to be 'expressly provided'. Such a rule was 'naturally and even necessarily indicated' in the Covenant; it was the 'rule natural to a body such as the Council of the League of Nations'. As the Court explained:

> Only if the decisions of the Council have the support of the unanimous consent of the Powers composing it, will they possess the degree of authority which they must have; the very prestige of the League might be imperilled if it were admitted, in the absence of an express provision to that effect, that decisions on important questions could be taken by a majority. Moreover, it is hardly conceivable that resolutions on questions affecting the peace of the world could be adopted against the will of those amongst the Members of the Council who, although in a minority, would, by reason of their political position, have to bear the larger share of the responsibilities and consequences ensuing therefrom.

Moving from these general and weighty considerations the Court concluded the first section of its argument. It dismissed the relevance of arbitration practices outside the League which allowed simple majorities to decide; and then gathered together its specific judgment in the instant case.

> Unanimity... is required for the decision to be taken by the Council... with a view to the determination of the frontier between Turkey and Iraq.

The question then remained, whether the representatives of the United Kingdom and Turkey could actually vote; and, if so, would this not then tend to defeat unanimity? The response of the Court was to permit 'the representatives of the interested Parties' a vote – but then to discount their votes in the assessment of unanimity. The Court was on reasonably firm ground in citing Paragraphs 6 and 7 of Article XV of the Covenant to support this view; but the Court's reference to Assembly resolutions was particularly unconvincing – if only because they were precisely the sort of legislation which the Permanent Council Members deplored. Nevertheless, however shaky their premises, the judges offered their deduction directly:

according to the Covenant itself, in certain cases and more particularly in the case of the settlement of a dispute, the rule of unanimity is applicable, subject to the limitation that the votes cast by representatives of the interested Parties do not affect the required unanimity.

In support of this interpretation of the Covenant the judges applied general principles. It was a 'well-known rule that no one can be judge in his own suit'. Moreover, simply from a

practical standpoint, to require that the representatives of the Parties should accept the Council's decision would be tantamount to giving them a right of veto enabling them to prevent any decision being reached....[97]

In this way the Court wove together League Covenant, Assembly resolutions, the Treaty of Lausanne and general principles and thus fashioned from the patterns of unanimity and majority the doctrine of qualified as opposed to absolute unanimity.[98]

Historically the doctrine of qualified unanimity had no practical effect on the League's reference of questions to the Court for advisory opinions. Even formally the doctrine was not accepted by the League – with the British government being the most persistent opponent of any clear legislative decision between the various categories of vote-counting.[99] Nevertheless the grounds for American apprehension can be appreciated. A critical examination of the Court's thinking in the Eastern Carelia case reveals a Court bypassing the 'topic' of an interested party's challenging the validity of the League's resort to the Court's advisory jurisdiction. Even the majority in that case had not agreed that the Russian objections ousted the Court's jurisdiction. Had they done so, the rebuke from the League might have been less firm; its tone suggested the dissident judges were not numerous. Such a frail decision could be easily overturned, as Moore often warned. And then it was. Not directly, but implicitly. In the Mosul decision the Court had decided, unanimously, that the votes of interested parties must necessarily be discounted; and that was a judgment brought against actual Members of the League as well as *ad hoc* adherents to the Covenant.

On the eve of the Senate debate on the Protocol the combined actions of the Court and Council suggested that the mere registering of dissent by the United States to a League request for an advisory opinion would be insufficient to oust the jurisdiction – though the most commonly held interpretation of the Eastern Carelia case was that such an American dissent would be absolutely and unconditionally effective. Nor could the United States government rely upon a simple unilateral reservation of traditionally privileged questions – the Nationality Decrees case had seen to that. Uniting both was the Mosul decision which automatically discounted the objections of an interested party – and did so on the grounds advanced by the Council in September 1923: the larger demands of war and peace. Such a line of reasoning was followed with foreboding by Moore and Borchard in private and by Borah in the columns of the *New York Times*.[100] Moore still desired American adherence to the Court; Borchard was somewhat ambivalent, any initial enthusiasm having weakened in the face of the pro-League lobbyists for the Court; while Borah felt vindicated in his earlier opposition to the working of the Court and its relationship to the League. The three men could not determine the outcome of the Senate debate; but between them they represented a perspective which would inform the Senate's analysis. Perhaps the one solution they and the Senate as a whole could agree upon lay in the United States' requiring all other members of the Court to accept explicitly, first, an American veto power over the use of the advisory jurisdiction; and, secondly, their agreement to respect traditionally reserved areas of American policy. It was a formidable request; but it was, essentially, what the United States Senate and Executive would require of the Court Signatories and League Members in the winter of 1925–6.

Notes

[1] Hughes to Harding, 17 February 1923 and 1 March 1923; Charles H. Hyde (Solicitor's Office) to Hughes, 28 February 1923; Harding to Hughes, 5 March 1923: NA500. C114/225a–228; *CR* 67:4, 5067–8. Some documentation is in *FRUS* (1923), I. 19–24. Hughes and his officials cited extensively from John Bassett Moore, esp. *Digest of International Law*, VII. 76–103.

[2] Hughes to Moore, 16 March 1923; Moore to Hughes, 4 April 1923: NA500. C114/247a, 441; Moore to Huber, 31 March 1923: Moore Papers.

[3] Moore to Sweetser, 10 March 1923; Hudson to Moore, 26 February 1923: Moore Papers.

[4] The William R. Castle, Jr., Papers are in the Houghton Library, Harvard University and in the Herbert Hoover Presidential Library, West Branch, Iowa. This paragraph owes much to the 'Unpublished and Untitled Manuscript by William R. Castle, Jr.' in the Hoover Presidential Library.

[5] Castle to Phillips, 11 May 1923: NA500. C114/263.

[6] Hudson to Moore, 26 February 1923: Moore Papers.

[7] 'Diary of Tour to the United States. March 21st to April 28th. Lord Robert Cecil', Cecil of Chelwood Papers, Department of Manuscripts, British Library, Add. Mss. 51071–51157, vol. 51131. Cecil's tour was well covered by *The Times* [*London*]; and on 10–12 May 1923 the paper printed three articles by Cecil on the League and Outlawry. See also *New York Herald* (29 April 1923), 2; 'Cecil Urges Disarmament', *Current Opinion* 74 (May 1923), 527–8.

[8] These next few paragraphs are based upon three main sources: the Hudson Papers, especially his numerous clippings from the Missouri press (Hudson was from Missouri); the Harding Papers; and the Herbert Clark Hoover Papers in the Hoover Presidential Library.

[9] *Address of the President of the United States at the Luncheon of the Associated Press, N.Y., April 24, 1923* (Washington, DC: GPO, 1923).

[10] *'Seeing Ghosts in the World Court'*, *Current Opinion* 74 (June 1923), 649–51; 'The World Peace Court as Political Dynamite' *Literary Digest* (28 April 1923), 5–7; 'The Republican Rumpus', *Literary Digest* (9 June 1923), 10–11;

New York Herald (29 April 1923), 1, 2; Lodge to Root, 27 April 1923: Jessup, *Elihu Root*, II. 429. Hover's speech of 11 April was reprinted in *International Conciliation* 186 (April 1923), 370–9; those of Root and Hughes in *PASIL* (1923), 1–15, 75–89.

[11] *St. Louis Post-Dispatch* (19 May 1923), II. 9, 11; *New York Herald* (19 May 1923), 1, 2.

[12] Johnson, *George Harvey*, pp. 393–7; Lodge to Scott, 26 April and 1 May 1924: Scott Papers; Clark to Harding, 15 June 1923; Harding to Clark, 20 June 1923: Harding Papers. Clark is today best known for his *Memorandum on the Monroe Doctrine*. Senate Document no. 114, Seventy-first Congress, Second Session (Washington, DC: GPO, 1930).

[13] Colcord to Hughes, 28 June and 30 July 1923; to Hoover, 29 July 1923: Hughes Papers.

[14] Lodge to Root, 27 April 1923: Jessup, *Elihu Root*, II. 429. Frank Walters, later the League's historian, sympathized with American complaints: Walters to Hudson, 17 July 1923: Hudson Papers.

[15] I have elaborated the preceding analysis in 'The Harding Administration and the World Court', unpublished paper to the Ohio Academy of History, Columbus, Ohio, April 1984. For the official text, see *Address of the President of the United States on the I.C.J. at St. Louis, Thursday Evening, June 21, 1923* (Washington, DC: GPO, 1923).

[16] Raymond B. Fosdick, *Secretary Hughes and the League of Nations* (New York: privately published, 1924.)

[17] *NYT* (29 June 1923), 10; *NYT* (1 July 1923), 1; Colcord to Hoover, 29 July 1923: Hughes Papers.

[18] Hudson, 'Problem of the International Court Today', *ABAJ* 10 (January 1924), 13–18, 49; Hudson to Cecil, 25 June 1923; to Drummond, 28 June 1923; Cecil to Hudson, 27 June 1923; Hammarskjöld to Hudson, 29 June and 9 July 1923: Hudson Papers.

[19] Russell, *Shadow of Blooming Grove*, ch. 20.

[20] Donald R. McCoy, *Calvin Coolidge: The Quiet President* (New York: Macmillan, 1967), 152, 185.

[21] Wickersham (President of the LNNPA) *et al.* to Harding, 24 June 1923: Harding Papers: Colcord to Hughes, 21 September 1923: Hughes Papers.

[22] Moore to Loder, 10 November 1923; to Finlay, 10 December 1923; to Huber, 10 December 1923: Moore Papers.

[23] Johnson, *George Harvey*, pp. 393–7; Frank Billings Kellogg to Hughes, 10 June 1924: Hughes Papers.

[24] Hudson to Drummond and Drummond minute, 28 June 1923: Hudson Papers.

[25] Castle to Hughes, 27 November 1923: NA500. C114/388.

[26] Correspondence of Hughes and Castle, December 1923: NA500. C114/321; William H. Beck (Secretary to Secretary of State) to W. C. Keirstead, 2 October 1923: Hughes Papers.

[27] *FRUS* (1923), I. vii–xxii at viii; Moore to Huber, 10 December 1923: Moore Papers.

[28] S. Res. 29, S. Res. 32, S. Res. 36: *CR* 68:1, 151–3.

[29] McDonald to Sweetser, 20 December 1923: Sweetser Papers. Lenroot's biographer is Herbert F. Margulies: see Margulies, *Senator Lenroot of Wisconsin: a Political Biography, 1900–1929* (Columbia and London: University of Missouri Press, 1977), esp. ch. 8. The Lenroot Papers are in the MD,LC.

[30] Moore to George Gray, 8 September 1921; to Huber, 9 March 1925; to Henry P. Fletcher, 21 June 1926; Huber to Moore, 13 January 1925: Moore Papers.

[31] See S. Res. 454, S. Res. 471: Sixty-seventh Congress, Fourth Session; S. Res. 220: Sixty-eighth Congress, First Session; *CR* 67:4, 4498–504, 4632–3, 5121, 5273, 5316; *CR* 68:1, 7904, 9144. The formal record of the Committee's actions is in US Senate, *Proceedings of the Committee on Foreign Relations, United States Senate: from the Sixty-eighth Congress (beginning December 3, 1923) to the Seventy-second Congress (ending March 3, 1933).* Printed for the Use of the Committee on Foreign Relations (Washington, DC: GPO, 1934), 20–1. This is cited below as SCFR, *Proceedings.*

[32] S.Res. 233: *CR* 68:1, 9144.

[33] Memo, 11 May 1924: Moore Papers. The WPF published a version of the Hearings as a *Pamphlet*, vol. 7, no. 2 (1924); so too the National Council for Prevention of War in their *Bulletin*, vol. 3, no. 6 (17 May 1924): 'Hearings Reveal Surprising Strength of World Court Sentiment'. For historians, see Fleming, *Treaty Veto*, 178–80; Accinelli, 'United States and the World Court', pp. 116–8. The official rcord is in US Senate, *Permanent Court of International Justice. Hearings before a Subcommittee of the Committee on Foreign Relations, United States Senate. Sixty-eighth Congress, First Session, Relative to the Adhesion of the United States to the Protocol under which the Permanent Court of International Justice has been established at The Hague. April 30 and May 1, 1924.* Printed for the Use of the Committee on Foreign Relations (Washington, DC: GPO, 1924).

[34] *NYT* (14 April 1923), 1.

[35] *CR* 68:1, 8084, 8322–3, 9393–4; SCFR, *Proceedings*, 21; Lodge to Scott, 26 April and 1 May 1924; Scott to Lodge, 30 April 1924: Scott Papers.

[36] *CR* 68:1, 9144; Eleanor E. Dennison, *The Senate Foreign Relations Committee*, Stanford Books in World Politics (Palo Alto, Ca.: Stanford University Press, 1942), 113.

[37] SCFR, *Proceedings*, 21.

[38] Ibid. 22.

[39] S. Res. 234: *CR* 68:1, 9157–8.

[40] Senate Report no. 634, Part 2: Sixty-eighth Congress, First Session: reprinted in SCFR *Proceedings*, 34–8.

[41] Ibid., 26–33: text of Senate Report no. 634 [Part 1]: Sixty-eighth Congress, First Session.

[42] Moore memo, 11 May 1924: Moore Papers; Hudson to Pepper, 5 May and 2 June 1924; Pepper to Hudson, 29 May 1924: Hudson Papers.

[43] *CR* 68:1, 9144.

[44] Republican Women's Club of Minneapolis to Hughes, 8 April 1924; reply of Assistant Secretary Leland Harrison, 25 April 1924: NA500. C114/353. Henrik Shipstead (Farmer–Labor) and Thomas D. Schall won the 1922 and 1924 senatorial elections in Minnesota.

[45] See the correspondence in *NYT*, 12 and 16 May, reprinted in *CR* 68:1, 8322–3, 9393–4.

[46] Taft to Root, 9 June 1924: Root Papers; 'Hiram Johnson's Opening Gun', *Literary Digest* (4 August 1923), 16; McCoy, *Calvin Coolidge*, chs 23 and 24.

[47] *National Party Platforms*, pp. 243 ff. For Root's role, see Hays to Root, 4 and 6 June 1924; Coolidge to Root, 16 June 1924: Root Papers.

[48] *National Party Platforms*, pp. 250–1. The John W. Davis Papers are in the Sterling Memorial Library, Yale.

[49] Taft to Hughes, 5 October 1924: Hughes Papers.

[50] Hudson to Gilchrist, 14 November 1924: Hudson Papers; Gilchrist, 'Some Reflections on the American Situation', 31 July 1923: Sweetser Papers.

[51] Herbert F. Margulies, 'The Senate and the World Court', *Capitol Studies* 4 (Fall 1976), 37–51 provides some detail on Lenroot's shift.

[52] *NYT* (11 January 1925), 1; *NYT* (12 January 1925), *1; NYT* (14 January 1925), 20.

[53] Borchard to Borah, 19 November 1924: Edwin M. Borchard Papers, Sterling Memorial Library, Yale. Taft praised Borchard's 'real authority on international law' but regarded him as a dangerous 'radical' on the Constitution: Taft to Root, 21 December 1922: Root Papers.

[54] Message to Congress: *FRUS*, 1924, I. vii–xxiii at xx–xxi.

[55] 'To End War, "Do It Now"', *Literary Digest* (14 February 1925), 12–13.

[56] Hudson to Hammarskjöld, 23 June 1924; to Drummond, 2 July 1924; to van Hamel, 2 July 1924: Hudson Papers.

[57] Lindsay Rogers, *American Political Science Review* (cited below as *APSR*) 19 (November 1925), 761–72 at 761; see also 'A Coolidge Congress', *Literary Digest* (22 November 1924), 10–11; *NYT* (2 January 1925), 1.

[58] *CR* 68:2, 2023, 4860–1.

[59] H.J. Res. 366: Sixty-eighth Congress, Second Session.

[60] H. Res. 426: Sixty-eighth Congress, Second Session: see *CR* 68:2, 2978, 5404–13; US House of Representatives, *Permanent Court of International Justice. Hearings before the Committee on Foreign Affairs, House of Representatives, Sixty-eighth Congress, Second Session on H. Res. 426, Favoring Membership of the United States in the Permanent Court of International Justice. January 21, 27 and 31, 1925* (Washington, DC: GPO, 1925); *Report.* House Document no. 1569, Sixty-eighth Congress, Second Session (Washington, DC: GPO, 1925).

[61] The details are in *CR* 69: Special Session, *passim.*

[62] Ibid. 10, 377; SCFR, *Proceedings*, 21–3, 34–8.

[63] Moore memo of conversation with Pepper, 10 July 1925: Moore Papers.

[64] Moore to Francis Colt de Wolf, 23 December 1930: NA500. C114 [Advisory Opinions Special File]/90; to Hughes, 5 April 1923: NA500. C114/387.

[65] Permanent Court of International Justice, *Acts and Documents concerning the Organization of the Court.* Publications of the Court, Series D, no. 2: Preparation of the Rules of the Court (Leiden: PCIJ, 1922), Annex no. 58a, 383–98. (This series is cited below as PCIJ, Series D, plus sequence number.) For the Rules adopted in 1922, see PCIJ, Series D, no. 1, 66–82. Moore's memorandum, 'The Question of Advisory Opinions', 18 February 1922 is in *The Collected Papers of John Bassett Moore*, 7 vols (New Haven: Yale University Press, 1944), V. 329–44.

[66] Hammarskjöld to Hudson, 4 February 1922: Hudson Papers.

[67] Bustamente y Sirven, *World Court*, pp. 253–4; Morellet, *Organisation de la Cour Permanente*, p. 128; Charles de Visscher, 'Les Avis Consultatifs de la Cour Permanente de Justice Internationale', *Recueil des Cours* (1929), I: vol.26, [1]–76 at 9.

[68] See citations at n. 64 above and Moore to Harlan Fiske Stone, 17 March 1932: Moore Papers. (Stone was one of the Republican 31.)

[69] The *Judgments and Orders of the Court* were published in serial form as PCIJ, Publications of the Court, Series A, nos 1–24, covering 1922–30. The *Advisory Opinions* for the same period were published as Series B, nos 1–18. For 1931–40 the two Series were amalgamated into Series A/B, nos 40–80. *Acts and Documents relating to Judgments and Advisory Opinions* constituted Series C: and *Annual Reports* were issued as Series E.

[70] Åke Hammarskjöld, 'Sidelights on the Permanent Court of International Justice', *Michigan Law Review* 25 (February 1927), 327–53.

[71] See joint Report of Moore, Loder and Anzilotti, adopted September 1927: PCIJ, *Fourth Annual Report of the Permanent Court of International Justice: June 15, 1927–June 15, 1928.* Series E, no. 4, 75–7; cf. Moore to Hughes, 27

September 1922: NA500. C114/269; to Hiram Johnson, 11 January 1936: Johnson Papers.

72 Drummond memo, 29 June 1924; Drummond minute, 3 July 1924 to Hudson's memo to van Hamel, 2 July 1924: Hudson Papers.

73 Dunne, 'Isolationism of a Kind', pp. 347–9.

74 Excellent, integrated analyses are: Gabriele Salvioli, 'La Jurisprudence de la Cour Permanente de Justice Internationale', *Recueil des Cours* (1926) II: vol. 12 [1]–114; J. H. W. Verzijl, 'Die Rechtsprechung des Ständigen Internationalen Gerichtshofes, 1922 bis Mai 1926', *Zeitschrift für Völkerrecht* 13, no. 4 (1926), 489–543.

75 PCIJ, Series B, nos 1–3.

76 Ibid., no. 4, 7–32. Fachiri, Counsel for the British government, discusses the case in *Permanent Court*, 2nd ed, pp. 150–60.

77 PCIJ, Series B, no. 4, 23–5, 31–2.

78 A theme developed in chs. 5–7 below; cf. ch. 2 above *passim*.

79 PCIJ, Series B, no. 4, 24.

80 H. Lauterpacht, *The Development of International Law by the Permanent Court of International Justice*. Publications of the Graduate Institute of International Studies, Geneva, no. 11 (London and New York: Longmans, Green, 1934), 58, 85 ff., 104; Louis L. Jaffe, *Judicial Aspects of Foreign Relations: in particular of the Recognition of Foreign Powers*, Harvard Studies in Administrative Law, (Cambridge, Mass.: Harvard University Press, 1933), 81.

81 For the 'dynamic' element of law, see e.g. Alejandro Alvarez, *Le Droit International Nouveau dans ses Rapports avec la Vie Actuelle des Peuples* (Paris: Pedone, 1959)

82 Kellor and Hatvany, *United States Senate and the International Court*, ch 14; Giblin and Brown, *World Court Myth*, chs 3, 9, 19.

83 Colcord to Hoover, 8 December 1924: Hoover Papers.

84 Moore to de Wolf, 23 December 1930 (cited at n. 64 above).

85 PCIJ, Series B, no. 5, 7–29 at 25–6.

86 Ibid. 27–9. The seven of the majority were: Anzilotti, Finlay, Huber, Loder, Moore, Oda and Wang; the minority were Altamira y Crevea, Bustamente y Sirven, Nyholm and Weiss.

87 Ibid. 27–9.

88 Moore, *Collected Papers*, VI. 103; cf. ibid., V 360–70.

89 Moore to Loder, 10 November 1923: Moore Papers.

90 Moore to Huber, 18 September 1926: Moore Papers.

91 Procès-Verbaux of Council meeting, 27 September 1923: *LNOJ* (November 1923), 1335–7; Annexe 576a: ibid. 1501–2.

92 Garner, 'Limitations on National Sovereignty in International Relations', *APSR 19* (February 1925), 1–24 at 10–11. Borchard later described Garner, who was then President of the American Political Science Association, as a nice man, but no lawyer! Borchard to Moore, 24 February 1931: Borchard Papers.

93 Fachiri, *Permanent Court*, 1st ed, 68, 155.

94 Moore to Huber, 18 September 1926 (cited at n. 90 above); cf. Moore to Senator Thomas F. Bayard of Delaware, 16 December 1925: Moore Papers.

95 PCIJ, Series B, no. 12, 6–35 at 6–18.

96 A good analysis was provided by Fachiri (Counsel to the British government), *Permanent Court*, 2nd ed, pp. 228–34.

97 PCIJ, Series B, no.12, 6, 26, 29–33.

98 C. Howard-Ellis, *The Origin, Structure and Working of the League of Nations* (London: Allen & Unwin, 1928), 395 ff.

[99] League of Nations, *Conditions of Voting on Requests for Advisory Opinions addressed to the Permanent Court of International Justice: Report Submitted by the First Committee to the Assembly*. A.68. 1935 V (Geneva: League of Nations, 1935)

[100] James G. McDonald to Frederick Keppel (of the CEIP), 3 December 1925: NA 500. C114/429; Borchard to Borah, 24 December 1925: Borchard Papers; *NYT* (30 November and 2 December 1925).

5 Reservations, understandings and conditions: the US Senate's terms for adherence, 1925–26

The Mosul question was not the only serious issue before the League Council in the closing months of 1925 – though it was serious enough. Vittorio Scialoja, the Italian delegate who had taken part in the Council's rebuke of the Court in the Eastern Carelia case, recalled in 1929 that the League had stood on the brink of war. From an even longer perspective, Frank Walters (then high in the Secretariat and later quasi-official historian of the League) described the 1925 crisis as graver than any until the disastrous year of 1931.[1] True, Walters had in mind the border warfare between Greece and Bulgaria; yet such acts of overt belligerence do not measure the full range of problems confronting the League of Nations. These problems might make our recent discussion of the Court's jurisprudence and its reception by the Council appear rather ornate, insubstantial and precarious – as though we have been examining the façade to a structure which was being substantially altered, even dismantled from within. This study of the Court Protocol in the United States can do no more than hint at the fundamental issues involved; but even a brief and highly selective review will serve two, interrelated purposes.

The first will be obvious to anyone studying the historiography of the Court Protocol. Historians have treated the question of American adherence in an essentially contradictory manner. As we noted in

Chapter 1, their predominant theme has been the 'symbolic' nature of the debate in the United States. In the words of the leading modern historian of the subject: 'the fight over the Court proposal was very much out of proportion to the significance of the proposal itself'.[2] Yet such an analysis – or rather, the suggestion of such an analysis – requires an examination at least of the relationship between the symbol and the reality; and, more profoundly, of the reality itself. Instead the historiography is characterized by a general neglect of the political dynamics of the League and its constituent Member States. Thus the presumption of symbolism encourages historians to ignore the very actuality which would justify an interpretation couched in symbolic terms. So much for the formal contradiction. Yet it must be admitted that the substantive question itself is hugely complex. Indeed the best examples of this complexity come from the historians of the League of Nations – the very writers who so often reveal, sometimes openly and with regret, more often inadvertently, the disjunction between the idealized image of the League and its mundane reality.[3]

Of course, the simplest sketch of the intersection of national, international and particularly League politics in the winter of 1925–6 would require many thousands of words and a global reference. Nevertheless a significant part of this complexity is revealed by the contemporaneous completion of the Locarno agreements. This package of undertakings between the United Kingdom, France, Belgium, Germany and Italy concerning the territorial settlement of Western Europe owed something to two previous diplomatic failures, each of which envisaged more extensive multilateral engagements to be negotiated under the auspices of the League of Nations. The first was the Draft Treaty of Mutual Assistance, deriving from the Fourth Assembly of 1923; the second, the abortive successor to its aborted predecessor, was the so-called Geneva Protocol for the Pacific Settlement of International Disputes, the product of the Fifth Assembly of 1924. The British Foreign Secretary, Austen Chamberlain, saw the Locarno agreements (which he had helped to complete) as gathering together and advancing the interests of the United Kingdom, the British Empire, Europe and the League – just as he and his predecessors had objected to the 1923 Draft Treaty and 1924 Protocol for rupturing this harmony.[4] The point of historical note is not that cabinets and governments disagree with one another, nor even that an idea favoured in conception will disappoint and be disowned by its originators. The relevance of this episode is more precise. At each stage of the process declared advocates, simple sceptics and even outright opponents of the League, both in the United Kingdom and elsewhere, encouraged or impeded the successive programmes by selective appeals to the Covenant. Either they mined (what one Council representative called) 'the infinite riches of that marvellous instrument' to promote the alternatives of loose and strict constructionalism (to use American terminology); or they searched in vain for textual support and therefore tried to 'fill the gap or gaps' in the Covenant (*boucher les fissures*) which appeared to expose League members to the risk of facing an enemy without the guarantee of collective support.[5]

The second task, then, is to bring these interpretations and uses of the Covenant into focus with an examination of the Court Protocol in the United States. For now we can see that the symbolic mode of analysis has acted less like a camera filter to bring out latent qualities or even like a distorting lens to intensify relationships but rather as a clouded glass to obscure points of illumination. For example: the jurisdictional reach of the Geneva Protocol was profoundly disturbing to some American supporters of Court adherence – and even to some who favoured the League.[6] Far more importantly, the Locarno agreements suggested to a number of pro-League commentators and activists that specific territorial commitments might first live alongside but then eventually displace the global, general obligations arising from the Covenant. In this way, unqualified, vaguely-phrased co-operation with the League (or more revealing, the League Powers) might contribute to the erosion of the League itself.[7]

It has long been said that no-one can step into the same river twice. The League of Nations was a peculiar river: no-one could step into the same river once. For the river changed as each person entered; it flowed and was shaped by the many diverse forces and obstacles which joined and departed. The river was not constant; it was dynamic: active and reactive. As we remarked at the beginning of this chapter, the crisis of 1925–6 was not simply one posed by belligerents to the authority and effectiveness of the League. Nor was it caused even primarily by the contemporaneous disputes surrounding the admission of Germany to the League, her claims to a permanent seat on the Council, the counter-demands of Poland, and the consequent dissatisfaction and withdrawal of Brazil and Spain.[8] The crisis was even more profound and concerned the very meaning of the League and its future direction. A short while ago we criticized the symbolic interpretation of the Court debate; within the last few sentences we have recalled Heraclitus's river. The difference and justification is that the League meant different things to different actors. Indeed some authoritative figures have suggested that by the winter of 1925–6 the fatal rupture within the League had already taken place; that the national interests of individual Member States had irrevocably diverged from the collective interests of the League; and that thereafter selfish ends were pursued under the slogans of co-operation and internationalism.[9]

Many of these issues will reappear in our account of the Senate debate on the Court Protocol. Before then, however, we must trace the changing and increasingly important role of Senator George Wharton Pepper, who in the summer of 1924 had established a reputation as a leading opponent of the Hughes–Harding–Coolidge conditions for adherence. The story is complex. The published writings of the principal characters involved are not helpful; the private papers of Moore are not exhaustive in details; there is no historiography of the main directions of movement. Nevertheless the scanty records do offer the beginnings of a coherent framework and lead us to understand the optimism of Moore and other Court supporters on the eve of the Senate debate. Alongside the principal characters were President Coolidge; his new Secretary of

State, Frank Billings Kellogg (formerly Senator from Minnesota and recently US Ambassador in London); and Dwight Whitney Morrow (who gained prominence later as Ambassador to Mexico). Morrow, a partner in J. P. Morgan & Co., had been a classmate of Coolidge's at Amherst, was highly respected by Moore and was reported to be putting pressure on Coolidge to advance the Court Protocol.[10]

The story begins in the spring of 1925, when Pepper raised no objections to Swanson's resolution displacing his own earlier scheme of Court-League 'disassociation'. As Pepper wrote to Senator Norris, a one-time Irreconcilable, and Esther Everett Lape, a senior member of the American Foundation and keen advocate of the Court and League: the 'difference' between his own former attitude towards the Court and that of Swanson's supporters could be 'reconciled'. The exact reasons for Pepper's reversal are unclear. He ignores the issue in his autobiographical writings; and his correspondence with Moore and Kellogg is uninformative on this point. But three possibilities emerge from the available evidence. One is that Pepper genuinely changed his mind and came to see that the League-sponsored Court offered the only practical hope for a world court worth the name. Great Power politics would inevitably enter his own scheme of 'disassociation'; so it was ultimately futile to break the League connection. The answer lay in bringing the influence of the United States into the electoral process and judicial proceedings and thereby contributing to the independence of the existing Court and the development of its jurisprudence. (This was, of course, the perspective and goal of Moore.) The second possibility is that Pepper attempted to get backing for his forthcoming campaign for Senate re-election: promoting the ratification of the Court Protocol might be an additional claim upon the Republican establishment in Pennsylvania for renomination in the 1926 congressional elections. A third possibility (which is not incompatible with the first two) is that Pepper saw too much of Borah's intransigence in his own initial position – the interpretation of his own motives which Pepper came nearest to stating publicly in his memoirs.[11]

Whatever the precise amalgam of causes, Pepper's change of mind held out hope to Moore. By the spring of 1925 Moore was seriously troubled by ill-health: his eyes were weakening and he had palpitations of the heart. He wanted to resign from the bench and return to the United States for good. Yet if he did so, this would lessen the chances of American adherence. On this Secretary Kellogg agreed; and both also apparently agreed that Pepper was now the best candidate to guide the Senate towards the goal of approving the Protocols. Pepper's anti-League background would help commend the project to the undecided – perhaps even to the former Irreconcilables.[12]

Later in the year Pepper and Moore (with the active support and encouragement of Coolidge and Kellogg) held a series of meetings and exchanged a number of memoranda. Their particular concern was the Court's advisory jurisdiction – a function which had become increasingly, and publicly, worrying to Coolidge, Kellogg and Root. Indeed, Coolidge had so retreated from his original support of the Walsh reservation that in May 1925 he wrote to Root saying that he could 'not see any great objection to having the Court abandon the practice of giving such opinions altogether'. By midsummer the fact if not the details of Pepper's new attitude had become known – perhaps leaked deliberately to the New York press, where Pepper and Dwight Morrow had good contacts. Indeed by early August the well-informed *New York Times* was referring to Pepper as leading the 'pro-Court Senators... arrayed against the faction headed by... Borah'. However Pepper's balancing act was difficult to sustain and he warned pro-Court lobbyists that their public pressure would weaken his credibility and effectiveness as both a leader and an intermediary.[13]

The substance of the Pepper–Moore negotiations did not emerge until the Senate debate was underway – and even then only in a most roundabout manner. Moreover areas of disagreement continued to exist between the two men and Pepper did not claim Moore's imprimatur. Even so, it is possible to construct the main elements in the negotiations, especially now that we have an understanding of the Court's use of the advisory jurisdiction and the response of the League Council.

Since the Pepper–Moore negotiations were directed mainly at overcoming the inadequacies they saw in Walsh's fifth reservation on the advisory jurisdiction it will be convenient to recall its text. The Walsh reservation, unanimously approved by the Foreign Relations Committee in May 1924 had stated:

> The United States shall be in no manner bound by any advisory opinion of the Permanent Court of International Justice not rendered pursuant to a request in which it, the United States, shall expressly join in accordance with the statute for the said Court adjoined to the protocol of signature of the same to which the United States shall become signatory.

Because Pepper and Moore did not see eye to eye in their criticisms and suggested amendments to Walsh's reservation, the following analysis is something of a merging of their different perspectives. Nevertheless a number of key elements do emerge with tolerable clearness.[14]

The first and most general is an apparently technical, procedural question; substantially, however, it was most important. Walsh's reservation suggested the advisory jurisdiction was lodged in the Court's Statute. We have seen, though, that this controversial function was omitted from the Statute but incorporated in the Rules. A primary concern of Moore and Pepper was to commit the Court Signatories, through their explicit acceptance of the American reservations, to the permanence of the proposed changes. As Moore constantly stressed, it was not sufficient, indeed it was unwise and dangerous, to rely upon precedent and the security of the Court's Rules to maintain the judicial and jurisdictional principles required by the United States. In this respect Pepper and Moore did not disagree with Swanson and his supporters who had quietly introduced the 'exchange of notes' reservation. But it was foolish to continue speaking (as Walsh's reservation did) of the advisory jurisdiction and the Court Statute in the same breath.

Certainly the advisory jurisdiction had to be controlled; but the Statute was not the instrument.

Secondly and relatedly: since the United States could not amend the Statute (though it should demand a veto upon its amendment) nor join in the political discussions of the League, its power to oust the advisory jurisdiction of the Court should be directed to the Court itself rather than against the League's referral. Moore and Pepper argued that this was not an unreasonable demand. It was, after all, the common interpretation of the Eastern Carelia Opinion. However (they both agreed) the common interpretation of the Eastern Carelia Opinion was ill-founded. It was a precarious majority decision; it had not decided the specific question of ouster; and the Council had challenged the legitimacy of the Court's demurrer. If, therefore, the Opinion in the Eastern Carelia dispute did constitute a precedent favourable to the American position (as was generally and glibly maintained), then there could be no harm in making this interpretation irreversible. The weakness of the Walsh reservation lay in its permitting the advisory reference to be entertained and adjudicated, and thus exposing the United States to the moral obloquy of an unfavourable judgment. Merely disclaiming that the United States would be 'bound' by an advisory opinion which it had not itself jointly requested was irrelevant. No State was 'bound' by any opinion. Likewise, no-one could ignore the moral weight of such a judgment. Therefore , if the United States was to avoid the potentially harmful impact of an advisory opinion, it must intervene and oust the jurisdiction before the case was entertained. (Later in 1925, that is after the Moore–Pepper negotiations, the decision in the Mosul case corroborated Moore's arguments that the Eastern Carelia Opinion had been rashly and complacently interpreted. In the Mosul Opinion the Court had unanimously ruled that interested parties *ipso facto* were to be discounted in the calculation of votes for and against action under the Covenant – and hence in the reference of cases for an advisory opinion.)

The legacy of the Eastern Carelia case had not been exhausted, for Moore and Pepper sought to maintain two further principles. First, that the right of the Court to decline to give an opinion should be enshrined. Moore had believed this discretion had been implicitly accepted by the judges when drafting the Court Rules in 1922; but the Eastern Carelia case had disabused him. Even his respected colleague Bustamente y Sirven had publicly if moderately joined in the criticism of the Court for not answering the League Council's question directly. The second principle, namely that the Court's advisory jurisdiction should always be used openly and without secrecy, had been incorporated explicitly in the Rules in 1922. During the drafting of the Rules the principle had been carried overwhelmingly. But after the delivery of the Eastern Carelia Opinion – though before the Council rebuke – an attempt was made to amend the Rules and permit secret opinions. The proposal failed; but it was another reminder to Moore that the protective wall around the inherently dangerous advisory jurisdiction derived from the frail Rules and relied upon the votes of individual and changeable judges.[15] If the Rules were too easily altered and the Statute altered only by unanimity among the Signatories, then judicial principle had to be defended through the reservations of the United States. One final point, though this was a goal sought by Moore rather than one in which Pepper had any special interest. Moore wanted to give statutory protection to Article 71 of the Rules providing for the declaration of dissenting opinions. The problem here – and it was not limited to the advisory jurisdiction – was that many Continental jurists, including Moore's colleagues Hammarskjöld and Altamira y Crevea, believed that the institution of dissenting opinions undermined the corporate authority of the bench.[16] What Moore failed to explain, either privately or in public, was why the Signatories – and behind them the League – should accept unanimously and explicitly conditions set by the United States – conditions which for some time had been unfavourably described as privileges.[17]

As the autumn of 1925 passed into early winter and the opening of the Congress came closer, Moore became increasingly confident. He wrote to various colleagues that Senator Pepper would play a determining role in the forthcoming debate; and the only real danger came from the unrestrained proponents of the League: individuals like Hudson, Holt, Wickersham and their 'tearful brethren' and the numerous lobby organizations they controlled, especially the League of Nations Non-Partisan Association.[18] But the situation was more complicated than Moore seemed to realize. The lobbyists were not united. For example, the World Peace Foundation was collectively worried by the growing support for the Outlawry of War movement. The latter was a vague, somewhat contradictory umbrella-group, which Borah had once seemed to champion. The Foundation was concerned that Outlawry offered an internationalist alternative to American membership in the Court and League, especially for those people who feared that armed sanctions lay behind the judgments of the Court. But while the forebodings of the Foundation showed a division within the ranks of the very lobbyists Moore had so frequently denounced, the contemporaneous emergence of the Outlawry movement posed a different danger to the progress of the Court Protocol. This was that Court membership would become subordinated to grandiose schemes and thereby arouse the suspicions of the Senate and Executive on one side and committed pre-Leaguers on the other, with the Court falling victim in the middle.[19]

Other pro-Court lobby-groups also showed signs of unease. The American Foundation and the Foreign Policy Association (FPA) wanted Elihu Root to join in an eve-of-Congress campaign in Washington. Root declined, saying the effort would be counter-productive. As he wrote to George Wickersham in late September:

> The gathering of distinguished gentlemen from the eastern seaboard at Washington for the perfectly plain purpose of overawing the Senate would inevitably cause resentment and give an excuse for a lot of wavering senators to vote against the Court as a personal declaration of independence.[20]

Faced with such a refusal, James McDonald of the FPA turned to the Department of State for help and advice. Would one of the senior officers undertake to brief the Senate? No, said Castle, resolutely trying to preserve an image of neutrality, for all the Department's sponsorship of ratification. The FPA went to the top of the hierarchy with an appeal to the White House. That was equally unsuccessful. Well then, suggested McDonald, in some despair: what about asking Manley Hudson to undertake the task? 'Nothing', Castle replied firmly, 'would be more unwise.'[21]

Yet for all Moore's new-found confidence in Senator Pepper and his optimism at the outcome of the Senate debate, his own position on the Court bench was being used against him personally and American adherence in general. What commentators called the 'opening gun' in this campaign had been fired in the early summer of 1925 by Senator James A. Reed (Missouri, Democrat) one of the few remaining Senate Irreconcilables. In speeches and articles Reed denounced the judges of the Court as 'aliens in tongue, and in every instance aliens in allegiance'. Every instance? Unquestionably, insisted Reed: Judge Moore simply

> perform[ed] the contemptible office of decoy, placed by foreign nations on the international pond in the hope that American geese may be induced to light.[22]

Moore knew of these abusive remarks; nor was Reed alone. Similar attacks were levelled by Reed's senatorial colleague, Cole L. Blease (South Carolina, Democrat), a newcomer, and George Holden Tinkham (a Republican Representative from Massachusetts), who had served ten years in Congress, kept a close watch on the Court Protocols and (like the late Senator Lodge) introduced legislation to establish a new court and provide for the codification of international law.[23] But Moore did not openly complain. Only later did he bother to respond at length to such personal and professional attacks; and then purely privately and in answer to questioning by Secretary Kellogg.

Kellogg was puzzled: could Judge Moore explain the slanders? He himself had always 'supposed that the [Court] personnel was of a very high order'. So it was, Moore reassured him. The members of the Court were all 'men of good repute'; and in his four years on the bench he had 'never heard any reports unfavourable to them in point of character'. The simple truth (Moore added) was that the virulent attacks were not only unjustified but completely disingenuous. Nine of the fifteen judges on the World Court were panel-members of the Permanent Court of Arbitration (namely Anzilotti, Beichmann, Bustamente y Sirven, Finlay, Huber, Nyholm, Oda, Weiss and Yovanovitch); and their presence on that panel had never to his knowledge been challenged in the United States – certainly not by Senator Reed & Company.[24]

Before we leave this one-sided slanging-match, a few comments are worth making, if only because Reed's invective has been readily mishandled. His attack on Moore was typically phrased: Reed was a chauvinist and an outspoken racist. Blease and Tinkham shared some of

Reed's views and something of his style. But racism was not confined to the opposition. In varying but significant degrees Swanson, Walsh and Root displayed similar prejudices.[25] Indeed, in their common argument for adherence we can detect the premise that the greatest White Power on earth should align with its racial equals. What of Japan? Here the exception confirms the general rule. Walsh's reservation on the advisory jurisdiction was directed primarily to reinforcing the Oriental exclusion-policy so popular in the Pacific and Mountain States of the Union – a concern also to Root.[26] Relatedly, the Court proponents' objections to schemes (such as those of Harding, Lenroot, Lodge and Pepper) to reduce the voting power of the British Empire were often couched as a defence of White votes in a multiracial entity, the League of Nations. Why cut down Australia and Canada (the proponents argued) only to increase the relative voting-strength of Haiti and Liberia?[27]

A second set of issues is raised by Reed's onslaught; for though xenophobia permeated his allegations there were substantive problems lurking beneath them. The Court's electoral process and the provision for national judges *ad hoc* in contentious proceedings acknowledged the political complexion of the Court. Some members of the Advisory Committee of Jurists tried to blame ignorant public opinion for these deviations from the judicial ideal; but that was an arrogant, self-justifying subterfuge. Moreover, as American critics of the Court pointed out, Root had opposed the idea of national judges when briefing the US delegation to the second Hague Peace Conference.[28] Nor could anyone doubt that the election of an American jurist did not have a political goal: Root had been guaranteed a seat on the bench – even promised the Court presidency – and Moore had confessed that his early retirement would impede the progress of the Court Protocol. But the clearest evidence of political considerations in the appointment of judges came from the Brazilian government, which made its insistence upon a seat on the bench quite open and unscrupulous.[29] On a slightly different tack, Moore in his private correspondence admitted the danger posed by a permanent court becoming permanently hostile to the United States. That was a major reason for his insistence upon controlling the use of the advisory jurisdiction. The argument and the risk had been publicly expressed by his close friend, Edwin Borchard. In reply, the more unrestrained advocates of American adherence minimized the danger by disavowing any obligation to implement the judgments of the Court or to be 'bound' by its advisory opinions – a type of moral flaccidity deplored by Hiram Johnson.[30]

A third set of considerations brings us back to the domestic setting of the Senate debate on the Court Protocols. Historians have generally taken Reed & Company's venomous rhetoric as typical of the opposition's case; and often they attach unexplained references to the shared hostility of the Ku Klux Klan, Irish-Americans and the Hearst press to the League and the Court.[31] Two observations are in order. The first and more obvious is that such a coalition requires investigation, for the middle of the 1920s registers the peak of the Klan's ethnocentricity, anti-urbanism and anti-Catholicism – the very points at which the Irish – Americans and Hearst press would appear to represent values, constituencies and material interests in conflict with the Klan. It is not that the existence of such a functional coalition is impossible; but rather that its paradoxical nature calls for analysis. After all, the Democratic convention which had endorsed the Court and League in 1924 was riven by just such dissensions.

The second observation is more specific to Reed himself and concerns the true weight of his contribution to the forthcoming debate. Reed was undoubtedly a powerful stump orator and brilliant debater, as his irreconcilable campaign in 1919–20 had shown. But even at a popular, mass-audience level his talents were being displaced by the technology of radio and increased English-language literacy. This is not to say skilful speakers could not exploit the possibilities of radio: the 1930s would prove that through such different political broadcasters as FDR and Fr. Coughlin. Rather, Reed was not one who adapted. Forensically, another type was required, particularly in the Senate debate. Someone who possessed knowledge and imagination and who commanded respect: the combination of qualities which constituted autoritativeness. Such a man was Borah. He, not Reed, was the Senate debater and tactician feared by the proponents; his were the arguments addressed at length by leading individuals, lobbies and the press; he was the Senator foreign governments regarded in the prelude to the Court debate.[32]

The chances, however, of Borah bringing about the Senate's rejection of the Protocol were very slim. There was a remote possibility that it might not be put to a vote. As we have seen, the agreement during the Special Session had placed it high on the calendar but had not set down a date for the final decision. If the Protocols did come to a vote, its passage was virtually guaranteed. Public press reports and confidental lobby-surveys showed more than seventy-five Senators in favour; never more than fifteen were listed as opposed. Even the Court's enemies admitted the numbers against them, though they deplored such 'propaganda' and called for its investigation by Congress.[33] On such polling, the necessary two-thirds majority looked certain. Borah, in fact, was relatively isolated. Former irreconcilable colleagues such as Frank Brandegee and Robert La Follette had died within a year of one another. Pepper had so shifted from his irreconcilable position that the press spoke of him as a leading pro-Court Senator; and Norris, another irreconcilable Senator, favoured ratification. This left Bert M. Fernald (Maine, Republian), George H. Moses (New Hampshire, Republican) and Hiram Johnson – the first two of whom thought Borah dangerously radical, while Johnson saw Borah succumbing to such conservative Republicans as Moses and Fernald – a style rather than a philosophy which Judge Moore called 'Coolidgism'.[34]

There was, however, one possibility – or rather two related but equally sinister possibilities, as Irvine Lenroot envisaged them. The resolution of adherence might become so encumbered with reservations that either the proponents would vote against it or the League would not accept it. This would be 1919–20 all over again. And what Lenroot also foresaw and deprecated was that it might be a majority of the proponents who compromised upon attaching such destructive reservations to the resolution.[35]

The First Session of the Sixty-ninth Congress opened on Monday, 7 December 1925. Ten days later S.Res. 5 became first order of business in the Senate and debate on the Court Protocol began. The remainder of this chapter is devoted to that debate and events behind the scenes. It may seem odd to justify a comparatively long analysis of these proceedings; but a number of reasons combine to make a compelling case for such a detailed review. First and perhaps most paradoxical is the defence of novelty. Nevertheless it is a stark fact that despite the frequent allusions to the course and effect of the debate, no systematic study has yet been published of the debaters' main and shared concerns – of which more in a moment. Secondly and relatedly: even a sceptic, though a shrewd and informed one, Lindsay Rogers, praised the argumentative level of the Court debate: it was reputedly far more thoughtful and focused than the debate on the Paris Peace Treaties in 1919–20.[36] Thirdly (and this is a consideration particularly for those habituated to the parliamentary dominance of the Executive), the debate shows the power of determined minorities to shape and even ultimately endanger legislation. The fourth and last reason is the most important of all. A careful examination of the words and structure of the debate demonstrates beyond any possible doubt that the final terms of the resolution were written and wholeheartedly approved by the self-proclaimed friends of the Court in the Senate and the Coolidge administration. Over the years the conditions set in the winter of 1925–6 have become notorious; but little if any attention has been paid to where the true responsibility for those conditions lay.

In the previous chapter we examined the two respects in which Swanson's S.Res. 5 differed from the conditions originally proposed and published by Secretary of State Hughes in February 1923. First was the well-publicized addition of a fifth reservation, sponsored by Senator Walsh, governing the Court's advisory jurisdiction. Before full debate began, President Coolidge emphatically endorsed Walsh's reservation – almost appropriated it – in his Annual Message to Congress. Such public support contrasted strongly with Coolidge's private doubts in the early summer. The second difference from the original Hughes formula was the far less open insertion of an unnumbered clause requiring the explicit acceptance by the Court Signatories of the American reservations *en bloc.*[37]

In the course of twenty days of debate and legislative action S.Res. 5 was amended in four respects. (The final terms are set out *verbatim* on pp. 146-47 below.) The first and least obvious was the addition of a clause to the fourth of the Hughes–Harding conditions reserving the right of the United States to 'withdraw its adherence' to the Court Protocol 'at any time'. The clause caused no controversy in the Senate or the Executive, since both assumed the existence of the right. What disagreement there was concerned the need to make the condition explicit.[38] The second amendment to S.Res. 5 was far more obvious and became notorious. This involved the redrafting of Walsh's original fifth reservation on the advisory jurisdiction. The substance and immediate circumstances of the new draft we shall examine later and in context. The amendment is noted here for two different but related reasons. First, the final terms of the reservation were sponsored by Swanson and the leading proponents of ratification. Secondly, the advisory jurisdiction and the phraseology of the relevant reservation were the crucial issues in the Senate debate. Ultimately all else turned on this – the 'central issue'.[39]

The two other changes introduced into S.Res. 5 were formally of a different and somewhat uncertain status. They were conceived less as conditions governing the United States and its prospective co-signatories but rather as reaffirmations of traditional unilateral policies and practices. Since neither amendment caused any serious dispute in the Senate chamber, it will not distort our examination of the main debate if we here cite their terms and recall their origins. On the contrary: Swanson's long, opening speech in support of his resolution contained a detailed discussion of both proposed amendments.

The first provision stated that

> recourse to the Permanent Court of International Justice for the settlement of differences between the United States and any other State or States can be had only by agreement thereto through general or special treaties concluded between the parties in dispute.

The language and purpose were familiar; the Senate, through the treaty-making power was to exercise a right of veto over the Executive's submission of disputes to arbitration or adjudication. The element of novelty in the amendment consisted simply in the specific reference to the PCIJ. As we saw in Chapter 1, from at least the end of the nineteenth century but most notably in the years immediately preceding World War I the Senate had attached comparable conditions to a whole series of bilateral and multilateral arbitration treaties. The Senate had qualified its endorsement of The Hague Conferences in such terms; and, most recently, Lodge's draft scheme for a new 'World Court' had contained a similar (though more restrictive) provision. A succession of administrations had agreed with the Senate that such a condition was an assertion of senatorial prerogative. Equally this reluctant admission by the Executive did not prevent bitter criticism from a number of Secretaries of State, notably John Hay, and constitutional objections from inside and outside government against the 'blackguard' one-third-plus-one minority which could defeat a treaty. Yet these well-known features of the condition were thrown into relief by one remarkable fact: Secretary of State Hughes had alluded to its reappearance in his original submission of the Protocol.[40]

The second provision added to S.Res. 5 stated that

> adherence... shall not be so construed as to require the United States to depart

> from its traditional policy of not intruding upon, interfering with, or entangling itself in the political questions of policy or internal administration of any foreign state; nor shall adherence... be construed to imply a relinquishment by the United States of its traditional attitude toward purely American questions.

Once again (as chapter 1 also shows) history was on the side of the Senate. The same language had been used in the American reservations to the Final Act of the first 1899 Hague Peace Conference and been repeated in respect of the second 1907 Conference. Root, Hughes and Taft (to name only three principals) had sought such an addition to the Draft League Covenant when it was published in February 1919. With minor changes the same terms had been incorporated into the Senate's reservations to the Treaty of Versailles containing the League Covenant. The 1924 schemes of Senators Lodge and Pepper had both explicitly reserved the Monroe Doctrine from the jurisdiction of their proposed World Courts – a purpose covered in the generalities of the phrasing, 'traditional attitude toward purely American questions'.[41]

From these explanatory remarks it is easy to realize that both these reservations had been widely and openly discussed before debate began. Far less apparent was the attitude of the Coolidge administration; but the official records suggest that the weak leadership exercised by the administration was prepared for the eventual incorporation of this pair of conditions into the resolution of adherence.[42] Swanson, however, used part of his long opening speech to deprecate their inclusion. Not because he objected to their substance; rather, they were both 'unnecessary'. In the first instance the Executive simply could not refer a dispute to any arbitral body without recourse to the two-thirds rule. As for the (so-called) Monroe Doctrine reservation, the traditional language was a proper statement of the unilateral American position on such other matters as the tariff and immigration; and adherence to the Permanent Court in no way altered its status or purpose. Swanson spoke in generalities: he did not, for example, make in public the well-known points he and Lenroot had made to the administration to the effect that Confederate Senators were arch-defenders of the two-thirds rule and constantly invoked the bogey of a hostile northern Republican administration permitting the international adjudication of the defaulted Southern Bonds.[43] Nor did he remind the Senate that in 1907 it was Secretary of State Elihu Root who instructed the American delegation to The Hague Conference to incorporate the Monroe Doctrine exclusion. But it was clear that Swanson's main concern was strategic. He did not want the amendment, however superfluous, of S.Res. 5, for fear it would destroy the principled argument against the addition of deliberately wrecking reservations.

Swanson handled the proposals firmly but briefly: to say too much might arouse suspicions. The two reservations then dropped from public view, only to re-emerge late in the debate as part of the proponents' bargain to achieve a favourable vote. Moreover the two clauses impeded the main flow of Swanson's speech, which was a presentation of the arguments for the Americanness of the Court; its independence of the

League; and the unexceptionableness of the Court's litigated and advisory work. Swanson spoke without complaint. The League was unconditionally praised; the judgments of the Court were endorsed in all particulars. The judgments were said to have no sanction but a 'moral sanction: the compelling power of public opinion'. This was a belief not shared by many pro-Leaguers abroad and their friends in the United States – but it was anyway contradicted immediately by Swanson himself.

The only sanctions that exist for the enforcement of the judgment of the court are... in the covenant of the league, and these are only binding upon its own members.

Not once did Swanson consider the substantive law to be declared by the Court, notably the Peace Treaties concluding World War I. Like so many advocates of adherence, Swanson favourably compared the Permanent Court of International Justice with the US Supreme Court. Like them, Swanson ignored questions about their respective legitimacy, their political composition, their popular support, their jurisprudential biases and their power of judicial review.[44]

Lenroot of Wisconsin spoke the following day. Though his speech was one-third the length of Swanson's, its relative brevity did not make it any more accurate or persuasive. After all, Lenroot had once sponsored a radical redrafting for the Court Statute. Consequently his major opening argument for the American origins of the Court and the independence of the bench jarred with the position he had taken in late 1923 and early 1924. His previous stance, however, coupled with his record as a Lodge Reservationist on the Treaty of Versailles, might be turned to advantage: his present support of Swanson's resolution could be interpreted as the action of a moderate. Thus the prelude and conclusion of Lenroot's speech worked variations on a common theme: he was the man in the middle denouncing the 'propaganda... upon both sides'. Signing the Court Protocol was not tantamount to entering the League nor would it bring a golden age of immediate and universal peace. What it would register was the 'endorsement and encouragement of the most powerful nation in the world to an instrument of peace'.[45]

Lenroot's general complaisance left him with no firm standpoint for himself. A case in point was his defence of Judge Moore in particular and the bench's corporate judicial impartiality. In an unwitting concession to chauvinistic opponents such as Senators Reed and Blease, Lenroot insisted that Moore's nationality could never influence his judgment. Within the hour, however, Lenroot acknowledged that the provision in the Statute for national judges had been designed to counterbalance existing national prejudices. Another, more subtle revelation of Lenroot's uncertainty came in his references to Germany under the Peace Treaties. Lenroot distinguished the League from the Court but held that both were responsible for Germany's subordinate, even abject condition. Yet he gave no grounds for believing that the Court, 'a judicial body', would act less reprehensibly than the League, 'a political body', in respect of Germany, even though it was his twofold argument that Germany must be restored to ensure peace and that the Court was the body to achieve this restoration. A third example of Lenroot's ambivalence lay in his urging of ratification as a contribution to peace. It illustrates our present analysis through its immediate coupling with Lenroot's denial that the United States would incur any obligation from adherence except to support the Court financially. Lenroot was not alone: many spoke like this. Senator Walsh went further and disclaimed benefits as well as duties: 'We incur no obligations... we acquire no rights'. But Lenroot's denial was implausible. It was not what pro-League advocates saw as the purpose of ratification; while foreign observers conceded this point in expressing the fear that such a miniscule obligation might indeed measure the true extent of American commitments. Small wonder that the blunt-speaking Hiram Johnson denounced such an argument as mean-spirited and a slander upon the United States – all the while convinced that the proponents were deluding themselves, if not deliberately deceiving their audience.[46]

Lenroot gave the floor to Borah, who rose to make the first of a number of speeches. Borah began by emphasizing the 'interdependence' of the Court and League; and it was an easy task for him to cite statements by leading politicians of the League, judges of the Court and, in particular, Elihu Root and James Brown Scott, to support his argument. As Borah pointed out, once upon a time no sensible person denied the closeness of the relationship. Then, for obvious, tactical reasons, the vital connecting links had been blurred, even denied in debate, especially in the United States. Furthermore, many of the authorities cited by Borah had openly shared the view expressed by Francis Hagerup of Norway in 1920 that American membership of the Court constituted 'the first step which will lead to the entry of the United States into the League'.

The second and far longer section of Borah's opening speech was devoted to the Court's advisory jurisdiction – a source of concern even to the proponents of ratification. A review of his arguments will add little to the analysis offered in previous pages; but we may note a number of areas in which Borah made a particular contribution. The first was Borah's readiness to use Judge Moore's position to support his opposition to the Court's performing an advisory role for the League. For Borah, Moore's memorandum of February 1922 still constituted an unanswerable case against the jurisdiction; and Moore's presence on the bench was less a reason for American adherence than an argument for American conditions to limit and ultimately abolish a judicial malpractice. This was, of course, Borah's second line of defence: his first was to attack and defeat adherence. To this end he concentrated his efforts on showing the potential of the advisory jurisdiction for extending compulsory jurisdiction and legitimating sanctions. Much of his evidence he drew from the recent advisory opinion in the Mosul case and from the earlier Geneva Protocol. Borah sought to unnerve the Senate by demonstrating the attempt of France and her Eastern European allies to extend the obligations of the Covenant and stiffen the judgments of the Court against so-called aggressors. Senator Walsh intervened to challenge Borah's conflation of the Covenant and Geneva Protocol with the developing jurisprudence of the Court as exemplified in the Eastern Carelia and Mosul cases. Walsh believed he had an irrefutable counter-argument: the failure of the Geneva Protocol, primarily at the hands of the British. Borah welcomed the objection: it corroborated his fundamental point. In reply to Walsh Borah insisted that the British case rested upon the adequacy of the Covenant and the existing competence of the League to maintain peace. Formal authority was not lacking but political will might be. That, of course, had been the fear of France and her allies. Borah concluded, in the face of cross-questioning from Walsh, that the Mosul case had made unmistakable what many pro-Court advocates had long stated, namely that armed sanctions lay behind the judgments and opinions of the Court. As Borah began, so he ended: a string of authoritative names was produced, each affirming that the League could enforce the Court's decisions – militarily, if need be. It was a powerful case, as Borah's critics had acknowledged even before the Senate debate.[47]

Senator Walsh now took the floor in his own right; and, on this second, crowded day of debate, began to deliver the longest speech on the Court Protocol.[48] Walsh was one of the few men in the Senate reckoned to approach Borah's legal and forensic skills. He had served in the Senate since March 1913 but had achieved national prominence and respect in 1922 for his prosecution of the Teapot Dome scandals. His widespread appeal had been put to the test in 1924, when he presided as permanent chairman of the bitterly divided Democratic convention in New York City. Walsh was the Western, insurgent, Roman Catholic whose presidential candidacy might help fuse the different sections in the Democratic party, as opposed to New York's Governor Smith who appeared to intensify centrifugal forces. What told against Walsh was the electoral insignificance of his home-State, Montana, which held only four electoral college votes.[49] In the debate on the World Court Protocol Walsh played a crucial but somewhat hidden role. The Republican proponents were led by Lenroot; the Democratic floor-manager was Swanson, with help from Joe Robinson of Arkansas, the Minority leader. Walsh's position was not that of a behind-the-scenes operator; rather it was that of a principled advocate of the League who would vouch for the acceptability of the reservations offered during debate. While Swanson appeared in the limelight as the effective Democratic leader, Walsh exercised a powerful, even determining influence as his party's moral arbiter, especially for the remaining Wilsonians and pro-League Senators.[50]

Walsh had voted for the Treaty of Versailles and the Covenant of the League; and, as he told the Senate in his opening remarks, he was 'not at all troubled about this court being an organ of the league'. That was a historic, indisputable fact. The real question was whether the Court could be 'safely intrusted' with 'international controversies' which were 'resolvable upon legal principles'. He was convinced that the Court could. Consequently there was no need explicitly to reserve the Monroe Doctrine from the Court's jurisdiction, for the Doctrine was a traditional declaration of unilateral policy and not a principle of international law. Throughout his long speech Walsh insisted upon this distinction. Adherence to the Court and the associated promotion of the judicial resolution of disputes could be categorically distinguished from supporting the League and the political determination of controversies. Yet this distinction was increasingly challenged by contemporary lawyers and politicians, particularly those who favoured the League and the Court's extensive view of its powers. It was, moreover, a scheme which Walsh's own analysis undermined. As he discussed the so-called unequal treaties applying to China, the Locarno agreements and the Mosul case he showed that political and legal categories overlapped. Even so, a far more revealing example had been his own sponsorship of a reservation governing the advisory jurisdiction to achieve a purpose once confidently stated to be exclusively within the political and legal competence of a sovereign State, namely the self-determination of its immigration policies and legislation.[51]

Admittedly these were contentious questions, to which Walsh gave conflicting answers. But surely no-one could accept the assertion on which Walsh completed his analysis of the advisory jurisdiction: 'the conclusion at which the court arrives is a matter of perfect indifference to the league as such.' Those who looked favourably on the erosion of the distinction between legal and political disputes were generally agreed that the great triumph of the Court had been its handling of the advisory function and its consequent aid to the League of Nations. And what was true in general terms was particularly true of the Mosul case, which Walsh himself had adduced on a number of occasions. To claim that the League was not interested, even disinterested, was plainly incorrect and could persuade only the completely ignorant.[52]

Time ran out on Walsh. The second day of debate ended; and he had to wait until Monday to finish his speech. Walsh returned to the Mosul case and discussed it at length; but he added nothing new to his previous interpretation. His most interesting remarks came when tackling two subjects which had already caused difficulties. In both instances he contradicted previous statements: in the first case he challenged Lenroot; in the second he reversed himself.

Walsh's reversal of himself was the more obvious and closer to our main focus on the advisory jurisdiction. Having denied the relevance of the Court's advisory opinions on Friday, on Monday Walsh spoke of their past, present and future importance – an importance which by definition concerned the conduct of the League. This was not a momentary lapse, for most of Monday's speech was a defence of the jurisprudence of the Court and the judicial rectitude of the advisory function itself. The other example of Walsh the contradictor came when he turned aside to the question which had defeated Lenroot: the provision for *ad hoc* national judges. Whereas Lenroot had protected Judge Moore against the possibility that he might favour the United States, Walsh argued that it was 'all but a foregone conclusion that [an *ad hoc* judge] will be an advocate for the cause of his country'. But Walsh did not stop with this contradiction of Lenroot's first position; he was, like Lenroot, led on to offer a second, conflicting analysis.

The provision attests the scrupulous care that was exercised in the drafting of the statute to insure an impartial consideration.[53]

Judge Moore found Walsh's marathon of a speech completely unsatisfactory. Moore was following the debate closely in the press; and as soon as he received news of Walsh's concluding remarks, Moore wrote a long letter to Senator Pepper giving his list of Walsh's omissions and mistakes. Moore ignored most of the points we have discussed and instead concentrated almost exclusively upon the advisory jurisdiction. *Pace* Walsh, the Eastern Carelia case had not guaranteed the Court's right to silence nor had it established impregnably a disputant State's right to oust the jurisdiction of the Court. Secondly, dissenting opinions under the advisory procedure were protected only by the Rules of the Court, not by the Statute. Thirdly, Walsh had neglected to fight for the United States' enjoying the same rights as the Permanent Members of the Council to prevent the reference of an issue to the Court under the advisory jurisdiction. Moore told Pepper that Walsh's behaviour had to be understood as a product of his original and fundamental complaisance towards the League – an outrageous sort of self and national abasement which not one of the Great Powers in the League would practise itself. Moore concluded his attack by deploring Walsh's failure to have advanced beyond his worthless reservation of May 1924: Walsh had not understood the development of politics within the League; nor had he appreciated the real drift of the Court's jurisprudence, particularly in the recent Mosul case.

Pepper agreed with Moore's catalogue of complaints. Nevertheless he well knew the esteem in which Walsh was held as a legal expert and a man of principle; as someone who was respected by both pro-League Democrats and insurgent Republicans in the irreconcilable camp. Pepper therefore suggested to Moore that they hold a joint conference with Walsh, Swanson and Lenroot. Lenroot was said to be ready to follow Pepper's lead; while Swanson was reported to believe that Walsh should acknowledge the broader goals that Moore was trying to achieve for the Court's independence and integrity by way of American adherence. If Walsh were induced to revise the terms of the fifth reservation, Robinson could be relied upon to bring over the vast majority of the Democrats and then the passage of the resolution would be virtually assured.[54].

As a step in this direction Pepper used the last full day of debate before the Christmas–New Year recess to publicize the basis of a compromise. He urged his credentials as a mediator. He shared the view of Walsh that the relationship between the Court and the League was undeniable; unlike Walsh he believed that his 1924 scheme of 'disassociation' was theoretically the best plan for a world court. Nevertheless he had to be realistic: the 1920 Statute was effectively the only answer. Pepper also distinguished himself from those like Swanson who praised the advisory jurisdiction in all particulars; at the same time he separated himself from those like Borah who damned it in the abstract, criticized specific decisions and thus tried to undermine the cumulative jurisprudence. Pepper readily agreed that the advisory jurisdiction was the 'essential matter' before the Senate and that they were rapidly approaching an impasse. He proposed, therefore, a method for resolving the controversy:

to analyze the jurisdiction and select the specific points which are really of importance to the United States.

Without revealing the details of his summer negotiations with Moore, Pepper reviewed the work of the Court and the Council and then put forward three elements for incorporation into Walsh's original fifth reservation. First, it was

now the rule and the practice of the... court... to give no confidential or secret advice. I believe that the United States will do well, in adhering to the court, to declare its understanding that this is a permanent and not a transient policy.

Secondly:

there should be an equally explicit declaration that the decision of the court in the Eastern Carelia case be likewise the expression of an acceptable and permanent policy –

namely, that the Court might decline to give an advisory opinion. As for a disputant State's power of ouster, this was left unclear by Pepper – except, that is, in regard to the United States. Thus Pepper supported Walsh's disclaimer of the binding power of an advisory opinion rendered without the explicit consent of the United States. He wished, however, to

go further, and request the assent of the signatories to the proposition that there shall be no advisory opinion on any matter directly affecting the United States unless the United States shall have consented that the court may take jurisdiction of that question and give an advisory opinion thereon.

Having offered this tripartite amendment to S.Res. 5, Pepper left the floor and the first stage of the Senate debate effectively came to a close.[55]

Moore was not happy even with Senator Pepper's contribution. One week after Pepper's initiative, Moore wrote a long letter to a close friend and former colleague explaining his objections. Moore's correspondent was Harlan Fiske Stone. Stone was a direct link to Coolidge. He had been a classmate of the future President at Amherst; he had been appointed by Coolidge Attorney General to succeed the disgraced Daugherty; and then elevated to the Supreme Court. Before holding these federal offices, Stone had been Dean of the Columbia Law School, Moore's academic base. Stone was also a member of the Republican

Thirty-One. He was, in short, a man respected by the east coast Republican establishment; a man sympathetic to an earlier conception of the League; and (as we shall see) he shared Moore's views on the proper role of the World Court and the potential of the United States for enhancing its independence. It was just along these lines that Moore now wrote to Stone. Whereas Moore had recently critized Walsh for subordinating the interests of the United States to those of the League of Nations, the charge against Pepper was that he had been more concerned to protect the United States than the Court. Even so, the main cause for complaint, Moore generalized, was the complaisance of the pro-League Senators. Stone agreed; and he expressed his shared pessimism at the course and style of the debate. There was

> really little discriminating, disinterested thought... devoted to this question by those whose first interest it should be to study the matter thoroughly and act in accordance with the realities of the situation.[56]

Full debate on the Protocols resumed on Monday, 4 January 1926.[57] A couple of days later Stone wrote again to Moore. He wondered whether Borah rather than Pepper ought not to be given the task of bringing Moore's criticisms and proposals to the Senate. Or was it the case, Stone asked Moore, that Borah was so closely 'identified with the irreconcilables' that no-one with an open mind would follow him? It was a desperate calculation. Certainly Moore's pessimism was increasing; but so too was his reluctance to become involved in any public lobbying. Pepper had resumed his efforts to get Moore to travel down to Washington from New York to confer with declared friends of the Court. Moore declined. He insisted that his views could be easily found in published articles, particularly his extensive 1923 essay on the Court.[58] Such a response to Pepper's request was obviously born of fatigue, impatience and depression; for the whole thrust of Moore's analysis of the advisory jurisdiction was that events since the publication of the Eastern Carelia Opinion both proved its precariousness and disproved the general interpretation of its meaning.

Then came the first signs of a breakthrough. Stone, using his very good contacts with the Coolidge administration and in the Senate, apparently leaked much of the substance of Moore's criticisms of Walsh and Pepper. Contemporaneously Walsh and Lenroot were making common cause with Borah in the publication of Moore's February 1922 memorandum arguing against an advisory jurisdiction for the Court. Shortly afterwards Walsh himself wrote to Moore and asked him to travel to Washington for a conference.[59]

Walsh and Moore, with Swanson in attendance, met in Washington on the night of 14 January. It was not an entirely satisfactory meeting for any of the participants. Walsh evidently did not want to go beyond his earlier phraseology and disliked (what Moore self-depreciatingly called) the 'provocativeness and verbosity' of his counter-proposals. Yet it was Swanson who caused Moore far greater distress, for Moore attributed his obduracy to partisan considerations and not principled objections to insulting (as Walsh put it) the League with American importunities.[60]

Moore appeared never to overcome the resentment – even contempt – he felt for Swanson's '"pussy-foot" attitude' at this critical moment – a form of cowardly circumspection that Stone (who first used the term 'pussy-foot') came to see as part of the 'moral aphasia' affecting many other Senators.[61] Walsh, however, gained Moore's long-lasting respect for his seriousness and candor. Moore acknowledged the force of his arguments and his senatorial leverage by responding with another lengthy memorandum. Moore's energy and optimism had revived. Whereas less than a fortnight earlier he had fobbed off Pepper with arguments from 1923, now he drew on the events of the intervening years to persuade Walsh that his May 1924 reservation was inadequate.[62]

Within a few days Walsh became convinced by Moore's arguments at a theoretical level; but, like Pepper, he believed that the practical course was to concentrate upon American concerns rather than dissipate effort by trying to affect and reform every aspect of the advisory jurisdiction.[63] The Senate leadership, however, was juggling with other factors. Swanson and Robinson for the Democrats were reluctant to look as though they had lost control to outside (especially anti-League) forces or to have been mistaken in their commitment to the 1924 formula. On the Republican side, Lenroot and Charles Curtis of Kansas, the Majority leader, wanted to clear any amendments with the White House and Department of State.[64]

But these delays had their own dangers. The day following the Walsh–Swanson–Moore conference the spectre of a filibuster was raised in the Senate when Blease and Fernald took the floor. A few days later, Borah acted unilaterally and without authority in leaking Moore's systematic criticism of the original Walsh reservation, which was still part of the resolution before the Senate. To the relatively detached judgment of Stone it seemed that a 'quiet undercurrent of opposition' was rising up and threatened eventually to overwhelm the Court Protocol. Samuel Colcord, viewing events from a diferent perspective, agreed. As he told Root, pro-Court Senators were going 'over to the opposition' in significant numbers and the two-thirds majority, once seemingly 'assured', was being eroded.[65]

To understand Stone's prediction and Colcord's anxiety we must go back a fortnight. The debate which had resumed on 4 January was noticeably different from the proceedings before the recess. In the first stage of the debate five leading Senators, closely identified with the legislative history of the Court Protocol, had delivered systematic expositions of the Court's career and jurisdiction and had sought to establish or disprove the dangers of the connection between the Court and the League. The five were Swanson, Lenroot, Borah, Walsh and Pepper. Their rather formal and studious contributions lacked verve; there was little drama. After the recess the atmosphere changed. There were many more actors involved; there was much more cut and thrust on the Senate floor. Some proponents of adherence now spoke boldly of the connections between the Court and the League. William Bruce (Maryland, Democrat) epitomized this style when he declared:

The more readily the features of the League of Nations can be seen in the face of the Harding – Hughes – Coolidge World Court, the better I like the child.

Even the more qualified proponents, such as the Republican Senators from Ohio, Frank B. Willis and Simeon D. Fess, were less inhibited than their leader on the Court issue, Lenroot. For the outright opponents, George Moses and Henrick Shipstead delivered particularly powerful and wide-ranging speeches. Conservative fought alongside radical. Their constitutional theory, their respective interpretations of international relations, their positions on domestic politics and economics were vastly different yet they came to a common conclusion on the Court issue. In their shared judgment, League of Nations internationalists were attempting to inveigle the United States of America into maintaining – by force, if necessary – the iniquitous and war-breeding imperialist systems consolidated by the World War I settlement. The Court advocates did not directly challenge this analysis; they ignored it. Instead they employed a different language and did not publicly examine structures. Bruce was representative when he inveighed against Moses and his alleged belief in 'a little America'. In Bruce's words:

I believe in a great America. [Moses] believes that this nation should shut itself out by a wall of selfish exclusion from all the interests of a common humanity.

I believe that its great power, its great wealth, its great prestige should be brought into relations of cooperation with the effort which the other civilized powers of the world are making to promote the cause of international peace and justice.[66]

Borah and Walsh continued to play the roles of opposing leading counsel – though, as we have seen, Walsh was beginning to shift ground. His second speech, delivered shortly after his opening to Moore, was markedly less pro-League, much more in the style of Pepper's realism than his marathon before the recess. Borah was far busier. Unlike Walsh, he did not have allies in the Republican and Democratic leadership. But Borah was in his element: a master in the chamber and behind the scenes. Press items reported his office crowded with Senators discussing tactics. The fears of a filibuster had grown stronger. Borah denied that was his method; and perhaps the denial was true, if literally construed. Others could play that role, notably Reed and Blease. Borah could then wait for the Senate as a whole to fear that an important tax-bill would be hazarded unless the Protocol was dropped – a very real possibility which the Republican leadership in Congress and the White House deprecated, especially in an election year.[67]

A filibuster had appeared to begin coincidentally with the Walsh–Swanson–Moore conference, when Reed and Blease spoke for the first time in the debate. Fernald's speech on the following day (Friday, 15

January) brought a genuine filibuster that much nearer.[68] Yet a filibuster had always been a possibility. Far more significant, therefore, was Borah's third speech, which he delivered just as the filibuster was gathering momentum.

At the resumption of debate after the recess, Harlan Fiske Stone had (as we have seen) asked Moore whether Borah could act as his counsel in the Senate. On Monday, 18 January, Borah assumed the role, but without clearance from Stone or Moore. In the single most dramatic event of the whole debate Borah introduced a long anonymous memorandum on the advisory jurisdiction. Borah declared that he was 'not at liberty to use the name of the author', who was 'in official life' and 'well known as an international jurist'. It was an open secret that this identity belonged to Judge John Bassett Moore.[69]

In a number of previous passages we have explained the burden of Moore's complaint against the Walsh reservation on the advisory jurisdiction. Even the most recent revisions offered by Pepper had not been entirely satisfactory. The nub of Moore's final contribution, handed to Stone and now broadcast by Borah, can be concisely stated. Moore required the United States to be on a 'footing of equality' with the Permanent Members of the League Council; for it was indisputable (Moore claimed) that no request for an advisory opinion had ever gone to the Court unless the Permanent Members had first individually and then collectively endorsed the referral. This was the deeper interpretation of the Tunis, Eastern Carelia and Mosul cases; and abstract and arid debates on the true meaning of the Court Statute and League Covenant missed this concrete, political fact. As Moore phrased his argument: the

> issue is simply whether the United States, which is not a member of the League of Nations, shall, in adhering to the Court, put itself in a position of national inferiority, by omitting to assure to itself a right of self-protection similar to that which other great powers, members of the league, possess.

The United States must not allow itself to be put 'in a subordinate and helpless position'. And not for selfish reasons; for such an imbalance was 'not in the interest of the court. On the contrary, it is likely to end in a catastrophe.'

Moore was never one to assert that the judicial resolution of disputes was a guarantee of peace: that was certainly not the lesson of the Dred Scott case. So far as the World Court Protocol was concerned, his foreboding was grounded in the possibility that the mere referral of contentious and allegedly purely political questions (such as immigration legislation or territorial spheres of interest without a specifically American aspect) would provoke fierce reaction in the United States to the Court itself and not just the League. Even if the Court declined to entertain the reference (the common interpretation of the Eastern Carelia precedent), the suspicion would never and could never be removed that the Court had bowed to political pressure – but this time from the United States. Thus the interests of the United States would be ostensibly served – but at the cost of the Court's reputation for integrity and independence.[70]

Borah's action and the authority of his anonymous counsel had immediate effect. Pepper recapitulated Moore's substantive points and announced that he would support ratification only if the fifth reservation were amended: first, to prohibit secret opinions; second, to make explicit the Court's right to decline to give an opinion; and, third, to permit the United States a *de jure* power of veto over the Court's entertainment of a reference corresponding to the *de facto* power of veto exercised by Permanent Members of the Council over the submission of a request. Though these three conditions essentially repeated Pepper's earlier proposals, their significance lay in the context of their repetition. Now Borah was seen to be dictating the terms of adherence.[71]

The proponents who took their lead from Walsh, Swanson and Lenroot appeared at a loss. None of these three Senators made a significant contribution to the debate for four days after Borah's dramatic intervention. Indeed the less committed, those not so closely identified with S.Res. 5, began to show signs of moving towards Borah and Pepper. William McKinley (Illinois, Republican) was the most conspicuous example. He described the gap between Borah's proposals and S.Res. 5 as 'differences in language [not] in spirit'. Even Hiram Johnson was induced to speak – if only to denounce the vitality and hypocrisy of the pro-League movement. Were the pro-Leaguers 'fooling the American people or… fooling the people across the sea?' They claimed there were no obligations arising from adherence: that was, at best naive, at worst deceptive. Alternatively they claimed that the obligations could be ignored: that was at best mistaken, at worst dishonourable. Johnson's speech against the 'poisonous propaganda' was direct and honest. Just as he had voted in the Committee on Foreign Relations against the Pepper 'disassociation' scheme as a diversion, so he would vote against adherence proper, 'with or without reservations'. As Johnson explained: he

> could not give [his] acquiesence to reservations except, in frankness, for the purpose ultimately by indirection of defeating that which I believe should be directly defeated.[72]

Lenroot, as we have seen, feared exactly such an outcome when the Protocol finally came to a vote – and he was not alone. In the words of the *New York Times*, such tactics would amount to 'crippling by reservations'.[73] Meanwhile even the chances of a vote appeared to lessen. The space left by the proponents was most obviously taken by Reed, who removed any last doubts that some Senators would wreck the Protocol by the procedural weapon of a filibuster. He spoke on four consecutive days, renewing his attacks on Judge Moore (the 'decoy duck') and his colleagues and including Marxist 'bolshevists' and capitalist 'internationalists' in his demonology of the Court and League – the enemies of America.[74]

Though silent, the leaders of the proposition were mounting their own procedural counter-attack: the introduction of a guillotine on debate. Under Senate Rule XXII a motion for cloture – the Rule requiring that it be debated the following Monday – required sixteen signatures for discussion and a two-thirds majority for passage; and the terms of the motion would specify the allocation of time in the remaining stages of debate and voting on an agreed resolution. On Friday, 22 January, Lenroot filed a motion for cloture. With 48 signatories, equally divided between Republicans and Democrats, its prospects looked healthy. Furthermore, if a two-thirds vote could be won for a procedural motion, then the passage of the resolution governing the Protocol (which also required a two-thirds majority) grew more likely. The Senate was notorious for valuing its procedures – even at the painful cost of losing substantial issues. In other words, some Senators might oppose a guillotine on grounds of principle even though they favoured ultimate ratification of the Court Protocol.[75]

A motion for cloture was not enough in itself: there remained the substantive question of S.Res. 5. McKinley had begun the public retreat from Swanson's original motion. At issue were the precise terms of its amendment. By Friday Lenroot had received clearance from the White House (which was setting the pace rather than the Department of State) that President Coolidge would 'accept anything that the Senate puts through'.[76] On Saturday, and as a prelude to debate on the cloture motion, Swanson introduced a revised version of S.Res. 5.

In setting the scene on the eve of the Senate debate we previously detailed the four areas in which the original S.Res. 5 would be amended before being put to the vote. On Saturday, 23 January, Swanson proposed the redrafting that was eventually submitted to the full Senate as the resolution of adherence. By way of recapitulation we can note that the preamble, the first five paragraphs or reservations, plus the 'exchange of notes' rider were identical to those of S.Res. 5 (and thus the Hughes–Harding–Coolidge terms), except in two respects. First was the inclusion of a clause in Paragraph IV affirming the right of the United States to revoke its adherence 'at any time'. Second and far more important was the redrafting of Paragraph V governing the advisory jurisdiction – the reservation originally introduced by Senator Walsh in May 1924. Finally there were appended two unnumbered paragraphs or 'further' conditions. The first required senatorial consent for the submission of cases to the Court; the second reserved a set of 'traditional' policies from the competence of the Court. Thus amended, the revised S.Res. 5 read as follows:

> *Resolved* (*two-thirds of the Senators present concurring*), That the Senate advise and consent to the adherence on the part of the United States to the said Protocol of December 16, 1920, and the adjoined Statute for the Permanent Court of International Justice (without accepting or agreeing to the optional clause for compulsory jurisdiction contained in said Statute), and that the signature of the United States be affixed to the said Protocol, subject to the following reservations and understandings, which are hereby made a part and condition of this resolution, namely:

I. That such adherence shall not be taken to involve any legal relation on the part of the United States to the League of Nations or the assumption of any obligations by the United States under the Treaty of Versailles.

II. That the United States shall be permitted to participate through representatives designated for the purpose and upon an equality with the other States, members, respectively, of the Council and Assembly of the League of Nations, in any and all proceedings of either the Council or the Assembly for the election of judges or deputy-judges of the Permanent Court of International Justice or for the filling of vacancies.

III. That the United States will pay a fair share of the expenses of the Court as determined and appropriated from time to time by the Congress of the United States.

IV. That the United States may at any time withdraw its adherence to the said Protocol and that the Statute for the Permanent Court of International Justice adjoined to the Protocol shall not be amended without the consent of the United States.

V. That the Court shall not render any advisory opinion except publicly after due notice to all states adhering to the Court and to all interested states and after public hearing or opportunity for hearing given to any state concerned; nor shall it, without the consent of the United States, entertain any request for an advisory opinion touching any dispute or question in which the United States has or claims an interest.

The signature of the United States to the said Protocol shall not be affixed until the powers signatory to such Protocol shall have indicated, through an exchange of notes, their acceptance of the foregoing reservations and understandings as a part and a condition of adherence by the United States to the said Protocol.

Resolved further, As a part of this act of ratification that the United States approve the Protocol and Statute hereinabove mentioned, with the understanding that recourse to the Permanent Court of International Justice for the settlement of differences between the United States and any other State or States can be had only by agreement thereto through general or special treaties concluded between the parties in dispute; and

Resolved further, That adherence to the said Protocol and Statute hereby approved shall not be so construed as to require the United States to depart from its traditional policy of not intruding upon, interfering with, or entangling itself in the political questions of policy or internal administration of any foreign state; nor shall adherence to the said Protocol and Statute be construed to imply a relinquishment by the United States of its traditional attitude toward purely American questions.[77]

The wording of the new Paragraph V was the work of Walsh, Swanson and Lenroot rather than Pepper and Moore, both of whom thought it should be more extensive. Borah, who was not directly involved in its formulation, tried to revise it to conform exactly to the terms of the anonymous memorandum; but a majority of the Senate would not support him.[78] Even so, the publication of Swanson's amendments achieved the first of its two sequential objectives, namely, passage of Lenroot's cloture motion. Debate on this procedural question was comparatively easy for the proponents. Nevertheless there were protests, notably from Reed but also from Southern Democrats and Middle Western Irregulars, who feared any restrictions upon free access to the Senate floor. They claimed this was their only weapon against the domination of party managers, the only defence of the sovereign State against the federal majority. A whole day's business was consumed by discussion of the cloture motion, which was carried late on Monday by a vote of 68:26 – the largest total of votes ever cast in the Senate until then and only the second time that such a motion had been put and won. Under the terms of the guillotine, speeches on the resolution of adherence were to be limited to an hour, with the final vote expected by mid February.[79]

In the event the remaining stages of the debate on the Protocol lasted only a couple of days. The administration had deferred to the collective judgment of Walsh, Swanson and Lenroot as to the final terms of the resolution of adherence; while the Senate's agreement to guillotine activity had been conditioned by the knowledge of what was acceptable to the leading proponents. Yet Borah, Blease and Moses kept up the attack. In terms reminiscent of President Harding and Senator Lenroot in 1923, Borah proposed an amendment to reduce the British Empire to one vote in the Council and Assembly elections to the Court's bench. Blease thereupon inverted this principle with a proposal to allocate a separate vote to 'each Sovereign State' within the Federal Union. Then in a gesture turned against Pepper, Moses introduced a motion to substitute the 1924 'disassociation' scheme for Swanson's amended S. Res. 5. Even proponents of ratification offered changes – if only for affect. Senator Overman (North Carolina, Democrat) moved that immigration, the Confederate debts and the Monroe Doctrine be specifically excluded from the Court's jurisdiction: the allusive though traditional language of Swanson's two final paragraphs might be inadequate. Overman did not press his objection to a vote. The message had been clearly registered. Southern Democratic Senators were catered for in the terms of two conditions that went back to The Hague Conferences.[80]

Such amendments were offered with small expectations of their success. They were rather acknowledgments of an audience outside the Senate. Indeed the Senate itself appeared to lose interest once the terms and timetable of the resolution of adherence had been accepted by two-thirds of the membership. Many places were empty as Walsh and Lenroot began their formal defence of Swanson's revisions. A careful observer would have noticed that Lenroot continued to ignore the Mosul case and based his argument for the redrawn Paragraph V on the commonly-held interpretation of the Eastern Carelia case. This was a deliberate attempt to avoid the impression that the proponents had been influenced by Borah's theatrical use of Moore's recent memorandum. As Lenroot insisted: there was 'nothing in [the new] reservations that is not entirely in harmony with the Harding–Hughes–Coolidge recommendations'. When Swanson himself spoke it was to undertake the easy task of explaining and justifying the clause governing the right of withdrawal. Then all three, Walsh, Lenroot and Swanson, joined to endorse the traditions which lay behind the two unnumbered paragraphs.[81] There could be no doubt in anyone's mind: S.Res. 5, as amended, had the wholehearted support of the proponents of American adherence to the Permanent Court of International Justice. As Colcord wrote exultantly to Root: the reservations had been endorsed 'by the warmest friends of the Court in the Senate'. The 'power of the irreconcilable group' had at last been broken.[82]

The following day, Tuesday, 26 January, the Senate met in Committee of the Whole to start line by line approval of the revised resolution. Moses would not desist from trying to embarrass Pepper by recalling the latter's 1924 scheme. Arthur Robinson, a very new Republican Senator from Indiana, did the same for Lenroot by reminding him of his previous objections to the multiple British Empire vote. For the proposition, the congressional veteran Frederick Gillett (Massachusetts, Republican) complained that the terms were 'somewhat suspicious and grudging'. Even so, they encountered no effective opposition when put to the vote individually, – certainly not from the proponents.[83]

The procedure for voting was complex, for the status of the 'reservations', 'understandings' and 'conditions' was unclear. For simplicity's sake it can be stated that the substantive consent of the Senate to the signing of the Court Protocol was contained in the preliminary enabling paragraph. Such consent was not formally and constitutionally necessary for the signature of a proposed international treaty; but it would be necessary in the subsequent legislative preliminaries to ratification. Through the reservations added to the enabling paragraph the Senate was notifying the Executive of the terms which it would later require for its final approval by a two-thirds majority. When the existing Signatories of the Court Protocol explicitly accepted the Senate's proposed conditions, the Executive could sign the Protocol and then come back to the Senate with a treaty to complete the penultimate stage before ratification.

This intricate arrangement did not exhaust the complexities of S.Res. 5 as amended in Committee of the Whole. The eight paragraphs which followed the enabling paragraph had no symmetry or agreed status. The first five were traditionally numbered as such (i.e. I–V) and corresponded to the so-called Hughes–Harding–Coolidge conditions as modified by Swanson, Walsh and Lenroot, first in May 1924 and then within the last few days. After these came the three paragraphs governing: (1) the 'exchange of notes' formula; (2) the treaty-making provision for the reference of cases to the Court; and (3) the exclusion of 'traditional' American policies from the Court's jurisdiction. It was these three paragraphs (which we shall refer to unofficially as Paragraphs VI, VII and VIII) whose status was problematical. Swanson, for example, argued that Paragraph VII (the two-thirds provision) simply recorded constitutional practice, while Paragraph VIII should not and indeed could not be 'incorporated in the body of international law'. As for Paragraph VI, the 'exchange of notes' formula, this was not part of the resolution so much as a requirement upon which subsequent ratification would be made. Vice-President Dawes, titular head of the Senate and *ex-officio* arbiter of the Senate's voting procedure, appeared to disagree with Swanson. He treated Paragraphs VI–VIII on all fours substantively with the five preceding Paragraphs, though he referred to them as sub-paragraphs or 'branches' of Paragraph V, the paragraph governing the advisory jurisdiction.[84]

The practical effect of these uncertainties emerged only later. For the moment they caused no problems to the Senate. Paragraphs VI, VII and VIII were passed by unanimous voice-votes. The contentious areas lay in Paragraphs I–V. Yet even here unanimity was not far away. One vote only was cast against Paragraphs I, IV and V; three votes were cast against Paragraph III; and eight Senators voted against Paragraph II – a protest against the British Empire and its alleged preponderance in the League. The one vote against Paragraph V was registered by Blease – a mark of his idiosyncrasy.[85]

The last day of debate on the Protocol was something of an anti-climax. The hard work had been done, the concessions already made. The proponents had offered their eight conditions for signing the Protocol; and they were no less insistent than the opponents that Paragraph V satisfied the legitimate demands of the United States. Moses and Reed persisted, however. First it was a question of the ultimate sanctions behind the Court's judgments. Lenroot and Walsh were obliged to admit that material rather than moral force lay behind the Court's decisions; but Moses's attempt to add a wrecking amendment to deny such enforcement powers was defeated by a vote of 69:22. As Underwood of Alabama correctly observed: such a condition would 'close the door itself before we have an opportunity to enter'. Reed pegged away at the British Empire. He too was unsuccessful. As a final fling at Pepper (who had objected to the sanctions reservation as unrealistic), Moses once again submitted the 'disassociation' scheme of 1924. It gathered only twenty-one votes; but there were straws in the wind. Both the New York Senators (the Republican Wadsworth and the Democrat Copeland) supported it; so too did Pepper's junior colleague from Pennsylvania, David A. Reed. The other Reed fought on in characteristic style: racist rhetoric was combined with procedural delaying-tactics.[86] All to no avail. In the early evening of Wednesday, 27 January 1926 (the twentieth day of debate) the revisions to S.Res. 5 offered by Swanson to expedite the Lenroot cloture motion were 'perfected... in Committee of the Whole', formally read for a final time and then by unanimous consent put to a vote, rather than postponed to the following day. Seventy-six Senators voted Aye, seventeen Nay: a clear two-thirds majority had been achieved.[87] It now remained for the signatory States to indicate 'through an exchange of notes, their acceptance of the [Senate's] reservations and understandings' so that the United States Executive could itself sign the Protocol of Signature of the Permanent Court of International Justice.

Notes

[1] Scialoja, 15 March 1929: quoted in Jessup, 'World Court – Geneva Trip, 1929': Jessup Papers; Walters, *History of the League of Nations*, 311–15, esp. 314.

[2] Accinelli, 'United States and the World Court', 434.

[3] For a participant's evidence, see Zimmern, *League of Nations and the Rule of Law*, Pt. III: 'The Working of the League'; cf. Dunne, 'Isolationism of a Kind', 346.

[4] A superb contemporary introduction is provided in *SIA* (1924), 1–64; *SIA* (1925), II. 1–75; *SIA* (1926), 1–80. My interpretation of Chamberlain is based upon his unpublished Papers, housed in the University of Birmingham Library.

[5] Walters, *History of the League of Nations*, 271, 315; cf. Philip J. Noel Baker, *The Geneva Protocol for the Pacific Settlement of International Disputes* (London: King, 1925); (Sir) Frederick Pollock, Bt., *The Covenant and the Protocol* (London: League of Nations Union, 1924),

[6] James T. Shotwell memo for LNNPA, 25 March 1925: copy in Sweetser Papers: Jesssup, *Elihu Root*, II. 429; George Wharton Pepper to Esther Everett Lape, 1 April 1925; to George W. Norris, 1 April 1925: Norris Papers, MD,LC.

[7] Austen Chamberlain to Robert Cecil, 19 November 1924: Chamberlain Papers; van Karnebeek (Dutch Foreign Minister), 11 May 1926: quoted in Richard M. Tobin (The Hague) to Secretary of State Kellogg, 11 May 1926: NA500. C114/519,

[8] Walters, *History of the League of Nations*, chs 18, 21–7, 33. Spain revoked its announced withdrawal.

[9] Chamberlain to Leo Amery, 10 November 1925: Chamberlain Papers. Barros in a number of works dates the fatal rupture to 1923: see esp., James Barros, *The Corfu Incident of 1923: Mussolini and the League of Nations*, (Princeton: Princeton University Press, 1965).

[10] T.R.B. in New Republic (2 September 1925), 43. Pepper's two major autobiographical works are *In the Senate* (Philadelphia: University of Pennsylvania Press, 1930) and *Philadelphia Lawyer: an Autobiography* (Philadelphia: Lippincott, 1944).

[11] Pepper to Norris, 1 April 1925; to Lape, 1 April 1925: Norris Papers; Edward W. Bok to Root, 5 June 1925; Pepper to Bok, 12 June 1925; Pepper to Root, 26 January 1926: Root Papers; Frederick Rasmussen (Chairman, Pepper Central Campaign Committee, Philadelphia) to Moore, 4 January 1926; Pepper to Moore, 15 January 1926: Moore Papers; Pepper, *Philadelphia Lawyer*, 133.

[12] Moore to Finlay, 21 March 1925; to Huber, 1 October 1925: Moore Papers; Pepper to Kellogg, 21 October 1925: NA500. C114/422.

[13] Pepper to Laura Puffer Morgan (National Council for prevention of War: NCPM) 13 October 1925; Charles Michelson in *The World* (New York), 29 May 1925; Fosdick to Hudson, 29 May 1925: Hudson Papers; Coolidge to Root, 16 May 1925: Root Papers; clippings from *New York Herald-Tribune* (cited below as *NYH-T*) (14 July 1925) and *NYT* (4 August 1925): Moore Papers; Pepper to Kellogg, 21 October 1925, NA500. C114/422.

[14] These next paragraphs draw heavily from Moore to Bayard, 16 December 1925; to Pepper, 21 December 1925; to Harlan Fiske Stone, 4 and 26 January 1926; to Walsh, 19 January 1926; Pepper to Moore, 27 July 1925 and 28 January 1926; Moore memo, 'Conference with Sen. Pepper', 10 July 1925;

Moore Papers; Root memorandum, 'The Objections to the Permanent Court of International Justice because it gives Advisory Opinions', 25 May 1925: Root Papers.

15 For the debate on secrecy during the drafting of the Rules, see PCIJ, Series D, no. 2, 293–6; Moore to Hughes, 5 April 1923: NA500. C114/387. For the events after the Eastern Carelia demurrer, see Moore to Stone, 28 January 1926; to Prof. J. L. Brierly, 15 February 1932: Moore Papers.

16 Hammarskjöld, 'Sidelights on the Permanent Court', 333–4; Altamira y Crevea, *Sociedad de las Naciones*, 293–4.

17 Epitacio da Silva Pessôa (a judge of the Court) in *O Jornal* (Rio de Janeiro), 28 February 1925, together with editorial matter of 3 March 1925: NA 500. C114/392–3. Pessôa, former President of Brazil and delegate to the 1919 Paris Peace Conference was an out-and-out political appointee to the Bench: Edwin V. Morgan (Rio de Janeiro) to Hughes, 22 and 26 June 1923; Root to Hughes, 1 June 1923; Hughes to Root, 9 June 1923: NA500. C114/281, 286, 276.

18 Moore to Prof. Joseph P. Chamberlain (Columbia) 12 and 31 August 1925; to Huber, 1 October 1925: Moore Papers.

19 Denys P. Myers to Everett Sanders, 3 and 13 July 1925: NA 500. C114/406, 410. For Borah and Outlawry, see pp. 74 ff. above.

20 Root to Wickersham, 26 September 1925; Wickersham to Root, 14 and 30 September: Root Papers.

21 McDonald to Frederick Keppel, 3 December 1925: to Kellogg, 4 December 1925; Castle to Beck, 9 December 1925; to Mrs W. F. Timlow, 4 September 1925: NA500. C114/429, 411.

22 Clipping from *New York American*, 4 May 1925: Moore Papers; clipping from *Kansas City Times*, 16 June 1925: as enclosure, Sen. Charles Curtis (Majority Leader) to Kellogg, 16 June 1925: NA500. C114/403¼.

23 Tinkham's resolution was H.J. Res. 221: Sixty-ninth Congress, First Session. Examples of the Blease and Tinkham attacks are on file in NA500. C114/408, 418, 426. See also press release of Tinkham, 30 November 1925: Hudson Papers.

24 Kellogg to Moore, 1 and 9 October 1925; Moore to Kellogg, 5 and 8 October 1925: Moore Papers.

25 Root to Madison Grant, 11 June 1934: Root Papers. For Reed, Swanson and Walsh, see, e.g., *CR* 68:1, 5075, 10975–6; *CR* 69:1, 1091–2.

26 Jessup, *Elihu Root*, II. 429; *NYT* (22–5 May 1925); SCFR, *Proceedings*, 21.

27 Ogden L. Mills, 'The Obligation of the United States toward the World Court', *Annals of the American Academy of Political and Social Science* (cited below as *Annals*), 114 (July 1924), 128–31; 'Crippling by Reservations', *NYT* (25 January 1926), 20.

28 PCIJ, *Procès-Verbaux*, 168–74, 197–200, 211–2, 529–39, 575–7, 614; Altamira y Crevea, *Sociedad de las Naciones*, 94–105, 249 ff.; Kellor and Hatvany, *United States Senate and the International Court*, 44.

29 For the Brazilian demands, see the citations at n. 17 above.

30 McDonald, memo of 1 December 1925, as enclosure to Kellogg, 4 December 1925: NA500. C114/429; for Borchard, see Chicago Council on Foreign Relations, *The International Court: Addresses by Edwin M. Borchard and Manley O. Hudson, Delivered December 29, 1923.* Pamphlet no. 3 (Chicago: Chicago CFR, 1924); for Johnson, see below pp.136, 145.

31 Fleming, Haynes, Accinelli and Margulies do so; cf. Evans C. Johnson, *Oscar W. Underwood: a Political Biography* (Baton Rouge and London: Louisiana State University Press, 1980), 423.

32 *Boston Herald* (12 May 1925), 1, 2; Manley O. Hudson, *Senator Borah and the World Court* (New York: LNNPA, 1925); Kellogg, memoranda of 2 April 1925:

NA500. C114/399, 401; 'The President, the Secretary of State and Senator Borah', *The Round Table* 15 (March 1925), 309–24.

33 Johnson, *Borah of Idaho*, 375–6; Giblin and Brown, *World Court Myth*, 319 ff.; *The Nation* (6 February 1926) 7. The *NYT* (29 November 1925) published such a survey.

34 Norris to W. F. Fisher, 29 January 1925: Norris Papers; Moore to Chamberlain, 12 August 1925: Moore Papers; Johnson to C. K. McClatchy, 23 December 1925; to Harold L. Ickes, 4 March 1926: Johnson Papers; Moses to James Brown Scott, 13 April 1925: Scott Papers.

35 Margulies, *Lenroot of Wisconsin*, 381; cf. Esther Everett Lape to Hoover, 14 December 1925: Hoover Papers.

36 Lindsay Rogers, *The American Senate* (New York: Knopf, 1926), 73, n.31.

37 Coolidge, Annual Message of 8 December 1925: *FRUS* (1925), I. vii–xxxi at xiv–xvii. See above pp. 101–2.

38 See the correspondence of Lenroot, Kellogg and the latter's two Assistant Secretaries, R. E. Olds and S. Phenix, late December 1925–mid January 1926: NA500. C114/428a–437½.

39 Margulies, 'Senate and the World Court', 46, an echo of an informed contemporary, Charles P. Howland: *Survey of American Foreign Relations* (1929), 333–86, esp. 350, 356 ff.

40 Swanson, *CR* 69:1 974–88 at 979. For Secretary Hay, see William Roscoe Thayer, *The Life and Letters of John Hay*, 2 vols (Boston: Houghton Mifflin, 1915), II. ch. 23–31,

41 Scott, *Instructions to the American Delegates*, 73–4; Scott, *Texts of the Peace Conferences at The Hague*, 90; Clark, *Memorandum on the Monroe Doctrine*. 173–5.

42 Myers to McDonald, 15 October 1925; 'Memorandum from Mr McDonald on the World Court Situation', 30 October 1925: Hudson Papers; memo of Beck, 20 January 1926; Castle to Olds, 1 February 1926: NA500. C114/437½.

43 Charles P. Howland, 'Our Repudiated State Bonds', *Foreign Affairs* 6 (April 1928), 395–407.

44 Two very different contemporary studies which emphasized the contrast between the Courts are Edward A. Harriman, *The Constitution at the Crossroads: a Study of the Legal Aspects of the League of Nations, the Permanent Organization of Labor and the Permanent Court of International Justice* (New York: Doran, 1925) and Lawrence D. Egbert, *Les Etats-Unis et la Cour Permanente de Justice Internationale* (Paris: Recueil Sirey, 1926).

45 *CR* 69:1, 1067–71.

46 Ibid. 1085–6, 1090–3 (Walsh); 2349–55 (Johnson).

47 Borah's major speeches are ibid. 1071–7, 2034–9, 2284–98, 2555–63; and these paragraphs are drawn from Borah and interlocutors, ibid. 1071–7, 1085–6, 1763–4, 2487–96. For Borah's critics, see 'Confidential' memorandum from the FPA, 1 December 1925: NA 500. C114/429.

48 *CR* 69:1, 1083–93, 1236–45.

49 Paul A. Carter, 'The Other Catholic Candidate: the 1928 Presidential Bid of Thomas J. Walsh', *Pacific Northwest Quarterly* 55 (January 1964), 1–8.

50 Tom Walsh is not to be confused with the Democratic Senator from Massachusetts, David Ignatius Walsh. The Tom Walsh Papers are in MD,LC; the David Walsh Papers in the Dinand Library, College of the Holy Cross, Worcester, Mass.

51 *CR* 69:1, 1083–8.

52 Ibid. 1092.

53 Ibid. 1236–45, esp. 1240–4.

54 Moore to Pepper, 21 December 1925: Pepper to Moore, 23 December 1925: Moore Papers.

55 *CR* 69:1, 1245–9.

56 Moore to Stone, 28 December 1925; Stone to Moore, 31 December 1925: Moore Papers.

57 *CR* 69:1, 1417 ff.

58 Stone to Moore, 6 January 1926; Pepper to Moore, 4 and 8 January 1926; Moore to Pepper, 5 January 1926: Moore Papers. The 1923 essay is printed in Moore, *Collected Papers*, VI. 79–140.

59 Walsh to Moore, 7 and 15 January: Moore Papers; *CR* 69:1, 1427–31.

60 These two paragraphs draw upon the correspondence of Moore, Stone, Pepper and Walsh, 15–28 January 1926: Moore Papers.

61 Stone to Moore, 21 January and 1 February 1926; Moore to Stone, [22–3] January 1926: Moore Papers.

62 Moore to Walsh, 19 January 1926; to Stone, 24 and 26 January, 1926; to Nyholm, 16 March 1926; Borchard to Moore, 14 October 1927: Moore Papers.

63 Moore to Stone, 26 January 1926; Pepper to Moore, 28 January 1926: ibid.; Senator Frederick H. Gillett to Root, 27 January 1926: Root Papers.

64 Stone to Moore, 23 January 1926; Moore to Stone, 26 and 28 January 1926: Moore Papers; Beck memo, 20 January 1926: NA 500. C114/437½.

65 *CR* 69:1, 2100–15, 2284; Stone to Moore, 21 January 1926: Moore to Stone, 28 January 1926: Moore Papers; Colcord to Root, 19 January 1926: Root Papers.

66 *CR* 69:1, 1479–84, 2195 (Bruce); 1417–26 (Willis); 1574–8 (Fess); 2190–5 (Moses); 1955–65, 8182–6 (Shipstead). Senators Tyson and McKellar (both Democrats from Tennessee) argued like Bruce: ibid., 2637–42, 2687.

67 Ibid. 1759–66, 2298, 2414, 2570–3, 2662–74; *NYT* (8 January 1926), 9; *NYT* (18 January 1926), 1, 2: Franklin L. Burdette, *Filibustering in the Senate* (Princeton: Princeton University Press, 1940), 146–7.

68 *CR* 69:1, 2022–49 (Reed and Blease); 2100–6 (Fernald); and, later, 2298–304 (Blease); 2358–62 (J. Thomas 'Tom-Tom' Heflin of Alabama); 2362–71 (Reed).

69 Ibid. 2284–95; Stone to Moore, 21 and 28 January 1926; Moore to Stone, 26 and 28 January 1926: Moore Papers; 'Judge Moore's Warning', *Washington Post* (26 January 1926); *NYT* (28 January 1926), 1. Borah's second major speech was on 14 January: *CR* 69:1, 2034–9.

70 Ibid. 2293–4; Moore memo in Moore to Walsh, 19 January 1926: Moore Papers.

71 *CR* 69:1, 2296–7; Moore to Stone, [22–3] and 26 January 1926; Stone to Moore, 1 February 1926: Moore Papers.

72 *CR* 69:1, 2248–656, esp 2356 (McKinley), 2349–55 (Johnson); SCFR, *Proceedings*, 26–33.

73 *NYT* (25 January 1926), 20.

74 *CR* 69:1, 2362–71, 2414–29, 2487–91, 2492–6, 2587–9.

75 Ibid. 2589–93; George H. Haynes, *The Senate of the United States: its History and Practice*, 2 vols (Boston: Houghton Mifflin, 1938), I. 396 ff.

76 Memo of Beck, 20 January 1926: NA500. C114/437½; Stone to Moore, 23 January 1926: Moore Papers.

77 *CR* 69:1, 2656–7; text here printed adapted from *FRUS*, 1926, I. 1–2.

78 *CR* 69:1, 2657; *NYT* (28 January 1926), 1; Borchard to Borah, 3 February 1926: Borchard Papers.

79 *CR* 69:1, 2662–79.

80 Ibid. 2657–8.

81 Ibid. 2679–92.

82 Colcord to Root, 1 February 1926: Root Papers.

83 *CR* 69:1, 2738–53, esp. 2738 (Moses); 2747 (Gillett); 2752–3 (Robinson).

[84] Ibid. 2756–63, esp. 2759–60.
[85] Ibid. 2756–9.
[86] Ibid. 2795 ff., esp. 2797, 2816–23.
[87] Ibid. 2824–5.

6 Textual language and political meanings: the League, the Court and the United States, 1926–31

The approval of the Court Protocol by the Senate was greeted with a wide variety of responses, public and private. Perhaps the only generalization which can be made with any certainty concerns the fifth of the Senate's eight separate conditions. Virtually all commentators predicted that the Fifth Reservation's second clause (requiring an American veto over the Court's entertainment of requests for advisory opinions) would cause difficulties. Even so, the weight of analysis suggested that these could be successfully negotiated. Fewer observers noted the possibilities for delay contained in the sixth condition (the 'exchange of notes' procedure); and there was also the doubt (less strongly expressed) that the Senate's conditions could be met only by amendments to the Court Statute. Since this was a multilateral engagement, signed and ratified by dozens of States, the amending process would be long, perhaps even never completed. Furthermore, there might be particular States with a decided interest in not accepting the American conditions. Whatever the status of the eighth condition – whether or not it was a provision which would technically be incorporated into the final treaty of adherence (as opposed to its being registered in the prenegotiations) – this last condition reserving (*inter alia*) the Monroe Doctrine was deeply offensive to a number of South American States. With Brazil poised to leave the League (if not the Court) and with public objections coming from Argentina and Chile against the presumptions of the United States for a privileged position, the chances of total and unanimous approval by the Court Signatories initially appeared remote.[1]

Manley Hudson was one of those who publicly expressed mild dissatisfaction with the Senate's final conditions (particularly the 'unfortunate' Fifth Reservation); but privately he rejoiced that the ultimate goal was that much nearer. The day following the passage of the resolution Hudson wrote to Secretary-General Drummond:

> We have jumped the hurdle, and now opinion in this country is in a position to be moved forward on the question of the League.

A few weeks later Hudson had the same argument and strategy repeated back to him by Arthur Sweetser: 'the Court victory [was] the greatest single victory in the whole League fight at home '. As Sweetser judged the significance of the vote for the future:

> The towering, outstanding fact of all is that the Senate has agreed to something – some very direct affiliation with the League. The rest will fall into place in shorter or longer time.

James G. McDonald (who had been so apprehensive before the Senate debate began) acknowledged the narrowness of the 'technical victory' while stressing the greatness of the 'moral victory' for the League cause.[2] This was a distinction well-understood in press and diplomatic circles in Europe. The Dutch Foreign Minister, van Karnebeek, let the American government know that the conditions of adherence would create problems – but none was 'in any degree comparable in importance to the fact of adherence'.[3] In the days immediately after the vote it was a judgment shared in the British and French Foreign Offices and repeated with many insignificant variations in the press. But it was not quite the whole story. An argument was forming to the effect that if the US Executive and Senate had surmounted a political and psychological barrier on the road from 'aloofness and isolation' (in Hersch Lauterpacht's phrase) but still carried the shackles of unacceptable conditions, then perhaps those same shackles should be struck off.[4]

John Bassett Moore was alive to this sort of thinking; and within days of the Senate vote he was writing to George Wharton Pepper predicting that, for all its reasonableness, 'an effort [would be] made to induce the United States to drop or to modify' Paragraph V on the advisory jurisdiction. Moore singled out the Fifth Reservation, for he saw its maintenance as a touchstone of whether the United States would 'radically reverse its policy and enter the League of Nations'. Pepper however was confident of the mood in the Senate and Executive and sought to allay Moore's forebodings on the Fifth Reservation. Its 'retention [was] essential'; and he did not believe 'any effective pressure [could] be exercised in the direction of change'.[5]

Senator Borah had no such confidence; nor could he take the risk that the Court Signatories would accept the Senate's conditions as they stood – let alone achieve their modification. Borah followed the same sequence of logic as Hudson, Sweetser, McDonald and many other lobbyists who believed that the United States was (in Sweetser's expression) joining the League on the 'instalment plan'. But Borah's political premises were different, his language more forceful. As he wrote to a friend a couple of days after the Senate vote:

> it is only the first step... to put this country into Europe.... A more wicked, corrupt, deceitful propaganda was never carried on than was carried on for this Court and will be renewed tenfold to get us formally and technically into the League.

Borah gave notice to his party organization in Idaho that 'every ounce of energy and ability' would now have to be spent in a political campaign to prevent the Senate and Executive from weakening the conditions of adherence. Indeed any amendments should be in the direction of stiffening the conditions, for they were still inadequate. In this way Borah hoped to dissuade the Court Signatories from the more remote possibility of their complete, unqualified and universal acceptance of the reservations. Thus Borah's two-pronged attack lay in dissuading the Signatories from agreeing to the Senate–Executive terms while preventing any American erosion of the terms themselves.[6]

The first stage in Borah's campaign was intervention in the primary elections of Senators who had approved the Court Protocol. Top of the list were Irvine Lenroot in Wisconsin and William McKinley in Illinois. But it was a form of attack which widened the gap between Borah and other Irregulars, particularly the more insurgent progressive Republicans. Robert La Follette (son of the more famous 'Fighting Bob', who had died in June 1925, and junior Senator to Lenroot) and Hiram Johnson, for example, refused to campaign against fellow Republican Progressives simply because they had supported the Court Protocol: men such as Norris of Nebraska and Peter Norbeck of South Dakota. Political acceptability was not to be measured by the Court issue alone. If it were, that would mean also opposing Progressives in the Democratic Party, notably Senators Walsh and Wheeler from Montana, and supporting men such as Reed of Missouri, Borah's chief ally.[7]

Borah no less than Hudson & Company saw the ultimate goal as American adherence to the League, not simply the Court. But, paradoxically, not all League Members were quite so eager to welcome the United States into the Court as these vocal fears and hopes suggested. The Dutch government did not speak for all the Member States. Diplomatic sources reported to Washington that the Dutch had selfish as well as altruistic motives in wanting to see the prestige of The Hague increased. Moreover, even their supranational goals could be interpreted as part of the desires of a neutral to counterbalance Great Power politics within the League.[8] Perhaps even more surprising to historians and certainly a critical consideration to contemporaries was the attitude of some of the Great Powers themselves, notably the British and French.

The attitude of successive British governments towards American membership of the Court had scarcely changed since the negotiations of 1922 which led to the four original Hughes–Harding conditions. But the essential constancy in attitude had become formalized in a more precise set of policies and priorities. The United States would be welcomed into the Court – provided the interests of the League (as defined by the British) were not sacrificed. Indeed, it would be best for the political work of the League to develop independently of the United States, with no presumption, even no wish for early American entry which might wreck the delicate structure represented by the Locarno agreements. Once Germany was safely in the League (and rightly accorded a permanent seat on the Council); the claims of Spain and Poland (and , if possible, Brazil) properly acknowledged by being accorded a status midway between the Great and Small Powers; after an 'Eastern Locarno' had been constructed – when all these problems had been resolved, then perhaps the United States might productively enter. In the meantime, the constitutional idiosyncrasies of the Americans, which prevented effective Executive action in multilateral organizations, together with the widespread antipathy to European politics in general, were an argument against American entrance into the League. Co-operation could and should take place in many spheres: disarmament; the renegotiation of debts and reparations; humanitarian and relief work. But none of these necessary international activities entailed American membership of the League of Nations.[9]

The logic of the British government may not have been irrefutable; it was assuredly not unreasonable. What is striking is the gap between this cautious approach and the clear-cut syllogisms of many pro-Court, pro-League advocates in the United States. In their thinking, adherence to the Court entailed membership of the League, while the Great Powers eagerly waited, pined even, for this consummation. On the contrary, as Judge Moore argued many times (in terms corroborated by diplomatic reports to Washington), it was rather the smaller States, the neutrals and the judges of an 'independent' mind (the three were not synonymous) who looked for American adherence to the Court – and largely to counterbalance the growing influence of the Great Powers.[10]

It was, therefore, in the context of these broader considerations that the British scrutinized the Senate's reservations and the debate which had preceded them. But it did not take long to form the judgment that the eight conditions and qualifications were unacceptable as they stood. The Fifth Reservation was the main objection: it threatened the effectiveness of the Council and seriously limited the use of the advisory jurisdiction as a substitute for compulsory adjudication. The French government completely agreed; and both sides pointed to the damage such a provision might have produced during the Mosul proceedings.[11] The Foreign Secretary, Austen Chamberlain, described himself as being a 'good deal disturbed' by the Reservation's possibilities; and, like many of his colleagues, he saw it and the other conditions inspired by American antipathy to the League. However, the British government was faced with a dilemma. American membership in the League – even in the Court – was not eagerly desired; yet American goodwill was necessary for the successful conclusion of many outstanding political issues. The British Ambassador in Washington, Esmé Howard, writing to Chamberlain, neatly expressed the problem posed by the Senate's actions.

For the moment... nothing better than these conditions can be expected from the Senate, and therefore the situation resolves itself into a choice of evils. Either the adherence of the United States to the World Court on the conditions laid down... must be rejected, which would be a triumph for the isolationists, and no doubt strengthen their position here for some time to come, or the conditions must be accepted... in the hopes that, as the World Court gains in prestige, they will become in practice inoperative and ultimately go by default....[12]

Howard's words were written on the day following the Senate vote. In the next weeks the policy of the British government emerged in its details. The United States should be encouraged into the Court – but not with 'privileges'. However, such firmness might produce a hostile reaction, even rebuff from the United States government; consequently it was important that the British government did not appear isolated in any action which could be termed intransigence. The wisest course, therefore, was to get the League itself to assume the responsibility for responding to the American conditions. (This diplomatic tactic had been offered by the Coolidge administration, which had communicated the terms of the Senate resolution directly to the four dozen Court Signatories and then notified the League Secretariat *qua* depository of the Protocol.)[13] It was agreed in Whitehall that the coming March Council Session would provide the proper forum for the League's first official discussion of the issue.

The British Foreign Office had not devised this solution on its own. There had been close contact with the Quai d'Orsay, where Aristide Briand, the Foreign Minister, and Henri Fromageot, the Legal Adviser, had good relations with their British opposite numbers, Chamberlain and Sir Cecil Hurst. The Dominions and India had been consulted; and their governments responded carefully and at length. (Even so, their replies reached London after the Council meeting – another sign that the meeting itself had been planned as part of a delaying process.)[14] With the terms agreed in advance, on 18 March Chamberlain successfully moved a motion in the Council that a Conference of Court Signatories be held in September at Geneva for the purpose of discussing the 'special conditions' proposed by the US government.

Chamberlain's motion defined much subsequent negotiation. He ignored the seventh and eighth conditions on the grounds that the Senate resolution required the Court Signatories to accept only Paragraphs I–V. Since, however, the signatory States were parties to a 'multilateral instrument', the 'special conditions' of American adherence should likewise 'be embodied in a multilateral instrument': they could not 'appropriately be embodied in a series of separate exchanges of notes' – as the sixth condition required. As ever, the nub of the problem was the Fifth Reservation. In the words of Chamberlain reported in the League Council Minutes:

> This paragraph is capable of bearing an interpretation which would hamper the work of the Council and prejudice the rights of Members of the League, but it is not clear that it was intended to bear any such meaning. The correct interpretation of this paragraph... should be the subject of discussion and agreement with the United States Government.[15]

The action of Chamberlain and its unanimous (and foregone) endorsement by his fellow Council delegates shocked, dismayed and even embarrassed a number of prominent figures, including Ambassador Howard, Secretary-General Drummond and the Registrar of the Court, Åke Hammarskjöld. Judge Max Huber, now President of the Court, described the initiative as a piece of 'stupid mismanagement' by an 'ill advised' Council. One of the major Swiss newspapers, the semi-official *Journal de Genève* (which wanted American membership of both the Court and the League), expressed editorial incredulity at the Council's 'tactical error'. The Senate's resolution had disclaimed the assumption of any 'legal relation' with the League – only for the Council to respond by proposing that the Court Signatories should discuss the resolution's acceptability to them *qua* Members of the League.[16]

Knowledgeable commentators and important actors, it is clear, were painfully surprised by the Council's behaviour.[17] But perhaps it was all-too-understandable. Such was the conclusion of two Americans working in the League Secretariat: Huntington Gilchrist and Arthur Bullard. In a series of letters they tried to impress upon a number of their pro-Court, pro-League allies that their lobby propaganda had been misconceived. As Bullard wrote some weeks after the Council meeting: Hudson, Fosdick, McDonald and their like had simply gone too far 'in pretending that the Court and the League were really separate'. Bullard continued:

> our friends have stretched the truth considerably in their efforts to prove that the Court and the League are absolutely independent of each other.... [S]ooner or later some of the member States would resent the implication that the parent was unworthy of the child.[18]

Bullard's correspondent was James T. Shotwell of Columbia. Shotwell, born in Canada but long resident in the United States, was closely identified with the League. He had served on the American delegation to the Paris Peace Conference, where he had contributed greatly to the establishment of the International Labour Organization. More recently in 1924 Shotwell had been prominent in devising the so-called 'American plan', one of the many proposals to stiffen the compulsory arbitration features of the League Covenant and so help to fill its perceived 'gaps'. Of course the political significance of the American plan lay precisely in its transatlantic origins and its potential for US co-operation in imposing League sanctions against designated aggressors – ideas which were to re-emerge in the Kellogg–Briand Pact of 1928 and which was itself heavily influenced by Shotwell. In short, the biography of Bullard's correspondent even more so than the letter itself was further evidence that the driving force behind the campaign for American adherence to the Court came from those who sought the ultimate goal of League membership.[19]

On 29 March Drummond communicated to Secretary Kellogg a formal invitation to attend the proposed Conference of Signatories. It was a futile action. As soon as informal reports of the Council's proposal reached the United States the opposition to any participation was voiced immediately and nation-wide. According to surveys conducted by British diplomatic officials, even the pro-Court Republican press was against sending an American representative to the Conference: the conditions approved by the Senate were not ambiguous and certainly not negotiable. Indeed a theme running through the news items and editorials was that the Conference and the invitation had been designed to produce an American rebuff.[20] Contemporaneously President Coolidge was openly insisting on the propriety and finality of the reservations. In a major address to the influential National Press Club Coolidge stated that the 'reservations... adequately safeguard[ed] American rights and also tend[ed] to strengthen the independence of the Court'.[21] Other, more equivocal evidence came from the Republican primary campaigns in Illinois and Wisconsin. Even after all these years the interpretation of the World Court issue and the effectiveness of the Borah-led campaign against Senators McKinley and Lenroot is problematical.[22] Nevertheless Ambassador Howard was in no doubt that the defeat of the two Republican incumbents was mainly due to their voting record on the Court Protocol – a judgment shared by McKinley, Lenroot and Borah themselves.[23]

The Department of State had decided on declining the invitation to the Conference within a matter of days of the notorious Council meeting. But a month elapsed before Secretary Kellogg responded officially. The delay is partly to be explained by the US government's desire to preserve the formalities of diplomatic convention – though the meticulousness ran the risk of seeming disdainful. Another factor lay in the Executive's wish both to prepare the ground for refusal while not appearing to be a mere follower of press and senatorial opinion. But whatever the precise combination of political forces Kellogg was trying to harness, there was no mistaking the directness of his words when they were finally delivered to Drummond on 18 April.

In the first paragraph of his letter Kellogg précised the events and decisions of the March Council meeting; the remaining second and third paragraphs explained why no American delegation would be attending the September Conference of Signatories. The 'invitation of the League' had been a 'courtesy', Kellogg acknowledged with a touch of impatience; but no 'useful purpose could be served' by American participation. The Senate had given its consent to adherence 'with certain specific conditions and reservations', and, Kellogg continued:

These reservations are plain and unequivocal and, according to their terms, they must be accepted by the exchange of notes between the United States and each one of the forty-eight States signatory to the Statute of the Permanent Court before the United States can become a party and sign the Protocol. The Resolution specifically provided this mode of procedure.

So much for the Senate. In the concluding paragraph Kellogg turned to the responsibilities and limitations of the Executive. He simply had 'no authority to vary this mode of procedure', namely the 'direct exchange of notes'; nor could he 'modify the conditions and reservations' or even 'interpret them'. In spite of the Council's decision, the US government did 'not consider... any new agreement [i.e., a multilateral treaty] necessary to give effect' to the Senate's terms; and Kellogg deprecated the possibility that 'the Council of the League should do anything to create the impression that there are substantial difficulties in the way of ... direct [i.e., bilateral] communication'. In his closing words Kellogg made a conciliatory gesture in wishing the Conference of Signatories well – but only on the understanding that it would precede acceptance of the Senate's conditions in the manner prescribed.[24]

Secretary Kellogg had two audiences: apart from the League there was opinion in the United States. Of course it would be naïve to imagine that Kellogg was just spontaneously addressing political forces in the United States and not already responding to them. Even so, his reply to the League received immediate and authoritative public endorsement. Kellogg's predecessor, Charles Evans Hughes, speaking only days afterwards to the American Society of International Law in Washington, unconditionally praised the substance and constitutional validity of the letter. Later, in the summer, Elihu Root offered private support to Kellogg's position. In a letter to this former collaborator, Lord Phillimore, Root wrote that the Senate's terms, while apparently 'formidable', were in fact reasonable so far as they affected the functioning of the Court. If he had a complaint it was the 'exchange of notes' formula, which he (unlike Coolidge, Kellogg and Hughes) regarded as an invasion of the Executive's prerogative to conduct foreign relations.[25]

The disagreement between Hughes and Root was characteristic of their approach to American adherence: Root was always more suspicious of the Senate and keen to reduce its role. As for the Senate itself, the spring and summer showed a number of Senators who went so far as to regret their previous approval of the Court Protocol. Among the recanters was Borah's Republican colleague from Idaho, the English-born Frank R. Gooding, who was facing re-election. More important still was the defection of the Democratic Senator from Florida, Park Trammell. He had voted not only for adherence to the Court but in 1919 and 1920 had favoured conditional ratification of the Treaty of Versailles. Yet even before these switches were nationally known Borah asserted in the early part of August that if a vote were now taken, 'the Senate would reverse its decision and decline to ratify the World Court'.[26]

Borah was seeking to shape events, not merely record them. But even if his forecast was deliberately overdrawn, an attempt to capitalize on his primary campaign against McKinley and Lenroot, his strategy was aided by prominent Senators in the pro-League wing of the Democratic party. Since the close of the Senate debate both Walsh and Swanson had publicly acknowledged that the United States was indeed demanding a right of absolute 'veto' over the Court's entertainment of a request for an advisory opinion. Consequently, when the Conference of Signatories was announced they both interpreted the proposal as a tactic to evade the Senate's conditions. More important still in the longer history of the Court Protocol was Walsh's deep embarrassment at the Council's actions. He had always insisted upon the effective independence of the Court from the League – an independence which the Great Powers represented on the Council appeared unprepared to allow. The disillusionment marked a stage in Walsh's increasing scepticism towards the value and safety of American adherence and a strengthening of his determination to maintain the substance of the January conditions.[27]

If this was intransigence on the part of Senators, the Coolidge administration and its political friends, counterparts existed in Europe. Certainly there were those judges and diplomatists who believed the League Council had mishandled the American conditions; but these individuals and their governments were not directing the movement of events. The Great Powers were, which meant effectively the British and the French. At the same time, Drummond (somewhat mistrusted earlier on by the British government) and leading officials in the League Secretariat (such as Paul Mantoux, Joseph Avenol and Arthur Salter) had moved appreciably closer to the Council's position.[28] Austen Chamberlain, his senior colleagues and advisers wanted American adherence ultimately – perhaps, indeed, as the mythic staging-post into a settled, more amenable League of Nations. But Chamberlain, like Drummond and others, would not 'sacrifice' present 'real advantages' for 'remote' possibilities. For all the arguments in favour of accepting the American conditions as the price of eventual entry into the League (a consideration strongly urged by the overseas members of the Empire), the Foreign Office grew convinced that there was nothing to gain from 'the United States coming in [to the Court] on special terms dictated by themselves'. Nor was there any virtue in 'hurry[ing] the question'. With the Coolidge administration and pro-Court Senators demanding a veto power which the British and French had determined not to allow to a non-Member State, the prospects for the Conference of Signatories were distinctly unpromising. The goal of the British government became limited to avoiding the public odium of leading the opposition to the American conditions.[29]

In Chapter 2 where we discussed the drafting of the Statute of the PCIJ in 1920, we alluded to the vast quantities of interesting documentary material recording that event. In 1926 the situation was noticeably different. Now the League of Nations sought secrecy; and the published records were not only far less detailed but even deliberately distorted. The official Minutes and Reports of the Conference of Signatories concealed policy decisions of the Great Powers in the League Council.[30]

The concealment is less important for its success in duping the US Executive and Senate: both parties soon made clear that they did not regard the Conference of Signatories as satisfying their joint requirements. (The Department of State received excellent reports of the Conference from the Consul General in Geneva, S. Pinkney Tuck.)[31] The significance of the deception lies elsewhere. First, in corroborating the case of those who insisted that the League exercised practical control over the Court and the Court's members, particularly in respect of the advisory jurisdiction.[32] Secondly and relatedly, the Foreign Offices of the Great Powers represented at the Conference of Signatories challenged the analysis of the Court's jurisprudence as it had been interpreted by the majority of American lawyers and pro-League advocates. Despite the statements and arguments which filled the pages of the published records of the Conference, the Great Powers (led by the United Kingdom and its spokesman Hurst) had determined that no State outside the League had the right to oust the advisory jurisdiction of the Court, even when that State was recognized as a party in dispute. In other and more specific words, the Eastern Carelia case could not bear this construction; and if the absolute and unqualified power of veto required by the United States was grounded upon the majority decision in that case, it was misconceived. In September 1923 the Council had challenged the Court's interpretation of its discretion; at the Conference of Signatories it was agreed that the substance of the Court's demurrer in the Eastern Carelia case should not be regarded as an established precedent. The Council's *de facto* rebuke of 1923 became in 1926 a *de jure* principle.[33]

Such an interpretation of the Conference's conclusions is at odds with the official Conference record. This was part of the concealment. The Conference publicly maintained that the American demand for a veto was met by the Eastern Carelia precedent in cases where the United States was a party in dispute. In private the Conference denied that that precedent would protect the United States. As for instances in which the United States only 'claimed' an interest, the Conference was prepared to concede 'a position of equality with States represented either on the Council or in the Assembly of the League of Nations'. In other words,

> in any case where a State represented on the Council or in the Assembly would possess the right of preventing, by opposition in either of these bodies, the adoption of a proposal to request an advisory opinion from the Court, the United States shall enjoy an equivalent right.

The Conference argued that the American demand for a veto in the second circumstance (i.e. the claim rather than possession of an interest) rested 'upon the presumption that the adoption of a request for an advisory opinion by the Council or Assembly requires a unanimous vote'. This was, perhaps, a plausible interpretation of the Senate's reservation; but it was completely untrue. Rather the Mosul case had demolished any argument that the principle of unanimity could prevent a request to the Court. If interested parties were *ipso facto* to be discounted, mere claimants, *a fortiori*, had no right to prevent the submission, if only the principle of unanimity were at issue. No: the Senate (followed by the Executive) had approached the question from a different direction. The Mosul opinion had cut the ground from under the presumption and defence of unanimity and thereby denied the veto power of a disputant State, Member of the League – in a manner analogous to the challenge posed by the Eastern Carelia case to the belief that a non-Member State, *qua* disputant, could oust the Court's advisory jurisdiction.[34] With disputant States, whether Members or not of the League, thus open to the Court's advisory jurisdiction, the response of the United States had been to claim the right of immunity from any possible advisory opinion. As Moore, leading Senator and the Department of State all acknowledged, the principle of unanimity was only 'incidental' to the discussion. Behind the Senate's Fifth Reservation lay (as the British and French governments realized) the American determination that the League should never, as a consequence of American adherence to the Court, be in a position to request an advisory opinion of the Court unless the United States approved of the reference.[35]

It was little wonder that even some proponents of American adherence (like the leading Brazilian jurist and diplomat, Raul Fernandes) described this determination as a simple claim for a privileged status. Nevertheless it was argued both inside and outside the Conference that such a legal privilege would be handled judiciously by a responsible Executive: practically and politically the American special status would be exercised on behalf of international peace and the interests of the League. Many delegates spoke openly in this way; Hurst used similar language in presenting his analysis of the Conference to Austen Chamberlain. But there were grumbles, notably from the Swedish, New Zealand and Canadian delegates.[36] The net effect of such complaints and the verbal resistance to according a 'privileged position' to the United States was to suggest that the American conditions had been met in full; that the United States had indeed been placed on a 'footing of equality' (as Moore and Root expressed it) with their prospective cosignatories.[37] The text of the Conference's Final Act, however, suggested otherwise. The response of the United States government was even less ambiguous.

The Conference of Signatories had learned a few lessons from the furore created by Chamberlain's initiative at the March Council. One was the determination to avoid, so far as possible, the appearance of meeting as a League-sponsored organization. Likewise, for all their collective decision-making, the terms of their response to the United States were to be delivered separately by every single Signatory. The 'basis of the replies' was set forth in the Conference's Final Act; and here again the events of the spring were influential. Partly to conciliate South American Member-States, partly as a result of the absence of some of the most important of these States, notably Brazil and Chile, the eighth (Monroe Doctrine) condition was deliberately excluded from discussion. So too was the seventh condition. By implication the sixth ('exchange of notes') condition was procedurally central to the Conference discussion.

Thus the boundaries drawn by Chamberlain in March were preserved: the League and Court Signatories would concern themselves only with the substance of Paragraphs I–V of the Senate's January resolution.

Paragraphs IV and V alone constituted potential difficulties, the Conference admitted; and even these were soluble. The right of withdrawal required by the US government should be conceded but on a reciprocal basis – especially because the terms of Paragraph V (on the advisory jurisdiction) might generate disagreements and ultimately deadlock. In the language of the Final Act:

> In order to assure equality of treatment, it seems natural that the signatory States, acting together and by not less than a majority of two-thirds, should possess the corresponding right to withdraw their acceptance of the special conditions attached by the United States to its adherence to the said Protocol in the second part of the fourth reservation and in the fifth reservation. In this way the *status quo ante* could be reestablished if it were found that the arrangement agreed upon was not yielding satisfactory results.

The Final Act stated that only the 'second part' of Paragraph V was contentious, for the 'first part' (governing notification of a reference and publication of the opinion) had been incorporated into the recently revised Rules of the Court and could easily be made the subject of a 'protocol of execution' between the United States and the existing signatory States. The Final Act concluded with a Preliminary Draft of such a protocol, running to a mere eight articles, chief of which was Article 4.

> The manner in which the consent provided for in the second part of the fifth reservation is to be given, will be the subject of an understanding to be reached by the Government of the United States with the Council of the League of Nations.
>
> The States signatories of the Protocol of December 16th, 1920, will be informed as soon as the understanding contemplated by the preceding paragraph has been reached.
>
> Should the United States offer objection to an advisory opinion being given by the Court, at the request of the Council or the Assembly, concerning a dispute to which the United States is not a party or concerning a question other than a dispute between States, the Court will attribute to such objection the same force and effect as attaches to a vote against asking for the opinion given by a Member of the League of Nations either in the Assembly or in the Council.[38]

Before the Conference assembled Hurst had confessed to great 'despair': the League was 'violently divided' over the response to make to the American conditions. At the conclusion of the Conference Hurst could congratulate himself on devising a programme which had won unanimous support from some forty delegations. He did not pretend the Final Act and the Preliminary Draft Protocol constituted an unqualified acceptance of the Senate resolution. That, after all, had not been his goal. But the United Kingdom had not been isolated as the leading antagonist to the United States. The Dominions and Whitehall had kept together, though often they diverged in policy towards the United States. Perhaps most remarkable of all, the Great Powers or Permanent Members of the Council had not openly split with the small or neutral Powers. The tendency of the latter to support the development of compulsory jurisdiction in the face of the general resistance of the Permanent Members to encouraging the Court's discretion met on the common ground of opposition to a non-Member State's being granted a *de jure* veto power over the advisory jurisdiction. Furthermore, the smaller, neutral Powers feared the potential of the Fifth Reservation in damaging the independence of the Court; the Permanent Members, for their part, deprecated any American obstacles to the flexibility and effectiveness of the League Council.[39] The language and procedure of the Draft Protocol, therefore, compromised the differing positions. But between this satisfactory compromise and the American terms there was a gap. The Final Act in this description could be seen as a 'bridge', the image used by the Dutch chairman, Willem van Eysinga, as he adjourned the Conference. It would remain with the US government 'only to pass over to meet' their prospective co-signatories. A few weeks later Hurst spoke less optimistically. The broader and more immediate imperatives of British and League interests had been successfully answered. Nevertheless, he added, it was

> useless to conceal the fact that the arrangements proposed... for giving satisfaction to the U.S.... might not work well in practice.

Hurst's forebodings as he faced the Conference reflected his fear that the League, and particularly the Permanent Members, would openly and decisively split on the response to be made to the US government. The French government was more sanguine – or, perhaps, more cynical: the Conference itself was rather an elaborate ruse politely but effectively to reject the American conditions for adherence to the Court.[40] It was a judgment not confined to leading participants; and it was one which made van Eysinga's conciliatory remarks essentially futile. Even before the publication of the Final Act many authoritative voices could be heard in the United States saying that the 'counter-reservations' from the Conference of Signatories were unacceptable.[41]

On 21 September the *New York Times* carried the headlines; 'Coolidge Opposes Compromise Plan on World Court'. In the news columns Senator Willis (incorrectly but significantly described as a leader in the Senate debate) was quoted as expressing total senatorial opposition to the 'scheme' being proposed at Geneva. This was only a foretaste of the coming reaction. With official publication of the Final Act the list of senatorial objectors multiplied. Borah and Moses were not surprisingly in the opposition; Senator Fess was one of the proponents-turned-critics. Then came press reports of Senators who wanted not to insist upon the January reservations but rather to rescind the resolution of adherence itself. Walsh and Swanson did not go that far; but both were deeply disillusioned. As Walsh wrote to Charles C. Bauer of the League of Nations Non-Partisan Association:

The position of those of us who must share responsibility in the matter is distressingly embarrassing at this juncture. We quite confidently assured the country that no question could be submitted to the Court in which we had or claimed an interest, like the Monroe Doctrine, for instance, without the consent of the United States. We must now back up and say that that view may be altogether wrong and we are powerless to prevent the submission of any such question.[42]

Bauer's organization was one of the lobby-groups represented in the Conference on the World Court – an *ad hoc* liaison committee. In late October the Conference agreed that the Final Act did not constitute (in James McDonald's phrasing) 'an acceptance...sufficient to justify the President's assuming that it meets the Senate's terms'. Nation-wide the pro-Court press was expressing the same judgment: the *New York Herald-Tribune* wrote in a common language when it declared that the US government 'could not accept membership [of the Court] at the Geneva Conference's price'. More idiomatically David Lawrence of the (Washington) *Star* wrote of the Court's being 'dead' and President Coolidge was not the man 'to resuscitate the issue'. It was less a scoop than an insider's authoritative comment: Lawrence was known to have good press relations with the White House.[43]

The epitaph from Coolidge was not delivered for many weeks; but when it came it was absolutely unambiguous. The occasion was Armistice Day, 11 November 1926; the place, Kansas City. Coolidge was not entirely accurate when he stated that he had 'advocted adherence to [the] Court... on condition that the statute... be amended to meet [American] views'; but the very nature of the claim was a mark of his identification with the Senate's terms and the 'resolution [adopted] for that purpose'. However, Coolidge added, the Conference of Signatories had shown itself 'unwilling to concur in [those] conditions'. Though 'no final decision' could be taken by the US government until the individual Signatories had all responded, he did

not intend to ask the Senate to modify its position. I do not believe the Senate would take favourable action on any such proposal, and unless the requirements of the Senate resolution are met, I can see no prospect of this country adhering to the Court.

Coolidge spoke with the complete support of Secretary Kellogg and the leading officers in the Department of State, especially Castle, who dismissively referred to the importunities of the 'pro-League crowd' and deplored the lobbyists' failure to read the mood of the American people and the 'League itself'.[44] Influential senators were equally in agreement: not just Borah, Moses and Johnson. Pepper, Lenroot, even Walsh and Swanson joined in endorsing Coolidge's speech.[45] The reaction of the French and British governments was, perhaps, predictable: they, after all, had been the leaders in the Conference of Signatories. The French were reportedly 'exasperated' by Coolidge's 'very self-righteous... tone'; but they were not, apparently, surprised by his message.[46] The British were, if anything, somewhat self-satisfied. The impossible demands of the US government had been firmly but courteously resisted at Geneva; and the British had not been singled out for public censure. However, as Chamberlain reminded his colleagues, the Court was not the only or even most important item on the international agenda. The British government should not exacerbate any ill-feeling towards itself or the League; accordingly it would

> be a mistake to choose this moment to send [our] reply [to the United States and] equally a mistake to take the initiative in getting a number of replies sent concurrently.

As so often in the history of the Court Protocol, procrastination was the safest policy.[47]

Among the major items on Chamberlain's agenda were inter-Imperial relations; the development of the Locarno system; preparations for the Naval Conference of 1927, in particular devising means to avoid a confrontation with the United States over belligerent rights; and the response to be made to the French government's initiative that led to the signing of the Kellogg–Briand Pact in August 1928. This list, drawn retrospectively and in British terms, is only a tiny record of the numerous diplomatic events of the months succeeding the Conference of Signatories.[48] (Nor should we forget, in our concentration upon foreign affairs, such domestic crises as the British General Strike of May 1926, which intervened between the March Council meeting and the September Conference.) So far as the Court Protocol was concerned, scarcely anything transpired between President Coolidge's Armistice Day address of 1926 and September 1928. In that month the Ninth Assembly of the League proposed a review of the Court Statute; and it was soon authoritatively suggested that such a review and possible revision of the Statute might provide an opportunity to re-examine the question and conditions of American adherence.

It would, however, be a mistake to deduce from these inter-governmental silences that the Court Protocol had vanished from the domestic American scene. Immediately upon the assembling of Congress in December 1926 the renegade Senator Trammell introduced a motion to rescind the January resolution. Though Colcord had predicted such senatorial reaction to the League's firmness, Trammell's resolution was treated more as a gesture of protest than an opportunity for serious legislative action. Proponents and opponents of adherence left the motion in abeyance and it died with the adjournment of Congress in

March 1927. When the new, Seventieth Congress (elected in 1926) convened in December 1927, Senator Blease introduced another motion to similar effect. Its tone and language, however, were noticeably different. Whereas Trammell had spoken in disillusionment, Blease was violently opposed to the 'so-called World Court' and censured the League, rather than the Court Signatories, for the inordinate and contemptuous neglect of the Senate's resolution and reservations. (In the House, Wilson of Mississippi and later Tinkham of Massachusetts introduced comparable resolutions to express a more general congressional antipathy to both the Court and the League.)[49]

Outside Congress the prospects for further action towards ratification could be interpreted more favourably. In the two and three-quarter years between the Senate's January 1926 vote and the League Assembly's resolution for reviewing the Court Statute the Carnegie Endowment for International Peace abandoned its earlier opposition to American membership. This meant that one of the wealthiest and most respected foreign-affairs organizations in the country had joined the ranks of the many pro-Court lobbies: groups such as the American Foundation, the Foreign Policy Association, the League of Nations Non-Partisan Association and the World Peace Foundation. It also brought the Carnegie Endowment's widely-circulating *International Conciliation* into the lists of pro-Court journals.[50]

Not that the American Foundation slackened its efforts. Collectively it decided that little could or need be done with the Senate; rather the Executive had to be encouraged to act independently. To this end one of the Foundation's leading officers, Esther Everett Lape, went on a visit to Northwest Europe and there conducted a series of lengthy interviews with diplomats, Court officials and members of the League Secretariat. Drummond, Hammarskjöld and Fromageot were only three of her interviewees. The result was a battery of memoranda, many running to several thousands of words, with the most substantial being sent to the White House and Department of State. In the autumn a compendium version was published in the *Atlantic Monthly* under Lape's own name and with a prophetic title: 'A Way Out of the Court Deadlock'. The nub of Lape's argument in its public form was that the Final Act of the September Conference of Signatories was itself misconceived. Since the Senate had never truly intended 'to establish equality between the U.S. and every member of the League Council', there was no question of an American veto. Consequently, the substantive portion of the Final Act could relate only to the first three Senate reservations; and these the Conference had explicitly accepted. Nothing, therefore, remained but for the President to declare that the Signatories had agreed to all the Senate's conditions; and on this basis subscribe the American signature to the Protocol. It was not even necessary for the President to resubmit the engrossed Protocol to complete the process of ratification.[51]

No senior officer in the Department of State thought anything of these perverse arguments – though they were allegedly endorsed by Root and John W. Davis, both senior members of the American Foundation. (The

British government was equally dismissive.) Former Senator Lenroot, a correspondent of Lape's, thought her completely wrong, both in her false analogies with domestic judicial practice – and, more importantly, in misunderstanding the mood of the Senate. Judge Moore also faulted Lape's judicial logic and political sensitivity. Indeed he appeared tempted by the notion of his friend Borchard that the *Atlantic Monthly* article should be widely distributed to embarrass the lobbists.[52]

They, however, kept up the pressure. As Blease's anti-League motion was being written into the Senate records in December 1927, a letter went to the White House signed by over five hundred public figures: presidents of universities; deans of law schools; editors of well-known papers and periodicals; and former cabinet members and diplomatists. Many of the signatories have already appeared in these pages: Edward M. House, Walter Lippmann, George Wickersham, Raymond Fosdick, Philip Jessup. Others we shall meet later: Eleanor Roosevelt, William Allen White, Newton D. Baker. The theme of the petition was becoming common: 'misunderstandings' separated the US Executive and the Court Signatories; therefore 'negotiations' should be resumed over language and procedures rather than concepts and substance.[53]

Such 'propaganda' was instanced by Senator Gillett in a letter written to Secretary Kellogg in late January 1928 describing the 'strong movement' to further US – League – Signatory negotiations. Gillett believed, however, that the 'Senate would never relax its insistence on the complete exemption from advisory opinions'. Consequently it was up to the parties to the Final Act to modify their position. Kellogg essentially agreed, except to register his doubt that the League-Court members would in fact alter their counter-reservations. It appeared a reasonable interpretation: in early April, Gilchrist and Sweetser both wrote to Lape and Hudson of there being 'mightily little interest' among the League Members for American adherence to the Court.[54]

Kellogg had made the obvious suggestion to Gillett that he test the mood of the Senate and not rely simply on impressions. To this end Gillett submitted a resolution requesting the Executive to undertake

> a further exchange of views... to establish whether the differences between the United States and the Signatory States can be satisfactorily adjusted.

The resolution, introduced on 6 February 1928, was not debated for a couple of months. Whether or not the Executive would eventually accept Gillett's suggestion, there could be no doubt about the Senate's commitment to the substance of the January 1926 reservations. Borah, as chairman of the Committee on Foreign Relations, had prepared the official materials for the debate on the Gillett resolution; but his contribution on the Senate floor was minimal and muted. The proponents of adherence made his case for him. Reed of Pennsylvania and Willis denounced the 'propaganda' of the lobbyists trying to change the January 1926 reservations – reservations they had both willingly supported. Swanson and Bruce, speaking for the pro-League Democrats, used the Senate chamber to reaffirm what Walsh had previously stated, namely that the Senate had indeed insisted upon a 'veto' power; and, added Reed, this was a power the September Conference had determined not to accord to the United States. The message which came from the Senate was clear. Whatever some pro-Court lobbyists maintained (the World Peace Foundation, through its Director of Research, Denys P. Myers, being the major exception) there was no 'misunderstanding'. Rather, as Gillett concluded, echoing the language of Lape in her *Atlantic Monthly* article, it was a question of 'deadlock'.[55]

Debate on Gillett's resolution had taken place in late spring, when congressional eyes were mainly focused on the forthcoming party conventions. The campaign platforms which the Republicans and Democrats constructed in 1928 contained no references to the World Court. Voters looking for commitment and qualifications would have to be satisfied with allusions by the Democrats to the promotion of 'international arbitration, conciliation [and] conference'. The Republicans, for their part, 'pledge[d themselves] to aid and assist in the perfection of principles of international law and the settlement of international disputes'.[56] In truth the Court issue played an insignificant role in the 1928 election. In narrowly organizational terms the problem for party managers, nationally and locally, was maintaining and possibly strengthening electoral support. Four years previously the Republican party had been close to a national split; in 1928 the Democrats did divide. Both elections can be seen as part of a long-term shift in voting allegiance: western, agrarian Republicans breaking traditional ties, while urban-based, second-generation Americans moved into the Democratic ranks. In 1924 it had been the western erosion within the Republican party which was so noticeable; in 1928 it was the breaking-up of the once Solid South, as a number of ex-Confederate States supported the 'dry', Protestant, Republican candidate, Herbert Hoover, against the 'wet', Roman Catholic, Democratic nominee, Governor Al Smith of New York.

Though the Court Protocol was (in Castle's phrase) 'dead' as an issue in the electoral campaign, the influential pro-League newspaper editor, William Allen White, thought he and his allies had scored something of a victory just by preventing Borah from writing an anti-Court plank into the Republican platform.[57] More important, though, than these debates was the occurrence of a number of disparate events which combined to loosen the 'deadlock' between the United States on the one side and the League and Signatories on the other. Contemporaneously with the Senate debate Judge Moore resigned from the Court Bench; but far from his resignation weakening the chances of eventual American adherence, it led to the nomination and subsequent election of ex-Secretary of State, Charles Evans Hughes. Informed observers described the League vote for such a distinguished American candidate as reversing the slackening momentum for adherence.[58]

Just before Hughes's election in September 1928 there had occurred an event of far greater significance in international politics: the signing in Paris of the multilateral General Treaty for the Renunciation of War as an Instrument of National Policy, known popularly but with many variations as the Kellogg–Briand Pact. Even today the origins, conflicting purposes and long-term value of the treaty still require careful analysis, not least in order to lift the charge of naïvety from politicians such as Borah and establish the responsibility of pro-Leaguers, such as Shotwell, for using the Pact to align the United States with the Permanent Members of the League Council.[59] Despite these complexities, however, in the common history of the Permanent Court of International Justice and the United States the meaning of the treaty is comparatively straightforward: its signing, speedy approval by the Senate and subsequent ratification by the Executive were taken by many people to be a major premise for consummating adherence to the World Court.[60]

This logic was not firmly constructed until after January 1929, when the Senate voted 85:1 in favour of ratifying the Kellogg–Briand Pact.[61] But such thinking could be seen in the previous autumn at the League Assembly which had elected Hughes to the Court bench. The context of the discussion was the decision to revise the Court's Statute in time for the new nine-year cycle to begin in 1930. The chief concerns of the Court Registry, the bench, the signatory States and the League lay in a broard range of matters from residency requirements for judges and the etiquette of secondary professional engagements to the advisability of giving statutory protection to provisions of the Court Rules, notably on the procedure for handling the advisory jurisdiction. The election of Hughes took place on 8 September; on 20 September the Assembly passed a motion requesting the Council to institute a review of the Court Statute; and four days later a rider was added suggesting a re-examination of the American conditions of January 1926 and the Final Act of September 1926.[62]

Among the Assembly's suggestions to the Council was a recommendation that the review of the Court's constitution and functioning should embrace the majority-unanimity controversy. In more precise words, were references to the Court for an advisory opinion to be made on the basis of neglecting the votes of disputant as well as (merely) interested parties; and, if so, had the other voters to be unanimous in their decision? This question had lain behind the framing of the Senate's Fifth Reservation and had been implicitly addressed in advisory Opinion no. 12, the Mosul case.

Arthur Sweetser, still sending lengthy communications from inside the League Secretariat to contacts in the Department of State, thought the conundrum would be solved satisfactorily to the United States. In Sweetser's account, the British, French, Japanese and Italian governments, that is the

> four Big Powers were definitely opposed to [the] majority vote as an infringement of the League's basic principle of unanimity, and as an unjustifiable extension of compulsory jurisdiction.

Consequently, he concluded:

they are in line with the American reservations which are based on the presumption of unanimity.

In fact the Big Powers held to a more complex analysis, the simplest element of which was that (as Cecil Hurst put it) 'the time [*was*] not yet ripe' to resolve any ambiguities.[63] Possibly more upsetting for Sweetser's optimism, however, was the position of the Little Powers (to adapt his terminology). The Swiss Government may fairly be taken as one of its leading members. They were definitely in favour of American adherence to the Court; yet they were also advocates of the majority principle. In short, Sweetser's mistake consisted in thinking that the Big Powers formed a 'united front' (as he put it) in support of the unanimity principle; while he ignored the opposition of the Little Powers to that very principle. Furthermore, behind the details, there lay the fundamental unwillingness of the Big Powers to extend what were seen as 'privileges' to the United States, particularly if such privileges would impede the flexibility and efficiency of the Council.[64]

Inside the United States the national elections of November 1928 which saw the triumph of the Republicans meant that Borah would continue as chairman of the Senate Committee on Foreign Relations. Later in the month a White House Conference attended by leading members of Congress confirmed that no Senate action would be taken on the Court Protocol during the remainder of Coolidge's term, that is until at least March 1929: after all, the initiative still rested with the Signatories. Nevertheless, influential pro-Court newspapers, such as the *New York Times* and the *New York Herald-Tribune*, continued to report pressure on Coolidge 'to sound out [the] leading powers with respect to' the 1926 Senate terms, in particular the 'veto' required over the advisory jurisdiction.[65]

The Dutch government (another of Sweetser's Little Powers) accurately translated the conflicting reports coming out of Washington and Geneva. It argued that Coolidge was unlikely to 'ask the… Senate to modify its reservations, and there [was] little reason to expect any action from the direction 'of the League.[66] However, in the short-term, a series of events occurred which initially challenged the Dutch analysis. From one side Elihu Root came back on to the scene and urged Kellogg against 'closing the door' on Court adherence. From somewhat different positions, Senators Borah and Swanson agreed to endorse an American approach to the Signatories – but only on the understanding that something should 'be done that would be acceptable to the United States Senate'. They were both quite definitely 'opposed to any negotiations'. Kellogg reported this obduracy to Root; but by the time Root and Kellogg were again in formal contact, the League Council meeting at Lugano in December had taken up the Assembly resolution and decided to appoint a second Advisory Committee of Jurists to review the 1920 Court Statute. Even more remarkably, the Council once more invited Root to serve as a member – though without formally placing the question of American adherence on the Committee's agenda.[67]

These few sentences compress issues and activities of great complexity; but if an authoritative defence is needed for such compression it can come from the Secretary-General of the League, Eric Drummond. Summarizing the situation in January 1929, Drummond wrote of the 'semi-initiative' which had originated within the United States and the League. 'Each side' had acted 'simultaneously but unconnectedly': the United States to see whether the League and Signatories would finally accept their conditions for adherence; the League was enquiring whether the United States truly sought 'greater privileges than the permanent Members'. Whatever the conclusions of the new Committee of Jurists, the subsequent action of the League and then the Signatories, only one thing was clear, Drummond concluded: the very uncertainty of the situation. In his words:

> neither side ... had committed itself in any very definite way either as to the lines on which it will act, or, indeed, as to whether it will act at all.[68]

Drummond's correspondent was Sweetser, an enthusiastic man, The wording, therefore, was as tenuous as possible: potentialities could be emphasized but no commitments or promises made. In fact the situation was fundamentally more certain though superficially more complicated than Drummond cared to reveal. The British government was convinced that Root could not bind the incoming Hoover administration or abandon the Senate's original demand for a veto. (Foreign Secretary Chamberlain and Ambassador Howard were generally distrustful of Kellogg anyway.)[69] For their part, Borah and the other Senators saw the limits of Root's task as constructing a method for implementing the right to oust the Court's advisory jurisdiction. Even so, discussion of the 1926 Final Act was not part of the Committee's initial brief: in this respect both the British and the Americans were anticipating the work of a Committee summoned simply to review the 1920 Statute.[70] One last point can be made – or rather, the implications of earlier remarks made more precise. Root was not an official representative of the US government, any more than he had been in 1920 at the meetings of the original Advisory Committee of Jurists. But then his private, unofficial status had been accurately assessed by his colleagues, while now his position was most ambiguous – and made more so by Kellogg's official communications with the League and Court Signatories.[71] Root himself was well aware that his 1929 colleagues represented ponderable, political force: Hurst from the British Foreign Office; Fromageot from the French; Gaus from the German; Scialoja from the Italian. It had been 'very different' nine years previously, when he had travelled with James Brown Scott: 'merely a gesture', Root told his new, young assistant, Philip Caryl Jessup. Now things had changed; 'practical politics' were involved.

> Somebody wants to get something very badly. But what it is, is being very carefully concealed.[72]

In such uncertainty, Root set sail once more for Europe. Not this time to

The Hague but, significantly, to Geneva – the only member of the Committee to serve both in 1920 and in 1929 as judicial adviser to the League.

A history devoted exclusively to the Permanent Court of International Justice would allot at least a chapter to the events of 1929. Among the items for inclusion would be the meeting of the Committee of Jurists in March 1929 and their formulation of a Draft Protocol of American Accession together with a complete rewriting of the 1920 Statute, the latter being embodied in a Draft Protocol of Revision. Then came the League Council's approval of both documents in June and their subsequent referral to the League Assembly and a second Conference of Signatories in September 1929, where the discussion and debate was less cursory than in the Council but equally to the same effect. The terms devised by the Jurists in March were accepted by all the intervening bodies with scarcely any modifications, certainly none of any significance.[73]

An observer is struck by the procedural similarities with 1920, when the Court's original Statute began life at The Hague in the Advisory Committee of Jurists and then passed through the hands of the Council, League Members, Secretariat and was given its final shape at the First Assembly. The striking difference in 1929 was the formality of the transmission – a conclusive sign of the authority of the second Jurists' Committee. In this respect Elihu Root's hopeful yet somewhat uncertain speculation was well-founded: his new colleagues had the confidence of their governments, the League and the Court. It would, however, have been incorrect to infer that they had gathered to negotiate the adherence of the United States on the conditions approved by the United States government in 1926. Throughout 1929 the League was collectively agreed that the American conditions could not be and had not been unequivocally accepted by the various, successive bodies – an interpretation which the US government came to share. Among those who argued differently, but unconvincingly, were Root and his assistant, Jessup.

In Chapter 2, where we discussed the drafting of the Court Statute in 1920, we focused upon the role of Elihu Root: not to suggest that the Court which emerged could be regarded as the 'Root Court', but rather to reveal the problematical nature of this title. Nine years later history repeated itself – but with complications. The new Protocol of American Accession was frequently referred to as the 'Root formula', even as the 'Root Protocol'; by which was meant a 'machinery' for harmonizing the League – US positions on the advisory jurisdiction.[74] Yet even superficially the term was misleading, since it referred both to Root's suggestions offered before the assembling of the Jurists' Committee and to the results of the Jurists' negotiations, in which the British representative, Cecil Hurst, was so influential. Indeed, the Committee's proposals for reconciling the US – League positions were known more properly as the 'Root–Hurst formula'.[75] This was a term little used in the United States, for two interrelated reasons. First it rightly suggested Root had compromised the original American conditions; secondly, Hurst had a particularly bad reputation as the most obstinate opponent of the 1926 conditions. Nor was the ill-feeling felt only by the enemies of adherence: Claude Swanson had been bitterly disappointed by Hurst's behaviour in 1926; so too Esther Everett Lape – to mention only actors already well known to us.[76]

Other substantive issues lay entangled in the 1929 negotiations – issues not suggested by the correct attribution of the 'formula' to Root or Hurst. The one which most concerned the League and Court was the timetable of revision. American accession was secondary to improving the functioning of the Court. If the Protocols of Accession and Revision were made interdependent, then revision of the Court's Statute would be hazarded if the Americans did not accept the new terms for American adherence. However, the US government might not accept the 'formula' for adherence if the substance of the 1926 Senate conditions were not incorporated textually into the new Statute.[77] The particular concern of the United States, of course, was the advisory jurisdiction; yet, paradoxically, this function of the Court was becoming less important to the League Council. The reason was twofold. First, the smaller Powers were increasingly urging the reference of questions by the majority principle – a development irksome to the Great Powers. Secondly, the procedural friction concealed a more substantial conflict, namely that the smaller Powers were more and more confident of the growing independence of the Court. While this confidence appeared to refute the indictments of the anti-Court campaigners in the United States, it did nevertheless corroborate their criticism that the League Council valued the Court as a docile source of judicial authority for legitimating political actions.[78]

With these broad considerations in mind it is possible to see the significance of events in 1929 for American membership in the Court. The Draft Protocol of American Accession which emerged from the Jurists' Committee and was later unanimously approved by the League and signatory States built upon the 1926 Final Act in a number of respects.[79] First, the absolute veto required by the United States over the advisory jurisdiction was denied. Secondly, however, the United States was permitted to register its objections to a reference; and, where the United States was reckoned to be a party in dispute, the objections would be considered in the light of the Eastern Carelia case; alternatively, if the United States merely claimed an interest, then the general principles governing voting procedures in the League would apply. In the event of an irreconcilable disagreement, that is, if the United States' objections were overruled, then the Signatories no less than the United States could revoke their agreement to the peculiar conditions of American adherence; in other words, each side could unilaterally rescind the Protocol of American Accession. This last provision, set out at length in the 1929 Protocol, had a detailed formality lacking in 1926. The far more substantial divergence from the Final Act of 1926 lay in the location of American action. The Senate's Fifth

Reservation had sought a veto power directed towards the Court itself. In 1929 the Jurists and their successors would allow the United States to register and then defend its opposition only before the bar of the League. The implication of this change, apparently so trivial, was that the League had the right to require the Court to deliver an advisory opinion on the merits of a question. Phrased differently, the precedent to be derived from the Eastern Carelia case also included the propriety of the Council's rebuke of the Court. It was an implication corroborated in the contemporaneous and ambiguous redrafting of the Court's Statute to deal with the advisory function. The crucial Article 68 in the Draft Protocol of Revision stated:

> In the exercise of its advisory functions, the Court shall further be guided by the provisions of the Statute which apply in contentious cases *to the extent to which it recognizes them to be applicable.* [Emphasis added.]

Later, during the League proceedings in September, the same point was made explicitly and in public; while confidential memoranda of Hurst in the spring and autumn gave further evidence of the important reasons for the change.[80]

Hurst was not the only witness for the Jurists. Even before the conclusion of their meetings, Scialoja and van Eysinga (President and Vice-President of the Jurists' Committee) expressed serious doubts that the US government would accept the terms emerging at Geneva.[81] Jessup's beguiling narrative in his biography of Root can be carefully interpreted to disclose the same meaning. Kellogg is there censured for retreating before the pressure of intransigent Senators and the rabid Hearst press. The message, however, is indisputable: whether for good or bad reasons Root had not constructed a 'formula' for implementing the American veto; rather he had joined with Hurst in devising what Root called a 'method of procedure' for registering and discussing an American objection.[82]

Long before Root arrived back in New York on 17 April 1929 it was clear that the Root–Hurst formula would not satisfy what Ambassador Howard called the ' "irreconcilable" element in the Senate'. Yet Howard was not entirely gloomy, for he believed that Hoover's new Secretary of State, Henry Lewis Stimson and Senator Swanson would both endorse the Jurists' Draft Protocol of American Accession.[83] Howard was proved right about Swanson; but Stimson was both more ambiguous and ambivalent. Stimson appeared to share the judgment of his senior officials that the Root–Hurst formula diverged from the Senate's original demands; but over the years he seemed to find it impossible to express his doubts openly to Root. If Kellogg had found plain-speaking difficult, so too did Stimson; yet the latter had been a close friend and colleague of Root's for many years (and been suggested for the Secretaryship by Root himself); while Kellogg was a man who exasperated Root with his flaccidity. On one point, however, Kellogg and Stimson agreed. The new terms would need to go before the Senate for approval as part of a draft treaty updating the resolution of January

1926. Simply on their own the provisions of the Accession Protocol were inadequate; and therefore, 'if any of the countries [were to] submit this form of acceptance of the reservations, the President [could not] sign'.[84]

The catalogue of influential actors and observers who denied that the Root–Hurst formula was (as Assistant Secretary Castle phrased it) 'synonymous' with the Senate's Fifth Reservation was extensive. Walsh, Pepper and Lenroot; Stone and Moore; Stimson and Kellogg (as we have seen); and, ultimately, even Root and Jessup denied the identity.[85] And these men were all proponents of adherence. Likewise a number of authoritative pro-Court newspapers alluded to the gap between Root's original position and the conclusions of the Committee of Jurists. Department of State officials wrote long memoranda to the same effect; and, in the case of Castle, earned Root's justified suspicion for the weakening of his commitment to adherence. But there was the more pressing problem of Senate approval for the changes. Granted the modifications, would they win a two-thirds majority? Castle and J. Theodore Marriner, his successor in the Division of Western European Affairs, thought the chances of success 'very slight'. 'Keen lawyers' would easily expose the concessions made by Root; and Swanson and any allies would have to 'fight hard and adroitly', with only an outside hope of success. Indeed, in his despair at the struggle which lay ahead, Castle wistfully suggested that Borah might be induced to support the Root–Hurst formula. Then 'the battle would be over'. It was an impossible idea: Borah's had been one of the first voices heard in denunciation of the Accession Protocol.[86]

The foregoing may be regarded as substantial problems but they intersected with more overtly procedural questions. The admission on all sides that the Root–Hurst formula was deficient naturally induced a reluctance within the Executive to express approval of the Draft Protocol of American Accession. Root, however, feared that unless the Executive encouraged the League Council, 'the whole business would go to pieces'; and (in rather ambiguous language) he put pressure on Stimson to notify the Council that the Draft Protocol 'would constitute a satisfactory basis for the adherence of the United States'. Stimson responded by urging the dangers to President Hoover's recovery programme in the current First (special) Session of Congress if the administration were to 'come out unequivocally and publicly' for the Accession Protocol. There would be 'bitter attacks'; the senatorial leadership was 'not prepared'; and the move 'would greatly endanger the ultimate chance of successful adherence'. To fail now, Stimson concluded, 'would set back adherence ... for half a generation'. Swanson repeated the same argument, adding that Root could trust Hoover and Stimson, a team whose commitment to the Court far outdistanced that of their predecessors. The administration and the Senate should wait until the Second Session of Congress assembled in December.[87]

This was precisely the tenor of the message which Stimson sent to Secretary-General Drummond in late May for transmission to the League Council. The proposed Protocol of American Accession was basically satisfactory; but the United States government could not anticipate the decisions of the League. The Council, Assembly and any Conference of Signatories must first approve the Protocol. Furthermore, no legislative action could be expected until December at the earliest. It was this last point which was so disturbing to Drummond. The Accession and Revision Protocols had been drafted in tandem. The League and Court would be embarrassed if both Protocols were approved by the Signatories, only for the United States Senate to challenge one or the other. As Hurst expressed the problem: there would be 'great confusion' if some Signatories accepted the new Protocols in the hope of inducing American adherence while others held to the original 1920 Statute out of a justifiable fear that the United States would reject the revisions to the Statute and the adaptation of the Senate's 1926 reservations made by the Committee of Jurists.[88]

Stimson's message of delay was a dark cloud on the horizon; but two concurrent events relieved the gloom. May 1929 also saw the installation of Charles Evans Hughes as a full judge of the Court – a sign for some observers of approaching American membership.[89] In the same month the vociferous Salmon O. Levinson, a leading figure in the Outlawry of War movement and one of the most energetic actors behind the Kellogg–Briand Pact, finally switched from opposing to endorsing American adherence to the Court. The grounds for Levinson's change lay in the Draft Protocol of Revision (rather than American Accession): he interpreted the new articles governing the advisory jurisdiction as ruling out military sanctions against recalcitrant States. It was an idiosyncratic view, one that the British and French Foreign Offices forcefully though discreetly dismissed and one which the Department of State thought groundless. But the temerity of Levinson as an advocate or the implausibility of many of his arguments are not the issue. Rather more important was the weight added to the pro-Court lobby in the United States. The split in the Outlawry movement registered in 1925 was largely repaired; Levinson's financial resources were extensive; he had access to friendly newspaper coverage via the *Chicago Daily News* in America's second city, where the McCormick *Tribune* and the Hearst *Herald-Examiner* were powerful anti-Court, anti-League newspapers; and it was widely (if erroneously) believed that Levinson had a strong hold over Senator Borah.[90]

The League Council had no desire to publicize Stimson's message – though its gist was widely known. At the June meeting in Madrid the work of the Jurists' Committee was approved without dissent, scarcely without discussion. As the American Minister, Ogden Hammond phrased it: the Draft Protocols were 'railroaded through in the most routine manner'. But Root grew increasingly anxious. Unless the US government acted in September, 'the last opportunity' would disappear, he told Stimson. Practically, it was now or never. Secretary-General Drummond wrote to Stimson in a different tone but to the same effect. Stimson responded by gaining clearance from the White House, then conferring with Root, and finally on 14 August he officially informed Drummond that the Draft Protocol of American Accession effectively [met] the objections represented in the reservations of the United States Senate and... constitute[d] a satisfactory basis for the adherence of the United States....

This, of course, was ambiguous language, designed to placate the vocal domestic opposition to the Drafts, cover the dissatisfaction within the Department of State, spare Root's feelings and still preserve reasonable relations with the League and its most influential members. Even so, there could be no avoiding the substantial gap and the Executive's need to fulfil the terms of the January 1926 resolution. Once the Protocols of Accession and Revision had been officially agreed by both the League and the Court Signatories and subsequently signed on the authority of the President, then, Stimson concluded, they would be 'submitted to the Senate for its consent to ratification'.[91]

Stimson did not commit himself to a timetable. Drummond continued to hope that the United States would sign during the parallel meetings of the Assembly and Conference of Signatories in September.[92] As for these two bodies, organizationally but only 'fictionally' separated from one another, it was rather like 1920 all over again.[93] Leading participants in the Jurists' Committee played prominent roles in the two gatherings: Hurst was one, Nicolas Politis of Greece another; but the most notable was van Eysinga, who now presided over the Conference and Assembly. As for the absent Root, his participation in the Jurists' Committee was taken as an American imprimatur. Consequently there was little surprise when the Conference of Signatories spent only a few hours debating and approving, 'unanimously and without change', the Protocol of American Accession.[94]

The vote was itself a response to discreet information that the United States accepted the Accession Protocol; but when Stimson made the administration's position public, he simultaneously informed Drummond that

it [was] not probable that it [would] be advisable to submit the [Accession Protocol to the Senate] for... advice and consent for a considerable period, possibly a year.

Stimson spoke confidentially – or so it seemed. But the purport of his latest message was readily detected in Geneva; and the subsequent meetings of the League Assembly displayed a 'restiveness' towards the United States.[95]

The description comes from Gilson Blake, the American Consul General in Geneva, who was assigned to monitor the proceedings; and its accuracy was attested by similar comments from Fosdick and Sweetser. Some weeks later in mid October Blake reflected on the events and their meaning for the future. At the very beginning of September the leading delegations, the British, French and Dutch in particular, had 'demonstrated their extreme anxiety to facilitate in every possible way the entry of the United States', especially by 'doing all in their power to influence the... recalcitrant delegates'. But immediately they had endorsed the Protocol of American Accession they were 'extremely disturbed' to learn of Stimson's procrastination. The sentiment among 'leading powers' now was not to ratify the Accession Protocol until the Americans signed it but rather to concentrate their efforts on implementing the Revision Protocol. Blake concluded by placing the blame implicitly upon his own government for being the main cause of an 'exceedingly unfortunate... deadlock'.[96]

This language was an echo of previous years; but if a 'deadlock' did exist, some senior officers in the Department of State were more ready to blame the signatory States and the League. Equally they reversed the alternative described by Blake and supported American signature of the Accession Protocol and neglect of the Revision Protocol. Where disagreement lay was over the timing of action. Only Assistant Secretary Castle favoured immediate signing; his new superior, Under Secretary of State Joseph P. Cotton, would delay signature until the late spring of 1930; Secretary Stimson was even more unsure. Consequently Stimson himself turned to the President for a broader analysis of international and domestic considerations. After all, Cotton's arguments for postponement hinged mainly on the impact of the Court question in the forthcoming primary elections: Illinois in particular appeared likely to offer an 'unpleasant' repetition of 1926, when pro-Court Senators were reckoned to have suffered at the polls.[97]

Hoover's first response was also to urge delay in signing the Protocols. He was well aware of the ill feeling caused in the League by Stimson's warning; but against that he weighed the popular and legislative opposition to signing and attempting to ratify the Protocols. The Senate was described as unmanageable, the press as hysterical and manipulative. Any apparent co-operation with the League would wreck the chances of gaining congressional approval for a new naval disarmament agreement, since this would be interpreted as an alignment with the British. Within a month, however, Hoover had changed his mind. Castle, Root, Sweetser and Fosdick had between them persuaded Hoover that his long-term goals were more likely to suffer than benefit from procrastination on the Court. Nothing worthwhile could be achieved internationally without the co-operation of the League; and (in the words of Sweetser, endorsed by officers of the Department) the delay in signing was

> generally considered in Geneva as the most serious snub yet administered to the League by the United States.

Reluctantly Hoover agreed. The 'good faith' of the United States government was in question; and on that all else depended. Despondently he authorized Stimson to prepare for signing the Protocols and submitting them to the Senate when Congress re-assembled in early December.[98]

On 18 November 1929, exactly a month after receiving Hoover's authorization, Stimson used the format of a letter to the President to make his public case for American adherence on the new terms. Stimson had sought Root's advice before drafting the final text; and the influence of his mentor, Root, and Root's protégé, Jessup, permeated Stimson's brief.[99] Apart from a fairly traditional review of the Court's origins and a history of American arbitration and judicial practice, an informed reader would note two major areas of argumentation. First, Stimson's brief largely incorporated (what may be called) the Jessup thesis on the relationship between the Senate's 1926 reservations, the Protocol of Revision and the Protocol of Accession. In a series of published essays, Jessup maintained that the Revision Protocol had textually incorporated the substantive demands of the Senate's Fifth Reservation. Under Articles 65–8 of the Revision Protocol secret opinions had been ruled out; interested parties could submit evidence and plead; and (implicitly) the power of a disputant to oust the Court's jurisdiction had been given statutory authority. As for the Senate's Fourth Reservation on withdrawal, that had been embodied in the Protocol of Accession. The third part of the triangle lay in the possibility that either the United States or the other Signatories might wish to void the treaty because of disagreement over the proper invocation and functioning of the advisory procedure by the League. In the Jessup thesis, so long as both sides maintained the Protocol of Accession, then the veto power existed; once it was revoked by either side, the veto power lapsed. (Bustamente y Sirven argued a similar case to an American audience.) In following the Jessup thesis, Stimson acknowledged that the veto power had not been accorded unconditionally to the United States; but he argued that the political weight and moral authority of the United States would tend to deter the League from pressing for an opinion at the risk of the United States revoking its adherence. However, what neither Jessup, Root, Stimson nor anyone else could explain was how this latter situation could come about if their understanding of the Eastern Carelia precedent had indeed been incorporated into the Revision Protocol. If Soviet Russia's disclaimer had been given statutory protection, how could a State's opposition to the use of the advisory jurisdiction be overridden? It was a fundamental objection – and one perceptively raised by President Hoover at the time. Stimson could provide no answer.[100]

The other novelty in Stimson's presentation was his tying adherence to the 'Pact of Paris', another title of the Kellogg-Briand Pact. Not that the logic itself was new; rather this was the first time the Executive developed the argument. Even so the connections between the Pact and the Court were ambiguously drawn. At one point Stimson praised the work of the Court 'in the interpretation of international treaty relations in Europe'; and he implied that the United States would aid concretely in maintaining the political system. At another moment he explicitly quoted and endorsed the Eighth (or Monroe Doctrine) Reservation of 1926 – though one of its key provisions was American abstention from European politics. Readers would decode the allusions in the light of their own politics. Thus Manley Hudson wrote to Stimson that his was the best analysis he had read (in English or French) in nearly a decade: 'nowhere [had he] seen a more satisfactory statement of the problems involved'. Borah, conversely, could gain Stimson's explicit agreement that the Kellogg–Briand Pact entailed no unilateral or collective sanctions, judicial or otherwise, if it were broken; and certainly no American participation in cooperative action for its enforcement.[101]

On 9 December 1929 the Court Protocols were signed by Jay Pierrepont Moffat, the acting chargé in Switzerland. (It was now correct to refer to three separate but interrelated documents: the original 1920 Protocol of Signature attached to the Court's Statute; the Protocol of Revision; and the Protocol of American Accession.) The site chosen for the signing ceremony was Bern, the federal capital, not Geneva, the seat of the League. This was yet another example of political delicacy by the administration and the League. But it had been obvious for some months that the three Protocols would not be submitted to the Senate for at least a year. As one Washington correspondent summed up the difficulties: the 'strained legislative and political situation' made this impossible.[102] Historians have generally ignored the evidence which shows the proponents of adherence to have counselled delay and the indictment is drawn against the opponents. However a number of counter-points must be made.

First, there is strong evidence to suggest that even if the Protocols had been incorporated in a new draft treaty and acted upon by the Senate the original Fifth Reservation would have been re-inserted. This, after all, would have been consistent with the judgment that the League and Signatories had indeed accepted the 1926 conditions.[103] Secondly, it was not at all certain that a draft treaty would have been approved and reported by the Committee on Foreign Relations, since fewer than half the twenty members of the Committee were said to be ready to accept the revisions and adaptations. The full Senate was estimated by the American Foundation to have a two-thirds majority for simple adherence; but this broad generalization ignored the exact conditions of adherence and the likely deference of the Senate to the advice of its Committee. Furthermore, the relative weakness of the dissidents concealed their growth in absolute terms. Seventeen Senators had voted Nay in 1926; now the prospective figure was in excess of twenty-two – and growing all the time.[104] Finally there is the question of individual Senators, their legislative independence and forensic significance. In a Senate where party control and regularity were weak, the authority of individuals was not equally shared, particularly on an issue with such a long history. Senators Walsh and Wheeler on the Democratic side, once advocates, were known to doubt the Accession and Revision Protocols; the Republicans Norris and Reed were similarly cautious. How they voted, what reservations or amendments they supported, would influence others. Nor was this the only determinant for the undecided Senator. The issue was alive in the constituencies, particularly in the Middle West primary campaigns. The prediction of Under Secretary Cotton was coming true: already it was being widely argued that a pro-Court stance would once again be an electoral liability.[105]

Without doubt the frequent charge of 'obstructionism' cannot be fairly laid solely and simply against those Senators who opposed ratification of the Court Protocols. Certainly the Committee on Foreign Relations did not discuss the matter for a year after the signing; but neither did the Executive present the Protocols to the Senate until a year had elapsed. Eventually, on 10 December 1930, President Hoover submitted them to the Third (lame-duck) Session of the Seventy-first Congress, with a request that they be considered 'as soon as possible after the emergency relief and appropriation legislation [*had*] been disposed of'. That, of course, was the legislative priority; and the opponents of the Court had no compelling reason to disagree. (Hoover's submission of the Protocols, with language to match, was no less a gesture than Harding's in February 1923.) Once the Protocols had been referred from the full Senate, the Committee voted 10:9 that 'the matter go over' until December 1931.[106]

Historians have usually cited the vote as further though redundant proof of destructive time-wasting by the opposition. But it was more complex than that, as even the public record shows. Reed of Pennsylvania moved the resolution; the influential Republican, Fess, voted for postponement; Borah voted against the delay; while Walsh absented himself from the meeting without explanation or offering a proxy. If Walsh had voted for senatorial action it might well have led to a 'needless black eye' for the Court – the verdict of his new Committee colleague, Arthur H. Vandenberg (Michigan, Republican), who favoured adherence and also voted for postponement.[107]

One other item in the Committee's proceedings is, however, widely recorded: the decision to invite Elihu Root to testify on behalf of the new Protocols. Five weeks later, on Wednesday, 21 January 1931, he appeared before the Committee. Major newspapers carried detailed accounts of the Hearing. Root was now nearly 86 years old; he was described as sitting wrapped in a heavy, fur-trimmed overcoat against Washington's wintry weather; but he was reported as having an 'excellent physical appearance' and remained 'vigorous' for the three-hour session. The main committee room of the Senate Office Building was crowded, with an eager audience overflowing into the corridors.[108] For almost two hours Root spoke without interruption; and then he answered a series of difficult, though gently phrased, questions from the Committee. In the course of his oral testimony Root circulated a five-thousand word memorandum to the Committee, a composition drafted with the help of Philip Jessup and backed with information and advice from legal staff in the Department of State.[109]

Senator Johnson had seen Root's task as explaining the 'unsolved mystery' of the compatibility between the American conditions of 1926 and the two Protocols of 1929.[110] After many thousands of words and hours of speaking, the mystery remained. Root categorically insisted that the American demand for a 'veto' had been accorded by the League; but then acknowledged that the Accession Protocol permitted the voiding of this provision and a return to the *status quo ante*. Against the last point he then further insisted that the Revision Protocol had incorporated into the Court's Statute his reading of the Eastern Carelia precedent, namely that a disputant's plea to the jurisdiction would defeat the Court's entertainment of a League request for an advisory opinion. Root, in other words, was rehearsing the Jessup thesis but with less precision than Jessup had shown in his scholarly articles.

A careful observer would note these formal discrepancies; but even a layperson would have noticed the major theme of Root's testimony. For all the textual intricacies traversed by Root, the weight of his current argument for ratification lay in his concern for the United States to more closer to the League – or, more accurately, the Council – in maintaining peace.

They are living under the consistent [*sic*] threat of breach of international peace all about them in all that vast region of eastern Europe, where there has been redistribution of territory, where territory had been taken from one power and given to another, where new powers have been created in that vast region. It is all seething with people who are dissatisfied with what they have got, dissatisfied with what they have lost.

Americans, Root continued, should cease to distance themselves from 'people on the other side of the Atlantic' – over the functioning of the Court, the role of the League, and, above all, 'the maintenance of peace, in the establishment of conditions which will make peace easier'. American 'idealism ha[d] a real desire, a strong desire' for peace, while the 'material interests of the United States demand[ed] peace'. How could the United States claim, let alone be granted, an absolute veto over the advisory jurisdiction and thereby irrevocably 'put a stop to a proceeding intended to secure peace in Europe, Asia, America, or wherever it might be [?]'.[111]

The Committee ignored such arguments: this was Root of the Appeal of Thirty-One Republicans, Root the advocate of conditional membership in the League, as the hostile *Chicago Tribune* complained. The Committee, in the persons of Swanson, Walsh, Reed and Johnson, was rather more concerned to extract Root's agreement that the 1926 American demand was for 'an absolute veto power'; that this stood 'unimpaired and unaffected' by the Protocols; and even if the *status quo ante* were restored through the unilateral or multilateral rescinding of the Accession Protocol, the Revision Protocol would still extend to the United States and 'other nations' the 'same sort of protection that [they had got] from the fifth reservation'.[112]

Senator Swanson thought that Root's 'conclusive' testimony had 'knocked the pins' from under the opposition; and he looked forward confidently to the Senate taking up a new resolution for adherence in December. Jessup was more restrained though equally satisfied with Root's performance. But these favourable judgments were not shared even by the supporters of adherence. Stimson, for example, confessed his uncertainty by telling Root that a resolution giving effect to the 1929 Protocol would need to differ from that passed in January 1926. Walsh was decidedly unhappy with Root's testimony and told John Bassett Moore that the contradiction between the Senate's reservations and the League's terms had still not been resolved: Root had simply rephrased the problem.[113] Inside the Department of State a new member of the Legal Section advised his senior colleagues that it would be 'unwise' to identify 'too strongly' with Root's 'independent' analysis. This cautious voice belonged to Francis Colt de Wolf, a firm believer in adherence (he later served in the Court's Registry) and the departmental officer who had been instructed to brief Root for the Committee Hearing. It all became too much for Castle, whose patience finally snapped. What he shortly described as a monumentally unimportant item was consuming senatorial and departmental energies; and the blame lay with those who perversely maintained that the League had accepted the American conditions. If proof of this last point was needed, it soon came. The Spanish Ambassador (acting as emissary for his more influential colleagues in Washington) personally visited the Department to protest at Root's claim that the veto power had been conceded by the League.[114]

Root did find support, as ever, in the powerful pro-Court lobby-groups: his own American Foundation, the World Peace Foundation, and the National World Court Committee (an umbrella-organization in which Jessup was prominent). But their collective concern was less with providing arguments in defence of Root than in bringing forward senatorial action. As Esther Everett Lape told Secretary Stimson: for the Protocols to wait until December 1931 would be 'disastrous'. 'Politics would be rampant', with all eyes fixed on the 1932 presidential conventions and campaign; and no one would take a risk on behalf of the Protocols and face rejection at the party primaries or in the November election. The lessons of 1926 and 1930 were still too frightening, particularly for Republican proponents.[115]

The briefs delivered by the lobbyists were little use to the Department. The calls for earlier Senate action were even more futile. The Foreign Relations Committee had made a decision; and the administration did not have the votes to reverse the postponement. If they had, this would mean a Special Session of the new Seventy-second Congress. In this Congress, elected in November 1930, the House would be organized by the Democrats (for the first time since 1919); and the Republicans would have a majority of only one in the Senate. Perhaps (as some lobbyists feared) the Protocols would be lost forever in the Congress beginning in December; but if a Special Session were summoned, a cross-party alignment of Democrats and irregular Republicans would push through a programme of agricultural aid, unemployment relief, public works programmes and labour law reforms. The administration had no intention of expediting such radical measures. Congress as a whole would stand adjourned for nine months after March 1931; and the idea of a Special Senate Session (as in the previous year, when the London Naval Treaty had been approved) was equally ruled out by Hoover, despite renewed pressure from the National World Court Committee.[116]

Less than three weeks later, the German and Austrian governments announced their intention to harmonize their customs regulations. The cry of *Anschluss* was heard – the political union of Germany and Austria. Europe was said to be on the brink of war.

Notes

[1] This paragraph is based upon Embassy reports to Washington esp. those from London, The Hague, Bern, Santiago de Chile and Buenos Aires: NA500. C114/444–71; Esmé Howard to Austen Chamberlain, 28 January 1926: Records of the (British) Foreign Office (File no. FO 371, Public Record Office, Kew), W924/30/98; minute of G. Villiers, 9 February 1926; minute of H. W. Malkin, 10 February 1926: ibid.; Moore to Stone, 28 January 1926: Moore Papers; Borchard to Moore, 28 January 1926: Borchard Papers; Hammarskjö ld to Hudson, 16 February 1926: Hudson Papers.

[2] Hudson, 'The United States Senate and the Permanent Court of International Justice', *AJIL* 20 (April 1926), 330–5; Hudson to Drummond, 28 January 1926; to Sweetser, 28 January 1926; Sweetser to Hudson, 16 February 1926; McDonald, 'Memorandum on the United States Adherence to the Permanent Court of United States [*sic*] Justice', 29 January 1926: Hudson Papers.

[3] Richard M. Tobin (The Hague) to Kellogg, 16 February 1926: NA500. C114/469.

[4] F. A. Sterling (London) to Kellogg, 17 February 1926: NA500. C114/468; Hersch Lauterpacht, 'The United States and the Permanent Court of International Justice', *SIA* (1926), 80–98, esp. 81.

[5] Moore to Pepper, 1 February 1926; Pepper to Moore, 6 February 1926: Moore Papers.

[6] Johnson, *Borah of Idaho*, 380; reports in *NYT* (22–24 February 1926); Sweetser to Fosdick *et al.*, 16 February 1926: Sweetser Papers; cf. Colcord to Root, 1 February 1926: Root Papers.

[7] *Chicago Daily Tribune* (29 January 1926), 2; *NYT* (25 July 1926), 1; Johnson to J. D. Fackler, 15 March 1926: Johnson Papers

[8] Tobin to Kellogg, 4 May 1926: NA500. C114/511

[9] This analysis derives from the Cecil Papers, vols for 1926–9; the correspondence of Chamberlain, Howard and Cecil, November 1924–July 1926, Containers 50–3: Chamberlain Papers; and the exchange between Chamberlain and Howard, 4 and 11 November 1925: GB Foreign Office, *Documents on British Foreign Policy, 1919–1939* (cited below as *DBFP*), Series 1A, II. 869–70.

[10] Moore to Henry P. Fletcher, 21 June 1926: Moore Papers. Cf. Tobin's reports of 22, 23 and 28 April: NA500. C114/501, 507, 508; R. Henry Norweb (The Hague) to Kellogg, 24 January 1927: NA500. C114/603.

[11] Minute of Chamberlain, 11 February 1926; Cecil Hurst to Henri Fromageot (Legal Advisers to the British and French Foreign Offices respectively), 17 February 1926: FO 371, W924/30/98; A. de Fleureau (French Ambassador) to William Tyrrell, 19 February 1926: FO 371, W1350/30/98.

[12] Howard to Chamberlain, 28 January 1926, with minute of Villiers, 9 February 1926 and Malkin, 10 February 1926: FO 371, W924/30/98.

[13] Kellogg *pro forma* to Edgar L. G. Prochnik (Austrian Minister), 12 and 19 February 1926; to Drummond, 19 February 1926: NA500. C114/445a, 445bbb.

[14] See esp. the memoranda from the governments of South Africa, India and Australia, 8 April–12 May: FO 371, W3047/30/98, W4115/30/98, W4130/30/98.

[15] *LNOJ* (April 1926), 536; see also Cmd. 2646, Misc. no. 4 (1926), *League of Nations, Thirty-ninth Session of the Council*. Report by the Rt. Hon. Sir Austen Chamberlain, KG, MP (London: HMSO, 1926).

[16] Howard to Chamberlain, 25 March 1926: FO 371, W2835/30/98; Alan F.

Winslow (Bern) to Kellogg, 24 March and 29 April 1926: NA500. C114/485, 505; Tobin to Kellogg, 22, 23 and 28 April and 4 and 11 May 1926: NA500. C114/501–19; S. Pinkney Tuck (Geneva) to Kellogg, 18 March 1926: NA500.C114/474; Norweb to Kellogg, 24 January 1927: NA500. C114/603; Moore to Fletcher, 21 June 1926; to Huber, 18 September 1926: Moore Papers; Hammarskjöld to Huntington Gilchrist, 25 January 1927: Gilchrist Papers, MD, LC.

[17] Hill, *Problem of a World Court*, 113–16.

[18] Bullard to James T. Shotwell, 26 April 1926: Deibel, 'League of Nations', 416–17.

[19] Shotwell's biographer is Harold Josephson, who provides an inventory of Shotwell's many written works: *James T. Shotwell and the Rise of Internationalism in America* (Rutherford N.J.; Fairleigh Dickinson University Press, 1975).

[20] Drummond to Kellogg, 29 March 1926: NA500. C114/490 (*FRUS* (1926), I. 8–10); Howard to Chamberlain, 25 March 1926: FO 371, W2835/30/98; British Library of Information (New York), 10 [April] 1926: FO 371, W3288/30/98.

[21] Speech of 8 April 1926: Text FO 371, W3264/30/98.

[22] Margulies, *Lenroot of Wisconsin*, 396.

[23] Howard to Chamberlain, 15 April 1926: FO 371, W3457/30/98; British Library of Information, 17 April 1926: FO 371, W3509/30/98; Johnson, *Borah of Idaho*, 381; Hiram Johnson to Harold L. Ickes, 15 April 1926: Johnson Papers; 'A World Court Defeat', *Literary Digest* (24 April 1926), 10.

[24] Kellogg to Drummond, 18 April 1926: NA500. C114/490 (*FRUS* (1926), I. 12–13); memo of Kellogg, 22 March 1926, NA500. C114/476; Kellogg to Coolidge, 1 April 1926: quoted in Ellis, *Kellogg and American Foreign Relations*, 227.

[25] Hughes, 'Some Observations on Recent Events', *PASIL* (1926), 1–14; Root to Phillimore, 27 July 1926: Root Papers.

[26] *NYT* (12 August 1926), 19; *NYT* (27 August 1926), 2; *NYT* (29 August 1926), 1.

[27] Walsh to Bullard, 8 March 1926: copy in Drummond to Hurst, 24 March 1926: FO 371, W2578/30/98; Accinelli, 'United States and the World Court', 381, 405–6.

[28] Deibel, 'League of Nations', 419–25.

[29] Chamberlain minute, 17 August 1926: FO 371, W7561/30/98; Hurst minute, 28 April 1926: FO 371, W3290/30/98; Drummond to Gilchrist, 28 August 1926: Sweetser Papers.

[30] League of Nations, *Conference of States Signatories of the Protocol of Signature of the Statute of the Permanent Court of International Justice: Final Act of the Conference*. League of Nations Publications, V: Legal, 1926. V 24 (Geneva: League of Nations, 1926); *Conference of States Signatories of the Protocol of Signature of the Statute of the Permanent Court of International Justice: Report by M. Pilotti, Rapporteur, Presented to the Conference on September 23rd, 1926*. League of Nations Publications, V: Legal, 1926. V 25 (Geneva: League of Nations, 1926); *Minutes of the Conference of States Signatories of the Protocol of Signature of the Statute of the Permanent Court of International Justice. Held at Geneva from September 1st to 23rd, 1926*. League of Nations Publications, V: Legal, 1926. V 26 (Geneva: League of Nations, 1926). These three works are cited below as Conference of Signatories (1926), *Final Act*, *Report by M. Pilotti* and *Minutes* respectively.

[31] See NA500. C114/544–68 *passim*.

[32] Van Karnebeek, cited in Tobin to Kellogg, 11 May 1926: NA500.C114/519.

[33] Conference of Signatories (1926), *Minutes*, 20–44.

[34] Conference of Signatories (1926), *Report by M. Pilotti*, 4; *Minutes*, 22, 34–5, 41–4; *LNOJ* (November 1926), 1561–82; Cmd. 2776, Misc. no. 11 (1926), *The Permanent Court of International Justice: the Question of Accession of the United States of America to the Protocol of December 16, 1920*. Report from the Legal Adviser to the Secretary of State for Foreign Affairs, 7 October 1926 (London: HMSO, 1926). This report is cited below as Hurst, *Permanent Court*.

[35] Moore to Nyholm, 16 March 1926; to Fletcher, 21 June 1926; to Huber, 18 September 1926: Moore Papers; *CR* 69:1 4203–5; *CR*, 70:1, 7509; Hurst to Fromageot, 17 February 1926, FO 371, W924/30/98; Fromageot to Hurst, 19 February 1926: FO 371, W1446/30/98.

[36] Raul Fernandes, *Les Etats-Unis et la Cour Permanente de Justice Internationale* (Brussels: Van Sulper, 1927). Fernandes had represented Brazil at the Paris Peace Conference and on the Advisory Committee of Jurists; Conference of Signatories (1926), *Minutes*, 28–35; Tuck to Kellogg, 14 September 1926: NA500. C114/565.

[37] For Moore, see citations in n. 35 above; Root to Phillimore, 27 July 1926: Root Papers.

[38] Conference of Signatories (1926), *Minutes*, 11–15; *Final Act*, Annex A; *LNOJ* (November 1926), 81; PCIJ, Series D, No. 1, 35–65; *FRUS* (1926), I. 30–8.

[39] Hurst to Villiers, 26 August 1926: FO 371, W7561/30/98; minute of Hurst, 6 October 1926; minute of Ivone Kirkpatrick, FO 371, W9423/30/98.

[40] Conference of Signatories (1926), *Minutes*, 64; Hurst, *Permanent Court*, 9; Fromageot, cited in American Foundation memo, sent as enclosure, E. M. Clark (Secretary to Coolidge) to Kellogg, 13 July 1927: NA500. C114/623.

[41] *NYT* (23 August 1926), 4; *NYT* (21 September 1926), 1; *NYT* (24 September 1926), 16; *NYT* (27 September 1926), 2; H. G. Chilton (Washington) to *Chamberlain*, 8 October 1926: FO 371, W9789/30/98 (DBFP Series 1A, II. 896–7).

[42] Walsh to Bauer, 9 November 1926: quoted in Accinelli, 'United States and the World Court', 406; *NYT* (5 October 1926), 9; Jessup to Moore, 30 November 1926: Moore Papers.

[43] 'Our World Court Membership in Peril', *Literary Digest* (9 October 1926), 9–11; W. H. Gardiner to Kellogg, 27 November 1926: NA500. C114/593.

[44] Memos of Assistant Secretary Harrison and Richardson of the Division of Western European Affairs (DWEA), 26 October and 29 November 1926: NA500. C114/583, 591; Castle to Beck, 2 December 1926: NA500. C114/593.

[45] *The World* (New York), the *New York Herald-Tribune* and the *New York Times* carried detailed reports on 12 and 13 November 1926; see also 'Giving up the Fight for the World Court', *Literary Digest* (27 November 1926), 7–9.

[46] Minute of Kirkpatrick, 23 November 1926: FO 371, W10862/30/98; Moore to Huber *et al.*, 19 September 1926: Moore Papers.

[47] Minute of Cecil, 5 November 1926: FO 371, W10235/30/98; minute of Robert Craigie, 15 November 1926: FO 371, W10608/30/98; minute of Chamberlain, 17 November 1926: FO 371, W11002/30/98; Chamberlain to Chilton, 29 November 1926: FO 371, A6304/6/45.

[48] The best introduction to the multitude of issues is provided by the Memoranda 'respecting the Foreign Policy of His Majesty's Government', annually revised and subsequently printed in successive volumes of DBFP Series 1A.

[49] See S. Res 282: *CR* 69:2, 37–8, 118–19; S. Res 34: *CR* 70:1, 355; SCFR,

Proceedings, 107, 115; H. Res. 323: *CR* 69:2, 16; H.J. Res. 274: *CR* 70:1, 6582–3; Colcord to Lape, 30 November 1926, cited in Colcord to Root, 20 December 1926: Root Papers.

50 Deibel, 'League of Nations', ch. 5.

51 The Root Papers contain much documentation: see, e.g., Lape to Root, 7 and 13 February 1927. The bulky memoranda are on file in NA500. C114/623, the quotation coming from 'Memorandum', 19. The public version is in *Atlantic Monthly* 140 (October 1927), 517–32.

52 Lape to Lenroot, 18 April and 11 October 1927; Lenroot to Lape, 20 April and 14 October 1927: Lenroot Papers; Clark to Kellogg, 13 August 1927: NA500. C114/623; Castle to Green H. Hackworth (Solicitor's Office), 15 August 1927; Hackworth to Castle, 16 September 1927: NA500. C114/635; Lenroot to Kellogg, 17 October 1927: NA500. C114/637½; Hurst to Campbell, 31 January 1929: FO 371, W1009/21/98; Moore to Ellery Sedgwick (Editor, *Atlantic Monthly*), 12 October 1927; Borchard to Moore, 23 October 1927: Moore Papers.

53 E. M. House *et al.*, to Coolidge, 12 December 1927: NA. 500. C114/644½.

54 Gillett to Kellogg, 30 January 1928; Kellogg to Gillett [early February] 1928: NA500. C114/653; Sweetser to Lape, 10 April 1928; to Hudson, 10 April 1928: Hudson Papers; Gilchrist to Hudson, 10 April 1928; to Lape, 10 April 1928: Gilchrist Papers.

55 S. Res 139: *CR* 70:1, 2503–4, 6075–8, 7505–10, esp. 7507; SCFR, *Proceedings*, 125; Gillett to Kellogg, 30 January 1928; Lenroot to Borah [mid February 1928]: Lenroot Papers; Kellogg to Borah, 10 and 11 February 1928: NA500. C114/656a–b; Myers to Kellogg, 12 April 1928; Kellogg to Myers, 25 April 1928: NA500. C114/668.

56 *National Party Platforms*, esp. 274, 284.

57 Walter Johnson, *William Allen White's America* (New York: Henry Holt, 1947), 404. Editor of the Emporia (Kansas) *Gazette*, White had been one of the Republican Thirty-one. Castle to Hoover, 11 July 1928: Castle Papers, Hoover Presidential Library.

58 Dionisio Anzilotti to Moore, 15 May 1928: enclosure in Moore to Root, 24 May 1928: Root Papers; Elbridge D. Rand (Geneva) to Kellogg, 8 and 15 September 1928: NA500. C114/700, 705.

59 E. M. Borchard, 'The Multilateral Treaty for the Renunciation of War', *AJIL* 23 (January 1929), 116–30; David Jayne Hill, 'The New International Alignment', *Saturday Evening Post* (9 November 1929), 37 ff.; James T. Shotwell, *War as an Instrument of National Policy and its Renunciation in the Pact of Paris* (New York: Harcourt, Brace, 1929), esp. ch. 20.

60 Norweb to Kellogg, 9 November 1928: NA500. C114/719; *CR* 70:2, 1135–6.

61 *CR* 70:2, 1062–731; 'After Ratifying', *NYT* (4 January 1929), 24; Norman H. Davis to Kellogg, 3 and 17 January 1929: NA500. C114/740½, 742½; 'League Paving our Way to World Court', *Literary Digest* (14 September 1929), 12.

62 *LNOJ* (October 1929), 1489, 1664–71; ibid., *Special Supplements*, nos 63, 64, 65.

63 Sweetser, 'The Permanent Court of International Justice' [September–October 1928]: copy in Castle to Hackworth, 13 November 1928: NA500. C114/730; memos of Hurst, 10 and 19 September 1928: FO 371, W1700/21/98.

64 Prentiss B. Gilbert (DWEA), memo of conversation with Lardy (Counselor, Swiss Legation), 11 December 1928: NA500. C114/731; Norweb to Kellogg, 10 and 12 December 1928: NA500. C114/734, 735; Theodore Marburg to Kellogg, 6 December 1928: NA500. C114/723.

65 *NYH-T* (25 November 1928), 1; Kellogg to Root, 26 November 1928: NA500. C114/737a; American Foundation press release, 1 December 1928: NA500.

C114/739. (The former unamalgamated *Herald* had been anti-Court.)

66 Norweb to Kellogg, 10 December 1928: NA500. C114/734.

67 Despatches of Norweb to Kellogg, 5–17 December 1928: NA500. C114/733–6; Kellogg to Root, 18 January 1929: NA500. C114/742; 'Mr Root and the Court', *NYT* (9 January 1929), 30; *LNOJ* (January 1929), 10, 35, 56; *LNOJ* (April 1929), 564–6.

68 Drummond to Sweetser, 30 January 1929: NA500. C114/747½.

69 Hurst to Campbell, 31 January 1929: FO 371, W1009/21/98; to Malkin, 9 March 1929: FO 371, W2135/21/98; Chamberlain to Howard, 13 and 14 February 1928; Howard to Chamberlain, 9 March 1928: Chamberlain Papers.

70 Kellogg to Root, 2 February 1929; Rand to Kellogg, 12 March 1929: NA500. C114/746a, 766.

71 Kellogg *pro forma*, 19 February 1929 and copy to Drummond: NA500. C114/445a, 445bbb (*FRUS* (1929), I. 1–4); Myron T. Herrick (Paris) to Kellogg, 21 March 1929: NA500. C114/776; Howard to Chamberlain, 8 February 1929: FO 371, W1381/21/98.

72 Memorandum, 'January 1929', Jessup Papers. Drummond and Hammarskjöld had vetoed Scott for his hostile and 'pronounced views': Norweb to Kellogg, 25 January 1929: NA500. C114/748.

73 A tiny fraction of the documentation is printed in *FRUS*, (1929), I. 4–31,

74 *United States Daily* (Washington) (cited below as *USD*) (14 March 1929), 1; *NYT* (6 September 1929), 1; *The World* (New York) (10 December 1929), 1, 2.

75 'World Court – Geneva Trip', 19–20 February; 5 and 11 March 1929: Jessup Papers; Drummond to Chamberlain, 6 March 1929: Chamberlain Papers; Hurst to Chamberlain, 4 March 1929: FO 371, W3108/21/98.

76 Kellogg to Root, 26 November 1928: NA500. C114/737a; Castle to Secretary of State Stimson, 16 May 1929: NA500. C114/791½; Lape to Borchard, 7 April 1927: Moore Papers.

77 Hurst to Campbell, 31 January 1929: FO 371, W1009/21/98; Howard to Chamberlain, 20 February 1929; minutes of Kirkpatrick and A. W. A. Leeper, 22 February 1929: FO 371 W1522/21/98; memos of Hurst, 10 and 19 September 1929: FO 371 W1700/21/98.

78 'World Court–Geneva Trip'; 12 and 14 March 1929: Jessup Papers; Castle, memo of conversation with Root and Jessup, 27 May 1929: NA500. C114/795; Tobin to Kellogg, 16 March 1929: NA500. C114/773; Blake to Stimson, 18 October 1929: NA500. C114/895.

79 The Draft Protocol of American Accession is to be found in League of Nations, Committee of Jurists on the Statute of the Permanent Court of International Justice, *Reports adopted by the Committee at its Session held at Geneva from March 11th to 19th, 1929*. League of Nations Publications, V: Legal, 1929, V 4. Official no. C 142. M.52. 1929 V (Geneva: League of Nations, 1929); the record of discussions was published as League of Nations, Committee of Jurists on the Statute of the Permanent Court of International Justice, *Minutes of the Session held at Geneva from March 11th to 19th, 1929*. League of Nations Publications, V: Legal, 1929, V 5. Official no. C 166 M.66. 1929 V (Geneva: League of Nations, 1929). These two compilations are cited below as League of Nations, Committee of Jurists, *Reports* and *Minutes* respectively.

80 The Australian delegate, W. Harrison Moore, wrote a perceptive account of the September Conference: sent as enclosure by R. C. Tredwell (Sydney) to Stimson, 25 June 1930: NA500. C114/1006; Hurst memorandum, 25 August 1929: FO 371, W8179/21/98: cf. Hurst to Malkin, 9 March 1929: FO 371, W2135/21/98; minute of Campbell, 17 July 1929: FO 371, W6875/21/98.

81 League of Nations, Committee of Jurists, *Minutes*, 20.

82 Ibid. 15, 20, 94; Jessup, *Elihu Root*, II. 438–42; Kellogg to Root *via* Rand, 14 March 1929: NA500. C114/768a (*FRUS* (1929), I. 10–11); Root press release of 20 March 1929: as enclosure in Sweetser to J. Theodore Marriner, 22 March 1929: NA500. C114/782.

83 Howard to Chamberlain, 22 March 1929: FO 371, W2963/21/98.

84 Memo of [DWEA], 27 March 1929: NA500. C114/779; for Root on Kellogg, see Jessup, *Elihu Root*, II. 439; while Stimson, *On Active Service*, avoids the problems of 1929.

85 Castle to Stimson, 16 May 1929: NA500. C114/791½; Walsh, cited in American Foundation 'Survey', 14 October 1930: NA500. C114/1158½; Pepper, radio speech of 6 March 1930: text in Norris Papers; Lenroot to Lape, 7 March 1930: Lenroot Papers; Stone to Moore, 23 March 1929; Moore to Stone, 5 April 1929: Moore Papers; Root and Jessup conversation, 18 January 1930: Jessup Papers.

86 Memo of Marriner, 6 May 1929; Castle to Stimson, 16 and 27 May 1929: NA500. C114/792a, 791½, 795; memo of Beck, 19 September 1929: NA500. C114/863½, *NYT* (21 March 1929), 1, 7; *USD* (21 March 1929), 1, 10.

87 Root to Stimson, 16 May 1929; Stimson to Root, 25 May 1929; Swanson to Stimson, 25 May 1929; to Root, 25 May 1929: NA500. C114/790½, 791¾, 797½.

88 Stimson to Hugh Wilson for Drummond, 27 May 1929: ibid./795 (*FRUS* (1929), I. 13–14); Hurst to Chamberlain, 4 April 1929: FO 371, W3108/21/98.

89 'Hughes in het Hof van Internationale Justitie', *Algemeen Handelsblad* (Amsterdam), 10 May 1929: copy in Hughes Papers; Tobin to Stimson, 24 May 1929: NA500. C114/801.

90 Levinson, 'In re: Article 68 of the World Court', 24–5 October 1929: copy NA500. C114/896½; Levinson to Stimson, 17 May 1929: NA500. C114/794½; Kellogg to Hoover, 27 July 1929: NA500. C114/825¼; memos of Hurst, 20 and 25 August 1929: FO 371, W8179/21/98 and W9616/21/98.

91 *LNOJ* (July 1929), 996–8; Hammond to Stimson, 17 June 1929; Root to Stimson, 5 July 1929; Drummond to Stimson, 12 June 1929; Stimson to Root, 2 August 1929; Root to Stimson, 12 August 1929; Stimson to Wilson, 14 August 1929: NA500. C114/808–830½.

92 C. Gross (Bern) to Stimson, 18 July 1929: NA500. C114/822.

93 The prescient description in Marriner to Cotton, 31 July 1929: NA500. C114/823. The official record of the proceedings is to be found in League of Nations, *Minutes of the Conference regarding the Revision of the Statute of the Permanent Court of International Justice and the Accession of the United States of America to the Protocol of Signature of that Statute. Held at Geneva from September 4th to 12th, 1929.* League of Nations Publications, V: Legal, 1929, V 18. Official no. C 514, M.173. 1929 V (Geneva: League of Nations, 1929). This volume is cited below as League of Nations, *Minutes of Conference* (1929). For the Assembly, see *LNOJ*, *Special Supplement*, no. 76. *Records of the Tenth Ordinary Session of the League: Meetings of the First Committee, Minutes of the First Committee (Constitutional and Legal Questions)*, 8–17; and League of Nations, *Records of the Tenth Ordinary Session of the Assembly: Plenary Meetings, Texts of the Debates*, 32, 53–4, 114 ff., 433–44. Assembly President Guerrero (of El Salvador) spoke of the two 'parallel' meetings: ibid. 122. See also League of Nations, *Question of the Revision of the Statute of the Permanent Court of International Justice. Report of the First Committee to the Assembly: Rapporteur, M. Politis (Greece). Annex: Projet de Protocole – Draft Protocol.* League of Nations Publications, V: Legal, 1929. V 16. Official no. A 50. 1929 V (Geneva: League of Nations, 1929) and League of Nations, *Question of the Adherence of the*

United States of America to the Protocol of Signature of the Statute of the Permanent Court of International Justice. Report of the First Committee to the Assembly: Rapporteur, M. Politis (Greece). Annex: Projet de Protocole – Draft Protocol. League of Nations Publications, V: Legal, 1929. V 15. Official no. A 49. 1929 V (Geneva: League of Nations, 1929).

[94] League of Nations, *Minutes of Conference* (1929), 16, 19; League of Nations, *Texts of the Debates*, 122.

[95] Hurst to Ronald Lindsay, 9 September 1929: FO 371, W8979/21/98; Stimson to Wilson, 5 September 1929; Gilson G. Blake (Geneva) to Stimson, 6 September 1929: NA500. C114/843a, 846.

[96] Blake to Stimson, 18 October 1929; memo of Marriner, 25 September 1929: NA500. C114/895, 863; Fosdick to Root, 26 September 1929: Root Papers.

[97] Memos of Cotton, Castle and Stimson, 9–16 September 1929; Francis Colt de Wolf, 'Accession of the United States to the PCIJ', 17 September 1929; Stimson to Beck, 16 September 1929: NA500. C114/848, 857½.

[98] Memos of Marriner and Noel H. Field, 25 September and 5 October 1929; Hoover to Stimson, 18 October 1929: NA500. C114/863, 871, 880½.

[99] Stimson to Hoover, 18 November 1929 (*FRUS* (1929), I. 31–40); to Root, 6 November and 4 December 1929; Root to Stimson, 18 November 1929: NA500. C114/913a, 902a, 910½.

[100] Hoover to Stimson, 27 November 1929: NA500. C114/913½; Philip C. Jessup, 'Mr. Root, the Senate and the World Court', *Foreign Affairs* 7 (July 1929), 584–99; 'The Permanent Court of International Justice: American Accession and Amendments to the Statute', *International Conciliation* 254 (November 1929), 524–76; *The United States and the World Court.* World Peace Foundation Pamphlet, vol. 12, no. 4 (Boston: World Beace Foundation, 1929); Antonio Sanchez de Bustamente y Sirven, *The World Court and the United States* (Atlanta: Emory University, 1929).

[101] Hudson to Stimson, 9 December 1929: NA500. C114/926; Stimson to Borah, 6 January 1930: Borah Papers.

[102] Howard to (Secretary of State for Foreign Affairs) Arthur Henderson, 12 September 1929: FO 371, W9235/21/98; *Christian Science Monitor* (Boston) (cited below as CSM), 10 December 1929, 2; *NYH-T* (10 December 1929), 1, 2; *The World* (New York) (10 December 1929), 1, 2.

[103] Lenroot to Lape, 20 May 1929 and 7 March 1930: Lenroot Papers; Lape to Root, 18 August 1930: Root Papers; Borchard to Borah, 24 November and 6 December 1929: Borchard Papers.

[104] The Root, Hoover and Davis Papers, together with the Department of State files, have numerous examples of the lobbyists' surveys, esp. those of the American Foundation: see esp. NA500. C114/921, 935, 1158½; survey in (anti-Court) *New York American*, 10 December 1929.

[105] Cotton to Stimson, 9 September 1929; Lape to Hoover, 22 March 1930: NA500. C114/848, 980; *USD* (19 April 1930), 1, 2.

[106] *CR* 71:3, 504; SCFR, *Proceedings*, 172; *USD* (11 December 1930), 1, 3.

[107] *USD* (18 December 1930), 1, 3; Senator Kenneth McKellar (Tennessee, Democrat) to Hoover, 23 December 1930: Hoover Papers.

[108] The documentation and official record is in US Senate, *World Court: Hearing before the Committee on Foreign Relations, United States Senate, Seventy-first Congress, Third Session. Relative to Protocols concerning Adherence of the United States to the Court of International Justice. January 21, 1931.* (Washington, DC: GPO, 1931); SCFR, *Proceedings*, 172–99.

[109] Jessup to Root, 18 December 1930; de Wolf to Root, 15 January 1931: Root Papers.

[110] *USD* (22 December 1930), 2, 4; *USD* (23 December 1930), 4, 10.

[111] SCFR, *Proceedings*, 181–5.

[112] Ibid. 192–7; 'The League and its Court', *Chicago Sunday Tribune* (25 January 1931).

[113] Swanson, quoted in Stimson to Root, 17 March 1931; Walsh to Root, 29 April 1931; Root to Walsh, 13 May 1931: Root Papers; Jessup to Hudson, 22 January 1931: Hudson Papers; Walsh to Moore, 29 April 1931: Moore Papers.

[114] De Wolf to Marriner, 22 January 1931; Stimson memo of conversation with Ambassador Alejandro Padilla y Bell, 29 January 1931: NA500. C114/1248, 1235; Castle, 10 February 1931: quoted in Robert H. Ferrell, *American Diplomacy in the Great Depression: Hoover–Stimson Foreign Policy, 1929–1933*. Yale Historical Publications, Studies no. 17 (New Haven: Yale University Press, 1957), 32.

[115] For the AF, WPF and NWCC, see materials on file in NA500. C114/1257, 1270, 1293, 1297; Stimson, memo of conversation with Lape, 16 February 1931; J. M. Hoyle to Hoover, 4 March 1931: NA500. C114/1254, 1267.

[116] Jessup to Root, 2 February and 13 March 1931: Root Papers; Senator Frederic C. Walcott (Connecticut, Republican and Jessup's uncle) to Hoover, 26 February 1931; Hoover to Walcott, 2 March 1931; Everett Colby to Hoover, 4 and 17 March 1931; press release of NWCC, 12 March 1931: Hoover Papers.

7 Legal phrases and active forces: the Austro-German Customs Union adjudication, the divided League and Roosevelt's New Deal, 1931–34.

In Chapters 4 and 5 we discussed in broad terms the nature and evolution of the World Court's advisory jurisdiction and its significance for the terms of American adherence finally agreed by the Senate and Executive in January 1926. Perhaps to some contemporaries and later historians the issues seemed rather abstract. Yet the response of the League, rather than the formal signatory States, and the counter-response of the US government in the following years conclusively proved that apparently technical and legal controversies had powerful political meaning. The events of 1931 were to make such a conclusion inescapable, even to the minds of the most complacent.

Historically 1931 registered a new benchmark for Senators, the Executive, lobbyists, lawyers in general and informed observers at large. Histyoriographically 1931 has been as neglected as the first years of the Court's existence from 1922 to 1925. This paradoxical silence, whether deliberate or not, has served two very useful purposes. It has allowed historians to ignore the contribution of the League and the Court to the case against American adherence; and, in another parallel to 1923–5, minimize the responsibility of the proponents for delaying debate on terms they had themselves endorsed. To redress the picture we must begin this chapter with a brief study of the most important case which ever came before the bar of the Permanent Court – a case which effectively ended its advisory function and undermined the prestige of the Court as a whole for the rest of its existence.

On 19 March 1931 the German and Austrian governments signed the Vienna Protocol, a 'preliminary agreement' (*Vorvertrag*) setting out the general principles by which they would later draw up a 'treaty to assimilate the tariff and economic policies of their respective countries'.[1] Enemies of the Vienna Protocol traced its origins to the *Zollverein* of nineteenth century Germany: as the *Zollverein* had paved the way for German unification under Prussia, so the proposed Austro-German Customs Union would lead to *Anschluss*, the incorporation of Austria into Weimar Germany, and thus constitute the first and easiest stage in demolishing the eastern half of the peace settlement established after World War I – a war itself fought, they argued, to prevent a German *Mitteleuropa*.

To understand the intensity of contemporary reaction we must remember that the Treaty of Saint-Germain-en-Laye (10 September 1919) followed the Treaty of Versailles in requiring the political separation of Germany and Austria: under Article 88, Austrian 'independence [*was*] inalienable, except with the consent of the Council of the League of Nations'. Even the name Austria was imposed by the victorious Powers: the designation German–Austria, adopted by the provisional governments in the two countries, was outlawed as a provocation to unification.[2] The restrictions upon Austria continued. In 1922 the prohibition of political incorporation into Germany was widened by the Geneva Reconstruction Protocols to exclude the possibility of a third party (Italy was the chief candidate) exploiting its economic and financial power to erode and eventually nullify 'the political independence, the territorial integrity and the sovereignty of Austria'. The Geneva Protocols (signed initially by Austria, the United Kingdom, France, Italy and Czechoslovakia) were only one of a series of international operations in the 1920s designed to bolster the Austrian economy and maintain her currency.[3] Politically excluded from Germany, economically cut off from her former partners in the Habsburg Empire, the Austrian 'rump' or 'carcass' (the contemporary metaphors were common) lacked the means of survival in a depressed and autarkic Central Europe. (In the winter of 1922–3 Senator Swanson had called Austria 'one of the wrecks left in [the wake] of the Great War'.) Here was a major material element in the ideological debate between supporters of *Anschluss*, Danubian confederation or integration with Hungary and Italy. Common to all such proposals was the premise that Austria's viability (*Lebensfähigkeit*) was minimal unless she became economically integrated with her neighbouring States.[4]

The Vienna Protocol of March 1931 had been the subject of immediate negotiations between the two Foreign Ministers, Julius Curtius of Germany and Johann Schober of Austria. Preparatory work, however, on such commercial harmonization had gone on for a number of years, particularly in the German Foreign Ministry, where the State Secretary, Bernhard von Bülow, was an articulate critic of the 1919 settlement and had long seen the possibilities of redrawing (as he put it) the political and territorial map of Central Europe by economic means. Curtius's predecessor, Gustav Stresemann, had never renounced the *Anschluss* as part of the reordering of Central and Eastern Europe. Indeed his co-operation in the Locarno agreements of 1925 was based upon the popular premise of revising Germany's eastern borders. Conversely, Stresemann's French opposite number and joint winner of the Nobel Peace Prize for negotiating the Locarno agreements, Aristide Briand, had sought to defend French and Belgian acquisitions from Germany in the West but not at the price of encouraging revision in the East. Throughout the 1920s Briand insisted that *Anschluss* meant war – a theme repeated even more intensely by his famous counterpart, Eduard Beneš, Foreign Minister of Czechosolovakia from 1918 to 1935 and one of the foremost statesmen in France's 'Little Entente' of Eastern European Successor States: Czechoslovakia, Yugoslavia and Romania.[5]

Granted that *Anschluss* was a nightmare to the governments of France and the Little Entente, not all Austrian politicians shared such pleasant dreams of union with Weimar Germany (*Anschlussträumen*). Schober was a Pan-German; but his major rival, the Christian Socialist, Mgr Ignaz Seipel, was at best sceptical. Indeed powerful evidence exists that some of the Christian Socialists released the news of the Customs Union negotiations to spike the scheme and discredit their opponents in government. Moreover, even sections within Schober's coalition were opposed to the Customs Union on economic grounds: in an enlarged German market their situation would be worsened rather than improved.[6]

Highly developed economic arguments against the Customs Union project were deployed by its foreign opponents to influence Austrian opinion and undermine the German claims to be aiding the peaceful restoration of the European economy. A common element in these attacks was the theme that German productive strength would distort and ultimately subordinate the Austrian economy and inevitably lead to formal, political *Anschluss*. It is precisely this latter stage which remains historically and historiographically at issue. Granted that the Austrians might successfully resist political incorporation into Germany, were German ministers and officials so exact and determined in their goals?

The answer comes as a qualified Yes. Curtius's published accounts of the events are incredibly naïve; but they can fairly be read as the apology of a man who did not want to be blamed for pursuing *Anschluss* in 1931, since the *Anschluss* of 1938 was (by his account) a definite step to aggressive war. Curtius's Chancellor, Heinrich Brüning, has left a record suggesting his virtual ignorance of the publicized scheme – and certainly no involvement in a covert strategy to bring forward political

Anschluss. Historians offer a different but compatible picture. Extremely able members of the Foreign Ministry, notably von Bülow and the Legal Adviser, Gaus, devised a scheme for commercial harmonization with Austria which could lay the ground for *Anschluss*, but which was not synonymous with *Anschluss*. Such a scheme could be legitimated internationally by reference to the current League-sponsored Commission of Inquiry for European Union; and, most importantly, the scheme could be capitalized upon domestically. Its substance, particularly if published boldly as a *fait accompli*, would 'take the wind out of the... sails' of the Nationalists, who had scored such spectacular successes in the September 1930 *Reichstag* elections and whose campaign programmes included the *Anschluss* and vigorous revisionism in Eastern Europe.[7] In this historiography Curtius and Brüning kept out of the limelight – and, indeed, somewhat out of the action – ready to come forward and claim governmental credit when the project was successfully advanced; alternatively they could disguise their involvement if the Austrians or third parties aborted the tentative scheme.

The preceding paragraphs provide only a skeletal history of the origins of the Vienna Protocol.[8] But there is no doubt about the fury of the French and their eastern allies at the announcement of the scheme. In contrast the Italian government was at first ambivalent. They wanted revision – but on their own terms; not Germany brought immediately to the Brenner. The British were possibly even more ambivalent. They appeared to favour the Customs Union scheme both as a potentially constructive programme for revitalizing the economy of Central Europe and as a political initiative which would strengthen Brüning against his enemies on the Left and Right. However the British government deplored the provocativeness of German diplomacy and had no wish to antagonize the French and Italians.[9]

Within a fortnight of the publication of the Vienna Protocol the 'first round in the international contest of wills' closed.[10] The British, French and Italians had agreed to support a reference to the League Council, though neither the French nor their eastern allies would ease their financial and economic pressure on Austria to renounce the Customs Union scheme. By mid-April the Austrian government succumbed: negotiations with Germany were suspended. Less than a month later the Austrian banking system collapsed, the victim (it was authoritatively said) of French undermining. By the time the Council met in mid May the Customs Union scheme was effectively dead; and now the French and their allies were demanding political concessions from Germany, notably on naval armaments and a recommitment to the 1919–20 territorial settlement in Eastern Europe.

A major part of the pre-Council bargain was an agreement to submit the Customs Union scheme to the Permanent Court for an advisory opinion on its legality under the Treaty of Saint-Germain and the 1922 Geneva Protocols. The full Council readily and unanimously approved, though not without bitter words from the Czech and Yugoslav representatives censuring German provocation and belligerence. The

German and Austrian representatives, none other than Curtius and Schober, acted like men who knew the scheme was doomed; but they were confident of the 'legal situation' and their endorsement of the proposal did not mean their governments doubted the compatibility of the Vienna Protocol with Austria's treaty obligations. On the contrary: they suggested that the Court's adjudication would prove that 'certain third Parties' (by which they meant France, her allies and Italy) would later use the political resources of the League to wreck a perfectly legal solution to the grievous economic problems of two Member States.[11]

A month after the Council meeting President Hoover declared a year's 'moratorium' on the repayment of intergovernmental debts due to the United States. Conceived as a temporary remedy for the international banking and financial crisis, Hoover's action evoked sharp criticism in France, which saw Germany as the main beneficiary, and from domestic opponents, such as his old adversary Hiram Johnson, who feared the moratorium would be an 'entering wedge' for total cancellation. (Borah's conditional support of Hoover reopened the latent rift between the two Senators.)[12] A month later the London Economic Conference convened, with representatives from the United States, France, Germany, Italy, Japan, Belgium and the host country. It was reputedly 'the most illustrious gathering of its kind' since the Paris Peace Conference. Even so the London Conference may be judged a failure, if the yardstick was the amelioration of the current crisis. The French continued to demand a 'political moratorium' of the German government; and the decline of the pound was leading the British, willy-nilly, to support the French terms for relieving political tension.[13] In such a setting and almost to the hour the Permanent Court began the adjudication of the Customs Union scheme.

Hoover himself compared the announcement of the Vienna Protocol to Sarajevo and the summer of 1914; but he was not alone in his sympathy for the scheme. Though, like Stimson and Castle, he deplored the German government's maladroit diplomacy, he was more disturbed by the condition of Austria under the Treaties of Peace – treaties which he himself had helped to shape as a member of the American Delegation to Paris in 1919. Throughout the 1920s the publications of members of the Delegation together with other revisionist writings has expressed this unease; and by spring 1931 it could fairly be stated that the balance of American opinion supported the Customs Union project.[14] But it was a delicate balance. Elihu Root, for example, in his January testimony to the Senate Foreign Relations Committee had implicitly sided with France and her eastern allies in their conception of the League's role and the foundations of peace in Europe. Pro-Court internationalists predominantly favoured the French position. In their geopolitical thinking they wove together League Covenant, Kellogg–Briand Pact and the Court Protocols into a net to involve the United States in maintaining the terms of the Paris Peace settlement.

Though the US government waived its right to appear before the Court it did not neglect the technical aspects of the Vienna Protocol or the question of its legality. A series of long memoranda inside the

Departments of State and Commerce contended that the Germans and Austrians had the better case at law. More worrisome was whether the provisions of the Protocol neatly avoided the obligation of the Signatories to extend most-favoured-nation treatment to the United States. Events were to overtake the anxiety – an outcome predicted within the Executive before the Court assembled. As the authors of one comprehensive memorandum phrased it: their analysis might well prove sterile, for the Customs Union would be defeated by a combination of external political and economic force and domestic opposition inside Germany and Austria.[15]

Perhaps this type of contemporary realism explains the neglect of the Customs Union case in the American historiography of the Court – and, indeed, in Stimson's own *Diary*, which records his main concern during these months as Nicaragua. A contributory factor may be the sheer volume of material: the written and oral testimony runs to a quarter of a million words. Yet the Court records repay close reading. Their vitality is striking. If history was indeed being made outside the Court, counsel matched the drama. The French, Czechoslovak and Italian prosecutors appeared borne along by their governments' political successes. (Indeed, nearly all the prosecuting counsel were or had been active and important politicians: Joseph Paul-Boncour, Massimo Pilotti and Vittorio Scialoja.) The Austrian and German advocates, Erich Kaufmann and Viktor Bruns, colleagues at the University of Berlin, countered with empassioned, eloquent and subtle resistance.

Defeat outside the Court seemed to inspire a determination to act with courage and pride. Nor were the debates simply talk: empty rhetoric and specious tropes. The factual detail and historical range, the textual exegesis and judicial construction were offered at the very highest levels by brilliant and informed lawyers and politicians; and the Court's proceedings have no superior as an introduction to the *Anschluss* question in the interwar period. Moreover, and of even greater importance to this present study, authoritative observers realized that the Customs Union project was the gravest case brought before the Court and that its judicial resolution would have momentous consequences.[16]

The reason was simple and concerns the basic agreement which both plaintiffs and defendants shared: the legal framework of international relations had been established by the World War I settlement. Opposing counsel drew different conclusions from this premise. The German and Austrian advocates, deploring the disposition of power embodied in the Peace Treaties, challenged the legitimacy of the settlement. Conversely the French, Czechoslovak and Italian advocates insisted upon the authority and morality of the settlement and showed the determination of their governments to maintain it. This fundamental, normative conflict, whether stated openly or only implicitly, was (to borrow the phrase used by both sides) the 'red thread' running through all the hundreds of pages of testimony.[17] It was an apt reminder to Americans of the day and later historians that few knowledgeable observers would interpret American adherence to the Court as being neutral towards the political system of the League and the jurisprudence of the Court.

The pleadings at The Hague began on 20 July and lasted for fourteen days. The judges deliberated for a month and published their conclusions on 5 September. But in the event, the advisory opinion came 'inevitabl[y]... as something of an anti-climax'. Two days before the Court ruled against the legality of the Vienna Protocol, the Austrian government announced that it had 'resolve[d] to pursue no further the project' outlined in March. France and her allies had finally triumphed. The Customs Union scheme was officially pronounced dead by both its originators and adjudicators.[18]

It is usually said that the Court found against the Vienna Protocol by the slimmest of margins: eight judges opposed to seven in favour. In fact the Court divided four ways. The seven judges who supported the Vienna Protocol were agreed in their arguments. Against them and ultimately outvoting them were eight judges who together held three different positions.[19]

What is generally regarded as the Court's majority Opinion was an argument advanced by only one judge, Bustamente y Sirven of Cuba. He alone distinguished between Austrian obligations under the Treaty of Saint-Germain and those deriving from the first Geneva Protocol. (The other fourteen judges held the two sets of obligations to be substantially the same.) Alongside Bustamente y Sirven and 'concurring' in his opinion were six judges who believed that the régime prefigured in the Vienna Protocol would 'be not only incompatible' with the Geneva Protocol (as Bustamente y Sirven maintained), 'but also and in itself incompatible' with the terms of the Treaty of Saint-Germain. These six were Guerrero (El Salvador), Rostworowski (Poland), Fromageot (France), Altamira y Crevea (Spain), Urrutia (Colombia) and Négulesco (Romania). In the 'operative portion' of the Opinion, that is the treaty incompatibility of the Vienna Protocol, one other judge concurred, Anzilotti of Italy; but he disagreed with the reasoning of his seven colleagues and lodged a separate opinion. Ranged against this eight-man coalition were the seven judges of the minority who filed their joint dissenting opinion. These seven were Adatci (Japan), Rolin-Jaequemyns (Belgium), Hurst (UK), Schücking (Germany), van Eysinga (Netherlands), Wang (China) and Kellogg (USA). (Charles Evans Hughes had resigned from the bench in 1930 – somewhat embarrassing the pro-Court campaigners. But, by the same token, ex-Secretary of State Kellogg was nominated and elected to maintain the momentum for American adherence.)[20]

Since the six judges 'concurring' with Bustamente y Sirven offered no grounds for their verdict, his arguments must stand for them all. But Bustamente y Sirven's reasoning was not very persuasive. He analysed the separate and combined provisions of the Vienna Protocol and concluded they did not, in themselves, 'constitute an act alienating Austria's independence'; they did not even 'endanger' her independence. However, since 'the régime projected by the [Vienna] Protocol' extended special and exclusive 'advantages' to Germany, it was *difficult to maintain* that [the] régime [was] not calculated to threaten the economic independence of Austria and that it [was], consequently, in accord with the undertakings specifically given by Austria in [the Geneva] Protocol with regard to her economic independence. [Emphasis added.][21]

The seven judges in the minority found this the most baffling part of the Court's Opinion – a term they used ironically to refer to the reasoning of one judge. In their words, no 'explanation [had been given] as to how and why that régime would threaten or imperil Austria's independence'. Bustamente y Sirven had suggested a test of reason; but though the plaintiff governments had frequently invoked the lessons of history to show that economic assimilation led to political unification, the Court's Opinion had not itself cited such evidence. But the real force of the minority opinion lay less in these rebuttals. Bustamente y Sirven had opened his arguments with suggestive allusions to Austria's 'existence, as determined by the treaties of peace', constituting a 'sensitive point in the European system'. The minority judges accepted the premise but drew different conclusions.

The numerous restrictions on Austria's liberty of action... are well known.... They affected Austria in matters military, financial [and] economic, which touch most closely on the national sovereignty. None of them were reciprocal in character. Yet they were all regarded as compatible with Austria's sovereignty and independence. *A fortiori* it seems to follow that a customs régime, such as that proposed in the Vienna Protocol, organized on a basis of parity and reciprocity, does not prejudice the independence of Austria.[22]

The 'individual opinion' submitted by Dionisio Anzilotti was the longest of the three reasonings rendered in the Austro-German Custom Union case. The judge who gained a reputation as the 'great dissenter' began by registering his 'agreement with the Court's conclusion', but added that his 'point of view [was] widely different' from that of Bustamente y Sirven and his six allies.[23]

Anzilotti started with a detailed examination of the determining treaties to establish his first principle, namely that the régime envisaged in the Vienna Protocol could

only be incompatible with the Geneva Protocol if it is incompatible with... the Treaty of Saint-Germain, since the [former] does not impose on Austria, as regards her independence, any obligation which does not already ensue from [the latter].

This was Anzilotti's major disagreement with Bustamente y Sirven. The second stage of his opinion was to establish that the restrictions upon Austrian independence were

not adopted in the interests of Austria, but in the interests of Europe as a whole, and thus it [would] be readily understood that Article 88 [of the Treaty of Saint-Germain], far from granting Austria rights, only imposes upon her obligations.

Nor was this all: Austria's residual independence was not sacrosanct. '[The] Council of the League of Nations, the sovereign judge of political situations and of the requirements of peace', was entitled to 'dispose' of this independence and permit its alienation. This was Anzilotti's first point of disagreement with the seven judges of the minority. The third part of Anzilotti's opinion was the most elaborate and subtle. Through it he distanced himself from what he saw (but did not call) the unreality of the minority. Over a number of paragraphs Anzilotti fashioned an intricate text to demonstrate that the immediate 'alienation of Austria's independence' was not the issue. Rather it was the Court's task to determine whether,

> in view... of the respective positions of Austria and Germany, and... of the consequences which the Customs Union would have on Austria's economic life, it can reasonably be foreseen that such a dangerous situation would ensue for the independence of Austria.

Adopting such a test, Anzilotti argued that the conclusion was unmistakable. The *Anschluss* movement was a 'fact', at the present no less than in the past. It was a movement 'based upon community of race, language and culture'; it was a movement given strength by the economic difficulties of Austria. These too were 'well known' facts which had been cited in the Court's proceedings. Given the 'great disproportion in the economic strengths of Germany and Austria', it was 'reasonably probable that Austria's economic life would sooner or later become dependent upon Germany's'. Customs unions might not always lead to political union; but in the instant case the dynamics could "reasonably" be predicted to move 'in that direction'. If the Court were to seek 'pertinent historic precedent', the 'only' example would appear to be the *Zollverein*; and if that were used as evidence, it would corroborate the case that the Vienna Protocol would promote political unification. In phrases echoing the language of his own government in the League Council and before the Court, Anzilotti dismissed the effectiveness of the clauses in the Vienna Protocol permitting its revocation by Austria.

> Man's will... has only a limited influence over social forces like those which are urging Austria towards fusion with Germany, and in all probability the consequences of the union would ensue despite the precautions taken in the Protocol.

The logic of facts was irresistible to a judge seeking to apply the 'letter and... spirit' of the determining treaties. Following a favourite judicial maxim, *pacta sunt servanda*, Anzilotti concluded his reasoning. There could be no doubt:

> The Austro-German Customs régime [was] incompatible with... the Treaty of Saint-Germain [and the Geneva Protocol] and... Austria [was] therefore obliged to abstain from it or to ask the consent of the Council of the League of Nations.

With these words Anzilotti endorsed the Court's majority advisory opinion and re-affirmed the supremacy of the Council of the League.[24]

Even if earlier in the year the balance of American opinion had tipped only slightly in favour of the Customs Union scheme, the response to the Court's verdict was far less ambivalent. Editorials in the minority of papers opposed to American adherence found conclusive evidence of the political role of the Court. McCormick's *Chicago Tribune* spoke for them all when it asserted that the judges had shown themselves the 'catspaw of the League'. It had become impossible to harbour any lingering 'illusion' that the Court was 'an independent and disinterested juridical body... free from the influence of nationalist interests and policies.[25] Such anti-Court judgments could not be dismissed simply as prejudice; for far more striking and important was the echo of such sentiments in the pro-Court, pro-League press, led by the *New York Times* and the *Herald-Tribune*. Numerous editorials were printed deploring the substance of the majority opinion; the nature and origin of the division within the Court were treated sceptically; the advisory jurisdiction was criticized in general terms, with calls for its complete abolition; and (it was widely agreed) the most that could be hoped for was the retrenchment of the Senate in its 1926 reservations. The alternative was the complete rejection of the 1929 Protocols. In the words of one editorial: 'the prospect of [adherence], never too brilliant, [had] been seriously dimmed'. It was a pessimistic conclusion drawn by all 'realistic friends of the World Court'.[26]

Press editorials and news reports are something of a blunt instrument for gauging popular opinion. Nevertheless some considerations suggest this medium can be used to register shifts in more general attitudes. For example, a number of pro-Court Senators recorded their own and constituents' dismay at the Customs Union Opinion. These included Dill of Washington and Gore of Oklahoma, two Democrats; Glenn of Illinois and Metcalf of Rhode Island, two Republicans; plus Norris of Nebraska.[27] Secondly, Frank Kellogg quickly came to express regret at the judgment, as did Lenroot and Root and, over time, Kellogg's colleague, Cecil Hurst.[28] Thirdly, the hostile reception in the United States should not be discounted as hypercritical; for it was nothing compared to the intensity and range of reaction in Europe. Whereas the American press and observers found some comfort that Judge Kellogg had taken (what was termed) an Anglo-Saxon, common-law and commonsensical stance for the legality of the Vienna Protocol, the press in France (in particular) censured the minority judges for being essentially pro-German, revisionist and excessively legalistic. Conversely the German and Austrian press attacked the racism and politics which, under the guise of legalism, had found against the Vienna Protocol. France, her Slavic eastern allies and Latin protégés, had conspired to strengthen the chains upon the Teutonic people. The one consolation was that the most respected and independent members of the Court had shared the judicial values and political goals of the German and Austrian governments.[29]

This type of interpretation was, of course, special pleading. In the French press Fromageot and his allies were seen as non-political and objective; in the British, Hurst was praised; in the German, Schücking was the virtuous judge. The only member of the bench to earn something approaching international credit was Anzilotti, whose arguments were seen as clear and honest. (Both Moore and Borchard deplored the Court's Opinion while commending Anzilotti for his openness and rationality.) However, Anzilotti was an Italian; he had once held high office in the League Secretariat; his individual opinion had paralleled his own government's case; consequently his contribution was sometimes taken as further proof that the Court's verdict represented the triumph of a 'Latin bloc' and the defeat of the 'Anglo-Saxons'.[30]

A fourth point is somewhat different, having less to do with attitudes and responses at the public level. Even so it is worth noting that Registrar Hammarskjöld and former Judge Loder had both complained forcefully to pro-Court Americans that the juridical quality of the bench had fallen following the 1930 elections. Now the judges were said to divide mainly into one of two categories: those who lacked 'judicial training' and those who were identified with their Foreign Ministries and (in Loder's words) were 'biased by the interests of their own countries'. In the second category, it was alleged, were Hurst and Fromageot. (Kellogg was exempted from this sort of criticism.)[31]

A final consideration brings us back to the specific question of the impact of the Customs Union Opinion on American attitudes, particularly the response of the Senate. Whatever the exact route through the complexities revealed by the European press, official statements, the pages of legal journals and private comments, the prevailing view was that held in the United States. The chances of American adherence had been seriously weakened; the conditions of any possible adherence would be more, not less, restrictive; and the timetable of Senate action had been greatly lengthened.[32]

The first stage in that timetable had been agreed at the Foreign Relations Committee meeting which had invited Root to testify: the Protocols would be taken up at the 'first meeting' in the incoming Seventy-second Congress, which meant 16 December 1931. Before then, however, and only a fortnight after the announcement of the Customs Union Opinion occurred an event which 'took the world by surprise', namely 'the Japanese *coup* of the 18th–19th September, 1931, in Manchuria'. The words are those of Arnold Toynbee, writing in the *Survey of International Affairs*; and the complex of forces surrounding the 'Mukden Incident' constitute the culminating section of his record of the '*annus terribilis*', 1931.[33]

There can be no doubt that the historiography of these events in Asia completely outweighs the study of the Court and the Customs Union case. As Esther Lape correctly predicted at the time: 'Manchuria' came to overshadow the issue of Court adherence.[34] It is impossible to offer here a detailed analysis of the antecedents to the Mukden Incident and its sequel in such well-known episodes as the publication of the Lytton Report in Autumn 1932 and Japan's withdrawal from the League of

Nations in the spring of 1933. When in Chapter 3 we discussed the Washington Conference of 1921–22 our perspective was that of the Court and American adherence; so now our comments on the latest stage of the decades-long Sino-Japanese struggle will be selective and drawn in relationship to the contemporaneous debate on the Court Protocols. Moreover, alongside the justifications of space we can range the more powerful arguments of words; for the Mukden Incident in its origins and results has generated a large number of first-rate studies.[35]

It is, indeed, the richness of this historiography which presents critical problems for a historian of the Court Protocols. The Mukden Incident became for many pro-Court, pro-League Americans an additional and immediate argument for joining or at least supporting the League – and, *a fortiori*, the League's Court. Among politicians and politically prominent people who argued in this way were Eleanor Roosevelt, Nicholas Murray Butler and Assistant Secretary of State, James Grafton Rogers.[36] (The latter was not backed, however, by the administration, which was careful to register its agreement with Borah that its commitment to the Kellogg–Briand Pact and the Washington Treaties did not mean an abandonment of isolationism.)[37] But what was the League? What were its purposes? What was the nature of its internationalism? If these were disturbing questions in 1925 on the eve of the first Senate debate, how much more problematical were they in the Autumn of 1931. The Austro-German Customs Union project had shown France and her eastern allies determining the politics of the League, with the British somewhat unwilling followers. The Italians has been characteristically independent but equally determined defenders of their rights under the Peace Treaties and the Covenant of the League. Now the actions of Japan against China posed a similar set of questions more disconcertingly. Historians provide abundant evidence of the split within the League; but much of this evidence is offered implicitly, often inadvertently. Usually the political division is characterized as a conflict between the Great and small Powers, between the Council and the Assembly.[38] More rarely is the sympathy of the British government for Japan acknowledged; or, even more generally, the priority of a number of western governments to support Japan as a stabilizing force against anarchy or socialism in China – both of which were seen to offer revolutionary potential for the Soviet Union.[39]

On another plane lay the uncertain status and effectiveness of a number of international engagements, notably the Nine Power Treaty, the Kellogg–Briand Pact and the Covenant of the League of Nations. As we have seen, a variety of arguments were spun around their existence, a common one suggesting that American adherence to one or more implied, even entailed, a commitment to the others. The British were generally more restrained; and a constitutional argument was always at hand, namely, the requirement of Parliamentary approval for acts of the Executive. But pro-League lobbyists in the United States did not desist: the United States had come and should continue to come closer to the League.[40] Yet it was precisely at this moment that the British, French, Italians and Japanese were theoretically and practically undermining the grounds of universalism and internationalism built into the abstract ideal of the League held by so many of its supporters in the United States. The bearing of these considerations on the history of the Court Protocols is clear. The pro-Court, pro-League advocates were resuming their efforts just when the League itself and the commitments of its Members were shown to be so ambiguous. (Diplomats in Washington and London wrily noted that such advocates were more enthusiastic than the 'sceptical' Europeans, 'more pro-League than the League itself').[41] Hardly had American observers time to reflect on the Customs Union case at the hands of the Council and before the bar of the Court when the League split even more profoundly over the Mukden Incident.

The pro-Court lobbyists and especially the lawyers among them, appeared untroubled by the Customs Union decision, Hudson, Jessup and John W. Davis particularly so. Lape and the American Foundation were as busy as ever, drafting surveys, republishing existing materials and importuning the Department of State and the White House. Wickersham used his influence in the ABA to gain endorsement of the Opinion from the American legal profession. This was all part of a carefully organized, 'nation-wide campaign, directed at the Senate', Colby told Hoover, and was backed by notable figures like Baker, Butler and John D. Rockefeller.[42] In a variety of articles, pamphlets and petitions they praised the realism of the Opinion (by which they meant Anzilotti) and the contribution of the advisory jurisdiction to the peaceful settlement of international disputes. Against them were those like Borah, who in the Spring had deprecated a judicial verdict against the Vienna Protocol, then monitored the Court proceedings *via* the Department of State and the American legation at The Hague and now described the Opinion as a 'miserable sophistry'. Though he continued to express his dismay at the condition of Germany and Austria under the Peace Treaties, Borah had two cold reasons for comfort. The chances of senatorial action on the Court Protocols had been virtually destroyed; and, even if debate were to take place, he and his allies were 'united in predicting [their] defeat'. It was a judgment reluctantly endorsed by the *New York Times* in early December.[43]

For nearly three months from the beginning of the Seventy-second Congress a 'consensus' within the Senate Committee on Foreign Relations held that 'domestic matters were too pressing' for action on the Court Protocols. Finally, however, and by a narrow vote of 11:9, the Committee resumed discussion on 2 March 1932. Even the lost vote could hearten the opposition: two supporters of adherence, Vandenberg and Bronson Cutting (New Mexico, Republican) had voted for postponement.[44] Nevertheless, their action was overshadowed by the next, well-prepared event. Senator Reed of Pennsylvania proposed the addition to the Protocols of a clause stating that they were ratified with the clear understanding that the Permanent Court of International Justice shall not, without the consent of the United States, entertain any request for an advisory opinion touching any dispute or question in which the United States has or claims an interest.

The motion was approved unanimously but on a recorded vote: each Senator wanted to be publicly identified with repeating the exact terms of the famous Fifth Reservation of 1926. In a matter of minutes the work and arguments of six years had been overturned.

The official minutes of the Committee speak of Reed's 'reservation'. The author disowned the term: he called it a

statement of understanding of the effect of the Root Protocol. In substance, it says to the other nations, 'we still insist on our original Fifth Reservation and we understand that you have accepted it in the Root Protocol.'

Senator Walsh agreed; so too did Minority leader Joe Robinson. Reed had not been influenced just by the Customs Union decision: he had been dissatisfied with Root's contradictory testimony in January 1931, as Stimson well knew. Outside the committee room Harlan Fiske Stone and John Bassett Moore backed the 'statement' and the reasoning behind it. As Stone wrote to Moore: Reed's wording was fine and its purpose unexceptional, provided Root, Stimson & Company were correct in arguing that the Fifth Reservation was indeed 'unaffected by the Root protocol'. However, the truth was dawning and some Senators were 'beginning to realize that [the] State Department and some others [had been] led astray by the protocol'.[45]

If the Committee was determined to repeat the text of 1926, it was completely divided about the mode of registering the reaffirmation. At the next Committee meeting on 9 March Walsh submitted a draft resolution of adherence incorporating Reed's 'statement'. Already press reports revealed the Committee 'split' in half. So-called friends of the Court were opposed to Walsh's drafting for fear this would constitute a substantive clause and require acceptance by the signatory States. Key Pittman (Nevada, Democrat), acting Minority leader on the Committee in the absence of Swanson, deprecated such a possibility, as did Pittman's immediate junior on the Committee, Joe Robinson.

Nevertheless Pittman was a dedicated supporter of the Fifth Reservation. His solution, therefore, was to delete the Reed 'understanding' in exchange for a separate motion requesting the Executive to gain diplomatic confirmation that the Signatories had indeed accepted the Fifth Reservation explicitly and unconditionally. It would have been a vain exercise. The British Foreign Office and diplomatic circles in Washington were already thrown into confusion. Small wonder that Borah and Johnson were reported to be 'gleeful'. The pro-Court Senators on the Committee were at odds with one another; and Pittman was referring to the arguments of Stimson and Root as unsatisfactory and mutually contradictory. The Democrats were splitting in an unprecedented way, with the acerbic Ham Lewis of Illinois involving himself on the side of the opposition. The predictions of Borah and his fellow opponents in November and December that the Protocols would be defeated were coming closer to realization.[46]

One other important decision was taken at the 9 March Committee meeting: an invitation to Secretary Stimson to testify on behalf of the Protocols. Never before in the history of the Court had such a request been made; and, in the light of the divisions between the proponents of adherence, it is not unreasonable to interpret the decision as ill-omened. Stimson, however, could not appear at the next scheduled meeting: absence from Washington and a 'heavy cold' were to blame. (Certainly Stimson had not wanted to face the Committee; but the illness was genuine.) Even so, in what he modestly called a 'brief résumé', Stimson explained his own position and his interpretation of the Protocols.[47]

Stimson could scarcely distance himself publicly from the arguments of Elihu Root. His January 1931 testimony, Stimson asserted, had been a 'clear exposition of [the] history and meaning' of the Protocol of Accession: everything had been 'luminously explained'. It was an implausible beginning, however, as Stimson's own invitation to testify had proved. But after this strategic mistake Stimson tactically blundered by mentioning Root's initial proposals to the 1929 Committee of Jurists and their 'modification' in the Root–Hurst draft. Not only was Hurst a bogey even to some pro-Court Americans; the very mention of the negotiations and 'condensing' Root's original terms was *prima facie* evidence of substantial change.

The first half of Stimson's defence was constructed around the guarantees offered in the Protocol of Accession; the second section resorted to the Protocol of Revision and its having 'frozen' the Eastern Carelia precedent, namely that

> the Court [would] not entertain a proposition for an advisory opinion in any dispute unless the parties to that dispute submit it to the jurisdiction of the Court.

Both defences were unsound, as we have seen; but in the most remarkable passage of the whole letter Stimson conceded the misgivings of the proponents when they read such arguments.

> It seems to me that... the much-discussed fifth reservation of the Senate is accepted in its entirety by the [Accession] protocol. But if there is the slightest doubt in the minds of the committee... the interpretative resolution... suggested by Senator Reed would make sure beyond peradventure that no other interpretation could in the future prevail. By Senator Reed's reservation it could be put beyond the possibility of future question that the interpretation which has been given to us by Mr. Root shall be the authoritative interpretation of the future.

Stimson concluded his letter in far more traditional style: the 'liabilities' deriving from adherence were purely financial; and, even so, they were 'insignificant'. At the same time the United States would gain a power to exercise... influence not only in the choice of the judges of the Court but in its method and procedure as well.... Never before was the world in greater need of the orderly development of international rules of conduct by the wise method of judicial decision which... Americans [were] so well acquainted with in the development of the common law of [their] country.

Stimson knew that both Root and Jessup supported him in endorsing Reed's 'interpretative resolution': and he sought maximum publicity for his arguments. This was perhaps to be expected. What *was* surprising, even for someone who claimed to relish struggle and understand the 'psychology of battle', was Stimson's attempt to isolate Pittman. This was an unwise move, especially if it had been inspired by annoyance at Pittman's complaints concerning earlier arguments of Stimson. Pittman's proposal for diplomatic soundings was at least a discreet method; Reed's 'statement', on the other hand, was objectively nothing short of a wrecking amendment. Inevitably Pittman was one of the many Committee members 'unsatisfied' with Stimson's written response; but it was on the motion of Johnson that the Committee decided to adjourn a full discussion until Stimson himself could attend and try to resolve the 'confusion' generated by his letter.[48]

The pejorative term was not just Johnson's. Moore used exactly the same language, even though he did not like Pittman's proposal, which he believed interfered with the Executive's proper and exclusive conduct of foreign relations. Stimson, however, thought his letter might have been too 'technical' and therefore too 'dull' to be appreciated! At all events the antagonism between Stimson and Pittman was not abated by face-to-face discussion – nor indeed was the 'confusion' resolved. Stimson continued to attack Pittman's proposal for diplomatic exchanges as 'exasperating' and 'humiliating' – for the United States no less than the signatory States; at the same time Stimson repeated his endorsement of Reed's 'statement'. But this sort of behaviour could not conceal Pittman's victory over Stimson in arguing that the latter's double reliance on the Accession and Revision Protocols conceded the case that neither had preserved the absolute veto over the advisory jurisdiction originally demanded by the United States. In other words Pittman exposed the weakness of the Jessup thesis and he then took his case to a much wider audience by publishing a long, personal rebuttal of Jessup in the *New York Times*.[49]

Walsh's manner was more conciliatory but his purpose was equally firm. He did not like Pittman's proposal: he was convinced it could only mean a third Conference of Signatories. But he was less troubled by that possibility than determined to maintain the veto he himself had come reluctantly to fashion and resolutely to defend. (Jessup now privately referred to Walsh as 'one of the chief sticklers for the prerogatives of the Senate'.) Vandenberg then joined in, puzzled by Stimson's references to the United States having to plead against the Court's jurisdiction rather than simply oust it by declaration. This became too much for Robinson. In his 'mind' it was 'clear' that under reservation 5 if we have an interest, or if we claim an interest, the Court is divested of jurisdiction; the Court has no power under that language... to pass upon the question.

Robinson thought that in such circumstances there would be an 'impasse', which could be broken only by implementing those articles of the Accession Protocol governing revocation and withdrawal. This was the plausible Jessup thesis; but it was not on all fours with its traditional partner, frequently repeated by Stimson, that the Revision Protocol had 'froze[n] into statute law... the doctrine of the Eastern Carelia case'.

The mutual complaisancy of Stimson and Robinson left both agreeing that the original Fifth Reservation envisaged 'the mere assertion of a claim of interest by the United States estop[ping] the Court from jurisdiction when an advisory opinion is requested'. However Stimson then added that the 1929 negotiations had maintained this power by arguments drawn from the unanimity rule. It was an unwise secondary argument; for, as he admitted to Johnson, there was only a 'presumption of unanimity'. The interchange between Johnson and Stimson became heated, with Stimson being forced to shift his defence to the practical ability of the United States to dissuade the League from proceeding with a request – he having by now realized that no one on the Committee would accept the argument that the jurisdictional veto had been incorporated into the Protocol of Accession. Stimson's shift brought Borah into the questioning. He wanted to know whether Stimson believed that the Root–Hurst negotiations had 'trade[d] or exchange[d] the right of veto for the right of withdrawal'. No: answered Stimson; and he drew the distinction between affecting the actions of the League and determining the competence of the Court.

In my opinion you never asked in your fifth reservation for a veto on the making of a request for an opinion; instead you expressly asked for a limitation on the jurisdiction of the Court to answer such a question when asked. *And that limitation you have obtained.* [Emphasis added.]

Borah thanked Stimson and appeared satisfied. It was a trial lawyer's trick. He did not believe Stimson; but the insistence could be exploited in debate. Cutting, however, wanted to be clear about Stimson's thinking. He addressed him directly.

Senator CUTTING: In the last analysis, we have an absolute and final right to veto, or prevent the Court from rendering an advisory opinion.

Secretary STIMSON: We have the right of raising the question on the limitation of the jurisdiction of the Court.

Stimson had turned again: the veto was not absolute. Lewis and Johnson pursued other questions; but now Pittman was obviously distressed by Stimson's tergiversations. In a long, carefully spelled-out example he once more posed the question: could the Court determine its jurisdiction if the United States objected? 'Absolutely no', Stimson insisted. They were his closing words – but they were not conclusive.[50]

Stimson's cross-examination or 'grilling' as he called it, had touched upon one other item apart from the advisory jurisdiction: the question of male–female equality under 'the code of law to be administered by the World Court'. At the previous meeting of the Committee Lewis had submitted a reservation drafted by the National Woman's Party (NWP) that adherence should be conditional upon the Court's abjuring treaties and engagements 'contain[ing] inequalities based on sex'. Lewis's support for the reservation was entirely disingenuous – as was Johnson's during Stimson's testimony. The reason for the Senators' support was not hard to find. With dozens of States, Members of the League of Nations, already opposed to such a commitment, the inclusion of such a principle in any resolution of adherence to the Court was tantamount to defeating ratification. At the same time, for the Committee on Foreign Relations to attach such a reservation would place the pro-Court lobby in a dilemma: so many members in the organizations were women and strong feminists at that. Either they continued to promote adherence but at the price of a principle which would be rejected by the Court's Signatories; or they tried to defeat the reservation from the NWP and so bypass one opportunity of fighting sexual inequality at home and abroad.[51]

The latter weeks of March and the beginning of April marked the start of a critical stage in the history of the Court Protocols. Stimson's testimony had been contradictory and quite clearly unconvincing – even to proponents of adherence. Meanwhile a powerful lobby within the feminist movement had become objectively enemies of adherence on terms the League could accept. The process continued on its intricate way. Carrie Chapman Catt of the League of Women Voters (LWV) wrote an open letter to Borah pressing for senatorial action and approval of the Reed 'statement'. (The LWV and the NWP were at odds over the sex-equality issue and the Court.) Denys Myers of the World Peace Foundation also advised acceptance of the Reed 'statement'. At the same time the Foreign Policy Association and the National World Court Committee were urging officers in the Department of State to help remove the Protocols from the agenda of the Committee on Foreign Relations. Pro-Court Senators were said to be 'frantically endeavouring' to postpone immediate action, though eager 'to put the blame for failure to act on somebody else's shoulder'. Robinson of Arkansas was more honest. He advised the proponents to defer action until the next Session of Congress in December; in other words, until after the party conventions and the national and presidential elections.[52]

On Wednesday, 13 April, a week after Stimson's testimony, the Committee took up a revised and conciliatory version of Pittman's original proposal for diplomatic soundings. Though it was defeated by 8:11, there were some encouraging signs for the dedicated opponents. Moses had opposed the motion – but this was tactical: he wanted to re-insert the Fifth Reservation and defeat adherence in that way. More importantly, Walter F. George of Georgia and Robert F. Wagner of New York (both Democrats) let it be known they supported Pittman's motion. Furthermore Vandenberg, who had voted against the motion, had been reported as allied to Pittman but somewhat afraid to stand up against the pro-Court lobby. Vandenberg might, therefore, be induced to take a firmer line for a version of the Fifth Reservation. Most encouraging of all was Robinson's repeating his call for postponement until December. In the more public record, however, the indictment against the opponents continued to grow. Pro-Court newspapers from New England to the Pacific published numerous editorials blaming the delay upon the anti-Court Senators; and such material was gathered up, reissued and sent to important individuals by the American Foundation.[53]

A month elapsed before the Committee returned to the terms of the resolution of adherence. Then, in a most unusual sequence of meetings on successive days, the Committee rewrote the resolution of January 1926. At the regular Wednesday morning meeting on 11 May 1932 a motion drafted by Reed and Walsh (originally introduced on 9 March and incorporating Reed's 'statement of understanding') was laid before a Committee, one third of which was absent. Given the importance of the issues to be decided and the number of proxy votes cast, it was clear that individual positions had already been taken and made known. Immediately Vandenberg moved the addition of Paragraphs VII and VIII from January 1926: the first to preserve a role for the Senate through the treaty-making power; the second being the (so-called) Monroe Doctrine clause and the reservation of domestic and political questions from the Court's competence. Vandenberg's motion was adopted on the nod.

Now the voting became important, but to exactly the same end. First Lewis moved the sex equality reservation: it was defeated 5:10. (No proxies were cast: a sign of its unexpectedness – or the disdain of the seven absentees.) Then Johnson proposed the restatement of the Fifth Reservation *verbatim*; i.e. not as an 'understanding' with, arguably, no binding effect but rather as an explicit condition of ratification. This was voted down 9:11. The two non-voters were George and Wagner – further indication to the opponents that the tide was moving their way. Even more obvious and encouraging, Cutting had backed Johnson, though formerly he had opposed Pittman's scheme for diplomatic soundings. The final vote of the morning would complete the pattern. On the motion of Moses it was proposed to repeat Paragraph VI of January 1926, namely the requirement that the signing of the Protocols be delayed until the existing Signatories had explicitly accepted the reservations stated by the Senate. The motion was carried 11:10. George continued to conceal his true position but it was implicitly hostile to the original Walsh–Reed resolution. Far more important was the backing of Cutting, Wagner and even Pittman for Moses's reservation.[54]

The Committee reconvened the next day, Thursday 12 May, and speedily disposed of its business. By a vote of 11:9 it agreed to report the resolution as amended. Substantially it was a bizarre event; and some interesting votes had produced this result. The Senators who had opposed the Moses Reservation were joined by Pittman and George in favour of action: after all, the 1926 terms had been restored. Robinson of Arkansas, however, who had opposed the Moses Reservation, was absent from Committee. No doubt, as Senate Minority leader, he could plead other business; and Swanson had returned to lead the regular Democratic advocates. But Robinson did not offer a proxy; and his preference for postponement was well known. More generally still, Robinson was highly ambitious – as Stimson knew. He had been vice-presidential candidate in 1928 and had even greater hopes for 1932. The mood in the Democratic Party was reported to be turning against the Wilsonian internationalist legacy, with progressive elements hardening against Newton D. Baker and becoming drawn to Governor Roosevelt of New York, who had gained the backing of William Randolph Hearst. For Robinson, silence rather than postponement might be the wisest policy. It is a speculation corroborated by another interesting vote – or, rather lack of vote. Wagner did not attend nor register a proxy, yet he had supported the Moses Reservation. Perhaps his re-election in the New York Senate campaign later in the year was assured with the Republicans so unpopular. But we do have the valuable evidence of Jessup that Wagner's fellow Democrat from New York, Royal S. Copeland, believed his own vote for ratification in 1926 'had wrecked his political career'.[55]

After the decision to report the Protocols the Committee turned to the question of authorship. Borah ruled himself out; and then Moses suggested a bipartisan approach: a 'joint report'. The Committee agreed and appointed Senators Walsh and Fess. It was a good balance: Walsh the advocate of the League, part-creator of the Fifth Reservation, a progressive Democrat; Fess the anti-Leaguer, advocate of the Court, a stalwart among regular Republicans. But, as usual, pro-Court sources ignored the substance and significance of the months of voting in Committee. Instead they concentrated upon Borah's honest reply when he was asked about the date of the *Report's* appearance. 'So far as I am concerned, never.' A few days later the *New York Times* published a famous editorial denouncing the opponents as simple obstructionists.[56]

The Walsh–Fes *Report* was published on 1 June. It was a remarkable document: quite the longest ever to be presented to or issue from the Senate on the subject of the Court Protocols. Thousands of words of argumentation were joined to extensive quotations from a veritable library of previously published material. Though the authors began briskly enough in dissociating themselves from Moses's reservation (since it prevented the resolution of adherence from being 'an unequivocal acceptance of the Protocol of Accession'), the numerous words which followed were consumed in a vain struggle to reconcile the conflicting interpretations surrounding that same Protocol. This is not a partisan judgment. As Walsh and Fess finally confessed:

> No attempt will here be made to resolve the controversy over the proper construction to be given to the Protocol. It must be admitted that, to say the least, it is ambiguous and one can not help regretting that in the preparation of treaties opportunity is so often left for either side plausibly to contend for such a

construction as seems to it best to suit its purpose.

If this was unusually honest, it was not the only novelty. Though Walsh and Fess wove in and out of the four basic methods of argumentation (reliance on either the Accession or the Revision Protocol; the Jessup thesis incorporating both; or the latest, Stimson-plan, to reaffirm the Fifth Reservation through the Reed 'statement'), it was their idiosyncrasy to invoke a host of astonishing allusions, suggestions and non-sequiturs. Thus Levinson's conversion to adherence *via* the text of the Revision Protocol was mysteriously linked to Borah's previous prominence in the Outlawry movement to imply that ratification was equally agreeable to both. Likewise, for apparently the first time in a Senate document, the origins of the Court in the Covenant were boldly proclaimed as part of Woodrow Wilson's handiwork – an interesting variant on the theme of Elihu Root's paternity, though one not used to exclude this traditional argument.[57]

Indeed it was Root who might come to the minds of informed readers studying the closing words of the Walsh-Fess *Report*. A year and a half previously Root had testified before the Committee that the League needed the help of the United States in preserving the peace in Eastern and Central Europe. The logic of his argument was that American adherence to the Court could help to prevent the wars which would inevitably involve the United States: prevention was better and safer than cure. It was not an unreasonable thesis; but the Senate had not appeared persuaded by it – least of all after the resolution of the Austro-German Customs Union project. Walsh and Fess echoed the same argument in their final words; but now the immediate costs of adherence were emphasized, the long-term benefits seemed even more remote.

It has come to be realized by the most painful experience that the whole world suffers from a war of any magnitude, and that every nation is consulting its own interest in contributing toward averting such a catastrophe. It is quite likely that Europe will continue largely to monopolize the attention of the Court with its unfortunate quarrels, that subject us to the chance of being again enveloped should they culminate in general hostilities. Whether the question be viewed selfishly or altruistically, our Government ought to give to the Court the moral support that would follow from association in maintaining it.[58]

The antecedents and content of the Walsh–Fess *Report* have been neglected in the most recent historiography – a tradition established by the first historians of the Court issue. Once again a form of historical realism might be employed to justify the neglect: early in the summer of 1932 the minds of Senators no less than the public at large and party leaders were fixed on more pressing and dramatic events. Veterans were mobilizing in the 'Bonus Army'; Congress and the White House were at odds over emergency relief legislation; the national conventions were only weeks away; repeal of Prohibition was a far more controversial subject; and, the most general consideration and the belief most widely held was the likelihood, the certainty almost of a Democratic victory in the presidential campaign and the return of a Democratic Congress for the first time since the election of 1916.

These last predictions were borne out. No student of American history is ignorant of President Hoover's defeat by Governor Roosevelt; the period of the so-called Interregnum and the last lame-duck Session of Congress from December 1932 to March 1933; and the famous 'Hundred Days' following Roosevelt's inauguration to the close of the First Session of the Seventy-third Congress in mid June 1933. Now the problems for the student of the Court issue are created by the sheer bulk of secondary material – not the writings on the Court but rather the historiography of Roosevelt and his presidency.

There is one tradition which depicts Roosevelt as a dangerous dictator at home and an irresponsible and covert meddler abroad – a tradition exemplified in the writings of Harry Elmer Barnes, Charles A. Beard, John T. Flynn and Charles C. Tansill. A related analysis, developed more abstractly within the methods of political economy, concentrates upon changes in the structural and dynamic elements of the American state under the impact of the interwar economic and social crisis and considers Roosevelt's New Deal administration as a particular historical phase in the concentration of capital and power in the United States, with necessary causes and consequences abroad – a form of historiography often referred to simply – if rather inaccurately – as the New Left or Wisconsin School of revisionism led by William Appleman Williams and Lloyd Gardner. Against both these types of interpretations can be ranged the more favourable, personalized accounts of the Roosevelt presidency characteristic of the postwar decades, such of Frank Freidel's multivolume study begun in the early 1950s to more recent biographies by Kenneth Davis and Ted Morgan. A fourth group of historians has investigated congressional and extra-congressional alliances and coalitions in their respective relationships to Roosevelt and his administration: scholars such as Otis Graham, James Patterson and George Wolfskill.

This historiographical typology is, of course, broadly drawn. As such it excludes what remains the single most stimulating modern study of the period by Ellis Hawley, not to mention the early brilliant comparative analysis by Robert Brady, *Business as a System of Power*.[59] The purpose of these four listings has not been to be comprehensive but rather to identify the main historiographical traditions which form the general scholarly context of modern World Court studies. Broadly speaking, the Second Generation has not been concerned to problematize the relationship of their own special investigations to the historiography of Roosevelt and the New Deal.[60] Rather the post-World War II specialists have followed the patterns established by Fleming: the Court issue was a battle between isolationists and internationalists, a continuation of the war whose first major engagement was the rejection of the League of Nations. This present study incorporates certain elements in that perspective; but one of its points of divergence lies in the nature of the relationship drawn between the Court–League issue and the Roosevelt presidency.

Without repeating in detail many of the points made in Chapter 1 or anticipating the narrative of the next chapter it may be fairly said that the most common explanation for the failure of the Senate to approve American adherence to the Court in January 1935 was the propaganda of the opposition – a propaganda barrage launched on the Senate by forces outside the Senate. This explanation was well established by the time the present generation of World Court historians began writing; and they have largely endorsed it. In this aetiology President Roosevelt is generally portrayed as either the reluctant isolationist or half-hearted internationalist. Under the first description Roosevelt is depicted openly leading the internationalist, pro-League forces towards the Court, only to be defeated by his irrational enemies. In the second portrayal – now the majority view – Roosevelt approved the goal but lacked the resolution to achieve it: his was a failure of 'leadership'.[61]

Two distinct points may be made about this mode of explaining Roosevelt's actions in their relationship to the Court – points which will bring us back to the events of 1932 and the main direction of our narrative. First, Roosevelt's repudiation of the League in the campaign of 1932 was public and unmistakable; and even privately and towards intimates he was not prepared to commit himself to pursue American membership of the Court.[62] In other words, if Roosevelt showed a lack of leadership, he had been practising the role for some years. Secondly the Democratic platform on which Roosevelt stood for office was ambiguous. Its relevant clause read: 'We advocate… adherence to the World Court with appending reservations'.[63] Did this mean the January 1926 conditions? the 1929 Protocols? or the Walsh–Fess *Report*? It was unclear. The net result, however, was not in doubt. A Democratic candidate advocating adherence on the basis of the 1932 party platform was either spurning the League's work of 1926 and 1929 or rejecting the legal analysis of the most authoritative Senators and Department of State officials.

If these complex problems have escaped historians, they have two defences. The most general is that foreign affairs were simply unimportant as an election issue in 1932.[64] The second and more specific would be the retort that contemporary lobbyists were equally remiss. Throughout the summer the American Foundation and the National World Court Committee pressed the Department of State to pursue adherence on the basis of the Walsh–Fess *Report* – a *Report* which the Department of State could not unravel. Esther Lape (a close friend of Eleanor Roosevelt) sent details to Secretary Stimson of those Senators who favoured debate in the lame-duck Session due to begin in December; but she was not careful to distinguish a readiness to debate from even qualified support for adherence. Philip Jessup also wanted action; so too did Senator Robinson.[65] Their keenness was largely to be explained by the realization that if the Protocols were not debated in the lame-duck Session they would automatically go back to the Committee on Foreign Relations and require a new report before reaching the floor of the

Senate. In this event, the Protocols would most probably not be acted upon until at least 1934.

When the lame-duck Session began on 5 December 1932, Borah knew he was serving his last term as chairman. The election results of November had returned a clear Democratic majority in both Houses of Congress and his post would pass to a Democrat. Within a week it was obvious that the Senate was opposed to any debate on the Protocols: Walsh followed Borah in making the news public. Still the petitions for action continued to reach the Senate and were printed in the newspapers, even after a coalition of Democrats and irregular Republicans formed in mid December to block an Executive Session and (consequently) prevent action on ratification of the Protocols. As Pittman wrote to Raymond Moley, a senior member of Roosevelt's transition team and soon to become Assistant Secretary of State: 'Adherence to the World Court is out of the question at this session.'[66]

In the new Seventy-third Congress, which began its First Session on 9 March, Pittman became chairman of the Committee on Foreign Relations. The ranking Democrat, Claude Swanson of Virginia, had resigned to become Secretary of the Navy. Immediately below Pittman in seniority was Joe Robinson of Arkansas, who now became Democratic Majority leader in the Senate after serving ten years as Minority leader. Below Robinson would have been Thomas J. Walsh; but he too had resigned from the Senate to take up the post of US Attorney General – only to die within hours of Roosevelt's inauguration. But if Borah had lost the chairmanship, his authority was undiminished. Even the hostile *New York Times* acknowledged his influence and stature – though praise from such an 'internationalist' source was sarcastically discounted by his fellow progressive Republicans, Hiram Johnson and George Norris.[67]

This rancour is another reminder of the divisions between the Senate Progressives – and a further challenge to any notion that Roosevelt represented the culmination of a unitary progressive tradition. Not that long-time Progressives such as Johnson and Norris did not support Roosevelt against Hoover in 1932 and give him the benefit of the doubt in 1933 and 1934. But such Progressives also swung away from Roosevelt – as did La Follette, Cutting and Borah. Furthermore, the turning point for Johnson and Norris was Roosevelt's eleventh-hour decision to endorse adherence to the World Court.[68]

It would be tempting to move straight on to the narrative of these events; but three items must briefly be mentioned. The first two are generally discussed in terms of the internationalist–isolationist dichotomy, with Roosevelt again depicted as the internationalist; both also serve to reveal the distance between the senatorial Progressives and those political vectors known under various synonyms for Roosevelt's New Deal. These two issues are the congressional proposals for an arms embargo in 1933 and the passage of the Reciprocal Trade Agreements Act in 1934. The third subject is the identity of the forces pressing for ratification of the Court Protocols.

From the complex antecedents and later history of the arms embargo movement (a history which includes the four Neutrality Acts of 1935–9) two sets of considerations are especially relevant to a study of the Court Protocols and the role of Roosevelt. First, the congressional initiative antedated Roosevelt's presidency; and, second, Roosevelt's own response was to side with the weight of senatorial opinion which sought to curb Executive discretion in the implementation of an embargo. In more direct and precise terms, the Senate would not agree to the Executive being empowered to impose a selective embargo against 'aggressors'. The limitation might be fairly regarded as a mark of senatorial isolationism; equally Roosevelt was not prepared publicly to repudiate the limitation. Even so the efforts of administration members and extra-congressional lobbyists to align the United States with the so-called peace-loving democracies caused great unease among many of Roosevelt's initial progressive allies. They feared a resurrection of the Wilsonian 'Messianic tradition': meddling unneutrality abroad combined with the growth of irresponsible governmental power at home. (The phrase comes from J. Pierrepont Moffat, the new Chief of the Division of Western European Affairs, trying to check the hopes of 'Sweetser and others' like him for any pro-League policies from Roosevelt and his new administration.)[69]

Such fears were increased in 1934 by the administration's success in passing the Reciprocal Trade Agreements Act (RTAA). The historiographical verdict on the RTAA is that it promoted political and economic internationalism; but the reality is more problematical. In our narrative, however, the relevance of the RTAA is quite different. First, the erosion of congressional, and particularly senatorial, powers in the framing and conclusion of commercial treaties was seen to mark a dangerous stage in the growth of Executive power – a process which had not begun in March 1933 but a process which had been intensified in and justified by the 'emergency legislation' of the Hundred Days. Second, tariff revision – implicitly downwards – was seen as a means of aligning the United States with the League.[70] On the RTAA many Progressives diverged from Roosevelt and his very partisan political allies: Robinson in the Senate and James A. Farley, Postmaster General, 'boss' of the Roosevelt section of the Democratic party, and a man with ambitions to match Roosevelt's all the way to the White House. Partly within the field of these forces the Court Protocols would be handled by the Senate.

Partly – but only partly. The other main determinants were the positive and negative forces behind ratification. With one exception the main extra-congressional lobbies for and against adherence had not noticeably changed since 1929. The exception was the *Washington Post*, which now supported American membership in the Court. Though small and with nothing like the coverage and international status of the major New York papers, the *Washington Post* was very influential in diplomatic circles. Such at least was Moffat's judgment. Certainly its pro-League orientation was obvious under its new editor, Felix Morley, himself a favourable authority on the League, a close friend of Sweetser's and on good terms with Drummond.[71] *Within* the extra-congressional coalitions, perhaps the most remarkable event was the financial weakness of the pro-Court lobbyists – a sign of the general economic depression. There is no objective evidence for any slackening of their efforts; but their senior officials appeared worried by lack of funds.[72]

Inside the Senate the pro-Court leadership had also weakened with the parting of Walsh and Swanson and the elevation of the sceptical Pittman to the chairmanship of the Committee on Foreign Relations. This was a paradoxical result with the Democrats now in control, for they had always been significantly more favourable to membership than the Republicans. Moses had been defeated in the 1932 elections; but he left strenuous and knowledgeable allies: Borah, Johnson, La Follettte and Shipstead among the Insurgents and Irreconcilables; and quasi-allies in Reed, Fess, Vandenberg and Arthur Capper of Kansas, Senators committted to the 1926 terms and likely to baulk at any move to make the Protocols a partisan issue. The Republican Robinson of Indiana was at best one of this latter group; while the Democratic Lewis of Illinois was openly hostile. All these Senators remained on the Committee. As Moffat correctly noted: there were few Senators who would fight for the Court; many who would fight against it.[73]

Roosevelt's cabinet contained no active supporters. Swanson apparently abandoned interest; Homer Cummings (Attorney General) had also supported adherence but he too gave no lead. Cordell Hull, the Secretary of State, kept a profile so low it bordered on neglect. His *Memoirs* do not require us to revise this judgement; and his own brief spell in the Senate (after years in the House) would have shown him how complicated and divisive was the question of adherence. Furthermore Hull had little authority with the Senate as a whole. As for the other members of the cabinet, the scattered evidence suggests they were at best lukewarm to adherence itself and particularly doubtful about the opportuneness of attempting to mobilize a two-thirds majority in the Senate.[74]

The lobbyists, however, wasted little time in pressing the Department of State, the White House and the Senate Democratic leaders to move forward on the Court Protocols. Lape did not have great confidence in Roosevelt's commitment – and even her qualified faith may have been a product of her friendship with Eleanor Roosevelt, who was a firm and public proponent. (Lape had also written off Pittman.) Jessup was even less sanguine about Franklin Roosevelt – a judgement endorsed by two senior and long-serving officers in the Department of State, Moffat of DWEA and Under Secretary of State William Phillips.[75]

Frederick J. Libby, Executive Secretary of the National Council for Prevention of War, was one of those lobbyists who argued that Roosevelt's forceful endorsement of the Court would stiffen Senators wavering before the electoral pressure of Hearst: Democrats such as Pittman and Lewis; Republicans such as Johnson and Robinson of Indiana. With victory in the Court battle (which Libby promised), Roosevelt would then be able to smash the obnoxious Hearst and free himself from the isolationist shackles imposed in the campaign bargain of 1932. By various ploys Roosevelt and Hull avoided giving direct statements of their own positions, though Hull did hint that the main problem lay in the Senate's opposition to ratification on the terms desired by the lobbyists themselves. But by early April (less than four weeks after the assembly of the new Congress) it was public knowledge that the Democratic leadership in the Senate and the Executive would not take any action on the Protocols before the Second Session convened in January 1934.[76]

Roosevelt's skill in disguising his real intentions was so great that one senior officer in the Department, the newly appointed Assistant Secretary, Francis B. Sayre, had to ask his friend Manley Hudson to interpret the evidence. (Sayre, son-in-law of Woodrow Wilson, was in favour of American membership of the League as well as the Court.) But 1934 was not far advanced before Roosevelt, Robinson and Pittman announced the renewal of their joint agreement to take the Court Protocols off the Senate calendar for a second year, that is until the mid-term elections of November 1934 had passed. The public reason given for postponement was striking. As Robinson explained:

> the situation in Europe is so complex that this is not the opportune time to proceed with ... the World Court.

This might be a rebuff to those like Hudson, Lape, Libby, Newton D. Baker and Nicholas Murray Butler who were contemporaneously calling for joint American action with the League to solve the problems of Europe. It was assuredly a gift for those opponents who had long insisted that the primary purpose and danger of adherence to the Court was precisely such political involvement with the League.[77]

At a less intense and more private level lay another powerful reason for postponement: Robinson doubted the votes existed in the Senate to secure a two-thirds majority for the Court Protocols. There were those like Butler who counted 80 (out of a theoretical maximum of 96) Senators favourable to ratification; but Lape and Jessup were more representative in thinking that a two-thirds majority could only be assured 'with leadership'. It was a significant qualification. The leadership had to come from the very top: from President Roosevelt himself. Robinson could not provide it. And, as it turned out, he would not provide it in 1934. His calculations, reported to Roosevelt to counterbalance more optimistic estimates showed over half the Senate opposed to debating and passing a resolution of adherence.[78]

One weakness of all these surveys was their generality: they did not provide information on the reasoning of individuals. Thus the absolute majority opposed to immediate action was composed of Senators who were outright, unconditional enemies of adherence; those who had different legislative priorities; and those who objected to the terms reported in June 1932, particularly the Moses Reservation. Since, however, the Protocols would require a new report (however perfunctory) to be discharged from the Committee on Foreign Relations and return to the Senate, it was procedurally correct and tactically sound to hold new Hearings. This gave the appearance of activity to the lobbyists but did not entail any swift response by the Committee and

Senate. By the end of January 1934 the solution had been accepted by Pittman; early in March he made the announcement publicly and with unconcealed disapproval.[79]

The pro-Court lobbyists were ready. When (as Hiram Johnson put it) Pittman named the actual day of the Hearings 'out of a clear sky', the stalwarts came in numbers: Hudson, Carrie Chapman Catt; a proxy for Root in the person of General Charles H. Sherrill, recently ambassador to Turkey; representatives of the American Bar Association and the US Chamber of Commerce; and a newcomer in the ranks, ex-Governor Al Smith of New York. Lape thought they had done well; Robinson and Pittman were discreetly non-committal. Both the White House and the Department of State had successfully kept out of view. Johnson's prejudices did not warp his judgment when he stated that this first day of Hearings had been remarkable for the numbers present, not the arguments deployed. Jessup's more private thoughts led to a similar conclusion: there would be no Senate action until at least January 1935 and the Reed' understanding' would be preserved from the 1932 *Report*. Where Jessup differed from Johnson was in desiring and predicting the elimination of the Moses Reservation.[80]

It took two months for the opposition to muster their lobbyists. The chronic antipathy between Johnson and Borah had somewhat abated in their common fight against the economic monopoly and Executive aggrandizement fostered by the New Deal; and the spring of 1934 saw them combining in a manner reminiscent of the anti-League campaign of 1919–20. Neither was able to persuade John Bassett Moore or Edwin Borchard to testify, particularly on the 'political character of the Court, as evidenced by the German-Austrian Customs decision' – though both Moore and Borchard believed the Court had indeed 'yield[ed] to political pressure'. Moore's suspicion of Borah's discretion still lingered from the embarrassment of the leaked memorandum in the January 1926 Senate debate; but the reason he gave for his absence was general ill-health. Borchard excused himself by saying that he did not like the role of 'gladiator'; and anyway (he added) his views could be found printed in numerous sources. Borchard's main argument, however, against testifying was a substantive one: the late Senator Walsh had defended the Fifth Reservation as well as anyone; and his collaborator in its formulation, former Senator Swanson, had endorsed Walsh's reasoning.[81]

Two rather different allies from the 1925–6 debate did respond to the appeals of Johnson and Borah: ex-Senators Pepper of Pennsylvania and Reed of Missouri. So too did Bainbridge Colby, Wilson's last Secretary of State, and J. Reuben Clark, Jr., who had served as Under Secretary of State in the late 1920s, then gone to Mexico as Ambassador but whose most important, if little known part in the Court saga had been his work in framing Harding's notorious St Louis speech of June 1923. Also present was the former Republican Senator from Illinois, Otis Glenn, whose presence was a powerful reminder of the continuing electoral importance of the Court issue. Collectively these anti-Court witnesses outweighed the previous pro-Court lobby in terms of Washington knowledge and political prestige. But, as Johnson admitted, the proponents' sheer numbers, energy and apparent expression of public opinion beyond the Senate won them the propaganda battle. The largely pro-Court press agreed and treated the second day of Hearings accordingly. Two weeks later, on Wednesday, 30 May, the full Committee unanimously voted to place the Court Protocols at the top of their agenda in the new Congress to assemble on Thursday, 3 January 1935, with 'consideration of the same [to] be concluded as early as practicable during that [First] Session'.[82]

Notes

1 Das Wiener Protokoll vom 19 März 1931: text in PCIJ, Series C, no. 53: *Customs Régime between Germany and Austria* (Protocol of 19 March 1931), 42–5. This volume is cited below as PCIJ, *Customs Régime*.

2 Francois Rodolphe and Pierre Dareste, *Les Constitutions Modernes*, 4th ed, rev. Joseph Delpech and Julien LaFerrière, 6 vols (Paris: Recueil Sirey, 1928–34), I. 58–98, 290–336.

3 League of Nations, *Treaty Series*, XII (1922), nos 334, 335, 336. W. T. Layton and Charles Rist, *The Economic Situation of Austria: Report Presented to the Council of the League of Nations*. Official no. C440 (1).M.162 (1). 1925 II (Geneva: League of Nations, 1925); League of Nations, *The Financial Reconstruction of Austria: General Survey and Principal Documents*. Official no. C568.M.232. 1926 II (Geneva: League of Nations, 1926).

4 *CR* 67:4, 2939; Archibald C. Coolidge, 'The New Austria', Temperley, *History of the Peace Conference*, IV. 462–84; Isaiah Bowman, *The New World: Problems in Political Geography*. rev. ed (London: Harrap, 1924), 206–15; 'Supplement', 86; Charles Seymour, 'The End of Empire: Remnant of Austria-Hungary', in Edward Mandell House and Charles Seymour, (eds), *What Really Happened at Paris: the Story of the Peace Conference, 1918–1919, by American Delegates* (New York: Scribner's, 1921), 87–111: cf. ibid. 452–7. Coolidge and Bowman had served with Seymour and House on the American Delegation to the Paris Peace Conference.

5 Johann Wolfgang Brügel, *Tschechen und Deutsche, 1918–1938* (Munich: Nymphenburger Verlagshandlung, 1967), 220–4.

6 Felix Kreissler, *Von der Revolution zur Annexion: Oesterreich, 1918 bis 1938* (Vienna: Europa, 1970), 178–9; Ludwig Zimmermann, *Deutsche Aussenpolitik in der Ära der Weimarer Republik* (Göttingen: Musterschmidt, 1958), 480.

7 Zimmermann, *Deutsche Aussenpolitik*, 408.

8 The literature is enormous: see the Bibliographical Essay to this study. For a general introduction, Stanley Suval, *The Anschluss Question in the Weimar Era: a Study of Nationalism in Germany and Austria, 1918–1932* (Baltimore and London: Johns Hopkins University Press, 1974).

9 Klaus Jaitner, 'Deutschland, Brüning und die Formulierung der britischen Aussenpolitik Mai 1930 bis Juni 1932', *Vierteljahrshefte für Zeitgeschichte*, 28 (no. 4, 1980), 440–86, esp. 454–9.

10 *SIA* (1931) 309.

11 Minutes of the Sixty-third Session of the Council, 18–19 May 1931: reprinted in PCIJ, *Customs Régime*, 10–40, esp. 21–5.

12 Johnson to Harold L. Ickes, 10 November and 28 December 1931; to W. W. Campbell, 25 November 1931: Johnson Papers.

13 *SIA* (1931) 86–7.

14 Herbert Hoover, *The Memoirs of Herbert Hoover*, 3 vols (New York: Macmillan, 1951), III. 61–5; Stimson *Diary*, 30 March and 16 September 1931: Henry Lewis Stimson Papers, Sterling Memorial Library, Yale; minute of Castle to Frederick M. Sackett (Berlin) to Stimson, 16 June 1931: NA 662. 6331/240. (This is the Department's file on the Customs Union scheme.) For public opinion, see the special pleading of Nathaniel P. Clough, *Beiträge zur Beurteilung der österreichischen Anschlussfrage in der öffentlichen Meinung der Vereinigten Staaten Nordamerikas* (Heidelberg: Hermann Meister, 1933).

15 Green H. Hackworth (Solicitor) to Stimson, 12 June 1931: NA 662. 6331/261; see also Joseph C. Green (DWEA), 'Austro-German Customs Union', 31 March 1931; Prentiss B. Gilbert (Geneva) to Stimson, 28 May 1931: memo of Stanley K. Hornbeck (Chief: Division of Far Eastern Affairs) [23 July] 1931: NA 662. 6331/143, 220, 311; Stimson, *Diary*, 25–30 March 1931: Stimson Papers.

16 Hallett Johnson (The Hague) to Stimson, 25 August 1931: NA 662. 6331/276; Borchard to Moore, 27 August 1931: Moore Papers. For the written and oral submissions of the disputants, see PCIJ, *Customs Régime*, 46–183; 210–591.

17 PCIJ, Customs Régime, 265, 432; cf. Josef L. Kunz, *Die Revision der Pariser Friedensverträge: eine völkerrechtliche Untersuchung* (Vienna: Springer, 1932).

18 *SIA* (1931) 319–33: *The Times* (London) (31 August 1931), 9; *Manchester Guardian* (4 September 1931), 12; *NYT* (6 September 1931), I. 6; *NYT* (7 September 1931), 2; Borchard to Borah, 5 and 7 September 1931: Borchard Papers.

19 The best analysis remains Franz Vali, *Die deutsch-österreichische Zollunion vor dem Ständigen Internationalen Gerichtshof* (Vienna: Manz, 1932).

20 George E. Morton to Lenroot, 18 March 1930; Lenroot to Morton, 24 March 1930: Lenroot Papers.

21 PCIJ, Series A/B, Fascicule no. 41: *Customs Régime between Germany and Austria* (*Protocol of March 19th, 1931*), 37–103, esp. 38–54 at 52. This volume is cited below as PCIJ, Series A/B *Customs Régime.*

22 Ibid. 74–87, esp. 82–6.

23 For Anzilotti's corpus of dissenting opinions, see his *Opere*, Part 2, II. 593–767.

24 PCIJ, Series A/B, *Customs Régime*, 55–73, esp. 64–8, 70–3; for Anzilotti and his maxim, see *Opere*, I. 43 ff.

25 'The Politics of the World Court', *Chicago Daily Tribune* (cited below as *CDT*) (8 September 1931), 12; 'A World-Court "Split" Stirs up its Foes', *Literary Digest* (26 September 1931), 9; *New York American* (11 October 1931), 2, 4.

26 *Evening Post* (Charleston, SC), cited in *CR*, 72:1, 5312; 'The Divided World Court' *NYT* (7 September 1931), 12; 'The Trouble with the World Court', *NYH-T* (10 September 1931), 20.

27 *USD*, (7 December 1931) 2; and see ch. 8 below.

28 Stimson, *Diary*, 7 December 1931: Stimson Papers; Lenroot to Lape, 26 January 1932: Lenroot Papers; Root to Kellogg, 7 September 1932: Root Papers; Hurst, 'World Court', in Philip Gibbs (ed.), *Bridging the Atlantic: Anglo-American Fellowship as the Way to World Peace* (London: Hutchinson, 1943), 180–203.

29 See the Mission reports from European capitals of press reaction: NA 662. 6331/284–302; cf. *NYT* (6 September 1931), 6; *NYH-T* (6 September 1931), 10; *NYH-T* (13 September 1931), II. 1, 2.

30 For the 'Latin bloc' see esp. *Corriere della Sera* (Milan) (6 September 1931):

copy in NA 662. 6331/290; Moore to Brierley, 15 February 1932; Borchard to Moore, 11 March 1932: Moore Papers; for scepticism about the Anglo-Saxons, see Lauterpacht, *Development of International Law*, 36–41.

31 Hammarskjöld to Hudson, 29 October and 29 November 1930: Hudson Papers; Lape to Stimson, 9 January 1931; Johnson to Stimson, 18 February 1931: NA 500. C114/1232½, 1265; Moffat, *Diary*, 16 July 1931: J. Pierrepont Moffat Papers, Houghton Library, Harvard University. Moffat was a well-connected career diplomat: see pp. 221 ff. above

32 *CSM* (5 September 1931), 1; *NYT* (6 September 1931), 6; *Deutsche Juristen-Zeitung* (Berlin) (1 October 1931), cols 1205–12; ibid. (15 November 1931), cols 1418–21; John G. Hervey, 'Advisory Opinions as an Obstacle to our Admission to the World Court', *Temple Law Quarterly* 6 (November 1931), 15–26.

33 *SIA* (1931) 61. Part IV of the *Survey* is a splendid introduction to events in East Asia.

34 Lape to Stimson, 28 October 1931: NA 500. C114/1365.

35 Christopher G. Thorne, *The Limits of Foreign Policy: the West, the League and the Far Eastern Crisis of 1931–1933* (London: Hamish Hamilton, 1972) maintains the fine historiographical tradition which began before World War II.

36 See the widely reported speeches of Roosevelt and Rogers, *NYT* (12 and 14 December 1931); and for Butler, *NYT* (21 February 1932), 13.

37 This is shown in the early study by Armin Rappaport, *Henry L. Stimson and Japan, 1931–1933* (Chicago: University of Chicago Press, 1963).

38 Alec Wilson, *The United States and the League* (London: Allen & Unwin, 1933), esp. 80–91.

39 Norman Rose, *Vansittart: Study of a Diplomat* (London: Heinemann, 1978), esp. 106–7, 126–7. Vansittart was Permanent Under Secretary at the British Foreign Office; and had served as Head of the American Department.

40 Raymond B. Fosdick, 'Our Foreign Policy in the Looking-Glass', *Atlantic Monthly* 148 (August 1931), 137–48; *United States in World Affairs,* 1931, ch. 14. This was the successor series to the Council on Foreign Relations, *Survey of American Foreign Relations*. It is cited below as *USWA*.

41 Moffat, *Diary*, 26 October 1931: Moffat Papers; minute of J. L. Dodds, 11 February 1932: FO 371, W1578/727/98; Fosdick to Root, 4 November 1931: Root Papers.

42 Colby to Hoover, 1 October 1931: Hoover Papers; circulars of Wickersham *et al.*, 11 August 1931 and 23 February 1932: copies in the Moore and Borchard Papers; Lape to Stimson, 14 December 1931; to Hornbeck, 20 January 1932: NA 662. 6331/312, 320: Hudson, 'The World Court and the Austro-German Customs Régime', *ABAJ* 17 (December 1931), 791–3; Jessup, 'The Customs Union Advisory Opinion', *AJIL* 26 (January 1932), 105–10; Davis, 'The World Court Settles the Question', *Atlantic Monthly* 149 (January 1932), 119–30.

43 Johnson, *Borah of Idaho*, 384; *NYT* (29 March 1931), I. 20; ibid. (18 October 1931), IV. 13; ibid. (21 November 1931), 9; ibid. (6 December 1931), 2; *CDT* (8 September 1931), 6; Borah in *Berliner Lokal-Anzeiger*, 25 December 1931: Borah Papers; Borah to Castle, 25 July 1931; Castle to US Legation, The Hague, 4 August 1931; to Borah, 21 August 1931: NA 662. 6331/265a, 266, 269; Borchard to Moore, 27 August 1931: Moore Papers.

44 *USD* (17 December 1931), 1; *NYT* (3 March 1932), 13; SCFR, *Proceedings*, 207–11.

45 *USD* (3 March 1932), 1; *NYT* (4 March 1932), 6; *NYT* (9 March 1932), 19; Reed to R. T. Rich (WPF), 1 June 1931: Hudson Papers; Stimson *Diary*, 25 January

and 25 May 1931: Stimson Papers; Stone to Moore, 5 and 24 March 1932; Moore to Walsh, 4 March 1932; to Stone, 25 March 1932: Moore Papers.

[46] SCFR, *Proceedings*, 211–13; *NYT* (17 March 1932), 7; *NYT* (24 March 1932), 1; *NYT* (7 April 1932), 1; *NYT* (14 April 1932), 17; Stimson, *Diary*, 8 March 1932: Stimson Papers; Moffat, *Diary*, 9 March 1932: Moffat Papers; Sir Ronald Lindsay (Washington) to Sir John Simon (Foreign Secretary), 3 March 1932; minutes of Dodds and Malkin, 15 March 1932: FO 371, W2983/727/98.

[47] Stimson to Borah, 22 March 1932: SCFR, *Proceedings*, 213–16; Stimson, *Diary*, 16 and 22 March 1932: Stimson Papers; Moffat, *Diary*, 16 and 28 March 1932: Moffat Papers; *NYT* (24 March 1932) 12.

[48] Memo of M. J. McDermott, 23 March 1932: NA 500. C114/1412; *NYT* (24 March 1932) 1, 12; minute of Beckett, 12 April 1932: FO 371, W3784/727/98; Moffat, *Diary*, 18 March 1932: Moffat Papers.

[49] SCFR, *Proceedings*, 218–42, esp. 222; *NYT* (7 April 1932), 1; *NYT* (13 April 1932), 17; Stimson, *Diary*, 22 and 24 March 1932: Stimson Papers; Moore to Myers, 6 April 1932; to Borchard, 27 April 1932: Moore Papers.

[50] Jessup to Hudson, 25 April 1932: Hudson Papers; SCFR, *Proceedings*, 236, 241.

[51] Stimson, *Diary*, 4 and 6 April 1932: Stimson Papers; Moffat, *Diary*, 23–27 March 1932: Moffat Papers; SCFR, *Proceedings*, 217, 238–43. The issues may be followed in the pages of the NWP's journal, *Equal Rights*, esp. 18 April 1932.

[52] *NYT* (23 March 1932), 14; *NYT* (7 April 1932), 1; *NYT* (14 April 1932), 17; Myers to Stimson, 19 March 1932; Memo of Field, 25 March 1932: NA 500. C114/1404, 1409.

[53] *NYT* (4 May 1932), 3; Lindsay to Simon, 14 April 1932: FO371, W4635/727/98; Broadsheet, 'Editors Urge the Foreign Relations Committee to Submit the Three World Court Protocols to the Senate': as enclosure, Lape to Hoover, 15 April 1932: Hoover Papers.

[54] SCFR, *Proceedings*, 243–4; *NYT* (12 May 1932), 10.

[55] SCFR, *Proceedings*, 245; *NYT* (13 May 1932), 6; Stimson, *Diary*, 20 June 1931: Stimson Papers; Philip C. Nash (Director, League of Nations Association) to Walter Lippmann, 2 June 1932: Lippmann Papers, Sterling Memorial Library, Yale; Jessup memo, 31 December 1931: Jessup Papers; Lape to Root, 30 July 1931: Root Papers.

[56] *NYT* (13 May 1932), 6; 'The Art of Delay', *NYT* (16 May 1932), 14.

[57] US Senate, Senate Report no. 758, Seventy-second Congress, First Session, *Touching Certain Protocols relating to the Permanent Court of International Justice* (Washington, DC: GPO, 1932), esp. 1–15; Walsh to Moore, 5 May 1931 and 4 March 1932; Borchard to Moore, 11 March 1932: Moore papers.

[58] The Walsh–Fess *Report* was covered in the *NYT* (2 June 1932), 22; *NYH-T* (2 June 1932), 8.

[59] Robert A. Brady, *Business as a System of Power* (New York: Columbia University Press, 1943); Ellis W. Hawley, *The New Deal and the Problem of Monopoly: a Study in Economic Ambivalence* (Princeton: Princeton University Press, 1966).

[60] The exception is Christer Olsson, *Congress and the Executive: the Making of United States Foreign Policy, 1933–1940.* Lund Studies in International History, no.16 (Solna: Scandanavian University Books, 1982).

[61] The literature is reviewed in Dunne, 'Isolation of a Kind', 337 ff.

[62] Lape to Root, 8 July 1932: Root Papers; Francis Bowes Sayre to Roosevelt, 13 October 1932: Sayre Papers, MD, LC. For Sayre, see ch. 8 below.

[63] *National Party Platforms*, 332. The Republicans were even more elusive: ibid., 345–6.

[64] *USWA* (1932), 159–65; Benjamin D. Rhodes, 'The Election of 1932 as Viewed from the British Embassy in Washington', *Presidential Studies Quarterly* 13 (Summer 1983), 453–7.

[65] Lape to Stimson, 3 June and 25 August 1932; memo of Pierre de Lagarde Boal (Chief: DWEA), 16 June 1932: NA 500. C114/1434-46: Lape to Jessup, 15 November 1932: Jessup Papers; Lape to Root, 7 June 1933: Root Papers.

[66] See *NYT* for the week 9-16 December 1932; Pittman to Moley, 18 January 1933: Kahn, 'Pressure Group influence', 62.

[67] NYT (2 February 1933), 3, 10; 'Burying the Dictator', *NYT* (24 February 1933), 16; Allan Nevins, 'Borah and World Politics', *Current History* 37 (February 1933), 513–19; Johnson to C. K. McClatchy, 5 June 1932; 8 January and 19 February 1933: Johnson Papers.

[68] Norris and La Follette swung back. Borah had never been very close: William Hard, 'Borah and '36 and Beyond', *Harper's Magazine* 172 (April 1936), 575–83. Cutting died in an air-crash in May 1935.

[69] Moffat to Hugh R. Gibson, 23 March 1933: Moffat Papers; cf. *Diary*, 17 March 1933: ibid; Borchard to Moore, 2 November 1932: Moore Papers; Borchard to Borah, 10 December 1934: Borchard Papers; William Phillips, *Diary*, 24 September and 20 December 1934: Phillips Papers; Root to Sweetser, 18 April 1935: Root Papers.

[70] P. G. Wright, 'The Bearing of Recent Tariff Legislation on International Relations', *American Economic Review* 23 (March 1933), 16–26; NYT (5 May 1934), 9; Ernest K. Lindley, *Half Way with Roosevelt* (New York: Viking Press, 1936), ch. 12; Allen W. Dulles and Hamilton Fish Armstrong, 'Legislating peace', *Foreign Affairs* 17 (October 1938), 1–12. Allen Dulles, brother of John Foster, was later Director of the CIA. The Progressive Senators disagreed over the Trade Agreements Programme, as the debates in *CR* 73:2 clearly show.

[71] Moffat to Norman H. Davis, 3 November 1934: Moffat Papers; Felix Morley to Sweetser, 1 July 1932: Sweetser Papers. The Morley Papers are in the Hoover Presidential Library, West Branch, Iowa. Morley's volume on the League is cited above, ch. 2, n. 11.

[72] Colby to Hoover, 1 October 1931: Hoover Papers; Nash to Root, 19 April 1931; Jessup to Root, 11 October 1932: Root Papers; Phillips, *Diary*, 8 January 1935: Phillips Papers.

[73] Moffat, *Diary*, 14 December 1934: Moffat Papers.

[74] This paragraph is corroborated by the memoirs of Roosevelt's Secretary of the Interior (and close friend of Hiram Johnson): Harold L. Ickes, *The Secret Diary of Harold Ickes*, 3 vols (New York: Simon & Schuster, 1953).

[75] Lape to Hull, 28 March 1933; Hull to Lape, 29 March 1933: NA 500. C114/1473; Lape to John W. Davis, 31 January 1933 and 13 January 1934: Davis Papers; Lape to Root, 10 and 24 April and 7 June 1933: Root Papers; Kahn, 'Pressure Group Influence', 85–6.

[76] Libby to Jessup, 23 May 1933; to Pittman, 24 May 1933; to Roosevelt, 26 May 1933; Hull to Robert Butler, 20 September 1933: NA 500. C114/1490–1506; *NYT* (28 March 1933), 2; *NYT* (30 March 1933), 2; *NYT* (5 April 1933), 5.

[77] Sayre to Hudson, 14 December 1933; Hudson to Sayre, 2 January 1934: NA 500. C114/1528a, 1531½; Jessup to Hudson, 10 February 1934: Hudson Papers; Phillips, *Diary*, 11 December 1933: Phillips Papers; Borchard to Borah, 13 April and 7 May, 1934: Borah Papers; *NYT* (5 January 1934), 16; *NYT* (7 January 1934), 29; *NYT* (12 January 1934), 25; *NYT* (29 January 1934), 16.

[78] Robinson to Roosevelt, 3 February 1934: Kahn, 'Pressure Group Influence', 105; Lape to Jessup, 3 and 12 January 1934; Jessup to Lippmann, 22 January

1934: Jessup Papers; Jessup to Root, 19 April 1934; Lape to Root, 1 May 1934: Root Papers.

79 Jessup to Hudson, 1 and 10 February 1934: Hudson Papers; Moffat, *Diary*, 22 March 1934: Moffat Papers.

80 Johnson to George Wharton Pepper, 19 and 24 March 1934; to Borchard, 16 April 1934: Johnson Papers; Jessup to Root, 24 March 1934: Jessup Papers; *NYT* (24 March 1934), 1, 9; *NYH-T* (24 March 1934), 4.

81 Johnson to Moore, 9 April 1934; to Borchard, 16 April 1934; to Borah, 23 April 1934: Johnson Papers; Moore to Borchard, 13 August 1932 and 29 April 1934; to Johnson, 17 April 1934; Borchard to Moore, 26 March and 6 April 1934: Moore Papers; Borchard to Borah, 5 April 1934: Borah Papers; Borchard to Johnson, 20 April 1934: Borchard Papers.

82 *NYT* (17 May 1934), 1, 17; *NYT* (18 May 1934), 1, 19; *NYT* (31 May 1934), 8; *NYH-T* (17 May 1934), 9. The Hearings were published in two parts: US Senate, *The World Court. Hearing before the Committee on Foreign Relations, United States Senate, Seventy-third Congress, Second Session, Relative to the Protocols concerning the Adherence of the United States to the Permanent Court of International Justice*, Part I, 23 March 1934; Part II, 16 May 1934 (Washington, DC: GPO, 1934).

8 Basic differences: the Senate, the Roosevelt administration and the Court defeat, 1934–35

The previous chapters may suggest that every aspect of American foreign policy during the interwar years was affected by the spectre of Geneva and that the Senate in particular was so paranoid that neither it nor the federal government as a whole had any constructive dealings with the League of Nations. Patently this was not so. Indeed, it was precisely the links and co-operation at the humanitarian level (as contemporaries described the League's work in areas such as narcotics and minority rights) that provided one argument for closer, political alignment, either through explicit provisions of the Covenant or by parallel, 'joint' action under such multilateral engagements as the Washington Treaties and the Kellogg–Briand Pact.[1] The question of American adherence to the Permanent Court of International Justice exemplifies this broader consideration; for the essential issue was whether membership would, from an American perspective, necessarily involve dangerous political relations or, in the alternative vision, hamper the Court's role in the League system. Yet an even sharper example was provided by the International Labour Organization, a branch of the League of Nations, which the United States formally joined in 1934 only months before the final Senate debate on the Court Protocols.

The massive congressional endorsement of American membership in the ILO is one clue to evaluating its true political significance. The House of Representatives approved the measure (H. J. Res. 368) by a comfortable 233 to 109 majority – only to be completely outdone by the

Senate, which passed its bill (S. J. Res. 131) on a voice vote with no dissenters. The ILO was purely an advisory body – a role emphasized by Congress in its traditional disclaimer of any obligations under the League Covenant. There were, of course, contemporaries who saw American membership in the ILO as a 'first step' which 'though neutral in itself, might lead still further' to full entry into the League; but historically the movement had been in a different direction. As Frank Walters, Felix Morley and other League authorities argued, since the establishment of the ILO in 1919 the 'separation' between the parent League and its anomalous offspring 'became wider'. If there was any doubt about this, the Roosevelt administration took great pains to follow congressional initiatives. (Even the notorious Lodge Reservations of 1919–20 envisaged membership in the ILO – conditional upon proper legislative action.) Roosevelt's Secretary of Labor, Frances Perkins, carefully consulted rather than led influential Senators; and the suspicions agitated by the contemporaneous drive for the Court were not even raised in the minds of Borah, Johnson and the anti-Leaguers. As Johnson himself commented: it was 'perfectly possible – in fact, a good idea – for the United States to adhere to this *one* organization'. It was his own emphasis and a crucial qualification.[2]

Where Johnson and his allies did detect a malign influence in the administration was in the Department of State. Culprits were rarely named; and when Secretary Hull was censured it was rather for his commercial policies than any concrete pro-League actions. The files of the Department are more revealing. They show Wallace McClure of the Treaty Division busily promoting League membership; attacking the Senate's treaty-making power; and so committed to ratification of the Court Protocols that he revived the discredited scheme of Kellogg's tenure and argued that the Signatories in both 1926 and 1929 had accepted the Senate's 1926 conditions *tout court* and President Roosevelt could therefore complete the ratification process without further ado.[3]

Francis Sayre, McClure's superior as Assistant Secretary of State, was another strong advocate of the Court, of the League, and of reining back the Senate (and Congress generally). He too had close links with the pro-League lobbyists. But the Department was not all of this mind. Under Secretary Phillips and DWEA Chief Moffat might have desired the ultimate goal; but this did not lead them to rash scheming. Assistant Secretary R. Walton Moore (once a Representative who had favoured adherence to the Court) moved closer to the thinking of Johnson in the Senate and John Bassett Moore and Edwin Borchard outside.[4] Lower down the hierarchy, officials in the key Office of the Solicitor and the Treaty Division successfully challenged the judicial reasoning and political judgment of Sayre and McClure. For example, Charles M. Barnes, Chief of the Treaty Division, summarized the objections to McClure's scheme for immediate ratification: it 'would be a very difficult if not wholly impracticable procedure'. As for McClure's alternative of a joint resolution, the Solicitor's Office cited Stimson's public repudiation of any congressional short-cut to displace and dishonour the Senate. For granted the joint resolution method had been used 'on numerous occasions', never had such 'legislation… been invoked to accomplish a matter… dealt with in a treaty *pending* in the Senate.' [Emphasis in original.][5]

Such was the setting in mid-September 1934 when Assistant Secretaries Sayre and Moore travelled out of Washington to the President's private home in Hyde Park, New York, for consultations on the Court Protocols. It was the usual story. Roosevelt gave nothing away. He said the Moses Reservation must go; but this was nothing new: it was the position of all the pro-Court lobby groups. More importantly, the consultation showed that the Department had not been working with Senator Pittman, Chairman of the Committee on Foreign Relations.[6] The significance of this would soon emerge.

Less than two months after the Hyde Park conference the mid-term national elections were held. For the first time since 1906 the incumbent party had gained seats – and huge numbers at that. It was, said William Phillips with some justifiable exaggeration, unprecedented. The results seemed a personal triumph for Roosevelt. An 'impressive victory', Hearst telegraphed: a magnificent 'popular endorsement'. Hiram Johnson agreed: and he sent his congratulations – another sign of their basic good-will in the early 1930s. Congratulations also came from Libby of the NCPW: the President could now smash Hearst, who provided the main opposition to the Court.[7] Historians seem to have fallen for Libby's way of thinking: The momentum was behind ratification; Roosevelt was poised to commit himself; the ratification process was set in train – but then failed, defeated by the propaganda of the Hearst press and its allies inside and outside the Senate.

In fact the situation was more complex, even in congressional terms. Certainly the Democrats nominally controlled the Senate: in the Seventy-fourth Congress there would be sixty-nine Democrats to twenty-five Republicans, plus one Farmer-Laborite and one Progressive. (In the House of Representatives the imbalance was even greater, with the Democrats holding more than three-quarters of the seats.) But party discipline was notoriously weak in the Senate, as the Minority leader Joe Robinson and Vice–President Garner well knew. Each deplored the prospect of working with a 'top-heavy' Democratic majority inclined 'to do some reckless things'. Political commentators phrased the same problem differently when they identified a plethora of groupings running across the political spectrum which more accurately reflected potential voting patterns than simple partisan alignments of Democrats and Republicans. More specifically, the insurgent coalition which had helped and led the Roosevelt administration with many so-called New Deal measures in the Seventy-third Congress was now seen to be reforming against the alleged abuses of this same New Deal. In this group were Johnson, Wheeler of Montana, the rapidly rising Cutting of New Mexico, Norris of Nebraska – and Borah, once again being tipped to run for the presidency and reckoned by some to command a national following even more broadly based than Roosevelt's.[9]

One of the chief complaints of this group was 'Farleyism', by which they meant the attempt of Jim Farley to claim all credit for his style and all patronage for his faction. It was a grievance held by many Democrats, conservative as well as progressive. If the Protocols were made an administration 'must', this kind of leadership might backfire. It was a risk recognized by Farley himself, who argued against Senate action and deplored any White House involvement if it took place.[10]

Within days of the elections officers in the Department of State began work on a draft resolution of adherence for use in the forthcoming Senate debate. Sayre was the most animated; his junior, McClure, was active but less visible; and Hull as usual stayed aloof.[11] The preparations were themselves remarkable for their deviousness. Ignorance could surely not explain the almost total neglect of the Austro-German Customs Union case and its political significance in a departmental memorandum on the history of the Court Protocols since Root's January 1931 testimony. As for the Department's proposed draft resolution there were other omissions and significant deviations from the terms reported by Senators Walsh and Fess in June 1932. These changes were quite deliberate. Sayre himself took responsibility for urging the President to consent to the deletion of the 'Monroe Doctrine proviso' (Paragraph VIII in 1926) and the reservation requiring senatorial consent to judicial referrals (Paragraph VII). Roosevelt did not dissent.[12]

Sayre was, of course, correct in arguing that Paragraph VIII would encounter opposition from Latin American States and thereby threaten to abort the ratification process. But it was surely worth raising the equally indisputable counter-argument that the Senate had unanimously agreed to the reservation in 1926 – as had the Foreign Relations Committee in 1932. Moreover, the Monroe Doctrine was not the only reserved topic in Paragraph VIII: immigration and the tariff were implicity covered. More troublesome still, to delete this reservation meant interpreting the 1932 Democratic platform to refer to the 1929 Protocols. This logic was reinforced by the deletion of Paragraph VII on the treaty-making power. Sayre justified his proposal on the grounds that the reservation had 'no legal effect', since the United States would not be subject to the Court's compulsory jurisdiction. The last point was true but completely irrelevant. Sayre's aim was rather to rein back the Senate. That Roosevelt offered no objection to Sayre's rationale was a mark of either complete ignorance or unruffled complacency on the Court issue. (Of course, Roosevelt had other political matters on his mind, as those close to him knew; but his present attitude goes some way to qualifying the belief in Roosevelt's wizardry.)[13]

Little if anything was said, apparently, between Sayre and Roosevelt about the Moses Reservation (Paragraph VI) or the Reed Understanding – though Sayre and his departmental colleagues were set on deleting the first and redrafting the latter. (It will be remembered that the Moses Reservation had been re-introduced in 1932 to make the Reed Understanding, renewing the veto on the advisory jurisdiction, binding on the signatory States.) The silence corroborates a picture of a devious Sayre and an ignorant or neglectful Roosevelt. Or rather a picture of a selectively careless Roosevelt.[14] For without mentioning the principle of Pittman's attachment to the 1926 and 1932 terms, Roosevelt again impressed upon Sayre that Pittman had to be consulted.

Assistant Secretary Moore was not entirely happy with events. He expressed his doubts about the policy of adherence, the opportuneness of the moment and the specific terms he and Sayre had presented to Roosevelt. William Phillips and Pierrepont Moffat were roughly the centre to the poles of Sayre and Moore. With lesser expectations about the results of adherence they both agreed that the Senate would approve a resolution consenting to ratification.[15] Sayre's meeting with Pittman would tell a different story.

Sayre met Pittman on Wednesday, 2 January 1935, the very eve of the new, Seventy-fourth Congress. In a favourite phrase of his, Sayre reported that Roosevelt wanted 'clean-cut adherence', which meant the elimination of 'the restrictive provisions... attached to the resolution' reported by Senators Walsh and Fess. Sayre chose to keep quiet about Roosevelt's agreement to removing Paragraphs VII and VIII; and he concentrated his energies on persuading Pittman to accept an amendment to the Reed Understanding and the deletion of the Moses Reservation.

Sayre was successful on the Reed Understanding. He got Pittman to agree that it should read 'over an objection by the United States', in place of 'without the consent of the United States'. In Sayre's argument it was unnecessary and burdensome to involve the United States in approving every League reference for an advisory opinion. It was sufficient that the ultimate power to object remained with the United States. Pittman conceded: he offered no resistance to the 'change... in the phraseology of this provision'.

On the Moses Reservation, however, Pittman was adamant. It was 'desirable' as a means of preserving the substance of the original Paragraph V on the advisory jurisidiction, to which he was personally 'committed in writing and in debate'. If the Moses Reservation were removed, Pittman commented, 'it would weaken [*the*] possibility of securing favorable action'. Pittman continued in this vein, overcoming his earlier reluctance to forecast the prospects of a two-thirds majority. He was a 'friendly neutral', yet he would resist any erosion of Paragraphs V and VI. The majority on the Committee might approve such changes and report them to the Senate; but 'at least four strong Senators' on the Committee would not desist: Borah, Johnson, La Follette and Shipstead. There would be a 'bitter fight'; and if the proponents were split over the terms, then these four Senators 'would have a good opportunity to pick up other recruits'. For all these reasons he thought it better that Senator Joe Robinson should manage the Protocols in Committee and on the floor.[16]

Even in the impersonal record of the Department of State, Pittman's annoyance at his neglect comes across; so too his aversion to the tactics of the Department and his belief that Roosevelt would eventually suffer. (Contemporaneously Under Secretary Phillips recorded his own dissatisfaction with the unco-ordinated workings of the Department, especially the direct access of Assistant Secretary Sayre to the President.) Two days after the interview with Sayre, Pittman wrote at length to Roosevelt explaining his position. He felt deep 'regret' at appearing to abandon the administration, for nothing would have given him 'more pleasure' than helping in the ratification of the Protocols. It was an 'unfortunate situation' and the prospects were even gloomier; for the 'failure to yield to the adoption of reservations that some of [the] leading Senators deem[ed] essential to the protection of the interest of the United States' would inevitably lead to the defeat of the Protocols.[17]

The day following Pittman's private letter to Roosevelt, the two men were in conference at the White House along with Hull, Sayre and Robinson. Now Robinson's assumption of the legislative task was made public; but perhaps the more striking feature was the determination he shared with Pittman to shelter Roosevelt from any criticism that he was promoting adherence. For once the editors of the *New York Times* were correct, their correspondents wrong. A story now appeared saying Roosevelt had pushed for adherence in the previous year; a few days later an editorial gave a more accurate account of Roosevelt's ambivalence and scheming.[18]

It had been a long conference; and Robinson was tactfully reticent. He predicted a favourable report from the Committee on Foreign Relations; but he offered no forecasts about the date or result of a final Senate vote. The pro-Court press was less restrained, and spoke of a general confidence that victory was assured. Inside and outside the Department of State pro-Leaguers were arguing that the logical progression was full membership in the League itself. Indeed the impetuous McClure suggested bypassing the Court – as he had once urged bypassing the Senate – and going directly for American membership of the League. However, opponents such as Borah and Johnson were not unduly troubled by such fantasies. In their calculations, such a clear indentification of the Court with the League system could only weaken the chances of senatorial approval.[19]

During the tenure of Secretaries Hughes, Kellogg and Stimson the Department of State had never guided the direction and details of Senate debate and action. Truly had the Executive proposed and the Senate disposed. Now the Department in the persons of Sayre and McClure provided Robinson with all the arguments and material they could.[20] Here was one piece of evidence, private though it was, of the developing partisanship in the process towards ratification. Granted that the senatorial Democrats had always shown more numbers for ratification than senatorial Republicans, this came about from the split within the Republicans. (After all, the history from 1923 to 1933 was of Republican Executives trying to work through a Committee led first by Lodge and then by Borah.) The situation had now altered: in advance of the first Committee meeting in the new Congress Robinson received lengthy and complex arguments in support of a resolution of adherence deleting Paragraphs VI, VII and VIII from the 1926 and 1932 terms and modifying Paragraph V in the manner suggested by Sayre to Pittman. The result of these changes was to seek the Senate's agreement to the ratification of the three Protocols signed in December 1929 and then submitted by Hoover in December 1930 (namely the Protocol of Signature of 1920 and the Accession and Revision Protocols of 1929), subject to the

> clear understanding of the United States that the Permanent Court of International Justice shall not, over an objection by the United States, entertain any request for an advisory opinion touching any dispute or question in which the United States has or claims an interest.[21]

Robinson's prediction of the Committee's action was correct. At its first business meeting on Wednesday 9 January the State Department's draft resolution of adherence was approved 14:7. Chester H. Rowell, a pro-Court Californian journalist hostile to Johnson, forecast that the neat two-thirds majority would be paralleled in the full Senate. Under Secretary Phillips also believed adherence was now assured; the British Ambassador, Sir Ronald Lindsay, thought as much. But Lindsay also saw that there could be problems. Like a number of pro-Court newspapers, he realized that the vote tended to obscure what the well-informed *Christian Science Monitor* described as a 'solid nucleus of opposition'.[22]

On one issue there was no dissent. Robinson and Pittman agreed with Johnson and Borah that the force of Paragraph V remained undiminished in the new draft. In Robinson's phrase: 'the legal import and effect of the original Reservation V has been preserved in full'. Johnson's variation was to say the Committee had unanimously 'reaffirmed the Senate's fifth reservation'. The 'solid nucleus' was revealed by the votes on unsuccessful motions to restore Paragraphs VII and VIII. Johnson moved to repeat Paragraph VII and gained eight supporters, including Capper and Vandenberg, both proponents of adherence. Vandenberg's own submission of Paragraph VIII confirmed the pattern: nine Senators favoured re-incorporation. This was strong evidence that the non-Democrats on the Committee would lead a senatorial attack on terms dictated by the administration. It is an inference corroborated by the voting on a motion submitted by Lewis. Its substance conformed to Paragraph VIII but the wording was different. It was defeated 15:5, Vandenberg and Capper (as might be expected) voting Nay – as did Borah (remaining faithful to 1926). The encouraging signs for the opposition were the votes of Cutting (now classed as an independent Republican) and the respective abstention and absence of two Democrats, the freshman James E. Murray from Montana and George of Georgia.[23]

Vandenberg gave immediate notice that he would resubmit Paragraph VIII during debate on the floor. The press reported that his action could be disruptive; and within days Secretary Hull was strongly urging Vandenberg to desist. Even so, like Assistant Secretary Sayre, Hull tried to conceal from colleagues the important divisions which had been revealed in the Committee proceedings. President Roosevelt (whom Sayre was protecting from unpleasant news) still managed to give the appearance of uninterest rather than disinterest; but privately he was telling Hudson that the final vote would 'be pretty close'. Assistant Secretary Moore used very similar language in writing to Ham Holt.

Even the normally optimistic Hudson was somewhat cautious. A number of newspapers were equally restrained and even admitted the possibility of failure. Other press sources wrote of 'apathy' and 'indifference' and predicted success for a measure borne along with 'passive acquiescence' rather than promoted by 'informed sponsorship'. And this was the language and perspective of the leading pro-Court press. In the background and setting the tone of the Senate debate were lobbyists such as the National Council for Prevention of War and the Women's World Court Committee calling for membership of the League after the ratification of the Court Protocols.[24]

The restrained and sometimes pessimistic forecasts in even the pro-Court press help us to resist the weight of the historiography drawn in terms of a propaganda victory for the opponents of adherence. Of course, public expressions of confidence can be found: Senator Charles McNary of Oregon, the Minority leader, spoke in these terms; his fellow Republican but opponent on the Court issue, Johnson, conceded the grounds for McNary's optimism in his own public and private denunciations of the 'increased propaganda' behind the drive *for* ratification. In truth, the situation seems more finely balanced than historians have argued. After all, Borah did not share Johnson's depressed forebodings; and he was not the only opponent to believe the votes existed to defeat ratification.[25]

This may appear paradoxical in the light of the many surveys showing an overwhelming majority of the Senators to favour adherence – surveys publicly available at the time in aggregate form and some later printed in detail. As on previous occasions, however, such surveys were not faultless. For example: on the question of strict accuracy in recording the position of individuals, even the most long-serving lobbyists could make mistakes. Likewise, the polls were not unambiguous. Thus even polls which showed up to seventy – perhaps more than eighty – Senators favouring ratification did not specify the precise conditions acceptable to these large numbers. Since Pittman and then Vandenberg, self-declared friends of adherence, had parted from the administration over the terms of the draft resolution, this factor was going to be crucial. A final consideration lies in the politics of publishing surveys: the larger the total registered as proponents the more likely would waverers and a cautious administration follow the crowd. It was a point obliquely made by editors and reporters in the pro-Court press.[26]

The draft resolution approved by the Committee on Foreign Relations was formally reported to the Senate by Robinson on Thursday 10 January. Immediately Vandenberg submitted a motion to restore Paragraph VIII; but full debate did not begin until Tuesday, 15 January, when Robinson himself delivered the opening speech. The press assessments of senatorial and public indifference were belied by reports of crowds on the chamber floor and in the galleries. Moreover, there were already some omens apart from Vandenberg's persistence. Senator Thomas P. Gore (Oklahoma, Democrat) published his intention to make ratification dependent on the resumption of war-debts payments. Gore's reservation was a specific application of the Johnson Act, which Hiram Johnson had sponsored in the previous Session 'to prohibit financial transactions with any foreign government in default on its obligations to the United States'. As such the Gore reservation tapped a reservoir of bipartisan support, particularly with maverick Democrats, and it constituted one of the first signs of a profound split within the nominal supporters of the administration.[27]

Joe Robinson of Arkansas was not known as a great orator or persuasive debater – though he fancied himself as a lawyer. (His ambitions had now apparently switched to a high judicial post: either on the US Supreme Court or perhaps even on the World Court, with Kellogg eager to resign and an American judgeship for the asking.)[28] Robinson began his case to the full Senate by insisting that adherence was a plank in both the Democratic and Republican platforms of 1932. It was an unwise reminder, given his sponsorship of a resolution which deviated from the terms implicitly endorsed by both parties. Partly to meet this objection Robinson claimed that the 1929 Protocols and the new draft confirmed the 'exact language' of Paragraph V on the advisory jurisdiction. This was both untrue and an encouragement to the opponents and undecided to repeat the text of 1926 *verbatim*. Finally, rebutting all allegations and resisting all invitations, Robinson denied the United States was moving closer to the League. Certainly the Court was already open for use by his country; but he feared the slanderous charge of 'sponger' if the United States government availed itself of the Court's facilities without contributing to its finances. (The Department of State estimated the annual cost between $40,000 and $70,000.) Financial obligations, indeed, were the only obligations assumed by the United States through adherence. On the credit side they would participate in the election of judges and share more directly in the development of the Court's jurisprudence and practice.[29]

Hiram Johnson led for the opposition on the following day, Wednesday 16 January. The floor and galleries were filled to hear Johnson; and he did not disappoint. Press reporters favourably compared the vigour and range of his speech to those he delivered in the Irreconcilables' campaign of 1919–20. This was his task: not to tackle the details of the proposition's case but rather to mount the broad indictment of the 'League of Nations Court'. Even when Johnson mentioned the controversy surrounding the Austro-German Customs Union Opinion his references were general: the sustained and close-reasoned prosecution would be conducted by his ally Borah. If there was a novel element in Johnson's speech it lay in his denunciation of the State Department for striking out three of the conditions set by the Senate in 1926. As he reminded his audience, until that month the one contentious area had been the advisory jurisdiction; now a struggle had been arranged between the Senate and the Executive.[30]

Johnson did not include Roosevelt in his public rebuke. He had, after all, stayed out of the fight, as Pittman and Robinson had advised; and throughout the Senate debate Johnson and Roosevelt remained on good personal terms. But on the day Johnson spoke Roosevelt committed his prestige to the cause of adherence. In a message drafted by Sayre, Roosevelt called on the Senate to ignore 'partisan considerations' while implying it should not append reservations opposed by the Democratic leadership. Whatever the logic of Roosevelt's invoking party platforms only to reject their content, press commentators were convinced his intervention was a sure sign of success. If the outcome had been in doubt, Roosevelt would have continued to stay aloof.[31] With little if any emotional or ideological interest in the Court, Roosevelt was now placing an apparently safe bet on Robinson's leadership in anticipation of recovering political capital for later legislative and patronage struggles. However, this favourable prediction was not the whole story. Before Johnson spoke proponents were quoted as believing the final vote lay only days ahead; afterwards Robinson talked in terms of two to three weeks of debate. And there was also a powerful argument from silence. Vice-President Garner studiously avoided taking the Senate chair throughout the debate: a reminder to his cabinet colleagues that he had predicted trouble and was convinced public opinion opposed adherence.[32]

Yet delay might not necessarily favour the opposition. For example, on the day following Johnson's speech and Roosevelt's message Senator Huey P. Long (Louisiana, Democrat) delivered a three-hour harangue against the League, the Court, Standard Oil, the Rockefeller interests in general – all foreign and domestic enemies of ordinary American citizens. Historians are apt to speak of Long's irrationalism and demagoguery. They imply that Long's frequent diatribes won, even forced votes for the opposition. In fact contemporary reports suggested Long's contributions were counter-productive, raising the spectre of a filibuster and thereby alienating independent and open-minded Senators. Yet whether Long's speeches were rational or irrational (Borchard and Moore knew Long was nobody's fool), their manner and context were decidedly important.[33] Long was not beholden to Roosevelt or to conservative Southern leaders such as Robinson, Pat Harrison of Mississippi and Carter Glass of Virginia; he touched a strong Populist, anti-establishment vein in Southern Democratic politics; many of his criticisms of Farleyism were shared by Northern Senators, Republicans and Progressives no less than Democrats; and he was known to be part of a strange but potentially powerful coalition for the 1936 elections – a coalition which included Borah and Cutting inside the Senate and men like Fr Coughlin and Dr Townsend outside.[34]

A less dramatic but more important event of this first Thursday of debate was Norris's submission of an amendment along the lines of Paragraph VII, but one couched in terms requiring senatorial approval of each single American reference to the Court. Historians who neglect Norris's action have the excuse that a number of usually acute observers were also remiss. But those commentators who did record the event stressed its significance: it was already clear that certain leading proponents of adherence were seriously at odds with Robinson and the Department of State.[35] The next day's debate on the Vandenberg amendment would confirm this interpretation.

As we mentioned earlier, Arthur Vandenberg's attempt during Committee to restore Paragraph VIII had been resisted by Robinson and later by Hull. All Vandenberg's previous actions no less than his current correspondence with Elihu Root showed him to be in favour of adherence – but only on the terms set in 1926. Vandenberg appeared shocked, even outraged, that the administration was dictating to the Senate, especially when its

> refusal to define and re-assert [the 1926 terms] invites the highly unfortunate implication that in some unknown way our American status is changed by the pending formula [for ratification].

As Vandenberg put it to Hull, Root and his senatorial colleagues: either there was a 'contradiction' between his belief that the Signatories had accepted the Senate's 1926 terms and the substantive reality; in this case the repetition of Paragraph VIII was 'vitally necessary'. Or, alternatively, there was no 'contradiction'; in that case, 'the only reason for rejection would be that it is needless surplusage'.[36]

Secretary Hull, with help from Robinson and Sayre, tried to turn this argument: to restate 'such an encumbering and unnecessary provision… could only have the effect of misleading the public in an irresponsible manner'. In other words (Hull was saying), to repeat Paragraph VIII would suggest that the 1926 reservation had indeed been weakened – and nothing could be further from the truth. On the contrary, Hull informed Vandenberg:

> without this provision we are left free to determine our policies as the circumstances may dictate and … we would acquire nothing by its inclusion except potential ill-will and embarrassment.

This last was a serious consideration, for Hull was alluding to the veto power of disgruntled and despised South American States. But Paragraph VIII embraced more than the Monroe Doctrine: and the curtness of Hull's response to a genuine advocate of adherence showed his notorious closeness even towards former colleagues, his lack of confidence and his unfamiliarity with the legislative history of the Court Protocols. After all, as Vandenberg had reminded Hull, Swanson and Walsh had both sponsored the reservation, first in 1926 and later in 1932.[37]

The first Friday of debate was highly significant. Vandenberg spoke for an influential group of pro-Court Republican Senators: Austin of Vermont; Barbour of New Jersey; Capper of Kansas; Couzens of Michigan; Hale of Maine; Keyes of New Hampshire; and McNary and Steiwer of Oregon. As we shall see, these men would oppose ratification on terms simply dictated by the Democratic administration. Though after Vandenberg spoke the proponents tried to wrest the initiative from the outright opponents, even this counter-attack had its weakness. First, all the speakers were Democrats: King of Utah, Logan of Kentucky and Pope of Idaho. Only King had any claims to seniority; while Pope was well known as a firm and vociferous advocate of American membership of the League – generally a taboo subject in the speeches of the proponents. More specifically, Pope was prominent in the campaign for the use of a congressional joint resolution to effect adherence and was contemporaneously arguing that entry into the Court logically required entry into the League.[38] But even if advocates of the Court were to rely on the strength of a purely partisan vote directed by the Democratic senatorial leadership their chances were faint: Ham Lewis, the Majority whip, used this Friday to restate his total opposition to adherence.[39]

The end of the first week of debate had been reached. Now the pro-Court lobbyists were less confident of success. The number of Senators estimated to favour adherence had fallen below two-thirds of the whole Senate. Individuals were singled out for direct canvassing – even for threatening. The freshman Democratic Senator from Ohio, Vic Donahey, was one candidate for political pressure.[40] Philip Jessup, always more circumspect than some of his fellow-campaigners, urged Manley Hudson to use his influence with the Department of State and the White House to re-insert Paragraphs VII and VIII for fear the whole resolution would fail. Hudson responded with qualifications. He thought the proposed Norris amendment 'most unfortunate' but nevertheless he acted, channelling his own petition through Jessup's mentor, Elihu Root. The public and private evidence is overwhelming: by the end of the first week of debate a two-thirds majority for the resolution sponsored by Robinson was far from assured.[41]

The Senate floor and galleries were crowded on Monday, 21 January as Borah delivered the main speech for the opposition. Here was the great orator and constitutionalist, the popular heir to Daniel Webster; and the public and congressional colleagues packed in to listen[42] Historians have prided themselves on seeing beneath Borah's rhetoric. The tradition had been established that Borah either bemused Senators with his verbal tricks or bored them into submission with stale arguments.[43] But in this historiography the accusers match the accused: no analysis is offered of Borah's case, least of all why such specious yet trite arguments should be so effective.

Johnson had already promised that the task of examining and interpreting the Austro-German Customs Union case would fall to Borah. It was an obvious choice, for that advisory opinion still remained the most contentious ever delivered by the Court. But Borah's method was idiosyncratic, one addressed to an American audience. He did not stress the legal wrong done to Austria and Germany in 1931; he did not even hark back insistently to the political wrong done to these States in 1919. Rather Borah developed concretely the argument he had used somewhat hypothetically and abstractly before the Senate vote of 1926. This argument turned on the dangers of the advisory jurisdiction for the United States. It would entangle the United States in the politics of the League, bringing the obligations of the covenant but none of its rights, notably a veto in the deliberations of the Council.

It was easy for Borah to prove the strong contemporary pressure for the United States to join the League; easy to cite examples of the call for armed sanctions to enforce the Court's decisions; easy to show the demands that the United States join with co-signatories of the Kellogg – Briand Pact in resisting 'aggressors'. Court historians have dismissed such charges as paranoia – and thus equally devalued the efforts of the self-styled internationalists and many in the heterogeneous peace-movement to align the United States with the League and then enter its ranks. Somewhat less surprising has been the widespread historiographical failure to analyse the policies and politics of the League and the so-called peace-loving Western democracies in the years since 1931. (Certainly Sweetser and Root were unable to state concretely what the League was in 1935 and both had recourse to speaking of the League 'ideal'.) Borah, however, could not be faulted: a major theme of his lengthy speech was condemnation and substantiation of the deviousness and hypocrisy of great power politics, including British and French complaisancy to Italian expansion in Africa and the shifts and turns which (as we now know) would lead to the Stresa Front of April 1935 – to be followed by the Anglo-German Naval Agreement in June of the same year.

Borah did not neglect, of course, a detailed critique of the Customs Union Opinion. Only Robinson tried to refute Borah's argument, with a brief drafted by Manley Hudson; but it was an uphill struggle. Many friends of the Court had deplored the political complexion of the decision; while those who favoured its substance did so largely on pro-League grounds that Robinson was reluctant to maintain. Even so, Borah's jurisprudential and political case against the Court and the League was familiar whatever his particular effectiveness on this Monday. Possibly more influential upon the outcome of the debate were events off the floor of the Senate. In the press it was rumoured that the administration, 'sensing the possibility of defeat', was about to concede on the Vandenberg Reservation (Paragraph VIII) – but not on that of Norris (a version of Paragraph VII).[45]

The rumours were correct. On Tuesday, 22 January, Vandenberg and Norris went to the White House and Roosevelt made the partial concession. But his public admission was ungracious. At his weekly press conference the next day, Wednesday, Roosevelt made a disingenuous attempt to suggest he did not know, let alone understand, Vandenberg's reservation – a clear sign he was unwilling to acknowledge that the administration had retracted. At the same time Roosevelt 'singled out' and attacked Norris's amendment as an encroachment upon the Executive's prerogatives in the conduct of foreign relations.[46] Clearly the administration was now trying to win the initiative. Behind the scenes Roosevelt took seriously the advice of his wife and Esther Lape to pressure individual Senators. On the public level Sayre worked with Robinson on Capitol Hill to co-ordinate strategy while Robinson worked with Eleanor Roosevelt to channel the massive lobbying of the Conference on the Cause and Cure of War, which was assembled in Washington. On this Tuesday and Wednesday the proponents took over the Senate floor, with speeches from three Democrats: Joe Robinson himself, Josiah W. Bailey of North Carolina and Elbert D. Thomas of Utah, the latter providing the clearest, most powerful statement of the pro-League case during the debate.[47]

Robinson's confidence, however, appeared to be slipping. He wanted an early vote, not least because the retraction on the Vandenberg Reservation had weakened the argument of principle against any modification of the draft resolution reported from the Committee earlier in the month. This was the debit to be set against any possible gains won by re-incorporating Paragraph VIII. And the move was underway for a complete restatement of 1926. Senator Davis of Pennsylvania (who had served in the cabinets of Harding, Coolidge and Hoover as Secretary of Labor) publicized a letter from George Wharton Pepper calling for the total repetition of the 1926 conditions.[48] The argument of Pepper, followed by Davis and developed by Henrik Shipstead in a brilliant, wide-ranging speech, was that the campaign for League membership was even stronger though more covert than in 1926. At the same time the Executive was bent upon an unprecedented policy of shackling the Senate, as the opposition to the Norris reservation proved. Irresponsible government was being increased at home while dangerous meddling was being encouraged abroad. The twin evils of Wilsonianism were once again powerful in Washington and only independently minded Senators could withstand the attack. Shipstead's polemic had, moreover, an even greater resonance; for he was the first to express the bitterness of those Senators under threat from the Democratic party establishment for not toeing the New Deal line and challenging the Roosevelt-Farley patronage system[49]

This Thursday, 24 January, marked the close of the second stage of the Senate's debate. Davis's use of Pepper's letter pointed to an increasing number of regular Republicans bridling at the Democratic administration's partisan handling of the Court Protocols. Shipstead's speech showed the insurgent, radical critique against the politics of the League to be as alive as ever; while the localism of domestic politics had been introduced in a Senate–Executive conflict. On the other side the Democratic proponents of adherence lacked the courage of their 1925–6 predecessors and with few exceptions did not openly advocate League membership or even praise its purposes. Outside the Senate the pro-Court lobbyists were making these connections, with the result that most of the pro-Court Senators (barring Vandenberg) looked naïve or deceitful.[50] In procedural terms this Thursday was also important. Johnson (acting as floor-leader for the opposition) agreed with Robinson that a guillotine should operate from the following Monday. But entangled in the timetable agreement were matters of substance. Vandenberg's motion to re-insert Paragraph VIII was accepted by Robinson and approved unanimously; while the next day, Friday, 25 January, was set aside for debate on Norris's amendment.[51] Clearly both sides intended to use the weekend for canvassing; less sure was the balance of votes. But one pro-Court paper now reported that the opposition was 'confident' of defeating the Protocols, 'despite aggressive administration pressure for the Court'.[52]

George W. Norris was the sole survivor in the Senate of the six members who had voted against the declaration of war in April 1917. Then his opposition had been based on the conviction that the Wilson administration had perverted the United States' neutrality policy by making impossible demands of the German government while conniving at British abuses of American rights and the general principles of international law. In January 1935 Norris was still influenced by those events. He insisted that his proposed amendment was not meant as an 'affront' to the office of the presidency nor was it inspired by personal antipathy. Certainly it was not designed, as Roosevelt had charged in his press conference, as a 'definite limitation of the Constitutional prerogatives of the Executive'. Rather it sought to maintain a proper senatorial check upon the enormous power of the Executive to embroil the United States in controversies and wars. The lesson of 1914–17 was the need for statutory congressional constraints upon the Executive; not because laws would guarantee peace or even wise policies, but simply because the number of participants involved would tend to inhibit emotional or partisan responses. A second and shorter set of reasons also prompted Norris to submit his reservation. The principle of senatorial involvement had not been challenged by the League in 1926 or 1929; and to abandon that principle now would impugn the good faith of the Court Signatories in acknowledging the constitutional imperatives of the United States.[53]

Norris's speech was short and gently phrased. He gave the benefit of the doubt to Roosevelt, despite Roosevelt's public intransigence; he spoke appreciatively of the Signatories, though we know there was impatience with American diplomatic practice; he had, of course, voted for adherence in January 1926 – the only Irreconcilable to do so. However Norris had indeed become increasingly worried by Executive attempts to limit senatorial prerogatives.[54] Other Senators were more outspoken than Norris. Vandenberg saw no reason why his success in rescuing a traditional principle should be bartered for one equally venerable and vital. Two other Republicans, Steiwer of Oregon and Wallace H. White of Maine joined in with appeals to the terms passed in 1926 and 1932 – both omitting to mention the changes in Norris's phrasing. The changes were not accidental: Norris's supporters had detected a 'loophole' in Paragraph VII which allowed references to the Court 'through general… treaties' rather than specific agreements covering a defined and single 'dispute or question'.[55]

Robinson could see the 1926 terms being reintroduced completely; but his response was strangely provocative. (After all, as Root reminded Roosevelt, the original Paragraph VII had a long tradition and had been sponsored by Senators Swanson and Walsh as the price of Southern Democratic support.) Robinson went on the offensive. If passed, he warned the Senate, the new Norris version would destroy 'the wholesome aim of the adherence resolution' by repeating the 'erroneous' and 'subversive' prerogative contained in Paragraph VII. Johnson was incensed: he retorted that Norris's reservation

simply preserves the prestige and the honor and the tradition of the American Senate. Why should we legislate the Senate out of the right to pass upon what is substantially a treaty and say we will delegate it to some other power or to some other individual?[56]

At his press conference two days previously Roosevelt had acknowledged that there were 'basic differences' between the terms set in 1926 and still favoured by the 'Senate Progressives' and those sponsored by his administration. It was now obvious that the crucial difference was not the advisory jurisdiction (covered in Paragraph V and the rephrased Reed Understanding) but rather the determination of the White House and Department of State to reduce senatorial participation in the conduct of foreign relations. Newspaper correspondents close to these Progressives and the White House realized the significance of the split. A week before Norris's speech William K. Hutchinson predicted that administration resistance to Norris's reservation would be opposed even by a sizeable number of Democrats, such was Norris's 'tremendous influence' in the Senate. Hutchinson was correct. In an atmosphere of great bitterness Norris's reservation was put to the vote, the first of the debate. It was defeated 47:37.[57]

The vote registered a skewed form of partisanship, whereby the administration was able to dictate to a majority of the Democrats (and even to an outright opponent of adherence: Lewis) and so win a majority in the roll-call; conversely, the non-Democrats (with the exception of Keyes of New Hampshire) united behind Norris and were joined by fifteen Democrats. The alignments on Norris's reservation suggested that Robinson and Roosevelt might have the numbers to enforce the terms of the resolution; but they could not, thereby, guarantee a two-thirds majority for passage of the completed resolution. On the contrary, the terms they specified might make rejection all the more probable.[58]

With the vote taken on the Norris Reservation Senators moved to other legislative business. Before they resumed debate on Monday under the terms of the guillotine agreed by Robinson and Johnson the notorious weekend of propaganda intervened. The historiography of this weekend is remarkable not simply for its volume and repetitiousness but also for its selectivity and inconclusiveness. A full exposure of its shortcomings cannot be given here: but some preliminary counterpoints can be established. First, it must be stressed that both sides in the Court debate took to the radio, campaigned through the press, mounted personal lobbies and petitioned individual Senators. In the words of the *San Francisco Chronicle*, a pro-Court paper: friends and foes of adherence both 'bludgeoned' the Senate with arguments that were equally 'isolationist' in their demands for American privileges and essentially unilateralist in their common disavowal of real political obligations.[59] When, however, historians do acknowledge the existence of two opposing campaigns they fall for the partisanship of their contemporary pro-Court sources and describe the leading personalities accordingly. In the typical phrasing of one Second Generation scholar:

> The blistering charges of Father Coughlin and William Randolph Hearst were truly staggering... The... appeal of the pro-Courters, by comparison, was mild, polite, and conscientious.

This account is in keeping with that of *Newsweek*, which wrote:

> Against the wit of [Cowboy Will] Rogers and the venom of Coughlin, Anna Eleanor Roosevelt bravely faced a microphone. Many listeners twirled dials to lighter entertainment from her serious, undramatic plea for aiding the cause of peace.[60]

Secondly, and somewhat more surprisingly, there has been no content-analysis made of the material which (in the common metaphors) poured, flooded, deluged and avalanched to swamp and blitz the Senators.[61] We are invited by nearly every historian to assume that the letters and telegrams all insisted upon the recipient's opposing ratification. More surprisingly still, we are rarely informed who the turncoats were or shown that the change of vote was dishonourable. After all, elected representatives are not obliged perversely to ignore the expressed wishes of constituents. Such problems go unregarded. Instead we have switches alleged in the abstract; and where names are offered, the suggestions are unconvincing.[62] In short, the traditional and widespread interpretation couched in terms of propaganda carries with it little if any of the evidence it so patently requires. But, as we shall see, the shape of the final vote against ratifying the Court Protocols can be detected by the end of the second week. This is not to say defeat was inevitable; it is to say success was not certain.

On Monday, 28 January debate began under the guillotine agreed by Robinson and Johnson the previous Thursday. The speeches were now shortened and intense versions of familiar themes. Johnson himself opened with a characteristic blend of invective against the League of Nations and reverence for the pantheon of nationalistic presidents from George Washington to his beloved Theodore Roosevelt. Long followed with a broadside against the enemies of the common people at home and abroad: his was a form of Populist internationalism. Yet though the language of the debate was familiar, important actions were taking place on the floor. The coalition which had gathered around Norris now supported a reservation from Long concerning the Monroe Doctrine, but one drafted in a form to nullify ratification by deviating from the text of 1926. As only one Republican (Keyes) had opposed Norris's amendment, so only one (Metcalf of Rhode Island) opposed Long's amendment. Here was an unmistakable sign that the non-Democrats could counter an administration whip; while the anti-administration Democrats also rallied behind Long. (Vandenberg, faithful to the 1926 terms, did not declare.)

The next significant event was the success of Davis in winning exactly one third of the votes (27:54) for his amendment to repeat the 1926 reservation (Paragraph V) on the advisory jurisdiction *verbatim*. (The generally astute reporters on the *New York Times* called this a 'minor amendment', since it was merely a change of language!) The roll-call on the Davis motion identified the bulk of the solid core of Democrats completely opposed to ratification and the administration's management: Donahey of Ohio, Gerry of Rhode Island, Gore of Oklahoma, Long of

Louisiana, McCarran of Nevada, McGill of Kansas, Murphy of Iowa, Reynolds of North Carolina and Trammell of Florida. But the vote was not unambiguous: some Senators committed to reaffirming the terms of 1926 had supported Long but opposed Davis. All were Democrats: Caraway of Arkansas, Thomas of Oklahoma, and Walsh of Massachusetts. To these three may be added Murray and Wheeler of Montana and Russell of Georgia. (Norris, who had been supported by Davis, voted against the Davis amendment – a sure sign that Norris still wanted to see the Protocols approved.)[63] But beneath the complexities the basic pattern could be distinguished. Fifteen or so Democrats could not be whipped into line for the final vote: the alignment of Friday had held. Johnson, Borah and their allies were in no doubt about the significance of the roll-calls; and they confidently demanded a final vote that evening. The proponents admitted the difficulties: reports in the pro-Court press spoke of ratification being 'desperately close', if not already lost. Privately William Phillips predicted defeat.[64]

Robinson moved an early recess. Though he told reporters the prospects for ratification now looked 'even better', it was public knowledge that he, Roosevelt and Hull were putting pressure on 'Democratic recalcitrants' and 'wavering' Senators. They were not the same people. The Democrats identified were Donahey, Gerry and Walsh; and there is strong evidence for including Caraway. The obvious non-Democrat was Cutting, the victim of quite unscrupulous and open pressure from the administration, which was threatening a straight party vote in the Senate to unseat him and install the defeated candidate in the 1934 New Mexico election, the Democrat Dennis Chavez. Perhaps an even clearer sign of the administration's worry was the agreement that Eleanor Roosevelt should hold a press conference to urge ratification. Senatorial resentment at her intervention was already well-known – and had been predicted even by supporters of adherence.[65]

The floor, galleries and lobbies of the Senate chamber were packed to overflowing on Tuesday, 29 January, the final day of debate. Pope led for the proposition – an unwise choice, given his prominence in the campaign for American membership in the League of Nations and his well-publicized efforts to weaken the Senate's role in treaty-making. Huey Long replied with his usual vehemence and sarcasm, but this time concentrating on the failure of the League to resolve the chronic Chaco War between Bolivia and Paraguay. It was a useful goad to the Senate's sensitivities about the Monroe Doctrine. But the force and bitterness of Long's speech were completely outdistanced by the Republican Thomas Schall of Minnesota. With language drawn from evangelical Christianity and Populism Schall denounced the conspiracy to draw the United States into the League and range it alongside the British Empire as it faced the threat of Japanese expansionism. Much of Schall's analysis was inadvertently corroborated by the pro-League lobbies, though their premises were different and their terminology not pejorative. Even so these elements of his latest diatribe were only an updating of Schall's opposition in the 1925–6 debate. The striking novelty was Schall's attack on the 'dictatorship' of the Roosevelt administration, which had invoked a national emergency to justify the arrogation of unconstitutional powers under the New Deal legislation.[66]

The most dramatic moments of the afternoon were still to come. First Thomas of Utah submitted an amendment to reinsert Paragraph VII requiring the submission of cases to the Court by 'general or special treaties between the parties in dispute', Johnson had moved this in Committee; the Norris amendment had been a stricter version of these terms; but Thomas now tried to foist the sponsorship upon Johnson. He vigorously resisted, well aware that Thomas was fronting for Robinson who lacked the courage to admit to the administration's retraction. Long sarcastically called the ploy 'a little backwater' to win votes. He was right. Hudson, Jessup, Shotwell and Root had all combined to lobby the White House for the concession, making it clear that many Southern Democratic Senators would make it a necessary condition of their support. (The *New York Times* reporters knew there had been a bargain but identified liberal Republicans and New England Democrats as the main beneficiaries.)[67]

Borah now intervened, detecting the chance of converting this reservation (acceptable to the League in 1926 and 1929) into a wrecking amendment. Borah's rewording required the formal and explicit consent of the Signatories to the substance of Paragraph VII and enlarged its purpose by foreclosing any possible and surreptitious use of the Court's compulsory jurisdiction. A contest between Borah's authority and Robinson's power was thus arranged. A vote was taken immediately and Borah's amendment defeated 44:40. This was the narrowest victory for the administration and a testimony to Borah's stature. Two Democrats who had opposed the Norris reservation stayed silent (namely Lewis of Illinois and Frederick Van Nuys of Indiana); while three other Senators simply followed Borah's lead. The trio were Gerry of Rhode Island, a Democrat; and the two Republicans, Keyes of New Hampshire and Warren Barbour of New Jersey[68]

Norris came back to try to remove the 'loophole' of 'general treaties' from Paragraph VII. The administration forces rallied again; and the second Norris reservation went down, 48:39. but these two victories were pyrrhic. Robinson had lost what bi-partisan support he began with, for the two votes showed all the non-Democrats voting Yea, only Democrats voting Nay; and the solid core of opposition within the Democratic ranks had not splintered. On the contrary: some opponents of ratification (notably Lewis and Bone of Washington) were following Robinson in resisting the amendments but were prepared to cast a final Nay.[69]

Paragraph VII was not quite done with. Long introduced an undisguised wrecking amendment; but even the opponents had no time to waste and it was lost on a voice-vote. (Long's reservation unwisely implied that the Monroe Doctrine might be justiciable – an idea anathema to both sides in the debate.) Thomas then succeeded in getting unanimous consent for the Paragraph's inclusion in the draft resolution. This meant that three of the four 1926 conditions had been restored:

Paragraphs VII and VIII – and Paragraph V on the advisory jurisdiction, for all sides agreed its substance had been reincorporated in the draft resolution's rephrasing of the Reed Understanding. Then Steiwer moved to add Paragraph VI, the Moses Reservation. For once Robinson had an argument which might carry weight with his nominal supporters: Walsh and Fess had explicitly dissociated themselves from repeating this condition. Steiwer's amendment was defeated 34:49; but again the voting patterns were preserved. All the Republicans supported Steiwer; all the votes against were from Democrats.[70]

Gore's amendment to make adherence conditional upon the resumption of payments on intergovernmental debts was then put to the vote – an obvious wrecking amendment, though one which pro-League activists such as Hudson, Sweetser and Shotwel, knew commanded more sympathy than the voting showed. The amendment was lost by 26:57. Nevertheless, Gore's speech was a powerful and eloquent argument that he had kept an open mind on adherence but had become disillusioned over the years. He produced evidence to prove the affect of the Austro-German Customs Union Opinion on his attitude; and others outside the chamber spoke in the same language of the Opinion's impact on neutral minds. More than any other Senator, Gore exposed the hollowness of the 'sponger' argument. As he rightly said, the drive for adherence was not a piece of sentimental symbolism. Its true proponents, not its complacent allies, were bent on American membership of the League.[71]

Contemporary political analysts frequently commented upon the intensity and unity of the progressive opposition to ratification of the Court Protocols and particularly to the legislative management of the Roosevelt administration. (Hudson and Moley spoke in comparable terms though Moley deplored Roosevelt's turning from his natural, progressive allies to 'Geneva internationalists'.) Farleyism had some responsibility; but the speeches of Shipstead, Schall and Gore showed their deep-seated antagonism to the centralization of Executive power when combined with an objectively pro-British and generally imperialist foreign policy. Here were the conceptual links to the late nineteenth-century; and it is easy to see how such programmes contained conservative as well as progressive elements. (One well-informed political commentator, Erwin Canham, wrote of the 'peculiar combination of conservatives and progressives' fighting against the Court Protocols.)[72] Historians, however, have inclined to emphasize the conservative side to the correlation and depicted the opposition as naï vely archaic. Two counterpoints may be offered. The first is more general and simply records the historiographical cliché that the solid, conservative Democratic South used to be regarded as the most 'internationalist' section of the Union. The second concerns more directly the course of the debate on the Court Protocols. For one of the heroes of those historians who divide Progressives into conservatives (archaic and isolationist) and moderns or liberals (adaptable, forward-looking and internationalist) is George Norris.[73] And it was he who took the floor to announce his intention to vote against the resolution of adherence.

The resolution of adherence was in its final form. Granted the argument that the League and Signatories had accepted the first four conditions (or Paragraphs) of the Senate from 1926; granted that Paragraph V (repeated in the Reed Understanding) had been reaffirmed in the Department of State's phraseology; given the fact of the *verbatim* repetition of Paragraphs VII and VIII; then the resolution set before the Senate on the evening of Tuesday, 29 January 1935 was substantially the same as that passed nine years before – with one obvious exception: the removal of Paragraph VI, the Moses Reservation. At this point Norris informed the Senate that he would oppose the redrawn resolution.

Norris's speech was simple and brief. He believed a two-thirds vote would be won for the Protocols; but two reasons had led him to change his mind and vote Nay. (This was the public rationale. Norris kept quiet about the Roosevelt-Farley attack on Cutting, which the Progressives as a group bitterly resented.) First, the administration's handling of Paragraph VII on the treaty-making power had convinced Norris that he had been naïve in 1926. He now realized the Paragraph's potential for abuse, especially from an Executive keen to cut down the powers of the Senate. Secondly, he had been persuaded by the argument (most forcefully put by Johnson and most subtly by Borah) that the danger of the advisory jurisdiction lay less in drawing European and specifically League Powers into American concerns but rather in entangling the United States in the maintenance of discredited empires and unjustifiable territorial settlements. He had reflected at length on the Austro-German Customs Union case; he had studied the determination of France and her allies to break the Customs Union, by military force if necessary; and he had become convinced that American membership of the Court would have led, willy-nilly, to active efforts to enforce the judgment of the Court if the German and Austrian governments had not themselves renounced the scheme.[74]

If later observers are tempted to dismiss Norris's reversal as a classic case of infectious paranoia, three considerations are apposite. The first is that we know that the real drive behind ratification of the Court Protocols came from those who wanted the United States to enter the League – and by congressional joint resolution if the Senate was to remain intransigent. Sayre, McClure and Pope were simply the newest names in a long list who so argued. The second consideration is the equally undeniable fact that the most influential proponents of American adherence wanted to place sanctions behind the decisions of the Court.[75] The third consideration is somewhat more intangible but none the less powerful. There might be no legal or textual obligation for a Court Signatory to join in the enforcement of judgments; but, as Woodrow Wilson himself had insisted, a moral obligation was nobler and more exacting than a legal one. That had been Wilson's response to Senators who tried to define the commitments deriving from the Covenant of the League of Nations; and Norris, a lesser-known but respected Irreconcilable from the League campaign, had touched the heart of the Court debate in 1935.[76]

Norris's declaration appeared to have immediate effect. William J.

Bulow, the Democratic Junior Senator from South Dakota and a man who rarely spoke on the floor, announced that he too had changed his mind and would oppose ratification. Since 'every Senator... in favor of going into the World Court [was] only in favor... provided certain reservations [were] made', Bulow deduced adherence was a 'dangerous thing'. It seemed an ingenuous remark but following so close upon Norris's recantation, Bulow's confession was seen to be the first sign of the shift in voting as a number of Senators came over into the opposition. As many commentators had foreseen, Norris would be most influential.[77]

Indeed, Norris's prediction that the Protocols would gather a two-thirds majority was put in doubt by Robinson's closing words as the revised resolution was read a third time before the final vote. Robinson denounced the propaganda barrage which had been levelled at the Senate: Hearst and Coughlin were the chief culprits. Schall and Long replied in kind, with complaints about Eleanor Roosevelt's efforts; but their colleagues called them off. These interchanges were a reminder of the personalities who had given drama to the debate *outside* the Senate but who were not, in themselves, decisive inside the chamber. With a maximum of 94 Senators able to vote and 89 physically present, the resolution sponsored by Robinson had to gather 60 votes for passage, the opponents needed to win only 30 votes. When the roll-call finished the result stood 52:36 in favour of ratification. The resolution was defeated.[78]

Evidence exists in the preceding narrative to challenge the need to resort to propaganda as a sufficient explanation for the defeat of the resolution. Robinson said as much after the final vote on at least two separate occasions; Roosevelt hedged his bets; the private correspondence of important pro-Court lobbyists shows they knew propaganda was not the sole or even the most important cause of failure.[79] In these pages it is impossible to give a detailed analysis of every Senator's intentions and actions during the debate. Impossible and unnecessary. The shape of the final vote can be detected and described with reasonable simplicity and brevity. The key evidence is to be found in the seven roll-call votes, supplemented and glossed by other authoritative sources.[80] (As we have seen, some Senators voted one way on amendments; but there was no doubt about their final position. The classic case here was Ham Lewis.)

Conceding, for the moment, the argument that only Nay votes have to be explained, we are presented with 36 names: 14 Republicans, 2 Independents and 20 Democrats. There was never any doubt that La Follette (Progressive) and Shipstead (Farmer–Labor) would oppose ratification; nor that Borah, Davis, Johnson, Gerald P. Nye (North Dakota), Schall and White would vote Nay, These last-named Senators comprise 6 of the 14 Republicans. The votes of the other 8 can be readily explained. Six of them cast identical votes to those of the opposition's leaders, Borah and Johnson; and, moreover, some of this sextet allowed their votes to be cast for them by proxies – a sure sign of their following an agreed path. The six were: Carey of Wyoming, Dickinson of Iowa, Frazier of North Dakota, Hastings of Delaware, Norbeck of South Dakota and Townsend of Delaware. Peter Norbeck had voted Yea in 1926 – as had Norris, of course, and the remaining Republican, Metcalf of Rhode Island. If Metcalf did switch, he was already moving before the notorious final weekend of propaganda and even before the administration's opposition to the Borah–Norris defence of the treaty-making power. Indeed, since Metcalf followed these authoritative Senators in the critical votes, the public and reasoned reversal by Norris may have been the last-minute determinant to his already ambivalent attitude – an attitude strongly and adversely affected by the Customs Union advisory opinion.[81]

Twenty Democrats voted against ratification; and they too displayed distinctive voting patterns. Eight followed the Johnson-Borah line on all proposed amendments – a sign of their complete separation from the administration. The eight were: Donahey, Gore, Long, McCarran, Murphy, Murray, Reynolds, and Russell. No actions of these Senators during debate suggested any was poised to vote Yea; no reports in the press described any as a surprise Nay. (Murphy worked closely with Borah.)[82]

This leaves twelve Democrats outside the Johnson–Borah pattern. One was Bulow, who justified his switch; another was Ham Lewis of Illinois. There could be no doubt of Lewis's total opposition to ratification; but if he was to be an effective Democratic whip , he could not constantly thwart his own Majority leader in a legislative struggle. Lewis, as all observers predicted, would cast one negative vote – against the final terms. There remain, therefore, ten votes to explain: Bone and Schwellenbach of Washington; Coolidge and Walsh of Massachusetts; Gerry of Rhode Island; McGill of Kansas; Smith of South Carolina; Thomas of Oklahoma; Trammell of Florida; and Wheeler of Montana.

The voting record of Bone was incomplete; but lobbyists rightly regarded him as an opponent of ratification and he was known to be at odds with the administration over policy and patronage. These latter considerations seem to have weighed with Schwellenbach, a freshman Senator from the progressive wing of the Democratic party in Washington. Certainly his Nay vote was listed as a surprise by one political correspondent. However Schwellenbach had attended the 1934 Committee Hearings as an opponent, claiming that most of his State was against adherence to the Court. Of the remaining eight Democratic Senators, four had supported adherence in 1926: Gerry, Smith, Trammell and Wheeler. Of these, only Ellison D. ('Cotton Ed') Smith was regarded as a surprise Nay; and he had been listed by the pro-Court lobbyists as favouring adherence. (It may be noted that Southern Democrats were usually classified as proponents.) However Smith had supported the Gore amendment – a protest against the Democratic leadership as well as the defaulting Europeans. The other three Senators all gave evidence of having shifted from their 1926 position: Trammell (as we have seen) within the space of a year; Wheeler not long afterwards (as the American Foundation discovered); and Gerry had been marked out for

White House pressure. The latter, therefore, had either already defected or was regarded as unreliable. This trio also had a common antipathy to the League, in the case of Gerry and Trammell reaching back to the Senate debates of 1919–20.[83]

Later analysis suggests that profound political realignments were taking place during the mid-thirties in Rhode Island, Gerry's State. Certainly his opposition to the League of Nations may have reflected ethnic group politics. In the Court vote Gerry was joined by his Massachusetts colleagues, Walsh and Coolidge, and both these two Senators cited great constituency pressure on them. (Indeed, the press commented on the pronounced hostility to the Court coming from Southern New England. Connecticut was *the* exception.) The final Nay vote of the two Massachusetts Senators elicited no surprise in the press; but it perhaps disappointed the administration. Walsh was another of the Democrat 'recalcitrants' summoned to the White House.[84]

This leaves Thomas of Oklahoma and McGill of Kansas. Once again Thomas disappointed the lobbyists but did not surprise the press: the newspaper prediction that he would vote Nay was corroborated by his help to his colleague Gore in the final stages of debate. Conversely McGill was listed by the lobbyists as an opponent; and his one deviation from the Johnson–Borah pattern was to oppose the Gore amendment on the intergovernmental debts.[85]

To summarize this analysis of the Democratic votes cast against ratification: only two were listed as surprises in the contemporary press, namely Smith and Schwellenbach – the latter being undoubtedly a simple mistake. The other ten were all tipped to oppose or recorded as very doubtful. If, therefore, we add Smith's name to the list of self-confessed recanters (that is George Norris and William J. Bulow), we have a maximum of three genuine switches to the opposition.

To complete the picture we can fill in the side always ignored but always implied by analyses couched in terms of presidential leadership: the names of those Senators who surprised observers by their Yea vote. (Joe Robinson claimed to have won some votes – though not, significantly, any converts.)[86] The two most obvious candidates are Hattie Caraway of Arkansas, a Democrat, and Bronson Cutting of New Mexico, an independent Republican, both of whom were subjected to extreme administration pressure and both of whom displayed a voting pattern compatible with rejection of the resolution. Each was forecast to vote Nay, Cutting being an odds-on certainty.[87] (The Yea vote of Cutting, so publicly extracted by a ruthless administration, *may* have induced Donahey, Gerry & Company to show their own independence – if any further argument is needed to explain their Nay votes.) George of Georgia was another Senator predicted to vote Nay. He had voted for ratification in 1926; but his absence from critical votes in the Foreign Relations Committee together with silence on most of the key roll-call votes on the floor appear a deliberate attempt to conceal his new intentions from the administration. (George's colleague, Russell, followed the Borah–Johnson voting pattern; and the Georgia legislature had petitioned both Senators to oppose adherence.)[88] The other Senators predicted to vote Nay were the Republicans: Hale of Maine and Keyes of New Hampshire. Both had a history of defending the Senate's independence of the Executive in the League of Nations struggle: they had both signed the March 1919 Round Robin; both had been mild Reservationists in the subsequent Versailles Treaty debates. If that earlier opposition did have a partisan edge against the Democratic Wilson, the parallel with 1935 is even more exact. In 1926 Hale and Keyes had both voted for the World Court when it was an administration measure; now they were reported as inclined to oppose a measure which was becoming identified with the Democrats. For both of them, apparently, the *quid pro quo* would be Roosevelt's retreat on Paragraph VII, the treaty-making reservation.[89] Finally we may note two other Senators in the list of potential Nay-voters, candidates in other words for the title of switcher to the proponents. Both were Democrats: one was Royal S. Copeland of New York; the other, William H. Dieterich of Illinois. Copeland did not vote in person or contribute to the final vote, being only paired as a Yea. He was, however, considered a possible opponent by the lobbyists; he was at odds with Roosevelt's faction in New York politics and the Congress; and he was widely reported as believing that his Yea vote in 1926 had ruined his political future. Dieterich did vote in person for ratification; but the lobby surveys listed him as an opponent and the press commented on the traditional State-wide opposition to the Court. If he did indeed shift to the proponents, perhaps this goes to confirm if not conclusively prove his susceptibility to administration pressure, as Frederick Libby had argued in the spring of 1933, when Dieterich first entered the Senate.[90]

Immediately after the vote on the Protocols Senator Robinson told reporters that the defeat 'foreclose[d] the entry of the United States into the World Court for an indefinite period'. But within days Hiram Johnson was writing to J. Reuben Clark that 'the snake [was] merely scotched'. A bill (H.R. 4668) came before the House of Representatives for adherence to the World Court by joint resolution; a bill (S. J. Res. 51) was soon presented to the Senate by Pope of Idaho for a constitutional amendment requiring only a simple 'majority vote of the United States Senate' to approve 'the ratification of treaties'. Pro-Court, pro-League advocates such as James Garner and Nicholas Murray Butler continued to attack the Senate's prerogatives and denounce the isolationism which had brought about the Court's defeat; and Jessup was one of the few who seemed to realize that the joint-resolution procedure was a confession of weakness which even some pro-Court Senators might oppose precisely to preserve senatorial rights and traditions.[91] (Senator Pope was not persuaded: in early May he introduced a bill for American membership of the League of Nations: S. J. Res. 119.) For some years the Protocols remained technically unfinished business in the Senate; then the Court and the issue of adherence both became defunct, to be resurrected and transfigured in the International Court of Justice of the United Nations Organization. Pro-League internationalists saw their dreams finally realized; the anti-League isolationists had seemed to lose the last and most desperate battle. Isolationism, which Arthur Vandenberg had scorned as unrealistic during the Court debate now became impossible for him after Pearl Harbor. As a French newspaper had presciently commented in the aftermath of the first World Court defeat in 1935: if the United States were ever to 're-enter Europe' to wage war again it would not be by the route of The Hague or even Geneva but by way of Asia and the Pacific.[92]

Whether isolationism truly ended at Pearl Harbor is another story.

Notes

1 Ursula P. Hubbard, 'The Cooperation of the United States with the League of Nations and with the International Labor Organization', *International Conciliation* 274 (November 1931), 675–825; cf. the arguments of Quincy Wright, Clarence Berdahl, and Arthur Holcombe in *APSR* 26 (February–June 1932), 45–526 *passim*; memo of Sweetser: as enclosure, Frank Walters to Cecil, 30 November 1934: Cecil Papers.

2 *USWA* (1934–5), 220–1; Johnson, *Borah of Idaho*, 492; Frances Perkins, *The Roosevelt I Knew* (New York: Viking Press, 1946), 343; Walters, *History of the League of Nations*, 194–7; Morley, *Society of Nations*, 621 ff.

3 Memo of McClure, 18 July 1934: NA 500. C114/1549.

4 Borchard to Borah, 13 April, 7 May, 14 November, 10 and 13 December 1934: Borah Papers; Johnson to McClatchy, 1 February and 11 March 1934: Johnson Papers; John Bassett Moore to R. Walton Moore, 7 December 1934: R. Walton Moore Papers, Franklin D. Roosevelt Library, Hyde Park, NY (cited below as R. Walton Moore Papers).

5 Memo of Barnes, 24 July 1934; Anna A. O'Neill (Solicitor's Office) to Jacob A. Metzger; Metzger to Moore, 6 September 1934: NA 500. C114/1557 ½.

6 Memo of John S. Dickey (Sayre's assistant) 11 October and 12 November 1934; Dickey to Sayre, 15 October and 15 November 1934: NA 500. C114/1558–64 ½; Moffat, *Diary*, 5–14 September 1934: Moffat Papers; Phillips *Diary*, 12–14 September 1934: Phillips Papers.

7 Phillips, *Diary*, 7 November 1934: Phillips Papers; Hearst to Roosevelt, 8 November 1934; Johnson to Roosevelt, 4 December 1934: Franklin D. Roosevelt Papers, Hyde Park, NY; Libby to Cordell Hull, 14 November 1934: NA 500. C114/1560.

8 Robinson to Louis Howe (President's Secretary), 9 November 1934; Garner to Roosevelt, 9 November 1934: Roosevelt Papers.

9 Levinson to Borah, 24 July 1934: Borah Papers; Marvin McIntyre (President's Secretary) to Roosevelt, 5 July 1934: Roosevelt Papers.

10 George W. Norris to Farley, 22 September 1933; Edward M. House to Roosevelt, 23 November 1934: Roosevelt Papers; Ickes, *Secret Diary*, I. 284 ff.

11 Phillips, *Diary*, 28 December 1934: Phillips Papers; McClure to Sayre, 3 January 1935: R. Walton Moore Papers; Jessup to Hudson, 21 January 1935: Hudson Papers; Castle to Kellogg, 2 February [1935]:Castle Papers, Hoover Presidential Library.

12 Memo of Hackworth, 13 November 1934: as enclosure, Phillips to Roosevelt, 15 November 1934; Sayre memo and Sayre to Roosevelt, 29 December 1934: NA 500. C114/1563–72A.

13 Eleanor Roosevelt to Esther Everett Lape, 24 January 1935: Root Papers;

John Morton Blum, *From the Morgenthau Diaries: Years of Crisis, 1928–1938* (Boston: Houghton Mifflin, 1959), 125–31.

14 Root to Hudson, 3 January 1935: Root Papers.

15 Moffat, *Diary*, 28 December 1934: Moffat Papers; Phillips, *Diary*, 28–31 December 1934: Phillips Papers; Borchard to Borah, 13 December 1934: Borah Papers: John Bassett Moore to Johnson, 12 January 1935: Moore Papers.

16 Dickey memo of Sayre–Pittman meeting, 3 January 1935: NA 500. C114/1578 (*FRUS* (1935), I. 383–5).

17 Phillips, *Diary*, 3 January 1935: Phillips Papers; Pittman to Roosevelt, 4 January 1935: reprinted in Edgar B. Nixon (ed.), *Franklin D. Roosevelt and Foreign Affairs, 1933–1937*, 3 vols (Cambridge, Mass: Belknap Press of Harvard University Press, 1969), II. 335–6.

18 *NYT* (6 January 1935), I. 1, 28; 'Again the World Court' *NYT* (11 January 1935), 22.

19 *San Francisco Chronicle* (cited below as *SFC*) (6 January 1935), 6; ibid. (11 January 1935), 14; *Los Angeles Times* (cited below as *LAT*) (17 January 1935), I. 1, 16; Phillips *Diary*, 31 December 1934: Phillips Papers; McClure to Sayre, 3 January 1935: R. Walton Moore Papers; Ham Holt to Moore, 14 January 1935: Moore Papers; John Bassett Moore to Borchard, 7 January 1935: to Borah, 11 January 1935: Borchard Papers; to Johnson, 12 January 1935: Moore Papers.

20 Sayre to Robinson, 8 January 1935; McClure to Sayre, 14 January 1935: NA 500. C114/1572D, 1587.

21 US Senate, Seventy-fourth Congress, First Session, *Senate Executive Report*, no.1 (Washington, DC:GPO, 1935).

22 Rowell in *SFC* (11 January 1935), 14; *CSM* (9 January 1935), 1; Phillips, *Diary*, 9 January 1935: Phillips Papers; Lindsay to Sir. John Simon (Foreign Secretary), 10 January 1935: FO 371, W707/55/98.

23 *NYT* (10 January 1935), 10; Johnson to Borchard, 11 January 1935: Johnson Papers; Phillips, *Diary*, 9 January 1935: Phillips Papers; memo of Dickey, 12 January 1935: NA 500. C114/1579; Lape to Eleanor Roosevelt, 17 January 1935: Root Papers.

24 Vandenberg to Hull, 11 January 1935; Hull to Vandenberg, 15 January 1935; to Prentiss B. Gilbert (Geneva), 9 January 1935; Sayre to Roosevelt, 9 January 1935: NA 500. C114/1573A–1576 (*FRUS* (1935), I. 385–9); Hudson to Root, 9 January 1935; Roosevelt to Hudson, 11 January 1935: Hudson Papers; Moore to Holt, 16 January 1935: R. Walton Moore Papers; *NYT*(11 January 1935), 7; *Washington Post* (cited below as *WP*) (11 January 1935), 3; *CSM* (12 January 1935), 2. For the NCPW and the WWCC, see NA 500. C114/1580, 1585.

25 *NYH-T* (13 January 1935), 20; Johnson to Borchard, 8 January 1935: Johnson Papers; Borah to Claudius O. Johnson (his biographer), 2 January 1936: Borah Papers; *NYT* (12 January 1935), 2; *San Francisco Examiner* (cited below as *SFE*) (16 January 1935), 1.

26 *SFC* (16 January 1935), 2: *NYH-T* (16 January 1935), 1, 8. The WWCC poll is reprinted in Nixon, *Roosevelt and Foreign Affairs*, II. 353–7

27 *CR* 74:1, 249, 432 ff.; *NYH-T* (16 January 1935), 1, 8: *SFE* (16 January 1935), 1. For the Johnson Act, see S.682: Seventy-third Congress, Second Session.

28 For Robinson and the Supreme Court, see Joseph Alsop and Turner Catledge, *The 168 Days* (Garden City, NY: Doubleday, Doran, 1938), 221–2; for Kellogg and the World Court, see Sayre's memo of conversation with Clark M. Eichelberger (Director: League of Nations Association), 18 July 1934: R. Walton Moore Papers; memo of McClure, 18 July 1934: NA 500.

C114/1549.

29 McClure to Sayre, 14 January 1935; Moore memo, 21 January 1935: NA 500.C114/1587, 1596; 'International Justice', *WP* (23 January 1935), 8; cf. Raymond Fosdick to Root, 10 October 1934: Root Papers.

30 *CR* 74:1, 479–90; *NYT* (17 January 1935), 1; *NYH-T* (17 January 1935), 6; *SFC* (17 January 1935), 5; *WP* (17 January 1935), 1, 2.

31 Sayre draft, 29 December 1934: NA 500. C114/1572A; Sayre to Roosevelt, 7 January 1935: Roosevelt Papers; Lindsay to Simon, 17 January 1935: FO 371, W544/55/98; Hudson to Hammarskjöld, 17 January 1935: Hudson Papers; Roosevelt message of 16 January 1935: Nixon, *Roosevelt and Foreign Affairs*, II. 363–64.

32 *NYT* (17 January 1935), 1; John Bassett Moore to Borchard, 3 February 1935: Moore Papers; Ickes, *Secret Diary*, I. 284.

33 *CR* 74:1, 563–79; Borchard to Moore, 23 January 1935; Moore to Borchard, 24 January 1935: Borchard Papers; *LAT* (18 January 1935), I. 11.

34 Boxes 1–4 of Official File 1403 in the Roosevelt Papers attest to the political importance of Long as a potential *broker* (rather than candidate) in 1936

35 *CR* 74:1, 893; *NYT* (18 January 1935), 5; *NYH-T* (18 January 1935), 7

36 Vandenberg to Root, 11 January 1935: Root Papers; *CR* 74:1, 636–40.

37 Hull to Vandenberg, 15 January 1935 (cited at n. 24 above); Robinson to Dickey, 14 January 1935; Dickey to Sayre, 14 January 1935: NA 500. C114/1576.

38 *CR* 74:1, 640–8; *NYH-T* (6 January 1935), 19; McClure to Sayre, 14 January 1935: NA 500. C114/1587.

39 *CR* 74:1, 639; *CSM* (8 January 1935), 1.

40 Eichelberger to Newton D. Baker, 20 January 1935: cited in Kahn, 'Pressure Group Influence', 196.

41 Jessup to Hudson, 21 January 1935: Hudson Papers; Root to Roosevelt, 28 January 1935: Nixon, *Roosevelt and Foreign Affairs*, II. 376–7; *SFE* (16 January 1935), 1; *SFE*, (20 January 1935), 1, 2; *SFC* (19 January 1935), 4; *SFC* (24 January 1935), 17.

42 *CR*: 74:1 695 ff.; *NYT* (22 January 1935), 5; *NYH-T* (22 January 1935), 1, 3; *SFC* (22 January 1935), 2.

43 Thomas N. Guinsburg, *The Pursuit of Isolationism in the United States Senate from Versailles to Pearl Harbor* (New York and London: Garland, 1982), 159 ff.

44 Sweetser to Hudson, 21 March 1935; Root to Hamilton Fish Armstrong, 11 May 1935: Root Papers; Phillips, *Diary*, 17 December – 6 January 1935: Phillips Papers.

45 Hudson to Robinson, 21 January 1935; to Sweetser, 30 January 1935: Hudson Papers; *SFE* (22 January 1935), 2.

46 *NYH-T* (23 January 1935), 6; *SFE* (24 January 1935), 1; *NYT* (24 January 1935), 18; Franklin D. Roosevelt, *Complete Presidential Press Conferences of Franklin D. Roosevelt*, 25 vols in 12 (New York: Da Capo, 1972), V 65–70.

47 *CR* 74:1, 765 ff.; *LAT* (24 January 1935), I. 18; Lape to Root, 17 January 1935; Eleanor Roosevelt to Lape, 24 January 1935: Root Papers.

48 *CR* 74:1, 877–9; *NYT* (24 January 1935), 14; *Washington Herald* (25 January 1935), 1.

49 *CR* 74:1, 873–7; *Springfield Republican* (25 January 1935), 2; *WP* (23 November 1934), 1, 6.

50 Borchard to Moore, 30 January 1935: Borchard Papers.

51 *CR* 74:1 893; *LAT* (25 January 1935), I. 5; *WP* (25 January 1935), 2.

52 *Springfield Republican* (25 January 1935), 2; *CSM* (23 January 1935), 1; *SFE* (24 January 1935), 2; *NYH-T* (24 January 1935), 6; *NYH-T* (26 January

1935), 14.

53 CR 74:1, 964 ff

54 Denna Frank Fleming had once sympathized with Norris: Fleming, 'The Advice of the Senate in Treaty Making', *Current History* 32 (September 1930), 1090–4.

55 *CR* 74:1 965 ff.; *Evening Star* (Washington) (25 January 1935), 1, 3; *CDT* (30 January 1935), 1.

56 *CR* 74:1, 968, 977; Root to Roosevelt, 28 January 1935 (cited at n. 41 above).

57 See Hutchinson's column in the *Washington Times* (18 January 1935); cf. *WP* (23 November 1934), 1, 6; *CR* 74:1, 977.

58 *NYH-T* (26 January 1935), 11; *CSM* (26 January 1935), 4; *SFE* (26 January 1935), 1; *NYT* (26 January 1935), 14.

59 'Senate Act Confirms America in Dangerous Nationalistic Isolation', *SFC* (30 January 1935), 10.

60 Kahn, 'Presidential Passivity', 155; *Newsweek* (9 February 1935), 6.

61 Part of this lexicon is given in *League of Nations Chronicle* (New York) (30 January 1935), 1, 4; *San Francisco Examiner* (28 January 1935), 1, 2. The *Examiner* was a Hearst paper.

62 Kahn suggests a total of 18 'switchers' and names four: Coolidge, Gerry, Metcalf and Walsh: 'Pressure Group Influence', 222. The press of Friday morning listed these four as likely Nays.

63 *CR* 74:1, 1039–56; *NYT* (29 January 1935), 1.

64 *SFE* (28 January 1935), 1, 2; *WP* (29 January 1935), 1, 3; *CSM* (29 January 1935), 1; *NYT* (29 January 1935), 1, 2, 20; Phillips, *Diary*, 28 January 1935: Phillips Papers.

65 Cordell Hull, *The Memoirs of Cordell Hull*, 2 vols (New York: Macmillan, 1948), I. 389; Ickes, *Secret Diary*, I. 217, 285; *LAT* (29 January 1935), I. 4; *LAT* (30 January 1935), I. 1, 5; *Springfield Republican* (30 January 1935), 1, 2,; Lape to Root, 27 January 1935: Root Papers.

66 *CR* 74:1 1112–23,

67 *CR* 74:1, 1123–5; memo of Jessup: 'Confidential: World Court' (28–29 January 1935): Jessup Papers; *NYT* (30 January 1935), 2.

68 *CR* 74:1 1126–7.

69 Ibid. 1127–31.

70 Ibid. 1131–4.

71 Ibid. 1134–40; Root to Sweetser, 18 April 1935: Root Papers; Hudson to Sweetser, 8 February 1935: Shotwell to Hudson, 18 February 1935: Hudson Papers; *SFE* (24 January 1935), 2; *SFE* (27 January 1935), 1.

72 *CSM* (30 January 1935), 1, 4; cf. T.R.B., *New Republic* (9 January 1935), pp. 244–5; Mark Sullivan, *LAT* (27 January 1935), II. 5; Hudson to Root, 30 January 1935: Root Papers; Moley to Roosevelt, 30 November 1935: Roosevelt Papers; Borchard to Borah, 10 December 1934: Borah Papers; Borchard to Moore, 30 January 1935: Moore Papers.

73 John C. Donovan, 'Congressional Isolationists and the Roosevelt Foreign Policy', *World Politics* 3 (April 1951), 229–316.

74 *CR* 74:1 1142–3.

75 Nicholas Murray Butler to Roosevelt, 9 October 1934: Roosevelt Papers; McClure to Sayre, 30 January 1935: R. Walton Moore Papers; and see the articles by Hudson, James Garner, Quincy Wright, Charles Fenwick and Arthur Kuhn in *AJIL* 29, 30 (January 1935–January 1936), *passim*.

76 Walter Lippmann, 'Defeat of the World Court', *NYH–T* (2 February 1935), 15; *CDT* (30 January 1935), 1; Hudson to Thomas W. Lamont: as enclosure, Lamont to Vansittart, 26 June 1935: FO 371, W5713/55/98; John Bassett Moore to Johnson, 20 March 1935: Johnson Papers.

[77] *CR* 74:1, 1143; *NYH-T* (30 January 1935), 1.

[78] *CR* 74:11 143–5. William Gibbs McAdoo (California, Democrat – and Woodrow Wilson's son-in-law) was abroad; Rush D. Holt (West Virginia, Democrat) was under-age and not yet sworn in.

[79] *NYT* (30 January 1935), 2; *NYT* (3 February 1935), IV. 3; *NYH-T* (30 January 1935), 1; *SFE* (30 January 1935), 2; Roosevelt to Hudson, 11 January 1935: Nixon, *Roosevelt and Foreign Affairs*, II. 350–1; Hudson, 'Memorandum Submitted to the Trustees of the World Peace Foundation on the Senate and the World Court', 16 February 1935: as enclosure, Raymond T. Rich to Root, 2 March 1935: Root Papers.

[80] The following analysis relies heavily upon reports in the dozen or so newspapers already cited. I refer to specific press items only in controversial cases.

[81] Libby to Norris, 30 January 1935: Norris Papers; *Washington Times* (30 January 1935), 2; *Springfield Republican* (30 January 1935), 1, 2.

[82] Richard Louis Murphy to Borah, 7 February 1935; Borah to Murphy, 20 February 1935: Borah Papers.

[83] The usually reliable *Christian Science Monitor* identified Schwellenbach and Smith as surprise Nays: *CSM* (30 January 1935), 1, 4.

[84] *SFE* (27 January 1935), 1; *SFE* (30 January 1935) 1, 2.

[85] *CR* 74:1, 1138 ff.

[86] *NYT* (3 February 1935), IV. 3.

[87] For Cutting, see Moore to Borchard, 30 January 1935; Borchard to Moore, 31 January 1935: Borchard Papers. For Caraway, see Raymond Clapper, *WP* (29 January 1935), 2.

[88] *SFE* (18 January 1935), 4.

[89] Keyes had a unique voting pattern during the Court debate; while Hale was a bitter political opponent of Borah's: Borah to Levinson, 30 July 1934: Borah Papers.

[90] For Copeland, see Lape to Root, 30 July 1931: Root Papers; *NYT* (14 January 1935), 9; *WP* (25 January 1935), 2; *SFE* (29 January 1935), 1; for Dieterich, see Libby to Jessup, 23 May 1933; to Roosevelt, 26 May 1933: NA 500. C114/1490, 1493.

[91] Johnson to Clark, 3 February 1935: Johnson Papers; *NYT* (30 January 1935), 2; *NYT* (10 February 1935), IV. 9: *NYT* (2 March 1935), 4; 'A Way Round' *The Sun* (Baltimore) (1 February 1935), 10; *Washington Daily News* (6 February 1935), 11; Jessup to Hudson, 6 February 1935: Hudson Papers. For the Senate valuing procedure over substance, see p.146 above.

[92] *Le Figaro* (Paris) (3 February 1935), 3. For Vandenberg in 1935, see *CR* 74:1, 636 ff.; for 1941, see Arthur H. Vandenberg, Jr., and Joe Alex Morris (eds), *The Private Papers of Senator Vandenberg* (Boston: Houghton Mifflin, 1952), 1.

9 Retrospect and prospect: the United States and the two World Courts

The United States failed to join the Permanent Court of International Justice – the first World Court – essentially because of its intimate connection with the League of Nations. Recent students of the Court campaign have acknowledged this fundamental truth, but somewhat reluctantly. So they write of a 'symbolic' struggle, a term which combines their own awareness that the League was the major factor with their uneasy realization that the League was a shifting coalition of political forces in no way synonymous with abstract internationalism, the slogans of peace and an undefined American national interest. Indeed some historians, impatient with these awkward realities, have complained that the pro-Court campaigners should have used their enormous energies directly for American membership of the League itself![1] Such had been the logic of Sayre, McClure and their kind – newcomers to the Court campaign and activists of a Wilsonian, uncompromising type. It was just this blatant, pro-League drive which convinced the open-minded (like Norris) or simple doubters (like Bulow) that Borah, Johnson, Shipstead and their allies had been right in 1926; and even John Bassett Moore had few regrets. From the beginning he had warned that the League connection was the crucial issue and constituted the most formidable obstacle to American adherence; and, like Borchard, Castle and Kellogg, Moore was not surprised that the Court campaign eventually failed in January 1935 once the League cause was revived and intensified in a flagrantly partisan manner.[2]

The Austro-German Customs Union adjudication, the Mukden Incident, the war-debts repudiation, the Italo-Ethiopian conflict – these were the main items in the catalogue of foreign events influencing

Senators in the winter of 1934–5. Such events only strengthened the determination of many proponents and all the opponents to maintain the terms for adherence set in 1926 and conditionally accepted by the League. But there were two important new domestic ingredients. One was the decision of Sayre and his allies to attack Paragraph VII of the 1926 terms, the clause providing for senatorial involvement in the submission of a case to the Court. Roosevelt's agreement to Sayre's initiative produced an Executive – Senate split unprecedented in the Court campaign. (The administration backed off in its opposition to Paragraph VIII, which covered the Monroe Doctrine, and partially limited the self-inflicted political damage.) The other disturbing novelty was the use of White House patronage. The Roosevelt – Farley threats directed successfully at Bronson Cutting and unsuccessfully at some of his colleagues showed that the administration had staked its own power and prestige on an issue which had previously been treated as a matter of individual judgment. In combination the two moves angered rather than cowed the Senate; and it responded by delivering the first 'agreed setback' to Roosevelt's presidency.[3]

Presidential leadership, Roosevelt's especially, constitutes a newer element in World Court historiography; but it is one which requires closer scrutiny. Two rather more traditional themes are the 'obstructionism' of the opposition and the American origins of the Court.[4] Both are highly problematical. To take 'obstructionism' first, as the simpler issue. Chapters 2–7 of this study show that it was the *proponents* who continually delayed legislative action on the Protocols, even though they were primarily responsible for drafting the conditions of American acceptance. Secondly and on a grander scale: historians have tended to portray the Court as a particularly American creation, fostered (if not necessarily engendered) by Elihu Root. Yet even Manley Hudson had to acknowledge the Court's more complex, multinational background when he addressed foreign legal scholars. In a familiar but justified phrase, Hudson described the Permanent Court as 'largely *sui generis*'.[5] In Chapter 2 the immediate origins of the Court have been described in some detail; but the belief in the Americanness of the Court will perhaps die hard, since it corroborates a widely held sentiment that American and global interests are synonymous. If this prediction seems somewhat speculative, there can be little doubt about the interpretive effects of the Americanness idea: what is always implied and frequently stated is that the Court had a peculiarly powerful claim upon American support. When that support was initially qualified (in 1926) and finally withheld (in 1935), the explanation lay in some malignity of the Senate or the people at large.[6]

So much by way of synopsis; but the question of the larger context remains. As we noted in Chapter 1, the Court campaign – like the inter-war years in general – continues to be viewed within the dichotomous framework of isolationism and internationalism. Though some Second Generation scholars have questioned the accuracy and utility of this bipolar model, the schema set by Denna Frank Fleming and the First Generation has persisted.[7] Basically the battle over American adherence was between internationalists and isolationists. In 1935 the isolationists won; and another huge step was taken on the road to war. The destructive sequence was classically expressed by Fleming when he commented on contemporary reports that the Roosevelt administration felt 'unconcerned' about the Court defeat. In Arthur Krock's words: 'Nothing like a pall hung over official Washington." No, added Fleming bitterly:

> The pall was to come a little later, on December 7, 1941. It was to be a great cloud of black smoke, heavy with the acrid fumes of a fine American air force suddenly destroyed on the ground, and of a greater battle fleet blasted while at anchor in harbor.[8]

With Pearl Harbor and the war came the end of isolationism; and isolationism understood not just as a set of beliefs about the scope and conduct of foreign relations. The objective or material bases of isolationism had been eroded to vanishing point. In a number of major studies by scholars such as Wayne Cole, Robert Dallek and Robert Divine, Roosevelt himself is taken to exemplify this social, geopolitical process: the tide of history bearing the great pragmatist willy-nilly from his isolationist instincts to responsible internationalism.[9]

The literature on Roosevelt is unending – though Hoover's judgment has never been bettered: Roosevelt was 'a chameleon on plaid'.[10] But the most obvious problem with the transition model is that isolationism did not disappear with World War II. *Prima facie* evidence comes from the many studies which either record the persistence of pre-war isolationist attitudes and policies or describe the emergence of neo-isolationism.[11] Of course, such data can be readily incorporated into a secular bipolar model, most obviously by conceptualizing the phenomena as examples of 'outward thrusts' succeeded by inward reactive 'impulses'. The variants are numerous.[12] Alternatively we may choose to distinguish American *policy* from *relations* and argue that while the United States is increasingly implicated by transnational forces – and hence its relations are becoming more international – its official actions have not adjusted to this reality – and hence its policy shows certain isolationist legacies. The common feature of these explanatory models and the implied programmatic strategies is a choice between internationalism and isolationism. Perhaps, however, the two positions are not true alternatives; and we shall understand both the history of American foreign relations and the contradictions of official policy by seeking consistency on a deeper plane.

An astute observer of the 1935 Court debate, Frank H. Simonds, noted that both the proponents and opponents of adherence had used essentially 'nationalistic' and 'isolationist' arguments. From the context of his remarks we can see that Simonds was stressing the fundamentally *unilateralist* attitudes common to both sides. Simonds's insight penetrated superficial appearances (the 1926 vote as the 'death-knell of isolationism'; the 1935 vote as a 'triumph for isolationism') and detected the continued insistence of *both* Senate *and* Executive that, in

Roosevelt's words, the 'sovereignty of the United States [would] be in no way diminished or jeopardized' by membership in the Court.[13] First, last and always the US government would set the conditions of its political dealings with the rest of the world. Behind the trappings of internationalism and multilateralism lay the determination to define and pursue American interests with no higher, external authority. Perhaps no other State would promise anything more; but, if so, such a simple truism will help observers to discount and thereby evaluate correctly the glib language of universalism prevalent in both American political and historical rhetoric. For it is not that the United States has passed from isolationism to internationalism; rather its leaders, political and intellectual, have cloaked their special goals in general terms. The example of the second World Court maintains the established pattern.

The first World Court, the Permanent Court of International Justice, was dissolved on 18 April 1946 – the very day on which its 'direct successor', the International Court of Justice held its inaugural session at The Hague.[14] Legal scholars have subtly debated the precise relationship of the two World Courts historically and jurisprudentially to one another; there has been far less disagreement about the relationship of the new Court to its political counterpart, the United Nations Organization. From our perspective, however, the mass of heterogeneous detail displays a clear configuration. In the story of United States relations with the two World Courts, the lines of continuity run strongly under the surface of change.

The evidence of change is, of course, undeniable. The creation of both the United Nations Organization (UNO) and the International Court of Justice (ICJ) was a classic example of learning from perceived mistakes. As Philip Jessup noted at the close of World War II: 'everyone thought of the fate of the Covenant before the Senate' in the aftermath of World War I.[15] Consequently senior Senators were prominent in the Roosevelt administration's planning for postwar organization. Chief among them were Tom Connally (Texas, Democrat), Chairman of the Foreign Relations Committee, and the ranking Republican Committee member, Arthur Vandenberg of Michigan. Whatever the Executive might be saying at the wartime Summits in Moscow, Cairo and Teheran (October –December 1943), Congress, *via* the Senate, was involved in the conferences at Dumbarton Oaks (August–October 1944) and San Francisco (April–June 1945) which produced the UN Charter and the ICJ Statute. Such bipartisanship and senatorial participation contrasted strongly with the Paris Peace Conference and the writing of the League Covenant during 1919. In the specific case of the new Court Statute there were some striking novelties – further testimony to the lost campaign of 1920–35. A few examples will give the picture. In April 1945 the latest Committee of Jurists worked directly and openly as a UN body; the Committee met in Washington not at The Hague; the members were explicitly governmental representatives; and in the particular instance of the United States, the delegation was led by the Legal

Adviser to the Department of State, Green H. Hackworth. (Jessup was one of his assistants.) As for the Court itself, unlike the PCIJ, it was established as 'the principal judicial organ of the United Nations'; in other words, it was to be 'an integral part' of the new international system. Moreover all Member States of the UNO were '*ipso facto* parties' to the Court Statute and formally obliged 'to comply with the decision of the International Court of Justice in any case to which it is a party'. Most importantly, the Security Council was empowered to 'make recommendations or decide upon measures to be taken to give effect' to decisions and judgments of the Court (UN Charter: Articles 92–4).[16]

When the Charter and the Statute reached the Senate for its 'advice and consent' to ratification, the contrast with 1919–20 was equally pronounced. On 28 July 1945 (between VE and VJ Day) the Charter was approved by 89 votes to 2; on 2 August 1946 the favourable vote for the Statute was 60 to 2.[17] Read against the background of struggle over the League and the Permanent Court, the message of this Executive–Senate co-operation was simple: as the United States had failed to join the Court of the League it had previously rejected (and by comparable voting tallies), so in 1945–6 the United States endorsed the Court of the United Nations it had created. The political logic was impeccable.

Logic, however, includes premises as well as systems of entailment; and it was in the maintenance of traditional principles that the continuity of American foreign policy was most marked. So while the US government narrowly declined the League system and overwhelmingly adopted the UNO, the basic terms remained unaltered. Formally and organizationally the bipartisan negotiators from the Executive and Senate won their key demands from the League–Court debate: a veto power in the Security Council; the preservation of the Monroe Doctrine; and the reservation of 'domestic' questions (UN Charter: Articles 27(3); 52; 2(7) respectively). The language of these principles was almost always couched in general terms; but there was no doubt about its particular reference. For example, in the Foreign Relations Committee's *Report* on the Charter, the Monroe Doctrine was identified as a principle which would be 'safeguarded' and 'strengthened' by the United Nations Organization. Even when a traditional demand failed to gain allusive recognition in the Charter, the Executive and Senate agreed that omission did not mean concession. Here the prime instance was the right to withdraw. In the Committee's formula: 'the legality of the right of withdrawal is not put in question through absence of specific permission in the Charter'. As one knowledgeable commentator noted, the remarkable feature of the United Nations system was 'the freedom of action left [to] the United States under the Charter'.[18]

In the drafting of the UN Charter, Vandenberg was prominent in the defence of the Monroe Doctrine – his own line of continuity with the prewar debate on American adherence to the Permanent Court. Connally's postwar fame was as eponymous defender of the so-called 'self-judging clause', by which the Senate conditioned its approval of the Court Statute, in particular the application of the Court's compulsory jurisdiction (ICJ Statute: Article 36). Under the Connally Amendment the Senate asserted the explicit right of the United States to determine the nature of 'domestic' matters and thereby reserve them from the jurisdiction of the Court – a line of continuity both to Paragraph VIII and the notorious Paragraph V governing the advisory jurisdiction. (The Statute of the ICJ, Articles 65–8, provided for advisory opinions – a striking omission from the original Statute of the PCIJ.) The result of the Connally-Vandenberg leadership was the Senate's consent to American membership of the International Court of Justice subject to the following exemptions:

(a) disputes the solution of which the parties shall entrust to other tribunals;

(b) disputes with regard to matters which are essentially within the domestic jurisdiction of the United States of America *as determined by the United States of America* [emphasis added];
or

(c) disputes arising under a multilateral treaty, unless (1) all parties to the Treaty affected by the decision are also parties to the case before the Court, or (2) the United States of America specifically agrees to jurisdiction.[19]

Twenty years after the passage of the Connally and Vandenberg amendments (sub-paragraphs (b) and (c) respectively) Denna Frank Fleming wrote in disillusionment: 'the Senate completed its "acceptance" of the [second World] Court... by backing away from it into the citadel of American sovereignty'.[20]

Throughout the 1950s any number of lawyers, corporately led by the American Society of International Law and the American Bar Association, called for the repeal of the Connally Amendment. The most common complaint was its 'boomerang effect': other States could invoke reciprocal disclaimers.[21] (The Vandenberg–Monroe Doctrine provisions were conveniently ignored.) Supporters of the Connally Amendment replied by stressing its role as a weapon against a 'polyglot' Court, which had become increasingly 'politicized' during the Cold War. The pejorative terms recorded a growing feeling that the International Court could not be relied upon to uphold American claims or follow American jurisprudence. In the most famous defence of the selfjudging clause Denison Kitchel wrote:

> The retention of the Connally Amendment–the guarding of our national sovereignty ourselves rather than placing it in the hands of the World Court for safekeeping–is essential to the ultimate victory of freedom in the present struggle....[22]

Kitchel's language and arguments were in keeping with the dominant consensus. Contemporaneously the Kennedy administration was describing the Soviet proposal for a judicial resolution of the Cuban missile crisis as a disingenuous ploy to represent a 'political attack' as a 'legal dispute' by embroiling the International Court in the 'Cold War' and 'the jungle of communist propaganda'.[23] On the Monroe Doctrine specifically, the Kennedy administration was in no doubt about its validity – though in public pronouncements the Doctrine was cloaked in multilateral form by the invocation of hemispheric treaties. As Louis Henkin correctly observed in a common metaphor: the 'malleability', the 'elasticity' of 'regional arrangements' under the UN Charter and the inter-American Treaties of Rio de Janeiro (1947) and Bogotá (1948) gave Washington unlimited scope for interpretation, self-justification and essentially unilateral action.[24] What was unmistakable was Washington's insistence, clearly expressed in the terms of American adherence in 1946, that the World Court had no *locus standi*, no competence unless the United States conceded the Court's intervention as an expression of its own national sovereignty.

Against such a background recent US policy towards the International Court reveals its fundamental consistency. The tradition stretches back not just to 1945–6 or even to the post-World War I years and the League–Court debates. Rather it goes back beyond the Roosevelt Corollary of 1904; the Cleveland–Olney *fiat* of 1895; the Polk Corollary of 1845 to the original Monroe Doctrine of 1823. The traditional pattern has two distinct motifs: one, the line of unilateralism; the other, the specific direction of that line drawn to embrace the Western Hemisphere. (The concept of the Western Hemisphere, in appearance simply geographical, is of course geopolitical.) This twofold, asymmetrical pattern expresses the secular essence of US foreign policy far more accurately than the isolationism –internationalism dichotomy. The Reagan administration's war against Nicaragua was made palatable to the Congress and the American public because legislators and the electorate share the same presumptions about the right of the United States to determine, by war if necessary, the political, economic and social systems of those Monroe patronized as the 'Southern brethren'. From this hemispheric, historical perspective the war for the Contras against the elected government in Managua can be seen as a bloody paragraph in a postwar chapter which includes Guatemala in 1954, Cuba in 1961, the Dominican Republic in 1965, Chile in 1973, and Grenada in 1983–to cite only the most notorious cases of US invasion and subversion.

As for the rule of international law adjudicated by an independent body, the United States will use the World Court instrumenally and cynically when such recourse serves American interests.[25] By such a test the United States appealed to the Court in the Teheran hostage case; and such instrumentalism explains its current use of the Court in controversies with Canada.[26] But when the World Court offers a jurisdictional challenge to Washington's claims, then the Court is denounced as politically inspired and ideologically hostile to the United States. Since 1984 the Reagan administration has sought to oust the jurisdiction of the Court from the suit brought by the Nicaraguan government to halt the 'paramilitary operations' waged by Washington in support of the Contras. Even the stages of the ouster parallel the general pattern of US foreign policy. First, in April 1984, came Washington's attempt to exclude or reserve Central America from the competence of the Court *vis-à-vis* the United States. Later, in October 1985, the United States tried to bar the Court from any case brought without Washington's specific agreement.[27] As we can see, these assertions are in keeping with the political principles of the Connally–Vandenberg amendments.

The International Court, to its great credit, entertained the Nicaraguan suit. In one of the most controversial judgments in its forty-year career the Court found against the United States on seven counts of violating international law. The verdict, handed down in June 1986, showed the Court divided even more dramatically than in the Austro-German Customs Union case – the case which ultimately undermined the first World Court. The Nicaraguan decision also showed the American judge, Stephen M. Schwebel, aligned solidly with his government and (it was said) its closest allies, in the persons of the British and Japanese judges.[28] Even more important, though less surprising, has been the Reagan administration's complete contempt for the Court's ruling. The undeclared American war against the elected government in Nicaragua continued – the war's termination a matter for political decision in Washington – not judicial resolution at The Hague. So it is, in general, with the use and abuse of the Court: how and when it will be employed or denounced by Washington remains a political decision not a judicial principle. (As with the Vietnam war, Congress collectively is close to the Executive: it responded to the Court's verdict by voting aid to the Contras.) One thing seems sure: the language of judicial internationalism will cloak the reality of political unilateralism. In the words of Abraham Sofaer, Legal Adviser to the Department of State, testifying before the Senate Committee on Foreign Relations: the American ouster meant no

> lessening of our traditionally strong support for the Court in the exercise of its proper functions, much less a diminution of our commitment to international law. We remain prepared to use the Court for the resolution of international disputes whenever possible and appropriate.[29]

Whenever possible, *whenever appropriate*. Neither side in the pre-war Court campaign would have settled for less.

Notes

1. See e.g. Guinsburg, *Pursuit of Isolationism*, 163.
2. Castle to Kellogg, 2 February [1935]: Kellogg to Castle, 6 February 1935: Castle Papers, Hoover Presidential Library; Borchard to Moore, 30 January 1935; Moore to Borchard, 30 January 1935: Borchard Papers.
3. *NYT* (30 January 1935), 1; cf. Phillips, *Diary*, 29 January 1935: Phillips Papers.
4. Dunne, 'Isolationism of a Kind', 332 ff.
5. Hudson, 'Les Avis Consultatifs de la Cour Permanente de Justice Interna-

tionale', *Recueil des Cours* (1925), III: vol. 8, 345–412 at 349.

[6] William E. Dodd to Joe Robinson, 30 January 1935: R. Walton Moore Papers; Roosevelt to Jessup, 2 February 1935: Nixon, *Roosevelt and Foreign Affairs*, II. p.387; Hull, *Memoirs*, I. 389.

[7] Deibel, 'League of Nations', II. 723.

[8] Fleming, *United States and the World Court*, 137; Krock in *NYT* (31 January 1935), 18.

[9] Epitomized in Dallek, 'Franklin D. Roosevelt as World Leader', *American Historical Review* 76 (December 1971), 1503–513 at 1513; cf. Thomas H. Greer, *What Roosevelt Thought: the Social and Political Ideas of Franklin D. Roosevelt* (East Lansing: Michigan State University Press, 1958), 171–7.

[10] James MacGregor Burns, *Roosevelt: the Lion and the Fox* (New York: Harcourt, Brace & World, 1956), 474.

[11] Norman A. Graebner, *The New Isolationism: a Study in Politics and Foreign Policy since 1950* (New York: Ronald Press, 1956); Robert W. Tucker, *A New Isolationism: Threat or Promise*? (New York: Universe Books, 1972).

[12] Frank L. Klingberg, *Cyclical Trends in American Foreign Policy Moods: the Unfolding of America's World Role* (Lanham, Md., and London: University Press of America, 1983).

[13] Message of 16 January 1935: Nixon, *Roosevelt and Foreign Affairs*, II. 363–4; Simonds, 'U.S. Nationalism Predominates', *SFC* (3 February 1935), F, 5.

[14] F. Blaine Sloan, 'Advisory Jurisdiction of the International Court of Justice', *California Law Review* 38 (December 1950), 830–59 at 831.

[15] Jessup, quoted in Ruth B. Russell and Jeannette E. Muther, *A History of the United Nations Charter. The Role of the United States 1940–1945* (Washington, DC: Brookings Institution, 1958), 888–9.

[16] US Department of State, *The International Court of Justice: Selected Documents relating to the Drafting of the Statute*, Publication no. 2491. Conference Series no. 84 (Washington, DC: GPO, 1946).

[17] Russell and Muther, History of the United Nations Charter, chs 33-35.

[18] Ibid. 939; US Senate, Seventy-ninth Congress, First Session, Senate Executive Report no. 8. *The Charter of the United Nations* (Washington, DC: GPO, 1945), 10–13.

[19] *FRUS* (1946), I. 59–60.

[20] Fleming, *United States and the World Court*, 197.

[21] Rudolf B. Schlesinger, 'The Connally Amendment–Amelioration by Interpretation?', *Virginia Law Review* 48 (1962), 685–97 at 693.

[22] Denison Kitchel, *Too Grave a Risk: the Connally Amendment Issue* (New York: Morrow, 1963), 105, 126.

[23] Adlai Stevenson, US Ambassador to the UN, quoted in Philip C. Jessup, 'The Development of a United States Approach toward the International Court of Justice', *Vanderbilt Journal of Transnational Law* 5 (Winter 1971), 1–46 at 6.

[24] Henkin, 'Comment', in Abram Chayes, *The Cuban Missile Crisis* International Crises and the Role of Law (London: Oxford University Press, 1974), 149–54. For the Kennedy administration's use of the Monroe Doctrine, see the legal briefs: ibid. 108–48.

[25] Jeane Kirkpatrick: *Time Magazine* (23 April 1984), 18; State Department source, *Newsweek* (28 January 1985), 45; Richard N. Gardner, 'U.S. Termination of the Compulsory Jurisdiction of the International Court of Justice', *Columbia Journal of Transnational Law* 24 (1986), 421–7.

[26] The detailed stories may be traced in the ICJ, *Yearbook*, from 1980 to the present.

[27] US, Department of State, *Bulletin* (cited below as *DSB*) April 1984–January 1986, *passim*; but the key texts are reprinted in Anthony Clark Arend (ed.),

The United States and the Compulsory Jurisdiction of the International Court of Justice (Lanham, Md., and London: University Press of America, 1986), 211–13.

[28] ICJ *Reports*, 1986: 'Case concerning Military and Paramilitary Activities in and against Nicaragua (Nicaragua v. United States of America)', 14 ff. Judge Schwebel's dissenting opinion runs to some 250 pages.

[29] Statement of 4 December 1985 to Senate Foreign Relation Committee: *DSB* (January 1986), 67–71 at 71.

Bibliographical Essay

Introduction

This essay begins with references to materials which are relevant at many points of the preceding narrative. So far as possible I avoid repeating citations already given in the Notes. (The major exception is the listing of theses and biographies.) In the second and much longer section of this essay I discuss sources and studies in relation to particular chapters; but the distinctions cannot be absolute. For example, works on the League of Nations are relevant to my arguments throughout Chapters 1–9 but they are gathered together at a number of places, notably Chapters 2 and 5.

1. Unpublished materials

Individuals' papers

Though I have consulted more than two dozen private manuscript sources in researching this book, not all have been equally rewarding. Senators' papers are often disappointing – sometimes incredibly thin: washed-out, no doubt, by careful laundering. Helpful finding-aids are: Kathryn A. Jacob, *Guide to Research Collections of Former United States Senators, 1789–1985* (Detroit: Gale, 1986) and John J. McDonough and Marilyn K. Parr, *Members of Congress: a Checklist of their Papers in the Manuscript Division, Library of Congress* (Washington, DC: GPO, 1980).

The most valuable sources for this study were the papers of the following: William E. Borah, Charles Evans Hughes, Philip C. Jessup, Irvine L. Lenroot, John Bassett Moore, Elihu Root and Arthur Sweetser: all in the Manuscript Division, Library of Congress; Edwin M. Borchard and Henry L. Stimson: Sterling Memorial Library, Yale; Manley O. Hudson: Harvard Law School Library; Hiram Warren Johnson: Bancroft Library, University of California at Berkeley; Herbert C. Hoover: Hoover Presidential Library, West Branch, Iowa and Hoover Institution on War, Revolution and Peace, Stanford; Jay Pierrepont Moffat and William Phillips: Houghton Library, Harvard; Franklin D. Roosevelt: Roosevelt Presidential Library, Hyde Park, NY; and James Brown Scott and Robert F. Wagner: Lauinger Library, Georgetown University.

In the UK my major private sources have been the Austen Chamberlain Papers: University of Birmingham Library; and the Robert Cecil (i.e. Cecil of Chelwood) Papers: Department of Manuscripts, British Library. An introduction to the latter depository is Margaret A. E. Nickson, *The British Library: Guide to the Catalogues and Indexes of the Department of Manuscripts,* 2nd ed rev. (London: British Library, 1982).

Governmental archives

The key American sources are in the records of the Department of State, Record Group 59: National Archives, Washington, DC, especially Files 500. C114 (PCIJ) and 662.6331 (Austro-German Customs Union Case). A helpful introduction is US National Archives and Records Service, *Guide to the National Archives of the United States* (Washington, DC: GPO, 1974).

In the UK the Foreign Office Papers are in the Public Record Office at Kew. The comparable guide is: Great Britain, *Records of the Foreign Office, 1782–1939*, Public Records Office Handbooks no. 13 (London: HMSO, 1969), which has a 'specimen search' on the Customs Union controversy.

Two valuable introductions to sources in modern British history are Cameron Hazelhurst and Christine Woodland, *A Guide to the Papers of British Cabinet Ministers, 1900–1951.* Royal Historical Society, Guides and Handbooks, Supplementary Series, no. 1 (London: Royal Historical Society, 1974) and Chris Cook *et al.*, *Sources in British Political History, 1900–1951,* 5 vols. (London: Macmillan, 1975–8).

2. Published materials

Official governmental and intergovernmental materials

In the text I have cited from the major American and British series, *Foreign Relations of the United States* (*FRUS*) and *Documents on British Foreign Policy* (*DBFP*). Not surprisingly, only a tiny fraction of the relevant documentation is printed. For the first World Court, the only special collection published by the US government was US Department of State, *The United States and the Permanent Court of International Justice. Documents relating to the Question of American Accession to the Court.* Department of State Publication, no. 44 (Washington, DC: GPO, 1930).

For the voluminous literature issued by the League, there are two main authoritative guides: Hans Aufricht, *Guide to League of Nations Publications: a Bibliographical Survey of the Work of the League, 1920–1947* (New York: Columbia University Press,1951) and Victor Yves and Catherine Ghebali, *A Repertoire of League of Nations Serial Documents, 1919–1947*, 2 vols (Dobbs Ferry, NY: Oceana, 1973). (Note: publications of the League system and of the ICJ can be found – though not always – in both English and French versions. Where possible I cite the English text.)

The records of both World Courts are extensive. At ch. 4, n. 65, 69 I cite PCIJ Series A–E; in ch. 9, n. 26, 28 I cite the ICJ *Yearbook* and *Reports*. For the bibliography of both Courts, see Edvard Hambro, *The Case Law of the International Court: a Repertoire of the Judgments, Advisory Opinions and Orders of the Permanent Court of International Justice and of the International Court of Justice, with a Bibliography prepared by J. Douma* (Leiden: A. W. Sijthoff, 1961), supplemented by J. Douma, *Bibliography on the International Court including the Permanent Court, 1918–1964* (Leiden: A.W. Sijthoff, 1966) and International Court of Justice, *Bibliography of the International Court of Justice* (The Hague: ICJ, 1947–), though this annual began as part of the ICJ *Yearbook*. For the first World Court, Manley Hudson produced important documentation and fine bibliographies: see *World Court Reports: a Collection of the Judgments, Orders and Opinions of the Permanent Court of International Justice*, 4 vols (Washington, DC: CEIP, 1934–43).

Reference works and bibliographical aids

For the Court itself the following have been useful: Académie Diplomatique Internationale, *Dictionnaire Diplomatique*, 3 vols (Paris: Académie Diplomatique Internationale, 1933–7); Hans-Jürgen Schlochauer, *Wö rterbuch des Völkerrechts*, 3 vols (Berlin: de Gruyter, 1961); Union Acadé mique Internationale, *Dictionnaire de la Terminologie du Droit International* (Paris: Recueil Sirey, 1960).

For US foreign relations generally a 'post-revisionist' base line has been drawn bibliographically with Richard D. Burns (ed.), *Guide to American Foreign Relations since 1700* (Santa Barbara, Ca. and Oxford: ABC-CLIO, 1983), though for our purposes it needs to be supplemented by works such as Berenice A. Carroll *et al.*, *Peace and War: a Guide to Bibliographies* (Santa Barbara, Ca. and Oxford: ABC-CLIO, 1983) and Linda Killen and Richard L. Lael (eds), *Versailles and After: an Annotated Bibliography of American Foreign Relations, 1919–1933*, Garland Reference Library of Social Science, vol. 135 (New York and London: Garland, 1983). The journal *Foreign Affairs* (see ch. 3 at n. 69) published excellent current bibliographies.

3 Biographical materials

Biographical reference

Two extremely helpful recent biographical guides – though by no means covering all our *dramatis personae* – are Harold Josephson (ed.), *Biographical Dictionary of Modern Peace Leaders* (Westport, Ct., and London: Greenwood Press, 1985) and Warren F. Kuehl (ed.), *Biographical Dictionary of Internationalists* (Westport, Ct., and London: Greenwood Press, 1983). For example, Anzilotti and van Hamel are absent; not so Sweetser. Esther Lape is also absent from both. For British actors (e.g. Cecil, Hurst and Phillimore) the *Dictionary of National Biography* remains useful; as, of course, for Americans is Scribner's *Dictionary of American Biography*. To trace non-Anglophones, 'foreign' language encyclopaedias and biographical sources are sometimes necessary: e.g. *Dictionnaire de Biographie Fransçaise* (1933–); *Neue Deutsche Biographie* (1953–); and *Meyers Enzyklopädisches Lexikon* (1971–9).

Biographical studies: published

Some recent biographies of important figures are extremely disappointing on the Court issue – no doubt a continuing legacy of the First Generation historiography. Whatever their other virtues, the major modern studies of Roosevelt fall into this category: e.g. Robert Dallek, *Franklin D. Roosevelt and American Foreign Policy, 1932–1945* (New York: Oxford University Press, 1979); Wayne S. Cole, *Roosevelt and the Isolationists, 1932–45* (Lincoln and London: University of Nebraska Press, 1983); Nathan Miller, *FDR: an Intimate History* (Garden City, NY: Doubleday, 1983); Ted Morgan, *FDR: a Biography* (New York: Simon & Schuster, 1985); and Kenneth S. Davis, *FDR: the New Deal Years, 1933–1937. A History* (New York: Random House, 1986).

Some biographers, however, are informative and accurate on the Court issue. Chief among them is Joseph P. Lash: see, especially, *Eleanor and Franklin: the Story of their Relationship, based on Eleanor Roosevelt's Private Papers* (New York: W. W. Norton, 1971). Lash is valuable in showing the role of Eleanor's friend, Esther Everett Lape, who merits her own biography. See also Jason Berger, *A New Deal for the World: Eleanor Roosevelt and American Foreign Policy* (New York: Columbia University Press, 1981) and Joan Hoff-Wilson and Marjorie Lightman (eds), *Without Precedent: the Life and Career of Eleanor Roosevelt* (Bloomington: Indiana University Press, 1984).

Two antagonists in the Court campaign are well discussed by Harold Josephson, *James T. Shotwell and the Rise of Internationalism in America* (Rutherford, NJ: Fairleigh Dickinson University Press, 1975) and Aubrey Parkman, *David Jayne Hill and the Problem of World Peace* (Lewisburg, Pa.: Bucknell University Press, 1975); while Harding's shifts through the election of 1920 are exhaustively covered in Randolph C. Downes, *The Rise of Warren Gamaliel Harding, 1865–1920* (Columbus: Ohio State University Press, 1970). All James Barros's works on the

League are instructive; and, apart from his major study of Eric Drummond (cited in ch. 3, n. 56), see *Betrayal from Within: Joseph Avenol, Secretary-General of the League of Nations, 1933–1940* (New Haven: Yale University Press, 1969). Two older biographies which remain very useful are Warren F. Kuehl, *Hamilton Holt: Journalist, Internationalist, Educator* (Gainesville: University of Florida Press, 1960) and Hoyt Landon Warner, *The Life of Mr. Justice Clarke: a Testament to the Power of Liberal Dissent in America* (Cleveland, Ohio: Western Reserve University Press, 1951). The flavour of Clarke's own arguments for adherence is given in John Hessin Clarke, *America and World Peace*. The Colver Lectures, Brown University, 1925 (New York: Henry Holt, 1925). As I noted in ch. 3, n. 80, the best biography of Borah remains that published in 1936 by Claudius O. Johnson, *Borah of Idaho*, which was reissued in 1967 with a new introduction by the author. Marian McKenna, *Borah* (Ann Arbor: University of Michigan Press, 1961) is exceptionally thin on the Court issue.

Biographical studies: unpublished

A sympathetic unpublished study of Borah is Orde Sorensen Pickney, 'William E. Borah and the Republican Party, 1932–1940' (PhD dissertation, University of California at Berkeley, 1957). Other actors are discussed by George Harry Curtis, 'The Wilson Administration, Elihu Root and the Founding of the World Court, 1918–1921' (PhD dissertation, Georgetown University, 1972); Leslie Brooks Hill, 'Charles Evans Hughes and United States Adherence to an International Court: a Rhetorical Analysis' (PhD dissertation, University of Illinois, 1968); James T. Kenny, 'The Contributions of Manley O. Hudson to Modern International Law and Organization' (PhD dissertation, University of Denver, 1976); Richard Megargee, 'The Diplomacy of John Bassett Moore: Realism in American Foreign Policy' (PhD dissertation, Northwestern University, 1963); Ralph Dingmann Nurnberger, 'James Brown Scott: Peace through Law' (PhD dissertation, Georgetown University, 1975); and Daryl L. Revoldt, 'Raymond B. Fosdick: Reform, Internationalism and the Rockefeller Foundation' (PhD dissertation, University of Akron, 1982). In a class of its own prosopographically is Terry Lattau Deibel, 'The League of Nations and American Internationalism, 1919–1929', 2 vols (PhD dissertation, Fletcher School of Law and Diplomacy, 1972). Deibel discusses the activities of Raymond Fosdick, Arthur Sweetser, Huntington Gilchrist, Manley O. Hudson, Howard Huston and Florence Wilson.

4 General works on the two World Courts, with particular emphasis upon jurisdiction

J. P. Fockema Andreae, *An Important Chapter from the History of Legal Interpretation: the Jurisdiction of the First Permanent Court of International Justice, 1922–1940* (Leiden: A. W. Sijthoff, 1948); Ijaz

Hussain, *Dissenting and Separate Opinions at the World Court* (Dordrecht: Martinus Nijhoff, 1984); Kenneth James Keith, *The Extent of the Advisory Jurisdiction of the International Court of Justice* (Leiden: A. W. Sijthoff, 1971); Michla Pomerance, *The Advisory Function of the International Court in the League and U. N. Eras* (Baltimore and London: Johns Hopkins University Press, 1973); Dharma Pratap, *The Advisory Jurisdiction of the International Court* (Oxford: Clarendon Press, 1972); and Ibrahim F. I. Shihata, *The Power of the International Court to Determine its own Jurisdiction* (The Hague: Martinus Nijhoff, 1965). The two very different but equally impressive contemporary accounts of the first World Court by Manley Hudson and Alexander Fachiri have been cited in ch. 1, n. 8.

Chapter 1

An excellent though little known critique of imprecise terminology in American historiography, especially on the interwar years, is James C. Malin, *On the Nature of History: Essays about History and Dissidence* (Lawrence, Kansas: privately published, 1954). In the same year William A. Williams published his classic essay, 'The Legend of Isolationism in the 1920s', *Science and Society* 18 (Winter 1954), 1–20. Representative essays from the Williams-Wisconsin school are in Lloyd C. Gardner (ed.), *Redefining the Past: Essays in Diplomatic History in Honor of William A. Williams* (Corvallis: Oregon State University Press, 1986); and a recent relevant monograph, dedicated to Williams, is Patrick J. Hearden, *Roosevelt Confronts Hitler: America's Entry into World War II* (Dekalb: Northern Illinois University Press, 1987). Very detailed historiographical reviews have been published by John Braeman: see e.g. 'The New Left and American Foreign Policy during the Age of Normalcy: a Re-examination', *Business History Review* 57 (Spring 1983), 73–104; though we may note that the new anti-consensus fashion is 'corporatism': see John Lewis Gaddis and Michael J. Hogan, 'The New School of American Diplomatic History: an Exchange [on] the Corporate Synthesis', *Diplomatic History* 10 (Fall 1986), 357–72.

The most scathing attack on the isolationists remains Adler, *Isolationist Impulse* (cited in ch. 1, n. 16). More sympathetic is the conceptual analysis by Manfred Jonas, *Isolationism in America, 1935–1941* (Ithaca: Cornell University Press, 1966); while the aetiology of isolationism is explored in multivariate terms by Leroy N. Rieselbach, *The Roots of Isolationism* (Indianapolis: Bobbs-Merrill, 1968). Diplomatic historians who follow the basic argument of Adler include John E. Wiltz, *From Isolation to War, 1931–1941* (New York: Thomas Y. Crowell, 1968) through Armin Rappaport, *A History of American Diplomacy* (New York: Macmillan; London: Collier-Macmillan, 1975) to Thomas G. Paterson *et al.*, *American Foreign Policy: a History since 1920,* 2nd ed (Lexington, Mass.: D.C. Heath, 1983).

My set of counter-propositions on the relationship of American isolationism to the outbreak of war in Europe in 1939 relies upon the evidence – if not the deductions – of the following representative texts: Karl Dietrich Bracher *et al.*, *Nationalsozialistische Diktatur, 1933–1945: eine Bilanz*. Bonner Schriften zur Politik und Zeitgeschichte, Band 21 (Düsseldorf: Droste, 1983); Jonathan Haslam, *The Soviet Union and the Struggle for Collective Security in Europe, 1933–1939* (London: Macmillan, 1984); Jiri Hochman, *The Soviet Union and the Failure of Collective Security, 1934–1938* (Ithaca and London: Cornell University Press, 1984); Wolfgang Michalka (ed.), *Nationalsozialistische Aussenpolitik*. Wege der Forschung, Band 297 (Darmstadt: Wissenschaftliche Buchgesellschaft, 1978); Wolfgang J. Mommsen and L. Kettenacker (eds), *The Fascist Challenge and the Policy of Appeasement* (London: Allen & Unwin, 1983); Simon Newman, *March 1939: the British Guarantee to Poland: a Study in the Continuity of British Foreign Policy* (Oxford: Clarendon Press, 1976); Anita Prazmowska, *Britain, Poland and the Eastern Front, 1939* (Cambridge: Cambridge University Press, 1987); and (summing-up his enormous research), Gerhard L. Weinberg, 'Response', *Journal of Modern History* 57 (June 1985), 316–20.

Roosevelt still had his defenders, of course: see e.g. Richard A. Harrison, 'Testing the Water: a Secret Probe towards Anglo-American Military Co-operation in 1936', *International History Review* 7 (May 1985), 214–34. In general, the thesis of Roosevelt's 'leadership' is marred by neglect (among other things) of politics abroad. In this category are Gloria J. Barron, *Leadership in Crisis: FDR and the Path to Intervention* (Port Washington, NY: Kennikat, 1973) and William E. Kinsella, Jr, *Leadership in Isolation: FDR and the Origins of the Second World War* (Cambridge, Mass.: Schenkman, 1979).

Studying events abroad – especially through the voluminous official documentation – has been made easier by the publication in 1981, from Scholarly Resources of Wilmington, Delaware, of four research guides. There are separate introductions to British, French, German and Italian materials; and each has the following model format: Sidney Aster, *British Foreign Policy, 1918–1945: a Guide to Research and Research Materials*. The other authors are Robert J. Young, Christoph M. Kimmich and Alan Cassels respectively. A companion volume on *International Organization, 1918–1945* is edited by George W. Baer, himself an authority on the League of Nations. It may be noted here that complacency towards the League has survived, despite much close investigation, and is not, of course, confined to Americans; see e.g. F.S. Northedge, *The League of Nations: its Life and Times, 1920–1946* (Leicester: Leicester University Press, 1986). An excellent critical analysis is George W. Egerton, 'Collective Security as Political Myth: Liberal Internationalism and the League of Nations in Politics and History', *International History Review* 5 (November 1983), 496–524.

Fleming's 'neo-isolationist' critique of the attempt to create a 'pax Americana' abroad and 'Fortress America' at home is briefly set out in *Annals* 360 (July 1965), 127–38 and at length in *The Origins and Legacies of World War I* (Garden City, NY: Doubleday, 1968); *America's Role in Asia* (New York: Funk & Wagnalls, 1969); and *The Issues of Survival* (Garden City, NY: Doubleday, 1972). A recent attempt to deal with such conceptual problems is Martin Ceadel, *Thinking about Peace and War* (Oxford and New York: Oxford University Press, 1987); while a sociological study of similar issues is Saul H. Mendlovitz and R. B. J. Walker (eds), *Towards a Just World Peace: Perspectives from Social Movements* (London: Butterworths, 1987).

Useful essays on arbitration, adjudication and many of the issues dealt with in ch. 1 can be found in two compilations: Alexander DeConde (ed.), *Encyclopedia of American Foreign Policy: Studies of the Principal Movements and Ideas*, 3 vols. (New York: Scribner's, 1978) and Jack P. Greene (ed), *Encyclopedia of American Political History*, 3 vols (New York: Scribner's, 1984). An excellent special study is John P. Campbell, 'Taft, Roosevelt, and the Arbitration Treaties of 1911', *Journal of American History* 53 (September 1966), 279–98.

For the *decline* of American recourse to arbitration, see Alex M. Stuyt, *Survey of International Arbitration, 1794–1970*, rev. ed (Leiden: A.W. Sijthoff; Dobbs Ferry, NY: Oceana, 1972), a work which updates accounts from the interwar years, e.g. Jackson Harvey Ralston, *International Arbitration from Athens to Locarno,* Stanford Books in World Politics (Palo Alto, Ca.: Stanford University Press, 1929); and the very detailed, multilingual study by Max Habicht, *Post-War Treaties for the Pacific Settlement of International Disputes* (Cambridge, Mass.: Harvard University Press, 1931). Contemporaneously appeared three other monographs, all relevant to the themes of ch. 1: A. C. F. Beales, *A History of Peace: a Short Account of the Organized Movements for International Peace* (London: G. Bell & Sons, 1931); Merle Curti, *The American Peace Crusade: 1815–1860* (Durham, N C: Duke University Press, 1929) to be followed by *Peace or War: The American Struggle, 1636–1936* (New York: W. W. Norton, 1936); and Christina Phelps, *The Anglo-American Peace Movement in the Mid-Nineteenth Century*. Studies in History, Economics and Public Law, no. 330 (New York: Columbia University Press, 1930). Two, more specialized monographs are still useful for their acuteness: Thomas Willing Balch, *The Alabama Arbitration* (Philadelphia: Allen, Lane & Scott, 1900) and Ruhl J. Bartlett, *The League to Enforce Peace* (Chapel Hill: University of North Carolina Press, 1944). The CEIP is discussed by a leading Second Generation scholar: see Martin David Dubin, 'The Carnegie Endowment for International Peace and the Advocacy of a League of Nations, 1914–1918', *Proceedings of the American Philosophical Society* 123 (December 1979), 344–68.

Anyone questioning the validity, let alone value, of the Anglo-American 'special relationship' theme must address the excellent account in David Reynolds, *The Creation of the Anglo-American Alliance, 1937–1941: a Study in Competitive Co-operation* (London: Europa, 1981); but counter-evidence, historical and political, can be found in such diverse works as John Bayliss, *Anglo-American Defence Relations, 1939–1984*, 2nd ed (London: Macmillan, 1984); Diana Johnstone, *The Politics of Euromissiles: Europe's Role in America's World* (London: Verso, 1984); and Kees van der Pijl, *The Making of an Atlantic Ruling Class* (London: Verso, 1984).

A final note on the 'symbolic' mode of interpretation. Dallek is indeed fond of the term: e.g., *Roosevelt and American Foreign Policy*, 95 and *Democrat and Diplomat: the Life of William E. Dodd* (New York: Oxford University Press, 1968), 251. Even more explicit is Dexter Perkins, *Charles Evans Hughes and American Democratic Statesmanship* (Boston: Little, Brown, 1956), 89–90.

Chapter 2

Temperley, *History of the Peace Conference* (cited in ch. 2, n. 5) remains an incomparable English-language introduction to the World War I settlement. Recent studies from an American perspective include Arthur Walworth, *Wilson and his Peacemakers: American Diplomacy at the Paris Peace Conference, 1919* (New York and London: W. W. Norton, 1986) and Lloyd E. Ambrosius, *Woodrow Wilson and the American Diplomatic Tradition: the Treaty Fight in Perspective* (Cambridge and New York: Cambridge University Press, 1987). An early study of British contributions to the formation of the League is Henry R. Winkler, *The League of Nations Movement in Great Britain, 1914–1919*. Rutgers University Studies in History, no. 7 (New Brunswick, NJ: Rutgers University Press, 1952); updated by George W. Egerton, *Great Britain and the Creation of the League of Nations: Strategy, Politics and International Organization, 1914–1919* (Chapel Hill: University of North Carolina Press, 1979). A recent study of Secretary Lansing is by Thomas H. Hartig, *Robert Lansing: an Interpretive Biography* (Salem, NH: Ayer, 1982). For the role of Viscount Bryce, see Leonard S. Woolf (ed), *The Framework of a Lasting Peace* (London: Allen & Unwin, 1917); Keith G. Robbins, 'Lord Bryce and the First World War', *Historical Journal* 10 (no. 2, 1967), 255–78 and Martin David Dubin, 'Toward the Concept of Collective Security: the Bryce Group's "Proposals for the Avoidance of War," 1914–1917', *International Organization* 24 (Spring 1970), 288–318. Lord Phillimore's ideas can be studied in Walter George Frank Phillimore, *Three Centuries of Treaties of Peace and their Teaching* (London: John Murray, 1917).

Works which downplay or totally ignore Root's contributions include John Eppstein (ed), *Ten Years' Life of the League of Nations: a History of the Origins of the League and of its Development from A.D. 1919 to 1929* (London: May Fair Press, 1929); League of Nations Secretariat, *Ten Years of World Co-operation* (Geneva: League of Nations, 1930); Démètre Négulesco (a judge of the Court), 'Cour Permanente de Justice Internationale', *Dictionnaire Diplomatique*, I. 587–95; Jean Ray, *Commentaire du Pacte de la Société des Nations selon la Politique et la Jurisprudence des Organes de la Société* (Paris: Recueil Sirey, 1930); Gabriele Salvioli, *La Corte Permanente di Giustizia Internazionale*. Pubblicazioni dell' Associazione Italiana per la Società delle Nazioni, no. 5 (Rome: Anonima Romana Editoriale, 1928); Walther Schücking and Hans Wehberg, *Die Satzung des Völkerbundes*, 2nd ed rev. (Berlin: Franz Vahlen, 1924). For the personal contributions of this pair of scholars, see Schücking, *Der Staatenverband der Haager Konferenzen* (Munich: Duncker & Humblot, 1912) and the companion volume on *Das Werk vom Haag* by Wehberg, *Das Problem eines internationalen Staatengerichtshofes* (Munich: Duncker & Humblot, 1912).

James Brown Scott was a prolific advocate, especially for the relevance of American domestic practice: see especially Scott, *Judical Settlement of Controversies between States of the American Union: an Analysis of Cases decided in the Supreme Court of the United States* (Oxford: Clarendon Press, 1919) and *The United States of America: a Study in International Organization* (New York: Oxford University Press, 1920). A counter-argument is Thomas Willing Balch, *A World Court in the Light of the United States Supreme Court* (Philadelphia: Allen, Lane & Scott, 1918).

The following works are helpful for understanding some of the technical debates in the evolution of the Court Statute: Helen Mary Cory, *Compulsory Arbitration of International Disputes* (New York: Columbia University Press, 1932); Edwin Dewitt Dickinson, *The Equality of States in International Law*. Harvard Studies in Jurisprudence, no. 3 (Cambridge, Mass.: Harvard University Press, 1920); and Max Habicht, *The Power of the International Judge to Give a Decision 'Ex Aequo et Bono'*, New Commonwealth Institute Monographs, Series B, no. 2 (London: Constable, 1935). Hudson, Jessup and Butler were involved in the London-based, pro-League New Commonwealth Institute.

Chapter 3

The contemporary study of the history of the interwar years from an anglophone, liberal internationalist perspective is brilliantly carried through in the *Survey of International Affairs* (*SIA*), published annually by the (British, later) Royal Institute of International Affairs in London. The RIIA's transatlantic sibling, the Council on Foreign Relations, based in New York City, followed with its own *Survey of American Foreign Relations* (*SAFR*), which became *United States in World Affairs* (*USWA*). For the establishment of the RIIA (also known as Chatham House), see Michael L. Dockrill, 'The Foreign Office and the "Proposed Institute of International Affairs, 1919" ', *International Affairs* 56 (Autumn 1980), 665–72. The Washington Conference in relation to the Paris Conference is analysed in Arnold J. Toynbee, *The World after the Peace Conference: being an Epilogue to the 'History of the Peace Conference of Paris' and a Prologue to the 'Survey of International Affairs, 1920–1923'* (London: Oxford University Press, 1925).

Buckingham, *International Normalcy* (cited in ch. 3, n. 37) is a brief, intelligent monograph; while Evans C. Johnson, *Oscar W. Underwood: a Political Biography* (Baton Rouge and London: Louisiana State University Press, 1980) corroborates my analysis. For Judge Straus, also one of the Republican Thirty-One, see Naomi W. Cohen, *A Dual Heritage: the Public Career of Oscar S. Straus* (Philadelphia: Jewish Publication Society of America, 1969). The prize-winning biography by

William C. Widenor, *Henry Cabot Lodge and the Search for an American Foreign Policy* (Berkeley and London: University of California Press, 1980) does not examine the Court issue. The same is true for the recent general study by Frank Costigliola, *Awkward Dominion: American Political, Economic and Cultural Relations with Europe, 1919–1933* (Ithaca and London: Cornell University Press, 1984).

For two other studies of the Senate battle over the Versailles Treaty written from the perspective of World War II (cf. Fleming and the First Generation), see Thomas A. Bailey, *Woodrow Wilson and the Great Betrayal* (New York: Macmillan, 1945) and Alan Cranston, *The Killing of the Peace* (New York: Viking Press, 1945).

The best historical introductions to the Department of State in the 1920s are Martin Weil, *A Pretty Good Club: the Founding Fathers of the U.S. Foreign Service* (New York: W. W. Norton, 1978) and Robert D. Schulzinger, *The Making of the Diplomatic Mind: the Training, Outlook, and Style of United States Foreign Service Officers, 1908–1931* (Middletown, Ct.: Wesleyan University Press, 1975). No-one seems to have yet studied the impressive officer, Anna A. O'Neill, who started as a clerk and became Assistant to the Legal Adviser. Higher up the scale was William Phillips, whose memoirs, *Ventures in Diplomacy* (Boston: Beacon Press, 1953) are uninformative on the World Court. A useful list of rather disparate materials is Robert U. Goehlert and Elizabeth R. Hoffmeister, *The Department of State and American Diplomacy: a Bibliography*. Garland Reference Library of Social Science, vol. 333 (New York and London: Garland, 1986).

Valuable though neglected contemporary sources for congressional politics are the *American Political Science Review* (*APSR*) and the *Political Science Quarterly* (*PSQ*). Both published detailed reviews of Congress, though *PSQ* discarded the practice. The *Annals of the American Academy of Political and Social Science* (*Annals*) provide good background material and analysis of domestic and foreign issues. *International Conciliation*, published by the Carnegie Endowment, is rich in documentation; so too the *American Journal of International Law* (*AJIL*). In 1923 *AJIL* began publishing Hudson's annual survey of the work of the Court.

Three other monographs may be mentioned here, which reopen the question of the survival of Progressivism in the 1920s: Stuart I. Rochester, *American Liberal Disillusionment in the Wake of World War I* (University Park and London: Pennsylvania State University Press, 1977); Eugene M. Tobin, *Organize or Perish: America's Independent Progressives, 1913–1933*. Contributions in American History, no. 114 (New York and London: Greenwood Press, 1986); and John A. Thompson, *Reformers and War: American Progressive Publicists and the First World War* (Cambridge: Cambridge University Press , 1987). Ham Holt, we may note, was the only Progressive of any consequence to carry on the fight for the League Court.

Chapter 4

Awkward questions of jurisprudence and legal-political theory are addressed in a number of contemporary monographs: J.L. Brierly, *The Law of Nations: an Introduction to the International Law of Peace*. 2nd ed (London: Oxford University Press, 1936); Margaret E. Burton, *The Assembly of the League of Nations* (Chicago: University of Chicago Press, 1941); T. P. Conwell-Evans, *The League Council in Action: a Study of the Methods Employed by the Council of the League of Nations to Prevent War and to Settle International Disputes* (London: Oxford University Press, 1929); Nicolas Politis, *The New Aspects of International Law*. A Series of Lectures delivered at Columbia University in July 1926. CEIP: Division of International Law, Pamphlet no. 49 (Washington, DC: CEIP, 1928); Cromwell A. Riches, *The Unanimity Rule and the League of Nations* (Baltimore: Johns Hopkins University Press, 1933); Charles K. Webster, *The League of Nations in Theory and Practice*. With some Chapters on International Co-operation by Sydney Herbert (London: Allen & Unwin, 1933). See also P. J. Baker, 'The Obligatory Jurisdiction of the Permanent Court of International Justice', *BYBIL* (1925), 68–102; J. L. Brierly, 'Matters of Domestic Jurisdiction', *BYBIL* (1925), 8–19; and John Fischer Williams, 'The League of Nations and Unanimity (with special reference to the Assembly)', *AJIL* 19 (July 1925), 475–88.

For the Court's early years and contemporary international law and relations in general, the serial *Recueil des Cours* of The Hague Academy of International Law provides a voluminous, diverse commentary. The Court's work has been abstracted in Vol. I of Krystyna Marek (ed.), *A Digest of the Decisions of the International Court of Justice* (The Hague: Martinus Nijhoff, 1974), not to mention Hudson's *World Court Reports*; and brilliantly analysed in Vol. I of J. H. W. Verzijl, *The Jurisprudence of the World Court: a Case by Case Commentary*. Publications of the Institute for International Law of the University of Utrecht, Series A: Modern International Law, no. 2 (Leiden: A.W. Sijthoff, 1965). Francophone scholars found particular interest in the advisory jurisdiction, to judge from the publication of a number of theses. Readers may follow the story in the arguments of M. Beuve-Méry, Gérard Bonvalot and Alexandre Daliétos of the University of Paris and Claude Dauvergne of the University of Montpellier. (All these works are in book-form.) More generally, see Bernard de Francqueville, *L'Oeuvre de la Cour Permanente de Justice Internationale*, 2 vols (Paris: Editions Internationales, 1928) and Eugène Remlinger, *Les Avis Consultatifs de la Cour Permanente de Justice Internationale* (Paris: Pedone, 1938).

A recent study of the background to the Mosul case is Michael L. Dockrill and J. Douglas Goold, *Peace without Promise: Britain and the Peace Conferences, 1919–23* (London: Batsford, 1981); while a friendly American view of British power is offered by the former Representative from New York and Minister to Spain, Perry Belmont in *National Isolation an Illusion: Political Independence not Isolation: Interdependence of the United States and Europe* (New York and London: Putnam's, 1924).

Harding's 'Voyage of Understanding' can be traced through *Speeches and Addresses of Warren G. Harding, President of the United States, Delivered during the Course of his Tour from Washington, D.C., to Alaska and Return to San Francisco, June 20 to August 2, 1923.* Reported and Compiled by James W. Murphy, Official Reporter, US Senate [1923]. One of his collaborators on the St Louis speech is the subject of Frank W. Fox, *J. Reuben Clark: the Public Years* (Provo, Utah: Brigham Young University Press and Deseret Book Co., 1980). For Harding's successor, see Donald R. McCoy, *Calvin Coolidge: the Quiet President* (New York: Macmillan, 1967). The most famous work of Coolidge's rejected nominee, Charles B. Warren, is his *Supreme Court in United States History*, 2 vols, 2nd ed rev. (Boston: Little, Brown, 1937). On a familiar theme, see Warren, 'The Supreme Court and the World Court: 1832 and 1932', *International Conciliation* 289 (April 1933), 175–90.

Tobin, *Organize or Perish*, 257 rightly calls the 'definitive account' of the 1924 election the old study by Kenneth Campbell MacKay, *The Progressive Movement of 1924* (New York: Columbia University Press, 1947), which is more wide-ranging than the title suggests. The biography of the Democratic candidate by William H. Harbaugh, *Lawyer's Lawyer: the Life of John W. Davis* (New York: Oxford University Press, 1973) is uninformative on the Court campaign.

I have discussed the context of Harding's New York and St Louis speeches in 'The Harding Administration and the World Court' (cited at ch. 4, n. 15). My conclusions differ from Accinelli, 'Was there a "New" Harding? Warren G. Harding and the World Court Issue, 1920–1923', *Ohio History* 84 (Autumn 1975), 168–81.

Chapter 5

For contemporary studies of the League, especially the various crises, see Max Beer, *Die Reise nach Genf* (Berlin: Fischer, 1932); José Carlos de Macedo Soares, *Brazil and the League of Nations* (Paris: Pedone, 1928); Harold S. Quigley, *From Versailles to Locarno: a Sketch of the Recent Development of International Organization* (Minneapolis: University of Minnesota Press, 1927); Georges Scelle, *Une Crise de la Société des Nations; la Réforme du Conseil et l'Entrée de l'Allemagne à Genève (mars-septembre 1926)* (Paris: Presses Universitaires de France, 1927); and J. M. Spaight, *Pseudo-Security* (London: Longmans, Green, 1928). For pro-League American forebodings, see Charles G. Fenwick, 'The Legal Significance of the Locarno Agreements', *AJIL* 20 (January 1926), 108–11 and David D. Burks, 'The United States and the Geneva Protocol of 1924: "A New Holy Alliance?" ', *American Historical Review* 64 (July 1959), 891–905. For more recent studies discussing the American involvement see Melvyn P. Leffler, *The Elusive Quest: America's Pursuit of European Stability and French Security, 1919–1933* (Chapel Hill: University of North Carolina Press, 1979); B. J. C. McKercher, *The Second Baldwin Government and the United States, 1924–1929: Attitudes and Diplomacy* (Cambridge: Cambridge University Press, 1984); S. A. Schuker, *The End of French Predominance in Europe: the Financial Crisis of 1924 and the Adoption of the Dawes Plan* (Chapel Hill: University of North Carolina Press, 1976). For one of the leading Second Generation historians on these issues, see Charles DeBenedetti, 'The Origins of Neutrality Revision: the American Plan of 1924', *The Historian* 35 (no. 1, 1972), pp. 75–87 and 'The First Détente: America and Locarno', *South Atlantic Quarterly* 75 (Autumn 1976), 407–23.

The problem of national judges was concisely stated by Pierre Crabitès, 'The World Court not a Judical Body', *Canadian Bar Review* 9 (February 1931), 117–18; while the background to the immigration issue is detailed in Maurice R. Davie, *World Immigration: with special reference to the United States* (New York: Macmillan, 1936); R. D. McKenzie, *Oriental Exclusion: the Effect of American Immigration Laws, Regulations and Judical Decisions upon the Chinese and Japanese on the American Pacific Coast* (New York: Institute of Pacific Relations, 1927); and Rodman W. Paul, *The Abrogation of the Gentlemen's Agreement* (Cambridge, Mass.: Harvard University Press, 1936). On the national salience of the Ku Klux Klan, see David Burner, *The Politics of Provincialism: the Democratic Party in Transition, 1918–1932* (New York: Knopf, 1968), ch. 3 and George H. Mayer, *The Republican Party, 1854–1964* (New York: Oxford University Press, 1964), ch. 11.

When anti-Courters complained of pro-Court propaganda, they had in mind such efforts as the American Peace Plan of the American Foundation: see Esther Everett Lape (ed), *Ways to Peace. Twenty Plans selected from the most representative of those submitted to the American Peace Award for the best practicable Plan by which the United States may co-operate with other Nations to achieve and preserve the Peace of the World* etc. (New York and London: Scribner's, 1924). For the sponsor of the Peace Plan, see Salme Harju Steinberg, *Reformer in the Marketplace: Edward W. Bok and the Ladies' Home Journal* (Baton Rouge and London: Louisiana State University Press, 1979) and Charles DeBenedetti, 'The $100,000 American Peace Award of 1924', *Pennsylvania Magazine of History and Biography* 98 (April 1974), 224–49.

George Wharton Pepper was something of a constitutional lawyer, with a special interest in foreign relations: see e.g. *Family Quarrels: the President, the Senate, the House*. William H. White Foundation Lectures, University of Virginia (New York: Baker, Voorhis, 1931). His papers are in the University of Pennsylvania Library; Dwight Whitney Morrow's are in the Amherst College Library; Frank B. Kellogg's are with the Minnesota Historical Society, St. Paul.

Rogers, *American Senate* (cited in ch. 5, n. 36), is an excellent introduction to the form and tone of the 1925–6 debate and has recently been reissued by the Johnson Reprint Corporation. For the particular issue of senatorial sectionalism, see Carroll H. Wooddy, 'Is the Senate Unrepresentative?', *PSQ* 41 (June 1926), 218–39. Tom Walsh is the subject of a forthcoming biography by J. Leonard Bates.

Chapter 6

For two rather complacent reviews of the American terms for adherence, see Claudio Baldoni, 'La Corte Permanente di Giustizia Internazionale e gli Stati Uniti d'America', *Rivista di Diritto Internazionale* (3rd series) 6 (no. 1, 1927), 17–33; and the more detailed study of Herbert Kraus, 'La Cour Permanente de Justice Internationale et les Etats Unis d'Amérique', *Revue de Droit International et de Législation Comparée* (3rd series) 7(nos 3–4, 1926), 281–320. Equally favourable is the pro-League David Hunter Miller, 'The Senate Reservations and the Advisory Opinions of the Permanent Court of International Justice', *Columbia Law Review* 26 (June 1926), 654–69. For the opposition view, see David Jayne Hill, 'The Relation of the United States to the Permanent Court of International Justice', *AJIL* 20 (April 1926), 326–30. The Senate-Executive demand for a veto was happily acknowledged by Arnold D. McNair, 'The Council's Request for an Advisory Opinion from the Permanent Court of International Justice', *BYBIL* (1926), 1–13. Lauterpacht's article (cited in ch. 6, n. 4) is what one would expect of the young lawyer, who was already highly regarded by Moore and Borchard. The Moore Papers are useful for their numerous clippings from the European press, notably the semi-official (Paris) *Le Temps*.

Chamberlain's policies and priorities can be readily understood from his own published writings: see, especially, *Down the Years* (London: Cassell, 1935) and the compilation by (Sir) Charles Petrie, Bt, *The Life and Letters of the Right Hon. Sir Austen Chamberlain, K.G., P.C., M.P.*, 2 vols (London: Cassell, 1940).

The 1926 primaries remain a puzzle, at least for generalization. The Lenroot Papers are inconclusive; but the Gerald P. Nye Papers, in the Hoover Presidential Library, suggest the anti-Court, anti-League campaign was effective – a conclusion borne out in Gilbert Courtland Fite, *Peter Norbeck: Prairie Statesman*. University of Missouri Studies, Vol. 22, no. 2 (Columbia: University of Missouri, 1948). Norbeck of South Dakota voted Yea in January 1926.

Helpful introductions to the events of 1929 are in Alexander P. Fachiri, 'The International Court: American Participation; Statute Revision', *BYBIL* (1930), 85–99; and the contributions by various authors in *PASIL* (1931), 61–91. For the League perspective on the political issues, see Henri Pensa, *De Locarno au Pacte Kellog* [*sic*]: *la Politique Européenne sous le Triumvirat Chamberlain-Briand-Stresemann, 1925–1929* (Paris: Roustan, 1930); Adriaan H. Philipse, *Le Rôle du Conseïl de la Société des Nations dans le Règlement Pacifique des Différends Internationaux* (The Hague: Martinus Nijhoff, 1929); and John Fischer Williams, *Some Aspects of the Covenant of the League of Nations* (London: Oxford University Press, 1934).

For the pro-League forces behind the Kellogg-Briand Pact, see (apart from Shotwell, *War as an Instrument of National Policy*, cited in ch. 6, n. 59): David Hunter Miller, *The Peace Pact of Paris: a Study of the Briand-Kellogg Treaty* (New York and London: Putnam's, 1928) and Denys P. Myers, *Origin and Conclusion of the Paris Pact: the as an Instrument of National Policy*, World Peace Foundation Pamphlet, vol. 12, no. 2 (Boston: World Peace Foundation, 1929). It will be obvious I disagree with the received wisdom on the Pact, especially the role of Borah. For his apparent ally, see the detailed biographical study by John E. Stoner, *S.O. Levinson and the Pact of Paris* (Chicago: University of Chicago Press, 1943).

An excellent account of the 1928 campaign has been given by Allen J. Lichtman, *Prejudice and the Old Politics: the Presidential Election of 1928* (Chapel Hill: University of North Carolina Press, 1979), which updates and challenges the earlier study by Ruth C. Silva, *Rum, Religion and Votes: 1928 Re-examined* (University Park: Pennsylvania State University Press, 1962).

Philip Caryl Jessup (whose 1929 volume on the *United States and the World Court*, cited in ch. 6, n. 100 is available in a Johnson Corporation reprint) is the subject of a forthcoming biography by Marshall Kuehl.

Chapter 7

Research on all aspects of the *Auschluss* has been aided by the multilingual study of Alfred D. Low, *The Anschluss Movement, 1918–1938: Background and Aftermath. An Annotated Bibliography of German and Austrian Nationalism*. Garland Reference Library of Social Science, vol. 151 (New York and London: Garland, 1984). However Low omits Vali, *Die deutsch-österreichische Zollunion* (cited in ch. 7, n. 19), which remains the best analysis of the Customs Union case. Two other works may be cited, the first for its contemporary range; the second for its specific, historical focus: Friedrich F. G. Kleinwächter and Heinz von Paller (eds), *Die Anschlussfrage in ihrer kulturellen, politischen und wirtschaftlichen Bedeutung* (Vienna and Leipzig: Wilhelm Braumüller, 1930); N. von Preradovich, *Die Wilhelmstrasse und der Anschluss Oesterreichs, 1918–1933* (Bern and Frankfurt am Main: Herbert Lang, 1971).

For the self-serving accounts of the German principals, see Heinrich Brüning , *Memoiren, 1918–1934* (Stuttgart: Deutsche Verlags-Anstalt, 1970) and Julius Curtius, *Bemühung um Oesterreich: das Scheitern des Zollunionsplans von 1931* (Heidelberg: Universitätsverlag, 1947). The enormous quantities of published official and unofficial materials covering the interwar years can be traced through Kimmich, *German Foreign Policy, 1918–1945* (cited at p.513 above). The Austrian Chancellor is the subject of a subtle biography by Klemens von Klemperer, *Ignaz Seipel: Christian Statesman in a Time of Crisis* (Princeton: Princeton University Press, 1972). Bernhard W. von Bülow's criticisms of the postwar settlement can be found in *Der Versailler Völkerbund: eine vorläufige Bilanz* (Berlin: Kohlhammer Verlag, 1923). Judical arguments for revision are given by a well-known duo: see Walther Schücking, *Die Revision der Völkerbundssatzung im Hinblick auf den Kelloggpakt*. Wissenschaftliche Beiträge zu aktuellen Fragen, Heft 1 (Berlin: Verlag Ebering, 1931); and Hans Wehberg, *Der Kampf um die*

Reform des Völkerbundes, 1920 bis 1934 (Geneva: Druckerei und Verlag Union, 1934). For the British government and the Customs Union, see David Carlton, *MacDonald versus Henderson: the Foreign Policy of the Second Labour Government* (London: Macmillan, 1970). The wider-ranging yet detailed study by Robert W. D. Boyce, *British Capitalism at the Crossroads, 1919–1932: a Study in Politics, Economics, and International Relations* (Cambridge: Cambridge University Press, 1987) describes British official reaction as far less ambivalent than I do.

The Department of State files, NA 662.6331/, are extremely rich in European sources for this period, especially the French and Italian press . For the allegedly American view of Europe and the League in particular, see the numerous citations in Pierre Mariotte, *L'Europe et les Etats-Unis devant la Société des Nations* (Paris: Editions Internationales, 1930). One of the merits of Clough, *Beiträge zur Beurteilung* (cited in ch. 7, n. 14), is the examination of the German-language press in the USA. This is the very tip of an iceberg of a problem; but we may note that the only published account, Carl Wittke, *The German-Language Press in America* (Lexington: University of Kentucky Press, 1957) does not discuss the Court and rather avoids the interwar years as a whole.

Research on topics such as the Austro-German Customs Union can usefully begin with the monumental compilation of Norman S. Field, *League of Nations and United Nations Monthly List of Selected Articles: Cumulative, 1920–1970. Political, Legal, Economic*, 10 vols (Dobbs Ferry, NY: Oceana, 1971–3). Apart from journals and newspapers cited in this and previous chapters, I have found the following serials helpful (I give place of publication for non-American titles): *Bankers Magazine*; *Commercial and Financial Chronicle; Economist* (London); *Economiste Européen* (Paris); *Europa-Wirtschaft* (Berlin); *Friedens-Warte* (Zurich); *Gerarchia* (Milan); *Oesterreichische Volkswirt* (Vienna); *Paneuropa* (Leipzig/Vienna); *Revue de Droit International de Sciences Diplomatiques et Politiques* (Geneva); *Revue des Deux Mondes* (Paris); *Zeitschrift für ausländisches öffentliches Recht und Völkerrecht* (Berlin); *Zeitschrift für Nationalökonomie* (Vienna); *Zeitschrift für Völkerrecht* (Breslau).

From the numerous articles in the American legal journals, I would recommend the retrospective and reflective study by Edward Dumbauld, 'Dissenting Opinions in International Adjudication', *University of Pennsylvania Law Review and American Law Register*" 90 (June 1942), 929–45. For the subordinate, 'unequal' condition of States such as Austria discussed as a theoretical problem by American legal scholars, see e.g. Hymen Ezra Cohen, *Recent Theories of Sovereignty* (Chicago: University of Chicago Press, 1937); Helen Dwight Reid, *International Servitudes in Law and Practice* (Chicago: University of Chicago Press, 1932); Stuart S. Malawer, *Imposed Treaties and International Law* (Buffalo, NY: Hein, 1977); and cf. Pieter Hendrik Kooijmans, *The Doctrine of the Legal Equality of States: an Inquiry into the Foundations of International Law* (Leiden: A. W. Sijthoff, 1964).

For Thorne's predecessors in the historiography of the 'Far Eastern Crisis' (ch. 7, n. 35), see Westel W. Willoughby, *The Sino-Japanese Controversy and the League of Nations* (Baltimore: The Johns Hopkins

Press, 1935); A. Whitney Griswold, *The Far Eastern Policy of the United States* (New York: Harcourt, Brace, 1938); and Reginald Bassett, *Democracy and Foreign Policy: a Case History. The Sino-Japanese Dispute, 1931–33*, Publications of the London School of Economics and Political Science (London: Longmans, Green, 1952). Secretary Stimson gave his own account in *Far Eastern Crisis: Recollections and Observations* (New York and London: Harper & Bros., 1936).

The pro-League American position is given in Clarence A. Berdahl, *The Policy of the United States with respect to the League of Nations*, Publications of the Graduate Institute of International Studies, Geneva, no. 4 (Geneva: Librairie Kundig, 1932).

I have reviewed Hoover and the Hoover historiography at some length in 'Herbert Hoover and the World Court' (cited in ch. 1, n. 26). For the World War I settlement specifically, see Lawrence E. Gelfand (ed.), *Herbert Hoover: the Great War and its Aftermath* (Iowa City: University of Iowa Press, 1979), esp. Royal J. Schmidt, 'Hoover's Reflections on the Versailles Treaty', ibid. 61–86.

The literature on Roosevelt and political coalitions in relation to the World Court has been enlarged by the detailed study of Ronald L. Feinman, *Twilight of Progressivism: the Western Republican Senators and the New Deal*. Johns Hopkins University Studies in Historical and Political Science, Ninety-ninth Series, no. 1 (Baltimore and London: Johns Hopkins University Press, 1981) and Ronald A. Mulder, *The Insurgent Progressives in the United States Senate and the New Deal, 1933–1939* (New York and London: Garland, 1979). I am not persuaded by Olsson, *Congress and the Executive* (cited in ch. 7, n. 60); but Olsson's is surely the best published analysis of the context of the Court vote. Many of the domestic determinants are identified – but not, I think, the important foreign ones.

Hiram Johnson's initial support of Roosevelt is discussed in Marty Hamilton, 'Bull Moose plays an Encore: Hiram Johnson and the Presidential Campaign of 1932', *California Historical Society Quarterly* 41 (September 1962), 211–21; his earlier career is the subject of Richard Coke Lower, 'Hiram Johnson: the Making of an Irreconcilable,' *Pacific Historical Review* 41 (no. 4, 1972), 505–26. One individual study helps to trace the emergence (or really reconstitution) of the Southern Conservative Democratic alliance – though without providing anything informative on the Court debate: see John Robert Moore, *Senator Josiah William Bailey of North Carolina: a Political Biography* (Durham, NC: Duke University Press, 1968). The special studies by George Q. Flynn, *American Catholics and the Roosevelt Presidency, 1932–1936* (Lexington: University of Kentucky Press, 1968) and David J. O'Brien, *American Catholics and Social Reform: the New Deal Years* (New York: Oxford University Press, 1968) confirm the general rule that historians are still dominated by the First Generation historiography.

The following works can be recommended for penetrating the rhetoric which still clouds Roosevelt and the New Deal: Edgar Kemler, *The Deflation of American Ideals: an Ethical Guide for New Dealers* (Washington, DC: American Council on Public Affairs, 1941); [John

Franklin Carter], *The New Dealers* (New York: Simon & Schuster, 1934); and the best of the edited memoirs, *The Secret Diary* by Ickes (cited in ch. 7, n. 74). On the early-mid 1930s, Senator Connally's memoirs are plausible – certainly in his assessment of Cordell Hull: see Tom Connally, *My Name is Tom Connally – as told to Alfred Steinberg* (New York: Thomas Y. Crowell, 1954). Moffat's edited Journals are uninformative on the Court – unlike the unpublished materials in the Houghton Library: see Nancy Harvison Hooker (ed.), *The Moffat Papers: Selections from the Diplomatic Journals of Jay Pierrepont Moffat, 1919–1943* (Cambridge, Mass.: Harvard University Press, 1956). Moffat was the son-in-law of Joseph C. Grew, on whom see Waldo H. Heinrichs, Jr, *American Ambassador: Joseph C. Grew and the Development of the United States Diplomatic Tradition* (Boston: Little, Brown, 1966).

The Papers of Felix Morley, editor of the *Washington Post*, are in the Hoover Presidential Library.

Chapter 8

James C. Shotwell was heavily involved in the establishment of the ILO: see esp. Shotwell, *The Origins of the International Labor Organization*, 2 vols. The Paris Peace Conference: History and Documents (New York: Columbia University Press, 1934). Useful for the American perspective is Francis Graham Wilson, *Labor in the League System: a Study of the International Labor Organization in relation to International Administration.* Stanford Books in World Politics (Palo Alto, Ca.: Stanford University Press, 1934). A review of 1934 in the Roosevelt context is Gary B. Ostrower, 'The American Decision to join the International Labor Organization', *Labor History* 16 (Fall 1975), 495–504. Margaret Hardy, *The Influence of Organized Labor on the Foreign Policy of the United States* (Liège: Vaillant – Carmanne, 1936) is broader than its title suggests.

Wallace McClure's long campaign against the Senate's 'treaty-making' power is evidenced in his *International Executive Agreements: Democratic Procedure under the Constitution of the United States* (New York: Columbia University Press, 1941) and the issue is updated in Elbert M. Byrd, Jr, *Treaties and Executive Agreements in the United States: their Separate Roles and Limitations* (The Hague: Martinus Nijhoff, 1960).

The context of the Gore reservation can be studied in J. Chal Vinson, 'War Debts and Peace Legislation: the Johnson Act of 1934', *Mid-America* 50 (July 1968), 206–22. Vinson is usually hostile to the Senate in general and the isolationists in particular; but this article is somewhat exceptional.

The 'propaganda-defeat' thesis is maintained in David H. Bennett, *Demagogues in the Depression: American Radicals and the Union Party, 1932–1936* (New Brunswick, NJ: Rutgers University Press, 1969) and Geoffrey Smith, *To Save a Nation: American Countersubversives, the New Deal, and the Coming of World War II* (New York: Basic Books,

1973). John Franklin Carter, *American Messiahs* (New York: Simon & Schuster, 1935), writing once more as the Unofficial Observer, may appear to share this demonology; but his work is thoughtful and informative, particularly in tracing the political alliances and feuds between Long, Caraway, Robinson and Harrison. The Long-Caraway relationship is just touched upon in Diane D. Kincaid (ed.), *Silent Hattie Speaks: the Personal Journal of Senator Hattie Caraway*. Contributions in Women's Studies, no. 9 (Westport, Ct., and London: Greenwood Press, 1979).

For question-marks over the tradition of Southern internationalism, see Alexander DeConde, 'The South and Isolationism', *Journal of Southern History* 24 (August 1958), 332–46 and Frank E. Smith, 'Valor's Second Prize: Southern Racism and Internationalism', *South Atlantic Quarterly* 64 (Summer 1965), 296–303.

Biographies are, in general, unhelpful on the Court debate and defeat: e.g., Rodney P. Carlisle, *Hearst and the New Deal: the Progressive as Reactionary* (New York and London: Garland, 1979) offers one paragraph. The study by Ferdinand Lundberg, *Imperial Hearst: a Social Biography* (New York: Equinox Cooperative Press, 1936) remains the most revealing analysis. The recent sophisticated double-portrait by Alan Brinkley, *Voices of Protest: Huey Long, Father Coughlin and the Great Depression* (New York: Knopf, 1982) opens up no new areas on the Court. Biographies of Senators Vandenberg, Gore and Wagner by C. David Tompkins, Monroe Lee Billington and J. Joseph Huthmacher are equally uninformative. Perhaps the authors are too ideologically close to their subjects – a fate Borah rarely shared. Huthmacher, *Senator Robert F. Wagner and the Rise of Urban Liberalism* (New York: Atheneum, 1968) avoids the 'Hearst factor' in Wagner's politics; while, more obviously still, Tompkins, *Senator Arthur H. Vandenberg: the Evolution of a Modern Republican, 1884–1945* (East Lansing: Michigan State University Press, 1970), 123–4 misses the history of Paragraph VIII! Key Pittman has sometimes been treated as a joke: certainly he had not the gravitas of his two predecessors, Borah and Lodge. Fred I. Israel, *Nevada's Key Pittman* (Lincoln: University of Nebraska Press, 1963) has not been superseded by the recent volume of Betty Glad, *Key Pittman: the Tragedy of a Senate Insider* (New York: Columbia University Press, 1986). Despite the evocative title, Glad simply gets much of the crucial detail wrong. On the Court issue, at least, Pittman was knowledgeable, shrewd and prescient, as even the public record shows.

Special biographical studies are often not much better on the Court issue. Robert C. Sims, 'James P. Pope, Senator from Idaho', *Idaho Yesterdays* 15 (Fall 1951), 9–15 says nothing about Pope's attack on the two-thirds rule; Ivie E. Cadenhead, Jr, 'Will Rogers: Forgotten Man', *Midcontinent American Studies Journal* 4 (Fall 1963), 49–57 is uniformative. A brief and far better portrait is William B. Evans, 'Senator James E. Murray: a Voice of the People in Foreign Affairs', *Montana: the Magazine of Western History* 32 (Winter 1982), 25–35. The literature on Robinson (though with nothing on the Court) can be gleaned from

Cal Ledbetter, Jr, 'Joe T. Robinson and the Presidential Campaign of 1928', *Arkansas Historical Quarterly* 45 (Summer 1986), 95–125.

For Long, the Monroe Doctrine and the League in Latin America, see Michael L. Gillette, 'Huey Long and the Chaco War', *Louisiana History* 11 (Fall 1970), 293–311; and more generally, the fine studies by Leslie B. Rout, Jr, *Politics of the Chaco Peace Conference, 1935–1939*. Institute of Latin American Studies, Latin American Monographs, no. 19 (Austin and London: University of Texas Press, 1970) and Bryce Wood, *The United States and Latin American Wars, 1932–1942* (New York and London: Columbia University Press, 1970).

Further contemporary evidence of divisions within the League from authoritative sources include Victor Margueritte, *Avortement de la S.D.N. (1920–1936)* (Paris: Flammarion, 1936); Auguste-Félix-Charles de Beaupoil, Comte de Saint-Aulaire, *Genève contre la Paix* (Paris: Plon, 1936) and H. M. Swanwick, *Collective Insecurity* (London: Jonathan Cape, 1937) – a title echoed by Ostrower (cited in ch. 3, n. 3).

Retrospective support for Borah's analysis of British policy can be found in numerous places (e.g. the materials listed on p.277 above): see also, Hines H. Hall, III, 'The Foreign Policy-Making Process in Britain, 1934–1935, and the Origins of the Anglo-German Naval Agreement', *Historical Journal* 19 (no. 2, 1976), 477–99.

On the Senate vote itself: the Bronson Murray Cutting Papers (MD,LC) are perhaps not surprisingly very thin on the Court campaign – as are the Franklin Roosevelt Papers. Even more unhelpful are those of Lewis B. Schwellenbach (MD,LC) and David I. Walsh (Dinand Library, College of the Holy Cross, Worcester, Mass.). We can record that three Democrats, Black (Alabama), Hatch (New Mexico) and Brown (New Hampshire) were noted by Esther Lape and the American Foundation as possible Nays – and so candidates for inclusion in the 'switchers' to the Robinson-Roosevelt leadership. But no other evidence corroborates this prediction. After the vote, two inconsequential sectional analyses were published, which show that the 'minority' defeat did not entail a popular (or rather electoral) majority. This was propaganda of a kind: see *Washington Daily News* (6 February 1935), 11; *Literary Digest* (9 February 1935), 5–6. The only scholars to have attempted to identify the 'switchers' to the opposition are Guinsburg, *Pursuit of Isolationism* (cited in ch. 8, n. 43); Kahn, 'Pressure Group Influence' (cited in ch. 1, n. 23) and Olsson, *Congress and the Executive* (cited in ch. 7, n. 60). My methods and conclusions differ from theirs.

I have consulted the *Springfield Republican*, partly because Fleming and Bailey did so. It was highly regarded: see John J. Scanlon, *The Passing of the Springfield Republican* (Amherst, Mass.: Amherst College, 1950) and Frank Luther Mott, *American Journalism: a History, 1690–1960*, 3rd ed (New York: Macmillan 1962). All historians will surely agree, though, that if the press at large is studied, *the* lead story during the World Court debate was the Hauptmann trial for the Lindbergh kidnapping – as the pages of the same *Springfield Republican* demonstrate. Fr Coughlin was, in fact, *attacking* Hearst and the rest of the press for the massive coverage of the trial as a diversion from important social issues, like the Court: see Charles E. Coughlin, *A Series of Lectures on Social Justice* (Royal Oak, Mich.: Radio League of the Little Flower, 1935), 122–51.

The Court campaign is not discussed in the recent study by Richard Steele, *Propaganda in an Open Society: the Roosevelt Administration and the Media, 1933–1941*. Contributions in American History, no. 111 (Westport, Ct. and London: Greenwood Press, 1985). (We may note that the term 'Open Society' is no less problematical than propaganda.) More analytical – but missing the Court issue – is Michael Leigh, *Mobilizing Consent: Public Opinion and American Foreign Policy, 1937–1947* (Westport, Ct., and London: Greenwood Press, 1976). Granted the Hearst press formed the largest newspaper opposition to Court and League, the *Chicago Tribune* was perhaps the single most influential hostile newspaper: see Jerome E. Edwards, *The Foreign Policy of Col. McCormick's Tribune, 1929–1941* (Reno: University of Nevada Press, 1971).

Chapter 9

For Robert A. Divine's synopsis of Roosevelt, see *The Reluctant Belligerent: American Entry into World War II*, 2nd ed (New York and Chichester, Sussex: John Wiley & Sons., 1979); but Wayne S. Cole is the most consistent historian for the argument that the material bases of isolationism were eroded: see Cole, 'Gerald P. Nye and Agrarian Bases for the Rise and Fall of American Isolationism', in John N. Schacht (ed.), *Three Faces of Midwestern Isolationism: Gerald P. Nye, Robert E. Wood, John L. Lewis* (Iowa City: Center for the Study of the Recent History of the United States, 1981), an update of Cole's major biography, *Senator Gerald P. Nye and American Foreign Relations* (Minneapolis: Minnesota University Press, 1962). The argument from the 'facts of geography' was advanced by Donald F. Drummond, *The Passing of American Neutrality, 1937–1941* (Ann Arbor: University of Michigan Press, 1955). Of course, it has long been argued that the practicality of isolationism had disappeared a generation before: e.g. John Milton Cooper, Jr, *The Vanity of Power: American Isolationism and the First World War, 1914–1917*. Contributions in American History, no. 3 (Westport, Ct.: Greenwood Press, 1969). For the treatment of Vandenberg and Johnson to support the transition model, see James A. Gazell, 'Arthur H. Vandenberg, Internationalism, and the United Nations', *PSQ* 88 (September 1973), 375–94 and Peter G. Boyle, 'The Roots of Isolationism: a Case Study', *Journal of American Studies* 6 (no. 1, 1972), 41–50, which deals with Johnson. More generally still, see Richard F. Grimmett, 'Who were the Senate Isolationists?', *Pacific Historical Review* 42 (no. 4, 1973), 479–98. Johnson was hospitalized during the UN vote. The two opponents were Shipstead and William Langer. On the latter, see Glenn H. Smith, *Langer of North Dakota; a Study in Isolationism* (New York and London: Garland, 1979).

George Norris is often cited as the classic transitional type (see pp. 250 ff. above). He has been sympathetically served by his biographer,

Richard Lowitt: see *George W. Norris*, 3 vols (1963–78, the last volume being published by the University of Illinois Press at Champaign).

For prosopographical studies of surviving isolationists, see Ronald Radosh, *Prophets on the Right: Profiles of Conservative Critics of American Globalism* (New York: Simon & Schuster, 1975) and Justus D. Doenecke, *Not to the Swift: the Old Isolationists in the Cold War Era* (Lewisburg, Pa.: Bucknell University Press: London: Associated University Press, 1979). A fine article, especially for its analysis of the ambiguous and ambivalent Roosevelt, is William C. Widenor, 'American Planning for the United Nations: Have we been asking the Right Questions?', *Diplomatic History* 6 (Summer 1982), 245–65.

Klingberg's models of 'mood cycles', 'cyclical trends' and swings from 'introversion to extroversion' (originally formulated in journals) were critically discussed in a valuable essay by Harvey Starr, 'Alliances: Tradition and Change in American Views of Foreign Military Entanglements', in Ken Booth and Moorhead Wright (eds), *American Thinking about Peace and War* (New York: Barnes & Noble; Hassocks, Sussex: Harvester Press, 1978), 37–57. Such cyclical modelling is to be found in Melvin Small, *Was War Necessary? National Security and U.S. Entry into War*, Sage Library of Social Research, vol. 105 (Beverly Hills, Ca. and London: Sage, 1980), which covers six American wars from 1812 to the 1950s. A more recent attempt to conceptualize the cycles of historiography is Richard A. Melanson, *Writing History and Making Policy: the Cold War, Vietnam, and Revisionism*. American Values Projected Abroad, vol. 6 (Lanham, Md., and London: University Press of America, 1983); though a more convincing, earlier study is Ernest R. May, *'Lessons' of the Past: the Use and Misuse of History in American Foreign Policy* (New York: Oxford University Press, 1973) on the American transition from 'Munich' to the 'domino-theory' as political patterns.

Arthur Sweetser's celebration of the 'complete reversal' in United States foreign policy is expressed in Sweetser, 'The United States, the United Nations and the League of Nations', *International Conciliation* 418 (February 1946), 51–9; cf. Sweetser, 'From the League to the United Nations', *Annals* 246 (July 1946), 1–8. Other so-called internationalists who wrote their own autobiographical accounts of the transition include Clark M. Eichelberger, *Organizing for Peace: a Personal History of the Founding of the United Nations* (New York and London: Harper & Row, 1977); Raymond B. Fosdick, *Chronicle of a Generation: an Autobiography* (New York: Harper & Bros., 1958); Frederick J. Libby, *To End War: the Story of the National Council for Prevention of War* (Nyack, NY: Fellowship Publications, 1969); James T. Shotwell, *The Autobiography of James T. Shotwell* (Indianapolis: Bobbs-Merrill, 1961).

My argument for political continuity and the persistence of unilateralism is supported by Leo Gross, 'The Charter of the United Nations and the Lodge Reservations', *AJIL* 41 (July 1947), 531–54; cf. Francis O. Wilcox, 'The United States accepts Compulsory Jurisdiction' and Lawrence Preuss, 'The International Court of Justice, the Senate, and Matters of Domestic Jurisdiction', *AJIL* 40 (October 1946), 699–736. The

Cold War perception of the proper function of the new Court is given in Oliver J. Lissitzyn, *The International Court of Justice: its Role in the Maintenance of International Peace and Security*. United Nations Studies, no. 6 (New York: CEIP, 1951); but as the Bricker Amendment controversy showed in the early 1950s, the Cold War attacks could come through domestic meddling – hence the continued relevance of the Connally Amendment. On the specific issue, see Duane A. Tananbaum, 'The Bricker Amendment Controversy: its Origins and Eisenhower's Role', *Diplomatic History* 9 (Winter 1985), 73–93; more generally, see M. S. Rajan, *The United Nations and Domestic Jurisdiction* (New Delhi: Orient Longmans, 1958). Wallace McClure kept up his own campaign with *World Legal Order: Possible Contributions by the People of the United States* (Chapel Hill: University of North Carolina Press, 1960).

Despite the American war in Southeast Asia (the 'Vietnam War') but because of growing détente at Superpower level, the early 1970s (like the late 1950s) was a time when American politicians spoke of *Strengthening the International Court of Justice*. Hearings before the Committee on Foreign Relations, United States Senate, Ninety-third Congress, First Session, on S.Res 74–78. May 10, 11, 1973 (Washington, DC: GPO, 1973). Meanwhile political scientists provided appropriate evidence: e.g. William D. Coplin and J. Martin Rochester, 'The Permanent Court of International Justice, the International Court of Justice, the League of Nations, and the United Nations: a Comparative Empirical Survey', *ASPR* 66 (June 1972), 529–50; John King Gamble, Jr, and Dana D. Fischer, *The International Court of Justice: an Analysis of a Failure* (Lexington, Mass.: Lexington Books, 1976). Proposals for enhancing the Court's work filled many legal pages: e.g. Leo Gross (ed.), *The Future of the International Court of Justice*, 2 vols (Dobbs Ferry, NY: Oceana, 1976), only one testimony to many years of work sponsored by the American Society of International Law. Such activity is reviewed by Margaret A. Rague, 'The Reservation Power and the Connally Amendment', *New York University Journal of International Law and Politics* 11 (Fall 1978), 323–58.

Some legal scholars, however, recognized the violent contradiction between the traditional American pretensions to being peaceful and law-abiding (as though the terms were synonymous): see especially Richard A. Falk, *The Status of Law in International Society* (Princeton: Princeton University Press, 1970). Such a critical perspective has been applied to the Reagan administration's actions in Central America and the Caribbean by scholars such as Francis Anthony Boyle, *World Politics and International Law* (Durham, NC: Duke University Press, 1985). As Boyle argues, *pace* Louis B. Sohn (ibid. ix–x), the 'gap' is not between academic disciplines but between value systems – or, as Americans express it, between ideologies. There are other continuities, as the Nicaragua case shows. Opponents of American policy spoke of the 'messianism and chauvinism in America's commitment to peace through law'; conversely Eugene Rostow likened the Court's judgment to the Dred Scott case as an example of 'hubris and an abuse of power': Lori Fisler Damrosch (ed.), *The International Court of Justice at a Crossroads*,

(Dobbs Ferry, NY: Transnational Publishers, 1987), 3 ff., 264 ff., 278 ff.

Whether or not the Court survives this crisis, historians and lawyers will remain indebted to the scholarship of Shabtai Rosenne, *The Law and Practice of the International Court*, 2nd ed rev. (Dordrecht, Boston, Lancaster: Martinus Nijhoff, 1985) and *Documents on the International Court of Justice*, 2nd ed (Dobbs Ferry, NY: Oceana; Alphen aan den Rijn, Sijthoff & Noordhoff, 1979). Continuing research on the ICJ and international law in general will rely upon the following invaluable indexing serials: *Current Law Index* and *Index to Foreign Legal Periodicals*, both sponsored by the American Association of Law Libraries; *Bibliographic Guide to Law*, published by G. K. Hall; *Index to Legal Periodicals*, published by H. W. Wilson; and *Public International Law: a Current Bibliography of Articles*, issued by the (Heidelberg) Max-Planck-Institut für ausländisches öffentliches Recht und Völkerrecht.

Index